SMP Further Mathematics Series

Statistics and probability

DOUGLAS QUADLING

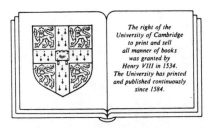

The right of the
University of Cambridge
to print and sell
all manner of books
was granted by
Henry VIII in 1534.
The University has printed
and published continuously
since 1584.

CAMBRIDGE UNIVERSITY PRESS

Cambridge

London   New York   New Rochelle

Melbourne   Sydney

Published by the Press Syndicate of the University of Cambridge
The Pitt Building, Trumpington Street, Cambridge CB2 1RP
32 East 57th Street, New York, NY 10022, USA
10 Stamford Road, Oakleigh, Melbourne 3166, Australia

First published 1987

Printed in Great Britain at
the University Press, Cambridge

British Library cataloguing in publication data
Quadling, D. A.
Statistics and probability.—(SMP
further mathematics series)
1. Mathematical statistics
I. Title   II. Series
519.5   QA276.12

ISBN 0 521 33615 5

Contents

Preface

This is a book on statistics for the mathematically competent reader, who expects to understand "why" as well as "how". It has been written in the first instance for students preparing to take A-level Further Mathematics examinations, but it could also be used as a supporting text for college and university mathematics courses. Although the books in this series have been prepared under the auspices of SMP, the ground covered is not restricted to that specified in SMP syllabuses; they should therefore meet equally well the requirements of those working towards other comparable examinations.

Many students at this level spend much of their time working on their own or in quite small groups, and access to advice from teachers is sometimes limited. I have tried to cater for this by writing a text which is intended to be read, and by providing fuller solutions to exercises than is usual in books of this kind. It is assumed that every reader will have a good scientific calculator available; and it is hoped that most will have access to a microcomputer, and are capable of writing short programs for themselves. These aids have an important part to play in presenting some of the key ideas in statistics vividly, without algebraic and numerical complication.

I have assumed that users of the book will have encountered previously some of the more elementary statistical measures and basic concepts of probability. A brief résumé of these starting points is given in the first chapter, with exercises to help to consolidate these before embarking on the course proper. It is recognised that at this stage some students will not have gone very far in pure mathematics, so that the mathematical demands of the first few chapters are slight. For example, the exponential function is not needed until Chapter 7, and integration until Chapter 11. Towards the end there are chapters in which more advanced topics such as eigenvectors and multiple integrals appear, but usually in quite straightforward applications. There is considerable emphasis on graphical and geometrical demonstrations, which can often be used to by-pass complicated algebraic arguments.

The book divides naturally into three parts, each terminating in a Revision exercise and a set of more extensive and open-ended Project exercises. The first part (Chapters 1-8) introduces fundamental ideas such as probability model, randomness, estimation and hypothesis testing; at this stage the models used are all discrete, such as binomial, Poisson and geometric probability. The second part (Chapters 9-16) brings in continuous models, and especially normal probability, which is used to develop more sharply focussed methods of hypothesis testing and estimation. The concept of expectation plays an important role at this stage. Finally, a third part (Chapters 17-21) goes more deeply into statistical theory, including many of the methods of statistical inference which originated in Britain during the first two decades of this century – chi-squared probability, t-probability, correlation and regression. The final chapter in this section, which deals mostly with Markov chains, stands somewhat apart from the rest, and could be taken earlier in the course if the supporting linear algebra is available.

The book is designed primarily as a teaching course, rather than as a work of reference or a systematic account of an area of mathematics. For this reason the material has been developed in a spiral manner: topics such as estimation, chi-squared probability, expectation and hypothesis testing are introduced early in the book, and then come back later for a deeper and more thorough treatment. This allows time for concepts to develop, and for relationships between concepts to be appreciated, before definitions and proofs are introduced. Teachers of more mature students who wish to bring forward the more theoretical aspects of the subject are, of course, at liberty to vary the order in which chapters are taken.

In planning and writing this book I have had invaluable support and advice from the Advisory Group set up by SMP: Jane Hamilton, Roger Pring, Colin Nye, Graham Howlett, Eric Door and Michael Dixon (who also read the text and checked many of the exercises in the final version). This group hammered out the shape of the book in a series of meetings, and contributed extensive and thoughtful comments in writing, often based on comments from students and discussions with colleagues. I am also much indebted to Peter Holmes, who read the first draft of the text and made many helpful suggestions. This first draft was duplicated and distributed by SMP to a number of schools, and I am especially grateful to the teachers and students who tried it out in the classroom and who reported their impressions with a friendly candour. Several of these teachers offered additional exercise material, which has found its way into the final version. In some exercises other questions have been reproduced from A-level examination papers: the School Mathematics Project wishes to thank the University of Cambridge Local Examinations Syndicate, the University of London School Examinations Board, and the Oxford and Cambridge Schools Examination Board (which provides examinations for both MEI and SMP) for permission to use examination questions in the text.

In addition to the sets of exercises, the text is interrupted from time to time with single questions, indicated by the letter "Q" and numbered consecutively through each chapter. The purpose of these is to give the student an opportunity to pause for thought about some point which has just been made in the text; it is an attempt to reproduce in print the give-and-take between teacher and student which is such an important feature of a good mathematics lesson. (Sadly, in the book the questioning is only one-way. We have yet to find how to simulate in print that equally important element, the questioning of the teacher by the student.) Students are urged to consider each of these questions as they appear in the text. Another feature of the exercise material is the recurrence of certain themes (for example, particular probability models) several times during the course. To avoid repeating ground which has been covered previously, students will find it helpful in such cases to keep their solutions for later reference. As a guide, the relevant questions are marked at the end, "(K)".

The SMP Further Mathematics series is the outcome of a long-standing and continuing partnership between the School Mathematics Project and the Cambridge University Press. It is difficult for an author to apportion his debt between project and publisher, and I am very conscious that without either partner this book would never have been contemplated, far less completed. It seems appropriate, therefore, to end these remarks with a reference to one individual who, more than any other, has symbolised and helped to cement this collaboration in recent years. So I would like to pay special tribute to John Hersee, formerly Executive Director of SMP, whose enthusiasm, energy and wisdom have been crucial in seeing this book through from an idea to a publication.

Douglas Quadling

1

Preliminaries

In this book it is assumed that you already know some of the basic ideas of probability and statistics. The purpose of this chapter is to collect together some of the definitions, results and notation which will be used later on. If any of them are completely new to you, it would be useful to refer back to some more elementary textbook and to do some of the examples in it. (Note 1.1)

This book also uses ideas from other branches of mathematics, especially calculus, algebra, and geometry of three dimensions using vectors. In the early chapters the knowledge you will need is quite elementary: differentiation of x^n, sigma notation and geometric progressions are typical topics. Later on you will want to know about certain more advanced topics, such as eigenvalues, multiple integrals, and reduction formulae for definite integrals. (Note 1.2)

1.1 MEAN, VARIANCE AND STANDARD DEVIATION

Suppose that, in carrying out a statistical survey, we make a certain measurement, or record a certain score, for each of n individuals. Some of the measurements may occur more than once – for example, if we are recording the age in years of 200 people on a railway platform, we shall not expect to get 200 different ages! Let us denote the number of different measurements by k. It is usual to choose a general capital letter, such as X, to describe the measurement (e.g. age) being made, and to attach suffixes $1, 2, 3, \ldots, k$ to the corresponding small letter to denote the k measurements which actually appear in the record. Thus the measurements will be called

$$x_1, x_2, x_3, \ldots, x_{k-1}, x_k.$$

The number of times that the particular value x_i comes up is called the *frequency* of x_i, and this is denoted by $f(x_i)$. This situation is illustrated in Fig. 1, where the height of each "stick" indicates the frequency of the measurement to which it corresponds. (To emphasize this, the sticks in this figure are shown split into unit segments, but usually they are shown as continuous lines.) Notice that the measurements are not necessarily listed in their current numerical order. (Note 1.3)

Q.1 Collect some statistical data of the form described above (e.g. the total number of goals scored in each game in last week's first division football matches). What are the values of n and k? Make a table of values of x_i, $f(x_i)$ for $i = 1$ to k for your data. (Keep your results to use in Q.3.)

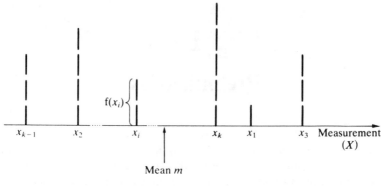

Figure 1

The sum of all the frequencies is, of course, the total number of individuals, that is n. We write this

$$n = \sum_{i=1}^{k} f(x_i).$$

This notation can now be used to write algebraic expressions for the commonest measures of the central position and the spread of the sample of measurements, the mean and the variance. The mean is found by adding the value of X for each of the n individuals, and dividing by n. However, in finding the sum, it is simpler to note that the measurement x_i will occur $f(x_i)$ times, so that altogether it contributes $x_i f(x_i)$ to the total. The *mean*, m, is therefore given by

$$m = \frac{1}{n} \sum_{i=1}^{k} x_i f(x_i).$$

In Fig. 1 the position of m has been indicated on the X-axis.

Q.2   Use the two equations just given to prove that

$$\sum_{i=1}^{k} (x_i - m)f(x_i) = 0.$$

Can you suggest a meaning for this equation?

In calculating the variance, each individual value of X contributes an amount $(X - m)^2$ to the sum (so that its contribution is always positive, whether the measurement is above or below the mean); that sum is then divided by n. But now the term $(x_i - m)^2$ occurs $f(x_i)$ times, contributing altogether $(x_i - m)^2 f(x_i)$ to the total. The *variance*, which is denoted by either v or S^2, is therefore given by

$$v = \frac{1}{n} \sum_{i=1}^{k} (x_i - m)^2 f(x_i).$$

The reason for having the alternative notation S^2 for the variance is that, since the frequency $f(x_i)$ is just a number, the quantity on the right has dimensions which are the square of the dimensions of x_i, and therefore of m. For example, if X is a measure of age in years, then

each x_i, and m, are in years; but
each $(x_i - m)^2$, and v, are in 'square years'.

In practice it is often more convenient to use a measure of spread which has the same dimensions as X and m. For this we define the *standard deviation*, S, by

$$S = \sqrt{v},$$

so that $v = S^2$. (But see the warning in Note 1.4!)

A very important result is that v can also be calculated as

$$v = \left\{ \frac{1}{n} \sum_{i=1}^{k} x_i^2 f(x_i) \right\} - m^2.$$

Q.3   Take the data you collected for Q.1, and use a calculator to find m. (It is convenient to store this in the "memory".) Then find v by means of each of the expressions given above in turn, checking that they give the same answer. Which of the two gives the simpler calculation?

To show that the two forms are equivalent, expand $(x_i - m)^2$ in the first expression for v, then separate the sum into three terms and use the equations for n and m given above.

Q.4   Do this for yourself!

If the measurements are taken from a value c rather than the origin, we get the equivalent but rather more general result

$$v = \left\{ \frac{1}{n} \sum_{i=1}^{k} (x_i - c)^2 f(x_i) \right\} - (m - c)^2.$$

Q.5   Prove this directly by expanding the expression on the right.

A quite different measure of central position is the *median*, which is defined so that just as many of the measurements lie above it as below it. If n, the number of individuals, is odd, then the median is just the measurement of the middle one when they are ranked in order of size. But if n is even, the median could be anywhere between the two middle measurements (if these are different); conventionally it is taken to be half-way between the two.

Q.6   How could it happen that the two middle measurements might *not* be different?

Exercise 1A

1   In a knock-out competition there are 32 competitors; half of the competitors remaining are eliminated in each round, so that in the fifth (final) round only two remain. Calculate the mean and variance of the numbers of rounds played by the individual competitors.   [SMP]

2   A university admissions officer interviews 30 candidates on Monday and 20 on Tuesday. On each day the mean length of all the interviews is exactly 15 minutes, but the standard deviations are 2 minutes on Monday and $2\frac{1}{2}$ minutes on Tuesday. Find the sums of the squares of the deviations from the mean on each day, and hence find the standard deviation for the two days taken together.   [SMP]

3   A test, in which the marks obtainable range from 0 to 100 inclusive, was sat by 30 boys who had been trained in such tests, and by 20 boys who had not. A summary of the results obtained is given in the table.

	Mean	Standard deviation
30 trained boys	62	10
20 untrained boys	52	12

Calculate the mean and the standard deviation of the combined set of 50 scores.

One of the boys was, in fact, ill during the test and scored only 1 mark. It was decided to exclude his result. Calculate the mean and standard deviation of the other 49 scores.   [London]

4   A weather recorder finds that during one September the mean minimum temperature is 9.2 °C, with standard deviation 1.5 °C. He wants to quote this information in a popular lecture, but would prefer to give the statistics in degrees Fahrenheit. Make the necessary calculations for him.

5   A history teacher gives a mark for a class test, described by the letter X. So that the marks can be compared with those for other subjects, she is required to scale her marks to a new mark Y by means of a formula $Y = a + bX$, where a and b are constants. The mean and standard deviation of the original marks are denoted by m_X and S_X, and those of the new marks by m_Y and S_Y. Write expressions for m_Y and S_Y as sums involving the values x_i, and deduce that

$$m_Y = a + bm_X, \quad S_Y = bS_X.$$

What values of a and b should she use if her original marks had mean 40 and standard deviation 5, but the scaled marks are to have mean 50 and standard deviation 15?

6   Write a computer program to input values of a particular measurement for any number of individuals and to print out the mean and variance. (K)

7   Explain why the variance can be described as the "mean of the squares of differences from m".

More generally, for any value p of the measurement in question, we can define a quantity q which is the mean of the squares of differences from p. Write an expression for q, using Σ notation, and show that

$$q = v + (p - m)^2.$$

Draw a graph to demonstrate how q varies with p. What is the minimum value of q, and for what value of p does it occur?

8 Instead of the quantity q in question 7, a quantity r can be defined as the mean of the *absolute* differences from p. (The absolute difference of x_i from p is $|x_i - p|$: that is, $x_i - p$ if $x_i \geqslant p$, and $p - x_i$ if $x_i < p$.) In a particular survey of 10 individuals the frequencies of the various results are as follows.

x_i	0	10	25	30
$f(x_i)$	1	4	3	2

Write expressions for r in terms of p, considering separately the cases $p < 0$, $0 \leqslant p < 10$, $10 \leqslant p < 25$, $25 \leqslant p < 30$, $p \geqslant 30$.

Draw a graph showing how r varies with p. What is the minimum value of r, and for what value(s) of p does it occur?

9 To investigate the situation in question 8 in general, suppose that the measurements x_i are arranged in ascending order of size, so that $x_1 < x_2 < \ldots < x_k$. Consider a value of p between x_u and x_{u+1}, and write an expression for the corresponding value of r. Show that in this interval the graph of r against p is a straight line, with gradient

$$\frac{1}{n}\left\{\sum_{i=1}^{u} f(x_i) - \sum_{i=u+1}^{k} f(x_i)\right\}.$$

What are the equivalent results when $p < x_1$ and when $p > x_k$?

Explain why r has its smallest value when p is at the median of the sample of measurements.

1.2 PROBABILITY

The theory of probability is usually regarded as having its origins in a correspondence between the French mathematicians Pascal and Fermat from June to October 1654 about the appropriate way of dividing the stakes in an unfinished game of dice. (Note 1.5) In the following century we find it being applied in more serious studies such as astronomy and political science.

The basic principle is that if some particular outcome of an experiment is denoted by the symbol C, then we can associate with this outcome a number between 0 and 1 called its *probability*, which is denoted by P(C). (Note 1.6) There are two main ways of finding probabilities:

(a) *Empirically*, based on past experience. Suppose that the experiment has been performed previously on a large number of occasions, say n times, and that the outcome C occurred with frequency F(C). Then the probability is taken to be equal to the *relative frequency* F(C)/n.

(b) *Theoretically*, by appealing to symmetry. If all the possible outcomes of the experiment can be broken down into a list of k exclusive "primitive outcomes" (such as the scores 1, 2, 3, 4, 5, 6 on a die, or heads and tails when a coin is tossed), and if it is reasonable to expect that each of them is "equally likely" to turn up, then the probability of each is taken to be $1/k$.

Q.7 Consider an experiment in which a pair of dice is rolled and the two scores recorded. Carry it out 20 times. If A denotes the outcome "at least one of the dice shows 6" and B denotes "both dice show the same score", estimate P(A) and P(B) empirically. (K)

Q.8 Suggest an appropriate set of primitive outcomes for the experiment in Q.7.

The word "exclusive" which appears in (b) means that no two of the primitive outcomes can result from the experiment on the same occasion. It can also be used in relation to any set of outcomes, primitive or not. For example, in the situation of Q.7, the outcomes "both dice show the same score" and "the sum of the scores is an odd number" are exclusive (since, if x is any score, $x + x$ is even). But the outcomes A and B in Q.7 are not exclusive: if a double-6 is rolled, then A and B occur simultaneously.

   Now the probability associated with an outcome which cannot occur is zero. It follows that, for two general outcomes A, B in any experiment,

$$\text{A, B are exclusive} \Rightarrow P(\text{A and B}) = 0.$$

   The term "A or B" is used to describe the possibility that either A or B (or both) occurs. An important law in probability theory is that

$$P(\text{A or B}) = P(\text{A}) + P(\text{B}) - P(\text{A and B}).$$

Q.9 From the results you obtained in Q.7, estimate P(A or B) and P(A and B) empirically, and verify this last equation using your answers.

Q.10 For general outcomes A, B of any experiment, use a Venn diagram to show that

$$F(\text{A or B}) = F(\text{A}) + F(\text{B}) - F(\text{A and B}).$$

From this establish the corresponding law for probabilities.

Putting the two statements together, it follows that

$$\text{A, B are exclusive} \Rightarrow P(\text{A or B}) = P(\text{A}) + P(\text{B}).$$

This is called the *addition law for probabilities*.
   With the aid of this law the theoretical definition of probability given in (b) can be generalised. If the outcome C is associated with r of the k primitive outcomes, then the law gives

$$P(C) = \underbrace{\frac{1}{k} + \frac{1}{k} + \frac{1}{k} + \ldots + \frac{1}{k}}_{r \text{ times}} = \frac{r}{k}.$$

So

$$\text{Probability of outcome C} = \frac{\text{number of primitive outcomes associated with C}}{\text{total number of primitive outcomes}}.$$

Q.11 Use this to find the theoretical probabilities P(A), P(B), P(A and B), P(A or B) for the situation in Q.7. On what assumption about the dice are these based? (K)

The probability associated with an outcome which is certain to occur is 1. This means that, if $\sim$A denotes the negative of the outcome A (usually read as "not-A"), then P(A or $\sim$A) = 1. Since A and $\sim$A are clearly exclusive, replacing B by $\sim$A in the statement of the addition law gives, for any outcome A,

$$P(A) + P(\sim A) = 1.$$

A more general result may be found by replacing A and B by "A and B" and "A and $\sim$B" in the addition law. You need to check that "A and B" and "A and $\sim$B" are necessarily exclusive; it then follows that, for any two outcomes A and B

$$P(A \text{ and } B) + P(A \text{ and } \sim B) = P(A).$$

Q.12 Write out this argument in full.

1.3 CONDITIONAL PROBABILITY AND STATISTICAL INDEPENDENCE

If we do not record the outcome ("A" or "not-A", as the case may be) every time the experiment is carried out, but only on those occasions when some other outcome B also occurs, then we may arrive at a different estimate of the probability of A. This is called the *conditional probability of A given B*, and denoted by $P(A \mid B)$.

Suppose, for example, that a team of market researchers is trying to find out how many men use aftershave. It may be that over the whole survey 30% of the men answer "yes", but of those asked by Brenda the proportion is 40%. Then if A denotes "the victim says he uses aftershave", and B denotes "Brenda is the interviewer", then one would estimate that P(A) = 0.3 but $P(A \mid B) = 0.4$.

If probabilities are being found by the relative frequency method, the number of occasions on which the result of the experiment is recorded is then reduced to F(B); and of these the outcome A is recorded when the combined outcome "A and B" occurs. So the conditional probability $P(A \mid B)$ would be evaluated as

$$\frac{F(A \text{ and } B)}{F(B)}.$$

Now this is equal to

$$\frac{F(A \text{ and } B)/n}{F(B)/n},$$

which suggests that the conditional probability should be defined by the equation

$$P(A \mid B) = \frac{P(A \text{ and } B)}{P(B)}.$$

A useful way of representing this is a *tree diagram* such as Fig. 2. (It is convenient to draw the tree growing out sideways!) The upper branch indicates the occasions on which the outcome B occurs; from this grow two twigs, according as A does or does not occur. So the route shown by the thick lines in Fig. 2 shows the combined outcome "A and B".

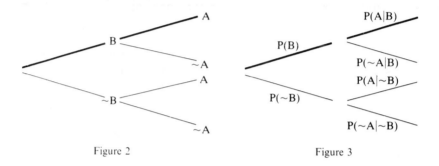

Figure 2   Figure 3

Now with each branch and twig is associated a probability, as shown in Fig. 3. The equation (rearranged from the definition above)

$$P(A \text{ and } B) = P(A \mid B) \times P(B)$$

then shows that the probability associated with the "thick" route in Fig. 2 is found by multiplying the probabilities associated with the branch and twig along that route in Fig. 3.

Q.13 Write down the equations of this form associated with the other three routes through the tree diagram.

Q.14 For the experiment you carried out in Q.7, calculate the conditional probabilities $P(A \mid B)$, $P(\sim A \mid B)$, $P(A \mid \sim B)$, $P(\sim A \mid \sim B)$, and draw the appropriate tree diagram.

Q.15 Repeat Q.14 using probabilities calculated from the theoretical definition (see Q.11).

Using two such equations, the law stated at the end of §1.2 can be written in the form

$$P(A) = P(A \mid B) \times P(B) + P(A \mid \sim B) \times P(\sim B).$$

Notice how this equation can be read off from the two routes ending in the outcome "A" in Fig. 2, using the probabilities shown in Fig. 3.

Q.16 Suppose that $B_1, B_2, B_3, \ldots$ is a set of exclusive and exhaustive outcomes of an experiment, and that A is some other possible outcome. Prove that
$P(A) = \Sigma\ P(A\,|\,B_i) \times P(B_i)$.

An important special case arises when $P(A\,|\,B)$ is equal to $P(A\,|\sim B)$. The outcome A is then said to be *statistically independent* of B, and both these conditional probabilities are then equal to $P(A)$. From this it follows that, if A is independent of B, then

$$P(A \text{ and } B) = P(A) \times P(B).$$

This is often called the *multiplication law for probabilities.*

It can be proved, by combining several of the laws given previously, that the converse is also true: that is, if $P(A \text{ and } B) = P(A) \times P(B)$, then $P(A\,|\,B) = P(A\,|\sim B)$. And in this case, by the symmetry of the condition, it must also follow that $P(B\,|\,A) = P(B\,|\sim A)$. Putting all this together leads to the important deduction

A is statistically independent of B

$\Rightarrow P(A \text{ and } B) = P(A) \times P(B)$

$\Rightarrow P(B \text{ and } A) = P(B) \times P(A)$

$\Rightarrow$ B is statistically independent of A.

This justifies the use of the alternative wording

"A and B are statistically independent".

Q.17 Construct proofs of the statements that (*a*) if $P(A\,|\,B) = P(A\,|\sim B)$, then both are equal to $P(A)$; (*b*) $P(A \text{ and } B) = P(A) \times P(B) \Rightarrow P(A\,|\,B) = P(A\,|\sim B)$.

Exercise 1B

1 Three dice are to be rolled. Find the probability of scoring a double but not a triple.
[London]

2 At a fête the vicar has a board in the shape of a circle having sectors coloured red and green, with an arrow which can be spun above it: you have to try to guess the colour on which the arrow will rest when it is next spun. It is made so that the results of successive spins are independent, and

P(the arrow rests on red) = 0.6.

Find the probability of guessing correctly
(*a*) if you always guess "green";
(*b*) if you toss a fair coin and guess "green" if it comes down "head" and "red" otherwise;
(*c*) if your guess is always the colour the arrow is resting on before the spin.
[SMP]

3 *The Daily Telegraph* carried a story about a couple who had three pairs of twins, describing this as a "512,000 to 1 chance". It was stated that the probability of twins in the population is 1 in 80, but that a couple who had had twins already were ten times as likely to have them again. Comment.

4 A sociologist wants to find out about children's smoking habits, but to protect them from having to incriminate themselves. So he asks them "Have you smoked during the last month?", but tells them before they answer to draw a card from a pack: if it is a picture card they should tell the truth, if it is a number they should lie. If the probability that a child selected at random is a smoker is s, what is the probability that he will answer "yes"?

5 A man has, by accident, mixed up two dud torch batteries with three new batteries of identical type. With a voltmeter he tests one battery after another until the two dud batteries are found. With the aid of a tree diagram, find the probability that he will have to test (*a*) 2 batteries, (*b*) 3 batteries, in order to be able to identify which two batteries are the dud ones.   [London]

6 An aircraft company identifies four possible sources of failure which may cause an aircraft to crash, and assigns to them the probabilities p_1, p_2, p_3, p_4. The probability that an aircraft will be at risk on a particular flight is then taken to be $p_1 + p_2 + p_3 + p_4$. Explain why this is not correct, but is an acceptable approximation.

7 The events A and B are such that $P(A) = 0.4$, $P(B) = 0.45$, $P(A \text{ or } B) = 0.68$. Show that the events A and B are neither mutually exclusive nor independent. [London]

8 Events A and C are independent. Probabilities relating to events A, B and C are as follows: $P(A) = \frac{1}{5}$, $P(B) = \frac{1}{6}$, $P(A \text{ and } C) = \frac{1}{20}$, $P(B \text{ or } C) = \frac{3}{8}$. Evaluate $P(C)$ and show that events B and C are independent.   [London]

9 A group of children takes examinations in Mathematics and English. The proportions passing are respectively 80% and 70%, while 10% fail both examinations. Find the probabilities that (*a*) a child passes both examinations; (*b*) a child who passes in Mathematics also passes in English.   [MEI]

10 The probability that a blue-eyed person is left-handed is $\frac{1}{7}$. The probability that a left-handed person is blue-eyed is $\frac{1}{3}$. The probability that a person has neither of these attributes is $\frac{4}{5}$. What is the probability that a person has both?   [SMP]

11 In a routine test for early warning of an unsuspected disease, 8% of those tested react (but do not all have the disease) while 7% in fact have the disease (but do not all react). The probability that a person neither has the disease nor reacts is 0.9. What is the probability that a person with the disease will be detected?

12 A bag contains 12 red balls, 8 blue balls and 4 white balls. Three balls are taken from the bag at random and without replacement. Find the probability that all three balls are of the same colour.
   Find also the probability that all three balls are of different colours.   [London]

13 Sampling of one object at a time with replacement is being carried out from a batch of N objects. Assuming that the selection is at random, find the probability that all of the first M objects sampled ($M \leqslant N$) are different. Deduce the probability that there is at least one 'repeat' among the first M objects, and show that the probability that the first 'repeat' occurs on the Kth drawing is

$$\frac{(N-1)!\,(K-1)}{N^{K-1}(N-K+1)!} \quad \text{for } 2 \leqslant K \leqslant N.$$

[MEI]

14 In a sequence of four digits, each digit is selected randomly (with equal probabilities) from the set $\{0, 1, 2, 3, 4, 5, 6, 7, 8, 9\}$. Calculate the probabilities that this process results in (a) four different digits, (b) three different digits (one occurring twice, the others once), (c) two different digits each occurring twice, (d) two different digits one occurring three times and the other once, (e) one digit occurring four times. (K)

15 Three golfers A, B, C take turns at sinking a 2 m putt with A starting. If A misses, the ball is replaced and B tries, and so on. If all three miss, A starts the cycle again. The winner is the first to sink the putt. Assuming that the probabilities that A, B, C sink any one putt are $\frac{1}{3}, \frac{2}{3}, \frac{2}{3}$ respectively, find for each player the probability that he wins.
[MEI]

16 Past experience shows that when a man A throws a dart at a dart-board the probability that he scores a bull is $\frac{1}{4}$. For men B, C, D the corresponding probabilities are $\frac{1}{3}, \frac{1}{2}$ and $\frac{3}{4}$ respectively. A game consists of the four men A, B, C, D in this order throwing a dart in turn, and the winner is the first person to score a bull. When all four throws are unsuccessful the procedure is repeated continuously until a bull is scored. Show that the probability that A wins is $\frac{4}{15}$. Find the probability of winning for the other three players.

Find the probabilities of each man winning if the probabilities of A, B, C, D scoring a bull are $\frac{1}{4}, \frac{1}{3}, \frac{1}{2}$, 1 respectively. [London]

17 Let a_n be the probability that in n tosses of a fair coin no run of two consecutive heads appears. Show that, for $n \geqslant 2$,

$$a_n = \tfrac{1}{2}a_{n-1} + \tfrac{1}{4}a_{n-2}.$$

Find the value of a_5. [SMP]

18 You are declarer in a hand of bridge, and can see that you and your partner (dummy) have 9 out of the 13 trumps between you. Before play begins, assess the probabilities that your opponents' trumps are split (a) evenly, (b) three–one or one–three, (c) four–zero or zero–four. (K)

1.4 INVERSE PROBABILITY AND BAYES' THEOREM

This topic is most easily introduced by an example.

Imagine that a pupil is taking a multiple-choice test in which five possible answers are given for each question, only one of which is correct. Past experience suggests that he works out two-fifths of the questions, on which he has a probability of 0.75 of selecting the right answer; the other three-fifths of the test he chooses an answer at random.

His teacher notices that he gets the question on ratio correct, and wonders "Did he work it out, or was it a lucky guess?" How should she assign probabilities to these two possibilities?

In this example we have two outcomes to deal with, which can be denoted by A and B (with their negatives $\sim$A and $\sim$B):

A: He works it out. $\qquad\qquad$ $\sim$A: He guesses.

B: He gets it right. $\qquad\qquad$ $\sim$B: He gets it wrong.

What the *teacher* knows is B, and she is interested on that basis in assigning a probability to A. So her problem is to find the conditional probability $P(A | B)$; and the definition gives us

$$P(A | B) = \frac{P(A \text{ and } B)}{P(B)}.$$

But it is more natural for us to think of this situation the other way round: the probability of getting it right depends on whether he works it out or guesses. The evidence of past experience suggests the probabilities

$P(A) = 0.4$, so that $P(\sim A) = 0.6$;

$P(B | A) = 0.75$;

$P(B | \sim A) = 0.2$ (since if he guesses all five answers are equally likely).

These are shown in Fig. 4 as a tree diagram.

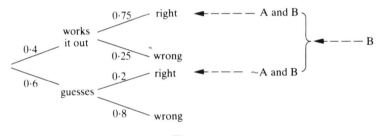

Figure 4

From this it is easy to deal with "A and B", by taking the upper branch and twig, and using

$$P(A \text{ and } B) = P(B | A) \times P(A) = 0.75 \times 0.4 = 0.3.$$

The outcome B is rather more complicated, since it comes from two separate routes through the diagram: "A and B", and "not-A and B". But these are exclusive –

Q.18   Why?

– so we can use the addition rule to calculate

$$P(B) = P(A \text{ and } B) + P(\sim A \text{ and } B)$$

$$= P(B | A) \times P(A) + P(B | \sim A) \times P(\sim A)$$

$$= 0.75 \times 0.4 + 0.2 \times 0.6 = 0.3 + 0.12 = 0.42.$$

The teacher now has all the information she needs, and can find the probability

$$P(A | B) = \frac{P(A \text{ and } B)}{P(B)} = \frac{0.3}{0.42} = 0.71 \left(\text{or } \frac{5}{7} \right).$$

Q.19 Find $P(\sim A | B)$ by a similar argument, and check that $P(A|B) + P(\sim A|B) = 1$.

Q.20 Go through the argument again on the basis that the pupil gets the question wrong, and find $P(A | \sim B)$ and $P(\sim A | \sim B)$.

Q.21 Use the answers to Q.19 and Q.20 to draw a tree diagram for this situation with B on the left and A on the right.

If we now drop the numerical data special to this example, it is easy to see that the calculation actually carried out was

$$P(A|B) = \frac{P(A \text{ and } B)}{P(B)} = \frac{P(B|A) \times P(A)}{P(B|A) \times P(A) + P(B|\sim A) \times P(\sim A)}.$$

This result can be applied to a whole class of problems, and it is known as *Bayes' theorem*. Thomas Bayes, an English philosopher, first gave it in a paper which was published by the Royal Society in 1763, two years after his death. One modern author has suggested that his theorem "is to the theory of probability what Pythagoras's theorem is to geometry". (Note 1.7)

Q.22 Verify Bayes' theorem for the experiment in Q.7, using (*a*) the empirical probabilities, (*b*) the theoretical probabilities.

We have to be careful, though, about the language we use when applying this theorem. It is wrong to refer to $P(A)$ as "the probability that the pupil worked the ratio question out" – for either he *did* work it out (in which case the probability is 1) or he guessed (in which case the probability is 0). But of course the teacher does not know which; and the problem is about her assessment of the probabilities based on the evidence available. What can be said is that, if we consider all the occasions on which the pupil gets the right answer, then in the long run he will have worked it out on $\frac{5}{7}$ of the times, and guessed on $\frac{2}{7}$. So, if the teacher selects one of the correct answers at random, the probability that the pupil worked it out is $\frac{5}{7}$. If she was a betting person, then she might be prepared to stake odds of "5 to 2 on" that the ratio question was worked out.

Exercise 1C

1 It is estimated that one-quarter of the drivers on the road between 11 p.m. and midnight have been drinking during the evening. If a driver has not been drinking, the probability that he will have an accident at that time of night is 0.004 %; if he has been drinking, the probability of an accident goes up to 0.02 %. What is the probability that a car selected at random at that time of night will have an accident?

   A policeman on the beat at 11.30 p.m. sees a car run into a lamp-post, and jumps to the conclusion that the driver has been drinking. What is the probability that he is right? [SMP]

2 The only bus routes that stop at a certain bus stop are numbers 10 and 25. The probability that the first bus to arrive at the stop is a number 10 is 0.6. Given that

30 % of all buses on the number 10 route are double-deckers while 50 % of the buses on the number 25 route are double-deckers, calculate the probability that

(*a*) a double-decker arrives first,

(*b*) if a double-decker arrives first, it will be a number 10 bus.   [London]

3   An automated engineering process for manufacturing components includes an automatic screening of the output to reject defective components. The process gives on average 5 % of defectives. The probability that the screening stage identifies correctly a defective component is 98 % but there is also a probability of 6 % that a component which is not defective is rejected at the screening stage. What is the proportion of all components which is rejected and what is the proportion of all components passed from the screening stage which is still defective?   [MEI]

4   Two dice are thrown. In each throw for which the total score is 6 or less, Alan attempts a given task. Otherwise the task is attempted by Brian. For each attempt at this task, the independent probabilities of success by Alan and Brian are 0.90 and 0.95 respectively.

(*a*) Find the probability that the first attempt at this task will fail.

(*b*) Given that an attempt did fail, find the probability that it was Alan who was making the attempt.

(*c*) Given that an attempt was successful, find the probability that it was Brian who was making the attempt.   [London]

5   The results of an experiment can be analysed according to one criterion into outcomes $A_1, A_2, \ldots, A_m$; according to another criterion they can be analysed into outcomes $B_1, B_2, \ldots, B_n$. Generalise Bayes' theorem so as to express $P(A_r | B_s)$ in terms of probabilities of the form $P(A_i)$ and conditional probabilities of the form $P(B_j | A_k)$.

2

Some probability models

A key idea whenever mathematics is used to investigate real life problems is that of a "mathematical model": that is, a theoretical piece of mathematics (such as a function, an equation or a matrix) which describes the actual situation closely enough to lead to useful predictions. (Note 2.1) In statistics this often takes the form of a "probability model", and this is a notion which will run right through this book. This chapter introduces some typical probability models: first in some semi-real life contexts such as dealing cards and rolling dice, and then in more important practical contexts.

2.1 A MODEL FOR CARD SUITS

Probability is not a subject to learn just by sitting at a table and thinking. To understand it fully, you need to do some experiments; and the author of this book hopes that, when an experiment is described, you will do it for yourself – either on your own or as a class. For the first experiment you need an ordinary pack of playing cards (without the "joker").

Deal one card, and note its suit (C, D, H or S). I dealt the jack of clubs, and therefore recorded

C.

When you do the experiment, you may get the same result or a different one; neither would be in the least surprising, and there is nothing of interest to say about it.

Suppose, however, that the experiment is repeated a large number of times (shuffling before each new deal). My results for 40 such deals were

HDSHH DDDHD SCHCH SHCHC SDDHS HSSDS CSSCH DCSDC.

When the fifth diamond came up in the first ten deals, and no clubs, I began to be suspicious, and checked the pack in case it had been "fixed". But these oddities were soon ironed out, as can be seen by making a table of the frequencies of the various suits after 5, 10, 15, ... deals:

Number of deals		5	10	15	20	25	30	35	40
	C	0	0	2	4	4	4	6	8
	D	1	5	5	5	7	8	8	10
Frequency of	H	3	4	6	8	9	10	11	11
	S	1	1	2	3	5	8	10	11

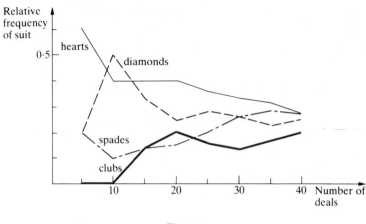

Figure 1

These frequencies have been converted into proportions, or relative frequencies, to give the graphs in Fig. 1.

Q.1   Draw a similar set of graphs for your own results. In what ways are they similar to mine, and in what ways do they differ?

The graphs illustrate a familiar situation in probability: that as the number of deals increases, the relative frequencies of the various suits get close to the theoretical probabilities –

Suit	C	D	H	S
Probability	0.25	0.25	0.25	0.25

– which we would assign in this experiment on the assumption that each suit outcome is equally likely. This table, illustrated in Fig. 2 by a "stick graph", describes what we call the *probability model* for the experiment. By this we mean

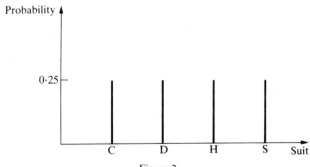

Figure 2

a function which associates a probability with each of a set of exclusive outcomes of the experiment.

Note that in the model the sum of all the probabilities is 1. This is an important check which applies to any probability model.

2.2 NEW MODELS FROM OLD

The purpose of this section is to show that we can use the laws of probability to find probability models for more complicated experiments.

With the same pack of cards, deal out two cards at a time and record the suits. In my experiment the first 50 results were

[SS] [CD] [SS] [CD] [HS]   [DD] [CS] [CH] [CD] [DD]
[CD] [DH] [HS] [CH] [CD]   [DS] [CH] [CH] [HS] [CH]
[DH] [DD] [DD] [HS] [DH]   [CD] [CC] [DH] [DS] [CD]
[HS] [SS] [HH] [CS] [CH]   [CH] [SS] [DH] [DH] [CS]
[CS] [CC] [CH] [SS] [DS]   [CS] [CS] [CH] [CS] [CD].

(Note that we have not recorded the order in which the two cards were dealt, but only the suits in the pair.) This gives these relative frequencies for the various possibilities:

[CC] [DD] [HH] [SS] [CD] [CH] [CS] [DH] [DS] [HS]
0.04 0.08 0.02 0.10 0.16 0.18 0.14 0.12 0.06 0.10

How do these compare with the theoretical probability model for the experiment? Is it true, as the results seem to indicate, that pairs with two different suits are more common than pairs with two cards of the same suit? To answer this, we need to calculate the theoretical probabilities of the various deals. One way of doing this is to imagine the cards to be dealt one at a time. The probabilities for the second card are then conditional probabilities (see §1.3) which depend on the suit of the first card. Suppose, for example, that the first card is a spade: then the second card is dealt from a pack consisting of 13 clubs, 13 diamonds and 13 hearts, but only 12 spades. It seems reasonable, generalising the previous probability model, that the probabilities of dealing cards of various suits from such a pack are proportional to these numbers, and are therefore $\frac{13}{51}$, $\frac{13}{51}$, $\frac{13}{51}$ and $\frac{12}{51}$ respectively. On this basis we calculate

$$\text{Probability of [SS]}$$
$$= P(\text{S first and S second})$$
$$= P(\text{S first}) \times P(\text{S second} \mid \text{S first})$$
$$= \tfrac{1}{4} \times \tfrac{12}{51} = \tfrac{1}{17} \approx 0.06.$$

For the combination [HS] we have to remember that the result can come in either of two mutually exclusive ways: S first and then H, or H first and then S.

So

Probability of [HS]

= P(S first and H second) + P(H first and S second)

= P(S first) × P(H second | S first) + P(H first) × P(S second | H first)

= $\frac{1}{4} \times \frac{13}{51} + \frac{1}{4} \times \frac{13}{51} = \frac{13}{102} \approx 0.13$.

Calculations of the other probabilities are obviously exactly similar, and it follows that the probability model for this experiment is:

[CC]	[DD]	[HH]	[SS]	[CD]	[CH]	[CS]	[DH]	[DS]	[HS]
0.06	0.06	0.06	0.06	0.13	0.13	0.13	0.13	0.13	0.13

(Check: do the probabilities sum to 1?)

It looks as if agreement with the experimental relative frequencies is quite good, considering that these were based on only 50 deals. If you are working in a group and each of you has done the experiment, then by pooling your results it would be possible to calculate relative frequencies for a larger sample; are these closer to the probabilities in the model?

Exercise 2A

1 The 'two-card deal' described in §2.2 could be varied by choosing to record the outcomes of the experiment in different ways. Give the probability models if the outcomes in which we are interested are
   (a) whether the two cards are of the same suits or different suits;
   (b) whether the cards are "two red", "one of each colour", or "two black".
   In each case compare the theoretical probabilities with the relative frequencies in the experiment.

2 Suppose that three cards are dealt from a standard pack. Make a list of all the possible combinations of suits, and calculate the probabilities for each of these possibilities. Deduce the probability models if the outcomes in which we are interested are
   (a) whether the cards are "all the same suit", "two of the same suit and one of another", "all different suits";
   (b) whether the cards are "three red", "two red and one black", "one red and two black", "three black".

3 In the single card experiment it was noticed that five diamonds came up in the first ten deals, but no clubs.
   (a) Calculate the probability that there would be no clubs in the first ten deals of a single card.
   (b) The five diamonds occurred in the pattern nDnnnDDDnD, where n stands for a non-diamond. Calculate the probability of this pattern of results. Given that there are 252 ways of arranging five n and five D in a row, deduce the probability of dealing a diamond five times in 10 deals.
   Are the answers to either (a) or (b) so small as to justify suspicions that the pack had been 'fixed'?

4 A committee consisting of 4 men and 6 women has to select a sub-committee. If the selection is made at random, investigate the probability model for the sex distribution of the sub-committee if this has (a) two members, (b) three members, (c) four members, (d) five members.

5 Five ball-point pens in a box of twenty were dud. Three pens were chosen at random from the box. Find the probability model for the number of dud pens picked.

Take a suitable set of twenty cards to represent the pens and use them to 'choose three pens' repeatedly. Draw a diagram of your results similar to Fig. 1. How do these compare with the probability model?

2.3 A MODEL FOR ROLLING DICE

Suppose that, instead of dealing two cards from a pack, we roll two dice. How will the probability models differ?

We cannot, of course, talk about "*the* probability model" for rolling a pair of dice until we have specified how the outcome is going to be recorded. There are various ways of doing this.

First, suppose that the two dice look exactly the same. Then we would probably record the result simply as "a 4 and a 5", "a double 6", and so on, very much as we did with the cards. Let us use a similar notation too, and denote these results by [45], [66], etc.

Q.2 Make a list of all the possible outcomes in this form. (Note that "a 4 and a 5" is no different from "a 5 and a 4", so we do not need both [45] and [54]. It is a good idea to fix on a definite order, such as 'smaller score first'.) Do all these outcomes have the same probability?

On the other hand, if the dice have different colours (black and white, say), so that we can distinguish between them, it may be better to record the outcome as an *ordered* pair "4 on the black, 5 on the white". This result could be denoted by (4, 5) – using a convention that the black score is written before the white one – and in this case (4, 5) and (5, 4) would represent different outcomes.

Q.3 Make a list of all the possible outcomes in this form. Do they all have the same probability?

Another way in which this could happen is by rolling just a single die twice. (Note 2.2) Then (4, 5) might stand for "4 on the first roll, 5 on the second". But there is a crucial difference between this and dealing two cards from a pack one after another. We saw in the previous section that the probability that the second card is a spade is $\frac{12}{51}$ if the first card was a spade, but $\frac{13}{51}$ if the first card was a club, diamond or heart. This is because the second card was dealt without putting the first card back in the pack: we call this *sampling without replacement*. When rolling the die, however, the probability of getting 5 on the second throw is the same whatever the result of the first throw, and is always equal to $\frac{1}{6}$. That is to say, the two scores recorded in the ordered pair are independent of each other, and we are therefore justified in applying the product law of probabilities:

the probability of rolling (4, 5)

is equal to

P(4 on the first roll) × P(5 on the second roll);

or, in the case of two distinguishable dice, it is

P(4 on the black) × P(5 on the white).

Q.4   What are the probabilities of getting the results (4, 5) and (6, 6)? What are the probabilities of getting [45] and [66] with the first method of recording?

The ordered pair notation for the scores on the black and white dice suggests an obvious graphical representation, taking the scores as coordinates as in Fig. 3. The 36 crosses represent the complete set of possible outcomes of the experiment, which we call the "possibility space"; and each of these outcomes has the same probability.

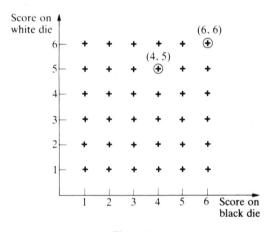

Figure 3

Yet another method of recording the result of rolling two dice is used in many games, and this is simply to count the total number of pips showing: so that instead of recording "a 4 and a 5" one simply records "9". In this case the possibility space is just the set of whole numbers from 2 to 12; but these outcomes certainly do not have the same probabilities. (Note 2.3)

If we think of all the ordered pairs which give a particular total – for example, (3, 6), (4, 5), (5, 4) and (6, 3) all give 9 – then on Fig. 3 these all lie on a line at 45° to the axes, and each cross on that line contributes $\frac{1}{36}$ to the probability of that total. This suggests a nice way of showing the graph for the probability model of the totals. In Fig. 4, Fig. 3 has been tilted through 45° so that the lines of

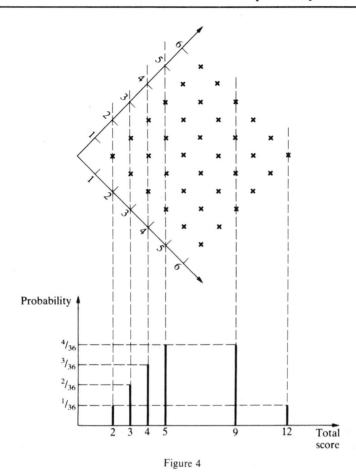

Figure 4

constant total become vertical, and the heights of the probability 'sticks' are just $\frac{1}{36}$ times the number of crosses on the corresponding verticals.

Q.5   Complete Fig. 4 for yourself, and check that the probabilities sum to 1.

The point made in this section is that a particular experiment may give rise to a number of different probability models, according to the outcomes we choose to record. The essential feature of any model is that, with each of the outcomes, a probability is defined; that is, we have a function which maps the outcomes (elements of the possibility space) to their probabilities (numbers between 0 and 1).

> A complete set of mutually exclusive outcomes of an experiment is called a *possibility space* for the experiment. The *probability model* corresponding to a given possibility space is a function which maps each outcome to its probability.

Exercise 2B

1   Roll a pair of dice 100 times (or more, if you are working in a class) and record the frequencies of the various outcomes in each of the ways described in the preceding section. Compare the relative frequencies with the probabilities given by the corresponding probability model. (K)

2   If X and Y denote the scores on two (distinguishable) dice, give the probability models if the outcomes recorded are (a) $X - Y$; (b) $|X - Y|$; (c) XY; (d) the greater of X and Y; (e) the number of sixes.

3   If X, Y and Z denote the scores on three dice, describe the possibility spaces if the outcomes recorded are (a) $X + Y + Z$; (b) the greatest of X, Y and Z; (c) the number of sixes.
   Find the corresponding probability models. (It may help to use a cubical array of $6 \times 6 \times 6$ dots to represent the set of primitive outcomes.)

4   In a set of dominoes there is only one "4 and 5" and only one "double 6", and similarly for all the other combinations of numbers 0 (blank), 1, 2, 3, 4, 5, 6.
   (a) How many different dominoes are there in a set?
   (b) If a domino is selected at random, find the probability model for the total number of spots on it.

5   If $C_1, C_2, \ldots, C_n$ is the possibility space for an experiment, what is the value of
   $$\sum_{i=1}^{n} P(C_i)?$$
   A spinner comes up with scores of $1, 2, \ldots, n$ with equal probabilities. If it is spun twice and the scores added, give the probability model for the sum of the scores. Show how this exhibits the algebraic result
   $$1 + 2 + 3 + \ldots + (n-1) + n + (n-1) + \ldots + 3 + 2 + 1 = n^2.$$

6   A spinner comes up with scores of 0, 1, 2 with probabilities $\frac{1}{6}, \frac{1}{3}, \frac{1}{2}$ respectively. Give probability models for the product of the scores on (a) two spins; (b) three spins.

7   A bag contains nine counters. Four are marked with the number 1, three with the number 2 and two with the number 4.
   (a) Two counters are taken out of the bag and the total of the numbers on them is noted. Give the probability model for this total.
   (b) One of the nine counters is taken out of the bag, its number noted and the counter is then replaced in the bag. This process is repeated. Give the probability model for the total of the two numbers noted.

2.4 PROBABILITY MODELS IN REAL LIFE

So far this chapter might have given the impression that probability theory is just about cards and dice. But although the subject originated in games of chance, its importance in the modern world lies in fields such as insurance, social planning, marketing and agriculture.

   For example, how many fire engines can a particular town manage with? With a fire engine costing perhaps £100 000 and a crew thousands of pounds a week – but with the potential cost of a fire running into millions – this is clearly a question to which a local authority doesn't want to get the wrong answer. But it is not a question that can be settled in absolute terms: fire calls occur in a random fashion, and they may take anything from half an hour to several hours to deal with. To reach a decision, we have to talk in terms of probabilities.

First, how do calls come in? The best way to find out is to keep a record of what actually happens over a period of, say, a month. This could be done by splitting each day into 24 intervals of an hour and noting the number of calls which come in during each hour requiring the despatch of a fire engine. Suppose that the month of December – a bad one for fires – produces the following statistics:

Number of calls per hour	0	1	2	3	4	5	*Total*
Number of one-hour intervals	240	253	157	71	20	3	744
							($=31 \times 24$)

Q.6   How many calls come in altogether during the month? What is the mean number of calls per hour?

Now what we need is a working probability model for this situation. The best we can do, in the absence of a theory, is to find this empirically: that is, to calculate the relative frequencies for these different numbers of calls, by dividing the frequencies by 744, and to use these as estimates of the probabilities. You can easily check that these relative frequencies are

$$0.3226, \quad 0.3401, \quad 0.2110, \quad 0.0954, \quad 0.0269, \quad 0.0040$$

(and that these add up to 1.0000). Since the probabilities are merely estimates, it would be unrealistic to retain so many decimal places in the model – this would suggest an accuracy quite unjustified by the evidence. So a reasonable probability model might be:

Number of calls per hour	0	1	2	3	4	*Total*
Probability	0.32	0.34	0.21	0.10	0.03	1.00

This information is not enough by itself to reach a decision about the provision of fire engines. For this we also need to know how long a fire engine spends out on a call; and this too is a question of probabilities. To estimate these, we need to monitor each of the 875 calls during the month and keep a record of the length of time that the fire engine and its crew are away.

There is no need to do this to the nearest minute – after all, a crew needs time to recuperate when it gets back from a call – so it should be good enough to list the possibility space in terms of half-hour blocks of time as follows:

Number of hours away	$\frac{1}{2}$ to 1	1 to $1\frac{1}{2}$	$1\frac{1}{2}$ to 2	2 to $2\frac{1}{2}$	$2\frac{1}{2}$ to 3	3 to $3\frac{1}{2}$	$3\frac{1}{2}$ to 4	4 to $4\frac{1}{2}$
Number of calls	69	167	222	181	125	69	28	14

Again these can be turned into relative frequencies (by division by 875), and approximated to give estimates of the probabilities. It is left to you to check that the result is the model:

Number of hours away	$\frac{1}{2}$ to 1	1 to $1\frac{1}{2}$	$1\frac{1}{2}$ to 2	2 to $2\frac{1}{2}$	$2\frac{1}{2}$ to 3	3 to $3\frac{1}{2}$	$3\frac{1}{2}$ to 4	4 to $4\frac{1}{2}$	*Total*
Probability	0.08	0.19	0.25	0.21	0.14	0.08	0.03	0.02	1.00

So now we have two probability models, on which an analysis of the calls on the fire service can be based. All that remains is to put these together to build up a picture of the way in which a town might manage its fire-fighting resources. With empirical models such as these the method used is 'simulation', a process which will be described in Chapter 5 – where this problem will be taken up again.

Exercise 2C

1 By collecting appropriate data over the next few weeks, devise probability models for the following random situations:
   (a) the numbers of letters delivered to your house each day;
   (b) the length of time it takes you to get to and from school or college;
   (c) the amount of rainfall in your area each day.

2 Use last year's football league tables to find a probability model for the results (home win/away win/draw) in league football matches. If on a randomly chosen Saturday a full programme of league games is played, and you pick out eight of them with a pin, what is the probability
   (a) that they will all be draws;
   (b) that seven of them will be draws and the eighth an away win? (K)

3 An insurance company has 20 000 customers with motor insurance policies. In one month it receives claims as follows:

Amount paid out	£50– £100	£100– £200	£200– £300	£300– £400	£400– £500	£500– £1000	£1000– £5000	over £5000
Number of claims	8	20	60	32	10	24	20	6

The company treats all its customers as equal risks, and regards this month as typical. Make a probability model for the amounts paid out to clients in a month.

To be entitled to a full no-claims bonus a client must have made no claim on his insurance policy in the previous three years. How many of its customers would the company expect to be getting a full no-claims bonus?

4 Get permission to survey the queueing system in a local post office, bank or supermarket. Make probability models for the numbers of customers joining a queue in one-minute intervals, for the length of time that it takes to attend to a customer, and for the length of time a customer spends in the queue before being served. (K)

3
Sequences of events

"Boast not thyself of tomorrow; for thou knowest not what a day may bring forth." This sentence from the book of Proverbs (chapter 27, verse 1) is a stark description of the raw material on which statisticians have to work. It also reminds us that many of the uncertainties with which we have to contend occur in sequences – perhaps daily or yearly, perhaps at less regular intervals: will there be any mail, will it be wet or dry, will the car pass its MOT test, will our Premium Bond win a prize, etc. But there is a good reason to believe that very often the probabilities associated with such events do obey certain recognisable rules; so that although the writer of the proverb was right about "tomorrow", it is possible to make predictions with greater confidence about what will happen in the long run.

In this chapter we shall look at two different kinds of rule, each of which seems to be applicable to a wide variety of sequences of events. It is worth while examining in detail the consequences of these two sets of rules, which are associated respectively with the names of the mathematicians Bernoulli and Markov.

3.1 BERNOULLI PROBABILITIES

If a couple's last child was a girl, is the next of their children more likely to be a boy or a girl?

Of course, we can't answer this question for the future; but there is plenty of past experience to go on. To see what this tells us, think of all the families you know with more than one child – friends, your own family, aunts and uncles, grandparents, etc. – and examine the statistics. It will be helpful to set them out in a table like this:

	Previous child	
	Boy	Girl
This child {Boy		
{Girl		
Total		

Then summarise your conclusions as follows:

Boy was followed by boy in ...%, by girl in ...% of the cases.

Girl was followed by boy in ...%, by girl in ...% of the cases.

26

If you are working in a group, compare your percentages with those found by others. Do they show a consistent pattern?

Many people believe that, before the moment of conception, any future baby is equally likely to be a boy or a girl, and that it makes no difference what sex the previous child was. Do your figures support these beliefs? (Note 3.1)

Q.1 Do these beliefs have a theoretical or an experimental basis? Are they equally true for horses, apes or gnu? What about pigs, mice, frogs, sparrows or bees?

Note that there are two separate issues here, which it is important to disentangle. The first is whether the sexes are split fifty–fifty, or whether there is a bias one way or the other. In fact, there is some evidence of slightly more male births than females in some human communities, and slightly more females than males in others. But some other species of animals and plants show no such symmetry between the sexes: for example, the Tasmanian native hen produces on average 3 males to 2 females, and only one-eighth of jojoba nut bushes are female.

The second question is whether or not the sex of a baby depends on that of its older brothers and sisters. Are boys more likely to be followed by another boy, and girls by another girl – or vice versa? If the answer to this question is no, but that the probabilities remain the same whatever the sex of the older siblings, then we have an example of a sequence of "Bernoulli type" – so named after Jacob Bernoulli, who wrote about probability in a book entitled *Ars conjectandi*, published in 1713 some years after his death. (Note 3.2)

A sequence of repetitions of an experiment is of *Bernoulli type* if
(a) the probability of each possible outcome is independent of the results of the experiment on previous occasions,
(b) the probability of each possible outcome is the same on each occasion.

In the example of the sex of babies there are just two possible outcomes, boy and girl, but this is not an essential feature of a Bernoulli sequence. There may be several different outcomes, and each of these may have a different probability, provided that all the probabilities remain fixed from one experiment to the next. (Note 3.3)

Q.2 Which of the following situations do you think give rise to Bernoulli sequences?
(a) Tossing a coin repeatedly and recording "head" or "tail".
(b) Drawing beads from a bag containing a lot of beads of several different colours, and recording the colour.
(c) Rolling a die repeatedly and recording the score.
(d) Rolling two dice repeatedly and multiplying the two scores.
(e) Driving through a town along a road with several sets of traffic lights and noting whether they show red, amber or green.
(f) Waiting for a no. 5 bus at the college bus stop and noting whether it is late or on time.

3.2 LENGTHS OF RUNS IN BERNOULLI SEQUENCES

To keep the discussion simple, we shall begin by supposing that the experiment has just two possible outcomes denoted by A and B, with probabilities a and b: for example, head or tail in tossing a coin, court card or number card in cutting a pack, a patient being late or on time for an appointment.

There are a number of interesting questions which we can ask about Bernoulli sequences. One of these is whether they give long runs of each outcome, such as

$$\underbrace{A\,A\,A\,A\,A}\;\underbrace{B\,B\,B\,B\,B\,B\,B}\;\underbrace{A\,A\,A\,A}\;\underbrace{B\,B\,B\,B\,B}\;\underbrace{A\,A}\;\ldots$$

or short ones, such as

$$\underbrace{A}\;\underbrace{B\,B}\;\underbrace{A}\;\underbrace{B}\;\underbrace{A}\;\underbrace{B\,B}\;\underbrace{A\,A}\;\underbrace{B}\;\ldots\;.$$

Obviously it is not possible to give a precise answer to this, such as "the outcome A will occur in runs of 5". In any truly random experiment the lengths of different runs will vary. For example, when I drew cards from a pack and recorded the suits (see §2.1) there were four runs of length 2 (one each of diamonds and hearts, two of spades) and one of length 3 (diamonds), whilst the rest were of length 1. So the best that we might expect is to find a model for the probabilities in the form "the probabilities of runs of A of lengths 1, 2, 3, ... are p, q, r, ... ".

Q.3   Roll a die 100 times and record the score each time. Make frequency tables for the numbers of runs of lengths 1, 2, 3, ... of (a) sixes, (b) non-sixes, (c) fives, (d) even numbers, (e) odd numbers. (K)

Q.4   Take a famous large family, such as that of Johann Sebastian Bach or George III, and make a list showing the sex of each child in order of birth. Make frequency tables for the numbers of runs of lengths 1, 2, 3, ... of (a) boys, (b) girls.

Suppose, then, that a run of the outcome A has just started. We record the first occurrence

$$\text{(A)}\quad.$$

The next outcome in the sequence will be either A or B, with probabilities a, b respectively. If it is B, then we record

$$\text{(A)}\quad B\;,$$

and the run has ended at length 1. So the probability that the run has length 1 is b.

Otherwise we record

$$\text{(A)}\quad A\;,$$

and the run of As continues. The next outcome may again be either A or B.

Arguing as before, if it is B, then we record

(A)   A   B ,

and the run has length 2; and the probability of this is ab. Otherwise ... and so on, and so on.

A good way to show this is in a tree diagram (see §1.3) such as Fig. 1. Notice that, since a run ends as soon as a B is recorded, there is no point in investigating what happens subsequently in that case – for by then the next run (of Bs) has already started. But since the run continues for as long as we go on recording the outcome A, the line of lower branches in the diagram extends indefinitely for as long as the experiment is repeated; there is theoretically no limit to the length of a run.

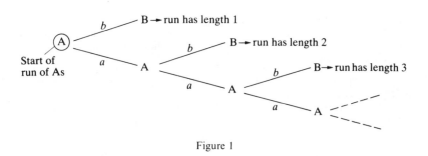

Figure 1

The probabilities of getting runs of As of various lengths can now be read directly off the tree diagram, using the method of multiplying the probabilities along the branches which lead to each twig-end. The results can be set out in a table, which defines the probability model for run lengths of the outcome A:

Run length	1	2	3	4	...	i	...
Probability	b	ba	ba^2	ba^3	...	ba^{i-1}	...

Note that the last entry gives a general formula for the probability of a run length of i, where i stands for any natural number.

Q.5 How are the two characteristic properties of Bernoulli sequences shown up in Fig. 1 and the probability calculations?

Q.6 Make a table showing the probability model for run lengths of the outcome B.

In this probability model each probability is just a times its predecessor, so that successive probabilities form a geometric progression with common ratio a and first term b. (Note 3.4) For this reason it is called a *geometric probability model*. Fig. 2 shows a stick graph for a typical model of this type.

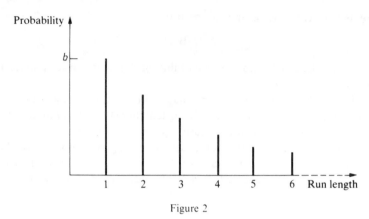

Figure 2

Exercise 3A

1 Draw diagrams similar to Fig. 2 for the probabilities of various run lengths of the outcomes A and B when (i) $a = 0.5$, (ii) $a = 0.8$.

2 Give an algebraic proof that the probabilities of all possible run lengths for the outcome A in the geometric probability model add up to 1.
   Find also the probability that a run of As selected at random has length less than 5. (This can be done in two ways; it is interesting to show that the answers obtained by the two methods are equivalent to each other.)

3 Each time Alan takes the driving test he has a probability 0.3 of passing. Find the probability that he will fail on his first two attempts and pass on the third. What is the probability that he will not have to take the test more than 10 times?

4 In the game of Ludo a player may not begin to move his counter until he throws a six. Find the probability model for the turn on which a particular player may first move his counter.
   If the number of players is small, each player may have two counters. Find the probability model for the turn on which a particular player may first move his second counter.

5 In a Bernoulli sequence of experiments with three possible outcomes A, B, C with respective probabilities a, b, c, what are the probabilities of runs of various lengths for the outcome (i) A, (ii) AB, (iii) ABC, (iv) AAB? (Start by assuming that the outcome has occurred once.) Verify that the probabilities sum to 1 in each case.

3.3 BINOMIAL PROBABILITY MODELS

A quite different kind of question which we can ask about Bernoulli sequences is:

> Suppose that we decided to do the experiment five times;
> how many As shall we get, and how many Bs?

Of course, this is another question to which it is impossible to give a definite answer; one might, for example, get all As or all Bs or any mixture between these extremes. So, as with the question of run length, the best we can hope for is to find a probability model, in the form:

Result	0A,5B	1A,4B	2A,3B	3A,2B	4A,1B	5A,0B
Probability						

Q.7   What are the first and last entries in this table?

As an example, consider the particular result 3A,2B. It is again helpful to use a tree diagram by way of illustration; and since the experiment is repeated just five times whatever the outcome, the appropriate form of diagram is that shown in Fig. 3. On the right side of this diagram is recorded the result corresponding to each route through the tree, and it is easy to count 10 routes (marked with heavier lines along the branches) which lead to the result 3A,2B. Also, by multiplying together the probabilities along the branches making up the route, it is clear that the probability of occurrence of the 3A,2B result is a^3b^2 in each case. Since these are 10 different (mutually exclusive) ways of achieving the result, the total probability of the 3A,2B result is $10a^3b^2$.

Q.8   Use a similar argument to complete the table of probabilities above.

Now this is simple enough when the number of repetitions is as small as five, but that is of very limited use. What we need is a general formula which gives the probability of getting i As and j Bs when the experiment is repeated n times (where, of course, $i + j = n$). By an obvious extension of the tree diagram, it is easy to see that each route corresponding to this result will have a probability of a^ib^j. What is not so easy is to count the number of routes through the tree in the general case.

The key to many counting problems is to find a way of 'coding' the objects being counted. To illustrate this, let us go back to the special case when $n = 5$, $i = 3$ and $j = 2$, and devise a way of describing each of the 10 routes. As an example, one of these is A B A A B, in which the first, third and fourth outcomes are As and the second and fifth are Bs. A possible description of this would be

$$1, 3, 4 \mid 2, 5$$

so that the numbers to the left of the vertical stroke indicate which of the repetitions have the outcome A, and those to the right indicate the repetitions with the outcome B. (Find this route for yourself on Fig. 3.) In this way, the 10 routes which give the result 3A,2B can be coded (reading from the bottom upwards in Fig. 3) as

1, 2, 3 | 4, 5	1, 2, 4 | 3, 5	1, 2, 5 | 3, 4	1, 3, 4 | 2, 5
1, 3, 5 | 2, 4	1, 4, 5 | 2, 3	2, 3, 4 | 1, 5	2, 3, 5 | 1, 4
2, 4, 5 | 1, 3	3, 4, 5 | 1, 2		

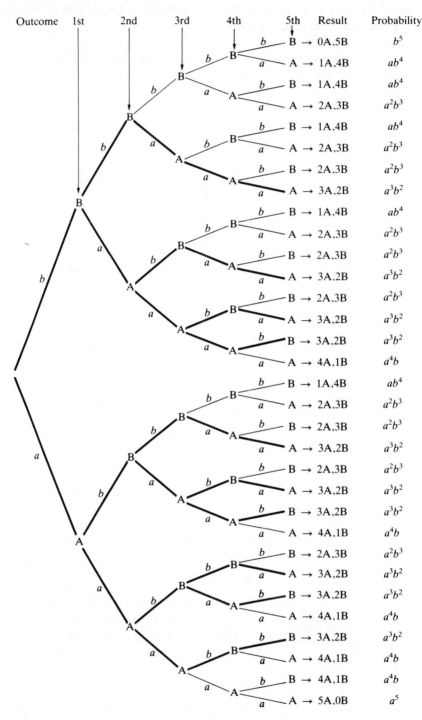

Figure 3

In effect, what we have done here is to partition the set $\{1, 2, 3, 4, 5\}$ into an ordered pair of subsets, the first having three elements and the second two.

Realising this gives the clue we need. For such a partitioning can be got by taking *any* ordering of the set $\{1, 2, 3, 4, 5\}$ and placing a stroke after the third number. For example, we could take the ordering 4, 1, 3, 5, 2 and derive from it the partitioning

$$4, 1, 3 \mid 5, 2.$$

But notice that this doesn't really give us a new partitioning into subsets: it is in fact just the same as

$$1, 3, 4 \mid 2, 5$$

which we considered before, since $\{4, 1, 3\}$ is the same subset as $\{1, 3, 4\}$ and $\{5, 2\}$ is the same as $\{2, 5\}$.

Q.9   Try writing down some more orderings of the set $\{1, 2, 3, 4, 5\}$ and then derive a partitioning from each in the way described. Show that in every case your partitioning is essentially the same as one of the ten in the list above.

Q.10   Write down all the orderings of the set $\{1, 2, 3, 4, 5\}$ which give the same partitioning into subsets as 1, 3, 4 | 2, 5. Do the same for 1, 2, 3 | 4, 5 and 2, 4, 5 | 1, 3. How many such orderings are there in each case? Why?

The important thing to notice is that all the orderings of $\{1, 2, 3, 4, 5\}$ which give the same partitioning as 1, 3, 4 | 2, 5 can be found by putting in the first three places some ordering of the subset $\{1, 3, 4\}$ and in the last two places some ordering of the subset $\{2, 5\}$.

To complete the argument we need a result from the theory of combinatorics:

> The number of ways of arranging k objects in order on a line is $k \times (k - 1) \times (k - 2) \times (k - 3) \times \ldots \times 3 \times 2 \times 1$. This product is called *factorial k*, and is denoted by the symbol $k!$.

(If you have not met this, you will find a proof in Note 3.5.) Applying this to the set of numbers $\{1, 2, 3, 4, 5\}$, the number of ways of ordering this is $5! = 5 \times 4 \times 3 \times 2 \times 1 = 120$; and each of these corresponds to some partitioning into a 3-set followed by a 2-set. But the 3-set can itself be ordered in $3! = 6$ ways, and the 2-set in $2! = 2$ ways, and any ordering of the 3-set can be combined with any ordering of the 2-set. So there are $3! \times 2!$ orderings of $\{1, 2, 3, 4, 5\}$ that correspond to the same partitioning. It follows that the number of essentially different partitionings, and therefore the number of routes leading to the result 3A,2B, is

$$\frac{5!}{3! \times 2!} = \frac{120}{6 \times 2} = 10$$

– the same answer as we got by direct counting.

But the advantage of reasoning in this way is that the argument can be generalised directly to the case when the experiment is repeated n times. The routes through the tree diagram which give a particular result iA, jB can be described by listing the i occasions on which the outcome is A, followed by the j occasions on which the outcome is B. The number of these routes can then be equated to the number of ways of partitioning an n-set into an i-set (the positions of the outcomes A) and a j-set (those of the outcomes B). The n-set can be ordered in $n!$ different ways; but $i! \times j!$ of these orderings correspond to each of the partitionings. So the number of partitionings is $n!/(i! \times j!)$. Putting this together with the probability of $a^i b^j$ for each route gives:

> In a Bernoulli sequence of n repetitions of an experiment with two possible (mutually exclusive) outcomes A,B having probabilities a, b, the probability of getting i As and j Bs (where $i + j = n$) is
>
> $$\frac{n!}{i! \times j!} a^i b^j.$$
>
> This is called the *binomial probability model*.

The quantity $n!/(i! \times j!)$, called a *binomial coefficient*, plays an important part in mathematics, and a special symbol $\binom{n}{i}$ is used to denote it. (The notation $_nC_i$ is also sometimes used; it can be read "n choose i", since it is the number of ways of choosing an i-set out of an n-set.) Notice that j does not appear in the notation; this is because $i + j = n$, so that once n and i are known j is determined. Its most important property, apart from its use in probability theory, is that it is the coefficient of $b^{n-i}a^i$ when the expression $(b + a)^n$ is multiplied out. (Note 3.6) We shall make use of this fact in Chapter 9.

Q.11   Verify this last statement when $n = 5$ by multiplying out $(b + a)^5$ directly.

Q.13   Show that, if $i + j = n$, then $\binom{n}{i} = \binom{n}{j}$.

When we come to calculate binomial coefficients, it is worth while to notice that the numbers $j, j - 1, j - 2, \ldots, 3, 2, 1$ whose product makes up $j!$ also appear in the expression for $n!$. These can therefore be cancelled in the fraction $n!/(i! \times j!)$, leaving only the factors $n, n - 1, n - 2, \ldots, j + 1$ in the top line. Since $j + 1$ can also be written as $n - i + 1$, it follows that

$$\binom{n}{i} = \frac{n(n-1)(n-2)\ldots(n-i+1)}{i!},$$

or $\dfrac{n}{1} \times \dfrac{n-1}{2} \times \dfrac{n-2}{3} \times \ldots \times \dfrac{n-i+1}{i}.$

One final detail. The definition originally given for $k!$, as the product of the numbers $k, k - 1, k - 2, \ldots, 3, 2, 1$, obviously has no meaning if k has the value 0. But for completeness it would be useful if the expression for the binomial probability model could also be applied to give the probability of getting n As and 0 Bs; that is, we would like

$$\frac{n!}{n! \times 0!} a^n b^0 \quad \text{to equal} \quad a^n.$$

Since $b^0 = 1$, this suggests that the symbol $0!$ should be understood to stand for 1. Another advantage of extending the definition in this way is that the equation $k! = k \times (k - 1)!$, which is obviously true for $k = 2, 3, 4, \ldots$, would also be true for $k = 1$. In fact, we can make this the basis of an alternative definition for factorial k:

If k is a natural number, then $k!$ is defined by

$$0! = 1, \quad k! = k \times (k - 1)! \quad \text{for} \quad k = 1, 2, 3, \ldots$$

Exercise 3B

1   In a series of six test matches between England and West Indies, calculate the probability that each side will win the toss the same number of times.

2   A die is rolled ten times. Find which of the following results has the higher probability: just one six, or just two sixes.   [SMP]

3   When a certain pair of blue-eyed snarks mate, there is for each offspring (independently) a probability $\frac{1}{4}$ that it will have green eyes. If the pair produces a litter of 5 young, calculate the probability that more than half of them will have green eyes.   [SMP]

4   The probability of a hurdler knocking down any particular hurdle in a race is $\frac{1}{5}$. Find a numerical expression for the probability that, in a race over 8 hurdles, she will knock down less than 3 hurdles.   [London]

5   In a certain population 20% are of Rhesus negative blood group. Find the probability of there being more than one of this blood group in a random sample of six people from this population.   [London]

6   Baseball fans reckon that, in a contest between the Biffers and the Smashers, the Biffers have a 60% probability of winning. In a World Series of seven matches, calculate the probability that the Smashers will win more often than the Biffers.

7   Five people taken at random are each asked to taste a sample of Brand A and a sample of Brand B margarine. Four of them prefer Brand A. Do you feel this provides conclusive evidence that "people prefer Brand A to Brand B"? Give your reason.   [SMP]

8   A coin is tossed six times. What is the probability that there will be more tails on the first three of these six throws than on the last three throws?   [SMP]

9   A canvasser knocks on the door of each house in a row of six. For each house the probability of there being a reply to his knock is $\frac{2}{3}$. Find the probabilities that (a) he receives exactly five replies; (b) he receives at least five replies.

Given that he receives a reply, the probability that it is satisfactory is $\frac{4}{5}$. Find the probability that he receives exactly five satisfactory replies.   [MEI]

10 Use the expression for $\binom{n}{i}$ given at the end of §3.3 to find the fraction by which $\binom{n}{i}$ must be multiplied to give $\binom{n}{i+1}$. Use this to write a computer program to calculate binomial probabilities. Use your program to compute the probabilities for various values of n, a, b. Adapt the program to display the probabilities (as a function of i) in the form of a stick graph. (K)

11 Explain why, if a and b are probabilities in a Bernoulli sequence of n experiments with two outcomes,

$$\sum_{i+j=n} \frac{n!}{i! \times j!} a^i b^j = 1.$$

By choosing special values for a and b, deduce that

$$\sum_{i+j=n} \frac{n!}{i! \times j!} = 2^n.$$

12 You probably know that the binomial coefficients $n!/(i! \times j!)$ can be found from *Pascal's triangle* (Note 3.7):

$$
\begin{array}{ccccccccccc}
& & & & 1 & & 1 & & & & \\
& & & 1 & & 2 & & 1 & & & \\
& & 1 & & 3 & & 3 & & 1 & & \\
& 1 & & 4 & & 6 & & 4 & & 1 & \\
1 & & 5 & & 10 & & 10 & & 5 & & 1 \\
\end{array}
$$

Verify this numerically for the entries in the table printed in bold type.

The law for making up Pascal's triangle is that each entry (except the 1s) is the sum of the two numbers diagonally above it in the previous row. Show that this corresponds to the relation

$$\binom{n}{i-1} + \binom{n}{i} = \binom{n+1}{i}$$

between the binomial coefficients, and prove this directly from the definition of $\binom{n}{i}$.

13 Consider a Bernoulli sequence in which the experiment has three possible outcomes A, B, C with probabilities a, b, c. Suppose that the experiment is repeated five times. List all the possible ways in which the result 2A, 1B, 2C would arise, and hence give the probability of this result. Show that each of these can be described by an ordering of the set $\{1, 2, 3, 4, 5\}$ partitioned as an ordered triplet $-, - \mid - \mid -, -$; and show that each such partitioning into a 2-set, a 1-set and a 2-set (for the outcomes A, B, C) can arise from four different orderings of $\{1, 2, 3, 4, 5\}$.

Now generalise this argument to the case when the experiment is repeated n times. Deduce that the probability of getting i As, j Bs and k Cs is

$$n!/(i! \times j! \times k!) \cdot a^i b^j c^k.$$

(This can be called the trinomial probability model. The general case, with any number of outcomes, gives the *multinomial probability model*.)

14 In the binomial probability model with $a = \frac{2}{3}$, $b = \frac{1}{3}$ and $n = 7$, prove that the probability of getting i As and j Bs is less than the probability of getting $(i + 1)$ As and $(j - 1)$ Bs provided that $3i < 13$. Deduce that the result with the highest probability is 5A, 2B.

15 Investigate the binomial probability model with $a = \frac{2}{3}$, $b = \frac{1}{3}$ and $n = 8$ using the method outlined in question 14. Show that in this case there are two results which equally have the highest probability.

16 Investigate the general binomial probability model using the method outlined in question 14. Show first that the probability of getting i As and j Bs is less than the probability of getting $(i + 1)$ As and $(j - 1)$ Bs provided that $i < (n + 1)a - 1$.

   Deduce that, if $(n + 1)a$ is *not* a whole number, then the most probable result is $[(n + 1)a]$As and $[(n + 1)b]$Bs, where the symbol $[x]$ denotes the 'whole number part' of x (strictly, the greatest integer not greater than x, sometimes denoted by int(x)). However, if $(n + 1)a$ is a whole number, then there are two results which are equally most probable: $(n + 1)a - 1$ As and $(n + 1)b$ Bs, and $(n + 1)a$ As and $(n + 1)b - 1$ Bs.

   Run the computer program that you wrote in question 10 with a number of sets of values of a, b and n to illustrate this result.

3.4 MARKOV CHAINS

A familiar example of a sequence of experiments is the Oxford and Cambridge boat race, which has been rowed regularly since 1839. (Note 3.8) Here is a list of the winners of each race up to 1982:

```
C C C O C   C C O O O   C O C O C   O O O O O   O O O O C
C C C C O   C O C O O   O O C O C   C C C O O   O O O O O
O O C C O   C C C O C   C C O O O   O O C C C   C O C C C
C C C C C   C C C C C   O O C O C   C C C C O   C O C C C
C O O C C   O C O O O   C C C C C   C O C O O   O O O O O
```

I was interested to find out if this could be described as a Bernoulli sequence. To do this, it was necessary to see whether the outcome of a race was influenced by the results in previous years. I therefore decided to compare the result of each race with that of the year before, and made out a table as follows:

		Winner of previous race	
		O	C
Winner of this race	O	35	23
	C	22	44
Total		57	67

Now altogether there were 58 Oxford wins and 67 Cambridge wins, that is 46% and 54% respectively. But the table shows that, of the races when Oxford won the previous year, 61% were won by Oxford and 39% by Cambridge; whereas when Cambridge won the previous year, 34% of the races were won by Oxford and 66% by Cambridge. This certainly suggests that, if you are going to row in the boat race, it is an advantage to row for the university which won the year before.

Q.13   Can you suggest any reasons for this?

Q.14   Why do the columns in the table (and the rows) not add up to 58 and 67?

As a contrast, I devised an experiment to give a Bernoulli sequence with two outcomes having probabilities 0.46 and 0.54 – the same as the proportions of Oxford and Cambridge wins – and from the sequence of results I selected a subsequence which had the same column totals as for the boat race statistics. (Note 3.9) The results were:

```
BBAAB  BAAAB  BBBAB  BBABB  BABBB
ABAAA  BBABB  AABBA  BBAAB  BBBAB
ABAAA  BABBA  BAAAB  BBBAB  AAABA
ABABB  BBBAB  BAAAA  BBBAB  BBAAB
AABBA  ABAAB  AAABB  AAABB  BABAB
```

Summarising these as we did before gives the table:

		Previous outcome	
		A	B
This	A	25	32
outcome	B	32	35
Total		57	67

That is, of the experiments where the previous outcome was A, 44% gave the outcome A and 56% the outcome B; whereas of the experiments where the previous outcome was B, the percentages were 48% and 52%. Although these proportions are not exactly the same as the probabilities on which the experiments were based – and some variability in the results must always be expected – they are certainly much closer than for the boat race.

Q.15   Look in more detail at the two sequences of results, and comment on any differences which you notice between them.

It seems, then, that if we wanted to predict the pattern of future boat race results on the basis of experience over the first 144 years, it would be very unwise to assume that they form a Bernoulli sequence.

A better theory might be to suppose that the probability of either outcome for a particular race depends on the result of the previous race – so that we are really dealing with conditional probabilities. Let us make a further assumption (a rather large one, perhaps!) that the probabilities remain constant over time. It would then be possible to use the percentages calculated earlier to suggest values for these conditional probabilities. It will be convenient to approximate to these by simple fractions, which suggests taking 61% to be $\frac{3}{5}$, 39% as $\frac{2}{5}$, 34% as $\frac{1}{3}$ and 66% as $\frac{2}{3}$. This then gives a table of probabilities:

		Winner of previous race	
		O	C
Winner of	O	$\frac{3}{5}$	$\frac{1}{3}$
this race	C	$\frac{2}{5}$	$\frac{2}{3}$
	Total	1	1

At this stage it is helpful to introduce some notation. Successive years in which the race is held can be numbered 0, 1, 2, 3, ..., year 0 being the last one for which a result is known. We can then use the symbol O_n to stand for the outcome "Oxford will win the race in year n", and similarly C_n for Cambridge. The conditional probabilities would be written

$$P(O_{n+1}|O_n) = \tfrac{3}{5}, \quad P(C_{n+1}|O_n) = \tfrac{2}{5}, \quad P(O_{n+1}|C_n) = \tfrac{1}{3}, \quad P(C_{n+1}|C_n) = \tfrac{2}{3}.$$

And this could be illustrated by a diagram such as Fig. 4. This figure is of course only one link in a whole chain of probability relationships beginning at year 0. The beginning of the chain is shown in Fig. 5.

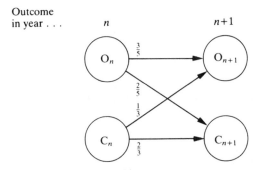

Figure 4

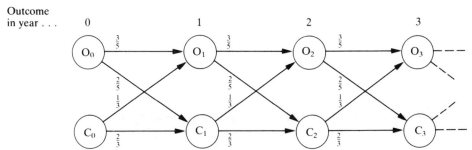

Figure 5

We can regard Fig. 5 as a kind of collapsed version of a tree diagram, and it is useful when we are interested more in the probabilities of the various outcomes than in disentangling the routes by which these outcomes have been arrived at. It is an example of a *Markov chain*, named after the Russian mathematician Andrei A. Markov, who lived from 1856 to 1922.

To make clear the difference between Markov and Bernoulli sequences, compare the following definition with the one given in §3.1:

A sequence of repetitions of an experiment is of *Markov type* if
(i) the probability of each possible outcome on each occasion is conditional only on the result of the experiment on the occasion immediately preceding it,
(ii) the conditional probabilities for each possible outcome are the same on each occasion.

For the rest of this chapter we shall investigate some features of such sequences.

3.5 CALCULATION OF SUCCESSIVE PROBABILITIES

Suppose that we already know that the boat race in year 0 was won by Oxford, and that we want to assign probabilities to the outcomes in years 1, 2, 3, ... Then we can write

$$P(O_0) = 1, \quad P(C_0) = 0.$$

Prediction for year 1 is therefore based simply on the left column of the probability table (i.e. on the arrows joining O_0 to O_1 and C_1 in Fig. 5) and we see that

$$P(O_1) = \tfrac{3}{5}, \quad P(C_1) = \tfrac{2}{5}.$$

Prediction for year 2, however, is more complicated. An Oxford win in year 2 might follow either an Oxford or a Cambridge win in year 1. Since these are exclusive, we can write

$$P(O_2) = P(O_2 \text{ preceded by } O_1) + P(O_2 \text{ preceded by } C_1).$$

The problem is now to calculate the two probabilities on the right, which can be done using the conditional probability equations

$$P(O_2 \text{ preceded by } O_1) = P(O_2 | O_1) \times P(O_1) = \tfrac{3}{5} \times \tfrac{3}{5} = \tfrac{9}{25},$$

$$P(O_2 \text{ preceded by } C_1) = P(O_2 | C_1) \times P(C_1) = \tfrac{1}{3} \times \tfrac{2}{5} = \tfrac{2}{15}.$$

So

$$P(O_2) = \tfrac{9}{25} + \tfrac{2}{15} = \tfrac{37}{75} \approx 0.493;$$

and since there are only two possible outcomes it follows that

$$P(C_2) = 1 - P(O_2) = \tfrac{38}{75} \approx 0.507.$$

So after 2 years the odds have swung marginally in favour of a Cambridge win.

Q.16   Obtain $P(C_2)$ directly by an argument like that used to find $P(O_2)$.

Now we can go on in the same way to find $P(O_3)$ and $P(C_3)$:

$$P(O_3) = P(O_3 \text{ preceded by } O_2) + P(O_3 \text{ preceded by } C_2)$$

$$= P(O_3|O_2) \times P(O_2) + P(O_3|C_2) \times P(C_2)$$

$$= \tfrac{3}{5} \times 0.493 + \tfrac{1}{3} \times 0.507 \approx 0.465,$$

$$P(C_3) = 1 - P(O_3) \approx 1 - 0.465 = 0.535.$$

The important thing to notice is that, because of the properties of Markov sequences, it is not necessary to carry the calculation back each time to year 0; the probabilities in any year can be found simply by using those of the two outcomes in the immediately preceding year. A good way of seeing what is going on is to adapt Fig. 5 and to set these calculations out in a chain as in Fig. 6.

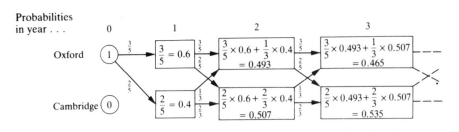

Figure 6

Q.17   Continue the calculations in this chain.

Q.18   Write a computer program to input the initial probabilities O_0 and C_0 and to print out the probabilities in successive years. Use this to calculate the probabilities if the race in year 0 was won by Cambridge.

The crucial point is that these calculations are repetitive, or *iterative* (to use the technical mathematical term). They may be summed up by the equations

$$P(O_{n+1}) = \tfrac{3}{5} \times P(O_n) + \tfrac{1}{3} \times P(C_n),$$

$$P(C_{n+1}) = \tfrac{2}{5} \times P(O_n) + \tfrac{2}{3} \times P(C_n),$$

which can be read directly off Fig. 4.

You will probably also have spotted, from the answers to Q.15 and Q.16, that as the calculation proceeds the probabilities seem to be settling down to steady values – and in fact this almost always occurs in Markov chains. What are these values?

The mathematician's usual response to such a question is to begin by inventing some notation for the unknowns he wants to find. We shall use the symbols P*(O) and P*(C) for the steady long-run probabilities that Oxford or Cambridge will win in a particular year. (Think of 'star' standing for 'steady'.)

The clue is then to use the iterative equations found above, replacing both $P(O_n)$ and $P(O_{n+1})$ by the steady probability $P^*(O)$, and both $P(C_n)$ and $P(C_{n+1})$ by $P^*(C)$. This then gives

$$P^*(O) = \tfrac{3}{5} \times P^*(O) + \tfrac{1}{3} \times P^*(C), \quad \text{and} \quad P^*(C) = \tfrac{2}{5} \times P^*(O) + \tfrac{2}{3} \times P^*(C)$$

– two equations for two unknowns. Unfortunately they both reduce to the same equation

$$\tfrac{2}{5}P^*(O) = \tfrac{1}{3}P^*(C),$$

so these are not sufficient by themselves to find the steady probabilities. But we also know another connection between $P^*(O)$ and $P^*(C)$: that

$$P^*(O) + P^*(C) = 1.$$

Putting the two equations together, it is easy to get the solutions

$$P^*(O) = \tfrac{5}{11} \approx 0.455, \quad P^*(C) = \tfrac{6}{11} \approx 0.545.$$

How does this square with the probabilities you found in Q.15 and Q.16?

Q.19   Show that the steady probabilities reflect the record of the numbers of wins of the two crews over the complete sequence of races to date.

These are, of course, the probabilities based on a knowledge of the sequence of results so far available, and on the rather naive assumption that history will repeat itself. To sum up, if we are trying to predict the results of future boat races on a basis of past experience, then for the next race after the sequence of known results we would lay odds of 3 to 2 on Oxford winning; but if we want to look further into the future, then these odds would gradually shift until, forecasting some years ahead, we would lay odds of 6 to 5 on Cambridge.

3.6   USING MATRICES TO DESCRIBE MARKOV SEQUENCES

Any well-brought-up mathematician seeing the iterative equations in §3.5 for $P(O_{n+1})$ and $P(C_{n+1})$ in terms of $P(O_n)$ and $P(C_n)$ will want to write them in matrix form, as

$$\begin{bmatrix} P(O_{n+1}) \\ P(C_{n+1}) \end{bmatrix} = \begin{bmatrix} \tfrac{3}{5} & \tfrac{1}{3} \\ \tfrac{2}{5} & \tfrac{2}{3} \end{bmatrix} \begin{bmatrix} P(O_n) \\ P(C_n) \end{bmatrix}. \quad \text{(Note 3.10)}$$

You will notice that this equation contains matrices of two kinds:

(1) An *outcome probability matrix*, which is a column matrix whose entries are the probabilities of the various possible outcomes in a particular year. Obviously the entries in this matrix must always add to 1. We will use the symbol $\mathbf{p}_n$ to denote the outcome matrix $\begin{bmatrix} P(O_n) \\ P(C_n) \end{bmatrix}$.

(2) A *transition matrix*, which is a square matrix whose entries are the

conditional probabilities exactly as they appear in the table of probabilities near the beginning of §3.4. Notice that the entries in each column of this matrix also add to 1. We will denote this matrix by $\mathbf{T}$.

So now the complete sequence of outcome probability matrices can be calculated from the equation

$$\mathbf{p}_{n+1} = \mathbf{T}\mathbf{p}_n,$$

beginning (in the boat race example) with the initial value

$$\mathbf{p}_0 = \begin{bmatrix} 1 \\ 0 \end{bmatrix}.$$

That is,

$$\mathbf{p}_1 = \mathbf{T}\mathbf{p}_0, \quad \mathbf{p}_2 = \mathbf{T}\mathbf{p}_1 = \mathbf{T}(\mathbf{T}\mathbf{p}_0) = \mathbf{T}^2\mathbf{p}_0, \quad \mathbf{p}_3 = \mathbf{T}\mathbf{p}_2 = \mathbf{T}(\mathbf{T}^2\mathbf{p}_0) = \mathbf{T}^3\mathbf{p}_0, \ldots$$

and in general

$$\mathbf{p}_n = \mathbf{T}^n\mathbf{p}_0$$

– a kind of 'geometric progression' with first term $\mathbf{p}_0$ and multiplier $\mathbf{T}$!

Q.20 For the matrix

$$\mathbf{T} = \begin{bmatrix} \frac{3}{5} & \frac{1}{3} \\ \frac{2}{5} & \frac{2}{3} \end{bmatrix},$$

calculate (working to an appropriate number of decimal places) the values of $\mathbf{T}^2$, $\mathbf{T}^3$, $\mathbf{T}^4$, ... Can you suggest a limiting value of $\mathbf{T}^n$ as $n \to \infty$?

Q.21 For the boat race model, plot on graph paper the outcome probability matrices $\mathbf{p}_0$, $\mathbf{p}_1$, $\mathbf{p}_2$, ... as vectors. Describe the transformation of the plane represented by the transition matrix $\mathbf{T}$. Plot also the steady probability matrix $\begin{bmatrix} P^*(O) \\ P^*(C) \end{bmatrix}$ as a vector, and state what property this has in relation to the transformation represented by $\mathbf{T}$.

These last two questions should give you some idea how matrices, and their corresponding geometrical representations, can offer a powerful way of investigating the properties of Markov sequences. These ideas are followed up further in the Project exercise A6 and in Chapter 21.

Exercise 3C

1 If I am late for work one day, the probability that I will be on time the next day is $\frac{3}{4}$. If I am on time one day, the probability that I will be late the next day is $\frac{1}{2}$. In one week I arrive on time on Monday. Calculate the probabilities that in the same week I shall be on time on (a) Wednesday, (b) Friday. In the long run, how many times in a (five-day) week would you expect me to be late?

2   If Mary stays in to work one evening, there is a probability of 0.7 that she will go out the following evening. If she goes out one evening, the probability that she will go out the following evening too is 0.6. In the long run, how often does she stay in to work?

3   A bowler bowls only leg breaks and googlies. When he has bowled a leg break, the probability that he next bowls a googly is $\frac{1}{6}$; and when he has bowled a googly, the probability that he next bowls a leg break is $\frac{7}{8}$. The first ball of an over is a leg break. Find the probability that the third ball is a googly.

4   Fred is what you would call a 'floating drinker'. If he goes to the Anchor one evening, then there is an 80% probability that he will patronise the Bull the next evening; and the evening after he is in the Bull, there is a 60% probability that you will find him in the Anchor. But of one thing you may be sure: every evening you will find him either in the Anchor or the Bull, and he will stay there until closing time. Denoting by $P(A_n)$, $P(B_n)$ the probabilities that he is in the Anchor or the Bull on evening n, write equations expressing $P(A_{n+1})$, $P(B_{n+1})$ in terms of these.

  Returning after an absence from the village, his choice of pub on evening 0 is decided by the toss of a coin. Calculate $P(A_n)$, $P(B_n)$ for $n = 1, 2, 3, 4$. Find also the steady values which the probabilities will approach once he gets back to his regular routine.

  Write the equations in matrix form, and calculate the first few powers of the transition matrix $\mathbf{T}$. Can you suggest a limiting value for $\mathbf{T}^n$ as $n \to \infty$?

5   A bag contains 4 red and 6 green beads. I draw a bead from this bag, hand it to my assistant, who records its colour. The experiment then proceeds as follows: I draw another bead, my assistant puts his back in the bag, I hand mine to my assistant, and he records the colour ... and so on. If R_n, G_n denote the outcomes that the nth bead after the first is red, green respectively, write down equations to find $P(R_{n+1})$, $P(G_{n+1})$ in terms of $P(R_n)$, $P(G_n)$. Calculate $P(R_n)$, $P(G_n)$ for $n = 1, 2, 3, \ldots$ and investigate how these probabilities vary as n increases. Investigate also whether steady probabilities exist, and if so calculate them.

6   Investigate the Markov chain defined by the equations

$$P(X_{n+1}) = \tfrac{5}{6}P(X_n) + \tfrac{1}{4}P(Y_n) \quad \text{and} \quad P(Y_{n+1}) = \tfrac{1}{6}P(X_n) + \tfrac{3}{4}P(Y_n),$$

with $P(X_0) = 1$, $P(Y_0) = 0$. Make up a problem which could be described by these equations, and interpret the steady probabilities in terms of your problem.

7   For the boat race example discussed in the text, let the quantities $P(O_n) - P^*(O)$, $P(C_n) - P^*(C)$ be denoted by x_n, y_n respectively. Explain why $x_n + y_n = 0$. By taking two of the equations in §3.5 and subtracting one from the other, prove that $x_{n+1} = \tfrac{4}{15}x_n$. Deduce that $P(O_n)$ is given by the formula $\tfrac{5}{11} + \tfrac{6}{11}(\tfrac{4}{15})^n$.

8   A document is repeatedly copied. At any stage the word WOAD has probability p of being copied correctly and probability q of being copied as WOOD, where $p + q = 1$. If it appears in the form WOOD it has probability r of being copied as WOOD and probability s of being copied as WOAD, where $r + s = 1$. In the original document the word appears as WOAD. Show that if u_n is the probability that after n copyings it reads WOAD, then $u_{n+1} = s + (p - s)u_n$.

  If x_n denotes the quantity $u_n - s/(q + s)$, prove that $x_{n+1} = (p - s)x_n$. Use this to find a formula for x_n, and hence for u_n. What value does u_n approach after many copyings?

9   I have three coins: one genuine, one double-headed and one double-tailed. First, I toss the genuine coin. After that, if the last toss resulted in a head, then I toss the double-tailed coin; if the last was a tail, then I toss the double-headed coin. Find the successive probabilities $P(H_n)$, $P(T_n)$.

Also write down the transition matrix, and describe it geometrically.

10 Repeat question 9, but with the rules changed so that
  (a) after a head I toss the double-headed coin, and after a tail I toss the double-tailed coin;
  (b) after a head I toss the double-headed coin, and after a tail I toss the genuine coin.

11 If $\begin{bmatrix} u \\ v \end{bmatrix} = \begin{bmatrix} a & b \\ c & d \end{bmatrix} \begin{bmatrix} x \\ y \end{bmatrix}$, and if $a + c = 1$, $b + d = 1$, $x + y = 1$, prove that $u + v = 1$.

What is the application of this result to the outcome and transition matrices for a Markov chain?

12 Mr Smart can get to work by bus, car or train. Fig. 7 shows the probabilities that he will use each of these modes of transport on day $n + 1$, depending on the way he went on day n. On 31 January he went by bus. Find the probabilities that he will go by the various modes of transport on 1, 2, 3, ... February.

His daughter hopes to use the car on 1 March. Estimate the probability that it will be available.

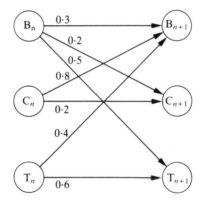

Figure 7

13 An animal cage has three boxes A, B, C in it, which are named in an anticlockwise order and are placed at the corners of an equilateral triangle; and the door of each box faces towards the interior of the triangle. A rat is placed in box A, and proceeds at random always towards a different box. The rat is twice as likely to move to the box on its right as to the box on its left. Show that after 4 moves the rat is most likely to be in box C, but otherwise is equally likely to be in box A or box B.

What is the situation after 6 moves? [SMP]

14 The probability of a team winning a match is 0.6 and of drawing 0.3 if the previous match was won. If the previous match was drawn the corresponding probabilities are 0.2 and 0.6, and if it was lost 0.2 and 0.4. Find the transition matrix, and hence the probabilities of winning or drawing any particular match in the distant future if the probabilities remain the same. [SMP]

3.7 RUN LENGTHS IN MARKOV SEQUENCES

Look back at the list of boat race results at the beginning of §3.4, and compare them with the results of the Bernoulli sequence of outcomes A and B. One thing that is very striking is the possibility of very long runs of consecutive wins in the boat race; for example, Oxford had two runs of 9 wins and one of 7 wins, whilst Cambridge once recorded a run of 13 wins. On the other hand, the outcome A occurred singly on 16 occasions, and had eight runs of length 2, seven of length 3 and just one of length 4. The difference shows up well in Fig. 8, which gives cumulative graphs of the proportions of runs of a given length or less for both outcomes in each of the two sequences.

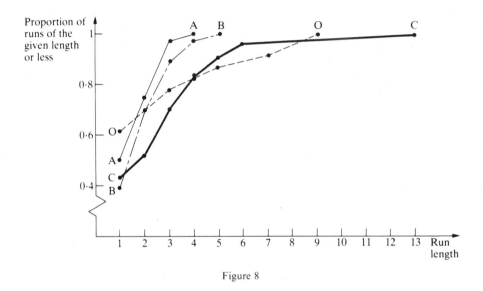

Figure 8

Does this mean that Markov chains give rise to longer runs than Bernoulli sequences? Certainly not. Anyone who has played Ludo knows that, when a die is rolled (a Bernoulli situation), runs of non-sixes can be very long indeed; but to compensate for this it is rare to have a run of sixes of length greater than 1. The difference with a Markov sequence is that it is possible for each outcome to have long run lengths – or, for that matter, for each to have short run lengths.

Q.22 Make up an example of a Markov sequence for which you would expect the run lengths for each outcome to be very short.

To see why this happens, consider a Markov sequence with two possible outcomes A and B, illustrated by Fig. 9. The probabilities a_1 and b_1 denote the conditional probabilities of these outcomes respectively when the previous outcome is A, that is $P(A_{n+1}|A_n)$ and $P(B_{n+1}|A_n)$. Similarly a_2 and b_2 denote $P(A_{n+1}|B_n)$ and $P(B_{n+1}|B_n)$.

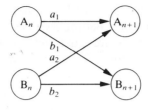

Figure 9

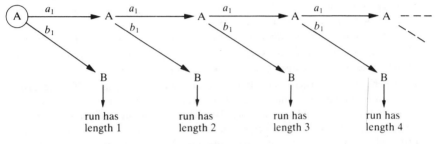

Figure 10

The probabilities of various run lengths can then be calculated from Fig. 10, which can be thought of as an 'extract' from a chain like Fig. 5 which gives a tree diagram similar to Fig. 1. Suppose that the circled "A" on the left is the first of a run of the outcome A. Then the run continues just as long as we remain in the top row of the chain, but stops as soon as we drop to the bottom row. So we can read off the following table of probabilities:

Run length	1	2	3	4	...
Probability	b_1	$b_1 a_1$	$b_1 a_1^2$	$b_1 a_1^3$	...

Q.23   Verify that the sum of the complete series of probabilities is 1.

Q.24   Obtain the corresponding table for runs of the outcome B:

Run length	1	2	3	4	...
Probability	a_2	$a_2 b_2$	$a_2 b_2^2$	$a_2 b_2^3$	...

From these two tables we can see an essential difference between the Bernoulli and Markov situations. Although the probabilities b_1 and a_1 are connected by the equation $b_1 + a_1 = 1$, and similarly $a_2 + b_2 = 1$, there is no such relation connecting the probabilities b_1 and a_2, or a_1 and b_2. So it is possible for both b_1 and a_2 to be small (as in the boat race example, where they had the values $\frac{2}{5}$ and

$\frac{1}{3}$), giving long runs of both A and B; also b_1 and a_2 can both be large, giving short runs of both outcomes. In a Bernoulli sequence, on the other hand, a_1 and a_2 are equal (to a), and b_1 and b_2 are equal (to b); so in this case the relationships $b_1 + a_2 = 1$ and $a_1 + b_2 = 1$ hold, which means that long runs of one outcome are compensated by short runs of the other.

Exercise 3D

1   Make tables for the theoretical probabilities for runs of various length of wins for Oxford and Cambridge in the boat race, based on the probabilities shown in Fig. 5. Make corresponding tables for lengths of runs of the outcomes A and B in a Bernoulli sequence with probabilities 0.46 and 0.54 respectively.

   Display your results in graphs similar to those in Fig. 8, showing the probabilities of getting runs of the given length or less. Compare these graphs of theoretical probabilities with the graphs of the proportions actually observed.

2   An experimenter has two icosahedral (20-faced) dice. The first has the five faces round one vertex painted black and the rest white. The second has the five faces round one vertex painted white and the rest black. By playing according to different sets of rules, he can arrange for the sequence of outcomes B and W to be determined by the probabilities in any of the diagrams (a), (b) or (c). Make up appropriate rules for each case.

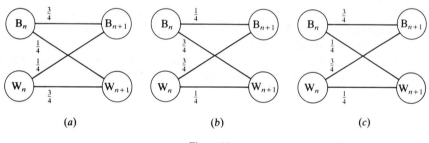

(a)   (b)   (c)

Figure 11

   For each set of rules, calculate the probabilities of getting runs of various lengths for each outcome. Illustrate your results with appropriate graphs.

4

The problem of estimation

There is not just one binomial probability model: there is an indefinite number of such models, with different numerical values for $a, b\,(= 1 - a)$ and n. Similarly there are infinitely many geometric probability models, or sequences of Markov type. But if we are to use probability theory to deal with real life situations, we need to choose particular models by substituting actual numbers for the letters used to describe the general model. The process of choosing these numbers is called "estimation", and in this chapter two methods of estimation will be described; the problem is one to which we shall be returning later in the book, especially in Chapters 8 and 15.

4.1 THE EXTRAPOLATION METHOD

No manufacturing process is perfect. Whether articles are produced by machine or by hand, there will always be some which do not come up to standard. For this reason many firms use "quality control", to make sure that the proportion of substandard goods does not become too large. Of course, you cannot usually test each single article as it comes off the production line – think of the problem in a chocolate factory! – so the checker has to test a sample and make a judgement about the whole batch on the basis of the results.

Imagine a factory which produces plates. Its output is, say, 1000 plates an hour, and 50 of these are picked out at random by the checker and examined for shape, glaze, paint, cracks, chips, etc. Suppose that she finds two plates in the sample to be faulty. What does this suggest about the total output of the factory?

Let us consider first what mental image we have of this factory. The process is obviously operating satisfactorily, but just occasionally it goes wrong: perhaps because a machine develops a slight wobble, or a new operator on the glazing machine has not yet got the knack of the controls, or a batch of clay is too dry. We might think of these as random imperfections in the system, resulting in a certain proportion of the plates being below standard. But the question we need to answer is, *what* proportion?

The most obvious answer is that the checker found two faulty plates out of 50, or 4% of her sample, so it seems reasonable that about 4% of the whole output was faulty. That is, she might work on the "extrapolation principle":

> The probability of an event occurring in the population as a whole is estimated by the proportion of occurrences of that event in the sample.

Note the distinction between the words "probability" and "proportion". The proportion is a number which we can actually calculate from an examination of the sample, as

$$\frac{\text{the number of faulty plates}}{\text{the number of plates in the sample}}:$$

it is an example of what we call a *statistic*. Other examples of statistics (using this word as the plural of "statistic" – not to be confused with the name of the subject) are the median, standard deviation or the largest of the heights of a sample of 8-year-old children, or the ratio of numbers of applicants to places for the statistics degree course in a particular university.

The probability, on the other hand, is a number which we use in describing a particular model and which may 'exist' only in the context of that model: we call it a *parameter*. Other examples of parameters are the mean and standard deviation of all the scores which will ever result from rolling a particular die, or the maximum age to which a tortoise can live.

Using these two words, we can state the principle more generally:

THE EXTRAPOLATION PRINCIPLE. The value of a parameter for the population as a whole is estimated by taking it to be equal to the value of the corresponding statistic in a sample.

This is the principle which we are using, for example, if we estimate the mean annual rainfall at a certain place (a parameter) as the average rainfall over the past 20 years (a statistic); the mean rainfall is a theoretical notion, based on certain modelling assumptions about the constancy of climate. Sometimes extrapolation offers a reasonable basis for estimation, but not always. For instance, you would not think of estimating the maximum height of members of the human race as the height of the tallest person you will meet in the next 24 hours.

Exercise 4A

1   Discuss whether you would use the extrapolation principle in the following situations:
   (a) Estimating the proportion of male to female births from the statistics in your county for the past month.
   (b) Estimating the mean size of clutches of eggs laid by wrens from the average number laid in all the nests recorded in Lancashire in May of last year.
   (c) Estimating the mean height of Martians from that of the occupants of a flying saucer which landed in Wiltshire last midsummer.

2   Suppose that, in the next three batches of 50 plates that she tests, the checker in the factory described in §4.1 finds 4, 1 and 3 faulty plates respectively. Should this cause her to revise her estimate of the probability of a plate produced by the factory being faulty?

3   In a Bernoulli sequence the outcomes A and B occurred as follows:

B B A A B	A A A B A	B A B B B	B A B B B	B A A A B
A A B A A	A A B A A	B A A B B	B A A B B	A A B A A
A A A A A	A A B B B	A B A B B	B A A A A	A A B B A
A A A B A	A B B A B	B A A A A	A B B B B	B A A A A

It was shown in Chapter 3 that the parameter *a* can be regarded either as (i) the probability of the outcome A, or (ii) the probability of runs of the outcome B of length 1. Apply the extrapolation principle with each of these interpretations in turn, to obtain two separate estimates of the parameter.

4   Animal populations are sometimes estimated by the "capture-recapture method". An experimenter goes out into the field and finds a number of the animals being investigated, which she marks before returning them to the wild. Some time later she goes out again and catches as many as she can, some of which will be marked. How could the extrapolation principle be used, from these data, to estimate the total population of the animals in the area investigated?

4.2 THE LIKELIHOOD OF A SAMPLE

The extrapolation principle proceeds *from* the sample *to* the model of the population as a whole: we measure the proportion of faulty plates in the sample, and 'infer' the number of faulty plates in the total output of the factory. But to go into the question of estimating parameters more deeply, we need to reverse this process and *discuss the sample in terms of the model*.

Let us go back to the problem of the plate factory. Notice that all we know *for certain* is that at least two of the 1000 plates were faulty, and that at least 48 were good. That is, we know that the probability of a plate being faulty, if it is selected at random from the hour's production, lies somewhere between 0.002 and 0.952 – not a very useful conclusion! So we must proceed on the basis of probabilities, not certainties.

Suppose that we are right in thinking that the probablity of a faulty plate is 0.04. The checker tests 50 plates: what would we expect her to find? Clearly she might get no faulty ones, or one, or two, or three ... there is a variety of possible outcomes, but they are not all equally probable. In fact, this is an application of the Bernoulli model: a test is carried out 50 times on a random sample of plates, and the probability of the result "faulty" is 0.04 on each occasion. You can check for yourself (using a calculator) that putting $a = 0.04$, $b = 0.96$ and $n = 50$ in the binomial formula (see §3.3) gives the following table of probabilities:

Number faulty	0	1	2	3	4	5	6	7	8	9	10	...
Probability	0.130	0.271	**0.276**	0.184	0.090	0.035	0.011	0.003	0.001	vs	vs	...

(The letters vs denote a very small probability – less than 0.0005.)

The figures printed in bold type draw attention to the fact that, on the hypothesis (or supposition) that the probability of a faulty plate selected at random is 0.04, the probability of getting the result that the checker actually recorded would be 0.276. But clearly, if she had picked out a different sample, she might easily have got a different result.

But suppose now that we had made some other hypothesis about the probability of a faulty plate – say $a = 0.05$. What would then be the probability of getting the result the checker recorded? To find this we can apply the binomial formula with $a = 0.05$, $b = 0.95$, $n = 50$, $i = 2$ and $j = 48$, giving the probability 0.261. This is not quite as high as with $a = 0.04$, but it still indicates that the result is almost as likely to occur on this hypothesis.

Indeed, we can carry out a whole batch of such calculations, finding the probabilities that the checker will get various numbers of faulty places based on various hypotheses about the probability. This has been done in Table 1, where a range of hypothetical probabilities from 0.007 up to 0.12 has been selected.

Q.1 Locate in Table 1 the probability 0.261 referred to in the last but one paragraph, and also the single row of probabilities calculated earlier.

Q.2 Table 1 contains two quite different sets of probabilities. Describe carefully in words what each of these signifies. Verify that the sum of the entries in each row of the table is equal to 1 (allowing for rounding errors, and obvious modifications in the last few rows), and explain why this should be so.

The entries of Table 1 have so far been described as "probabilities", and this is precisely what they are so long as we think of the table as being built up row by

Table 1

		Number of faulty plates in a sample of 50									
		0	1	2	3	4	5	6	7	8	9	10
Hypothetical probability (a)	0.007	0.704	0.248	**0.043**	0.005	vs	vs	vs	vs	vs	vs	vs
	0.008	0.669	0.270	**0.053**	0.007	0.001	vs	vs	vs	vs	vs	vs
	0.009	0.636	0.289	**0.064**	0.009	0.001	vs	vs	vs	vs	vs	vs
	0.01	0.605	0.306	**0.076**	0.012	0.001	vs	vs	vs	vs	vs	vs
	0.02	0.364	0.372	**0.186**	0.061	0.015	0.003	vs	vs	vs	vs	vs
	0.03	0.218	0.337	**0.256**	0.126	0.046	0.013	0.003	0.001	vs	vs	vs
	0.04	0.130	0.271	**0.276**	0.184	0.090	0.035	0.011	0.003	0.001	vs	vs
	0.05	0.077	0.202	**0.261**	0.220	0.136	0.066	0.026	0.009	0.002	0.001	vs
	0.06	0.045	0.145	**0.226**	0.231	0.173	0.102	0.049	0.020	0.007	0.002	0.00(
	0.08	0.015	0.067	**0.143**	0.199	0.204	0.163	0.106	0.058	0.027	0.011	0.0(
	0.10	0.005	0.029	**0.078**	0.139	0.181	0.185	0.154	0.108	0.064	0.033	0.01
	0.12	0.002	0.011	**0.038**	0.083	0.133	0.167	0.171	0.147	0.108	0.068	0.03

row – that is, starting from various theoretical models and calculating the probabilities of the different possible outcomes. But this does not correspond to the estimation problem we began with, where what is known is that the checker found two faulty plates in her sample. This suggests that we really want to read the table by columns rather than by rows, and in particular we are interested in the column of figures in bold type corresponding to two faulty plates. The question is then

"How likely are we to get this result if we make such-and-such a hypothesis about the probability of a faulty plate?"

You will see that the entries in the column rise to a maximum when a is taken to be 0.04, and then drop again. This provides a reason for choosing this hypothesis in preference to the others.

This approach to the problem of estimation is called "maximising the likelihood". This last word is used in statistics in a technical sense: the entries in the column for the outcome "2 faulty plates" are called the "likelihoods" of that outcome of the sampling experiment corresponding to various hypotheses about the probability.

The *likelihood* of an outcome, for a certain value of a parameter, is the probability of obtaining that outcome on the hypothesis that the parameter takes the chosen value.

So in our example, the likelihood of the sample of two faulty plates is greatest when $a = 0.04$, and takes the value 0.276.

Q.3   Suppose that the checker takes another sample of 50 plates, and finds five faulty. Use Table 1 to find the value of a which maximises the likelihood of this sample.

This procedure can be summarised in the form of a general principle:

THE MAXIMUM LIKELIHOOD PRINCIPLE. The value of a parameter for the population as a whole is estimated to be that which maximises the likelihood of the outcome in the sampling experiment.

4.3 APPLYING THE MAXIMUM LIKELIHOOD PRINCIPLE

The fact that the entries in Table 1 can be called "probabilities" or "likelihoods", according to the way in which the table is being used, should not cause any confusion. You can compare it to the fact that you call your parents "mother" and "father", whereas your cousin calls them "aunt" and "uncle". And in practice, we calculate likelihoods as probabilities, by using some probability model.

Let us stay a little longer with the example of the plate factory. In Table 1, although the columns list all the possible outcomes from 0 to 10 (because the number of faulty plates must be a whole number), the tabulated values of a can only be a selection of all the possible probabilities; there is no reason why the best probability should be taken from one of the values 0.007, 0.008, 0.009, 0.01, 0.02, ..., 0.10, 0.12 for which we have chosen to do the calculations. So to investigate the problem mathematically, it would be better to use algebra.

If the hypothetical probability (which is the parameter we are trying to estimate) is denoted by a, then the likelihood of the sample of 2 faulty plates is given by the formula

$$\binom{50}{2} a^2 b^{48}, \quad \text{where} \quad b = 1 - a,$$

using the binomial probability model. This is of course a function of the variable a, so let us denote it by the symbol $L(a)$. Then

$$L(a) = 1225 a^2 (1 - a)^{48}.$$

We want to find the value of a which maximises this, and this is a situation where we can use calculus. The method is therefore to differentiate $L(a)$, making use of the product rule and the chain rule: (Note 4.1)

$$L'(a) = 1225\{2a(1 - a)^{48} + a^2 \cdot 48(1 - a)^{47} \cdot (-1)\}$$

$$= 2450a(1 - a)^{47}\{(1 - a) - 24a\} = 2450a(1 - a)^{47}(1 - 25a).$$

Obviously $L(a)$ has its smallest value, that is zero, when $a = 0$ or $a = 1$, so it is greatest when $1 - 25a = 0$, or $a = 0.04$. Note that this is the value suggested by Table 1.

Notice that in this example the maximum likelihood principle leads to the same estimate as the extrapolation principle – which is encouraging. But this does not always happen.

Exercise 4B

1   Use calculus to verify the answer to Q.3 in §4.2.

2   A loaded die is rolled 20 times and three sixes turn up. If the probability of a six turning up in a single throw is denoted by s, write down an expression in terms of s for the likelihood of this outcome. Use the maximum likelihood principle to estimate the value of s.

3   Consider again the situation described in question 2 of Exercise 4A, in which the checker finds 2, 4, 1, 3 plates faulty in four successive batches of 50 plates. Assuming that the probability of a plate selected at random being faulty remains constant (denoted by a), explain why the likelihood of this succession of outcomes is

$$\text{constant} \times a^{10}(1 - a)^{190}.$$

Use this to make a new estimate of the value of a. What general result does your answer suggest?

4   A certain experiment is performed n times, and the outcome C occurs on r occasions. Assuming that the succession of experiments can be modelled by a Bernoulli sequence, and denoting P(C) by x, write down the likelihood of this result. Use this to estimate x in terms of r and n.

What light does this throw on the empirical method of finding probabilities described in §1.2?

5   Suppose that the experiment in question 4 is performed n_1, n_2 and n_3 times respectively on three successive days, and that the outcome C occurs r_1, r_2 and r_3 times. Use the maximum likelihood principle to estimate x from these data.

6   A spinner in a fruit machine is divided into 18 equal sections, and is arranged so that only one section is visible at a time. The sections are marked with lemons and other fruits; you would like to know the number, n, that are marked with lemons.

In nine spins a lemon turned up twice. Calculate the likelihood $L(n)$ of this outcome in terms of n. Find the value of n for which this likelihood is greatest.

Repeat this calculation if a lemon turned up twice in (a) ten spins, (b) eleven spins.

7   A bag contains 100 beads, all of the same size but some black and some white. A bead is taken out, its colour noted, and returned to the bag; this is repeated again and again, until ten beads have been taken. It turns out that four are white and six are black.

If the bag contained w white beads, express the likelihood of this result in terms of w. Hence use the maximum likelihood principle to estimate w.

8   The experiment in question 7 is varied by taking all ten beads out of the bag at once. Show that the likelihood is now given by

$$L(w) = \binom{w}{4}\binom{100-w}{6}\bigg/\binom{100}{10}.$$

Find the condition for $L(w + 1)$ to be greater than $L(w)$, and hence find the value of w which maximises the likelihood in this case.

9   Repeat questions 7 and 8 if, from the bag of 100 beads, a sample of eight is taken of which three are white.

10   A model can be made from Table 1 in §4.2, using a nailboard with the nails in a rectangular pattern and straws, cut to lengths proportional to the probabilities, placed over the nails. Make such a model, and use it to illustrate (a) the probabilities of getting different numbers of faulty plates in the sample for a given probability in the population as a whole, (b) the likelihood of getting a particular sample for different values of the probability. Alternatively, adapt the computer program which you wrote in question 10 of Exercise 3B to illustrate the distinction.

11   An ecologist is trying to estimate the number of squirrels in a wood, using the capture-recapture technique (see question 4 of Exercise 4A). On the first occasion she succeeds in catching and marking 20 squirrels. A week later she catches 30 squirrels, and finds that four of them are marked. Find the likelihood of getting this result in terms of the total population, n, of the squirrels in the wood. Find the value of n which maximises this likelihood. How does this compare with the estimate which would be given by the extrapolation principle?

12   An elderly man was watching his granddaughter playing a game with a die. Here is a snippet of the conversation between them:
"Mary: Another six! That makes five sixes I've got already, Grandad!
Grandad: Well done! How many throws did it take you to get them?
Mary: Ooh! ... I've lost count."
Use the maximum likelihood principle to estimate the answer.

13 Use Table 1 of §4.2 to find, for different values of a,
    (i) the probability that the number of faulty plates in a sample of 50 will be 2 or fewer,
    (ii) the probability that the number of faulty plates in a sample of 50 will be 2 or more.
    If, in estimating the probability a, we reject as "unreasonable" any value which makes either of these probablities less than 0.05, what values does this leave?

5

Random numbers and simulation

In previous chapters it has been suggested that you should carry out various experiments, such as drawing a pair of cards from a pack 50 times, noting the suits and shuffling after each draw. If you did this conscientiously, it will have taken quite a time. Later we are going to suggest that you carry out such experiments not just once but many times. To avoid provoking a sit-down strike, we intend in this chapter to describe some less laborious ways of carrying out experiments like this – or, to be more accurate, of 'simulating' them without using a pack of cards at all.

5.1 THE BINGO METHOD

To make a game of bingo or a raffle fair to all the competitors, there must be a way of drawing each of the numbers 1 to 99 – or whatever the range of numbers marked on the cards or tickets happens to be – with equal probability. You can arrange this with elaborate electronic equipment, like ERNIE which selects Premium Bond winners, (Note 5.1) or with a mechanical device which tosses numbered balls into the air randomly, or simply by having counters numbered 1 to 99 in a bag and picking one out by hand. The probability of a particular number – say 57 – coming up is then $\frac{1}{99}$; and this is the same as the probability of getting 5, or 83, or 31, or any other number in the possibility space.

In bingo or a raffle, once a number has been selected we do not usually want it to come up again, so after being drawn the counter or ball can be left on the table and the next draw made from those that remain. This is therefore an example of sampling without replacement. However, in other applications we often want to have the possibility of the same number or result coming up again with its probability unchanged, and this is arranged by putting the counter or ball back after its number has been recorded; this is sampling with replacement. Examples of the two methods of sampling were given in §2.3. In any sampling experiment it is important to decide whether the sampling is carried out with or without replacement.

Suppose that we want to imitate, or simulate, our experiment of drawing a pair of cards from a pack using a random ball-tossing device. It might be suggested that we could do this by using ten balls and marking them respectively [CC], [DD], [HH], [SS], [CD], [CH], [CS], [DH], [DS], [HS]. We could then imagine that picking the ball [HS] is equivalent to drawing a pair of cards consisting of one heart and one spade from the pack. Would this be a fair comparison?

Clearly not. If the machine tosses the balls into the air genuinely 'at random', then with this device the probability of getting the outcome [HS] would be $\frac{1}{10}$; but it was shown in §2.2 that the probability model for the card-drawing experiment assigns to this outcome the probability $\frac{13}{102}$. It is an essential feature of any simulation that each outcome in the simulation should have the same probability as the corresponding outcome in the experiment it is simulating – that is, *the experiment and its simulation should be described by the same probability model.*

Indeed, the probability model is the essential link between any experiment and its simulation. In this example, the ball-tossing device must be modified so that it gives probabilities of $\frac{6}{102}$ for outcomes such as [CC], [DD], ..., and $\frac{13}{102}$ for outcomes such as [CD], [CH], ... How can this be done in practice?

The simplest method is to use not 10 balls but 102, each with an equal probability of being picked, and to mark six of them [CC], six [DD], ..., thirteen [CD], thirteen [CH], ... Then, if a ball is taken at random, the probabilities of recording each of the ten possible outcomes will be the same as in the card-drawing experiment.

But this is hardly progress! If we have to go to the trouble of marking 102 separate balls before beginning the simulation, this will take even longer than the original experiment. The answer is of course to have a standard simulation device which can be used for any such experiment – consisting, for example, of a set of *numbered* balls – and to combine this with some code which associates with each number a particular outcome of the experiment being simulated. (Note 5.2) For example, the card-drawing experiment could be simulated by placing 102 balls in the machine, numbered consecutively from 1 to 102, and then interpreting the numbers which come up so that

balls numbered	1–6	7–12	13–18	19–24	25–37	38–50	51–63	64–76	77–89	90–102
correspond to	[CC]	[DD]	[HH]	[SS]	[CD]	[CH]	[CS]	[DH]	[DS]	[HS].

The probability of recording the outcome [SS], for example, is then the probability of picking a ball numbered *either* 19 *or* 20 *or* 21 *or* 22 *or* 23 *or* 24, that is $\frac{1}{102} + \frac{1}{102} + \frac{1}{102} + \frac{1}{102} + \frac{1}{102} + \frac{1}{102} = \frac{6}{102}$, just as required for a true simulation.

Q.1   Verify that this procedure would give the correct probabilities for all the outcomes of the experiment.

5.2 RANDOM NUMBERS

The next step is to ask whether we actually need to do the experiment at all. Could we not have a set of 'standard draws' made once for all, and take one off the shelf when we need it? This may not be as exciting as doing the draw on the spot, but it could save a lot of time – and be just as fair.

The answer is that we can and do: a table of "random numbers" is just that. The table consists simply of a large number of digits from 0 to 9 (which can be used singly or in blocks of any length we choose) such as you might get if you repeatedly drew a counter at random out of a bag. You can use these – starting wherever it takes your fancy, or better by selecting the row and column of the first digit by some random method – to save the work of doing the experiment.

There are many ways of making a collection of random numbers. If all you want is a single random digit, you could not do better than to go to the electric meter in your house and read the last digit; but this would be difficult to extend if you wanted a string of 100 random digits. More practically, you (or the class working together) could produce some with a spinner having sectors numbered 0 to 9, or with a 20-sided die having each of these digits on two of its faces. But if you do not want to make your own set, you can use a ready-made one. (Note 5.3)

If what you want is a sequence of numbers selected from the integers 0 to 9, then the table of random numbers can be used directly. The same is true if it is to be selected from the integers 0 to 99, provided that you take two digits at a time and remember to interpret 00 as 0, 01 as 1, 02 as 2, and so on. For a sequence of random numbers between 1 and 100, you can use the same method but interpret 00 as 100. Even if you want random numbers between 1 and 50, or 1 and 200, or 1 and 2500, this is quite easy, since the sizes of these sets divide exactly into some power of 10. For example, to pick a winner for a raffle in which you have sold just 50 tickets numbered 1 to 50, you can use two-digit random numbers and count 00 as 50, 01 as 1, 02 as 2, ..., 50 as 50, 51 as 1, 52 as 2, ..., 99 as 49.

Q.2   Check that this corresponds to the rule: "divide the random number by 50 and take the remainder as the number of the winning ticket, counting a zero remainder as 50."

It is rather more complicated, however, to use the table of random numbers in a case such as the card-drawing experiment, for which we required a sequence of random numbers selected from the integers from 1 to 102. Here are two possible methods, both illustrated by using the sequence of random numbers in four-digit blocks

$$8990 \quad 2636 \quad 2274 \quad 7113 \ldots.$$

taken from the top row of the SMP table of random numbers (see Note 5.3).

First method
Divide each four-digit random number in turn by 102 and take the remainder, counting a zero remainder as 102; then use the table in §5.1 to translate this into a pair of card suits.

$$8990 \div 102 = 88 \text{ remainder } 14, \text{ corresponding to [HH]}$$
$$2636 \div 102 = 25 \text{ remainder } 86, \text{ corresponding to [DS]}$$
$$2274 \div 102 = 22 \text{ remainder } 30, \text{ corresponding to [CD]}$$
$$7113 \div 102 = 69 \text{ remainder } 75, \text{ corresponding to [DH]}$$

So the simulated draw is [HH], [DS], [CD], [DH], ...

Second method
Treat each block of random numbers as a four-place decimal, multiply it by 102 and take the next greater integer, then use the table in §5.1 as before.

$$.8990 \times 102 = 91.6980, \text{ and } 92 \text{ corresponds to [HS]}$$
$$.2636 \times 102 = 26.8872, \text{ and } 27 \text{ corresponds to [CD]}$$
$$.2274 \times 102 = 23.1948, \text{ and } 24 \text{ corresponds to [SS]}$$
$$.7113 \times 102 = 72.5526, \text{ and } 73 \text{ corresponds to [DH]}$$

So the simulated draw is [HS], [CD], [SS], [DH], ...

Exercise 5A

[It may be appropriate for questions 1 to 3 in this exercise to be carried out in groups rather than individually.]

1   This question is about the experiment in which two cards are dealt from a pack and the suits recorded.
   (*a*) In §2.2 the results of carrying out the experiment 50 times are given. Display these in a bar chart. (If you did the experiment yourself and kept the results, use these instead of the ones printed in the book.)
   (*b*) Simulate the experiment by drawing numbered counters from a bag (or some other convenient method), using the coding described in §5.1. Make a bar chart to illustrate the results.
   (*c*) Repeat (*b*), but interpreting the numbers so that

balls numbered   1-6   7-19   20-32   33-45   46-51   52-64   65-77   78-83   84-96   97-102
correspond to   [CC]   [CD]   [CH]   [CS]   [DD]   [DH]   [DS]   [HH]   [HS]   [SS].

   (*d*) Simulate the experiment using a table of random numbers, translating these by means of the first method described in §5.2. Make a bar chart to illustrate the results.
   (*e*) Repeat (*d*), but using the second method described in §5.2.
   Compare your five bar charts, and make any comment you think appropriate.

2   Make one or other of the following pieces of equipment:
   (i) A spinner in the shape of a regular decagon, with its sides numbered 0, 1, 2, ..., 9.
   (ii) An icosahedron (20 faces), with pairs of opposite faces numbered 0, 1, 2, ..., 9.
   Use this to generate a sequence of random numbers.
      Test your digits for randomness by
   (*a*) finding the frequency of occurrence of each of the ten digits,
   (*b*) finding the number of 'doubles' 00, 11, 22, ..., 99 in your list, and comparing these with what you would expect on the basis of probability theory.

3   Make a list of all the families you know in which the parents have three children. Make a table showing the numbers of these families with 3 boys, 2 boys and a girl, 2 girls and a boy, 3 girls.
      Simulate this situation
   (*a*) by repeated tossing of three coins, making "tail" correspond to "boy" and "head" to "girl",

(b) using a table of random numbers with some appropriate coding.
Compare the results of your simulations with the evidence you collected of actual families.

4 Suggest ways of adapting a table of random numbers so as to produce sequences of random numbers with equal probabilities between (a) 0 and 249, (b) 1 and 200, (c) 1 and 80, (d) 34 and 58.

5 Use each of the two methods described in §5.2 to generate a sequence of random numbers between 1 and 37.

6 In the first method described in §5.2 for devising a sequence of random numbers between 1 and 102, some remainders occur more frequently than others, so that the simulation is not quite true. Investigate the difference between the probabilities assigned to the various outcomes in the simulation and the corresponding probabilities in the original experiment.
Suggest a way of modifying the simulation so as to correct this fault.

7 In the second method described in §5.2 for devising a sequence of random numbers between 1 and 102, some numbers occur more frequently than others, so that the simulation is not quite true. Explain why this is so, and investigate the difference between the probabilities assigned to the various outcomes in the simulation and the corresponding probabilities in the original experiment.

8 Use the tests for randomness suggested in question 2, and any others you can think of, to test the possibility of using (a) the final digits, (b) the last-but-one digits, of a sequence of numbers in the telephone directory as a sequence of random numbers.

9 Use a table of random numbers to simulate sequences of (a) throws of a die, (b) days of the week, (c) draws of a card from a pack.

10 Devise a method of using a table of random numbers to award first, second and third prizes at random to *different* members of your class.

5.3 PSEUDORANDOM NUMBERS

Nowadays there is an even simpler way of obtaining sequences of random numbers: we just get a computer to produce them for us to order when we need them.

Precisely what form the numbers come in depends on the particular model of computer available. Some machines will print out sequences of random integers between any limits which we wish to specify; others will print random decimal numbers between 0 and 1 to a given number of places. Both of these have their uses in statistical applications. But if your computer prints out random numbers in a form which is different from the one you want, it is usually quite simple to adapt them to fit your purpose.

Q.3 Write programs to get your computer to print out sequences of random numbers in as many different forms as possible. Try adapting your programs to produce the random numbers in alternative forms.

The idea of using a computer or a calculator to produce random numbers seems at first sight to be a contradiction in terms; for a computer can only do programmed calculations, and it is difficult to see how these can have a random result. However, what actually comes out of the computer is a sequence of numbers which *looks* totally random, and which satisfies any practical test for randomness – so that although they are not made by a genuinely random process they are just as good as if they were. Indeed, tables of random numbers are constructed by just such a method. Such sequences are called "pseudorandom".

Various algorithms have been suggested for making pseudorandom sequences, and they need to be checked carefully to ensure that they do not follow a concealed pattern. The biggest danger is that after a time the numbers get into a 'loop' which continually repeats itself. Here is a suggestion for one way in which you could construct your own 'personalised' set of random numbers:

Step 1. Write down your telephone number (or that of your college or school) as a number x, with a decimal point inserted so that the final digit comes in the sixth decimal place. Delete any digits which come in front of the decimal point.

Step 2. Map the letters of the alphabet cyclically onto the numbers from 1 to 9, so that $A \to 1$, $B \to 2$, ..., $I \to 9$, $J \to 1$, $K \to 2$, ..., $R \to 9$, $S \to 1$, ..., $Z \to 8$. In this way convert the first three letters of your last name into a multiplier m.

Step 3. Use the same method to convert the first six letters of your first name, and write it after the decimal point to give an adder c. (If your name is too short for this, put a suitable number of zeros after the decimal point.)

Step 4. Form $y = mx + c$, delete any numbers in front of the decimal point, and record the first four digits after the point as a random number.

Step 5. Using y (with the front digits deleted) in place of x, repeat the process.

For example, the telephone number of Cambridge University Press is 0223312393, so that their sequence of random numbers would be calculated as follows:

	$x = 0223.312393$	248.666734	530.367829
PRE$$→795	$m = 795$	795	795
	248.352435	530.053530	292.424055
CAMBRIDGE→314299	$c = .314299$	$.314299$	$.314299$
	$y = 248.666734$	530.367829	292.738354

The random numbers therefore begin

$$6667 \quad 3678 \quad 7383 \quad .... \quad ....$$

and these can now be used in the way described in §5.2.

Q.4 Write and run a computer program to produce your own sequence of pseudorandom numbers according to this algorithm.

5.4 MAKING FULL USE OF THE COMPUTER

Using a table of random numbers removes some of the drudgery from statistical experiments, but – as you will have found – the business of recording, coding, tabulating and counting is still time-consuming. One big advantage of using a computer to produce random numbers is that we can then arrange for all these other processes to be done automatically without any intervention on our part.

Suppose, for example, that we want to simulate the experiment of throwing a die 1000 times. Then this could be done by a program such as:

```
FOR THROW = 1 TO 1000
PRINT RND(6)
NEXT THROW
```

(Note 5.4) But this would present us with 1000 scores, which would still need to be sorted and counted – and these are tasks for which the computer is ideally suited! All that is needed is to set up an array of six stores, denoted by FREQ(S) for S = 1, 2, ..., 6, in which a tally of the frequencies of the six possible scores can be kept. If these are set initially to zero, then the program

```
FOR THROW = 1 TO 1000
S = RND(6)
FREQ(S) = FREQ(S) + 1
NEXT THROW
```

counts the numbers of occurrences of each score – and we would never even have seen the individual scores displayed. The process can then be completed with a sequence of print-out commands:

```
FOR S = 1 TO 6
PRINT "The frequency of the score"; S; "is"; FREQ(S)
NEXT S
```

Q.5 Write and run this program. Then adapt it for use with a 'die' having any number of faces, thrown any number of times. (K)

The advantage of using the computer to simulate the experiment is now obvious. In a fraction of the time that it would take to roll the real die 1000 times the experiment can be simulated over and over again – so that you could get an idea whether the first set of results is typical, and how much variation you might expect to find between different runs of the same experiment.

But there is just one drawback. Doing an experiment 'for real' gives one a feel for the situation, and the experience we get in this way sometimes leads us to modify or to re-think the experiment itself. If we go straight to the computer, we shall lose this experience – with possible unfortunate consequences. It is often worth while to do a short run of an experiment by hand in the first instance, before having recourse to the computer. In this way we get the best of both worlds.

Exercise 5B

1   Write a computer program to simulate the experiment of dealing two cards from a pack and recording the suits (see Exercise 5A, question 1), arranging for the suit-pairs to be printed out directly.

 Adapt your program so that the frequencies of the ten possible suit-pairs are printed out.

2   Use a computer to print out random sequences of (a) throws of a die, (b) days of the week, (c) draws of a card from a pack.

3   Program a computer to award first, second and third prizes to *different* members of your class.

4   Write and run a computer program to generate a sequence of 1001 random digits (from 0 to 9) and to count the number of 'doubles' 00, 11, 22, ..., or 99.

5   One method that has been suggested for making up a sequence of pseudorandom four-digit numbers is as follows. Take any four-digit number, square it and retain the middle four digits; repeat this process indefinitely. Write and run a computer program to carry out this procedure.

 Suggest a weakness in the method proposed.

6   Combine the computer program which you wrote in question 6 of Exercise 1A with that in Q.5 of §5.4, so as to generate a sequence of n random integers between 1 and q and print out their mean m and variance v.

 For some chosen values of n and q, run this program several times and comment on the results. (K)

7   Adapt the program in Q.5 of §5.4 so as to produce the output in the form of a stick graph showing the frequencies of the various possible scores as the experiment proceeds.

8   Write and run a computer program to simulate a sequence of tosses of a coin, and to produce the output in the form of a table of frequencies of runs of various lengths of each of the outcomes "head" and "tail".

9   In §3.4 a sequence of outcomes A and B of an experiment of Bernoulli type was generated artificially using a table of random numbers (see Note 3.9). Use a computer to generate such a sequence, based on the same probabilities 0.46 and 0.54, and to produce the output in the form of a table of frequencies of runs of various lengths of each outcome.

 Now simulate a sequence of outcomes of the Oxford and Cambridge boat race in a similar manner, basing it on the probabilities 0.61 and 0.39 following an Oxford win, and 0.34 and 0.66 following a Cambridge win.

10   Use a computer to simulate the Markov type situation described in question 1 of Exercise 3C, arranging the program so as to print out the number of times I am late in each successive week.

11   In a sequence of 20 two-digit random numbers, how many would you expect to contain the digit 7 (e.g. 57, 73, 77)?

 Use the computer to generate a succession of such sequences, and to display in the form of a stick graph how many of the sequences have 0, 1, 2, 3, ... of their members which contain the digit 7.

5.5 USING SIMULATION TO INVESTIGATE REAL-LIFE PROBLEMS

Experiments with coins, dice or cards are usually described by simple probability models, and they can often be analysed theoretically. For example, we have already seen that some problems of this kind can be related to a binomial probability model; in later chapters other models with simple equations will be introduced. The simulation methods described in this chapter are useful in getting a first idea of how the models are likely to work out in practice, and may give us a lead in the direction of the appropriate theory.

But when we are concerned with a problem in the real world – designing a pension scheme, reorganising the queueing system in a bank, or tracing the progress of an epidemic – the probability models are likely to be too complicated for theoretical analysis. Then simulation really comes into its own.

To illustrate this, we will return to the problem which we started to investigate in §2.4, of deciding how many fire engines are needed to provide adequate cover for a town. On the basis of data collected over a month, two probability models were suggested:

Number of calls per hour	0	1	2	3	4	*Total*
Probability	0.32	0.34	0.21	0.10	0.03	1.00

Model 1.   Number of calls per hour

Number of hours away	$\frac{1}{2}$ to 1	1 to $1\frac{1}{2}$	$1\frac{1}{2}$ to 2	2 to $2\frac{1}{2}$	$2\frac{1}{2}$ to 3	3 to $3\frac{1}{2}$	$3\frac{1}{2}$ to 4	4 to $4\frac{1}{2}$	*Total*
Probability	0.08	0.19	0.25	0.21	0.14	0.08	0.03	0.02	1.00

Model 2.   Time taken to service a call

Now with empirical results like this, there is no possibility of devising a set of algebraic formulae to determine the number of fire engines needed. So instead, the use of fire engines in the town is simulated by 'playing' these two probability models with the help of sequences of random numbers.

To do this, it is first necessary to devise a method of coding the random numbers in terms of the possibility spaces for each model. Since the probabilities are given to two decimal places, the obvious choice is to use two-digit random numbers. One possible choice of codings which give the right probabilities is:

Random numbers	00–31	32–65	66–86	87–96	97–99	
correspond to	0	1	2	3	4	calls during the hour.

Model 1

Random numbers correspond to	00–07	08–26	27–51	52–72	73–86	87–94	95–97	98–99	
	$\frac{1}{2}$ to 1	1 to $1\frac{1}{2}$	$1\frac{1}{2}$ to 2	2 to $2\frac{1}{2}$	$2\frac{1}{2}$ to 3	3 to $3\frac{1}{2}$	$3\frac{1}{2}$ to 4	4 to $4\frac{1}{2}$	hours away.

Model 2

We now start to 'run' the fire station from time 0000 on day 1 using two sets of random numbers. In Fig. 1 this has been done using the SMP random numbers (see Note 5.3) – reading the numbers across the page from the top left corner for model 1, and up the page from the bottom right corner for model 2.

There are certain practical details which have to be settled before we can start:

(a) In model 1, at what precise times during the hour are the calls supposed to come in? The solution adopted in Fig. 1 is to divide the hour into equal sub-intervals, and to suppose that the call comes in at the middle of each sub-interval – so that, for example, with three calls in an hour the sub-intervals have duration 20 minutes and the calls come in at 10, 30 and 50 minutes past the hour. (An alternative, possibly more realistic method would be to use a third set of random numbers between 00 and 59 to decide the minute in which each call arrives.)

(b) In model 2 there is a half-hour tolerance in stating the length of time the fire engine is out. In Fig. 1 the upper bound of this has been taken: for example, "$1\frac{1}{2}$ to 2 hours" has been interpreted as "2 hours", so that the crew can usually reckon on getting a short break before they are on call again. But here too it would have been possible to assign this time by a further random process.

This is how the system operates. The first of the model 1 random numbers is 89, giving three calls in the first hour. By (a), these come in at times 0010, 0030 and 0050. We therefore need three of the model 2 random numbers, and the first of these are 11, 63 and 16 – indicating that these calls require the use of the fire engines for $1\frac{1}{2}$, $2\frac{1}{2}$ and $1\frac{1}{2}$ hours respectively. They are shown by the top bars in the columns headed A, B and C in the chart on the right side of Fig. 1.

It is left to you to follow through the rest of the first day's operation. It needs to be explained that, in the chart, each bar has been put successively in the column as far to the left as possible at the time; from this it is easy to see how many fire engines are in use at any one time. (Each column does not, though, correspond to a particular engine and crew; which one to send out on a call is a scheduling question, which cannot really be decided until the number of available fire engines is known.)

Notice that the largest number required at any one time during the first day is five, but that the time during which they are all out together is very short – only $1\frac{1}{2}$ hours – and there is in fact one period of $\frac{3}{4}$ hour when none of them is in use. The total duration of all the 31 calls on that day is only $68\frac{1}{2}$ hours (plus $1\frac{1}{2}$ which spill over into day 2). So, if the fire station is equipped to cope with the maximum demand the fire engines are standing idle for 43% of the time.

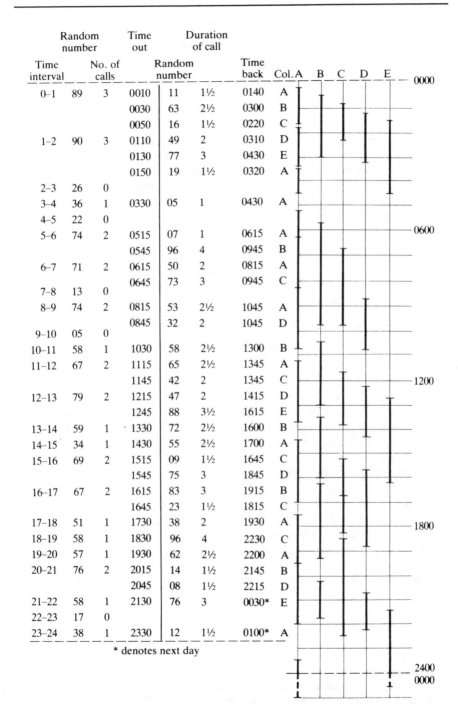

Time interval	Random number — No. of calls	Time out	Random number	Duration of call	Time back	Col.
0–1	89 3	0010	11	1½	0140	A
		0030	63	2½	0300	B
		0050	16	1½	0220	C
1–2	90 3	0110	49	2	0310	D
		0130	77	3	0430	E
		0150	19	1½	0320	A
2–3	26 0					
3–4	36 1	0330	05	1	0430	A
4–5	22 0					
5–6	74 2	0515	07	1	0615	A
		0545	96	4	0945	B
6–7	71 2	0615	50	2	0815	A
		0645	73	3	0945	C
7–8	13 0					
8–9	74 2	0815	53	2½	1045	A
		0845	32	2	1045	D
9–10	05 0					
10–11	58 1	1030	58	2½	1300	B
11–12	67 2	1115	65	2½	1345	A
		1145	42	2	1345	C
12–13	79 2	1215	47	2	1415	D
		1245	88	3½	1615	E
13–14	59 1	1330	72	2½	1600	B
14–15	34 1	1430	55	2½	1700	A
15–16	69 2	1515	09	1½	1645	C
		1545	75	3	1845	D
16–17	67 2	1615	83	3	1915	B
		1645	23	1½	1815	C
17–18	51 1	1730	38	2	1930	A
18–19	58 1	1830	96	4	2230	C
19–20	57 1	1930	62	2½	2200	A
20–21	76 2	2015	14	1½	2145	B
		2045	08	1½	2215	D
21–22	58 1	2130	76	3	0030*	E
22–23	17 0					
23–24	38 1	2330	12	1½	0100*	A

* denotes next day

Figure 1

Exercise 5C

1   Run day 2 of the fire station simulation. (If possible, use the continuation of the same sets of random numbers. Remember that two fire engines are out already.)

2   Write a computer program to simulate the fire station situation. Include in the print-out (*a*) the largest number of fire engines out at any one time, and (*b*) the total duration of all the calls. Use your program to simulate the working of the fire station over a period of four weeks.

3   A garage uses one petrol pump attendant who can deal with two customers in a 5-minute interval. It has been found that, in any non-rush hour period, custom is subject to random variations and that, in periods of five minutes, the probabilities of 0, 1, 2, 3, 4 cars stopping for petrol are 0.05, 0.15, 0.40, 0.30, 0.10 respectively. Simulate this situation for three one-hour runs, assuming that a new arrival will not wait if there are two cars already waiting to be served. How much custom is lost as a result of having only one attendant?   [Cambridge]

4   The probabilities of different numbers of ships arriving at a seaport on any day are as follows:

Number of arrivals	1	2	3	4
Probability	0.1	0.3	0.4	0.2

The turn-round time for a ship is four days, including the day of docking; thus if a ship arrives on day x and docks on day y, it will occupy a berth on days y, $y + 1$, $y + 2$, $y + 3$. If there is a berth vacant on the day of arrival, it can dock straight away (so that $y = x$).

There are ten berths altogether, and at the beginning of 1 January one berth is free, four are occupied by ships which docked on 31 December, two by ships which docked on 30 December, and three by ships which docked on 29 December. Simulate the situation in the port on the first 20 days of the new year. Find the numbers of ships waiting idle or the numbers of berths unoccupied on each day, and show the results on a graph.

Investigate the effect of having different numbers of berths on the operation of the port.   [Cambridge]

5   Use the data on post office arrival and service times which you collected in Exercise 2C, question 4 to simulate the processing of customers with various numbers of service points. Assume that each new arrival joins the queue which is shortest at the time. Compute the average length of time a customer has to wait, and the standard deviation.

With the same data simulate the service if the "separate queue" system is replaced by the "single queue" system. Again find the average waiting time and the standard deviation.

6   Choose a stretch of two-way road along which traffic flows freely and where it is sometimes difficult for pedestrians to cross. Make observations of the time-intervals between successive vehicles in each direction, and use this to construct a simplified probability model for the traffic flow in each direction.

Simulate this traffic flow, and hence compute the average time that a pedestrian would have to wait before he can cross the road safely. Then repeat your simulation with a pedestrian refuge built in the middle of the road. Do your results suggest that a significant improvement could be made in the ease of crossing the road if such a refuge were provided?

6

Testing the model

A probability model is a piece of theory: but we can use it to predict what will happen in practice. The difficulty with statistics is that what actually happens rarely agrees with what we predict. This is because statistics is all about *variability*.

Of course, if what we actually observe is close to what we expect, nobody is very worried. But if the two are very different, then there are two possible conclusions: either something is wrong with the experiment (for example, we may have taken a very untypical sample), or the theory is wrong. In that case we must go back to the drawing board.

But the crucial question is, how close is "close"?

6.1 THEORY AND PRACTICE

To get the most out of this chapter, you will need to begin by doing a small experiment. If you are working in a class, then it is best if you all do the experiment independently; for it is the comparison of a number of different sets of experimental results that may suggest how a theory of "goodness of fit" can be constructed.

Take a pencil with a hexagonal cross-section, and with coloured pens mark successive faces as follows: blue, green, red, blue, green, red. Then roll the pencil on the table 30 times and record the colour that comes up on the top face each time. Count the frequencies of each colour.

Are your results what you would expect?

What *would* you expect?

Hopefully, your answer to that question was "It's impossible to tell." It would not be surprising if you went on to say: "I suppose you're hoping that I'll answer that I expect to get 10 of each colour. Mathematicians are like that! If you insist, I'll (grudgingly) go along with you; but I don't really believe it. In fact, if someone said that he actually got 10, 10, 10, I would suspect him of fiddling the results."

Quite right. When I did the experiment, the result was:

Colour	blue	green	red
Frequency	11	8	11

This amount of deviation from the 'equal frequencies' result seemed acceptable, and in line with experience. But in another experiment I got:

Colour	blue	green	red
Frequency	17	6	7

This looked distinctly unlikely. (Not surprisingly: the pencil was in fact 'loaded' deliberately.) Our problem is, what results might quite reasonably occur with an unbiased pencil, and at what point would we say "It looks as if that pencil is loaded"?

In this discussion, what is the status of the 'equal frequencies' result? It would certainly be going too far to say that this is what we would 'expect' to get. On the other hand, with an unloaded pencil we would be surprised if the frequencies came out very different from these. It therefore provides a kind of standard against which an actual result can be compared.

It is useful to remind ourselves where these frequencies come from. In §1.2 it was pointed out that two different ways are used to find probabilities – empirical and theoretical. Either of these can be used to obtain a set of standard frequencies for an experiment, as follows:

EMPIRICAL APPROACH   THEORETICAL APPROACH

Experiment, leading to calculation of relative frequencies for the various possible outcomes.

Identification of equally likely primitive outcomes.

Observation that relative frequencies appear to approach limiting values.

Proportion of these primitive outcomes associated with each recorded outcome.

Probabilities of the various outcomes in the possibility space (probability model).

Calculation of standard frequencies as probabilities × number of repetitions.

In our experiment the probabilities are found theoretically, as:

Colour	blue	green	red
Probability	$\frac{1}{3}$	$\frac{1}{3}$	$\frac{1}{3}$

The standard frequencies are then calculated by multiplying these probabilities by 30 (the number of repetitions) to give:

Colour	blue	green	red
Standard frequency	10	10	10

In statistics it is customary to refer to these standard frequencies as "expected frequencies", or "expectations", but it is important to realise that these results are not those we actually expect to get – statisticians have more common sense than this! However, it is difficult to think of any other term which is not equally misleading. So, with this warning, we shall adopt the conventional terminology, and define:

In an experiment of Bernoulli type, the *expected frequency* of each outcome is the product of its probability and the number of repetitions.

The notation $F_e(C)$ will be used to stand for the expected frequency of an outcome C, and $F_o(C)$ for the actual, or "observed", frequency of the outcome in the experiment. (See Note 1.6) Thus if the experiment is performed a number of times (for example, if each member of your class did the pencil experiment independently) the values obtained for $F_o(C)$ will probably be different, but $F_e(C)$ will stay the same provided that the conditions do not change. Also, the letter k will be used to denote the number of different outcomes in the possibility space, and n the number of repetitions: in the rolling pencil experiment, $k = 3$ and $n = 30$.

Q.1   Use this notation to write the definition of expected frequency in the form of an equation.

Q.2   When you did the experiment, what were the values of $F_e(\text{blue})$ and $F_o(\text{blue})$?

Q.3   If the outcomes of an experiment are denoted by C_i, where i takes the values 1, 2, 3, ..., k, explain why

$$\sum_{i=1}^{k} \{F_o(C_i) - F_e(C_i)\} = 0.$$

6.2 A MEASURE OF NONCONFORMITY

Of the members of your class who carried out the pencil experiment, whose result came closest to the expected frequencies? Whose came furthest away?

You may not find it easy to agree about the answers to these questions. How can we measure how close the observed frequencies come to 10, 10, 10? Is a person who got 4 blue, 10 green and 16 red closer than one who got 7 blue, 17 green and 6 red, or not? To answer this, what we need is a single number which will indicate how well one's results conform to the expected frequencies – a kind of 'distance' between the two.

Use of the word 'distance' suggests the possibility of a geometrical approach. In fact, we deliberately began with an experiment having just three outcomes, so that it is possible to represent the result by a point in three-dimensional space having coordinates (F_o(blue), F_o(green), F_o(red)), which it will be convenient to abbreviate to (b, g, r). My own result is illustrated in this way in Fig. 1; the point marked E shows the 'expected' result (10, 10, 10).

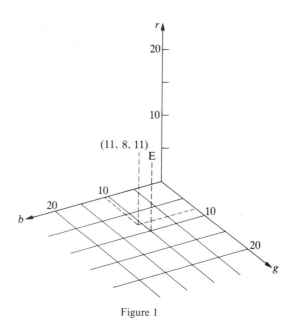

Figure 1

A nice way of showing this practically is to make a physical model. You can do this by taking a base of some softish flat material such as corkboard or polystyrene, and pasting on top of this a sheet of squared paper. A cocktail stick is then pushed into the surface at the point with coordinates (b, g) on the squared paper, and a drinking straw is slipped over the stick and cut to a length r (on the same scale as the coordinates b and g). The point (b, g, r) can conveniently be marked at the top of the straw with a felt-tip pen. It may also help to stick a knitting needle upright into the base at (0, 0) to represent the r-axis.

Q.4   Make such a model, with a separate straw for the result obtained by each member of the class. Also insert a straw of a different colour to show the expected frequencies (10, 10, 10). What do you notice about all the points? Does this model help to settle the questions at the beginning of this section?

There is a simple check on the accuracy of your model: since the frequencies add up to 30, the tops of all the straws should lie in the plane whose equation is $b + g + r = 30$. You can test this with a piece of flat card.

Now, with this model, there is a natural way of displaying the difference between one's own result and the expected frequencies: that is, by means of the vector from E to the point representing the observed result. For my result, illustrated in Fig. 1, this vector is

$$\begin{bmatrix} 11 \\ 8 \\ 11 \end{bmatrix} - \begin{bmatrix} 10 \\ 10 \\ 10 \end{bmatrix} = \begin{bmatrix} 11 - 10 \\ 8 - 10 \\ 11 - 10 \end{bmatrix} = \begin{bmatrix} 1 \\ -2 \\ 1 \end{bmatrix}.$$

The length l of this vector then provides a distance which could be used to measure the nonconformity of the result – the larger the distance, the less good the match. For my result,

$$l^2 = 1^2 + (-2)^2 + 1^2 = 6.$$

Q.5 Calculate l^2 for your own result, and put the values for all the members of the class in order of closeness on this basis. Does this order correspond to your earlier impression?

Q.6 For a general result, write expressions for the vector and the value of l^2 in terms of the frequencies (b, g, r). Then rewrite these expressions using the notation $F_o(\text{blue})$, $F_e(\text{blue})$, etc. What relationship always holds between the three components of the vector?

6.3 WHAT IS "REASONABLY CLOSE"?

A small difference between an observed result and the expected frequencies, measured by a small value of l^2, is clearly acceptable. But there comes a point where l^2 becomes so large that we begin to suspect that something is amiss, either with the experiment or the theory. For example, my second set of results

(17, 6, 7) is represented by a vector from E of $\begin{bmatrix} 7 \\ -4 \\ -3 \end{bmatrix}$, so that

$$l^2 = 7^2 + (-4)^2 + (-3)^2 = 74;$$

and this gave rise to suspicions that the pencil might be loaded. The problem is, where to draw the dividing line between values which are acceptable without question and values which – though not impossible – make us uneasy. This is a matter of probability.

The pencil experiment consists of a sequence of 30 trials, each of which has three possible outcomes – blue, green, red – with fixed independent probabilities $\frac{1}{3}, \frac{1}{3}, \frac{1}{3}$ (provided that the pencil is not loaded). This is therefore a Bernoulli sequence, so that the probabilities of getting various frequencies (b, g, r) in the complete experiment are given by the multinomial probability model (see

Exercise 3B, question 13) as

$$\frac{30!}{b! \times g! \times r!} (\tfrac{1}{3})^{b}(\tfrac{1}{3})^{g}(\tfrac{1}{3})^{r}.$$

For example, the probability that the experiment will throw up the expected frequencies (10, 10, 10) is

$$\frac{30!}{10! \times 10! \times 10!} (\tfrac{1}{3})^{10}(\tfrac{1}{3})^{10}(\tfrac{1}{3})^{10} \approx 0.0270:$$

that is, we expect to get this result not every time, but on average once in just under 40 times!

Q.7   Calculate the probability of your own result when you did the experiment. Compare this with the probabilities for the results obtained by other members of the class.

Q.8   Calculate the probability of my first result (11, 8, 11). Show that there are five other results which give rise to a value $l^2 = 6$, and that two of these have the same probability as mine, whilst the other three have a different probability.

Q.9   Calculate the probability of my second result (17, 6, 7), for which $l^2 = 74$. What is the probability of getting a result such that $l^2 = 74$?

The calculation of these probabilities for all the possible results is a somewhat tedious process, but the geometrical representation in Fig. 1 provides a convenient way of displaying these. Since all the results (b, g, r) are represented by points in the plane $b + g + r = 30$, they can be shown in a two-dimensional diagram at the vertices of a triangular grid bounded by the triangle in which this plane intersects the planes $b = 0$, $g = 0$ and $r = 0$; the vertices of this triangle have coordinates (30, 0, 0), (0, 30, 0) and (0, 0, 30).

Q.10   To which results do these points correspond? What are their probabilities? What is the value of l^2 for these points?

In Fig. 2 this triangle has been drawn out. You can imagine it as being a view of the plane looked at from a point far out along the vector in the direction $\begin{bmatrix} 1 \\ 1 \\ 1 \end{bmatrix}$; the b-, g- and r-axes would then appear to be coming out of the plane at an angle, and the origin (0, 0, 0) would be hidden behind the centroid of the triangle.

Also in Fig. 2, at the points of the triangular grid with integer coordinates, have been marked the probabilities of the corresponding results for the pencil experiment. For ease of reading, these probabilities have been multiplied by 10^4 in the diagram. For example, the figure of 270 shown at the centroid of the

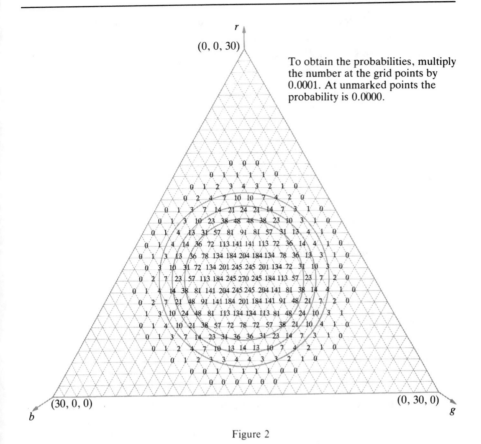

Figure 2

triangle indicates the probability of 0.0270 for the expected frequencies (10, 10, 10) as calculated earlier.

Q.11   Locate in Fig. 2 the results referred to in Q.7, Q.8 and Q.9, and verify the probabilities shown in the diagram.

Q.12   Find in Fig. 2 all the points for which $l^2 \leqslant 6$. Use the given probabilities to find the probability of getting a set of frequencies in the pencil experiment which is as close (or closer) to the expected frequencies (10, 10, 10) as my first result (11, 8, 11).

What is obvious from Fig. 2 is that there is a high probability of getting a result which is quite close to the expected frequencies. To demonstrate this, three circles have been added to Fig. 2, enclosing the points of the plane for which $l^2 \leqslant 46, l^2 \leqslant 59$ and $l^2 \leqslant 92$. It can be calculated that the probabilities of getting a result represented by a point within these circles are about 0.90, 0.95 and 0.99 respectively. So, although none of the results represented on the grid is absolutely impossible, on average only 10%, 5% and 1% respectively will lie outside these circles. This means that, if we do the experiment and get frequencies for the three colours shown outside one of these circles, then there is good reason to suspect that there is some mismatch between theory and practice. For example, the frequencies of (17, 6, 7) which I obtained in my second experiment (when the pencil was loaded) give a point which lies outside the two smaller circles and only just inside the largest one; so we were justified in regarding them with suspicion.

To verify this theory, I wrote a computer program to simulate the pencil experiment and ran it 100 times. On each occasion the frequencies of the three colours were counted and a value of l^2 was calculated: the program then recorded where the point lay in relation to each of the three circles. When the program was run, the result was:

Point outside the circle	smallest $(l^2 > 46)$	middle $(l^2 > 59)$	largest $(l^2 > 92)$
Number of occasions in 100 runs	12	4	0

This seems to agree well with the 10%, 5% and 1% figures suggested by the theory.

Q.13 By adding the probabilities shown in Fig. 2 at points inside the smallest circle, verify that the probability of getting a result in this region is about 0.90.

Q.14 When members of your class did the experiment, what proportion of the points were outside (*a*) the smallest circle, (*b*) the middle circle, (*c*) the largest circle?

Q.15 Write your own program to carry out the simulation described in the last paragraph. (Keep this until after Q.17.)

6.4 APPLICATION TO OTHER EXPERIMENTS

The trouble with the method described in the last section is that it only applies to experiments in which the number of trials is 30 and the probabilities are equal. The next step must be to extend the theory so that it can be applied to a wider range of experiments.

First, consider what difference it might make if the pencil were rolled a different number of times – 3000, say. In theory it would still be possible to calculate the probabilities and show them in a diagram such as Fig. 2, but the labour would now be enormous. Fortunately, it turns out that this is unnecessary.

It will be helpful to concentrate on a particular experimental result, for example the frequencies (11, 8, 11) which I obtained in my first experiment. We have seen that this differs from the expected frequencies by $\begin{bmatrix} 1 \\ -2 \\ 1 \end{bmatrix}$, and (from Q.12) that just under 0.3 of all the experiments would come out as close to (or closer than) the expected frequencies as this.

Now with 3000 rolls the expected frequencies are (1000, 1000, 1000), and the result which differs from this by the same vector $\begin{bmatrix} 1 \\ -2 \\ 1 \end{bmatrix}$ is (1001, 998, 1001). Would you expect about 0.3 of all the experiments to come out as close to the expected frequencies as this? Surely not – indeed, if anyone claimed to have got such a result you would probably suspect that they had rigged the experiment. I adapted my computer program to simulate rolling the pencil 3000 times, and the smallest value of l^2 I achieved in 100 runs was 42. So clearly with 3000 rolls the radii of the circles which net any given proportion of the results must be much larger than they were with 30 rolls.

Another possibility suggested by the geometrical approach is that the radii might be scaled up in proportion: that since with 3000 rolls the triangle has sides 100 times as large as Fig. 2, the radii should also be multiplied by 100, which would mean that a vector of $\begin{bmatrix} 1 \\ -2 \\ 1 \end{bmatrix}$ would be magnified to $\begin{bmatrix} 100 \\ -200 \\ 100 \end{bmatrix}$, giving frequencies of (1100, 800, 1100) and a value of 60 000 for l^2. Would you expect about 0.3 of all the experiments to come as close as this? Again, this seems most improbable: whilst we expect some variability, surely most of the results will be much nearer than this to the expected frequencies. Indeed, in the 100 runs of my computer simulation, the largest value of l^2 which came up was 17 658.

The right answer would seem to lie somewhere between these extremes: the radii must be increased, but not in proportion to the number of rolls. It turns out that the appropriate scaling is to make the radii increase in proportion to the square root of the number of rolls: so that with 3000 rolls the dimensions should be 10 times what they were with 30 rolls. This means that the vector $\begin{bmatrix} 1 \\ -2 \\ 1 \end{bmatrix}$ would become $\begin{bmatrix} 10 \\ -20 \\ 10 \end{bmatrix}$, making frequencies of (1010, 980, 1010) of equivalent closeness to (11, 8, 11) in the smaller experiment. With this modification the value of l^2 would be 100 times as large.

For a proof of the statements in the last paragraph you will have to wait until Chapter 18; but meanwhile they can be made credible by computer simulation. The program described at the end of 6.3 was changed so that it simulated an experiment in which the pencil was rolled 3000 times, and the critical values of l^2 were changed from 46, 59, 92 to 4610, 5990, 9210. (Note 6.1) When the program was run, the result was:

Point outside the circle	smallest	middle	largest
Number of occasions in 100 runs	14	7	1

These figures are only slightly higher than the 10%, 5% and 1% suggested by the theory, so they provide encouragement that the values of l^2 have been scaled up in the right proportion.

Q.16   Change the computer program which you wrote in Q.15 so that you can carry out this simulation for yourself. (*Warning*. This involves selecting 300 000 random numbers, so running the program may take a considerable time.)

But it is not very satisfactory to have a procedure which involves using different critical values according to the number of times the pencil is rolled; and this drawback can be got over by applying the scaling instead to the quantity which we use to measure closeness. That is, in place of l^2 a different measure of closeness is defined by *dividing each term by the corresponding expected value*. We call this quantity the "discrepancy" between the observed and the expected frequencies. So for 30 rolls, when the expected frequency of each colour is 10, the discrepancy is given by the formula

$$\frac{(b - 10)^2}{10} + \frac{(g - 10)^2}{10} + \frac{(r - 10)^2}{10},$$

which is of course just $l^2/10$; and for 3000 rolls, with expected frequencies of 1000, it is given by

$$\frac{(b - 1000)^2}{1000} + \frac{(g - 1000)^2}{1000} + \frac{(r - 1000)^2}{1000},$$

which is $l^2/1000$. For example, the frequencies (11, 8, 11) and (1010, 980, 1010), which seemed to be of equivalent closeness to the respective expected frequencies, would have discrepancies of 6/10 and 600/1000 – and these are both equal to 0.6. So we expect that, in different experiments, *results with the same discrepancy are of equivalent closeness in terms of probability*.

In that case, if the circles in Fig. 2 are defined in terms of discrepancy rather than distance, then the critical values are also independent of the number of times the pencil is rolled. These values are found by dividing 46, 59, 92 by 10, or by dividing 4610, 5990, 9210 by 1000; and we find that, for any sequence of trials having three outcomes with probabilities $(\frac{1}{3}, \frac{1}{3}, \frac{1}{3})$ in which the frequencies of each outcome are recorded, there is a probability of

$$\left\{ \begin{array}{l} \text{0.10 that the discrepancy will exceed 4.61,} \\ \text{0.05 that the discrepancy will exceed 5.99,} \\ \text{0.01 that the discrepancy will exceed 9.21.} \end{array} \right.$$

Q.17   Adapt the computer program which you wrote in Q.15 so that it operates in terms of the discrepancy rather than l^2. (K)

Q.18   Write an expression for the discrepancy using the notation $F_o(\text{blue})$, $F_e(\text{blue})$, etc.

6.5 GENERALISATION TO UNEQUAL EXPECTED FREQUENCIES

There is an even more important reason for measuring closeness by the discrepancy rather than by l^2: that is when the probabilities of the outcomes are unequal, so that the expected frequencies are different from each other.

To investigate that I carried out another experiment in which the faces of the pencil were coloured in succession blue, green, blue, red, blue, red. Then, if the pencil is fairly balanced, theory suggests for 30 rolls:

Colour	blue	green	red
Probability	$\frac{1}{2}$	$\frac{1}{6}$	$\frac{1}{3}$
Expected frequency	15	5	10

But in practice my results were 11 blue, 7 green and 12 red. So the vector indicating the difference between the observed and expected frequencies is

$$\begin{bmatrix} 11 \\ 7 \\ 12 \end{bmatrix} - \begin{bmatrix} 15 \\ 5 \\ 10 \end{bmatrix} = \begin{bmatrix} 11 - 15 \\ 7 - 5 \\ 12 - 10 \end{bmatrix} = \begin{bmatrix} -4 \\ 2 \\ 2 \end{bmatrix}.$$

Now this is certainly further out than my previous experimental result, but you would probably think that it is not too unlikely.

Suppose however that the big difference had occurred in the frequency of the green rather than the blue, so that the results had been 17 blue, 1 green and 12 red. The vector would then have been $\begin{bmatrix} 2 \\ -4 \\ 2 \end{bmatrix}$, which has the same length as before; but you would probably think that this is a less likely result. We can check this by calculating the probabilities.

Q.19 Use the multinomial probability model to calculate the probabilities of (a) the expected frequencies (15, 5, 10), (b) my frequencies (11, 7, 12), (c) the frequencies (17, 1, 12).

Q.20 Calculate the discrepancies from the expected frequencies of (a) my frequencies (11, 7, 12), (b) the frequencies (17, 1, 12).

Notice that, although the vectors have the same length, mine has the smaller discrepancy and a correspondingly larger probability.

To show what is going on, Fig. 3 gives the triangular grid of Fig. 2 adapted for the unsymmetrical case. You can see from this that the expected frequencies (15, 5, 10) have the highest probability of occurring (0.0310), but that it is possible for points at the same distance from (15, 5, 10) to have very different probabilities associated with them. It is therefore more appropriate to replace the circles of Fig. 2 by ellipses, and these are curves on which the *discrepancy* takes the

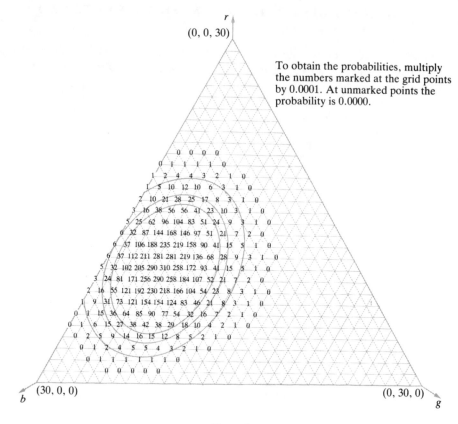

To obtain the probabilities, multiply
the numbers marked at the grid points
by 0.0001. At unmarked points the
probability is 0.0000.

Figure 3

constant values 4.61, 5.99 and 9.21 respectively. And it then turns out that, as
before, 10%, 5% and 1% of the results will fall outside these ellipses as a
consequence of random variation.

Q.21 Locate the points corresponding to frequencies (11, 7, 12) and (17, 1, 12)
in Fig. 3, and compare their positions relative to the small ellipse.

Q.22 Repeat Q.13 for the smallest ellipse in Fig. 3.

Q.23 If the pencil were rolled 3000 times, what comparable frequencies would
produce the same discrepancy from the expected frequencies as (11, 7, 12)
does with 30 rolls?

Q.24 Use a computer to simulate the pencil experiment with expected frequencies (15, 5, 10), and run it 100 times. How many times do you get
discrepancies exceeding 4.61, 5.99 and 9.21 respectively?

6.6 CHI-SQUARED PROBABILITY TABLES

In the experiments discussed so far, there have been three possible outcomes (blue, green, red) for each trial. However, almost all that has been said about these can be generalised to experiments in which there are any number of possible outcomes.

In a Bernoulli sequence of n trials, each having k possible outcomes $C_1, C_2, \ldots, C_k$, the *discrepancy* between the observed frequencies $F_o(C_i)$ and the expected frequencies $F_e(C_i) = P(C_i) \times n$ is defined as

$$\sum_{i=1}^{k} \frac{\{F_o(C_i) - F_e(C_i)\}^2}{F_e(C_i)}. \qquad \text{(Note 6.2)}$$

If in a particular experiment the value of the discrepancy is large, then we may judge that the mismatch between theory and experiment is unacceptable. To help in making this decision, we find the discrepancies which will only be exceeded by chance with probabilities 0.10, 0.05 and 0.01. We have seen that for $k = 3$ these are 4.61, 5.99 and 9.21.

The only difference in the procedure for a general value of k is that these critical values for the discrepancy are changed: the critical values depend on k. It is therefore necessary to have a table of these critical values, so that the right ones can be selected for the experiment in hand. This is called a *table of chi-squared probability*. (Note 6.3)

But before looking at such a table, one more new idea will have to be introduced – that of "degrees of freedom". The reason for this is that chi-squared probability can be used to handle a wide range of different problems, and it turns out that in deciding the critical values what really matters is not the number of possible outcomes, but the number of *independent* observed frequencies. Now in the pencil-rolling experiment, the frequencies $F_o(\text{blue})$, $F_o(\text{green})$ and $F_o(\text{red})$ were not in fact independent, since they satisfied the equation

$$F_o(\text{blue}) + F_o(\text{green}) + F_o(\text{red}) = 30.$$

This means that, once two of these frequencies are known, the third could be calculated from them; and this showed itself geometrically by the fact that the points representing all the results were found to lie in a plane, which is two-dimensional. We therefore say that in this experiment there are "two degrees of freedom".

The number of *degrees of freedom* in an experiment is the number of independent recorded observations.

It is customary to use the greek letter v to denote the number of degrees of freedom. For experiments of the kind that have been discussed so far in this chapter, $v = k - 1$; but we shall see later that this relationship does not always hold.

In a chi-squared probability table, the critical values of the discrepancy are given corresponding to certain selected probabilities for various numbers of degrees of freedom. Here is a small extract from such a table (Note 6.4):

Probability →		10%	5%	1%
	1	2.71	3.84	6.63
	2	4.61	5.99	9.21
$v =$	3	6.25	7.81	11.34
	4	7.78	9.49	13.28
	5	9.24	11.07	15.09
	6	10.64	12.59	16.81

You will recognise the critical values already quoted in the row of the table for $v = 2$.

Q.25   State in words the meaning of the entries (a) 6.25, (b) 15.09 in this table. Give an example of an experiment in which each entry might be relevant.

Notice that in the table the probabilities are often given as percentages. It is not of course possible to print tables which cover every value of v that might arise, but most tables give critical values for those which occur most commonly in practice; if you find that you need them for some untabulated number of degrees of freedom, it is good enough to use "proportional interpolation" between the two nearest entries in each column.

Example 1
A survey of families is carried out in a large mixed school. It is found that 72 families of three children are represented, made up as follows:

all boys	14	two boys and one girl	18
all girls	11	two girls and one boy	29

Is this distribution surprising?

How would you expect a family of three children to be made up? If the probabilities for each child of being a girl or a boy are $\frac{1}{2}$, $\frac{1}{2}$, then the binomial probability model suggests that the probabilities of having all girls or all boys are $\frac{1}{8}$, $\frac{1}{8}$, and of the other two types of family $\frac{3}{8}$, $\frac{3}{8}$. So the expected frequencies amongst the 72 families are:

all boys	9	two boys and one girl	27
all girls	9	two girls and one boy	27

This gives a discrepancy between the observed and expected frequencies of

$$\frac{(14 - 9)^2}{9} + \frac{(18 - 27)^2}{27} + \frac{(29 - 27)^2}{27} + \frac{(11 - 9)^2}{9} \approx 6.37.$$

We next need to know the number of degrees of freedom – that is, the number of independent observed frequencies. Since the total number of families is known, this number is three. Referring to the table of chi-squared probabilities for $v = 3$, the discrepancy of 6.37 is just above the critical value of 6.25 which corresponds to a probability of 10%. So there is a probability of less than 0.1 that the composition of the families in the school should be as unbalanced as this as a consequence of chance variation.

This is not really exceptional – after all, 1 in 10 chances do come up in other contexts without our thinking anything of them – but it is perhaps just interesting enough to justify looking for an explanation. In this case, it is the families where the children all have the same sex which seem to be rather more numerous than the mixed families: might this reflect a tendency for parents who already have two boys to try for a third child, with the (fifty-fifty) chance that it might be a girl, and vice versa? If so, then perhaps the binomial probability model was not really an appropriate one to use in calculating the expected frequencies. But the evidence is certainly not strong enough to force such a conclusion.

The statistician's way of describing the result in this example is to say that "the discrepancy is significant at the 10% level".

If in a Bernoulli sequence of trials the discrepancy between the observed and expected frequencies exceeds the tabulated critical value for $P\%$, then the probability of getting a discrepancy as large as (or larger than) this by chance variation is less than $P\%$. The discrepancy is then said to be *significant at the $P\%$ level.*

Q.26   Conduct and analyse a survey on the lines of Example 1 in your own school or college.

Q.27   What changes would you expect in the data, and what changes would you need to make in the analysis, if such a survey were conducted in an all girls school?

Q.28   Suppose that the law of the land required parents to stop having more children once they had a child of each sex. What would the expected frequencies of different kinds of three-child families in Example 1 be then?

Exercise 6A

1   It has been suggested that a suitable way of getting a sequence of random digits would be to use the final digits of telephone numbers. Take a column of such numbers at random from the telephone book, and find how often each digit occurs as the final figure. What would be the expected frequencies of each digit in a random sequence of this length? Calculate the discrepancy between the observed and expected frequencies, and use a chi-squared probability table to test whether this discrepancy is acceptable.

2   Take 100 pairs of digits from a table of random numbers (or generate them with a computer). How many would you expect to have (*a*) both digits odd, (*b*) both digits even, (*c*) one odd and one even? What results do you actually get? Calculate the discrepancy between the actual results and the expected ones, and use a chi-squared probability table to test the closeness between them.

3 If two dice are rolled together and the scores totalled, the sum may be any number from 2 to 12. What are the expected frequencies if this is done 180 times? Carry out this experiment and calculate the discrepancy between the actual frequencies and the expected ones. Is this discrepancy significant at the 1%, the 5% or the 10% level?

4 A pair of guinea pigs has produced a total of 64 offspring of which 30 have been red, 9 black and 25 white. A geneticist has predicted that, in a cross of this type, such progeny should occur in the ratios $9:3:4$. Use a chi-squared test to determine whether or not the observed numbers are in agreement with his theory.   [SMP]

5 A firm manufactures men's pyjamas in three sizes: small, medium and large. The firm's production is based on the assumption that the numbers of men requiring small, medium and large pyjamas will be in the ratio $1:3:2$. To test this assumption the firm measures its 60 male employees and the numbers requiring small, medium and large pyjamas are 5, 29 and 26 respectively. Use a chi-squared test to determine whether the results of this sample are consistent, at a 5% significance level, with the firm's assumption.   [Cambridge]

6 Get the most recent list of Premium Bond winning numbers from the newspaper and use chi-squared probability to test whether there appears to be any bias in the digits in any particular position.

7 At a public library, during a given week, the following numbers of books were borrowed:

Monday	204	Thursday	283
Tuesday	292	Friday	252
Wednesday	242	Saturday	275

Is there reason to believe that more books are generally borrowed on one weekday than another?

8 Ask a large number of people each to choose a number between 100 and 1000, and classify their answers according to the (a) first, (b) middle, (c) final digit of the number chosen. Do the answers indicate a significant preference for certain digits?

9 In Example 1 of §6.6, show that you get the same value for the discrepancy by using the formula

$$\sum_{i=1}^{k} \frac{\{F_o(C_i)\}^2}{F_e(C_i)} - n.$$

Prove algebraically that this expression is equivalent to the one given at the beginning of that section.

Can you suggest any advantages or disadvantages of using this alternative formula for the discrepancy?

10 One difference between Figs. 2 and 3 is that in Fig. 2 the vector from the origin $(0, 0, 0)$ to the point representing the expected result $(10, 10, 10)$ is perpendicular to the plane $b + g + r = 30$; whereas in Fig. 3, when the expected result is $(15, 5, 10)$, this is no longer true. But it is possible to transform the unsymmetrical case by introducing new coordinates

$$b' = ub, \ g' = vg, \ r' = wr$$

and to choose the multipliers u, v, w so that the transformed vector is perpendicular to the transformed plane.

(a) Write down the image of (15, 5, 10) under this transformation, and the vector from the origin to this image point.

(b) Write down the image of the plane $b + g + r = 30$ under the transformation, and deduce the normal vector to the transformed plane.

(c) By equating the vectors in (a) and (b), obtain the relation $15u^2 = 5v^2 = 10w^2$. Verify that these equations are satisfied by taking $u = 1/\sqrt{15}$, $v = 1/\sqrt{5}$, $w = 1/\sqrt{10}$.

(d) Since the transformation has restored the perpendicularity, it seems reasonable to use the value of l^2 in the transformed plane as a measure of the closeness of an experimental result to the expected result. Write an expression for l^2 *in terms of b', g' and r'*.

(e) Deduce an expression for l^2 in terms of b, g and r, and verify that it is equivalent to the discrepancy for the experiment described in §6.5.

6.7 CAN THE DATA FIT TOO WELL?

There was at one time a broadcaster on BBC children's programmes who used to end his talks with this piece of advice: "And now, be good – but not so *frightfully* good that someone says, 'And now what have *you* been up to ?'" (Note 6.5) It is a warning that applies in statistics too.

In §6.4 it was suggested that, if someone did the pencil-rolling experiment with 3000 trials and got frequencies of (1001, 998, 1001), then you would think there was something fishy about the result. But how could you justify your suspicions? And how close would the frequencies need to be to (1000, 1000, 1000) to make you suspicious ... would you be unhappy, for example, with (1000, 995, 1005), (1003, 993, 1004), or (1010, 994, 996)? Can we answer these questions scientifically, or must we just rely on a subjective 'hunch'?

The answer is that the theory of chi-squared probability can be adapted to deal with questions such as these. For the frequencies (1001, 998, 1001) the discrepancy from the expected frequencies is

$$\frac{(1001 - 1000)^2}{1000} + \frac{(998 - 1000)^2}{1000} + \frac{(1001 - 1000)^2}{1000} = 0.006.$$

This certainly seems very small; is it unreasonably small? The statistician's way of asking this question is:

> "What is the probability of getting a discrepancy as small as (or smaller than) this by chance variation?"

Now it is to answer questions like this that tables of chi-squared probability have columns for probabilities such as 99 % and 95 %, as well as 10 %, 5 % and 1 %. For example, the tables show that, in an experiment with 2 degrees of freedom, the critical value for a probability of 99 % is 0.0201. This means that, in a genuinely random experiment, the probability of getting a discrepancy greater than 0.0201 is 0.99; so the probability of getting a discrepancy *less* than 0.0201 is only 0.01. And our discrepancy of 0.006 is well under this critical value. So we can say that

"The probability of getting a discrepancy as small as (or smaller than) 0.006 is less than 1%."

The closeness of (1001, 998, 1001) to the expected frequencies is then described as "significant at the 1% level".

Q.29   Investigate similarly the results (1000, 995, 1005), (1003, 993, 1004) and (1010, 994, 996).

Q.30   When I did the pencil-rolling experiment with 30 trials, the frequencies were (11, 8, 11). Is the closeness of this result to (10, 10, 10) significant?

6.8   A WARNING: SMALL EXPECTED FREQUENCIES

One of the methods sometimes used to test a set of supposedly random numbers is the "poker test". The idea of this is to group the sequence of digits into blocks of four, and to put each block into one of five classes according as it contains

(A) four different digits,
(B) three different digits (one occurring twice, the others once),
(C) two different digits, each occurring twice,
(D) two different digits, one occurring three times and the other once,
(E) one digit, occurring four times.

If you refer back to Exercise 1B, question 14 you will recall that, if the numbers are genuinely random, then the probabilities associated with these classes are

(A) 0.504, (B) 0.432, (C) 0.027, (D) 0.036, (E) 0.001.

I used this test with 100 such blocks taken from the table of random numbers in the *SMP Advanced Tables*, with the following results:

	(A)	(B)	(C)	(D)	(E)
Actual frequencies	58	35	4	3	0
Expected frequencies	50.4	43.2	2.7	3.6	0.1
Difference $F_o - F_e$	7.6	−8.2	1.3	−0.6	−0.1

This gives a discrepancy of

$$\frac{(7.6)^2}{50.4} + \frac{(-8.2)^2}{43.2} + \frac{(1.3)^2}{2.7} + \frac{(-0.6)^2}{3.6} + \frac{(-0.1)^2}{0.1} \approx 3.53,$$

which is in fact (for $v = 4$) well within the range of values which could occur reasonable by chance. There is no reason to suppose, on this evidence, that the numbers are anything but random.

Notice, though, that the probabilities, and therefore the expected frequencies, for each of the last three classes are very small, and this could cause problems. Suppose, for example, that amongst the digits selected there had been just one

(E) block – and, unlikely though this outcome is, we should certainly expect it to occur *sometimes* in a true random sequence. Changing $F_o(E)$ from 0 to 1 would have the effect of changing the last term in the calculation of the discrepancy from $(-0.1)^2/0.1 = 0.1$ to $(0.9)^2/0.1 = 8.1$; and that would be almost enough by itself to take the discrepancy into the range where we would question the randomness of the sequence.

Now perhaps it is right that we should (see Note 6.6) – but what is unsatisfactory is that the value of the discrepancy should be so sensitive to such a small change. You will see that the difficulty arises because the expected frequency is very small, and because the actual frequencies have to be whole numbers. For this reason, statisticians are generally agreed that it is misleading to calculate the discrepancy in situations where some of the classes have very small expected frequencies associated with them. Some make a general rule that "one should never allow expected frequencies of less than 5", but this is probably over-cautious; opinion nowadays is moving towards acceptance of lower expected frequencies than this. The issue is not so much a mathematical one, but is rather about the interpretation which is put on the results of the statistical calculations. (There *are* mathematical approximations involved in the method – these are discussed in Chapter 18 – but that is another story.) Perhaps the best advice is that if, in calculating the discrepancy, a substantial part of the total comes from terms for classes with small expected frequencies, you should be suspicious about drawing firm conclusions from the evidence.

Is there anything else we can do about the problem? One obvious answer is to do more trials in the experiment, thereby increasing the total frequency n and hence the expected frequencies in each class. For example, had I taken 5000 blocks from the random number tables rather than 100 the expected frequency for class (E) would have been 5. But this may not be practicable (in this case the tables only contain 600 blocks!) and anyway it may be very extravagant. An alternative way round the problem is to combine two or more classes with small expected frequencies into a single class. For example, in applying the poker test classes (C), (D) and (E) might be put together:

	(A)	(B)	(C, D, E)
Actual frequencies	58	35	7
Expected frequencies	50.4	43.2	6.4
Difference $F_o - F_e$	7.6	−8.2	0.6

We then calculate the discrepancy as

$$\frac{(7.6)^2}{50.4} + \frac{(-8.2)^2}{43.2} + \frac{(0.6)^2}{6.4} \approx 2.76,$$

where of course this now has to be related to chi-squared probability with $v = 2$, since there are only three classes. Again, this is comfortably within the 'reasonable' range, so the conclusion is in fact unchanged.

Inevitably, combining classes in this way suppresses some of the detail in the results, and it is always possible that it suppresses important detail; that is a risk which we take. However, in an example such as this the discrepancy method probably leads us to more reliable conclusions if the classes are combined.

Exercise 6B

1   A student is set to do Exercise 6A, question 3 for homework and records the following set of experimental frequencies:

Sum	2	3	4	5	6	7	8	9	10	11	12
Frequency	4	12	15	19	26	28	24	21	16	9	4

The teacher suspects that the student has saved himself trouble by making up his "experimental" results. Is the evidence strong enough to make such an accusation?

2   Suppose that the survey described in Example 1 (§6.6) had produced the results:

all boys   9   two boys and one girl   26
all girls   11   two girls and one boy   26

Would you be surprised?

3   Gregor Mendel, the originator of modern genetic theory, used certain characteristics of peas in his experiments. In one experiment, for example, the proportions of yellow to green seeds, and of round to wrinkled seeds, were both expected to be $3:1$. If these bred independently, then the proportions of the four combinations yellow and round, green and round, etc. should be $9:3:3:1$. In three such experiments the following numbers of seeds were counted:

(a) 315, 108, 101, 32; (b) 51, 11, 16, 2; (c) 860, 315, 340, 117.

Comment on the match between the experimental results and the theory.

4   In a table of random numbers the digits are grouped in blocks of four. If a block is chosen at random, what are the probabilities that it contains (a) no nines, (b) one nine, (c) two nines, (d) three nines, (e) four nines? Test this out in such a table by counting the numbers of blocks in each category.

5   Take a sequence of random numbers (either from a table or computer generated) and record the lengths of runs of digits of the same parity (i.e. all odd or all even). How well do the numbers of runs of different lengths correspond to the frequencies which you would expect on theoretical grounds?

6   A six-sided die with faces numbered as usual from 1 to 6 was thrown 5 times and the number x of sixes was recorded. The experiment was repeated 200 times with the following results:

x	0	1	2	3	4	5
Frequency	66	82	40	10	2	0

On this evidence, would you consider the die to be biased?   [MEI]

7   Examine the following data to see whether, in litters of rats, the sex of the offspring fits
    a binomial probability model with $a = \frac{1}{2}$:

Number of males per litter	0	1	2	3	4	5	6	7	8
Litters of six	0	10	14	27	18	11	0	–	–
Litters of seven	1	6	25	36	35	20	9	1	–
Litters of eight	1	7	15	42	46	44	22	5	3

7

A model for queueing

So far we have dealt with a variety of examples of events which occur "at random", but in every case these have arisen from experiments carried out on separate, or "discrete", occasions – such as rolling a die, crossing a road, or selecting a random number. For such situations the Bernoulli model (see Chapter 3) often gave a suitable description. It is now time to generalise this to events which may occur at any instant of continuous time (or space). The corresponding models are associated with the name of the French mathematician Poisson, who introduced them into his book *Recherches sur la probabilité des jugements* in 1837.

To understand this chapter you will need to be acquainted with some of the properties of the "exponential function" $x \mapsto e^x$. The important parts of the theory for our purposes are summarised in §7.1; if you are already familiar with this, then you need only skim quickly through this section and Exercise 7A, and pick up the thread in §7.2.

7.1 THE EXPONENTIAL FUNCTION

The symbol e stands for a particular number between 2.7 and 2.8 which has many special properties (rather like π): you can find its value to more decimal places by keying in succession

$$\boxed{1} \, , \, \boxed{e^x}$$

on your calculator (this calculates it as e^1). The power e^x is also often written as exp x, and this is how you would normally call it up in a computer program. An important application of the function $x \mapsto \exp x$ is to provide a mathematical description of the phenomena of "exponential growth" (such as a population explosion) and "exponential decay" (as when the bath water gets cold). A more detailed treatment can be found in books on pre-university calculus. (Note 7.1)

The most important property of the function is:

(1)   If $y = e^x$, then $\dfrac{dy}{dx} = e^x$.

Other properties which are important in this chapter are:

(2)   If n is large, $\left(1 + \dfrac{x}{n}\right)^n \approx e^x$; and, in the limit,

as $n \to \infty$, $\left(1 + \dfrac{x}{n}\right)^n \to e^x$.

(3)   The sum of the infinite series $1 + \dfrac{x}{1!} + \dfrac{x^2}{2!} + \dfrac{x^3}{3!} + \ldots$ is e^x.

Exercise 7A

1   Take $x = 1, n = 1024 (= 2^{10})$ and use a calculator to evaluate $(1 + x/n)^n$. (The point of taking n as a power of 2 is that you can do this by repeated squaring.) Compare your answer with the value of e.

   Now repeat the calculations for $x = 2, 0.5, -1, -0.5$ and (in each case) for $n = 1048576 (= 2^{20})$. Compare each of your answers with the corresponding value of e^x.

2   The sum $1 + \dfrac{x}{1!} + \dfrac{x^2}{2!} + \cdots + \dfrac{x^{10}}{10!}$ can be found simply with a calculator or a computer by considering what each term needs to be multiplied by to give the next. Carry out this calculation for $x = 1, 2, 0.5, -1, -0.5$, and compare your answer in each case with the corresponding value of e^x.

3   Use a calculator to find e^x for a range of values of x, and use the results to plot the graph of e^x. From your graph, verify property (1) by drawing tangents.

4   Draw sketches to show the relation between the graphs of $y = e^x$, $y = e^{-x}$, $y = e^{2x}$, $y = e^{-\frac{1}{2}x}$.

5   Find the derivative of $1 + \dfrac{x}{1!} + \dfrac{x^2}{2!} + \cdots + \dfrac{x^k}{k!}$. Use your answer to connect properties (1) and (3) in §7.1.

6   If $f(x) = (1 + x/n)^n$, write down the value of $f'(x)$. Show that, when n is a large number and x is not too large, $f'(x) \approx f(x)$. Hence connect properties (1) and (2) in §7.1.

7   Use the binomial theorem to write out the first four terms of the expansion of $(1 + x/n)^n$. Show that, when n is large, these can be approximated by $1 + \dfrac{x}{1!} + \dfrac{x^2}{2!} + \dfrac{x^3}{3!}$. Hence connect properties (2) and (3) in §7.1.

7.2   A PROBLEM FOR HOSPITAL ADMINISTRATORS

Most of us go through life without ever having our appendix removed. But if someone's appendix does 'blow up', it often happens quite suddenly and he needs to be moved to hospital quickly – day or night. This presents a problem to the hospital, which needs to have a bed ready whenever the emergency arises.

   Suppose that a hospital in a large city admits on average four appendicitis cases every day. Of course this does not mean that each day there are four new appendicitis patients – if life were as tidy as that, then the hospital would have no problem! Sometimes there may be only one or two, on other days the hospital must be able to cope with six or seven. What is the largest number that might be expected in any day, and how often will such an eventuality arise? This is obviously a statistical question, and the fact that there are "on average four cases a day" has something to do with the probability of getting appendicitis – but what? Before reading further, you might try to think how this number could be used as the basis of a "probability model". For example, could you devise an experiment using random numbers to simulate this situation?

Four cases a day means, of course, an average of one every 6 hours; but again, there is not a probability of 1 that in any 6-hour period a case will arrive. It is quite possible that on a bad day there might be two, or even three, cases between 6 a.m. and noon.

However, at least the number "1" *could* be a probability – so this seems a useful way of proceeding. Thus four cases a day means on average $\frac{1}{6}$ cases an hour; would it be reasonable to say that there is a probability of $\frac{1}{6}$ that a case arrives in any hour, and a probability of $\frac{5}{6}$ that no case arrives in the hour? Probably not, for it is still conceivable that more than one case might arrive within the hour ("it never rains but it pours"!) and we have not allowed for this.

But if we take an even shorter time, say a minute, then it might be said that for more than one case to arrive within any one minute would be a remarkable coincidence – an event with negligible probability. We might therefore make a reasonable model of the situation by dividing the day into $60 \times 24 = 1440$ minutes, and supposing that in any minute

$$P(\text{a case arrives}) = \tfrac{1}{360}, \ P(\text{no case arrives}) = \tfrac{359}{360}.$$

What will happen in the next minute ... and the next ... and the next? The population served by the hospital is so large that the arrival of a case in one minute can scarcely affect the probabilities for the next minute; that is, the outcome in each minute is independent of what has happened previously. And if this is so, we can think of a day as made up of 1440 separate minutes, with constant and independent probabilities in each of a case arriving or not – and this is the characteristic of a Bernoulli sequence (see §3.1). The probabilities of 0, 1, 2, 3, ... cases in the day can therefore be written down as binomial probabilities, using the formula

$$\binom{n}{i} a^i b^{n-i}$$

(see §3.3) with $n = 1440$, $a = \tfrac{1}{360}$ and $b = \tfrac{359}{360}$:

Number of cases in the day	Probability	
0	$\left(\dfrac{359}{360}\right)^{1440}$	$= 0.0182$
1	$\dbinom{1440}{1} \times \left(\dfrac{359}{360}\right)^{1439} \times \left(\dfrac{1}{360}\right)$	$= 0.0731$
2	$\dbinom{1440}{2} \times \left(\dfrac{359}{360}\right)^{1438} \times \left(\dfrac{1}{360}\right)^2$	$= 0.1464$
...	...	...

Q.1   Extend this table of probabilities by three more lines, and use a calculator to evaluate them.

Exercise 7B

1   In a post office, customers join a queue at the stamp counter at an average rate of 3 a minute. By breaking down into seconds, and supposing that two people are very unlikely to arrive within the same second, find the probability that someone will join the queue in any particular second. Then use the binomial probability model to calculate the probabilities of 0, 1, 2, 3, ... people joining the queue within any minute.
   Have you made any assumptions about the way in which people join queues? Are these reasonable?

2   Simulate the situation described in question 1, using random numbers (either from a table or using a computer). How can you arrange for certain numbers to be selected to represent "a customer arrives in a particular second" with the correct probability? Run the simulation second by second to show a typical pattern of customers arriving over a period of 5 minutes. Plot the arrivals on a time scale. What is the largest number of customers joining the queue in any period of a minute? What is the smallest? What is the longest time interval between successive arrivals?

3   Customers arrive at the barber's shop on average once every 10 minutes. What is the probability that a customer arrives in a particular second? Calculate the probabilities of 0, 1, 2, ... customers arriving within any minute.

7.3 SIMPLIFYING THE CALCULATION

You may have found it somewhat laborious, even with a calculator, calculating the probabilities in Q.1. Fortunately, it is possible to simplify this with very little sacrifice of accuracy. We do this in two steps.

First, each probability can be derived as a multiple of the one before, and the multipliers simplified by using an approximation. Writing the probabilities of 0, 1, 2, 3, ... cases as p_0, p_1, p_2, p_3, ..., the table at the end of §7.2 becomes:

Number of cases in the day	Probability
0	p_0
1	$p_1 = \dfrac{1440}{1} \times \dfrac{1}{359} \times p_0 \approx \dfrac{1440}{360} \times p_0 = \quad 4p_0$
2	$p_2 = \dfrac{1439}{2} \times \dfrac{1}{359} \times p_1 \approx \tfrac{1}{2} \times \dfrac{1440}{360} \times p_1 = \tfrac{1}{2} \times 4p_1$
3	$p_3 = \dfrac{1438}{3} \times \dfrac{1}{359} \times p_2 \approx \tfrac{1}{3} \times \dfrac{1440}{360} \times p_2 = \tfrac{1}{3} \times 4p_2$
...	...

The explanation of this is as follows. The first multipliers after the first " $=$ " sign in each row are the multipliers for the binomial coefficients (see Exercise 3B, question 10). Taking $n = 1440$ and $i = 0, 1, 2, \ldots$ in turn gives

$$\binom{1440}{1} = \frac{1440}{1} \times \binom{1440}{0}, \quad \binom{1440}{2} = \frac{1439}{2} \times \binom{1440}{1},$$

$$\binom{1440}{3} = \frac{1438}{3} \times \binom{1440}{3}, \text{ etc.}$$

The second multiplier arises from the fact that, in the expression for the probability, there is each time one fewer factor of $(\frac{359}{360})$ and one more of $(\frac{1}{360})$, so that the expression in the previous row must be multiplied by $\frac{1}{360} \div \frac{359}{360}$, or $\frac{1}{359}$. Then, after some rearrangement, the fractions $\frac{1440}{359}, \frac{1439}{359}, \frac{1438}{359}, \ldots$ are all taken as approximately equal to $\frac{1440}{360}$, or 4.

Q.2   Fill in the next two rows of the table, finding approximations for p_4 in terms of p_3, and for p_5 in terms of p_4. Then put the results from all the lines together to show that the probabilities are given approximately by

$$p_0, \; p_1 \approx \frac{4^1}{1!} p_0, \; p_2 \approx \frac{4^2}{2!} p_0, \; p_3 \approx \frac{4^3}{3!} p_0, \text{ etc.}$$

What meaning was attached to the number 4 in the original problem?

The second step is to simplify the calculation of p_0. This was

$$\left(\frac{359}{360}\right)^{1440}, \text{ or } \left(1 - \frac{1}{360}\right)^{1440}, \text{ or } \left(1 - \frac{4}{1440}\right)^{1440}.$$

This is where the approximation for e^x given at the beginning of the chapter comes in. The last of these three expressions is of the form $(1 + x/n)^n$, with $x = -4$ and $n = 1440$; and when n is large, property (2) of §7.1 states that this is approximately equal to e^x. So

$$\left(1 - \frac{4}{1440}\right)^{1440} \text{ is approximately equal to } e^{-4}.$$

This suggests that we could take p_0 to be e^{-4}.

Q.3   Use a calculator to compare the values of $\left(\frac{359}{360}\right)^{1440}$ and e^{-4}.

Putting the two steps together, the probabilities of the hospital having to admit $0, 1, 2, 3, \ldots$ cases in a day can be taken as

$$e^{-4}, \frac{4^1}{1!} e^{-4}, \frac{4^2}{2!} e^{-4}, \frac{4^3}{3!} e^{-4}, \ldots.$$

Fig. 1 shows these probabilities on a stick graph. It is worth noticing that the

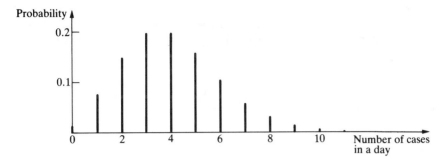

Figure 1

probability function has quite a long 'tail': although on average there are only 4 cases a day, there is a fair probability (more than 1 %) that from time to time the hospital will have to cope with as many as 9 cases in a day. This is typical of situations of this kind.

7.4 POISSON PROBABILITIES

The probabilities found at the end of the previous section for the number of hospital admissions are an example of the probability model discovered by Poisson. The conditions under which the model applies are:

(*a*) The events must occur *singly*. For example, the model would not be appropriate for casualty admissions, for which several cases may have to be admitted at the same time as a result of the same accident.

(*b*) The events must occur *independently*. A case of appendicitis does not arise as a consequence of a previous case, but is a separate independent event.

(*c*) The events must occur at a *uniform average rate*. This does not mean, of course, that they occur at exactly equally spaced instants of time – if that were so, there would not be a statistical problem! But the probability of one of the events occurring in a short time-interval of given length must be the same, whenever that interval is taken. The greek letter λ is often used to denote this uniform rate; in the hospital admissions example, if we take the unit of time to be a day, λ is equal to 4.

> If a certain event occurs randomly, singly and independently, at a uniform average rate of λ occurrences per unit of time, then the probabilities of $0, 1, 2, \ldots, i, \ldots$ occurrences within a time-interval of unit length are
>
> $$e^{-\lambda}, \frac{\lambda^1}{1!}e^{-\lambda}, \frac{\lambda^2}{2!}e^{-\lambda}, \ldots, \frac{\lambda^i}{i!}e^{-\lambda}, \ldots.$$
>
> This is called the *Poisson probability model*.

Example 1

Calls come into a telephone switchboard at an average rate of 150 an hour. Calculate the probabilities of having to cope with 0, 1, 2, ... calls within any minute.

Taking a minute as the unit of time, the switchboard receives on average $150 \div 60 = 2.5$ calls a minute. We therefore take λ to be 2.5, and calculate the Poisson probabilities

$$e^{-2.5}, \frac{2.5}{1!} e^{-2.5}, \frac{(2.5)^2}{2!} e^{-2.5}, \ldots.$$

The simplest way of actually doing the calculation is to begin by using tables or a calculator to find $e^{-2.5}$, and then to find each successive probability from the one before by multiplying in turn by 2.5/1, 2.5/2, etc. This gives the following table of values:

Number of calls in a minute	Probability
0	$e^{-2.5}$ $= 0.082$
1	$\times \dfrac{2.5}{1} = 0.205$
2	$\times \dfrac{2.5}{2} = 0.257$
3	$\times \dfrac{2.5}{3} = 0.214$
4	$\times \dfrac{2.5}{4} = 0.134$
5	$\times \dfrac{2.5}{5} = 0.067$
6	$\times \dfrac{2.5}{6} = 0.028$
7	$\times \dfrac{2.5}{7} = 0.010$
8	$\times \dfrac{2.5}{8} = 0.003$
9	$\times \dfrac{2.5}{9} = 0.001$

As a check, add up all the calculated probabilities; the sum comes to 1.001, which is near enough to 1 within the margin of rounding errors.

Q.4 Show these probabilities on a stick graph similar to Fig. 1.

Exercise 7C

1   A Geiger counter records α-particles striking a sensor. If the average rate is 0.6 particles a second, calculate the probabilities of 0, 1, 2, ... particles striking the sensor within a one-second interval. Check that the sum of the probabilities is 1.

2   Use property (3) of §7.1 to show that the Poisson probabilities for the number of occurrences within a time-interval of unit length, when the average rate is λ, have a sum of 1.

3   Cars travelling randomly along a road at an average rate of two a minute arrive at a level crossing. If the crossing gates are closed for a minute to allow a train to pass, what is the probability that more than two cars will be held up?

4   On average I get 30 letters a week (Monday to Saturday). Would you expect a Poisson probability model to be a suitable way of finding the probabilities of getting various numbers of letters in each day's mail? On this assumption, calculate the probability that on a particular day I shall get fewer than three letters.

5   Telephone calls coming in to a switchboard follow a Poisson probability model with an average rate of 3 a minute. Find the probability that in a given minute there will be 5 or more calls.

   If the duration of every call is exactly three minutes, and at most 12 calls can be connected simultaneously, find the probability that at a given instant the switchboard is fully loaded.

6   The probabilities that a company will require 0, 1, 2, 3, ... articles of a certain kind in any one month are given by a Poisson distribution with mean 2. Find the least number of articles that the company should have in stock at the beginning of the month so that the probability of having no stock left at the end of the month is less than 0.02.   [London]

7   If an event is occurring randomly at an average rate of λ occurrences in unit time, which number of occurrences in unit time has the highest probability (a) if λ is not an integer, (b) if λ is an integer?

8   Write a computer program which, when a given value of λ is input, will calculate the Poisson probabilities and produce a stick graph like Fig. 1. (K)

9   In a simplified probability model of the service in a barber's shop it is supposed that all haircuts take exactly six minutes and that a fresh batch of customers arrives at six-minute intervals. The number of customers in a batch is described by a Poisson probability function, the mean number being 3. Any customer who cannot be served instantly goes away and has his hair cut elsewhere. The shop is open for 40 hours a week. Calculate the theoretical frequencies with which batches of 0, 1, 2, 3, 4, 5, and more than 5 customers will arrive.

   The proprietor reckons that it costs him £200 a week to staff and maintain each chair in his shop, and he charges £2 for each haircut. Calculate his expected weekly profit if he has (a) 3, (b) 4, (c) 5 chairs.   [SMP]

10 Cars arrive at a motorway filling station at an average rate of 3 a minute. Devise a simulation using random numbers, based on the Poisson probability model, for the arrival of cars in successive minutes.

   Suppose that it takes two minutes to serve a car with petrol. Use your simulation to investigate whether a queue will build up at the filling station if there are (a) 6 pumps, (b) 7 pumps, (c) 8 pumps. (You may find it simplest to begin to do this 'concretely', using counters for cars; once you have found out how this works, devise a method for recording the simulation, or for running it on a computer.)

11 From the formula for Poisson probabilities, find the probabilities of getting, in a time-interval of two units length,
    (a) no occurrences (i.e. none in either interval),
    (b) one occurrence (i.e. one in the first and none in the second, or vice versa),
    (c) two occurrences,
    (d) three occurrences.
    Simplify your answers. Are the results what you would expect?

12 Women enter a shop randomly at an average rate of λ_1, and men enter it at an average rate of λ_2. Find the probabilities that, in a unit interval of time,
    (a) nobody enters the shop,
    (b) just one person (either a man or a woman) enters the shop,
    (c) just two people enter the shop,
    (d) just three people enter the shop.
    Could you have got your answers another way?

13 The machines in a certain factory break down independently and at random. In one section of the factory there is an average of one breakdown a day. In another section one breakdown occurs on average every two days. Calculate the probability that in the two sections together there will be
    (a) no breakdowns on a given day,
    (b) at least three breakdowns on a given day.   [Cambridge]

14 At the 'hot drinks' counter in a cafeteria both tea and coffee are sold. The number of cups of coffee sold per minute may be assumed to be a Poisson variable with mean 1.5, and the number of cups of tea sold per minute may be assumed to be an independent Poisson variable with mean 0.5.
    (a) Calculate the probability that in a given one-minute period exactly one cup of tea and one cup of coffee are sold.
    (b) Calculate the probability that in a given three-minute period fewer than 5 drinks altogether are sold.
    (c) In a given one-minute period exactly three drinks are sold. Calculate the probability that these are all cups of coffee.   [Cambridge]

15 A fire station serves a rural area and a small town. Calls from them arrive independently, and the number of calls in a given interval in each case is a Poisson variable. In the summer, a call is made once in six days in the town, and once in four days in the country, on average. What is the probability that on a given day there will be more than one call?

16 Two machine shops, A and B, in a factory are known to be dangerous places to work in, with accidents occurring randomly at a rate of 2 accidents in three months in A, and 3 accidents in four months in B. A safety officer is appointed on 11 January in shop B. In fact he has no effect on the accident rate; what is the probability that he will nevertheless be able to report "no accidents so far" on 1 March? As a result of such a report he is transferred to shop A, where he still has no effect. What is the probability that there will be no accidents in shop A in the next month and 1 or more accidents in shop B?

17 One problem, for an event occurring randomly in continuous time, is to estimate the "average rate of occurrences per unit of time". A possible way of doing this is to use the principle of maximum likelihood (see Chapter 4). In the hospital admissions example, suppose that on ten successive days the numbers of appendicitis cases were

7, 4, 1, 3, 2, 5, 3, 4, 6, 4.

Show that, on the hypothesis that the average number of cases per day is λ, the likelihood of this outcome is

$$\frac{\lambda^{39}}{7!\,6!\,5!\,(4!)^3(3!)^2 2!\,1!}\,e^{-10\lambda}.$$

What value of λ maximises this?

Generalise the argument to the situation where the average has to be estimated from the fact that $a_1, a_2, \ldots, a_n$ cases are admitted on n successive days.

18 If an event occurs randomly at an average rate of λ occurrences per unit of time, what is the average rate of occurrence "per t units of time"? Deduce that the probabilities of 0, 1, 2, ... occurrences in a time-interval of length t units are

$$e^{-\lambda t},\ \frac{(\lambda t)^1}{1!}\,e^{-\lambda t},\ \frac{(\lambda t)^2}{2!}\,e^{-\lambda t},\ \ldots.$$

Taking λ as 4, and the unit of time as 1 day, draw graphs of these probabilities as functions of t. For various values of t, investigate which of the graphs is 'highest'. Use the graphs to discuss the relative probabilities of various numbers of appendicitis cases in a given period of time in the hospital admissions example.

7.5 DISCRETE EXPERIMENTS *v.* CONTINUOUS TIME

Siméon Poisson was born in 1781 and died in 1840. He was on the staff of the Ecole Polytechnique in France, an institution originally established by Napoleon to promote the study of military engineering. He did important work in the application of mathematics to the behaviour of continuous media, for example in the theory of elasticity and the flow of heat. This switch of emphasis from the 'discrete' (or separate) to the 'continuous' also shows up in his contributions to the theory of probability.

Compare some of the situations to which we have applied Bernoulli and Poisson probability respectively:

Bernoulli	*Poisson*
Throws of a die – how many sixes?	Queues – how many join in a minute?
Sex of babies – how many boys?	Appendicitis cases – how many in a day?
Testing plates – how many faulty?	Traffic – how many cars in a minute?

There is one obvious difference between the two lists. For the Bernoulli situations there is a succession of separate hazards (throws, births, tests), and on

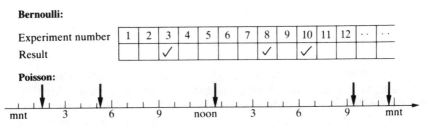

Figure 2

each occasion a certain outcome (six, boy, faulty) may or may not occur. In the Poisson situations, the events may occur at any instant in a continuous 'stream of time'. Fig. 2 shows the comparison in a diagram.

7.6 ARE POISSON PROBABILITIES EXACT OR APPROXIMATE?

At this stage, you may well object: did we not get the Poisson probabilities as approximations based on the Bernoulli model? True – but this was simply because at that stage we had no machinery for dealing with continuous time. For this reason, the appendicitis problem was solved by splitting the day into separate minutes and using an approximation. But there is no special reason to use minutes; any short time-interval would have done, provided that the probability of getting more than one case in that time is negligible.

Q.5   Suppose that we choose to use 10 seconds as the length of the time-interval. Show that the Bernoulli probabilities of 0, 1, 2, ... cases would then be

$$p_0 = \left(\frac{2159}{2160}\right)^{8640}, p_1 = \frac{8640}{2159} \times p_0, p_2 = \tfrac{1}{2} \times \frac{8639}{2159} \times p_1, \ldots$$

Use your calculator to evaluate these, and compare your answers with the values given in the table at the end of §7.2. Show that approximations similar to those made in §7.3 would still lead to the probabilities

$$e^{-4}, \frac{4^1}{1!} e^{-4}, \frac{4^2}{2!} e^{-4}, \ldots$$

What is at the heart of this argument is not really approximation, but a *limiting process* – just as we deal with tangents to curves in calculus as the limiting forms of chords. Let us investigate this for the general case in which an event occurs on average λ times in a time-interval of unit length.

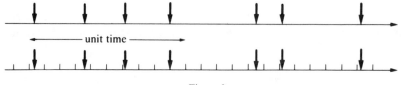

Figure 3

The situation in continuous time – the 'real situation' – is illustrated by the top diagram in Fig. 3. Since we do not (as yet) know how to deal with this directly, we devise a Bernoulli model which approximates to it. This is done by dividing each unit time-interval into n small intervals, as in the lower diagram of Fig. 3, and saying that there is a probability λ/n that the event occurs in any one of these intervals. Thus in any of these intervals the probability that the event does *not* occur is $1 - \lambda/n$. It is now possible to calculate the probabilities in the appropriate binomial probability model, just as before, taking $a = \lambda/n$ and $b = 1 - \lambda/n$. These are set out in the table: you should check the details for yourself.

Number of cases in unit time	Binomial probabilities		Limiting Poisson probabilities as $n \to \infty$
0	$p_0 = (1 - \lambda/n)^n$		$p_0 = e^{-\lambda}$
1	$p_1 = \dfrac{n}{1} \times \dfrac{\lambda/n}{1 - \lambda/n} \times p_0$	$= \dfrac{1}{1} \times \dfrac{n}{n} \times \dfrac{\lambda}{1 - \lambda/n} \times p_0$	$p_1 = \dfrac{\lambda}{1} p_0 = \dfrac{\lambda^1}{1!} e^{-\lambda}$
2	$p_2 = \dfrac{n-1}{2} \times \dfrac{\lambda/n}{1 - \lambda/n} \times p_1$	$= \dfrac{1}{2} \times \dfrac{n-1}{n} \times \dfrac{\lambda}{1 - \lambda/n} \times p_1$	$p_2 = \dfrac{\lambda}{2} p_1 = \dfrac{\lambda^2}{2!} e^{-\lambda}$
3	$p_3 = \dfrac{n-2}{3} \times \dfrac{\lambda/n}{1 - \lambda/n} \times p_2$	$= \dfrac{1}{3} \times \dfrac{n-2}{n} \times \dfrac{\lambda}{1 - \lambda/n} \times p_2$	$p_3 = \dfrac{\lambda}{3} p_2 = \dfrac{\lambda^3}{3!} e^{-\lambda}$
...	...		...

The first step in each line is to express the binomial probability as a multiple of the previous one, using the method of Exercise 3B, question 10. The trick is then to rearrange the multipliers in a particular way, so that each is shown as the product of

(a) a number of the sequence $1, \frac{1}{2}, \frac{1}{3}, \ldots$;

(b) a number of the sequence $\dfrac{n}{n}, \dfrac{n-1}{n}, \dfrac{n-2}{n}, \ldots$, all of which tend to 1 as n tends to infinity;

(c) the number $\dfrac{\lambda}{1 - \lambda/n}$, which tends to λ as n tends to infinity.

The multipliers in the final (Poisson) column can then be written down as the products of the limits of the numbers in (a), (b) and (c); that is, as $\lambda, \frac{1}{2}\lambda, \frac{1}{3}\lambda, \ldots$.

So the Poisson probabilities do in fact give an exact model for describing the continuous situation – not an approximation. In Chapter 21 it will be shown that they can also be obtained directly, without going through the binomial probabilities; but in any case the connection between the two models has a useful application, which is discussed in the next section.

7.7 POISSON PROBABILITIES AS AN APPROXIMATION FOR BINOMIAL PROBABILITIES

One great advantage of Poisson probabilities is that they are very simple to calculate – simpler than binomial probabilities. Since in some circumstances the two are very near to each other, it is sometimes convenient to calculate the Poisson probabilities and to use these as approximations to the binomial ones.

We can only do this when the probability of an event occurring (a, or λ/n) is very small, although λ itself ($= na$) need not be small. (Think of the appendicitis example, where the probability of a patient arriving in any minute was only 1/360.) An important example is in quality control, where one is concerned with sub-standard products in a production process. Hopefully there are not many of these, so there is only a small probability of a particular article selected at random being faulty.

Suppose, for example, that 2% of the oranges in a consignment are soft, and that they are inspected in sample batches of 20 selected at random. What are the probabilities of getting various numbers of soft oranges in the batch? (Note 7.2) This is obviously not a situation where events occur randomly in continuous time – so one would not expect to use Poisson probability. An exact solution would be calculated by means of the binomial probability model, with $a = 0.02$ and $n = 20$. However, if the words "unit interval of time" are replaced by "batch" in the description of the Poisson probability model in §7.4, and if the average number of soft oranges in a batch is taken to be 20×0.02, or 0.4, then the Poisson probabilities

$$e^{-0.4}, \frac{0.4}{1!} e^{-0.4}, \frac{(0.4)^2}{2!} e^{-0.4}, \frac{(0.4)^3}{3!} e^{-0.4}, \ldots$$

$$= 0.670, 0.268, 0.054, 0.007, \ldots$$

should give good approximations to the probabilities of getting 0, 1, 2, 3, ... soft oranges in a sample batch. Not only are these easier to calculate than the exact binomial probabilities, but they are also easy to tabulate – since they depend only on the single number $\lambda = 0.4$ – and this is a considerable advantage when one is designing a statistical procedure which is to be operated by checkers who are not expert statisticians.

Exercise 7D

1   For the example of the soft oranges in §7.7, calculate the binomial probabilities corresponding to the approximate Poisson probabilities given in the text.

2   For the example in Chapter 4 about the inspection of plates for faults, use Poisson probabilities to approximate to the entries in Table 1 of §4.2 (previously calculated as binomial probabilities).

3   Given that 5% of a population are left-handed, use the Poisson distribution to estimate the probability that a random sample of 100 people contains 2 or more left-handed people.   [London]

4   2% of the toy cars produced by a factory are defective. They are packed in cartons of 50. What is the chance that a retailer gets a carton containing (a) no defectives, (b) more than two defectives?

5   A machine generates 3-digit random numbers from 000 to 999. A 'success' is scored whenever three identical digits are obtained (i.e. 000 or 111 or 222 etc). Use an

appropriate probability distribution to estimate the probability of obtaining more
than 4 successes in 200 tries.   [Cambridge]

6 The probability of a baby being born with a certain type of congenital abnormality is
1 %. In one week 200 babies are born in a particular hospital. Write down, but do not
evaluate, an exact expression for the probability that four or fewer of them will have
the abnormality. Use a suitable Poisson approximation to give a numerical estimate
of this probability.

In the given week five such abnormalities occur. What statistical conclusion can
you draw from this?   [SMP]

7 In 200 shifts in a factory the following record of accidents is made:

Accidents per shift	0	1	2	3	4	5
Frequency	130	51	12	4	2	1

Calculate the mean number of accidents per shift.

Use the Poisson probability model with this mean to calculate the probability of
three or more accidents occurring in a single shift.

8 Over a number of months in the second world war, 576 squares with $\frac{1}{2}$ km sides were
observed, and many flying bomb hits were recorded. The table gives the number of
squares in which r hits were recorded:

r	0	1	2	3	4	5
Frequency	229	211	93	35	7	1

Calculate the frequencies which would be expected from a Poisson model having the
same mean, and compare these with the observed frequencies.

9 In a data transmission link between two computers, each character (i.e. letter, digit or
other symbol) is transmitted separately and there is a constant small probability that
a transmission error will occur; the mean failure rate is 1 error per ten million
characters transmitted.
(a) If 2 500 000 characters are transmitted, calculate the probability of no errors
occurring, and the probability of more than 2 errors occurring.
(b) N characters of data are to be transmitted. Find an approximate value for the
maximum value of N such that the probability of no errors occurring is at least
0.999.
(c) If an error occurs in transmitting a character, there is a probability p that it will be
discovered and corrected automatically. Prove that if N characters are transmitted the probability of no errors finally remaining is $e^{-\mu(1-p)}$, where $\mu = N \times$
10^{-7}.   [Cambridge]

8

Probability in practice

The study of probability oscillates between theoretical development and practical application. In this chapter we shall examine how various theoretical probability models, such as the binomial and Poisson, can be put to practical use in a world in which uncertainty rules the day.

8.1 SOME TYPICAL APPLICATIONS

In the France of Louis XIV, the question which brought probability theory into prominence – how the stake should be divided when a game of chance is interrupted before it has run its course – was an issue of great importance to the aristocratic contemporaries of Pascal and Fermat. (See Note 1.5. A modern equivalent might be the "pools panel" which invents imaginary results for postponed football matches.) In seventeenth-century England the more commercially minded inhabitants – in particular Sir Edmond Halley, discoverer of the comet – collected statistics about ages of death and then used probability arguments to calculate how much should be charged for life annuities. One hundred years later, astronomy had advanced to the point where more accurate determinations of the paths of the planets were urgently needed, and new techniques in probability were developed by Legendre, Laplace and Gauss for the analysis of observational errors. Further advances in the theory in the early years of the present century, associated with the names of Karl Pearson and Sir Ronald Fisher, were motivated by an interest in using methods of selective breeding to improve the quality of crops and livestock.

In this book two real-life problems have been discussed whose solution can only be expressed in terms of probabilities. The analysis of the fire engine usage in §5.5 showed that during the month in question all the demands could be met by employing a fleet of five vehicles. But there is always the remote possibility that the town might have to cope with a petrochemical disaster, a train crash and a bomb scare in the town hall at the same time. Administrators have consciously to accept that such risks exist, and to plan on the basis of uncertainty. A possible principle of decision-taking might be:

"A fire service will be set up such that there is at least a 95% probability of meeting all the demands on it in any month"

– or, which is the same thing,

"... such that the probability that it will *not* meet the demands on it in any month is less than 0.05".

In the hospital admissions problem in Chapter 7, it is clearly possible that there might be as many as 20 cases of appendicitis in one day; but, even on a remote island, it is unthinkable that anyone would plan hospital provision on the basis of such an improbable eventuality. More likely, one would set a level of provision such that the probability of the standard provision being inadequate on any day is less than, say, 0.01, and reckon to make do (for example, by using an alternative hospital or a private nursing home) on the occasional days when this occurs. To find out what this implies in practice, it would be necessary to calculate the Poisson probabilities (with $\lambda = 4$ in this example; see §§7.1–3) *cumulatively*:

Number of cases	0	1	2	3	4	5	6	7	8	9	10 ...
Probability	0.018	0.073	0.147	0.195	0.195	0.156	0.104	0.060	0.030	0.013	0.005 ...
Probability of more than this number in one day	0.982	0.909	0.762	0.567	0.372	0.216	0.112	0.052	0.022	0.009	0.004 ...

Q.1   How is the bottom line of this table calculated from the line above?

The entry picked out in the 'box' indicates that, by having 9 spare beds available at the beginning of each day, the probability of not being able to meet the demand that day is less than 0.01 – which was the criterion laid down.

8.2 THE LEVEL OF ACCEPTABILITY

Suppose that you are the 'declarer' in a hand of bridge. (If you are not familiar with the game, you will find an explanation in the answer to Exercise 1B, question 18.) When your partner's cards are laid down (dummy), you see that you have 9 of the trump cards between you, so that your opponents have the other 4. You plan to play in the hope that three rounds of trumps will clear your opponents out of that suit. Is this a reasonable risk to take?

Your plan will work provided that the trumps are not split 0–4 or 4–0 between your opponents. The probabilities that the trumps will fall in various ways are shown in Fig. 1; these were calculated in Exercise 1B, question 18, and the probabilities for each of the unfavourable outcomes were found to be $\frac{55}{1150} \approx$ 0.048. So the probability that three rounds of trumps will not be enough is 0.096, or just under 10%.

But this is as far as probability theory will take you. The question whether this is a risk worth taking is one to which there is no right answer: it depends on your temperament, and probably also on what is at stake – whether it is just a family game or the final match of a tournament, whether this game will decide the rubber, and so on.

If we were perfectly rational human beings, then we should for every situation lay down in advance the level of risk – that is, the greatest probability of an unfavourable outcome – which we are prepared to accept. We should then work

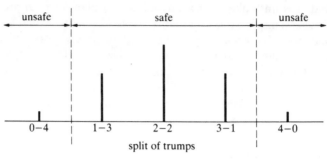

Figure 1

out that probability, and if it is too high we should take some alternative course of action. Of course, in practice people do not behave in this way – which is why there are so many road accidents, and why betting shops stay in business. But if you are in the statistics business, working perhaps as an actuary or in market research, then the success of your career may depend on submitting yourself to statistical disciplines of this kind.

8.3 STATISTICS AND SCIENTIFIC EXPERIMENTS

A friend claims, "It's easy to distinguish real ale from keg." How could you tell whether he really can, or whether he is just shooting a line?

The obvious answer is to set up a scientific trial, by giving him a sequence of different beers to taste and identify.

Q.2 Suggest a way of making sure that the test is set up randomly: that is, that there is no detectable pattern in the sequence.

Suppose that in the trial there are 12 different glasses, and that the results are as follows:

Content of glass	R	R	K	K	K	R	K	K	R	K	R	K
Friend's verdict	R	R	K	R	K	R	K	R	K	K	R	K
Right or wrong?	r	r	r	w	r	r	r	w	w	r	r	r

How would you evaluate your friend's performance?

Since he got the right answer nine times, it is tempting to conclude that "he is right three times in four" – and on the evidence it is certainly possible that this is so. But it is also possible that he has just made some lucky guesses, and rather than attempting to assign precise numerical proportions it would be more realistic to investigate how likely that is.

There are then two alternative theories, or "hypotheses" (the technical word used by statisticians), that we might consider:

Hypothesis 1. He guesses each time, so that the probability of being right is equal to the probability of being wrong.

Because this is contrary to your friend's claim, this is sometimes described as the "null hypothesis". Against this we set the "alternative hypothesis":

Hypothesis 2. Your friend has some ability to discriminate, so that the probability of being right is greater than the probability of being wrong.

Now it is a fundamental tenet of English law that a person is innocent until proved guilty. Similarly, it is a fundamental principle of statistical inference that:
   A hypothesis remains tenable until it has been shown to be unacceptable.
In this example, this means that if the alternative hypothesis 2 is to be established, then the null hypothesis 1 must be discounted. To do this, we have to calculate, on the assumption that the probabilities of being right and wrong are equal, the probability of getting the result observed in the trial; and if this probability is less than a certain acceptable level, then the null hypothesis will be rejected – in which case the alternative hypothesis is left alone in the field.

   But what is this "certain acceptable level" of probability? Here we are back where we were with the bridge ploy: what will convince you in one situation may not convince someone else, and might not even convince you in different circumstances. However, in evaluating scientific hypotheses statisticians do have certain conventions, and a probability below 0.05 is often regarded as "significant" evidence that an experimental result is out of line with the hypothesis being investigated. The evidence for rejecting the hypothesis, and therefore accepting the alternative hypothesis, is then said to be "significant at the 5% level". Other critical probabilities which are often used are 0.01 ("significant at the 1% level", or "very significant") and 0.001 ("significant at the 0.1% level", or "highly significant").

   The next step, then, is to do a calculation based on the null hypothesis, taking the probabilities of getting each beer right or wrong as both equal to $\frac{1}{2}$, and to find the probability of getting 9 right out of 12 ... or rather, we find the probability of getting 9 *or more* right – for it is not the exact number right that is important, but being "as far out from the norm" as this. So, as in the hospital beds example in §8.1, the probabilities are reckoned cumulatively. This time, however, the appropriate probability model is binomial, with $n = 12$ and $a = b = \frac{1}{2}$, as follows:

Number right	0	1	2	3	4	5	6	7	8	9	10	11	12
Probability	0.000	0.003	0.016	0.054	0.121	0.193	0.226	0.193	0.121	0.054	0.016	0.003	0.000
Probability of at least this number	1.000	1.000	0.997	0.981	0.927	0.806	0.613	0.387	0.194	0.073	0.019	0.003	0.000

The probability we are interested in, corresponding to your friend's observed performance, is shown in the box, with value 0.073. Since this is greater than 0.05, we argue that the evidence is not strong enough to reject hypothesis 1: he has not performed well enough on the test to establish his claim to be able to distinguish real ale from keg.

Q.3   Draw suitable graphs to illustrate the calculations in the above table, and describe the criterion for rejecting the null hypothesis in terms of these graphs.

Q.4   How many beers would your friend have had to identify correctly for the evidence to be significant (*a*) at the 5% level, (*b*) at the 1% level?

Q.5   What are the probabilities of (*a*) getting zero in a spin of a roulette wheel, (*b*) throwing a double-six with two dice? Are they greater or less than 5%? Have you ever known these events to happen? What implication does your answer have for the procedure for rejecting hypotheses described in the text?

Q.6   In August 1975 the births of 38 boys and 66 girls were registered in Cambridge. On the hypothesis that a new-born baby selected at random is equally likely to be of either sex, the probability of getting so many more girls than boys in a month can be shown to be less than 0.004. Do you consider that this imbalance was due to local genetic peculiarities or to chance?

8.4 SOME IMPORTANT REMARKS

If you found the argument in the last section complicated, that is hardly surprising – for it took many years for statisticians to evolve this form of reasoning, usually called "hypothesis testing". It is, however, central to the whole process of applying probability theory to practical situations. You have already met it in a special form when you used chi-squared probability to test whether the discrepancy between observed and expected frequencies was significant, in Chapter 6. The purpose of this chapter is to show that it can be used more generally. It is therefore important to stress certain fundamental points about the method.

First, there is no question of "calculating the probability of the theory being true". Your friend either can distinguish real ale from keg (though he is clearly not 100% reliable at doing so), or he cannot. It is meaningless to say that "there is a ... % probability that he can". The aim is merely to find whether or not the hypothesis that he cannot is a tenable one. (Note 8.1)

Second, we are not asking which of the two hypotheses is "more probable". We have seen that the evidence is not strong enough to reject hypothesis 1; but there is clearly no cause to reject hypothesis 2 either. So the only verdict we can bring in is the Scottish one: his claim is "not proven on the evidence submitted".

This analogy with the law may be taken further. When I served on a jury, the judge summing up the case addressed us in the following terms: "It is not a question of whether you think the defendant committed the crime or not. Only if (on the evidence you have heard) you consider it established beyond reasonable doubt that the defendant could not have been innocent of the crime should you bring in a verdict of guilty." In the court of the statistician, "beyond reasonable doubt" means that there is a probability of less than 5% (or 1%, or 0.1%, as you have decided in advance) that the evidence is consistent with an assumption of innocence.

To sum up, then, the standard procedure for making statistical inferences about the validity of a theory is as follows:

(1)   A hypothesis is proposed, which usually takes the form of a "null hypothesis"; that is, a hypothesis that the theory under investigation is not true.

(2)   This is set alongside an alternative hypothesis, that the theory is true.

(3)   A level of significance is decided upon.

(4)   An experiment is designed to test whether the null hypothesis is acceptable.

(5)   The experiment is carried out and the result recorded.

(6)   If, on the assumption of the null hypothesis, the probability of the result obtained (calculated cumulatively) is greater than the level of significance, then the null hypothesis is not rejected, and the theory is "not proven".

(7)   If the probability of the result obtained (calculated cumulatively) is less than the level of significance, then the null hypothesis is rejected, and the theory is considered established by the evidence.

Q.7   The author was once consulted by a teacher who was investigating the disparity which he had observed between the "mock" examination results in his school and the grades achieved in the following summer's certificate examination. A statistical analysis showed (contrary to what he had expected) that the difference between the two sets of results was not significant. The disappointed teacher then asked "What can I do to make the results significant?" Compose a suitable answer to this question.

8.5 ONE-TAIL AND TWO-TAIL TESTS

In the previous example, the null hypothesis was evaluated by calculating the probability of identifying nine or more beers correctly. You will have found from Q.3 that this is shown graphically by the sum of the heights of the sticks to the right of a mark placed between the coordinates 8 and 9. For this reason the test is said to be *one-tail*, since it uses only the right tail of the graph.

Sometimes, however, a situation calls for calculation of the probabilities in both the left and right tails of the graph. The test is then described as *two-tail*. The text example illustrates the use of such a test.

Example 1

Jean is employed by a company which leases electronic gaming machines, to empty the cash trays in the pubs and cafés. When she does this she is required also to check the performance of each machine by playing it 20 times. One type of game is designed so that it allows players to win 3 times out of 10 on average.

What results should cause Jean to report the machine as faulty?

The difference between this and the beer-tasting experiment is that an error either way – too generous to the player (so not enough profit to the company), or too unfavourable (insufficient player motivation) – would be regarded as a fault. As a null hypothesis we assume that the machine is set correctly:

Hypothesis 1. The probability of a single play being successful is 0.3.

The alternative hypothesis is that the machine needs servicing:

Hypothesis 2. The probability of a single play being successful is not equal to 0.3.

A significance level of 5% again seems appropriate.

The next step is to calculate the probabilities of various possible results, using a binomial probability model with $n = 20$, $a = 0.3$ and $b = 0.7$:

Number of successes	0	1	2	3	4	5	6	7
Probability	0.001	0.007	0.028	0.072	0.130	0.179	0.192	0.164

Number of successes	8	9	10	11	12	13	14 or more
Probability	0.114	0.065	0.031	0.012	0.004	0.001	vs

Q.8 Show these probabilities graphically. (If convenient, use the computer program you wrote in Exercise 3B, question 10.)

Now we want to exclude those results which – reckoned cumulatively – have a probability of less than 0.05. But here a new question arises: how does one "reckon cumulatively" when values both to the right and left are to be included?

To answer this a further convention is required: the significance level of 5% is split evenly between the two ends, as $2\frac{1}{2}\%$ on the right and $2\frac{1}{2}\%$ on the left. That is, we exclude results to the right such that the probability of getting that number of successes *or more* is less than 0.025; and we exclude results to the left if the probability of getting that number *or less* is less than 0.025. A table is therefore produced showing these probabilities calculated cumulatively from either end:

Number of successes	0	1		2	...	10		11	12	13	14 or more
Cumulative probability	0.001	0.008		0.036		0.048		0.017	0.005	0.001	vs

The broken lines separate off those results which, on the basis of the null hypothesis, are unacceptable.

The conclusion is therefore that Jean should recommend the machine for service if, in her 20 plays, she gets 1 success or fewer, or 11 successes or more. Otherwise she should regard any discrepancy from the expected value of 6 successes as consistent with the hypothesis that the machine is functioning normally.

Exercise 8A

1   At last term's Student Union elections 40% of the members supported Anna for president. Recently the college magazine selected ten members at random, and eight of them said they would vote for Anna next time. Does this provide evidence of a significant increase in her support?

2   A psychologist is doing research in the colour preferences of children. In one experiment he offers each of 20 children a choice from three balls – one white, one blue and one yellow. Ten of the children choose the yellow. He deduces that, of these three colours, children have a preference for yellow. Is this conclusion justified?

3   Stephen suffers from migraine from time to time; the attacks appear to occur randomly. For some years he has had attacks at an average frequency of about ten a year. Last year he started taking tablets to combat it, and he had only four attacks during the year. Does this indicate that the tablets did some good?

4   Scientists have been keeping a volcanic island under observation for some years. Minor eruptions occur from time to time, at an average rate of five a year. However, last year ten such eruptions were recorded. Does this indicate a significant increase in volcanic activity?

5   At a medical inspection it was found that two people out of a group of 50 were colour-blind. Test whether this number is significantly high given that 1% of the population as a whole is colour-blind, using
   (a) the exact relevant distribution,
   (b) a suitable Poisson approximation.
    Using the Poisson approximation for a group of size n, write down the probability that two or more out of the group are colour-blind. Show that when $n = 35$ this probability is approximately 0.05.   [SMP]

6   A local newspaper remarked that driving standards must have significantly improved in the last year, since the number of fatal accidents recorded in the area was four, as against an average figure of eight over the past several years. Use the Poisson probability model to test the paper's claim.   [SMP]

7   During the seven years from 1950 to 1956 inclusive, electric traction was used on 2500 miles of railway line. During these years, 35 child trespassers were fatally electrocuted. In a succeeding year, 3 children were fatally electrocuted on one 100-mile stretch in separate incidents. Assuming that the numbers of children fatally electrocuted have Poisson distributions, investigate whether this stretch of line requires additional protection.   [London]

8   A die is rolled 20 times. How many sixes would you need to get to be persuaded, using a test of significance at the 5% level, that the die is biased in favour of six?
    Write a computer program to simulate the throws of a biased die, in which the probability of a six is (a) 0.2, (b) 0.3, (c) 0.5; the probabilities of all the other scores

are equal in each case. Count the number of sixes in 20 throws. Does your test reveal that the simulated die is biased?

9 At the final of a chess championship the players toss a coin to decide which of them shall play white in the first match. To make sure that the coin is fair, each player has the right to toss it himself 15 times, and to reject it if he can produce evidence of bias (at the 1% significance level). What numbers of heads or tails would justify him in making such a claim?

10 The individuals eligible for jury service in a city are 54% women and 46% men. Juries of 12 people are supposed to be selected at random from this population. The men's rights lobby will object to a jury if it has evidence (at the 5% significance level) that it has not enough men (on the grounds of under-representation) or too many men (on the grounds of exploitation). How must a jury be made up if it is to avoid such an objection?

11 On a roulette wheel the probability of a zero should be $\frac{1}{37}$. From time to time the government's Inspector of Casinos tests all the wheels in a gaming house by running each 250 times, and he requires a wheel to be withdrawn if there is evidence (at the 5% significance level) that it is biased. How many zeros must show up in the test if a wheel is to satisfy the inspector?

12 A researcher is testing a hypothesis that, in an experiment, the probability of a certain event is a. He carries out the experiment n times, and decides to use a $P\%$ significance level as his criterion for rejecting the hypothesis. Taking account of various possible alternative hypotheses, write a computer program to input a, n and P and to print out a rule of thumb (in terms of the number of times that the event occurs) for determining whether or not the hypothesis is rejected. (K)

8.6 INTERVAL ESTIMATION

The arguments used to test hypotheses can also be adapted to throw more light on the problem of estimating the properties of a population from a sample, which was discussed in Chapter 4. There we considered the example of a factory in which a sample of 50 plates was inspected, and two were found to be blemished. The principle of maximum likelihood gave 0.04 as the best estimate for the probability of a fault being found in a plate selected at random.

But while this may be the "best", it is certainly not the only reasonable estimate that might be made. For example, if the probability of a faulty plate were 0.03 or 0.05 rather than 0.04, it is still quite possible that, in inspecting a sample of 50, two would be found flawed. However, if a rival firm asserted that the probability of a faulty plate in this factory was 0.4, that is clearly quite unreasonable on the evidence of the sample. The situation is illustrated in Fig. 2, which suggests that there must be some interval surrounding the value 0.04 which includes all the reasonable estimates of the probability on the basis of the sample. A quality control supervisor would need to know what this interval is, so that clear assurances can be given to the management about the reliability of the product.

Now to ask whether an estimate is "reasonable" or "unreasonable" brings us back to the language of hypothesis testing. The only difference now is that, instead of having just two hypotheses – the null hypothesis and an alternative

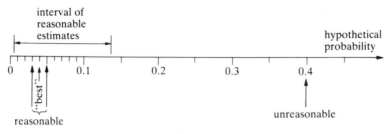

Figure 2

hypothesis – every separate possible value of the probability becomes a hypothesis in its own right. On the evidence of the sample, some of these hypotheses will be reasonable, others not; the aim is to separate the one from the other.

What about 0.08, for example? Would this be a reasonable value for the probability of a faulty plate? To find out, we put up a hypothesis:

Hypothesis 1. The probability of a plate selected at random being faulty is 0.08.

The alternative hypothesis is just the denial of this:

Hypothesis 2. The probability of a plate selected at random being faulty is not 0.08.

This is familiar territory: it is just the same kind of situation as Example 1 of §8.5, so we can proceed in the same way as we did there. This means using a two-tail test, and calculating the cumulative probability from either end. (Note 8.2) Now in the present example the individual probabilities have already been calculated; they are given in Table 1 of §4.2, the fourth line up from the bottom. So the cumulative probabilities can be found simply by adding up in the directions of the two arrows (Note 8.3):

Number faulty in sample	0	1	2	...	7	8	9	10	11
Probability	0.015	0.067	0.143	...	0.058	0.027	0.011	0.004	0.001 ...
Cumulative probability	0.015	0.082	0.225	...	0.101	0.043	0.016	0.005	0.001 ...

$\longrightarrow$ $\longleftarrow$

Q.9 State in words precisely what these cumulative probabilities stand for (*a*) on the left, (*b*) on the right.

We have not yet settled on a significance level. Suppose that we take this to be 5 % as before. Since the test is two-tail, this means $2\frac{1}{2}$ % at either end; that is, the hypothesis will be rejected if, when the sample is taken, the number of faulty plates is such that the cumulative probability (from the appropriate end) is less than 0.025. Notice that this is a decision that needs to be made in advance; it is not an acceptable practice to take the sample first and then to choose where to draw the line between "significant" and "not significant".

On this basis, then, the estimate of 0.08 would be regarded as unreasonable if a sample of 50 turned up no faulty plates, or nine or more faulty. But given that the sample actually taken contained just two faulty plates, we have to conclude that 0.08 is a perfectly reasonable estimate for the probability of a faulty plate – even though it is not the "best" one.

Q.10 Use Table 1 of §4.2 to investigate similarly whether other estimates for the probability of a faulty plate (0.007, 0.008, ... 0.10, 0.12) are reasonable, given that in the sample of 50 plates actually taken there were just two faulty. Can you determine the complete interval of reasonable estimates (see Fig. 2)?

8.7 SIMPLIFYING THE CALCULATION

You probably found the first part of Q.10 easy to do, since most of the calculation had already been done for you when Table 1 was constructed, and all that was needed was to change the probabilities given there into cumulative probabilities from the left and the right – a matter of simple addition. But the question at the end is much harder, and involves a "trial and error" approach: first you have to decide what hypothetical probability to try, then calculate from scratch the probabilities of getting the various number of faulty plates in the sample, adapt these to cumulative probabilities ... before you can decide whether that particular estimate is reasonable or not. So it is worth while finding ways of reducing the labour in carrying out this procedure. Two ways will be suggested in this section, which can be used either separately or in combination.

The first is to use a computer. You already have a program for calculating binomial probabilities, and for showing these in the form of a stick graph (Exercise 3B, question 10). It is a simple matter to insert into this program extra lines to calculate the cumulative probability from the left (the probability of i or fewer As) and from the right (the probability of i or more As, which is $1 -$ the probability of $(i - 1)$ or fewer As), and then to draw the corresponding sticks in a different colour (red, say) if either of these cumulative probabilities is less than 0.025 – or some other value if a significance level different from 5% is chosen. The trial and error process can then be carried out very quickly: if the stick corresponding to the known sample is red, then the estimate is unreasonable, if it is white then the estimate is reasonable.

Q.11 Adapt your program in the way suggested, and use it to investigate the last question in Q.10.

The other simplification makes use of the fact that, in certain circumstances, binomial probabilities are approximately equal to Poisson probabilities (see §7.7). For example, going back to the situation discussed in §8.6, the hypothesis that the probability of a plate selected at random being faulty is 0.08 could be expressed by saying that the expected number of faulty plates in a sample of 50 is 50×0.08, or 4. The probabilities, in an actual sample, of getting various numbers faulty can be found approximately as Poisson probabilities with $\lambda = 4$ (see Exercise 7D, question 2). This gives the following table in place of the one set out in §8.6:

Number faulty in sample	0	1	2	...	7	8	9	10	11	12	...
Probability	0.018	0.073	0.147	...	0.060	0.030	0.013	0.005	0.002	0.001	...
Cumulative probability	0.018	0.091	0.238	...	0.111	0.051	0.021	0.008	0.003	0.001	...
	$\longrightarrow$									$\longleftarrow$	

(Note 8.4) You will notice that the correspondence is quite close, and in this case gives just the same cut-off points where the cumulative probability is less than 0.025.

The advantage of replacing binomial by Poisson probabilities is that the Poisson model depends on just one parameter, the expected number λ. This makes it possible to make a single chart (for a chosen level of significance, such as 5%) showing which samples are consistent with which hypotheses. For example, the table above shows that, on the hypothesis that the expected number of faulty plates in a sample of 50 is 4, it would not be remarkable in an actual sample to get anything between 1 and 8 faulty (since for these numbers the cumulative probability exceeds 0.025). Fig. 3 shows the result of carrying out a similar calculation for a range of expected numbers λ. The vertical lines in this chart then indicate the range of hypotheses about the expected number, and therefore about the probability λ/n, which would be considered reasonable at the 5% significance level following a sampling experiment in which particular numbers of faults were found.

There is, though, one very important restriction on the use of this method. The close approximation of the binomial and Poisson models only holds when the probability λ/n is small; it would be unwise to rely on it for probabilities much greater than one-tenth. Now this is rarely a problem in quality control applications, like the one we have been discussing: a mass-production process in which more than 10% of the output is sub-standard is unlikely to survive very long! But the restriction does mean that the Poisson approximation could not be used, for example, to find the margin of error in political opinion polls; for this purpose a different approximation is used, which will be described in Chapter 16.

Example 2
A checker in an electronics factory tests a batch of 500 resistors and finds three faulty. What does this indicate about the proportion of faulty resistors coming off the production line as a whole?

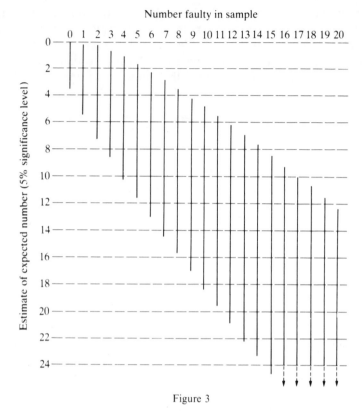

Number faulty in sample

Figure 3

Since 3 in 500 is a small proportion, the Poisson approximation can be used. The vertical line in Fig. 3 corresponding to a sample with three faults contains values of λ from 0.7 to 8.7. So, using a 5% significance level as the basis for estimation, the probability of a resistor selected at random being faulty may be as small as $0.7/500$, and as large as $8.7/500$; that is, the estimated proportion of faulty resistors lies in the interval from 0.14% to 1.74%.

Exercise 8B

1   In Exercise 8A, question 1, eight of the ten members polled by the college magazine said they would vote for Anna. Consider various estimates for her support within the Union as a whole, and investigate which of them are consistent with the poll at the 5% significance level. Find the interval of "reasonable" estimates.

2   A bag contains 100 beads, all of the same size but some black and some white. A bead is taken out, its colour noted, and returned to the bag; this is repeated again and again, until ten beads have been taken. It turns out that four are white and six are black. Make an interval estimate of the number of white beads in the bag.

3   A zoologist working on a remote island succeeds in capturing fifteen specimens of a rare species of mouse, and notes that three of them are of the striped tail variety. What can he say about the proportion of striped tail mice on the island?

4   Twenty people are stopped in the street, and fifteen of them express a preference for Sudz washing powder. What does this suggest about the popularity of Sudz in the population as a whole?

5   A volcano, unknown to science until 100 years ago, has erupted seven times during the past century. Assuming that eruptions occur independently and at random, make an interval estimate of the average number of eruptions per century.

6   In the past 50 years a tropical island has suffered four severe droughts. Estimate the probability that a year will be a drought year.

7   In a sample of 1000 oysters nine are found to contain pearls. Estimate the proportion of oysters in that locality which contain pearls.

Revision exercise A

1 People in a properly conducted marketing exercise taste two brands of margarine, Flamingo and Yodel. The two brands are indistinguishable except for the packing, and this is removed prior to tasting. Each taster expresses a preference for one of the brands. Assuming that the first 10 people to taste react independently, find the probabilities that
   (a) exactly 8 of them prefer Flamingo to Yodel;
   (b) at least 8 of them prefer Yodel to Flamingo.
   It is known that 85% of the population prefer butter to Flamingo. How many people, acting independently, should take part in a marketing exercise of the sort described above for there to be a better than evens chance of at least one person preferring Flamingo to butter? [MEI]

2 A counter lies on the x-axis and is initially at $x = 0$. A fair coin is tossed: the counter is moved along the x-axis one unit in the positive direction or one unit in the negative direction according as the result is heads or tails. This process is repeated at each new position and continued indefinitely. Find the probability that after two tosses the counter is again at $x = 0$. State the positions that the counter can be in after three tosses, and the associated probabilities.
   Calculate the mean squared distance from $x = 0$ after (a) 1 toss, (b) 2 tosses, (c) 3 tosses, (d) 4 tosses. Suggest a general result.
   If the coin has probabilities p of heads and $(1 - p)$ of tails, show that the mean squared distance from $x = 0$ after three tosses is $9 - 24p + 24p^2$ and determine the value of p for which this is least. [SMP]

3 I select three eggs from a box of ten and find that two of the three are bad. Find the probabilities of this happening for the various possible numbers of bad eggs in the whole box. Would you discard any of these possibilities on the grounds that they make the observed result too improbable? [SMP]

4 A population consists of 100 men and 900 women and it is known that exactly 10 men and 30 women have red hair. A person is chosen at random from the population. Find the probability that the selected person (a) is male, (b) has red hair, (c) is male given that the person has red hair.
   In a further selection, five people are chosen at random and with replacement. Find the probability that exactly two of the people have red hair. Find also the probability that at least two have red hair. [London]

5 At a large fruit farm plums are coming continuously on a conveyor belt into a packing shed. A proportion p of them are unripe. I select a batch of twenty plums at random and find that three of them are unripe. For what range of values of p is this the most probable number of unripe plums in the sample? [SMP]

6 Three machines A, B and C produce 25%, 25% and 50% respectively of the output of a factory manufacturing a certain article. A sample of three articles is selected at

random from the total output. Find the probabilities (*a*) that they are all from C, (*b*) that at least two are from B.

If a second independent sample of three articles is selected, find the probability that both samples have the same number of articles produced by A.

Of the articles produced by A, B and C, 1%, 2% and 5% respectively are defective. A single article is selected at random. If **D** denotes the event "defective" and **C** the event "produced by machine C", find P(**D**) and P(**C** and **D**).

An article is examined and found to be defective. What is the probability that it was produced by C?   [SMP]

7   A chess match between two grandmasters A and B is won by whoever first wins a total of two games. A's chances of winning, drawing or losing any particular game are p, q, r respectively. The games are independent and $p + q + r = 1$. Show that the probability that A wins the match after $(n + 1)$ games $(n \geq 1)$ is

$$p^2\{nq^{n-1} + n(n - 1)rq^{n-2}\}.$$

By considering suitable operations on the infinite geometric series $(q + q^2 + \ldots)$, or otherwise, show that the probability that A wins the match is $p^2(p + 3r)/(p + r)^3$. Find the probability that there is no winner and comment on your result.
                                                                                    [MEI]

8   An ordinary die is thrown n times and the greatest and smallest numbers obtained are recorded. By considering the events (*a*) that all throws result in numbers less than or equal to 5, and (*b*) that all throws result in numbers greater than or equal to 2, or otherwise, determine the probability p_n that the difference between the greatest and smallest numbers is 5. Verify that your result is correct for $n = 1$ and $n = 2$. Also evaluate, and comment on the value of,

$$\lim_{n \to \infty} p_n.$$
                                                                                    [MEI]

9   In a bag there are ten discs numbered 0 to 9. Two, selected at random, are removed from the bag and the one with the larger number is then returned. A disc is now selected at random from the bag. What is the probability that it bears the number (*a*) 9, (*b*) 4?

Simulate this problem on a computer which has a routine for generating random digits, to obtain an approximation after 10 000 trials to the probability (*b*).
                                                                                    [SMP]

10 An examiner is required to set one question each year that must be either on Markov chains or else on the Poisson probability model. If he sets a question on Markov chains one year, then the probability that he will set a question the following year on the Poisson model is 0.7, while if he sets a question on the Poisson model one year the probability that he will set a question the next year on Markov chains is 0.8. Set up a transition matrix for this system and, using this matrix (or otherwise), calculate the probabilities that he will set a question on the Poisson model (*a*) in three years' time, (*b*) in four years' time, given that this year's question is on the Poisson model.

11 Six dice were thrown together 1000 times. At each throw, the number of ones obtained was noted and the frequency is shown in the table:

Number of ones in a single throw	0	1	2	3	4	5	6
Number of throws	370	380	150	90	9	1	0

(a) Calculate the mean and variance of the number of ones obtained in the experiment.

(b) Produce a corresponding table of the expected frequencies, to the nearest integer in each case, based on the assumption that the six dice are unbiased and that the 1000 throws are independent.

(c) Comment on the closeness of the experimental results to the theory.

[London]

12   The number of calls per day to the fire brigade at town A is distributed as a Poisson variate with mean 1, and the number of calls per day to the fire brigade at town B is independently distributed as a Poisson variate with mean 2. Find the probability that on   particular day

(a) both fire brigades have exactly two calls,

(b) the fire brigade from town A receives no calls but the brigade from town B receives at least one call,

(c) between them the two fire brigades have less than 3 calls.

Find an expression for the probability that on a particular day both fire brigades have the same number of calls.   [London]

13   In a certain football league it was noted after a long period of observation that the number of goals scored per match has a Poisson distribution, the mean number of goals per match being 3. Calculate the probability that

(a) more than five goals will be scored in a particular match,

(b) at least two out of three matches will be goal-less.   [London]

14   A random sample of 500 people born in 1961 is being studied. It can be assumed that birthdays are uniformly distributed throughout the year.

(i) Use the Poisson distribution to find the probabilities that there are (a) exactly two people, and (b) no more than two people, with birthdays on 1 January.

(ii) Also find the probability that, if two of the sample are chosen at random, they have birthdays in the same month.   [MEI]

15   In a certain windy desert, sandstorms occur randomly at an average rate of one every two days. Calculate

(a) the probability that, on a randomly chosen day, there will be two sandstorms,

(b) the probability that, in a randomly chosen week, there will be more than two sandstorms,

(c) the probability that, on a randomly chosen day, there will be a sandstorm,

(d) the probability that, in a randomly chosen week, there will be exactly two days on which there are no sandstorms.   [Cambridge]

16   Samples of 40 are taken of mass-produced articles of which 1 % are defective. Using (a) the binomial distribution, (b) the Poisson distribution, estimate the probability that a sample contains less than two defective articles.

Using the Poisson distribution find also the probability that, of 60 such samples, more than one contains two or more defective articles.   [London]

17   One suggested test for deciding whether a coin is fair or not is to toss it four times and call it "biased" if four heads or four tails are obtained. A second suggested way is to toss it seven times and call it biased if six or seven heads, or six or seven tails, are obtained. Show that both these tests would be equally likely to conclude wrongly that a fair coin was biased.

Which of these two suggested tests would be better for correctly judging as biased a coin whose probability of coming down heads was $\frac{2}{3}$?   [SMP]

18 It is known that 0.1% of people having an influenza injection of type A suffer an adverse reaction. If 2250 people are to receive an injection, what is the probability that

(*a*) exactly 2 people will suffer an adverse reaction,

(*b*) more than 3 people will suffer an adverse reaction?

Given that 2000 people receive an injection of type B and no one suffers an adverse reaction to this injection, is this sufficient evidence to suggest that there is a smaller probability of an adverse reaction to type B than to type A?   [London]

Project exercises A

A1 A BITING PROBLEM

A full adult set of teeth consists of 16 in the upper gum and 16 in the lower, positioned more or less opposite each other to make 16 biting pairs. Unfortunately, with age the total number of teeth that a person has decreases, and this also reduces the number of biting pairs.

1   If a person has n teeth left, then there are $\binom{32}{n}$ different ways in which these might be placed in the gums. Find an expression for the number of these in which there are r biting pairs and $n - 2r$ singles (i.e. teeth without matching partners). Deduce the probability p_r that a person having n teeth in all will have r biting pairs. On what assumption is your calculation based?

2   Evaluate these probabilities when $n = 10$, $n = 20$ and $n = 13$, for all the relevant values of r in each case, and for these values of n deduce which is the most probable number of biting pairs.

3   Consider the inequality $p_r > p_{r-1}$, and show that this is equivalent to a simple algebraic relationship connecting r and n. Check this numerically for the three values of n investigated numerically in question 2.

4   Make a table, or find a formula, which gives the most probable number of biting pairs for any value of n from 0 to 32.

A2 WORLD SERIES

In many sports, the winner is decided not by a single game but by finding which player wins most often in a series of games. For example, the US baseball World Series is given to the team which wins at least 4 games in a series of 7; men's tennis matches are decided on the most wins in a series of 5 sets; and so on. To avoid draws, the number of games in the series is always taken to be odd. (Often, of course, the series is cut short when one team has won more than half of the total number of games in the series.)

1   Suppose that when two teams A and B play each other, their respective probabilities of winning are a and b, where $a + b = 1$ and $b < a$. Write down the probabilities that B will win a tournament in which the result is decided as (i) the best of 3 games, (ii) the best of 5 games, (iii) the best of 7 games.

2   By multiplying b by $(b + a)^2$, and comparing the result with the answer to (i), show that the probability that B will win in a 3-game series is smaller than in a single game.

3   Use a similar argument to show that B's probability of winning in a 5-game series is smaller than in a 3-game series, and that B's probability of winning in a 7-game series is smaller still.

4 Write down sums which give B's probabilities of winning in a $(2n + 1)$-game series and a $(2n - 1)$-game series, beginning with the terms

$$b^{2n+1} + \ldots \quad \text{and} \quad b^{2n-1} + \ldots$$

respectively. Explain why, if the second of these is multiplied by $(b + a)^2$, the result only differs from the first expression in the terms involving $b^{n+1}a^n$ and $b^n a^{n+1}$.

5 Hence prove that B's chance of winning in a $(2n + 1)$-game series is smaller than in a $(2n - 1)$-game series: that is, the more games that are played, the higher the probability that the best team will win.

A3 VOLLEYBALL

In volleyball a team can only score a point if it is serving. If the opposing team is serving and you win the rally, then your team takes the service but does not get a point.

To make the model as simple as possible, imagine that A and B are equally matched teams, and that for either team having the service gives no advantage in winning the rally.

1 Suppose that A has the service. Draw a tree diagram showing the sequences of rallies until the next point is won. Show that A's probability of winning the next point is

$$\frac{1}{2} + \frac{1}{8} + \frac{1}{32} + \ldots$$

and evaluate the sum of this series.

Write a similar series for B's probability of winning, and evaluate its sum.

2 Another way of calculating A's probability of winning the point, given that it has the service, is to restrict attention to a part of the tree diagram and to note that the situations are exactly the same at the two points marked * in Fig. 1.

Denoting the required probability by p, use this diagram to write an equation for p. Show that this leads to the same result as the series in question 1.

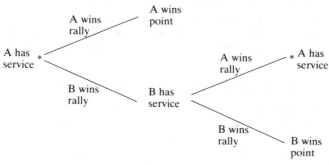

Figure 1

3 If A_n denotes the outcome "A wins the nth point", and B_n denotes "B wins the nth point", write equations for $P(A_{n+1})$ and $P(B_{n+1})$ in terms of $P(A_n)$ and $P(B_n)$. Evaluate the probabilities for $n = 1, 2, 3, 4, 5$, and guess general expressions for $P(A_n)$ and $P(B_n)$. Use mathematical induction to prove these correct. Show that the advantage of first service 'wears off' after a number of points, but that it never totally disappears.

4   Suppose that A and B play a mini-game, the winner being the first to score 3 points. Draw a tree diagram showing the sequence of *points* (not rallies) until this occurs. If A serves first, find the probabilities of A and of B winning the game.

5   In the real game, if the scores reach 14-all, the teams continue to play until one or other gets 2 points ahead. Fig. 2 is a tree diagram illustrating this.

   Denoting by q the probability (for either team) that it wins the game from an even-points situation (14-14, 15-15, etc.) in which it holds the service, use the diagram to write an equation for q. Hence find the probability that A will win from the score 14-all with A serving.

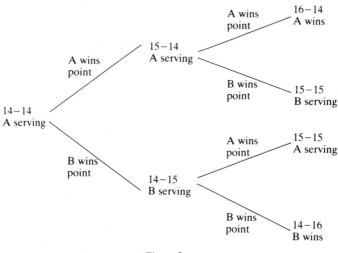

Figure 2

6   Try generalising this model in some of the following ways:
   (i)   A and B have different probabilities a, b of winning a rally.
   (ii) Service affects the probabilities of winning a rally.
   (iii) Consider longer games in question 4, or a game like that in question 4 but in which, if the score reaches 2-all, the teams play on as described in question 5.

A4   FERTILISATION "IN VITRO"

In the late 1970s a technique was developed which made it possible for some women who had previously been barren to have children. A number of eggs were taken from the women, fertilised outside the body in favourable conditions, and then replaced. In the early applications only about 30 % of the embryos replaced grew to full maturity; so the usual practice was to replace several embryos rather than just one, to give a greater chance of a live birth resulting from the procedure. Unfortunately this also increased the probability of a multiple birth (triplets, quadruplets, or even more), which was regarded as undesirable. The problem was therefore how many embryos it was best to replace.

1   Calculate, for different numbers of embryos replaced, the probabilities of the process leading to (*a*) at least one child, (*b*) exactly one, (*c*) two or more children, (*d*) three or more. (Assume the embryos develop independently.)

2 One possible criterion for deciding how many embryos to replace is to try to maximise the probability of getting exactly one child. On that basis, what practice should be adopted? Does this lead to acceptable values for the probabilities (a) to (d) calculated in question 1?

3 As experience increases, it is to be expected that the technique will improve, and a higher success rate will be achieved. Repeat the calculations in questions 1 and 2 on the hypothesis that a proportion p of the embryos replaced grow to full maturity.

4 Can you suggest some other criterion which might be used for making the decision, which gives proper weight to the two factors – achieving at least one child, but avoiding multiple births? Investigate the consequences of this criterion, and compare these with the answers to questions 2 and 3.

A5 TWELVE GOOD MEN AND FALLIBLE

In a country which is about to become independent the lawyers are trying to devise a new legal code. They have decided that criminal cases should be decided by juries of twelve citizens, and are considering what majority (f to g, where $f + g = 12$) should be sufficient to secure a conviction. Every juror is required to vote either for or against, but unfortunately no juror is completely reliable in his judgement; it is assumed that each has (independently) a probability x of deciding that an innocent person is guilty, and a probability y of deciding that a guilty person is innocent.

1 Write expressions, in terms of x, y, f and g, for the probabilities that an innocent person will be convicted, and that a guilty person will go free.

2 Write a computer program to input values of x and y, and to print out the values of these probabilities for all possible values of f and g.

3 The lawyers would like to get the probabilities in question 1 at least as low as 0.0001 and 0.1 respectively. The criminologists estimate that realistic values of x and y are 0.2 and 0.3 respectively. Is it possible to choose values of f and g compatible with the lawyers' requirements and the criminologists' data?

4 If not, then either the lawyers must lower their standards of justice or the jurors must be better trained. Use your computer program to investigate compromise values for the four probabilities which would make the system workable.

A6 MARKOV SEQUENCES AND MATRICES

In Chapter 3 we looked at a Markov sequence (the boat race results) with transition probability matrix

$$\mathbf{T} = \begin{bmatrix} \frac{3}{5} & \frac{1}{3} \\ \frac{2}{5} & \frac{2}{3} \end{bmatrix}$$

and initial outcome probability matrix

$$\mathbf{p}_0 = \begin{bmatrix} 1 \\ 0 \end{bmatrix}.$$

1 On a sheet of graph paper, draw the vectors $\mathbf{p}_0$, $\mathbf{p}_1 = \mathbf{T}\mathbf{p}_0$, $\mathbf{p}_2 = \mathbf{T}\mathbf{p}_1$, ... as far as you can. What prevents you from going on indefinitely?

2   By considering its effect on $\begin{bmatrix} 1 \\ 0 \end{bmatrix}$ and $\begin{bmatrix} 0 \\ 1 \end{bmatrix}$, prove that the matrix **T** maps the line $x + y = 1$ to itself. What is the significance of this if **T** is regarded as a transition matrix?

3   In Chapter 3 it was shown that $\mathbf{p} = \begin{bmatrix} \frac{5}{11} \\ \frac{6}{11} \end{bmatrix}$ is a 'steady' matrix. Show that $\mathbf{Tp} = \mathbf{p}$.

4   Show that the matrix $\mathbf{q} = \begin{bmatrix} 1 \\ -1 \end{bmatrix}$ has the property that $\mathbf{Tq} = \lambda\mathbf{q}$. What is the value of the multiplier λ? (We call 1 and λ, the multipliers in the equations $\mathbf{Tp} = \mathbf{p}$ and $\mathbf{Tq} = \lambda\mathbf{q}$, *eigenvalues* of the transition matrix; the corresponding matrices **p** and **q** are *eigenvectors*. See, for example, the book *Linear Algebra and Geometry* in this series.). Plot **q** on your graph paper.

5   Show that $\mathbf{p}_0$ can be expressed in the form $\mathbf{p} + \beta\mathbf{q}$, and illustrate this relationship in your diagram. Prove that in this case $\mathbf{p}_1 = \mathbf{p} + \beta\lambda\mathbf{q}$, and more generally $\mathbf{p}_n = \mathbf{p} + \beta\lambda^n\mathbf{q}$. Deduce that (as should be clear from your diagram) $\mathbf{p}_n \to \mathbf{p}$ as $n \to \infty$.

6   Prove that, if **E** denotes the matrix $\begin{bmatrix} \frac{5}{11} & 1 \\ \frac{6}{11} & -1 \end{bmatrix}$ whose columns are eigenvectors, then $\mathbf{T}^n\mathbf{E} = \mathbf{E}\begin{bmatrix} 1 & 0 \\ 0 & \lambda^n \end{bmatrix}$. Use this to write an expression for $\mathbf{T}^n$. What is the limiting form of this matrix as $n \to \infty$?

7   Now repeat questions 1–6 with the transition matrix $\mathbf{T} = \begin{bmatrix} \frac{3}{5} & \frac{2}{3} \\ \frac{2}{5} & \frac{1}{3} \end{bmatrix}$. What similarities and what differences do you notice? (The steady matrix **p** is, of course, different from that given in question 3, and this means that a different matrix **E** must be taken in question 6.)

8   Finally, consider a general transition matrix of the form

$$\mathbf{T} = \begin{bmatrix} a & 1-b \\ 1-a & b \end{bmatrix} \text{ where } 0 \leqslant a \leqslant 1 \text{ and } 0 \leqslant b \leqslant 1,$$

with an initial outcome probability matrix

$$\mathbf{p}_0 = \begin{bmatrix} k \\ 1-k \end{bmatrix} \text{ where } 0 \leqslant k \leqslant 1.$$

Follow through questions 1–6 (with appropriate changes in questions 3 and 6) for this transition matrix. What is the difference between the cases $a + b > 1$ and $a + b < 1$? Explain this in probability terms.

9   What happens if $a + b = 1$? To what special kind of sequence does this correspond? Other special cases arise when $a = b = 0$ and when $a = b = 1$. Discuss these.

9

Mean and variance in probability models

When we carry out a statistical experiment, the results often come in the form of measurements or scores. This produces a lot of numbers, far too many to use individually; so a common practice is to reduce the data to a few key numbers, such as the mean and variance whose calculation was described in §1.1.

But experiments of this kind can also be described theoretically, by means of probability models. Instead of actually rolling a die and counting the frequencies of the scores 1, 2, 3, 4, 5, 6, we construct a model in which a probability is associated with each of these scores. In this case we cannot calculate an actual mean and variance, since we have no frequency data to substitute in the formulae; but there are clearly numbers which can be calculated for the model, indicating the central score and the spread of the scores, which closely resemble the mean and variance which would be found from experimental data.

This chapter is concerned with defining such numbers, and using mathematical techniques to calculate them for some of the well known types of probability model.

9.1 THE THEORETICAL MEAN

Example 1
A local lottery offers one £100 prize each week, and ten prizes of £20 each. The number of tickets sold in one week is 1000. If I buy one 50p ticket, how much should I expect to win?

Unless one is incurably optimistic, the short answer to this question is "nothing". Certainly this is the result with by far the largest probability – the 'modal' return for my investment.

But the question could be looked at another way. The probability of winning the £100 prize is 1 in 1000, and of winning of £20 prize 1 in 100. So if I were to go on buying one ticket a week for 1000 weeks, and the number sold each week remains the same, then I might reasonably hope (if the gods are just) that one week I might get the £100 prize, and that in ten other weeks I might win £20. That is, over the 1000 weeks I might hope to win £100 + 10 × £20, or £300. On that basis, my 'average' weekly expectation of return is £300 ÷ 1000, that is 30p.

Q.1 Why can I not be sure of winning the £100 once in the 1000 weeks? What are the probabilities of winning it (*a*) at least once, (*b*) more than once?

This way of calculating the expectation can be based directly on the probabilities, without having to imagine the experiment repeated 1000 times. We reason as follows:

Probability of winning £100 is 0.001 : expected return £0.10

Probability of winning   £20 is 0.01   : expected return £0.20

Probability of winning   £0 is 0.989 : expected return £0.00

Total expectation is £0.30

Here the words "expected return" are used in much the same way as "expected frequency" in §6.1, as the product of the value of the prize and the probability of winning it. In this sense the expected return is a kind of long-run average, rather than any actually possible win. It might in fact be better to describe it as the "theoretical mean return". It bears the same relation to the probability model as does the actual mean of the results to a series of experiments.

To see this, consider an experiment each of whose possible outcomes is described by a 'score'. (For the lottery example the scores are £100, £20 and £0.) Suppose that there are k different scores, denoted by $x_1, x_2, \ldots, x_k$, and that when the experiment is repeated n times these scores occur with frequencies $f(x_1), f(x_2), \ldots, f(x_k)$, as described in Note 1.3. The mean score would then be calculated as

$$m = \frac{x_1 f(x_1) + x_2 f(x_2) + \cdots + x_k f(x_k)}{n},$$

which can be written in the form

$$m = \sum_{i=1}^{k} x_i \frac{f(x_i)}{n}.$$

Suppose now that we make a probability model for this experiment. With each score x_i we need to associate a probability $p(x_i)$. (Note 1.6) How is this done?

We have seen that there can be more than one answer to this question. The probabilities may be found theoretically, either by identifying a set of equally likely outcomes (e.g. the scores 1, 2, 3, 4, 5, 6 when a die is rolled) or by using probability theory (e.g. the probabilities given by a binomial probability model); alternatively they may be found by experiment, as when an insurance company estimates the probabilities of various kinds of accident. But in either case, if the model is a good one the probabilities $p(x_i)$ should come out close to the relative frequencies (i.e. the actual proportions of occurrences of the various scores), which are calculated as $f(x_i)/n$.

Q.2   What is $\sum_{i=1}^{k} f(x_i)/n$? To what does this correspond in the probability model?

This is the clue to defining a theoretical mean for a probability model, which is usually denoted by the greek letter μ. (Note 9.1) We merely take the formula for m and replace each relative frequency $f(x_i)/n$ by the corresponding probability, to give

$$\mu = \sum_{i=1}^{k} x_i p(x_i).$$

You will see that this expresses generally the method used to calculate the total expectation in the lottery example.

9.2 THEORETICAL VARIANCE AND STANDARD DEVIATION

Would you prefer to take a ticket in the lottery described above, or in one with 60 prizes a week of £5 each? This would give just the same expectation of return, since the probability of winning a prize in any week would be 60 in 1000, or 0.06, so that

$$\mu = £5 \times 0.06 + £0 \times 0.94 = £0.03.$$

But the difference lies in the spread of prizes – the choice between a few good prizes with a small chance of winning anything, or a small prize which you might hope to win three or four times a year.

To distinguish these we need to introduce the idea of "theoretical variance", which is the parameter for a probability model corresponding to the variance of the scores obtained in an actual experiment. Putting n inside the summation in the formula for variance given in §1.1 produces

$$v = S^2 = \sum_{i=1}^{k} (x_i - m)^2 \frac{f(x_i)}{n}.$$

As before, we replace the relative frequency $f(x_i)/n$ by the probability $p(x_i)$, and m by μ, to obtain

$$\sigma^2 = \sum_{i=1}^{k} (x_i - \mu)^2 p(x_i). \qquad \text{(Note 9.2)}$$

For example, for the two lotteries this gives the theoretical values

$$\sigma_1^2 = \{£(100 - 0.30)\}^2 \times 0.001 + \{£(20 - 0.30)\}^2 \times 0.01$$
$$+ \{£(0 - 0.30)\}^2 \times 0.989$$
$$= (£)^2 \ 13.91,$$
$$\sigma_2^2 = \{£(5 - 0.30)\}^2 \times 0.06 + \{£(0 - 0.30)\}^2 \times 0.94$$
$$= (£)^2 \ 1.41.$$

So although both lotteries have the same theoretical mean, the more risky one has a theoretical variance nearly ten times as great as the other. (Which you would prefer to indulge in – if either – is of course a matter of temperament!)

As a unit, "square pound" is not very familiar. So for practical purposes a better idea of spread is conveyed by taking the square root, and giving the "theoretical standard deviation" σ. In these examples the standard deviations are respectively £3.73 and £1.19.

One last point. You will recall from §1.1 that, when calculating a variance, it is often simpler to use the equivalent formula

$$v = S^2 = \left\{\frac{1}{n} \sum_{i=1}^{k} x_i^2 f(x_i)\right\} - m^2, \quad \text{or} \quad \left\{\sum_{i=1}^{k} x_i^2 \frac{f(x_i)}{n}\right\} - m^2,$$

which can easily be derived from the definition. Not surprisingly an exactly similar argument can be applied to the theoretical variance, leading to the expression

$$\sigma^2 = \left\{\sum_{i=1}^{k} x_i^2 p(x_i)\right\} - \mu^2.$$

Q.3   Use this to recalculate the variances σ_1^2 and σ_2^2 for the two lotteries.

Q.4   Derive the alternative expression for σ^2 from the definition, by expanding $(x_i - \mu)^2$, splitting the summation into three separate parts and taking out any common factors.

To sum up:

If an experiment can result in any one of k different scores $x_1, x_2, \ldots, x_k$, and if the probabilities of these scores are $p(x_1), p(x_2), \ldots, p(x_k)$, then the *expectation* or *theoretical mean* of the scores is defined as

$$\mu = \sum_{i=1}^{k} x_i p(x_i),$$

and the *theoretical variance* is defined by

$$\sigma^2 = \sum_{i=1}^{k} (x_i - \mu)^2 p(x_i), \quad \text{which equals} \quad \left\{\sum_{i=1}^{k} x_i^2 p(x_i)\right\} - \mu^2.$$

The square root of the theoretical variance, σ, is the *theoretical standard deviation*.

In practice, when the meaning is unambiguous, the word "theoretical" is usually omitted when referring to these parameters.

Exercise 9A

1   In a sideshow at a fair, customers are invited to place their stakes (in multiples of £1) in any of twenty numbered containers. An electronic device then selects one of the numbers at random. If your number comes up, the stall-holder gives you ten times the amount you staked on it; but he keeps all the cash in the containers. Fred wants to wager £3, which he can do in three ways: all in one container, £1 in each of three separate containers, or £2 in one and £1 in another. Compare the means and variances of the loss incurred using the three strategies.

2   In your pocket you have three 1p pieces, two 2p, two 5p and one 10p piece. You take two coins out at random and put them in a collecting box. What is the expected amount that you give?

3   Two unbiased dice are rolled and the greater score (or either, if they are the same) is recorded. State the set of possible scores and the probabilities associated with these scores. Find the expected value and the variance of the recorded scores.   [SMP]

4   A spinner is made so that the probability of its landing on any of the numbers 1, 2, 3, 4, 5 is proportional to that number. Suggest a method of designing the spinner, and calculate the mean and variance of the score when it is spun.

5   Calculate the theoretical mean, variance and standard deviation of the scores when a fair die is rolled.
    Calculate the same parameters for the sum of the scores when two dice are rolled simultaneously. Do you notice anything of interest about the results?
    Carry out the same calculations for the product of the scores when two dice are rolled simultaneously.

6   The scores on a spinner are $1, 2, 3, \ldots, n$, and all of them have the same probability of coming up. Calculate the mean score and the variance.

7   Five pennies are tossed, and the 'score' is the number of heads showing. Calculate the theoretical mean, variance and standard deviation.
    Repeat the calculation for different numbers of pennies. Do your results suggest a general rule?

8   Five dice are rolled, and the 'score' is the number of sixes. Calculate the theoretical mean, variance and standard deviation.
    Repeat the calculation for different numbers of dice. Do your results suggest a general rule?

9   In Example 1 of Chapter 7 (§7.4) a table of probabilities is given for various possible numbers of calls per minute coming into a telephone switchboard. Verify from the table that the mean number of calls per minute is 2.5 (making allowance for a small rounding error), and calculate the variance. What property of Poisson probability is suggested by your results?

10 Mary, who is totally non-psychic, takes part in a telepathy test. On each trial she has a probability a of succeeding in identifying a picture selected by Mark, and a probability b of failing. What is her expectation for the number of successes on a single trial, and the variance? Simplify your answer by using the relationship $a + b = 1$.
    If she takes two trials, she may get 0, 1 or 2 right. Write down the probabilities for each of these, and calculate the mean and variance for the number of successes.
    Repeat these calculations for the cases when Mary takes three and four trials. Do your results suggest a general rule?

11 A large batch of manufactured articles is accepted if either
    (a) a random sample of 10 articles contains no defective article, or
    (b) a random sample of 10 articles contains one defective article only, and a second sample of 10 is then drawn and found to contain no defective article.
    Otherwise, the batch is rejected. If, in fact, 5% of the articles in the batch are defective, find the probability of the batch being accepted.
    Find the expected number of articles that will have to be sampled to reach a decision on a batch.   [London]

12 When baggage is unloaded from an aircraft, the pieces of luggage are placed one at a time on a conveyor belt by the baggage handlers, and are then carried on the belt into the baggage reclaim hall. Suppose that there are n pieces of luggage on the aircraft, of which r belong to me.

(a) Prove that the probability that my last bag is the kth to appear is

$$\frac{r(n-r)!}{n!} \times (k-1)(k-2)\dots(k-r+1).$$

(b) By summing this for values of k from r to n, check that the formula gives a total probability of 1.

(c) What value of k has the largest probability?

(d) Prove that the expected value of k is $\dfrac{r}{r+1}(n+1)$.

9.3 APPLICATION TO SOME SPECIAL PROBABILITY MODELS

You will have gathered from the questions in the last exercise that for some of the standard types of probability model the calculation of the mean and variance is especially simple. Most of the rest of this chapter will be concerned with exploring this.

The 'scores' in these probability models are almost always natural numbers 1, 2, 3, ..., k (or sometimes 0, 1, 2, 3, ..., $k-1$ or even 0, 1, 2, 3, ... continued indefinitely). In such cases the symbol x_i can be replaced simply by i, and the probability of getting this score can be denoted by $p(i)$. So the expressions for μ and σ^2 take the simpler forms

$$\mu = \sum ip(i)$$

and

$$\sigma^2 = \sum(i-\mu)^2 p(i), \quad \text{or} \quad \sum i^2 p(i) - \mu^2.$$

For example, the scores when a die is rolled can be 1, 2, 3, 4, 5, 6; the runs in a Markov sequence can be of lengths 1, 2, 3, ... (the possibilities, in theory at least, continuing indefinitely); the number of customers arriving in a coffee bar between 8 and 8.15 p.m. can be 0, 1, 2, 3, ...; the number of girls in a family of four children can be 0, 1, 2, 3, 4; and so on. In each of these examples there is a probability associated with each of the possible numbers. The Σ signs in the formulae are to be taken to indicate summation over the relevant set of natural numbers – though in fact we may if we like interpret them always as $\Sigma_{i=0}^{\infty}$, and make a convention that $p(i)$ is equal to 0 for any natural number not in the possibility space of the model.

Q.5 Suggest what types of probability model might be appropriate in the examples given in the previous paragraph.

Q.6 With the convention just described, what would be the values of $p(0)$, $p(3)$ and $p(6)$ for (a) the die-rolling example, (b) the four-child family example?

Before going on to discuss some particular probability models, it will be helpful to notice one more expression for the variance σ^2 which can be used when the scores are natural numbers. It turns out that in practice it is often simpler to find the sum $\Sigma i(i-1)p(i)$ rather than $\Sigma i^2 p(i)$. This is no problem. Since

$$\sum i(i-1)p(i) = \sum i^2 p(i) - \sum ip(i) = \sum i^2 p(i) - \mu,$$

the equation $\sigma^2 = \Sigma i^2 p(i) - \mu^2$ given above can be written as

$$\sigma^2 = \sum i(i-1)p(i) + \mu - \mu^2.$$

A first opportunity to use this form will appear in the next section.

9.4 DIRECT CALCULATION: POISSON PROBABILITY

For some of these probability models it is quite simple to find μ and σ directly from the formulae. Poisson probability is a good example. Consider an event which takes place randomly at a uniform average rate λ per unit of time; what are the mean and standard deviation of the number of occurrences in unit time? The answer for the mean is surely obvious – it must be equal to λ. But it is not so easy to guess the standard deviation.

We saw in §7.4 that for this model

$$p(0) = e^{-\lambda}, \; p(1) = \frac{\lambda^1}{1!} e^{\lambda}, \; p(2) = \frac{\lambda^2}{2!} e^{-\lambda}, \ldots, \; p(i) = \frac{\lambda^i}{i!} e^{-\lambda}.$$

Using the form for σ^2 at the end of §9.3, we have to find the sum of terms

$$i(i-1)p(i) = i(i-1)\frac{\lambda^i}{i!} e^{-\lambda}.$$

Now when $i = 0$ or 1, this clearly has the value 0. (Remember the convention that $0! = 1$; see §3.3.) For $i \geqslant 2$, the fact that $i! = i(i-1) \times (i-2)!$ makes it possible to cancel the factor $i(i-1)$ to give

$$i(i-1)p(i) = \frac{\lambda^i}{(i-2)!} e^{-\lambda}.$$

So

$$\sum_{i=1}^{\infty} i(i-1)p(i) = 0 + 0 + \frac{\lambda^2}{0!} e^{-\lambda} + \frac{\lambda^3}{1!} e^{-\lambda} + \frac{\lambda^4}{2!} e^{-\lambda} + \ldots$$

$$= \lambda^2 e^{-\lambda} \left(1 + \frac{\lambda^1}{1!} + \frac{\lambda^2}{2!} + \ldots \right)$$

$$= \lambda^2 e^{-\lambda} \times e^{\lambda} = \lambda^2,$$

because the expression in the brackets is the series expansion for e^{λ} (see §7.1).

Using also the fact that $\mu = \lambda$ gives

$$\sigma^2 = \sum i(i-1)p(i) + \mu - \mu^2$$
$$= \lambda^2 + \lambda - \lambda^2 = \lambda.$$

So, for the Poisson probability model with parameter λ the standard deviation is equal to $\sqrt{\lambda}$. This is an important result, which we shall make use of from time to time. A numerical illustration was suggested in Exercise 9A, question 9.

Q.7   In the above argument we have taken it as obvious that $\mu = \lambda$. It is, however, possible to prove this directly from the definition $\mu = \Sigma ip(i)$, using the fact that, for $i \geqslant 1$, $i! = i \times (i-1)!$. Write out the calculation in detail.

Exercise 9B

1   In the geometric probability model (see Q.6 of §3.2) the probability that a run of the outcome A will have length i is given by $p(i) = ab^{i-1}$. Write an expression for $\Sigma ip(i)$ in terms of a and b, and use the power series

$$(1-x)^{-2} = 1 + 2x + 3x^2 + \ldots + ix^{i-1} + \ldots$$

to find μ in as simple a form as possible.
    Also write $\Sigma i(i-1)p(i)$ in terms of a and b, and show that a simple form for σ^2 can be found by using the power series

$$(1-x)^{-3} = 1 + 3x + 6x^2 + \cdots + \frac{i(i-1)}{2}x^{i-2} + \ldots.$$

2   Prove that $i\binom{n}{i} = n\binom{n-1}{i-1}$ and that $i(i-1)\binom{n}{i} = n(n-1)\binom{n-2}{i-2}$.
    In a Bernoulli sequence of n repetitions of an experiment with two outcomes A and B having probabilities a, b, the probability that the outcome A will occur i times is given by the binomial probability model as $p(i) = \binom{n}{i}a^i b^{n-i}$ (see §3.3). Use the above relations to write the sums $\Sigma ip(i)$ and $\Sigma i(i-1)p(i)$ in alternative forms, and deduce simple expressions for μ and σ in terms of n, a and b.
    The Poisson model can be deduced from the binomial by writing $a = \lambda/n$, $b = 1 - \lambda/n$ and letting n tend to infinity (see §7.6). Show that your expressions for μ and σ then tend to λ and $\sqrt{\lambda}$ respectively, as found in §9.4.

9.5   GENERATING FUNCTIONS

It was a stroke of luck that the series which had to be summed in the Poisson probability calculation was simply related to the well-known exponential series for e^{λ}. Other probability models are not so well disposed in this respect, and even if the series can be summed the algebraic details are often quite complicated – as you will have found from Exercise 9B. For this reason it often pays to use an indirect method of calculating the mean and variance, rather than tackling the problem head on.

At this stage it will help to pick up an idea from algebra, that of a "generating function". This is a device for producing the numbers in a sequence by expanding a function as a power series. (Note 9.3)

One way of doing this is to use the long division process. You probably know how to apply this to divide one polynomial by another, beginning with the highest powers of x. (Note 9.4) Have you ever tried beginning at the other end? As an illustration, follow through the division set down here:

$$
\begin{array}{r}
1 + 2t + \ldots \\
1 - 2t \overline{)1} \\
\underline{1 - 2t} \\
2t \\
\underline{2t - 4t^2} \\
4t^2 \\
\ldots \quad \ldots
\end{array}
$$

Q.8   Carry this on for a few more steps. What will be (*a*) the quotient, (*b*) the remainder after n steps? Write this in the form $A = BQ + R$, where A, B, Q, R are polynomials.

You will have found that this produces in turn the terms $1, 2t, 4t^2, 8t^3, \ldots$ in the quotient. The mathematical way of describing this is to say that the function $1/(1 - 2t)$ "generates" the sequence of coefficients $1, 2, 4, 8, \ldots$.

Q.9   Show that the same result can be obtained (*a*) by summing the geometric progression $1 + 2t + (2t)^2 + \cdots + (2t)^{n-1}$ by the usual method, (*b*) by applying the binomial power series for $(1 + x)^n$ with $x = -2t$ and $n = -1$.

Q.10   Investigate in the same way the application of the long division process to

$$(a) \quad 1 - 2t + t^2 \,\overline{)1} \qquad ; \qquad (b) \, 1 - t - t^2 \,\overline{)1} \quad .$$

What sequences are generated by the functions $1/(1 - 2t + t^2)$ and $1/(1 - t - t^2)$? Could you get (*a*) another way by applying the binomial power series?

Q.11   Use the power series expansion for $\ln(1 + x)$ to express $\ln\left(\dfrac{1}{1 - t}\right)$ as a series of powers of t. What sequence is generated by this function?

You should by now have seen enough examples to generalise the notion in the form of a definition:

If a function f has a power series expansion of the form

$$f(t) = u_0 + u_1 t + u_2 t^2 + \ldots,$$

then we say that f is a *generating function* for the sequence $u_0, u_1, u_2, \ldots$.

Students often ask what the number t stands for in this definition. The answer is that it has no meaning of itself; but it is impossible to talk about a function without having some symbol to represent the variable. Any letter could be used equally well: whether we write $f(t) = u_0 + u_1 t + u_2 t^2 + \ldots$ or $f(z) = u_0 + u_1 z + u_2 z^2 + \ldots$, the function generates the same sequence $u_0, u_1, u_2, \ldots$. The letter t in the definition is for this reason sometimes called a "dummy variable".

9.6 PROBABILITY GENERATORS

The link between generating functions and probability theory is made by choosing the terms of the sequence $u_0, u_1, u_2, \ldots$ to be the probabilities p(0), p(1), p(2), $\ldots$ of getting scores of 0, 1, 2, $\ldots$ in various probability models. This turns out to be a remarkably powerful device. The generating functions are then called "probability generators", and they are usually denoted by the letter G.

Example 2
Find a probability generator for the scores when a fair die is rolled.

The possible scores are 1, 2, 3, 4, 5, 6, each with probability $\frac{1}{6}$. The power series $u_0 + u_1 t + u_2 t^2 + \ldots$ therefore takes the finite form

$$\frac{1}{6} t + \frac{1}{6} t^2 + \frac{1}{6} t^3 + \frac{1}{6} t^4 + \frac{1}{6} t^5 + \frac{1}{6} t^6,$$

since the coefficients for all the other powers of t are zero. This is a geometric progression, and its sum can be found in the usual way to give the probability generator

$$G(t) = \frac{1}{6} t \times \frac{1 - t^6}{1 - t} \quad \text{(provided that } t \neq 1\text{).}$$

Q.12 Write $G(t)$ in Example 2 as $\frac{1}{6} t (1 - t^6)(1 - t)^{-1}$, expand $(1 - t)^{-1}$ by using the binomial power series for $(1 + x)^n$ with $x = -t$, $n = -1$, and multiply out the brackets. Does this lead back to the original probabilities?

It is important to find the probability generators for the three special types of probability model which we have already met – Poisson, geometric and binomial. By good fortune, all of them can be recognised as quite simple, familiar functions.

(1) Poisson probability
If u_i is taken to be the Poisson probability $p(i) = (\lambda^i/i!)e^{-\lambda}$, then the power series has the form

$$e^{-\lambda} + \frac{\lambda^1}{1!} e^{-\lambda} t + \frac{\lambda^2}{2!} e^{-\lambda} t^2 + \ldots,$$

which can be written as

$$e^{-\lambda}\left\{1 + \frac{(\lambda t)}{1!} + \frac{(\lambda t)^2}{2!} + \cdots\right\}.$$

You will recognise the expression in the curly brackets as the power series expansion of the function $e^{\lambda t}$. So the Poisson probabilities are generated by

$$G(t) = e^{-\lambda} \times e^{\lambda t}, \text{ or } e^{\lambda(t-1)}.$$

(2) Geometric probability

This has been introduced as the probability model for runs of various lengths of one outcome (B, say) in a Bernoulli sequence. A slightly different way of regarding this is to ask which trial in the sequence will be the first in which the other outcome (A) occurs. In either case the appropriate formula for the probability is $p(i) = ab^{i-1}$. (Note 9.5) Substituting this for u_i in the power series gives

$$at + abt^2 + ab^2t^3 + \cdots,$$

which is an infinite geometric progression with first term at and common ratio bt. Using the standard formula for the sum, it follows that the geometric probabilities are generated by

$$G(t) = \frac{at}{1 - bt} \text{ (provided that } t \text{ is restricted so that } |bt| < 1).$$

Q.13 In a Bernoulli sequence with two outcomes A and B, what is the probability model for the number of trials before the first occurrence of the outcome A? Write down the corresponding probability generator.

(3) Binomial probability

The probability that the outcome A occurs just i times in a Bernoulli sequence of n trials is $p(i) = \binom{n}{i}a^ib^{n-i}$, where i can have any integer value from 0 to n. The power series then takes the finite form

$$b^n + \binom{n}{1}ab^{n-1}t + \binom{n}{2}ab^{n-2}t^2 + \cdots + a^nt^n$$

$$= b^n + \binom{n}{1}b^{n-1}(at) + \binom{n}{2}b^{n-2}(at)^2 + \cdots + (at)^n,$$

which you will recognise as the binomial expansion of

$$G(t) = (b + at)^n.$$

The label B(n, a) (where the B stands for "binomial") is sometimes used as a shorthand notation to describe this model.

9.7 CALCULATING MEAN AND VARIANCE WITH PROBABILITY GENERATORS

It is worth noting that there is a useful check on any expression which we obtain as a probability generator. If t is put equal to 1, then the power series for $G(t)$ becomes

$$p(0) + p(1) + p(2) + \ldots,$$

the sum of the probabilities of all the possible scores – and this, of course, must be 1. So, for any probability generator,

$$G(1) = \sum p(i) = 1.$$

Q.14   Use this to check the probability generators for Poisson, geometric and binomial probabilities found in §9.6.

The problem now is this. We have an expression $G(t)$ for the sum $\sum p(i)t^i$, and we know how to evaluate the mean and variance if we can find the sums $\sum ip(i)$ and $\sum i(i-1)p(i)$. One technique available is to substitute a particular number for t, as we did in the check just now – but there is no substitution which will solve the problem directly, because it cannot produce the multipliers i and $i(i-1)$ which are needed. How else can the series be connected?

The clue lies in introducing calculus – in particular the idea of differentiation. From

$$G(t) = \sum p(i)t^i$$

we can derive

$$G'(t) = \sum ip(i)t^{i-1}$$

and then

$$G''(t) = \sum i(i-1)p(i)t^{i-2}.$$

(Note 9.6) Now you will notice that the series we want are almost the same as the right sides of these last two equations, except for the powers of t. To remove these, we can do just as we did in the check above – that is, put t equal to 1. This gives

$$G'(1) = \sum ip(i) \quad \text{and} \quad G''(1) = \sum i(i-1)p(i),$$

which are exactly the sums required.

So all we have to do to evaluate these sums is to differentiate the expression for the probability generator and then substitute $t = 1$. Putting these equations together with the expressions for the mean and variance given in §9.3 (using the second form for the variance at the end of the section), the argument can be summarised as follows:

> If to each outcome in a probability model there corresponds a score i which has probability $p(i)$, then the model can be described by means of a *probability generator* $G(t) = \Sigma p(i)t^i$. The theoretical mean and variance of the scores are then given by
>
> $$\mu = G'(1) \quad \text{and} \quad \sigma^2 = G''(1) + \mu - \mu^2. \text{ (Note 9.7)}$$

Amongst the models to which these results can be applied are the Poisson, geometric and binomial. For ease of reference, the details are set out in Table 1, and you are strongly encouraged to work through this column by column to make sure that you fully understand the method. In fact, it is possible to find the mean and variance for these models without using the probability generator (see §9.4 and Exercise 9B); but you will probably agree it is easier to apply the generator method than to go back each time to the definitions of mean and variance.

Table 1

Model	Poisson	Geometric $(a + b = 1)$	Binomial $(a + b = 1)$
$p(i)$	$\dfrac{\lambda^i}{i!}e^{-\lambda}$	ab^{i-1} $(i \geqslant 1)$	$\dfrac{n!}{i!j!}a^i b^j$ $(i + j = 1)$
$G(t)$	$e^{\lambda(t-1)}$	$\dfrac{at}{1 - bt}$	$(b + at)^n$
$G'(t)$	$\lambda e^{\lambda(t-1)}$	$\dfrac{a}{(1 - bt)^2}$	$na(b + at)^{n-1}$
$G''(t)$	$\lambda^2 e^{\lambda(t-1)}$	$\dfrac{2ab}{(1 - bt)^3}$	$n(n-1)a^2(b + at)^{n-2}$
$\mu = G'(1)$	λ	$\dfrac{1}{a}$	na
$G''(1)$	λ^2	$\dfrac{2b}{a^2}$	$n(n-1)a^2$
$\sigma^2 = G''(1) + \mu - \mu^2$	λ	$\dfrac{b}{a^2}$	nab
σ	$\sqrt{\lambda}$	$\dfrac{\sqrt{b}}{a}$	$\sqrt{(nab)}$

Some of the results in Table 1 deserve a comment. For the binomial model $B(n,a)$, the expression for the mean should come as no surprise: if the probability of the outcome A in a single experiment is a, then in n repetitions one would expect to get the outcome *na* times. This is precisely how "expected frequency" was defined in §6.1. However, the form $\sqrt{(nab)}$ for the standard deviation is much more interesting. Although, as one would expect, the standard deviation increases with the number of repetitions, it is not proportional to *n* but only to $\sqrt{n}$. For example, if a coin is tossed 4 times, the standard deviation of the number of heads is 1; but if it is tossed 400 times, the standard deviation is only 10, not 100. This property has important consequences for the practice of statistical sampling, and we shall meet it frequently in later chapters. (In fact, it has been mentioned once already in §6.4, where it was found that the radii of the circles for various significance levels should be enlarged in proportion to the square root of the number of times the pencil was rolled.)

The mean of the geometric probability model is perhaps more surprising. It tells us, for example, that on average one will have to roll a die 6 times in order to get a six (since the outcome "six" has probability $a = \frac{1}{6}$). People often think that, because with reasonable luck you might hope to get one six in the first 6 rolls, the mean number of rolls necessary would be less than 6; but this does not take into account that one may not have "reasonable luck", and that it is sometimes necessary to wait a long time before the first six appears – and this puts up the average.

Q.15 Write a computer program to simulate the rolling of a die and to record the number of rolls up to the appearance of a six. Adapt it to run a large number of times, and to calculate the mean number of rolls up to a six. How closely does your answer agree with the theoretical value of 6?

Exercise 9C

1 The driving instructor reckons that Sam has a probability 0.4 of passing the driving test, and that he will never get any better. Write down the probabilities that he will have to take the test 1, 2, 3, ... times, and find a simple expression for the probability generator. Use this to find the mean and standard deviation for the number of times that he will have to take the test altogether.

2 In a multiple-choice examination there are 50 questions. For each question five possible answers are suggested, only one of which is right. Jim answers the paper by guessing randomly one of the choices in each question. What are the probabilities that he will get (*a*) none right, (*b*) all right, (*c*) just one right, (*d*) *i* right? Write down a probability generator for the number of questions that he will get right. Use this to calculate the mean and standard deviation for his total number of correct answers.

3 Alice and Brenda play a game in which they take it in turns to throw a quoit over a peg. At each throw Alice has a probability $\frac{1}{3}$ of succeeding, whilst Brenda has a probability of $\frac{1}{4}$. The game continues until one or other of them is successful. Find the probability generators for the total number of throws in a game (*a*) if Alice throws first, (*b*) if Brenda throws first. Use these to find the expected number of throws in a game in each case.

4 The probability that any electric bulb produced by a certain factory is defective is 0.01. A shipment of 10 000 bulbs from this factory is sent to a wholesaler. Find (*a*) the expected number of defective bulbs, (*b*) the standard deviation of the number defective.   [London]

5   A barman breaks on average three glasses a fortnight. He is allowed one breakage each week without penalty; for a second breakage 50p is stopped from his wages, and for a third breakage a further £1.50. If he breaks four glasses in a week he gets the sack.
(a) How long should he expect to remain in employment?
(b) What is his expected weekly penalty in the first week?

6   Draw graphs to illustrate each of the following probability models:
   (i) Binomial, $a = 0.6$, $b = 0.4$, $n = 6$.
   (ii) Binomial, $a = 0.6$, $b = 0.4$, $n = 24$.
   (iii) Poisson, $\lambda = 5.76$.
   (iv) Geometric, $a = 0.2$, $b = 0.8$.

Calculate for each the mean and standard deviation, and mark on your graphs the values of μ and of $\mu \pm \sigma$. What is the probability of getting a score which lies within the interval from $\mu - \sigma$ to $\mu + \sigma$ in a random trial?
   How might you define (a) the median, (b) the mode of a probability model? Calculate these in the four examples specified.

7   In a Bernoulli sequence of experiments with two outcomes, let the mean lengths of run for the two outcomes be r_A and r_B. Prove that $1/r_A + 1/r_B = 1$. Deduce that one of the outcomes has a mean run length less than or equal to 2, and the other has a mean run length greater than or equal to 2.
   Generalise this to Bernoulli sequences with more than two outcomes.
   Why may the situation be different in a Markov sequence?

8   If $G(t)$ generates probabilities $p(0)$, $p(1)$, $p(2)$, ..., write out expressions for $G(1)$ and $G(-1)$ in terms of these probabilities. Deduce that the probability that the score is even is $\frac{1}{2}\{1 + G(-1)\}$, and write down the probability that the score is odd.
   The rules of a football competition state that, if a match ends in a draw, each side will take a penalty kick in turn until one or other is successful. If every kick has a probability 0.2 of succeeding, write down a probability generator for the number of penalties that will be needed to settle the match, and deduce from this the probability that the team which has first kick will win the match.

9   In §7.6 it was shown that the Poisson model can be derived as the limiting case of a binomial with $a = \lambda/n$ and $b = 1 - \lambda/n$. Write down the probability generator for this binomial model, and show that the generator for the Poisson model can be obtained from this by letting n tend to infinity.   [SMP]

10   Two children toss fair coins simultaneously (one coin each). They continue tossing until each of them has thrown at least one head. Show that the probability that the game is still unfinished after each child has made n tosses is

$$2(\tfrac{1}{2})^n - (\tfrac{1}{2})^{2n} \quad (n = 1, 2, 3, \ldots).$$

Hence, or otherwise, show that if the game ends with the Nth pair of tosses then

$$P(N = n) = 2(\tfrac{1}{2})^n - 3(\tfrac{1}{2})^{2n} \quad (n = 1, 2, 3, \ldots).$$

Show that the generator for these probabilities can be written in the form

$$\frac{4}{2 - t} - \frac{12}{4 - t} + 1$$

and hence, or otherwise, find the mean and variance of N.

11   In a game with possible scores 0, 1, 2, ... the corresponding probabilities are p(0), p(1), p(2), ... and these are generated by G(t). Probabilities q(0), q(1), q(2), are defined by equations

$$q(n) = \sum_{i=0}^{n} p(i).$$

State in words what q(n) means as a probability.
     Show that the probabilities q(0), q(1), q(2), ... are generated by K(t), where

$$K(t) = \frac{G(t)}{1 - t}.$$

Explain why $K(1) \neq 1$.   [SMP]

12   Let a_n be the probability that in n throws of an unbiased die an even number of sixes is obtained. Explain why $a_0 = 1$ and prove that, for $n \geqslant 1$, a_n and a_{n-1} satisfy the recurrence relation

$$a_n = \frac{5}{6} a_{n-1} + \frac{1}{6}(1 - a_{n-1}).$$

The generator, G(t), for the probabilities a_n is defined by

$$G(t) = \sum_{n=0}^{\infty} a_n t^n \quad (|t| < 1).$$

Multiply both sides of the above recurrence relation by t^n, and sum over an appropriate range of values of n to prove that

$$G(t) = \tfrac{1}{2}(6 - 5t)(1 - t)^{-1}(3 - 2t)^{-1}.$$

Express G(t) in partial fractions and hence, or otherwise, prove that $a_n = \tfrac{1}{2}(1 + (\tfrac{2}{3})^n)$.   [SMP]

13   A boy tosses a coin repeatedly and scores 3 for each head and 2 for each tail and adds up the scores he gets. Let p_n denote the probability that his score will ever equal n. Give the values of p_0, p_1, p_2, p_3. Show that, for $n \geqslant 3$,

$$2p_n = p_{n-2} + p_{n-3}.$$

Multiply this equation by t^n and sum over n to show that the generator for the probabilities p_n is

$$G(t) = \frac{2}{2 - t^2 - t^3}.$$

9.8 THE MULTIPLICATION PROPERTY

Probability generators have one more very important property, which accounts for their usefulness in probability theory.
     Suppose that we have two independent experiments, each of which may give scores of 0, 1, 2, ... This could involve, for example, drawing one card from each of two packs, or a pupil's mark in two successive tests, or the numbers of boys in

two families of children. Let the probabilities of the score i be denoted by $p(i)$ and $q(i)$ respectively, and the probability generators by $G(t)$ and $H(t)$, so that

$$G(t) = \sum p(i)t^i \quad \text{and} \quad H(t) = \sum q(i)t^i.$$

Now consider the result of multiplying the two series together. (Note 9.8) A convenient format for doing this is to set out the terms in an array:

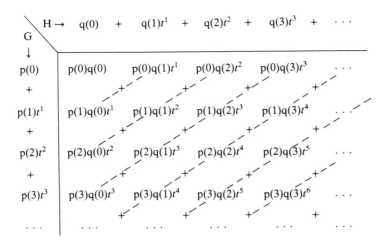

Now collect together terms with the same degree in t, as indicated by the broken lines. This gives another series

$$\begin{aligned}
K(t) = {} & p(0)q(0) + \{p(1)q(0) + p(0)q(1)\}t^1 \\
& + \{p(2)q(0) + p(1)q(1) + p(0)q(2)\}t^2 \\
& + \{p(3)q(0) + p(2)q(1) + p(1)q(2) + p(0)q(3)\}t^3 + \ldots .
\end{aligned}$$

Notice that this series also has positive terms, and that $K(1) = G(1)H(1) = 1 \times 1 = 1$. So $K(t)$ might also be a probability generator. What meaning do the coefficients in this series have as probabilities?

To answer this, let us look first for example at the coefficient of t^2, and examine each term separately. These all have the form of products, and *since the experiments are independent* these products give the probabilities of both the associated outcomes occurring. So we can argue:

$p(2)q(0) = P(2$ on first experiment *and* 0 on second experiment$)$,

$p(1)q(1) = P(1$ on first experiment *and* 1 on second experiment$)$,

$p(0)q(2) = P(0$ on first experiment *and* 2 on second experiment$)$.

Now the three events on the right sides are clearly exclusive; so the sum of the three terms gives the probability that one or other of them occurs. But they are in fact the three ways of getting a total score of 2 in the two experiments taken together. So

$$p(2)q(0) + p(1)q(1) + p(0)q(2)$$

$$= P(\text{the sum of the scores in the two experiments is 2}).$$

Q.16   Write out similar arguments for the coefficients of t and t^3.

Applying similar arguments to all the coefficients in turn, what this shows is:

The product of the probability generators for the scores in two independent experiments is the probability generator for the sum of the scores in the two experiments taken together.

Example 3

Two dice are rolled and the scores added together. Find a probability generator for the results.

In Example 2 (§9.6) the probability generator for the score on a single die was found to be $\frac{1}{6}t(1 - t^6)(1 - t)^{-1}$. The scores on the two dice are, of course, independent; so the generator for the sum of the scores is

$$\frac{1}{6}t(1 - t^6)(1 - t)^{-1} \times \frac{1}{6}t(1 - t^6)(1 - t)^{-1} = \frac{1}{36}t^2(1 - t^6)^2(1 - t)^{-2}.$$

Q.17   By expanding this expression in powers of t, obtain the probabilities of getting totals of 2, 3, 4, ..., 12 when two dice are rolled. What are the coefficients of powers higher than t^{12} in the expansion?

Q.18   Find the corresponding probabilities for the possible totals when (a) three, (b) four dice are rolled. Draw stick graphs showing your results.

Exercise 9D

1   In the Football League championship a team gets 3 points for a win, 1 point for a draw. One club has two matches over Easter weekend; experts predict probabilities 0.3, 0.2 for a win and a draw respectively in the first match, and 0.5, 0.3 in the second. Write down probability generators for the number of points the club will get (a) from each of the two matches, (b) from the two matches together. Hence find the probability model for the number of points the club will get over the weekend.

2   Write down the probability generator for the number of heads which will show if you toss (a) one penny, (b) two pennies, (c) n pennies.

3   Mr and Mrs Smith both have blood group A, but their children may have blood groups O or A, with probabilities $\frac{1}{4}, \frac{3}{4}$ respectively. Write down the probability generator for the number of children with blood group O, if there are (a) two children, (b) three children, (c) n children in the family.

4 In a Bernoulli sequence of experiments there are two outcomes A, B with probabilities a, b. Write down the probability generator for the number of occurrences of the outcome A in a single experiment. Use the multiplication property to deduce the probability generator for the number of occurrences of A in n repetitions of the experiment.

5 The traffic along a road consists of cars and trucks, with average frequencies of 3 per minute and 2 per minute respectively. Assuming that the flow of both sets of vehicles separately is described by Poisson probability models, write down probability generators for (a) the number of cars in a randomly selected minute, (b) the number of trucks in a randomly selected minute, (c) the number of vehicles in a randomly selected minute, (d) the number of trucks in a randomly selected hour.

6 Use probability generators to solve Exercise 7C, question 12 in a different way.

7 A die is thrown repeatedly. Write down the probability generators for (a) the number of the throw on which the first six appears, (b) the number of the throw on which the second six appears, (c) the number of the throw on which the rth six appears. Calculate the probabilities that (d) the second six occurs on the tenth throw, (e) the fifth six occurs on the 20th throw.

   Find the mean and standard deviation for the number of the throw on which the rth six appears.

8 In a machine game of chance, when a lever is pulled, one of the numbers 1, 2, 3 appears in a window. The lever is pulled five times and the total score is recorded. If the probabilities associated with the numbers 1, 2, 3 are $\frac{1}{6}, \frac{1}{3}, \frac{1}{2}$ respectively, write down an expression for the probability generator, $G(t)$, for the possible total scores. Evaluate $G(-1)$ and hence, or otherwise, find the probability that the total score is even. [SMP]

9 A symmetrical spinning top has five edges numbered $-2, -1, 0, 1, 2$. Show that the probability generator for the scores when the top is spun once can be written

$$\frac{1}{5}t^{-2}(1 - t^5)(1 - t)^{-1}. \qquad \text{(See Note 9.7.)}$$

   Hence, or otherwise, find the probability of getting a total score of zero when the top is spun three times. [SMP]

10 In a multiple-choice test, there are five suggested answers for each question, only one of which is correct. There are 25 questions in all. There are two schools of thought about the marking of such tests. One simply favours giving 4 marks for a correct answer, 0 for a wrong one. The other, in an attempt to discourage guessing, gives 4 marks for a correct answer but *deducts* 1 mark for a wrong answer. Suppose that a candidate takes the test and simply guesses the answer to all 25 questions. Show that the probability generator for his score on question 1 is $(t^4 + 4)/5$ or $(t^5 + 4)/5t$ according to the method of marking adopted. Calculate the mean and variance of his total marks on the test as a whole in each of the two cases. Is there any advantage in using the second method except for the psychological effect on the candidate?

11 In the notation of §9.8, is it possible to interpret $G(t) + H(t)$ as a probability generator?

12 In a game, the probability generator for the various possible scores is $G(t)$. The game is played n times, and the scores on the separate plays are added to give a final result.

If the probability generator for this final result is $K(t)$, express $K(t)$ in terms of $G(t)$. Prove that

$$K'(1) = nG'(1) \quad \text{and that} \quad K''(1) = n(n-1)\{G'(1)\}^2 + nG''(1),$$

and hence express the mean and variance for the final result in terms of μ and σ^2, the mean and variance of the score on a single game.

13 If in two independent experiments the theoretical means and variances for the scores are μ_1, μ_2 and σ_1^2, σ_2^2, and if the mean and variance for the sum of the scores are μ, σ^2, prove that

$$\mu = \mu_1 + \mu_2 \quad \text{and that} \quad \sigma^2 = \sigma_1^2 + \sigma_2^2.$$

10

Matching models to data

Now that a method is available for finding theoretical parameters (such as mean and variance) for probability models, it will no longer be necessary for so many of the examples to be about dice, random numbers, card suits and sex distribution.

The point about these is that probabilities can easily be selected by assuming that various possible outcomes are equally likely: scores from 1 to 6, digits from 0 to 9, clubs/diamonds/hearts/spades, male/female. But if we have some experimental data, which we think it may be appropriate to describe by a particular type of probability model, then probabilities can be calculated by adapting the "extrapolation principle" introduced in §4.1: that

> "the value of a parameter for the population as a whole can be estimated by taking it to be equal to the value of the corresponding statistic in a sample".

This chapter deals with the application of this principle to models of various kinds.

Notice, though, that it is still necessary to have an idea of the type of model – whether it is binomial, Poisson, geometric or whatever. This is usually decided by knowing the kind of situation that each of these models has been invented to describe. For example, the binomial model is based on the assumption of a Bernoulli sequence (§3.1), that the probability of each outcome remains constant and is independent of the result on previous occasions; the Poisson model applies to an event which occurs randomly, singly and independently at a uniform average rate; and so on. So once the extrapolation principle has been used to calibrate the model, we shall want to check whether it gives a good fit. We already know a way of doing this, by calculating the discrepancy between the observed and the expected frequencies and finding if this is less than the critical value given by the chi-squared probability tables (see §6.6). If not, then the assumptions on which the choice of model was based must be called into question.

10.1 CHOOSING A PARAMETER

The process can probably be best explained with the help of an example.

Example 1
Imported peaches come in boxes each holding six peaches. A batch of 100 boxes

examined in a supermarket revealed the following distribution of imperfect fruit amongst the boxes:

Number of imperfect peaches in box	0	1	2	3	4	5	6
Frequency	50	25	14	8	2	1	0

If the imperfect fruit were randomly distributed amongst the boxes, would you expect to get such a result?

The first question to ask is: if the imperfect peaches were randomly distributed, what type of probability model would describe the number of imperfect fruit in the various boxes?

Q.1 What do you think?

There would be a certain probability that a peach selected at random would be found to be imperfect; and on the assumption of random distribution, this would have no effect on the condition of the other peaches in the box. So we have an experiment – examining a peach – repeated 6 times, with a certain independent probability each time of getting the result "imperfect". These are just the conditions for a Bernoulli sequence with two possible outcomes, so this suggests looking for a binomial model with $n = 6$.

But to fix on a particular binomial model it is necessary to decide on the probability of a peach being imperfect. Obviously there is no theoretical way of doing this; so we can only estimate it from the data. This is where the extrapolation principle comes in, and the simplest "parameter" to base it on is the mean number of imperfect peaches in a box. From the sample of boxes examined, this mean is

$$\frac{1}{100}(0 \times 50 + 1 \times 25 + 2 \times 14 + 3 \times 8 + 4 \times 2 + 5 \times 1 + 6 \times 0) = 0.9.$$

So this is equated to the theoretical mean for a binomial model. If a is the probability of a single peach being found imperfect, this theoretical mean is na (see Table 1 in §9.7). This gives the equation

$$6a = 0.9,$$

from which $a = 0.15$.

Q.2 Calculate the total number of imperfect peaches in the batch of 100 boxes examined. Check that the relative frequency of imperfect peaches in the batch is equal to 0.15.

10.2 DOES THE MODEL FIT THE DATA?

The investigation does not end with the calculation of the probability. We now have to find out whether the binomial model, on which that calculation was based, does in fact give expected frequencies which correspond well with those found experimentally.

The first step is to use the estimated value of a to find the probabilities of getting various numbers of imperfect peaches in a box, according to the binomial model. Taking $n = 6$, $a = 0.15$, $b = 0.85$, you can check for yourself that these are:

Number of imperfect peaches in box	0	1	2	3	4	5	6
Probability	0.377	0.399	0.176	0.041	0.005	0.000	0.000

These probabilities can now be converted into expected frequencies of boxes containing various numbers of imperfect peaches, by multiplying by 100, and these can be compared with the frequencies actually observed:

Number of imperfect peaches in box	0	1	2	3 or more
Observed frequency	50	25	14	11
Expected frequency	37.7	39.9	17.6	4.6

(Notice that the last four classes have been combined into one, to avoid the problem of dealing with very small expected frequencies. See §6.8.)

This does not look a very good fit; and to confirm this we can calculate the discrepancy between the observed and expected frequencies, which is

$$\frac{(50 - 37.7)^2}{37.7} + \frac{(25 - 39.9)^2}{39.9} + \frac{(14 - 17.6)^2}{17.6} + \frac{(11 - 4.6)^2}{4.6} = 18.32.$$

What we have to decide is whether or not this is "too large". In effect, this involves (in the language of Chapter 8) testing

Hypothesis 1. The imperfect fruit is randomly distributed, so that the binomial model is valid.

against the alternative hypothesis

Hypothesis 2. The imperfect fruit is not randomly distributed.

Hypothesis 1 will be rejected if the discrepancy is too large, at the chosen level of significance – say 5% – and this means that a one-tail test should be used. We therefore compare the calculated value of the discrepancy with the critical value given in the table of chi-squared probability, for $P = 5$ and the appropriate number of degrees of freedom.

But the question is, how many degrees of freedom are there? Usually with four classes v has been taken to be 3; the justification for this being that

> "the number of degrees of freedom is the number of independent recorded observations",

and the four frequencies $F(i)$ – both observed and expected – of getting i imperfect peaches in a box (for $i = 0, 1, 2, 3$ or more) are not independent, since they are connected by the equation

$$F_o(0) + F_o(1) + F_o(2) + F_o(3 \text{ or more}) = F_e(0) + F_e(1) + F_e(2) + F_e(3 \text{ or more}),$$

both sides being equal to 100. (Note 10.1) In this example, however, there is a *second* equation connecting the four frequencies; this is because the probability a was chosen so as to make the mean of the expected frequencies equal to the mean of the observed frequencies, which is 0.9.

Q.3   Write out this second equation in full.

This means that once two of the frequencies have been chosen, the rest of them can be found by making the total equal to 100 and the mean equal to 0.9. The number of degrees of freedom is therefore $4 - 2$, or 2.

This argument can be generalised, and stated as a general rule:

> If, in devising a probability model to compare with actual data, one or more parameters are determined from the data, then in a subsequent test of goodness-of-fit the number of degrees of freedom is reduced by 1 for each parameter found in this way.

So to complete discussion of the example, the tables of chi-squared probability give a critical value of the discrepancy for $P = 5$ and $v = 2$ to be 5.99. Since the value calculated from the data was 18.32, the hypothesis can be decisively rejected.

It is not difficult to find an explanation for the fact that the imperfect peaches are not randomly distributed. It is likely that at the packing station the distribution was random, but that in transit the good fruit in boxes containing one or more bad peach was affected. This would upset the assumption on which the model was based, that the probability of any peach being imperfect is independent of that for any other peach.

Q.4   Show that in this example the discrepancy is significant even at the 0.1% level.

Exercise 10A

1   Groups of six people are chosen at random and the number, x, of people in each group who normally wear glasses is recorded. The results obtained from 200 groups

of six are shown in the table:

Number in group wearing glasses	0	1	2	3	4	5	6
Number of occurrences	17	53	65	45	18	2	0

Calculate, from the above data, the mean value of x.

Assuming that the situation can be modelled by a binomial distribution having the same mean as the one calculated above, state the appropriate values for the binomial parameters. Calculate the theoretical frequencies corresponding to those in the table, and comment on the comparison.   [Cambridge]

2   A student was required to carry out an experiment in probability by tossing four similar drawing pins onto a table and recording how many landed with the point uppermost. He was to continue until he had completed 200 trials, and then estimate the probability p that drawing pins of this type land point up. The results he gave were as follows:

Number landing point up	0	1	2	3	4
Frequency	5	32	67	70	26

Estimate p from these results, and, using an appropriate probability distribution, calculate the corresponding theoretical frequencies.

Carry out a test of goodness of fit and comment on the implications of your result.
                                    [Cambridge]

3   A six-sided die with faces numbered as usual from 1 to 6 was thrown 5 times and the number x of sixes was recorded. The experiment was repeated 200 times with the following results:

x	0	1	2	3	4	5
Frequency	66	82	40	10	2	0

On this evidence, would you consider the die to be biased?

Fit a suitable distribution to the data and test and comment on the goodness of fit.
                                        [MEI]

4   It has been suggested that the numbers of goals scored in football matches might be described by a Poisson probability model. On a particular Saturday in November 1984 the numbers of goals scored in 44 matches in the English Football League were:

Number of goals	0	1	2	3	4	5	6	7	8	9
Frequency		3	7	8	9	9	4	3	0	0	1

Find the mean number of goals per match, and calculate the frequencies you would expect to get if the theory were correct. Do your results suggest that the Poisson model is a suitable one in this case?

5   A piece of electronic equipment has been designed to cause a light to flash at random. The number of flashes per minute produced by the apparatus is recorded for 100 separate one-minute intervals, and the following results are obtained:

Number of flashes	0	1	2	3	4	5	6	7
Frequency	21	20	27	15	8	6	2	1

What probability model is it reasonable to use to describe the above data? Do the results cast any doubt on the randomness of the flash-producing mechanism?

[SMP]

6   A record was made of the number of visits made by each of the vehicles in an army unit to a repair depot, with the following results:

No. of visits	0	1	2	3	4	5	6 or more	Total
No. of vehicles	295	190	53	5	5	2	0	550

Fit a Poisson distribution with the same mean as the observed data and test for goodness of fit.   [MEI]

7   Over a period of a year (52 weeks) at a certain hospital, the numbers of patients admitted per week for treatment of a fairly rare disease were as follows:

Number of admissions	0	1	2	3
Number of weeks with that number of admissions	26	15	9	2

Examine whether these data provide evidence against the assertion that the number of admissions per week is well modelled by a Poisson distribution.   [MEI]

8   On 40 consecutive weekdays the numbers of letters I received in my mail were as follows:

3 5 1 1 3   3 2 4 6 1   4 0 1 3 1   2 5 4 2 1
7 4 2 5 1   3 4 1 6 5   5 1 3 4 2   5 1 3 2 4

Calculate the mean and variance.

Compare the frequencies with those which would be expected on the assumption of an appropriate Poisson probability model. Use a suitable test to investigate whether the difference could reasonably be attributable to chance.   [SMP]

9 A small firm's switchboard was on duty one day from 8.40 a.m. to 1.10 p.m. and from 1.40 p.m. to 5.30 p.m. The table below gives the frequency distribution for telephone calls that were answered during the 100 five-minute intervals that made up the day.

No. of calls	0	1	2	3	4	5	6	7	8 or more
Frequency	5	22	28	24	11	5	4	1	0

(a) Find the mean and standard deviation of these data.

(b) Find the corresponding frequencies that would be predicted by a Poisson model with equal mean, and test the agreement between observed and predicted frequencies.

(c) Are there any features of the situation that would cause you to doubt the suitability of a Poisson model?   [SMP]

10.3 TWO-WAY TABLES

How do men and women compare as mathematicians?

We know of course that (sadly) fewer girls choose to do mathematics than boys; but of those who do, and who get to the top, how do they get on? To help to investigate this, here are the results of the mathematics finals (the Mathematical Tripos, Part II) for one particular year at Cambridge University: (Note 10.2)

	Firsts	Seconds	Thirds	Total
Men	43	94	24	161
Women	6	17	7	30
Total	49	111	31	191

You could easily make out a case from these figures that the women didn't do too well. For example, women accounted for nearly 16% of the entries, but they got only 12% of the firsts (or "wranglers", as they are called at Cambridge) and nearly 23% of the thirds. But "the devil can cite percentages to his own purpose"; so let us examine the figures more closely.

The enquiry can be set up as a test of the null hypothesis:

Hypothesis. There is no difference in quality between men and women students as mathematicians.

This hypothesis asserts the statistical independence of two properties of mathematics students: their sex, and their class of degree. So the appropriate probability model is the "multiplication law for probabilities" (see §1.3), and this can be used to calculate the expected frequencies in the various categories.

Of course, it is not possible to assign theoretical values to the probabilities of the various classes, or of the students' sex: the university does not allocate a fixed proportion of first, second and third classes, nor is there a fixed proportion of men and women. But, from the totals in the table of results, it is possible to find the probabilities that a mathematics student selected at random from this particular year-group obtained a certain class of degree, or was of a certain sex. For example, the probability that a student selected at random was awarded a first class is $\frac{49}{191}$, and the probability that the student is male is $\frac{161}{191}$. So, on the basis of the hypothesis, the multiplication law gives, for a student selected at random,

$$P(\text{student is a man and got a first}) = \frac{161}{191} \times \frac{49}{191}.$$

Since there are 191 students in all, the expected frequency for the category "man and first class" is

$$191 \times \left(\frac{161}{191} \times \frac{49}{191} \right), \text{ or } 41.3.$$

(It is obviously simpler to work this out as $\frac{161}{191} \times 49$, or as $\frac{49}{191} \times 161$, and this is how one would normally do it, as a straight proportion calculation. The more complicated, but more symmetrical, method has been used here to emphasise the theoretical basis on which the argument rests.)

Working in a similar way, the complete table of expected frequencies is:

	Firsts	Seconds	Thirds	Total
Men	41.3	93.6	26.1	161
Women	7.7	17.4	4.9	30
Total	49	111	31	191

Q.5   Check the entries in this table for yourself, and make sure that they add up to the correct totals.

This table provides a theoretical standard against which to test the hypothesis of independence. It can be combined with the table of actual results to give the differences $F_o(C_i) - F_e(C_i)$ (using the notation of §6.6):

	Firsts	Seconds	Thirds
Men	+1.7	+0.4	−2.1
Women	−1.7	−0.4	+2.1

(As a further check on accuracy, notice that the sums in each row and each column are zero.) From these we can compute the discrepancy

$$\frac{(1.7)^2}{41.3} + \frac{(0.4)^2}{93.6} + \frac{(-2.1)^2}{26.1} + \frac{(-1.7)^2}{7.7} + \frac{(-0.4)^2}{17.4} + \frac{(2.1)^2}{4.9} = 1.53.$$

Q.6   Use the result of Exercise 6A, question 9 to work this out another way.

Before we can decide whether a discrepancy of 1.53 is large enough to reject the hypothesis being tested, it is necessary to find the number of degrees of freedom. In this example the known quantities which are common to the tables of observed and expected frequencies are the totals in the rows and columns. The question is therefore: given these totals, how many entries can be made in the table without restriction, before the rest of the entries are determined by the totals? In this case it should be clear that the answer is 2: for example, once the numbers of men getting firsts and seconds have been written in -

43	94	*	161
*	*	*	30
49	111	31	191

- the remaining frequencies (marked with asterisks) can be found by simple addition and subtraction.

So the discrepancy is compared with the critical value given in the table of chi-squared probability for $v = 2$. Taking the usual significance level of 5%, this critical value is 5.99, which is far more than the calculated discrepancy. There is therefore no reason whatsoever to reject the hypothesis; on the evidence of these results, there is no support for the suggestion that mathematical ability is sex-related.

10.4 A GENERAL EXPRESSION FOR v

When individuals are described according to two properties (in the example in §10.3, sex and class of degree), the table in which the frequencies are recorded is often called a *contingency table*. If the table has r rows and c columns, then it is an "$r \times c$ table".

The argument used to find the number of degrees of freedom in the example can be generalised in an obvious way. If the totals of the rows and columns in an $r \times c$ table are given, then it is possible to write in the entries in the first $r - 1$ rows and $c - 1$ columns without restriction (provided that their sums do not exceed the totals); but then the frequencies in the last row and the last column can be found by arithmetical methods. It therefore follows that:

> In a test for independence of two properties based on frequencies shown in an $r \times c$ contingency table, the number of degrees of freedom is $(r - 1)(c - 1)$.

Q.6   Obtain this result by a slightly different argument, as follows:
(a) The total number of entries in the table is rc.
(b) These entries must satisfy $r + c$ linear equations.
(c) These equations are connected by one relation.
(d) Therefore $v = rc - (r + c - 1)$, which is $(r - 1)(c - 1)$.

Exercise 10B

1   The total undergraduate numbers by subject at Cambridge University in 1983–4 can be analysed as follows.

	Arts	Social science	Science & technology
Men	1760	921	3637
Women	1448	403	1095

Do these figures provide evidence that sex and choice of subject are related?

2   A survey was carried out to investigate the performance of cars in a roadworthiness test. Of 56 randomly chosen cars which were taking the test for the first time, 44 passed and 12 failed. Of 24 randomly chosen cars which were undergoing a second or subsequent test, 13 passed and 11 failed. Test at the 5% level of significance whether these data provide evidence of an association between the pass/fail rates of the test and whether or not the car is taking the test for the first time. State carefully the conclusions reached in your analysis.   [MEI]

3   The following table summarises the total notifications in London of the diseases poliomyelitis and polioencephalitis as a function of age group during the period 1937–46 and also during the epidemic year 1947. Is there any statistical evidence to show that the age distribution of those attacked in the epidemic year was significantly different from that previously experienced?

	1937–46	1947
Age group ⎰ 0–14 years	467	453
attacked ⎱ 15 and over	131	249

[SMP]

4   A margarine firm has invited 200 men and 200 women to see if they can distinguish margarine from butter. It is found that 120 of the women, but only 108 of the men, can. Investigate whether there is any evidence of a sex difference in taste discrimination.   [SMP]

5   Carry out, and analyse the results of a test similar to that in question 4 amongst the students of your own school or college.

6   As part of the National Child Development Study, a report by Pringle, Butler and Davie recorded the numbers of boys and girls aged 7 who had had a temper tantrum in the previous three months.

	Yes	No
Boys	1209	2849
Girls	1064	2863

Do these figures indicate a significant difference of behaviour between boys and girls?

7   Examine the following data on the performance of candidates in the Sociology honours degree for two colleges.

College	Grade 1	2	3	4	Total
A	6	66	114	56	242
B	5	40	86	49	180

8   The numbers of home wins, draws and away wins in the four divisions of the English Football League in the 1982–3 season were:

	Division 1	2	3	4
Home wins	255	220	297	283
Draws	111	144	137	142
Away wins	96	98	118	127

Do these figures suggest a difference in the pattern of results from one division to another?

9   A 2×2 contingency table has frequencies for the various combinations of properties as follows:

a	b	$a + b$
c	d	$c + d$
$a + c$	$b + d$	n

Show that the expected frequencies all differ from the observed frequencies by δ/n, where $\delta = ad - bc$ and $n = a + b + c + d$. Deduce that the discrepancy between the observed and expected frequencies is

$$\frac{\delta^2 n}{(a + b)(a + c)(c + d)(b + d)}.$$

11

Continuous random variables

Anyone reading this book so far might think that probability theory dealt only with situations with discrete outcomes which can be described by 'scores' x_1, x_2, ... This is, of course, far from true. The length of a centipede, the time between successive blips on a Geiger counter, the mass of a can of beans – these are all measurements which vary randomly, but they take values which can be chosen from the whole set of real numbers within some interval.

At least, that is the 'mathematical model' that we find convenient to use for such examples. In practice we can only measure any of these quantities to a limited degree of accuracy, so we usually assign the measurements to some interval bounded by rational numbers: for example, "$26\,\text{mm} < l < 27\,\text{mm}$", or "$t = 0.73\,\text{s}$ to the nearest hundredth of a second". But it is theoretically preferable to suppose that measurements can be represented by any real number, even though we have no conceivable practical way of finding what this number is. Measurements of this kind are known as *continuous random variables*, in contrast to the isolated 'scores' which we have discussed so far and which are known as *discrete random variables*. (Note 11.1)

The introduction of continuous random variables makes it necessary to reconsider the meaning of probability, and to introduce a new concept – probability density. New expressions also have to be devised for the theoretical mean and variance in terms of probability density. These form the subject-matter of the present chapter.

11.1 GRAPHING DATA

To illustrate this theme, statistics were collected of the masses at birth of infants delivered under normal conditions in a medical practice in Guildford. (Note 11.2) For the 20 most recent deliveries these were, in kg:

3.315	3.150	3.840	4.400	3.450	3.405	3.730	3.680	3.770	3.190
3.410	3.960	4.270	3.515	3.310	3.765	3.850	3.165	2.385	3.895

How should such data be represented graphically?

One possibility would be to draw the usual stick graph, putting a vertical line above the scale at each measurement recorded in the sample (Fig. 1). But if we do this, the result has a different form from that when the random variable is discrete. With a discrete possibility space one soon begins to get repetitions, so that the sticks start to vary in height. But for a continuous random variable an exact repetition would be a very rare event; we would not expect two babies,

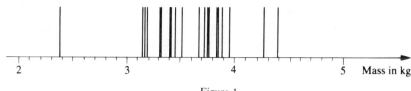

Figure 1

even identical twins, to weigh exactly the same. So as more and more babies are weighed, a true representation would have a greater density of sticks along the line, but with uniform height. (Note 11.3)

How tall should the sticks be? Of course, it doesn't really matter; but since the purpose of this chapter is to generalise the idea of probability, it is most helpful to make the heights of the sticks represent the *relative* rather than the actual frequency – so that, since there are no repetitions, the height of each stick is $1/n$ where n is the number of measurements. (One could imagine a single stick of fixed length being used to represent the whole population, which is cut into n pieces; the more babies there are, the less of the stick there is to represent each one.) So in Fig. 2, which shows the masses at birth for the last 100 deliveries recorded, the sticks are each one-fifth as tall as those in Fig. 1; but, to compensate this, they are more densely packed along the scale.

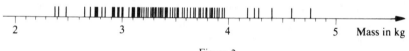

Figure 2

Now imagine what the graph would look like if we had records of 1000 babies, or 10 000 babies. Clearly the heights of the sticks would diminish to virtually nothing, but they would be packed along the scale very densely indeed.

This is not a very practical way of representing large samples of measurements; in fact, this type of graph is not in itself very important. But it does suggest two features of the probability models that are likely to emerge when the random variable is continuous. If we think of probabilities as numbers which relative frequencies get close to when the number of readings becomes large, then:

(a) The probability of a continuous random variable taking any particular real value is usually zero! In this example, if the 100 infants born in Guildford in 1984 are considered as a sample (not at all random) from the population of all the infants who ever have been or might be born at any time anywhere in the world, then for that population

P(a baby's mass is 4 kg) = 0,
P(a baby's mass is 3.45678 kg) = 0,
P(a baby's mass is π kg) = 0, and so on.

There can, however, be exceptions to this; see Exercise 11A, questions 3 and 4.

(b) For a continuous random variable, what is of interest is the density of the distribution of probability, or relative frequency, along the scale. For example, in Fig. 1 the average density of relative frequency over the interval from 3.0 kg to 3.5 kg is

$$\tfrac{8}{20} \div (0.5\,\text{kg}) = 0.8\,\text{kg}^{-1},$$

because $\tfrac{8}{20}$ of the sample is to be found within an interval of extent 0.5 kg. (Note the curious unit: because probability, or relative frequency, is a pure number, the unit of probability density, or relative frequency density, is the inverse of the unit of measurement of the random variable. But see Note 11.4.)

Q.1   Use Figs. 1 and 2 to calculate the average relative frequency density for the samples of 20 babies and of 100 babies, over the intervals from 2.0 to 2.5 kg, 4.0 to 5.0 kg, 2.5 to 4.0 kg.

11.2 HISTOGRAMS

It is clear that, to calculate relative frequency density, all the measurements which fall within a chosen interval have to be grouped together. This is the basis of representing such data in a histogram. The simplest form of (relative frequency) histogram is made up of rectangles standing on a set of equal intervals spaced along the scale, with heights proportional to the relative frequency densities in these intervals. In the present example, we might choose intervals of extent 0.5 kg, for which we calculate, for the sample of 100 babies:

Interval boundary (kg)	2.0		2.5		3.0		3.5		4.0		4.5		5.0
Frequency		5		17		45		27		4		2	
Relative frequency		0.05		0.17		0.45		0.27		0.04		0.02	
Interval extent (kg)		0.5		0.5		0.5		0.5		0.5		0.5	
Relative frequency density (kg^{-1})		0.1		0.34		0.9		0.54		0.08		0.04	

The quantities in the last line of the table determine the heights of the rectangles in the histogram, which is drawn in Fig. 3. (Note 11.5)

Q.2   Calculate the total area of the rectangles in Fig. 3.

In Fig. 3 the heights of the rectangles are also proportional to the actual frequencies, as in a simple bar chart. But this is not always so.

One important feature of this form of representation is that the choice of the intervals into which the measurements are grouped is entirely arbitrary. We

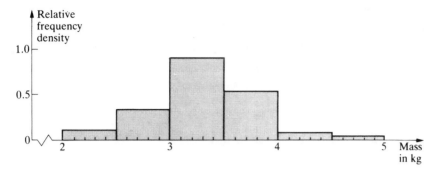

Figure 3

could, for example, choose a lot of very short intervals (say of extent 0.1 kg), which would give a histogram looking like the Chicago skyline; or we could choose wide intervals (say of extent 1 kg), giving a bland, featureless appearance.

Q.3   Sketch the histograms with these interval widths.

Another possibility is to use intervals of different widths in different parts of the scale, so that more detail can be brought out where there are enough measurements to justify it. For example, the domain of masses from 2.0 kg to 5.0 kg might be split up like this:

Interval boundary (kg) 2.0	2.5	2.75	3.0	3.1	3.2	3.3	3.4	3.5	3.75	4.0	4.5	5.0
Frequency	5	2	15	4	11	8	9	13	12	15	4	2
Relative frequency	0.05	0.02	0.15	0.04	0.11	0.08	0.09	0.13	0.12	0.15	0.04	0.02
Interval extent	0.5	0.25	0.25	0.1	0.1	0.1	0.1	0.1	0.25	0.25	0.5	0.5
Relative frequency density (kg^{-1})	0.1	0.08	0.6	0.4	1.1	0.8	0.9	1.3	0.48	0.6	0.08	0.04

This gives the histogram in Fig. 4. (It is interesting to compare this with Fig. 2.)
   The dotted lines in this figure indicate the outline of the histogram in Fig. 3, in the places where the two histograms differ. Notice that the total area is the same for both histograms; the difference between them is in the distribution of the area. This points to another way of regarding a histogram, as a diagram in which relative frequency is represented by area. This is because the area of any rectangle in the histogram is

relative frequency density × interval width = relative frequency.

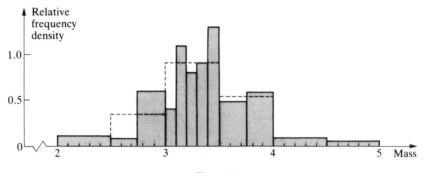

Figure 4

Q.4   Cut out a rectangle of paper of unit area, according to the scale of Figs. 3 and 4. Show that this rectangle can be dissected into smaller rectangles which exactly fit over the histograms in these figures.

To sum up:

> If measurements are made of experimental values of a continuous random variable, and the domain is split into a set of intervals, then the relative frequency of the measurements within any interval divided by the extent of the interval gives the *relative frequency density* in that interval. A diagram made up of rectangles standing on these intervals of heights representing the density is a *relative frequency histogram*. The area of each rectangle represents the relative frequency in the corresponding interval. The total area of all the rectangles in the histogram is 1.

These definitions have been given in terms of relative rather than absolute frequencies, because it is these that lead to probabilities. But if the word "relative" is deleted everywhere that it occurs in the above statement, we get a definition of the more familiar type of histogram which is constructed directly from the frequencies. The only other modification required is that the number "1" which comes in the final sentence must be replaced by "n", the number of measurements in the sample.

Exercise 11A

1   Collect some data giving measurements which could be regarded as sample values of a continuous random variable, and represent them by means of a histogram. Here are some suggestions.
   (a) The length of time that people can hold their breath.
   (b) Reaction times. (It is not difficult to devise a suitable experiment using a visual or aural stimulus produced on a computer at a random instant.)
   (c) The width that people can span with their left hands.
   (d) The annual rainfall for your locality over a period of years. (This is often given in the reports of local natural history societies, which are available in public libraries.)

(e) Buy a bag of nuts and measure the mass or the length of individual nuts.

(f) For members of your college or school, how far they have to travel to get there from home, or how long it takes.

(If some members of your class are studying a subject such as biology or geography, work in these subjects may suggest some interesting possibilities.) (K)

2   From the histogram in Fig. 4, how could you find directly (a) the proportion of babies weighing between 2.75 and 3.75 kg, (b) the proportion of babies weighing between 2.8 and 3.2 kg?

3   From local records, find out the rainfall each day over a period of several months and represent this graphically. Why is it more difficult to do this than to make a histogram for the annual rainfall over a period of years, as suggested in question 1(d)?

4   When you arrive at the kerbside and want to cross the road, you may be able to cross at once or you may have to wait a considerable time before it is safe to cross. If this experiment were repeated a large number of times, and the "waiting time before crossing" recorded, how could the results be shown graphically?

It would be unwise to carry out this experiment practically, but it would be possible to simulate it using random numbers to identify the flow of traffic and the instants of arrival at the kerbside. Carry out such a simulation, and represent the results graphically.

5   Write a computer program to read in a set of values of a continuous random variable and to construct a histogram with specified interval boundaries.

11.3 PROBABILITY DENSITY

In Chapter 2 we saw how the idea of the relative frequencies of particular values of a discrete random variable could lead to a theoretical probability model for that random variable – expecting that, if the experiment is repeated a large number of times, the relative frequencies will turn out to be very close to the probabilities in the model. It is now necessary to ask the question: how can the idea of a probability model be extended to continuous random variables?

For example, from the data in §11.1, could we suggest a way of assigning probabilities to particular values of the mass of a new-born baby? (Note 11.6)

Enough has been said already to indicate that it will not be helpful simply to try to assign a probability to each separate value of the continuous random variable – since in most cases the probability of getting any *particular* value is zero! (This does not mean that the outcome is impossible, but that if it does happen to occur in a sample of n measurements, the relative frequency of its appearances is almost certain to be very small if n is a large number.)

So the model will not be found by making an abstraction from the relative frequencies of particular values in a random sample. Instead, it is derived from the idea of the relative frequency densities over intervals of the possibility space.

But the problem then is, what intervals? We have already seen that, in drawing histograms, the intervals can be chosen as we please (compare Figs. 3 and 4). However, if a large sample of experimental results is available, the intervals can be made very small. For example, if we had the masses of 100 000

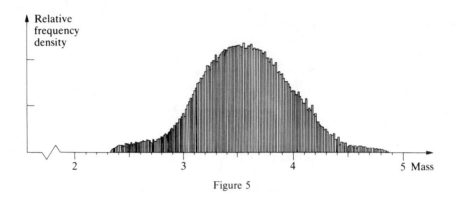

Figure 5

new-born babies rather than 100, it might be possible to draw a reasonable histogram like Fig. 5 with intervals whose extent is only 0.01 kg.

The histogram would, of course, still be made up of rectangles having total area 1; and every different sample of 100 000 babies weighed would give rise to a different histogram. Nevertheless, it is tempting to replace the outline of Fig. 5 by a continuous curve such as Fig. 6, and to regard this as a probability model for the distributions of the masses of new-born babies in the south of England towards the end of the twentieth century. And since the heights of the rectangles of the histogram represent relative frequency density, it seems appropriate in the model to describe the height of the curve by the term "probability density".

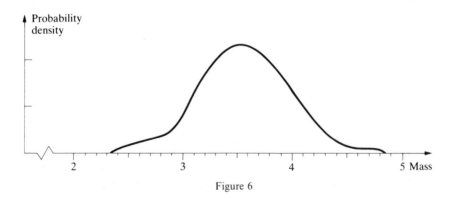

Figure 6

But what exactly is probability density? This is not an easy question to answer directly. It is of course measured in the same units as relative frequency density (i.e. the inverse of the unit in which the quantity under discussion is measured), and can be thought of as a kind of "probability per unit ...", where the dots are replaced by "mass", "time", "length", etc as appropriate. But the important property of the probability density graph, which carries over from the corresponding property of the histogram, is that the area under the graph for any interval within the possibility space of the experiment measures the probability that the continuous random variable lies in that interval. We can use this as the basis for a definition of a probability density function: (Note 11.7)

> If, for a continuous random variable defined over a possibility space U, a non-negative function ϕ is defined so that, for any interval $a \leqslant x \leqslant b$ within U, $\int_a^b \phi(x)\, dx$ gives the probability that the random variable lies inside this interval, then ϕ is called a *probability density function* for the random variable. In particular, ϕ has the property that, taken over the whole of U, $\int_{x \in U} \phi(x)\, dx = 1$.

Example 1
Signs on a motorway give distances of destinations correct to the nearest mile. This means that the error (the amount by which the stated distance exceeds the correct distance) always lies between -0.5 and $+0.5$ miles. What is the probability density function for the error?

We have to suppose that the destination point is precisely defined (e.g. the market cross in the centre of the town) and that the distances are capable of measurement to any desired accuracy. Once these modelling assumptions are made, there is no good reason for any one value of the error to occur more than any other. We can then use intuitive arguments to find the probability that the error lies within any given interval.

Q.5   What are the probabilities of a distance having an error which lies between (a) -0.5 and $+0.5$ miles, (b) 0 and $+0.5$ miles, (c) 0 and $+0.1$ miles, (d) $+0.1$ and $+0.3$ miles?

In general, the probability of an error between a miles and b miles (where $-0.5 \leqslant a < b \leqslant +0.5$) is found by expressing the extent of the interval $a \leqslant x \leqslant b$ as a proportion of the interval $-0.5 \leqslant x \leqslant +0.5$; that is,

$$\frac{b-a}{(+0.5)-(-0.5)}, \text{ or } b-a.$$

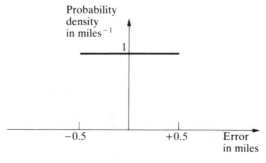

Figure 7

So we have to look for a function ϕ defined for $-0.5 \leqslant x \leqslant +0.5$ with the property that

$$\int_a^b \phi(x)\, dx = b - a.$$

The obvious answer is to take $\phi(x) = 1$ within this interval. The graph of the probability density function therefore has the form shown in Fig. 7.

Exercise 11B

1   A psychologist carries out an experiment in which she asks a large number of subjects to estimate the position of the mid-point of a line. She finds that nobody is more than 2 cm out to the left (negative) or 3 cm to the right (positive); and she postulates a probability model for the distribution of the errors, x cm, by means of a probability density function

$$\phi(x) = \frac{6}{125}(2 + x)(3 - x),$$

where $-2 \leqslant x \leqslant 3$. Verify that this satisfies the condition $\int_{-2}^{3} \phi(x)\, dx = 1$, and use the model to calculate the probabilities that a subject selected at random will (a) err to the right of the true mid-point, (b) get within 1 cm of the true position.

2   A person asks a friend to "ring me sometime between 10 and 11 o'clock". The probability model for the time, t minutes after 10, at which the friend actually makes the call is described by the probability density function

$$\phi(t) = \frac{\pi}{120} \sin\left(\frac{\pi t}{60}\right),$$

where $0 \leqslant t \leqslant 60$. Find the probability that the friend will not ring until after $\frac{1}{4}$ to 11.

3   In a medical practice, the receptionist devises a probability model for the time, t minutes, after she has last put the telephone down that it will ring again, using the probability density function

$$\phi(t) = \tfrac{1}{4}e^{-\frac{1}{4}t}.$$

Verify that $\int_0^\infty \phi(t)\, dt = 1$.
   What is the probability that, if she slips out for two minutes to make a cup of coffee immediately after putting the telephone down, it will ring again while she is out?

4   A new town is being planned, on a circular site of radius 5 km. The planners base their calculations on a probability model for the distance, x km, of residents from the centre of the town, with probability density function of the form

$$\phi(x) = kx\sqrt{(5 - x)}.$$

What value must they take for k?
   If a resident is selected at random, what will be the probabilities that he or she will live (a) within 1 km of the town centre, (b) within 1 km of the town boundary?

5   Fig. 8 shows a double-ended spinner arm, with its axis of rotation placed at a distance c from a graduated scale. When the spinner stops, the arm points at a mark x on the scale, the zero being the point of the scale closest to the axis of the spinner. Show that the probability that the mark x lies between a and b (where $a < b$) is

$$\frac{1}{\pi} (\tan^{-1}(b/c) - \tan^{-1}(a/c)).$$

Hence find a probability density function for x.

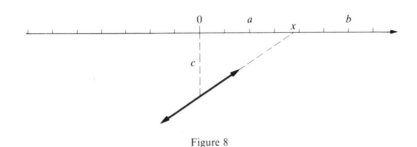

Figure 8

11.4   MEAN AND VARIANCE FOR A CONTINUOUS RANDOM VARIABLE

It seems natural to want to extend the idea of theoretical mean and variance to probability models in which the random variable is continuous. But clearly the formulae

$$\mu = \sum_{i=1}^{k} x_i \mathrm{p}(x_i), \ \sigma^2 = \sum_{i=1}^{k} (x_i - \mu)^2 \mathrm{p}(x_i) = \sum_{i=1}^{k} x^2{}_i \mathrm{p}(x_i) - \mu^2 \ (\text{see §9.2})$$

cannot be used directly, since we no longer have discrete scores $x_1, x_2, \ldots, x_k$. So the problem is, how can they be adapted in terms of the probability density function ϕ for a continuous random variable?

The clue lies in the interpretation of integration as a method of "summation". (Note 11.8) The argument, applied to the formula for the mean, then runs as follows.

To find the mean, we can 'lump together' small intervals of values of the continuous random variable and consider them as if they were single values of a discrete variable. (You might imagine, for example, all the masses in Fig. 6 to be rounded to two places of decimals; then all the values between 2.305 kg and 2.315 kg would be replaced by the single value 2.31 kg.) Fig. 9a shows all the values of the continuous random variable between x and $x + \delta x$, and the graph of the probability density function ϕ within this interval of extent δx. The probability that the random variable lies within this interval is given by the shaded area δA. If all these values are lumped together, this is the probability which will replace the factor $\mathrm{p}(x_i)$ in the discrete formula for μ.

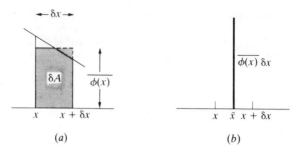

Figure 9

Now think of δA as the area of a rectangle having the interval from x to $x + \delta x$ as base (see Fig. 9a again). Clearly

$$\delta A = \overline{\phi(x)}\, \delta x,$$

where $\overline{\phi(x)}$ stands for a kind of average value of the function ϕ over this interval. This is shown by the height of the 'stick' in Fig. 9b, which forms part of a discrete stick graph corresponding to the continuous graph in Fig. 9a.

What should be written for x_i in the formula for the mean? We cannot tell for certain, but it must certainly be some value between x and $x + \delta x$. Let us call it $\bar{x}$. Then the expression for μ becomes a sum of the form

$$\mathbf{S}\bar{x} \times \overline{\phi(x)}\, \delta x.$$

The theory of integration now tells us that, if the extents of the intervals δx tend to zero, so that $\bar{x}$ tends to x, and $\overline{\phi(x)}$ tends to $\phi(x)$, then such a sum becomes the integral

$$\int x\phi(x)\, dx,$$

evaluated over the possibility space U.

A similar argument can be used for the variance, and so the required results are:

For a continuous random variable defined over a possibility space U with probability density function ϕ, the theoretical mean μ and variance σ^2 are defined by the integrals

$$\mu = \int_{x \in U} x\phi(x)\, dx$$

and

$$\sigma^2 = \int_{x \in U} (x - \mu)^2 \phi(x)\, dx = \int_{x \in U} x^2 \phi(x)\, dx - \mu^2.$$

11.5 SOME MATHEMATICAL CONVENTIONS

It was mentioned in §1.1, with reference to a set of measurements $x_1, x_2, \ldots, x_k$, that it is common practice to use the corresponding capital letter X to describe the measurement being made – that is, the "random variable" which can take the particular realisations x_1, x_2, etc. When there is need of a symbol to designate a random variable, this convention is adopted more generally wherever possible. For example, we write $P(X = x)$ to denote the probability that the continuous random variable X takes the particular value x.

Another useful convention enables us to drop the reference to "the possibility space U" in the definitions of the preceding sections. Since the values taken by a continuous random variable are real numbers, or possibly quantities measured by real numbers – of which U is a subset – it is sometimes helpful to think of the domain of the function ϕ as being not just U, but the whole set of real numbers or real number quantities, and to define $\phi(x)$ as zero when x does not belong to U.

For example, in Example 1 of §11.3, the error x miles could be regarded as having any value between $-\infty$ and ∞; but we would then define

$$\phi(x) = \begin{cases} 0 & \text{if } x < -0.5, \\ 1 & \text{if } -0.5 \leqslant x \leqslant +0.5, \\ 0 & \text{if } x > +0.5. \end{cases}$$

Its graph would then have the form shown in Fig. 10.

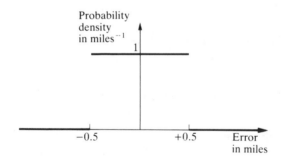

Figure 10

If this convention is followed, then the condition $\int_{x \in U} \phi(x)\, dx = 1$ would be replaced by

$$\int_{-\infty}^{\infty} \phi(x)\, dx = 1;$$

and the expressions for mean and variance would become

$$\mu = \int_{-\infty}^{\infty} x\phi(x)\, dx$$

and

$$\sigma^2 = \int_{-\infty}^{\infty} (x - \mu)^2 \phi(x)\, dx = \int_{-\infty}^{\infty} x^2 \phi(x)\, dx - \mu^2,$$

whatever the actual nature of the possibility space U.

This modification does not affect the actual process of calculating the mean and variance. If U is not itself the complete set of real numbers, then to calculate $\int_{-\infty}^{\infty}$ it will be necessary to split the interval of integration into a number of parts, over some of which ϕ takes the value 0. But there are advantages in the simplification of certain theoretical results which make the introduction of the convention worth while.

Exercise 11C

1   Calculate the theoretical mean and variance for the model of motorway distance errors described in Example 1.

2   In a game a wooden block is propelled with a stick across a flat deck. On each attempt the distance, x metres, reached by the block lies between 0 and 10 m, and the variation is modelled by the probability density function

$$\phi(x) = 0.0012x^2(10 - x).$$

Calculate the mean distance reached by the block.   [SMP]

3   In Exercise 11B, question 3, calculate the mean time between the receptionist putting the telephone down and the next call.

4   In Exercise 11B, question 4, calculate the mean distance of residents from the centre of the town, and the variance.

5   Sketch the graph of the function ϕ defined by

$$\phi(x) = \begin{cases} kx^3(1 - x) & \text{for } 0 < x < 1, \\ 0 & \text{otherwise.} \end{cases}$$

If ϕ is a probability density function for a continuous random variable X, use the fact that $\int_{-\infty}^{\infty} \phi(x)\, dx = 1$ to find the value of k. Then find the mean and variance of X, and mark the lines $x = \mu - \sigma$ and $x = \mu + \sigma$ on your graph.

Calculate the probability that X lies between $\mu - \sigma$ and $\mu + \sigma$.

6   Repeat question 5 for the function ϕ defined by

$$\phi(x) = \begin{cases} ke^{-x} & \text{for } x > 0, \\ 0 & \text{otherwise.} \end{cases}$$

7   A mathematical model for the fraction x of the sky covered with cloud $(0 < x < 1)$ assigns to this a probability density function

$$\phi(x) = k/\sqrt{\{x(1 - x)\}}.$$

Calculate:
(a) the value of k,
(b) the expected fraction covered by cloud,
(c) the probability that not more than $\frac{1}{4}$ of the sky is covered.   [SMP]

8   The possibility space for a continuous random variable is the interval $-b < x < b$, and within this interval the probability density function ϕ is given by

$$\phi(x) = a(b^2 - x^2).$$

Prove that $a = \frac{3}{4}b^{-3}$. Write down the mean, and calculate the standard deviation.
   Find the interval $-c < x < c$ such that the random variable has a probability of 0.95 of lying within this interval. Express your answer in the form:
   "There is a probability of 0.95 that the random variable lies within ... standard deviations of the mean."

9   The probability density function of the random variable X is

$$\phi(x) = \begin{cases} kxe^{-\lambda x}, & x \geq 0, \\ 0 & \text{elsewhere} \end{cases}$$

where k, λ are constants ($\lambda > 0$).
   Determine k in terms of λ, and show that the mean and variance of X are $2\lambda^{-1}$ and $2\lambda^{-2}$ respectively.
   Determine the probability that the value of X lies within two standard deviations of its mean.
   [MEI]

10   Suggest ways of defining (a) the mode, (b) the median, for a continuous random variable X. Find these quantities for the random variables with the probability density functions ϕ defined in questions 5 and 6.

11   The random variable X can take all values between 0 and a inclusive, where $a > 0$. Its probability density function $\phi(x)$ is zero for $x < 0$ and $x > a$, and, for $0 \leq x \leq a$, satisfies

$$\phi(x) = (A/a) \exp(-x/a),$$

where A is a positive constant. Show by integration that $A = 1.582$ to 3 decimal places.
   Also use integration to find
   (i) the probability that X is less than $\frac{1}{2}a$;
   (ii) the number λ for which there is a probability $\frac{1}{2}$ that X is less than λa.
   [MEI]

12   It has been suggested that a flat circular island of radius 10 miles could accommodate the whole human population sitting down. If people were uniformly spread over the whole island, explain why the probability that a person selected at random would be sitting at a distance from the centre between a miles and b miles is $\frac{1}{100}(b^2 - a^2)$.
   Taking as the random variable the distance R miles of a person from the centre of the island, write down an equation for the probability density $\phi(r)$. From what you know about integration, find a function ϕ which satisfies this equation. Hence find the mean distance of the population from the centre of the island, and the variance of the distance.

13   Bees are densely and uniformly packed in a swarm of radius c with the queen at its centre. Find the mean and the variance for the distance of a random bee from the queen.

14   Prove directly from the integral definitions the equivalence of the two expressions for σ^2.

15 Write out in full the argument justifying the integral formula for the variance.

16 (For readers who have studied some mechanics.) A rod extends along the x-axis from $x = a$ to $x = b$. It has variable density (mass/unit length) $\phi(x)$ along its length. You are given that the mass of the rod is 1.
   (i) Write this last item of data as an equation involving an integral.
   (ii) To what would the statistical formulae for μ and σ^2 correspond in the mechanical example?
   (iii) To what would σ correspond?
   (iv) What interpretation in mechanics could be given to the equivalence of the two expressions for σ^2?

17 An observer records the time intervals between the passages of successive vehicles along a motorway. He obtains the following frequency distribution.

Time interval (s)	0–15	15–30	30–45	45–60	60–75	75–90
Frequency	69	25	12	7	5	2

Find the mean of this distribution.

The exponential distribution with parameter λ $(\lambda > 0)$ has probability density function $Ae^{-\lambda t}$ for $t \geqslant 0$, where A is suitable constant whose value depends on the value of λ. Determine A, and show that the exponential distribution has mean λ^{-1}.

Suppose that the parameter λ is chosen so as to fit the mean of the traffic data in the first part of this question. Show that it is then predicted that 63.3 passage times (correct to one decimal place) will lie in the range 0–15 seconds. Determine the corresponding frequencies for the other ranges of passage times, and test the agreement between the observed and predicted frequencies.   [SMP]

18 A distribution has probability density function

$$\phi(x) = \begin{cases} \lambda e^{-\lambda x} & x \geqslant 0, \\ 0 & \text{otherwise.} \end{cases}$$

Prove that $P(a \leqslant X \leqslant b) = e^{-\lambda a} - e^{-\lambda b}, 0 \leqslant a \leqslant b$.
   The times to failure of 500 batteries are given in the following table:

Time (hours)	0–	50–	100–	150–	200–	250–	300–	350–	400–	450–	500–
Frequency	192	120	76	45	31	15	10	6	3	2	0

Estimate λ by putting λ^{-1} equal to the sample mean and test the data for goodness of fit with the given distribution.   [MEI]

11.6 CUMULATIVE FUNCTIONS

"72.5 % of those in full-time work earn less than £5000 a year, whilst 99.1 % earn less than £10 000."

"23 % of the population of this town are under 18, and 86 % are under 60."

Statements of this kind remind us that there is an alternative way of giving information about the distribution of a continuous random variable (in these cases, salary and age). Instead of splitting the possibility space into intervals and giving the relative frequency density in each interval, we may select various measurements along the scale and state what proportion of the population falls below these; this proportion is called the *cumulative relative frequency*.

For example, consider the data about the masses of infants at birth given in §11.2. The statistics in the second table of that paragraph could be organised cumulatively as follows:

Calibration point (kg)	2.0	2.5	2.75	3.0	3.1	3.2	3.3	3.4	3.5	3.75	4.0	4.5	5.0
Cumulative relative frequency	0	0.05	0.07	0.22	0.26	0.37	0.45	0.54	0.67	0.79	0.94	0.98	1

Notice that the relative frequencies in this table apply to specific masses – not to intervals, as was the case in §11.2 – so they can be plotted as points on a graph, as in Fig. 11. This diagram shows, for certain selected masses, what proportion of the babies had a mass at birth less than these masses.

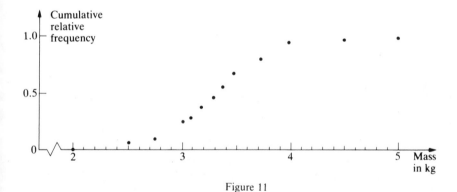

Figure 11

Q.6   Make a similar table and graph based on the first of the two tables in §11.2 and compare them with the table and graph printed here.

How should this graph be completed?
    There are several possible answers to this question which are worth considering; before reading on you might find it worth while trying to decide for yourself the most appropriate method.

(1) 'Correctly' for the given sample
If, for each mass *m* kg, one plots the proportion of the sample which has a mass

less than m kg, then the graph would be made up of a sequence of horizontal lines, separated by 'jumps' at those values of m corresponding to the mass of a baby in the sample.

Q.7   Using the data in §11.1 for the masses of the 20 babies most recently delivered, draw the graph of the cumulative relative frequency for the sample. How is this graph related to Fig. 1 ?

(2) With straight lines joining the points
In doing this we are, in effect, discarding knowledge about the particular masses in each interval which occur in the sample, but indicating a general trend. This is what we also did in constructing the histogram (Fig. 4): each mass is assigned to an interval rather than to its particular position on the scale. Some important relations emerge when these two representations are put together, as in Fig. 12.
    The key questions are:
(*a*) Given the histogram, how can we draw the cumulative graph?
(*b*) Given the cumulative graph, how can we draw the histogram?

(*a*) As an example, look at the point 3.0 kg on the scale. The cumulative relative frequency at this point is the proportion of the sample with masses less than 3.0 kg, i.e. the sum of the proportions in the intervals $2.0 < m < 2.5$, $2.5 < m < 2.75$ and $2.75 < m < 3.0$. These proportions are shown in the histogram by the

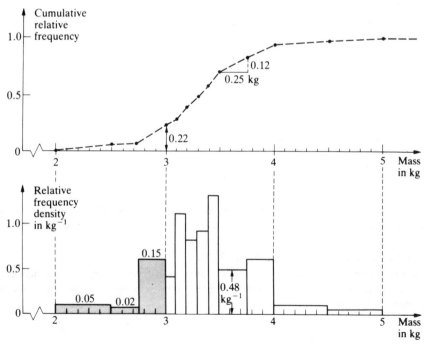

Figure 12

areas of the rectangles covering these intervals, shown shaded in the diagram. So the height of the cumulative frequency graph is equal (on the appropriate scale) to the area to the left of that point in the histogram.

Q.8   Explain why this is true even if one selects a point, such as 2.9 kg, which is not a boundary point on the histogram.

(*b*) Now look, as an example, at the interval $3.5 < m < 3.75$ on the scale. The height of the histogram over this interval is found by dividing the proportion of the sample which falls in the interval by the extent of the interval, which is 0.25 kg; that is,

relative frequency density

$$= \frac{\text{proportion less than } 3.75 \text{ kg} - \text{proportion less than } 3.5 \text{ kg}}{0.25 \text{ kg}}$$

$$= \frac{0.79 - 0.67}{0.25 \text{ kg}} \text{ (using the table at the beginning of this section)}$$

$$= 0.48 \text{ kg}^{-1}.$$

Fig. 12 shows clearly that, on the cumulative graph, this is the *gradient* of the chord spanning the interval.
    To sum up:

The cumulative relative frequency at any point of the scale is equal to the area of the histogram to the left of that point. The height of the histogram at any point is equal to the gradient of the chord of the cumulative graph at that point.

Q.9   Verify these statements at other points and over other intervals.

(3) With a curve
Imagine what the cumulative relative frequency graph would look like if the histogram had the form shown in Fig. 5, for a sample of masses of 100 000 babies. The plotted points would then be very close together, and would appear to define a curve. Now it is impossible for the true cumulative graph for any finite sample to be a continuous curve; but by drawing such a curve through the plotted points one is making a conjecture about the shape that the cumulative graph might have if a very large sample of readings were available. It therefore gives a hint how the connection between cumulative relative frequency and relative frequency density might be carried over into a connection between cumulative probability and probability density. We take up this point in the next section.

Exercise 11D

1 Draw cumulative graphs corresponding to the histograms you drew for the data collected in Exercise 11A, question 1. (K)

2 A small factory employs 100 people. It publishes the following statistics, giving the numbers of employees whose basic weekly wage is less than various amounts:

Basic weekly wage (£)	40	50	60	80	100	150	200
Number of employees getting less than this amount	0	6	31	65	85	95	100

Draw a histogram showing the distribution of the employees into various wage-bands; indicate clearly on your diagram the scales to which it is drawn.

It is not possible to calculate the mean wage exactly from these statistics, but it can be stated that the mean weekly wage lies between £x and £y, for certain values of x and y. Give the values of x and y which are as close together as the data allow.   [SMP]

3 The table below gives a cumulative frequency distribution of the masses of 100 geese:

Mass in kg, not greater than	2	4	6	8	10	12
Cumulative frequency	10	26	46	75	93	100

Derive the corresponding frequency distribution, and hence calculate estimates for the mean and variance of these masses.   [Cambridge]

11.7 CUMULATIVE PROBABILITY

Just as probability is an idealisation of relative frequency, so the idea of cumulative probability is carried over directly from that of cumulative relative frequency. In a model for the distribution of a continuous random variable, the *cumulative probability function* associates, with each measure x on the scale, the probability that the random variable is less than or equal to x. (Note 11.9) Because this is a probability rather than a "probability per unit . . .", this is often in practice an easier idea to deal with than probability density.

The standard convention is to use a capital letter to denote this function, corresponding to the small letter used for the probability density function. So, if the probability density function is ϕ, the cumulative probability function is denoted by Φ. (Note 11.10) That is,

$$\Phi(x) = P(X \leqslant x).$$

As an illustration, look again at Example 1 in §11.3 about errors in motorway distances. If x miles is some error between -0.5 miles and $+0.5$ miles, then the probability of getting an error less than or equal to this is found by expressing the extent of the interval -0.5 miles $\leqslant$ error $\leqslant x$ miles as a fraction of the extent of the complete interval of possible errors, -0.5 miles $\leqslant$ error $\leqslant +0.5$ miles. So

$$\Phi(x) = \frac{x - (-0.5)}{1} = x + 0.5 \quad \text{if} \quad -0.5 \leqslant x \leqslant +0.5.$$

Obviously, if x is less than -0.5, then the probability of getting an error less than x is zero (since all distances are to the nearest mile); and if x is greater than $+0.5$, the probability is 1. So we can write

$$\phi(x) = \left\{ \begin{array}{l} 0 \\ 1 \\ 0 \end{array} \right. \quad \text{and} \quad \Phi(x) = \left\{ \begin{array}{ll} 0 & \text{if } x < -0.5, \\ x + 0.5 & \text{if } -0.5 \leqslant x \leqslant 0.5, \\ 1 & \text{if } x > 0.5. \end{array} \right.$$

Q.10 Draw the graph of $\Phi(x)$ for this example. How is it related to that of $\phi(x)$?

11.8 CUMULATIVE PROBABILITY AND PROBABILITY DENSITY

Another way of finding the cumulative probability function is to obtain it from the probability density.

The definition of probability density was based on the idea that the probability of the random variable lying in any particular interval is found from the integral which gives the area under the probability density graph over that interval. Now to ask the question "What is the probability that the random variable is less than or equal to x?" is equivalent to asking for the probability that the random variable lies in the interval stretching from the left end of the domain (or from $-\infty$ if we follow the convention described in §11.5) up to x. It follows that

$$\Phi(x) = \int_{-\infty}^{x} \phi(t) \, dt. \text{ (Note 11.11)}$$

Q.11 Verify this relationship in the case of Example 1.

This is the equation used to obtain the cumulative frequency from the probability density. To carry out the reverse process, the key is to use the property known as the "fundamental theorem of analysis" (Note 11.12), which states that the opposite process to integration is differentiation: that is,

$$\Phi'(x) = \phi(x).$$

So if the cumulative probability function is known, the probability density function is found by differentiating.

Q.12   Verify this in the case of Example 1. What happens at $x = -0.5$ and $x = +0.5$?

Expressed geometrically, these relationships are exactly analogous to those for the relative frequency histogram and the cumulative relative frequency:

The cumulative probability at any point of the scale is equal to the area under the probability density graph to the left of that point. The height of the probability density graph at any point is equal to the gradient of the cumulative probability graph at that point.

Exercise 11E

1   A random variable is defined over the interval $0 < x < \pi$ with probability density function given by

$$\phi(x) = \tfrac{1}{2} \sin x.$$

Find an expression for the cumulative probability function Φ.
   Draw the graphs of ϕ and Φ.

2   A random variable can take any positive real value. The probability that its value is less than or equal to x, where $x > 0$, is given by

$$\Phi(x) = 1 - e^{-kx},$$

where k is a positive constant. Find an expression for the probability density function ϕ.
   Draw the graphs of ϕ and Φ.

3   In Exercise 11C, question 2, calculate the probability that the block does not travel farther than x metres.

4   Sketch the graph of the cumulative probability function for the probability model whose probability density graph is shown in Fig. 6.

5   Explain why any cumulative probability function Φ must have the following properties:
   (i) Φ is an increasing function; that is, if $a < b$, then $\Phi(a) \leqslant \Phi(b)$.
   (ii) $\Phi(x)$ tends to 0 as $x \to -\infty$, and to 1 as $x \to +\infty$.

6   The probability that a light bulb lasts longer than t hours is $e^{-t/\mu}$. Find the probability density function for the lifetime of a bulb.
   Show that the mean lifetime is μ.
   If the mean lifetime is 1500 hours, how unlikely is it that a bulb will last more than 3000 hours?
   If the manufacturer wants to ensure that less than 1 in 1000 bulbs fail before 5 hours, what is the lowest mean lifetime he can allow his bulbs to have?   [SMP]

7   The cumulative distribution function for a continuous random variable X is given by

$$\Phi(x) = \begin{cases} 0 & \text{for } x < -2, \\ k(4x - \tfrac{1}{3}x^3 + \tfrac{16}{3}) & \text{for } -2 \leqslant x \leqslant 2, \\ 1 & \text{for } x > 2. \end{cases}$$

Find (a) the value of k, (b) $P(-1 < X < 1)$, (c) the probability density function for X, (d) the mean and variance of X. [Cambridge]

8 In an electronic game a spot moves very rapidly at constant speed along a line-segment (the x-axis) from 0 to b; when it reaches b it returns instantaneously to 0 and starts again. When a player presses a key the spot stops where it is at that instant. The player's aim is to stop the spot as close to b as he can. The spot moves so fast that his shot is in effect random.
   (i) What is the probability that the coordinate of the point where the spot stops is less than x, where $0 < x < b$?
   (ii) Suppose that the player is allowed three shots, and to count as his score the largest of the three coordinates. What is the probability that his score is less than x, where $0 < x < b$?
   (iii) Find the probability density function for his score, and sketch its graph.

9 In a shooting gallery at a funfair a customer tries to get his shots as close to the target's nose as possible. He is allowed 5 shots in all. His shots are in fact scattered randomly with uniform probability in a circular area of radius r with the nose at its centre. Calculate (a) the probability that a single shot will come within a distance x of the nose (where $0 < x < r$), (b) the probability that the best of his five shots will come within a distance x of the nose.
   Hence find the probability density function for the distance from the nose of the best of his five shots.

10 A random variable X is defined over the real numbers with probability density

$$\phi(x) = \frac{1}{\pi}(1 + x^2)^{-1}.$$

A new random variable Y is defined by the relation $Y = X^2$. If y is a positive real number, express $P(0 < Y < y)$ in terms of y.
   Deduce the probability density function for Y.

11 Fig. 13 shows the graph of the cumulative probability function Φ for a random variable X defined over the interval $a < x < b$, where $b > a > 0$. Express the mean value of X in terms of Φ, a and b, and hence show that it is represented by the shaded area in the figure.
   Generalise this result for the case $b > 0 > a$.
   How could the median and the mode of X be found from the figure?

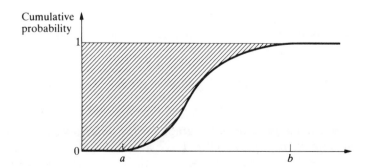

Figure 13

12
Some models for a continuous random variable

You have already met a number of different types of probability model. In Chapter 2 the dice-rolling experiment led to the "uniform" model for the score from a single die, and the "stepped triangular" model for the sum of the scores on two dice. In Chapter 3 Bernoulli sequences of experiments produced the "geometric" model for the lengths of runs of a particular outcome, and the "binomial" model for the number of times a particular outcome occurs in a sequence of fixed length. Chapter 7 introduced the "Poisson" model for the number of occurrences within a unit interval of time of an event which strikes randomly in continuous time.

In all of these models the random variable is discrete: in fact, it can only take values 0, 1, 2, ... But there are also some important types of probability model for which the random variable is continuous, ranging either over all the real numbers or over some interval of real numbers. The purpose of this chapter is to examine some of these in detail.

12.1 THE RECTANGULAR MODEL

You are already familiar with a special case of this model, from the example of the errors in recording motorway distances in Chapter 11. In that example, the possibility space consisted of the interval from $-\frac{1}{2}$ mile to $+\frac{1}{2}$ mile. More generally, if a continuous random variable can take values between a and b, and if any value within this interval is as likely to occur as any other, then we get the general form of the *rectangular probability density model*, given by the equations

$$\phi(x) = \begin{cases} 0 & \text{if } x < a, \\ 1/(b-a) & \text{if } a < x < b, \\ 0 & \text{if } x > b. \end{cases}$$

The graphs of both the probability density function and the cumulative probability function are shown in Fig. 1.

Q.1 Write down equations for the cumulative probability function.

Q.2 Check that $\int_a^b \phi(x)\, dx = 1$, and calculate the mean and standard deviation.

Q.3 Draw the cumulative probability graph for the (discrete) uniform model for the scores when a die is rolled. Draw also the cumulative probability graph for the stepped triangular model for the sum of the scores when two dice are rolled together (see §2.3).

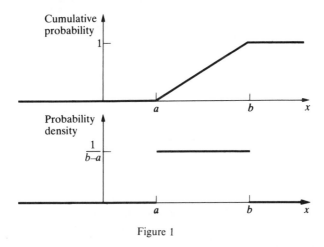

Figure 1

12.2 THE TRIANGULAR MODEL

There is an obvious similarity between the rectangular model for a continuous random variable and the uniform model for a discrete random variable, such as we get for the score when a die is rolled.

However, when two dice are rolled and the scores added, the appropriate probability model is no longer uniform, since the middle totals have a greater probability than the extreme ones. This situation leads to the stepped triangular model (see §2.3). We now ask the question: what is the model corresponding to this when the random variable is continuous?

Suppose that we have two random variables X and Y, each having a rectangular probability density function. The problem is to find the probability model for the sum, $X + Y$. (As an example, go back to the model for the errors in motorway distances given to the nearest mile. If two such distances are added, the total error can vary between -1 mile and $+1$ mile. What is the probability model for the total error?)

To simplify the problem, let us suppose that the possibility space for both X and Y is the interval from 0 to b; that is, in Fig. 1 we take a to be 0. For a start, what is needed is to find a way of representing this in a single diagram. An obvious idea is to take (X, Y) to be the coordinates of a random point in a plane. The conditions $0 < X < b$ and $0 < Y < b$ then confine this point to a square, as shown in Fig. 2.

Now consider two strips parallel to the edges of the square, with widths δx and δy, as shown in the figure. Since the probability density for X in the interval $0 < x < b$ has the constant value $1/b$, the probability that the random point (X, Y) lies in the 'vertical' strip is $(1/b)\delta x$. By similar reasoning, the probability that (X, Y) lies in the 'horizontal' strip is $(1/b)\delta y$. Therefore, if the two random variables are independent – and this is an essential condition for the theory to hold – the multiplication law can be applied to give the probability that (X, Y)

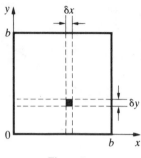

Figure 2

lies in both strips (that is, in the small shaded rectangle) as

$$\frac{1}{b}\,\delta x \times \frac{1}{b}\,\delta y = \frac{1}{b^2}\,\delta x\,\delta y$$

$$= \frac{1}{b^2} \times \text{the area of the shaded rectangle.}$$

This result can now be extended to apply to any region inside the square, not necessarily rectangular in shape. By approximating to this region by a figure made up entirely of rectangles, which can be done as closely as we please, and adding the probabilities for each rectangle given by the rule above, it follows that

$$\text{P}((X,\ Y)\ \text{lies in the region}) = \frac{1}{b^2} \times \text{the area of the region.}$$

In this case the random point $(X,\ Y)$ is said to have constant "area probability density" of $1/b^2$ over the square. The idea of an area probability density, for a point representing a pair of continuous random variables, is one which will be important in later chapters.

The next step is to bring in the random variable $S = X + Y$, for which the probability model is required. There are two ways of approaching this – either through the cumulative probability function or through the probability density. There is something to be learnt from both methods, so it is worth describing them in some detail.

Method 1, by cumulative probability
The question to be asked is: for any real number s, what is the probability that $X + Y$ is less than s?

Notice first that, if $s < 0$, then the answer is obviously zero; and if $s > 2b$, it is obviously one. So it is only necessary to consider the interval $0 \leqslant s \leqslant 2b$.

The procedure is to find which parts of the square in Fig. 2 satisfy the inequality $x + y \leqslant s$. Now this relation defines a region within the square; Fig. 3 shows that if $0 < s \leqslant b$ this region is a triangle, whereas if $b < s < 2b$ it has a more complicated shape which can be thought of as the whole of the square *less*

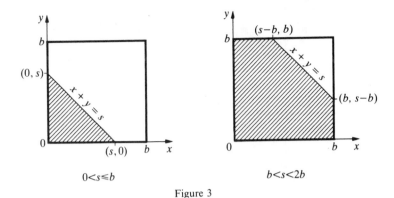

Figure 3

a triangle. In each case, the probability is found by multiplying the area of the region by the area probability density $1/b^2$.

It is easy to calculate that the sides of the triangles bounding the right angles are s in the left figure, and $b - (s - b)$, or $2b - s$, in the right figure. So the cumulative probability function Φ is given by

$$\Phi(s) = \begin{cases} \dfrac{1}{b^2} \cdot \tfrac{1}{2}s^2 & = \dfrac{s^2}{2b^2} & \text{if } 0 < s \leqslant b, \\[3mm] \dfrac{1}{b^2} \cdot \{b^2 - \tfrac{1}{2}(2b - s)^2\} = 1 - \dfrac{(2b - s)^2}{2b^2} & \text{if } b < s < 2b. \end{cases}$$

The probability function can then be found by differentiating, which gives

$$\phi(s) = \begin{cases} \dfrac{s}{b^2} & \text{if } 0 < s \leqslant b, \\[3mm] \dfrac{2b - s}{b^2} & \text{if } b < s < 2b. \end{cases}$$

Fig. 4 shows the graph of Φ, which is made up of segments of two parabolas over this interval, joined at the point $(b, \tfrac{1}{2})$; and of ϕ, which consists of a pair of lines meeting at $(b, 1/b)$. From the shape of the probability density graph, this is named the *triangular probability model*.

Q.4 Verify that the area of the triangle is 1.

Method 2, by probability density
The method, which produces the probability density directly, uses the idea that the probability of a random variable S lying between s and $s + \delta s$ is approximately $\phi(s)\delta s$, if δs is small.

Now the condition

$$s < X + Y < s + \delta s$$

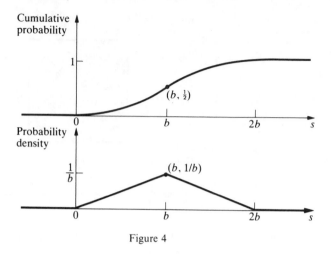

Figure 4

restricts the random point (X, Y) to a narrow band bounded by the two lines $x + y = s$ and $x + y = s + \delta s$ (see Fig. 5). The probability of this is $1/b^2$ times the shaded area within the band and the square.

Now the thickness of this band, measured perpendicular to the two lines, is

$$\delta s \cos 45° = \frac{1}{\sqrt{2}} \delta s.$$

The shaded area is therefore approximately

$$l \times \frac{1}{\sqrt{2}} \delta s,$$

where l is the length of the segment of the line $x + y = s$ within the square. (In making this approximation the shaded region is taken as a parallelogram rather than the trapezium which it really is.) This gives

$$P(s < X + Y < s + \delta s) = \frac{1}{b^2} \times l \times \frac{1}{\sqrt{2}} \delta s;$$

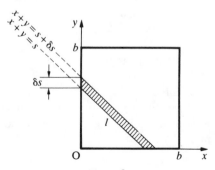

Figure 5

and since this is equal to $\phi(s)\,\delta s$, it follows that

$$\phi(s) = \frac{l}{b^2\sqrt{2}}.$$

This leads directly to the shape of the probability density graph in Fig. 4. As s increases from 0 through b to $2b$, the length l increases from 0 to $b\sqrt{2}$ and then decreases back to 0; so $\phi(s)$ increases from 0 to $1/b$ and then decreases to 0.

Q.5   From this expression, obtain the formulae for $\phi(s)$ found by the first method. Deduce from these the formulae for $\Phi(s)$.

Q.6   Find the exact formula for the area of the shaded region in Fig. 5, and deduce that the mean value of ϕ over the interval from s to $s + \delta s$ is $(s + \tfrac{1}{2}\,\delta s)/b^2$. What does this approach as $\delta s \to 0$?

Exercise 12A

1   Adapt the argument in §12.2 to the case in which X and Y vary within the interval from $-\tfrac{1}{2}$ to $+\tfrac{1}{2}$, as in the example on errors in motorway distances (Example 1 of §11.3).

2   Random variables X and Y both have rectangular probability density over the interval from 0 to b. A random variable G is defined as the greater of X and Y. Show that, if g is any number between 0 and b, the random points (X, Y) for which $G \leqslant g$ lie in a square of area g^2. Hence find an expression for $P(G \leqslant g)$, and draw the graphs of cumulative probability and probability density for the random variable G.

3   With the notation of question 2, a random variable Q is defined as the gradient of the line joining the origin to the random point (X, Y). Show that, if q is any number between 0 and 1, the random points for which $Q \leqslant q$ lie in a triangle of area $\tfrac{1}{2}b^2q$. Find expressions for $P(Q \leqslant q)$ in each of the cases (i) $0 < q \leqslant 1$, (ii) $q > 1$. Draw the graphs of cumulative probability and probability density for the random variable Q.

4   With the notation of question 2, a random variable T is defined as the product XY. If t is any number between 0 and b^2, sketch the region within the square (Fig. 2) for which $T \leqslant t$. Deduce that

$$P(T \leqslant t) = \frac{t}{b^2}(1 + \ln(b^2/t)).$$

Draw the graphs of cumulative probability and probability density for the random variable T.

5   For the situations in questions 2 and 3, use the second method described in §12.2 to find expressions for the probability density directly.

6   If X is a random variable having rectangular probability over the interval 0 to b, and Y is a random variable having rectangular probability over the interval from 0 to c, where $b < c$, investigate the probability model for the random variable $S = X + Y$.

7   Calculate the mean and standard deviation of $X + Y$, where X and Y are rectangular random variables over the interval from 0 to b. What are the probabilities that the value of $X + Y$ lies within (i) one standard deviation, (ii) two standard deviations of the mean?

8 Using a cube in three dimensions, investigate the probability model for the sum of three random variables X, Y, Z, each of which has rectangular probability density over the interval from 0 to b. (Consider separately the intervals $0 \leqslant s \leqslant b$, $b < s \leqslant 2b$, $2b < s \leqslant 3b$.) Draw graphs of the cumulative probability and the probability density, and calculate the mean and standard deviation of $X + Y + Z$.

9 Combining the results of questions 7 and 8, show that there are formulae

$$\text{mean} = \alpha n, \text{ standard deviation} = \beta \sqrt{n},$$

which hold whether n, the number of random variables added, is 2 or 3. What meaning is attached to the constants α and β?

12.3 THE NEGATIVE EXPONENTIAL MODEL

The account of Poisson probability in Chapter 7 concentrated on a discrete random variable, the number of occurrences of the 'event' [the arrival of an appendix case at the hospital, in our illustration] in a given period of time [one day]. But the same situation can also raise questions about a continuous random variable – the length of time that will elapse before the next occurrence [how long will it be before the next patient arrives?]. This variable may in theory have any positive value, so the possibility space is the set of times represented by positive real numbers.

To investigate the probability model for this random variable, it is simplest to begin with the cumulative probability function. That is, we ask:

> For some time $t(>0)$, what is the probability that the event will have occurred – at least once, but possibly more than once – by this time?

The words "at least once" should act as a signal to anyone experienced in probability theory. "At least one" means the same as "not none". So let us turn the question round, and ask for the complementary probability:

> For some time $t(>0)$, what is the probability that the event will not have occurred before this time?

Or, what is the same thing:

> What is the probability that there will be 0 occurrences of the event in a time-interval of length $t(>0)$?

The point of adapting the original question in this way is that, in this last form, you should recognise the standard question of Poisson probability. Suppose that on average there are λ occurrences of the event in *unit* time. Then in time t there will be on average λt occurrences (see Exercise 7C, question 18). The Poisson model then gives the probability of i occurrences in time t as

$$\frac{(\lambda t)^i}{i!} e^{-\lambda t};$$

and, in particular, the probability of no occurrences in time t is just $e^{-\lambda t}$. So it follows that:

For any time $t(>0)$, the probability that the event will not have occurred before this time is $e^{-\lambda t}$.

And so, finally:

For any time $t(>0)$, the probability that the event will have occurred (at least once) before this time is $1 - e^{-\lambda t}$.

This then is the required cumulative probability function, and we can write

$$\Phi(t) = 1 - e^{-\lambda t} \quad \text{for} \quad t > 0;$$

and so, by differentiation,

$$\phi(t) = \Phi'(t) = \lambda e^{-\lambda t} \quad \text{for} \quad t > 0.$$

From the equation for probability density, the probability model described by these equations is called *negative exponential probability*. The graphs are shown in Fig. 6.

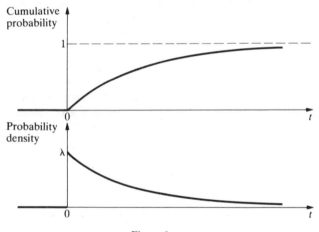

Figure 6

Q.7 Explain (in terms of the hospital admissions illustration if you wish) why the probability density is greatest when t is small.

Q.8 Show that the mean and standard deviation for this model are both $1/\lambda$.

12.4 SIMULATION FOR A CONTINUOUS RANDOM VARIABLE

To carry out a simulation experiment when the possibility space is discrete and finite, random numbers can be associated with each of the possible outcomes in such a way as to make the probabilities in the experiment match those in the real situation. Various methods for doing this were described in Chapter 5. But if the random variable is continuous, this is clearly not possible.

However, there are ways of approximating to a probability density function using random numbers. Some computers, for example, have a facility for producing on command a random 6-digit decimal number between 0 and 1. (The same effect can be achieved by taking sequences of six digits from a table of random numbers, and dividing the resulting number by 10^6.) In reality this still gives a discrete uniform probability model, with a million possible outcomes each having probability 10^{-6}; but it is an acceptable approximation to a continuous rectangular probability model over the interval $0 < x < 1$ with probability density 1 throughout the interval. (Note 12.1)

But often the random variable whose values we want to simulate is modelled by some other probability density function. The problem then is, how to adapt this approximate rectangular model to produce the desired distribution. In this section, two possible procedures are suggested.

Method 1, using cumulative probability

Suppose that the continuous random variable X to be modelled has a cumulative probability function Φ. Then the aim is to find a method of simulation such that, if x is any particular real number,

$$P(X \leqslant x) = \Phi(x).$$

Now the technique described above enables us to call up values of a random variable Y with rectangular probability density in the interval from 0 to 1. The method is then to map each such value to a value of X by means of the function Φ^{-1}, as indicated in Fig. 7. (Note 12.2) This gives a sample of values of X which fits the required probability model.

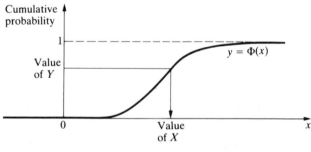

Figure 7

The reason is simple. Let y be any number between 0 and 1, and let $x = \Phi^{-1}(y)$. Since the random variable Y has rectangular probability density,

$$P(Y \leqslant y) = y.$$

But Φ is an increasing function, so that $Y \leqslant y \Leftrightarrow X \leqslant x$. Therefore

$$P(X \leqslant x) = y = \Phi(x),$$

which is just the property required.

This method is very efficient and simple to apply, but it does require two conditions to be satisfied. First, we have to know a formula for the cumulative probability function Φ; since this involves integrating the probability density function ϕ, it is not always possible. Second, we have to find Φ^{-1}, which means turning the relation $y = \Phi(x)$ inside out so as to make x the subject; again, this may not be possible. So it is important to have an alternative method available in case this one fails.

Method 2, using probability density
The principle underlying this method is to fill the region beneath the graph of $\phi(x)$ with random points having constant *area* probability density, and then to select the x-coordinate of each point as a value of the random variable X. The probability that X lies in any particular interval is then proportional to the area under the probability density graph in that interval, as required.

To achieve this even spread of points, the trick is to frame the probability density graph in a rectangle, as shown in Fig. 8 – the closer it fits, the better. (Note 12.3) The rectangle is then peppered with points by defining the two coordinates of a random point (X, Y), such that the random variable X has rectangular probability density across the width of the rectangle, and Y has rectangular probability density through its height. To do this, we adapt the method described at the beginning of this section, separately for X and for Y. Then, for each particular point (x, y), a test is applied:

If $y \leqslant \phi(x)$, then the value of x is recorded.

If $y > \phi(x)$, then the point is discarded and not counted in the sample.

This ensures that only points in the region below the probability density graph are included.

Clearly this is a less efficient method than the first one, since to get each value of X two separate random numbers have to be used — and even then some are discarded. However, the great merit of the method is that it can be used for any probability model. It is an example of a technique known as the "Monte Carlo method".

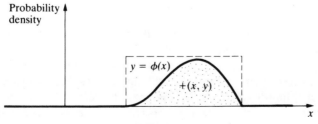

Figure 8

Exercise 12B

1   For the negative exponential probability model with $\lambda = 4$, prove that $\Phi^{-1}(y) = -\frac{1}{4}\ln(1 - y)$.

Use this, with a table of random numbers (or a computer), to generate values for the times between successive appendicitis cases in the hospital admissions example in Chapter 7. By accumulating these, calculate the numbers of cases which arrive in successive days, and hence make a frequency table for the numbers of days on which there are 0, 1, 2, ... cases.

Compare this with the frequencies predicted by the Poisson probability model.

2   Use whichever method of simulation is most appropriate to generate sequences of values of random variables with the following probability density functions:
(a) $\phi(x) = \frac{1}{2} \sin x$ over the interval $0 < x < \pi$;
(b) $\phi(x) = \frac{1}{36}(9 - x^2)$ over the interval $-3 < x < 3$;
(c) $\phi(x) = 20x^3(1 - x)$ over the interval $0 < x < 1$.
From your values construct a relative frequency histogram, and compare it with the graph of the probability density function.

3   Use the first method of simulation described in §12.4 to generate a sequence of values of a random variable with the triangular probability of §12.2, taking b to be 1. Calculate the mean and variance of these values, and compare them with the theoretical mean and variance of the model.

4   Use both methods of simulation to generate sequences of values of a random variable with probability function given by

$$\phi(x) = \frac{1}{\pi(1 + x^2)},$$

the domain being the set of all real numbers. Construct the relative frequency histograms in both cases. Compare the ways in which the two processes get round the difficulty of the infinite possibility space.

5   In a village post office there is just one person serving. The time S minutes taken to serve a customer is modelled by a probability density function $\psi(s) = \frac{1}{2}s^2e^{-s}$. The time-interval T minutes between successive arrivals of customers is modelled by a probability density function $\phi(t) = \lambda e^{-\lambda t}$. Simulate the arrival, service and departure of customers in the cases (a) $\lambda = \frac{1}{4}$, (b) $\lambda = \frac{1}{3}$, (c) $\lambda = \frac{1}{2}$. Investigate whether, and how quickly, a queue builds up. Are the results as you would expect from a consideration of the means of the two random variables?

12.5 LINKS BETWEEN DISCRETE AND CONTINUOUS MODELS

It will not have escaped your notice that the three continuous models described in this chapter are very similar to three of the standard discrete models used in earlier chapters. This comparison is shown diagrammatically in Fig. 9.

But we can go further than this. By making suitable changes of scale and then carrying out a limiting process, it is possible to derive the continuous model from the corresponding discrete one. This is a useful device which will be used in Chapter 13 to obtain an important new model. As an introduction to the

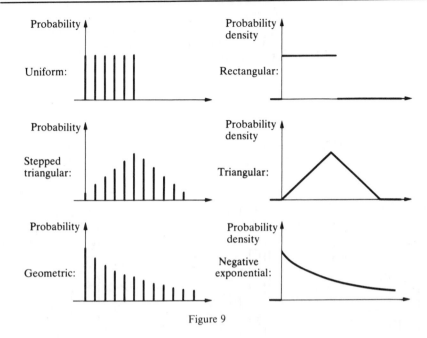

Figure 9

method, it will be used here to transform the geometric probability function (which we first met in §3.2 in connection with Bernoulli sequences) into the negative exponential probability density function.

The transformation is carried out in four steps, and the stages are illustrated in Fig. 10. We use the form of the geometric model given in §9.6, with $p(i) = ab^{i-1}$.

Step 1. This converts the probability function into a probability density function, by replacing each value i of the discrete random variable by the interval of real numbers between $i - \frac{1}{2}$ and $i + \frac{1}{2}$. That is, the probability that the discrete random variable is equal to i is re-interpreted as the probability that a continuous random variable lies between $i - \frac{1}{2}$ and $i + \frac{1}{2}$. Since this interval is of length 1, the probability density is numerically equal to the original probability.

Step 2.   Each rectangle of the histogram (as it now is) has width 1. Now eventually, to produce the continuous probability density curve, the widths of the rectangles will be made to tend to zero. In preparation for this, the values of the random variable are multiplied by a scale factor $1/n$. But we cannot do this by itself; to keep the total area of the histogram equal to 1, we must compensate by multiplying the probability densities by n.

One effect of this change of scale is to multiply the mean and standard deviation by $1/n$, so that the mean becomes $1/(na)$ and the variance $b/(n^2a^2)$, as shown in the third frame of Fig. 10.

Step 3.   One snag about this change of scale is that the quantity na, which is now the height of the histogram when the random variable equals zero, tends to

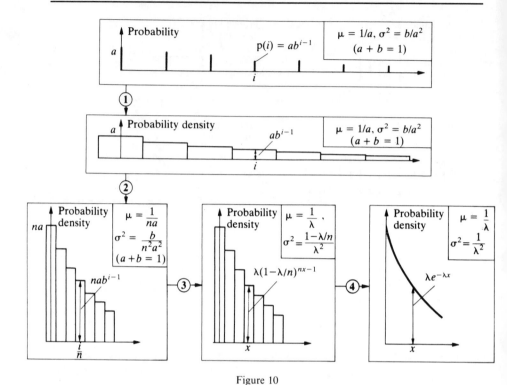

Figure 10

infinity as $n \to \infty$. To get round this, we choose a *fixed* value λ for this height, and arrange for the probability a to get smaller as n increases, in such a way that the product na always has the value λ. (Note 12.4)

This means taking a to equal λ/n, so that $b = 1 - a = 1 - \lambda/n$. Also, the value i/n of the random variable is written as x. The probability density nab^{i-1} therefore becomes

$$\lambda(1 - \lambda/n)^{nx-1}.$$

The mean and variance also take new forms, as indicated in the fourth frame of Fig. 10.

Step 4. Finally, we take limits as $n \to \infty$. The key property is the one used earlier in §7.6, that $(1 - \lambda/n)^n$ tends to $e^{-\lambda}$, so that $(1 - \lambda/n)^{nx}$ tends to $e^{-\lambda x}$. Clearly also $1 - \lambda/n$ tends to 1; therefore $(1 - \lambda/n)^{nx-1}$ also tends to $e^{-\lambda x}$.

It follows that the limiting process leads to probability density function given by

$$\phi(x) = \lambda e^{-\lambda x}$$

defined over the domain $x \geqslant 0$, which is precisely the form of the negative exponential model. Also the mean and variance tend to the values $1/\lambda$ and $1/\lambda^2$, as previously calculated for the model (see Q.8). So this completes the transformation.

Exercise 12C

1   Draw a stick graph for the probability function for a spinner which gives equally likely scores of 0, 1, 2, ..., n. Transform this into a rectangular probability density function by the following process: carry out step 1 as described in §12.5, multiply the random variable by a scale factor of $1/n$, and finally let n tend to infinity.

Verify that the mean and variance for the scores on the spinner are transformed into the mean and variance for the rectangular model.

2   If the spinner in question 1 is used twice and the scores added, a stepped triangular probability function is obtained. Transform this into a triangular probability density function.

3   A discrete random variable has the probability function

$$p(i) = \tan\left(\frac{\pi}{2n}\right)\sin\left(\frac{i\pi}{n}\right) \quad \text{for } i = 1, 2, \ldots, n-1.$$

Verify for $n = 2, 3$ and 4 that $\Sigma_{i=1}^{n} p(i) = 1$. Assuming that this is true for all integral values of n greater than 1, transform this probability model into a model for a continuous random variable whose possibility space is the interval of real numbers between 0 and 1.

13

Normal probability

In the list of transformations from discrete to continuous probability models at the end of Chapter 12 there was one notable absentee – binomial probability. The reason is that this leads to a probability density function which is so important that it deserves a chapter to itself.

This function, the "normal" probability density function, was first identified by de Moivre in 1733, just twenty years after the formula for binomial probability had been published in Jacob Bernoulli's *Ars conjectandi* (see §3.1). His method was in essence that given in §13.5. A quite different derivation was subsequently given by Laplace (1749–1827), using the idea of a "characteristic function" (see §17.9). The function is also associated with the name of Gauss (1777–1855), who gave it as a "law of errors" and applied it to errors in astronomical observations. (Note 13.1)

Normal probability will feature prominently in most of the later chapters of this course. In this chapter its equation will be obtained first numerically and then theoretically, and some of its immediate applications will be described.

13.1 A NUMERICAL APPROACH

Binomial probability functions come in many shapes and sizes, according to the values of a, b ($= 1 - a$) and n. (For the notation, see Chapter 3.) Some have graphs which are skewed to the left, others to the right. Some have greater width, some have greater height. Fig. 1 shows graphs of four typical binomial probability functions which exhibit these differences; if you have kept your computer program for producing binomial graphs (Exercise 3B, question 10) you can easily carry this investigation further.

However, these differences are not as great as they seem, if the value of n is reasonably large – as in these four examples. This can be seen by transforming the graphs so that they have the same mean and standard deviation, which we do in three steps:

Step 1. Convert the probability function to a probability density function, as described in §12.5.

Step 2. Translate the mean to the origin, by reducing the random variable by na (see §9.7, Table 1).

Step 3. Divide the new random variable by $\sqrt{(nab)}$, with a corresponding multiplication of the heights by $\sqrt{(nab)}$ so as to keep the total area equal to 1.

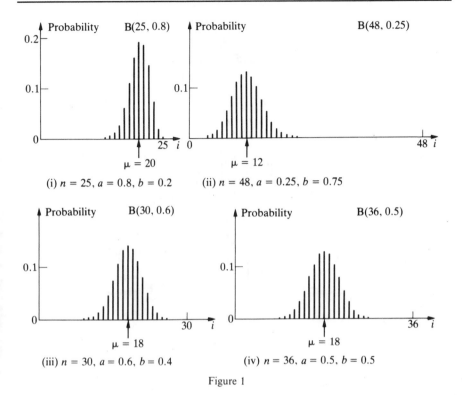

Figure 1

Fig. 2 shows the result, and indicates a remarkable similarity between the transformed graphs. The apparent skewness has almost vanished, and so have the differences in scale. This suggests that, as $n \to \infty$, the limiting probability density curve will be the same whatever the values of a and b.

This turns out to be true, and in §13.5 it will be proved. In the meantime, we can investigate the conjecture numerically. It is slightly simpler to do this for the fourth graph, since this has no skewness at all; but very similar results will be obtained if one of the others is used.

The original binomial probability function is given by the equation

$$p(i) = \binom{36}{i} (\tfrac{1}{2})^i (\tfrac{1}{2})^j \text{ where } i + j = 36$$

$$= \binom{36}{i} (\tfrac{1}{2})^{36}.$$

This gives the table of values:

i	18	17	16	15	14	13	12	11	10	9
		19	20	21	22	23	24	25	26	27
$p(i)$		0.1321	0.1251	0.1063	0.0810	0.0552	0.0336	0.0182	0.0087	0.0037	0.0014

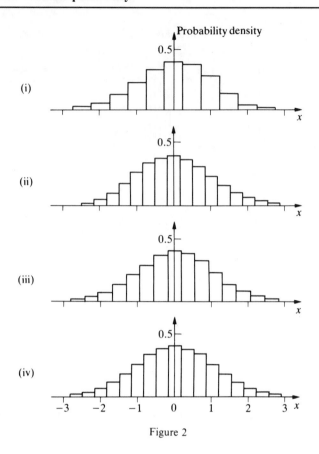

Figure 2

The entries are now changed by translating the mean ($\mu = 18$) to the origin and dividing by the standard deviation ($\sigma = \sqrt{(36 \times \frac{1}{2} \times \frac{1}{2})} = 3$), so that the new variable is

$$x = \tfrac{1}{3}(i - 18).$$

In compensation p(i) is multiplied by 3 to give the probability density, which is denoted by $\phi(x)$:

x	0	$\pm\frac{1}{3}$	$\pm\frac{2}{3}$	±1	$\pm1\frac{1}{3}$	$\pm1\frac{2}{3}$	±2	$\pm2\frac{1}{3}$	$\pm2\frac{2}{3}$	±3
x^2	0.000	0.111	0.444	1.000	1.778	2.778	4.000	5.444	7.111	9.000
$\phi(x)$	0.396	0.375	0.319	0.243	0.166	0.101	0.055	0.026	0.011	0.004

Notice the extra line in this table, giving values of x^2. This is suggested by the symmetry about the 'vertical' axis, which indicates that ϕ is an even function with an equation involving even powers of x.

Q.1   Plot $\phi(x)$ against x^2. Is the shape of the resulting curve familiar?

The answer to the question in Q.1 is that the standard curve most resembling the graph is that of a negative exponential function. To test this possibility, the *logarithm* of $\phi(x)$ can be set against x^2:

x^2	0.000	0.111	0.444	1.000	1.778	2.778	4.000	5.444	7.111	9.000
$\ln \phi(x)$	−0.93	−0.98	−1.14	−1.41	−1.80	−2.29	−2.91	−3.65	−4.50	−5.47

These points are plotted in Fig. 3, and – encouragingly – they appear to lie very close to a straight line. If you have a calculator which is programmed to find lines of regression automatically, the 'line of best fit' can be read off directly in the form

$$\ln \phi(x) \approx -0.50x^2 - 0.91. \text{ (Note 13.2)}$$

In exponential form, this is

$$\phi(x) \approx e^{-0.50x^2} \times e^{-0.91}$$

$$\approx 0.4e^{-0.5x^2}.$$

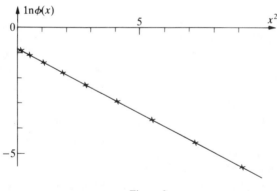

Figure 3

A numerical argument can, of course, only suggest an approximate equation. When the theory is investigated algebraically, it will turn out that the number −0.5 in the exponent is in fact exactly right, but the multiplier 0.4 is an approximation to the exact value $1/\sqrt{(2\pi)}$. The correct equation for the limiting curve is thus

$$\phi(x) = \frac{1}{\sqrt{(2\pi)}} e^{-\frac{1}{2}x^2}. \text{ (Note 13.3)}$$

Q.2 Use a calculator to evaluate $1/\sqrt{(2\pi)}$.

Q.3 Draw a graph of this equation on the same scale as Fig. 2. Using tracing paper, find out how well it fits the graphs in Fig. 2.

This is called the *standard normal probability density function*. It is the most important function in statistics, and it is important to be able to write down and recognise its equation. Many books of statistical tables include a table of values of this function, but nowadays with a calculator it is a simple matter to calculate them when required.

There is, however, no simple way of evaluating the associated cumulative probability function, given by

$$\Phi(x) = \int_{-\infty}^{x} \frac{1}{\sqrt{(2\pi)}}\, e^{-\frac{1}{2}t^2}\, dt \quad \text{(see Note 11.11)}.$$

It is therefore essential to have a table of values of Φ available, and all books of statistical tables contain one in some form or other. (Note 13.4)

Exercise 13A

1   Values of the cumulative normal probability function Φ are usually tabulated only for positive values of x. Use a sketch of the probability density function ϕ to show $\Phi(x)$, where $x < 0$, as an area, and hence show that

$$\Phi(x) = 1 - \Phi(-x).$$

Use this rule to find $\Phi(-\frac{1}{2})$ from your tables.

2   Use tables to find the probabilities that a random variable with standard normal probability density lies between (a) 1 and 2, (b) 0 and 1.5, (c) -0.6 and $+0.6$, (d) -1 and 0.5, (e) -1.5 and -1.

3   Find the number q such that a standard normal random variable has probability $\frac{1}{2}$ of lying within the interval $-q < x < q$.

4   Locate the points of inflection on the graph of the standard normal probability density function ϕ.

5   By writing σ^2 as an integral and using integration by parts, verify that the variance of a standard normal random variable is 1.

6   Find the probabilities that a standard normal random variable lies within n standard deviations of the mean, when $n = 1$, 2 and 3.

7   Use a step-by-step method of integration to solve numerically the differential equation

$$\frac{dy}{dx} = \frac{1}{\sqrt{(2\pi)}}\, e^{-\frac{1}{2}x^2}, \text{ with } y = 0.5 \text{ when } x = 0.$$

Compare your values with the table of the cumulative normal probability function Φ.

8   Calculate the binomial probabilities for the case $a = 0.64$, $b = 0.36$, $n = 25$, and show these on a stick graph. Carry out the transformations on this as described in the text, and hence obtain graphs comparable to those in Figs. 2 and 3. Obtain the equation of the line of best fit, and convert it to exponential form.

13.2 NORMAL PROBABILITY AS A MODEL

Before reading further, refer back to the data which you collected in Exercise 11A, question 1, and the histograms which you constructed from it.

The chances are that, whichever experiments you did, the resulting histograms were 'hump-shaped' – rather like those in Fig. 2. That is, there were probably relatively few individuals at the extremes and more in the middle. For this reason, if we want to devise a theoretical probability model to describe such a situation, and if the histogram looks reasonably symmetrical, then the normal probability density function seems an obvious candidate.

But a word of caution is needed here. There are plenty of other functions with symmetrical hump-shaped graphs besides that of normal probability density; examples are $1/(\pi \cosh x)$ and $1/\{\pi(1 + x^2)\}$ over the domain of all real numbers, or $\frac{3}{8}(1 - \frac{4}{25}x^2)^2$ and $\frac{2}{5}\cos^2(\frac{1}{5}\pi x)$ over the interval $-\frac{5}{2} < x < \frac{5}{2}$. And although in some of the experiments theoretical arguments can be suggested to justify the choice of a normal probability model (see Chapter 16), in others the only evidence is empirical – that is, when we do the experiment it "looks normal". Contrary to popular belief, the converse of the statement "normal probability has a hump-shaped graph" is false!

Q.4   Use a graph program to display on a computer screen the graphs of the four functions mentioned in the previous paragraph, together with the graph of the normal probability density function. Which ones do your own histograms most resemble?

In any case, even if the models for reaction times, hand spans or masses of nuts are of 'normal type', there is one respect in which they all differ from the function $\phi(x)$ described in §13.1: that is, their means are certainly not zero, and it is very unlikely that their standard deviations are 1. So when we speak of data of this kind being "described by a normal probability model", we cannot be referring to the *standard* normal probability model so far defined.

The idea of normal probability must therefore be extended to cover models with a general mean (μ) and standard deviation (σ). This can be done in much the same way as has also been used to adjust binomial models to fit the form of standard normal probability (steps 2 and 3 of §13.1), but in reverse: that is, by enlarging the scale of measures in the ratio $\sigma : 1$ (with corresponding multiplication of the probability density by $1/\sigma$ to maintain the area as 1), and then translating the graph through a displacement μ. These transformations are illustrated in Fig. 4.

The third of these graphs gives the general normal probability density model. By varying μ and σ it offers a wide choice of possible models to describe a variety of situations. The label $N(\mu, \sigma^2)$ is sometimes used to indicate this model; with this convention, the first two graphs in Fig. 4 would be denoted by $N(0, 1)$ and $N(0, \sigma^2)$ respectively.

The quantity $(x - \mu)/\sigma$ which appears in the equation for $N(\mu, \sigma^2)$ is simply, in words, "the number of standard deviations by which x exceeds the mean". So,

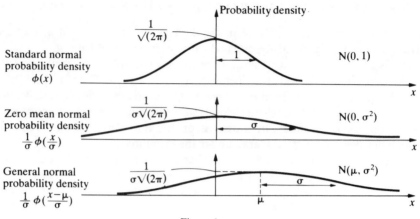

Figure 4

to compute the normal probability density for a particular value of the measured quantity, we merely calculate by how many standard deviations this exceeds the mean, compute the corresponding *standard* normal probability density, and multiply this by $1/\sigma$.

A similar remark applies to the cumulative probability function, except that in this case there is no final multiplication by $1/\sigma$. This is because the cumulative probability is given by the area under a part of the probability density graph, and both the transformations in Fig. 4 leave the area unchanged. The cumulative probability function for general normal probability is therefore just $\Phi((x - \mu)/\sigma)$; one finds by how many standard deviations the particular value of the measured quantity exceeds the mean, and the table for Φ then gives directly the probability that the random variable falls short of this.

Q.5 Draw a sequence of graphs similar to Fig. 4 for the cumulative functions $\Phi(x)$, $\Phi(x/\sigma)$ and $\Phi((x - \mu)/\sigma)$.

To sum up:

The general *normal probability model* with mean μ and standard deviation σ, denoted by $N(\mu, \sigma^2)$, has probability density function $\dfrac{1}{\sigma} \phi\left(\dfrac{x - \mu}{\sigma}\right)$ and cumulative probability function $\Phi\left(\dfrac{x - \mu}{\sigma}\right)$, where $\phi(x) = \dfrac{1}{\sqrt{(2\pi)}} e^{-\frac{1}{2}x^2}$, and $\Phi(x) = \displaystyle\int_{-\infty}^{x} \phi(t)\, dt$.

Another way of expressing this is:

X has general normal probability $N(\mu, \sigma^2)$

$\Leftrightarrow \dfrac{X - \mu}{\sigma}$ has standard normal probability $N(0, 1)$.

Example 1

The labels on packets of butter state that the mass is 200 g. At a particular time the machine is producing packets of mean mass 205 g with standard deviation 2 g. Assuming a normal probability model, what is the probability that a packet selected at random will be found to be underweight?

The situation can be illustrated by either a cumulative probability graph or a probability density graph (Fig. 5). In the former the probability of getting an underweight packet is shown by the height of the graph when the mass is 200 g, in the latter it is shown by the area under the graph to the left of 200 g.

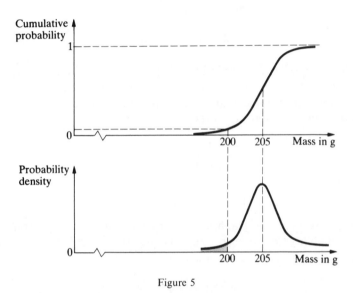

Figure 5

The nominal mass of 200 g is 2.5 standard deviations below the mean; that is, when $x = 200$,

$$\frac{x - \mu}{\sigma} = \frac{200 - 205}{2} = -2.5.$$

So the probability that a random packet will have mass less than 200 g is $\Phi(-2.5)$. This is not given in the tables directly, but it can be found from the relation

$$\Phi(-x) = 1 - \Phi(x)$$

(compare Exercise 13A, question 1), which gives

$$\Phi(-2.5) = 1 - \Phi(2.5) = 1 - 0.9938 \approx 0.006.$$

The probability of an underweight packet is therefore about 0.6%.

13.3 DOES A NORMAL MODEL FIT THE DATA?

Now we can come back to the question raised at the beginning of the last section: given the histogram for a set of experimental data, is normal probability a suitable model to describe it?

It is not at all easy to judge this by eye – especially since, as you will have noticed in your own experiments, histograms can look quite erratic even when quite a large number of readings is available. So in practice it turns out to be more convenient to plot the graph of cumulative relative frequency rather than the histogram of relative frequency density. This transformation was described in §11.6, and you may already have carried it out with your own data in Exercise 11D, question 1. The question is now whether this gives a reasonable fit to an equation of the form

$$\text{cumulative relative frequency} = \Phi\left(\frac{x - \mu}{\sigma}\right),$$

where Φ is the cumulative probability function for normal probability.

This is where we can take a leaf out of the book of experimental science. You probably know, for example, that if you suspect that two variables x and y may be connected by a relationship of the form

$$y = a \times b^x,$$

then this can be tested by plotting the logarithm of y against x, since the corresponding relationship

$$\log y = \log a + x \log b$$

would have a straight line graph. A similar device can be used to test data for normal probability, by transforming the equation for cumulative relative frequency (c.r.f.) given above into the form

$$\Phi^{-1}(\text{c.r.f.}) = \frac{x - \mu}{\sigma}.$$

If then there is a normal model which gives a good fit to the data, the plot of $\Phi^{-1}(\text{c.r.f.})$ against x should give a set of points which all lie close to a straight line.

The method is illustrated by Example 2, and it is suggested that you might carry out a similar analysis of your own experimental data.

Example 2
The marks awarded (grouped by grades) in an A-level examination in mathematics taken by 580 candidates were as follows.

Mark range	0–49	50–104	105–129	130–159	160–181	182–214	215–300
Number of candidates	17	106	88	98	66	115	90

Investigate whether a normal probability model fits this mark distribution.

The first step is to organise these figures to give the cumulative frequency, and thence the cumulative relative frequency, below each grade boundary. A fourth line has been added to the table, giving the values of Φ^{-1}(c.r.f.).

Grade boundary	$49\frac{1}{2}$	$104\frac{1}{2}$	$129\frac{1}{2}$	$159\frac{1}{2}$	$181\frac{1}{2}$	$214\frac{1}{2}$
Cumulative frequency	17	123	211	309	375	490
Cumulative relative frequency	0.029	0.212	0.364	0.533	0.647	0.845
Φ^{-1}(c.r.f.)	-1.89	-0.80	-0.35	-0.08	0.38	1.01

The hypothesis of a normal probability model can then be tested by plotting Φ^{-1}(c.r.f.) against the grade boundaries, to see whether the points lie approximately on a straight line.

In practice, however, it is possible to avoid calculating the last line of the table, by obtaining a sheet of commercially produced "normal probability paper". This is graph paper with a variable scale up the 'vertical' axis, so that the line corresponding to any particular value of the c.r.f. is drawn at a distance from the x-axis proportional to Φ^{-1}(c.r.f.). Fig. 6 shows the data plotted on such paper; in this figure, though, a second vertical axis has been drawn to show how the scale on the graph has been devised. (Note 13.5)

The figure shows that, in this example, the points fit a straight line only moderately well. This could be due to sampling factors, or to bad luck in the choice of the points of subdivision. But the divergence from the 'best straight line' (drawn with a broken line in the figure) has a suspiciously S-shaped form which may indicate that normal probability is not a very suitable model in this case. Although examination results are often discussed on the assumption of a normal probability model, in practice this is rarely applicable to selective examinations such as A-level.

Q.6   The points $(-\frac{1}{2}, 0)$ and $(300\frac{1}{2}, 1)$ clearly do not fit well on the 'best straight line'. Why is a normal probability model certain to be unsuitable at the extremes of the mark range?

Any straight line drawn on normal probability paper corresponds to some normal probability model (except for a line drawn parallel to one of the axes). The values of μ and σ can be read directly from the graph, using the facts that

$$\Phi^{-1}(\text{c.r.f.}) = 0 \Leftrightarrow \frac{x - \mu}{\sigma} = 0 \Leftrightarrow x = \mu$$

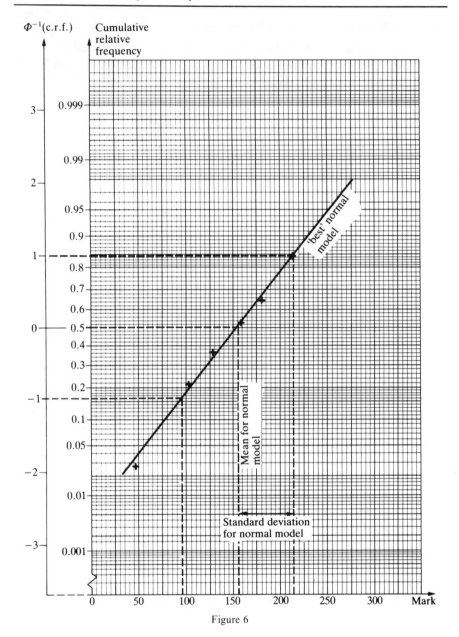

Figure 6

and

$$\Phi^{-1}(\text{c.r.f.}) = 1 \Leftrightarrow \frac{x - \mu}{\sigma} = 1 \Leftrightarrow x = \mu + \sigma.$$

These correspond to values of the cumulative relative frequency of $\Phi(0) = 0.5$ and $\Phi(1) \approx 0.841$ respectively. In the example illustrated in Fig. 6, these are the values for marks of 156 and 215, so that $\mu = 156$ and $\sigma = 215 - 156 = 59$.

Therefore, *if the mark distribution is reasonably described by a normal model,* the best estimates for the mean and standard deviation are about 156 marks and 59 marks respectively.

Q.7   Test your own experimental data for normal probability, and if this model seems suitable estimate the mean and standard deviation.

Exercise 13B

1   The heights of adults may be assumed to be normally distributed with a mean of 175 cm and a standard deviation of 10 cm. Find the percentage of adults having heights (*a*) greater than 186 cm, (*b*) between 170 cm and 180 cm.   [London]

2   Given that the lifetimes in hours of electric light bulbs are normally distributed with mean 2040 and standard deviation 60, estimate the proportion of bulbs which can be expected to have a lifetime exceeding 1960 hours.   [London]

3   The mean survival period of daisies after being sprayed with a certain make of weed killer is 24 days. If the probability of survival after 27 days is $\frac{1}{4}$, estimate the standard deviation of the survival period.   [SMP]

4   Packets of semolina are nominally 226 g in weight. The actual weights have a normal distribution with $\mu = 230.00$ g and $\sigma = 1.50$ g. What is the probability that a packet is underweight?
   A decision is taken that the probability of an underweight packet should not exceed 0.001. To change the distribution of weights of the semolina packets to conform to this decision, two methods are considered:
   (*a*) to increase μ, leaving σ unaltered;
   (*b*) to improve the packing machine, thus reducing σ, while leaving μ unaltered.
   Find the new values (of μ and of σ respectively) required for each method to succeed.   [SMP]

5   Hens' eggs have mean mass 60 g, with standard deviation 15 g, and the distribution may be taken as normal. Eggs of mass less than 45 g are classified as Small. The remainder are divided into Standard and Large, and it is desired that these should occur with equal frequency. Suggest the mass at which the division should be made.   [SMP]

6   Each weekday a man goes to work by bus. His arrival time at the bus stop is normally distributed with standard deviation 3 minutes. His mean arrival time is 8.30 a.m. Buses leave promptly every 5 minutes at 8.21 a.m., 8.26 a.m., etc. Find the probabilities that he catches the buses at (*a*) 8.26 a.m., (*b*) 8.31 a.m., (*c*) 8.36 a.m., assuming that he always gets on the first bus to arrive.
   The man is late for work if he catches a bus after 8.31 a.m. What mean arrival time would ensure that, on the average, he is not late for work more than one day in five?   [MEI]

7   In a certain country the heights of adult males have mean 170 cm and standard deviation 10 cm, and the heights of adult females have mean 160 cm and standard deviation 8 cm; for each sex the distribution of heights approximates closely to a normal probability model. On the hypothesis that height is not a factor in selecting a mate, calculate the probability that a husband and wife selected at random are both taller than 164 cm.   [SMP]

8 In a particular school 1460 pupils were present on a particular day. By 8.40 a.m. 80 pupils had already arrived, and at 9.00 a.m. 12 pupils had not arrived but were on their way to school. By assuming that the frequency function of arrival times approximates to normal form, use tables to estimate
(a) the time by which half of those eventually present had arrived,
(b) the standard deviation of the times of arrival.
If registration occurred at 8.55 a.m. how many would not have arrived by then?
   If each school entrance permitted a maximum of 30 pupils per minute to enter, find the minimum number of entrances required to cope with the 'peak' minute of arrival.   [SMP]

9 X is a normal variable. Calculate the mean and standard deviation of X given that $P(X > 10) = 0.1$ and $P(9 < X < 10) = 0.2$.   [Cambridge]

10 A marketing organisation grades onions into 3 sizes: small (diameter less than 60 mm), medium (diameter between 60 mm and 80 mm) and large (diameter more than 80 mm). A certain grower finds that 61 % of his crop falls into the small category and 14 % into the large category. Assuming that the distribution of diameters of the onions in his crop is described by a normal probability function, sketch a graph showing the information given above.
   On this basis, calculate the standard deviation and the mean of the diameters of the onions in his crop.   [SMP]

11 A man leaves home at 8 a.m. every morning in order to arrive at work at 9 a.m. He finds that over a long period he is late once in forty times. He then tries leaving home at 7.55 a.m. and finds that over a similar period he is late once in one hundred times. Assuming that the time of his journey has a normal distribution, before what time should he leave home in order not to be late more than once in two hundred times?   [SMP]

12 A characteristic of the shape of a human skull is measured by a number n. People are classed into three groups: A (for which $n \leqslant 75$), B ($75 < n \leqslant 80$) and C ($n > 80$). In a certain population the percentages of people within these three groups are 58, 38 and 4 respectively. Assuming that n is distributed normally within this population, determine its mean and standard deviation.
   Three people are chosen randomly from this population. Determine the probabilities that
(a) each of the three has a value of n greater than 70;
(b) at least one of the three has a value of n less than 70.

13 Use the table of cumulative relative frequency in §11.6 to test the hypothesis that the masses of babies at birth can be described by a normal probability model. Assuming this is so, estimate the mean and standard deviation.   [MEI]

14 Rule out sheets of 'probability paper' for the probability density functions $1/\{\pi(1 + x^2)\}$ and $1/(\pi \cosh x)$. Try plotting your own experimental data, the data of A-level marks in Example 2, and the data about masses of babies at birth from §11.6, on these. Is the 'straight line fit' better or worse than it was on normal probability paper?

15 Use the substitution $s = (t - \mu)/\sigma$ to show that, if $\sigma > 0$,

$$\int_{-\infty}^{x} \frac{1}{\sigma\sqrt{(2\pi)}} e^{-(t-\mu)^2/2\sigma^2} \, dt = \int_{-\infty}^{(x-\mu)/\sigma} \frac{1}{\sqrt{(2\pi)}} e^{-\frac{1}{2}s^2} \, ds.$$

Explain the significance of this equation.

13.4 TESTING THE FIT

Plotting on normal probability paper gives a simple, quick way of finding out whether normal probability might be a good model to describe a situation when a sample of experimental values is available. But it can be misleading – particularly since there is no way of showing how large a sample has been used; one would expect to get a better approximation to a straight line graph with a large sample. So it needs to be backed up with a more precise test instrument.

The obvious approach is to adapt the method developed in §10.2, based on the chi-squared probability tables, so that it can be applied to cases where the random variable is continuous. As an illustration, let us examine whether the masses of babies at birth might fit a normal model, on the evidence of the data summarised in Fig. 2 of §11.1. (But see Note 11.6.)

First, then, we need to form a hypothesis, of the form:

"The masses of infants at birth (in the south of England in the last quarter of the 20th century) are described by a normal probability model with mean μ and standard deviation σ."

But the question is, what values of μ and σ to take; we cannot apply a numerical test until this is settled. Perhaps the most natural choice would be to use the mean and standard deviation of the sample of 100 masses which we know. These have been calculated as 3.360 kg and 0.463 kg respectively. So the hypothesis to be tested becomes

Hypothesis 1. The masses of infants at birth are described by a normal probability model with mean 3.360 kg and standard deviation 0.463 kg.

with the alternative hypothesis

Hypothesis 2. The masses of infants at birth are not described by a normal probability model with this mean and standard deviation.

Now the method of §10.2 depends on splitting the experimental data into categories and comparing the observed frequencies with the expected frequencies in each category. With a discrete random variable the choice of categories is usually simple, but when the random variable is continuous it has to be made artificially. The histograms in Figs. 3 and 4 of §11.2 give a clue: by splitting the possibility space into intervals with convenient boundaries, a number of categories can be defined such that the mass of each infant falls into just one of these categories. In what follows we will use the same intervals as in Fig. 4 of §11.2, with the frequencies set out in the second table of that section.

The next problem is to calculate the expected frequencies in each interval, based on the model in hypothesis 1. To do this, we use the property that, for a *standard* normal random variable, the probability of lying within the interval $a < x \leqslant b$ is $\Phi(b) - \Phi(a)$. So the masses m kg are standardised for the given mean and standard deviation by means of the transformation

$$x = \frac{m - 3.360}{0.463},$$

Interval boundary (kg)	$x = \dfrac{m - 3.360}{0.463}$	$\Phi(x)$	Interval	Difference $\Phi(b) - \Phi(a)$	Expected frequency	Observed frequency
2.5	−1.857	0.031	$m \leqslant 2.5$	0.031	3.1	5
2.75	−1.317	0.094	$2.5 < m \leqslant 2.75$	0.063	6.3	2
3.0	−0.778	0.219	$2.75 < m \leqslant 3.0$	0.125	12.5	15
3.1	−0.562	0.287	$3.0 < m \leqslant 3.1$	0.068	6.8	4
3.2	−0.346	0.365	$3.1 < m \leqslant 3.2$	0.078	7.8	11
3.3	−0.130	0.448	$3.2 < m \leqslant 3.3$	0.083	8.3	8
3.4	0.086	0.534	$3.3 < m \leqslant 3.4$	0.086	8.6	9
3.5	0.302	0.619	$3.4 < m \leqslant 3.5$	0.085	8.5	13
3.75	0.842	0.800	$3.5 < m \leqslant 3.75$	0181	18.1	12
4.0	1.382	0.916	$3.75 < m \leqslant 4.0$	0.116	11.6	15
4.5	2.462	0.993	$4.0 < m \leqslant 4.5$	0.077	7.7⎫ 8.4	4⎫ 6
			$m > 4.5$	0.007	0.7⎭	2⎭

Table 1

and the probabilities are then calculated using this property. Finally, the probabilities are converted to expected frequencies by multiplying by 100, the number of masses in the experimental sample. The full calculation is set out in Table 1.

All is now set to test the fit of the model to data, by calculating the discrepancy between the observed and expected frequencies. In Table 1 the last two entries have been combined, to avoid having a category with a very small expected frequency (see §6.8), so that there are eleven pairs of frequencies for comparison; you can check for yourself that the discrepancy is 13.2.

Before we can decide whether this is unacceptably large, the number of degrees of freedom has to be found, using the principle set out in §10.2. In this application both the parameters μ and σ have been determined from the experimental data; the total of the expected frequencies has been made equal to 100, the same as the total of the observed frequencies. So the number of degrees of freedom is three fewer than the number of categories, that is

$$v = 11 - 3 = 8.$$

Now the tables of chi-squared probability give the critical value of the discrepancy, for $P = 5$ and $v = 8$, as 15.51. Since 13.2 is smaller than this, the hypothesis 1 is acceptable at the 5% significance level. That is, a normal probability model with mean and standard deviation equal to those in the sample is consistent with the experimental data.

Q.8 Copy the histogram in Fig. 4 of §11.2, and superimpose on it the graph of normal probability density with mean 3.360 kg and standard deviation 0.463 kg.

Q.9 Does the above argument prove that
"the masses of infants at birth have a normal probability distribution
with mean 3.360 kg and standard deviation 0.463 kg",
or simply that
"the masses of infants at birth have a normal probability distribution"?

Q.10 If hypothesis 1 had been rejected, would this have justified the conclusion
that
"the masses of infants at birth do not have a normal probability
distribution"?

Exercise 13C

1 In an A-level mathematics paper the numbers of candidates in the mark ranges 1-10,
11-20, 21-30, ..., 171-180 were

0 0 12 15 23 26 30 40 45 29 25 33 16 15 18 15 16 9.

A statistical analysis of the marks showed that they had a mean of 94.57 and a
standard deviation of 38.85. Investigate whether this mark distribution could
reasonably be described by a normal probability model having this mean and
standard deviation.

2 Over a period of time a store sold 500 pairs of trousers. The numbers sold in various
waist sizes were:

Waist (cm)	70	75	80	85	90	95	100	105	110
Frequency	5	13	37	88	114	123	82	29	9

Estimate the mean and standard deviation of the waist measurements, and find
whether the figures support the theory that waist measurement follows a normal
probability model. (Note that a customer with, for example, a waist measurement
between 80 and 85 cm requires trousers with an 85 cm waistband.)

3 In the National Child Development Study the heights of children aged between
7 years 3 months and 7 years 4 months were measured to the nearest inch, with the
following results:

Height (in.)	35	36	37	38	39	40	41	42	43	44	45	46	47
Number of { boys	0	0	0	4	8	13	9	20	33	54	129	220	318
of { girls	1	1	0	2	7	12	19	16	41	74	152	269	326

Height (in.)	48	49	50	51	52	53	54	55	56	57	58	59	60
Number of { boys	424	389	275	142	73	27	11	0	0	1	4	2	1
of { girls	396	325	229	110	59	30	7	5	0	1	2	1	3

Investigate how well these measurements fit a normal probability model.

4   The activity of a starch-splitting enzyme in human blood serum in 100 normal healthy adults was measured (Street & Close, in *Nature*, Vol. 179), with the following results:

Activity	3	4	5	6	7	8	9	10	11	12	13
Frequency	3	12	16	19	16	12	11	3	5	1	2

Can we produce a reliable model against which other adults may be judged?

5   Investigate whether the distribution of A-level mathematics marks given in Example 2 of §13.3 are a good fit to a normal probability model.

6   A statistics teacher makes up a question about the length of time that light bulbs last. She uses normal probability tables to invent the following data:

Lifetime of bulb (hours)	Below 1000	1000 -1100	1100 -1200	1200 -1300	1300 -1400	1400 -1500	Above 1500
Frequency	4	34	175	366	305	101	15

Do her figures differ sufficiently from the theoretical values to carry credibility?

7   In an experiment, a continuous random variable having normal probability with mean μ and standard deviation σ takes the value x, measured correct to within a small interval of length h units. Explain why the probability of this result can be taken as $h\phi\left(\dfrac{x-\mu}{\sigma}\right)$, where ϕ denotes the standard normal probability density function.

In n independent repetitions of the experiment the variable takes the values $x_1, x_2, \ldots, x_n$, each measured within an interval of reliability of length h units. Write down the probability that this will occur, and prove that it can be expressed in the form

$$\frac{h^n}{\sigma^n(2\pi)^{\frac{1}{2}n}} e^{-\{nS^2 + n(m-\mu)^2\}/2\sigma^2},$$

where m and S are the mean and standard deviation of $x_1, x_2, \ldots, x_n$.

Regarding this probablity as a likelihood function of μ and σ, where $x_1, x_2, \ldots, x_n$ are known, prove that the likelihood is greatest when $\mu = m$ and $\sigma = S$. How is this relevant to the procedure described in §13.4?

13.5 A THEORETICAL JUSTIFICATION OF NORMAL PROBABILITY

So far the use of the equation for normal probability density has been based solely on the numerical argument in §13.1. Now that we have seen how the model works in practice, it is time to return to the link between binomial and normal probability, and to establish the equation algebraically. (Note 13.6)

To do this, it will be helpful to draw on a result from pure mathematics,

known as *Stirling's approximation*. This is a formula which gives approximations to factorial numbers, and it states that, if n is a not-too-small positive
integer, then

$$n! \approx \sqrt{(2\pi)} n^{n+\frac{1}{2}} e^{-n}.$$

This is proved in books on advanced calculus (Note 13.7), but here it will simply
be assumed. Before going on, however, it would be worth while trying it out
numerically.

Q.11   Use a calculator to find the percentage error in Stirling's approximation
numerically.

Q.12   Show that the ratio of the expressions for $(n + 1)!$ and $n!$ in Stirling's
approximation can be written in the form

$$(n + 1) \times \left(1 + \frac{1}{n}\right)^n \times \left(1 + \frac{1}{n}\right)^{\frac{1}{2}} \times e^{-1}.$$

Use property (2) in §7.1 to explain why this ratio is approximately equal
to $(n + 1)$ when n is large. How does this help to make Stirling's
approximation plausible?

We begin, then, with the general binomial probability function $B(n, a)$, in which
the probability that a discrete random variable takes the value i is

$$p(i) = \frac{n!}{i!\,j!}\, a^i b^j, \text{ where } i + j = n \text{ (see §3.3).}$$

Applying Stirling's approximation to this expression (supposing that n, i and j
are not too small) gives

$$p(i) \approx \frac{\sqrt{(2\pi)} n^{n+\frac{1}{2}} e^{-n}}{\sqrt{(2\pi)} i^{i+\frac{1}{2}} e^{-i} \times \sqrt{(2\pi)} j^{j+\frac{1}{2}} e^{-j}}\, a^i b^j.$$

You can easily check that the powers of e cancel out, because $i + j = n$, so that

$$p(i) \approx \frac{1}{\sqrt{(2\pi)}} \frac{n^{n+\frac{1}{2}}}{i^{i+\frac{1}{2}} j^{j+\frac{1}{2}}}\, a^i b^j.$$

The procedure is now to follow through the three steps set out in §13.1 for
converting binomial probability into normal probability density. The first of
these is to change the probability function into a probability density histogram;
this associates the probability $p(i)$ with the interval from $i - \frac{1}{2}$ to $i + \frac{1}{2}$ rather
than just the point i, but it does not involve any algebraic modification. Next,
steps 2 and 3 reduce the random variable by na and then divide the result by
$\sqrt{(nab)}$, and the effect of this is to define a new random variable

$$x = \frac{i - na}{\sqrt{(nab)}}.$$

In order to substitute this into p(i), it must be turned round to give

$$i = na + x\sqrt{(nab)} = na\left\{1 + x\sqrt{\frac{b}{na}}\right\},$$

and

$$j = n - i = n - na - x\sqrt{(nab)} = nb - x\sqrt{(nab)} = nb\left\{1 - x\sqrt{\frac{a}{nb}}\right\},$$

using the fact that $b = 1 - a$. At the same time (in step 3) the probability density is multiplied by $\sqrt{(nab)}$, so as to preserve the area. The effect of all these transformations is to replace the probability p(i) by the probability density

$$\frac{1}{\sqrt{(2\pi)}}\left[\frac{\sqrt{(nab)}n^{n+\frac{1}{2}}a^i b^j}{(na)^{i+\frac{1}{2}}(nb)^{j+\frac{1}{2}}}\right]\frac{1}{\left\{1 + x\sqrt{\frac{b}{na}}\right\}^{i+\frac{1}{2}}\left\{1 - x\sqrt{\frac{a}{nb}}\right\}^{j+\frac{1}{2}}}.$$

There has been a great deal of rearrangement at this stage, and you should check that you can account for each factor in this expression. The point is that the fraction in the square brackets cancels down to 1, so that the probability density reduces to the much simpler form

$$\frac{1}{\sqrt{(2\pi)}}\frac{1}{P_1 P_2},$$

where P_1 and P_2 denote

$$\left\{1 + x\sqrt{\frac{b}{na}}\right\}^{na+x\sqrt{(nab)}+\frac{1}{2}} \quad \text{and} \quad \left\{1 - x\sqrt{\frac{a}{nb}}\right\}^{nb-x\sqrt{(nab)}+\frac{1}{2}}$$

respectively.

At this stage of the calculation it is worth remembering what we are aiming for, which is the density function for standard normal probability. So what is left to prove is that $1/(P_1 P_2)$ approaches $e^{-\frac{1}{2}x^2}$ when n becomes large. This suggests taking logarithms (to base e), as follows:

$$\ln P_1 = (na + x\sqrt{(nab)} + \tfrac{1}{2})\ln\left(1 + x\sqrt{\frac{b}{na}}\right)$$

$$\approx (na + x\sqrt{(nab)} + \tfrac{1}{2})\left(x\sqrt{\frac{b}{na}} - \tfrac{1}{2}x^2\frac{b}{na} + \tfrac{1}{3}x^3\frac{b}{na}\sqrt{\frac{b}{na}}\right),$$

where in the last line the Taylor approximation $\ln(1 + h) \approx h - \frac{1}{2}h^2 + \frac{1}{3}h^3$ has been used. This is now multiplied out, omitting any terms which contain n to a negative power, since these will tend to zero as $n \to \infty$. The result is

$$\ln P_1 \approx x\sqrt{(nab)} - \tfrac{1}{2}x^2 b + x^2 b = x\sqrt{(nab)} + \tfrac{1}{2}x^2 b.$$

It is left to you to carry out the similar process for $\ln P_2$, which leads to

$$\ln P_2 \approx -x\sqrt{(nab)} + \tfrac{1}{2}x^2 a.$$

We are now home. Adding these two expressions gives

$$\ln(P_1 P_2) = \ln P_1 + \ln P_2 \approx \tfrac{1}{2}x^2(b + a) = \tfrac{1}{2}x^2,$$

so that

$$P_1 P_2 \approx e^{\tfrac{1}{2}x^2}.$$

Substituting this into the expression for the probability density found earlier shows that the limiting value of the probability density is

$$\frac{1}{\sqrt{(2\pi)}}\, e^{-\tfrac{1}{2}x^2},$$

as expected. So it has been established that:

> If any binomial probability function is interpreted as a probability density and transformed to zero mean and unit standard deviation, the limiting form of the probability density function as $n \to \infty$ is that of the standard normal probability density function.

13.6 APPROXIMATING TO BINOMIAL PROBABILITY BY A NORMAL MODEL

One of the advantages of normal probability is that it is very easy to compute: one set of tables serves to calculate the cumulative probabilities for any normal model, whatever its mean and standard deviation.

For binomial probability the situation is very different: the probabilities for each different binomial model have to be calculated separately. Things are even worse when the cumulative probability is needed: to find the probability that a binomial variable I is less than or equal to some value i, there is no alternative to laboriously calculating the probabilities for $I = 0, 1, 2, \ldots, i$ and adding them.

This is where the result stated at the end of §13.5 is very useful. If it is re-interpreted as a statement about approximations when n is large, rather than limits as n tends to infinity, then a simpler normal model can be used as an approximation to a binomial model.

Of course, we have to take account of the translation and rescaling which had to be carried out (steps 2 and 3) in going from the binomial model to the limiting normal form. If I is a binomial random variable with probability model $B(n, a)$, then it is the random variable

$$X = \frac{I - na}{\sqrt{(nab)}},$$

regarded as continuous, which has standard normal probability $N(0, 1)$ in the limit. Following the argument in §13.2, this means that, when n is large, I has approximately general normal probability $N(\mu, \sigma^2)$ with $\mu = na$ and $\sigma = \sqrt{(nab)}$; that is, $N(na, nab)$.

If the general binomial probability function is interpreted as a probability density, then when n is large it approximates to a general normal probability density function with mean na and standard deviation $\sqrt{(nab)}$.

This is a very useful result. A typical application is given in the following example.

Example 3
A psychical research investigator carries out an experiment in which subjects are asked to pick the ace out of five cards placed face downwards on the table. Each subject is tested 100 times. How many successes would the subject need to achieve for the investigator to conclude, at the 5 % level of significance, that she has a special gift for detecting aces?

As usual, we begin by putting forward a null hypothesis:

Hypothesis 1. The probability that the subject will select an ace on each test is 0.2.

If the subject has a special gift, then this probability would be greater than 0.2, so the alternative hypothesis is:

Hypothesis 2. The probability that the subject will select an ace is greater than 0.2.

On hypothesis 1, the probability model for the number of successes in 100 trials is B(100, 0.2), with mean $100 \times 0.2 = 20$ and standard deviation $\sqrt{(100 \times 0.2 \times 0.8)} = 4$. This null hypothesis will be rejected if the subject picks the ace a certain number of times, r say, such that the probability of getting r or more right is less than 0.05 (see Fig. 7(a)).

It would clearly be very laborious to calculate r directly, which would involve adding the probabilities of getting 100, 99, 98, ... right until the sum exceeded 0.05. It is far simpler to approximate to the binomial probability by the normal probability with the same mean and standard deviation (Fig. 7(b)). The condition that then has to be satisfied by an unacceptable score x is

$$1 - \Phi\left(\frac{x - 20}{4}\right) < 0.05.$$

Tables of the cumulative normal probability function can now be used to give the condition

$$\frac{x - 20}{4} > 1.6449 \quad \text{(Note 13.8)},$$

so that $x > 26.58$.

You might be tempted to think from this that, in the discrete problem, $r = 27$ would be the critical number of successes; but some care is needed at this stage of the argument. This is because, in moving from the binomial model to the approximate normal form, the first step was to replace the stick graph by a histogram with rectangles 1 unit wide and the same height. The probability

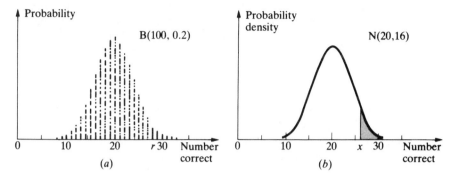

Figure 7

P(number correct $\geqslant$ 27) for the discrete model should therefore be interpreted as P(number correct > 26.5) when it is replaced by the continuous model; and the calculation shows that this is just greater than 0.05. (Note 13.9) So the criterion for rejecting the null hypothesis must be "28 or more correct", whose probability corresponds to P(number correct > 27.5) in the continuous model, which is certainly less than 0.05.

This modification of the inequality condition when a probability model for a discrete random variable is replaced by one for a continuous random variable is called a *continuity correction*. It arises quite frequently when applying normal probability to situations in which the random variable can take only whole number values, not just in the case of approximation to binomial probability. A diagram showing the probability function in the form of a histogram can often help to clarify the argument.

Exercise 13D

1   Find the probability that, of 10 000 digits each chosen at random from the digits 0 to 9, (a) the digit 7 appears at most 1030 times, (b) the digit 7 appears at most 980 times.
                                                                                                [London]

2   A nurseryman found over a long period of years that the proportion of his broad bean seeds that germinated was 0.9. This year he planted 500 seeds and found that only 439 of them came up. Is this number significantly less than he would expect from past experience?   [SMP]

3   During August 1975 the numbers of live births registered in Cambridge were 64 boys and 38 girls. Comment on these figures.

4   A bus company allots a certain time for a particular bus journey. One hundred bus journeys are timed by a dissatisfied consumer organisation and they find that 35 of these journeys take longer than the allotted time. The company protests that there is no need to alter their timetable schedules since on about a quarter of all occasions some external factor (such as level crossings, road works, etc.) makes a vehicle late. Examine their claim.   [SMP]

5   In an experiment to investigate extra-sensory perception one card is drawn at random from an ordinary pack of 52 by the 'sender'; he then concentrates on the suit of the card drawn, trying to communicate the name of the suit to a second person, the 'receiver', who is in another room. The card is returned to the pack and the pack is shuffled after each trial. In an extended series of trials the receiver correctly identifies the suit of the card in 291 trials out of 1000. Explain carefully, with supporting calculations, whether you regard this result as contradicting the supposition that results are obtained entirely by guesswork.   [Cambridge]

6   A machine produces screws, some of which are known to be faulty. An inspection scheme is devised by taking random samples of 1000 screws from a large batch produced by the machine and noting the number x of faulty screws in the sample. If $x > 80$ the batch is rejected, but if $x \leqslant 80$ the batch is accepted. Find the probabilities of
(a) accepting a batch containing 5% faulty screws,
(b) rejecting a batch containing 10% faulty screws.   [MEI]

7   If the probability of a male birth is 0.514, what is the probability that there will be fewer boys than girls in 1000 births?
    How large a sample should be taken to reduce the probability of fewer boys than girls to less than 5%?   [SMP]

8   A grain merchant has a batch of seed which he knows is either of strain A or of strain B. On average 60% of strain A and 90% of strain B will germinate. He plans to plant n seeds, selected at random from the batch, and to regard the batch as strain A if y or fewer germinate, and as strain B if more than y germinate.
    If the seed is strain A, the merchant wishes to plant just sufficient seed to be 99% certain that his test does not mislead him into regarding it as strain B. Show that n and y must satisfy

$$y + \tfrac{1}{2} \approx 0.6n + 1.14\sqrt{n}.$$

The merchant also wishes to be 95% certain that, should the seed be of strain B, his test does not mislead him into regarding it as strain A. Show that

$$y + \tfrac{1}{2} \approx 0.9n - 0.49\sqrt{n},$$

and hence find suitable values for n and y.   [SMP]

9   In the experiment described in Example 3 of §13.6, explain why the probability of picking *exactly* r aces can be found approximately as $\phi(z)$ for an appropriate value of z. Calculate this for $r = 20$, 25 and 30, and compare the results with the exact values.

10   In a certain book the frequency function for the number of words per page may be taken as approximately normal with mean 800 and standard deviation 50. If I choose three pages at random, what is the probability that none of them lies between 830 and 845 words each (inclusive)?   [SMP]

11   The intelligence of an individual is frequently described by a positive integer known as an IQ (Intelligence quotient). The distribution of IQs amongst children of a certain age-group can be approximated by a normal probability model with mean 100 and standard deviation 15. Write a sentence stating what you understand about the age-group from the fact that $\Phi(2.5) = 0.994$.
    A class of 30 children is selected at random from the age-group. Calculate the probability that at least one member of the class has an IQ of 138 or more.   [SMP]

12   Ornithologists reckon that, of the birds which they ring, about 1 in 50 are recovered and reported back to them. If n birds of one species are ringed at a particular site (where n is a large number), what is the expected number which will be reported back, and the variance of that number?

How large should n be to give a 95% probability of getting at least 20 reports back?

14

Expectation – a useful shorthand

The fact that in probability theory there are two kinds of random variable, discrete and continuous, could be rather tiresome. It ought not to be necessary to work through all the theory twice, with two different sets of formulae.

For this reason a notation has been devised which can be applied equally to random variables of either type. The immediate effect of this is that you will be asked to take on board yet another system of symbols for dealing with concepts such as mean, variance, probability generator, etc. But in the long term it will prove well worth while, since it will greatly simplify the presentation of the theory of estimation and sampling, which are two of the central themes of statistics.

This chapter will concentrate on the algebraic rules needed to work with this notation, which will then be applied to statistical problems in the chapters which follow.

14.1 SOME DEFINITIONS

As an example of the parallel formulae used with discrete and continuous random variables, consider the defnitions of the theoretical mean given in §§9.2 and 11.4:

$$\mu = \sum_{i=1}^{k} x_i \mathrm{p}(x_i) \quad \text{and} \quad \mu = \int_{x \in U} x\phi(x)\, dx.$$

What is needed is a notation which describes the right side of either of these equations, and which conveys the idea (see §9.1) of the "expected value" of the random variable X, with the probability function p or the probability density function ϕ as appropriate. The symbol used for this is $E[X]$, where the letter E stands for expected value or (as we usually say) "expectation". (Note 14.1)

Obviously the introduction of this notation does not achieve anything of itself. The advantage lies in two consequences:

(a) The same notation can be used to describe a wide range of probability parameters.

(b) A simple set of rules can be found for manipulating the symbol.

To illustrate (a), consider the formulae for variance:

$$\sigma^2 = \sum_{i=1}^{k} (x_i - \mu)^2 \mathrm{p}(x_i) \quad \text{and} \quad \sigma^2 = \int_{x \in U} (x - \mu)^2 \phi(x)\, dx.$$

218

The only difference between these expressions and the corresponding ones for μ is that the multipliers of the probabilities are now $(x_i - \mu)^2$ or $(x - \mu)^2$ rather than x_i or x. This suggests that the expectation notation could be applied to these formulae as well, describing σ^2 as the "expectation of $(X - \mu)^2$", and writing

$$\sigma^2 = E[(X - \mu)^2].$$

Actually, this is such an important quantity that it is also given a symbol of its own within the system: it is common to write

$$\sigma^2 = V[X], \quad \text{(Note 14.2)}$$

the letter V being chosen to stand for "variance". Thus, by definition,

$$V[X] = E[(X - \mu)^2].$$

More generally still, the notation is extended to define the expectation of *any* function of the random variable X:

If f is a function of a random variable X, the *expectation* of f is defined as

$$E[f(X)] = \sum_{i=1}^{k} f(x_i)p(x_i) \quad \text{or} \quad \int_{x \in U} f(x)\phi(x)\, dx$$

according as the random variable is discrete or continuous.
   In particular, if $f(x) = (x - \mu)^2$, then $E[f(X)]$ is called the *variance* of X, and is written as $V[X]$.

As for the point (b) above, the algebra of the expectation notation is explored in the following exercise.

Exercise 14A

1   If X is any random variable, discrete or continuous, and c is constant, what value do the definitions suggest for $E[c]$?
   Prove also that $E[X + c] = E[X] + c$ and that $E[cX] = c\,E[X]$. Interpret these equations in terms of transformations of the random variable.

2   Use the definitions to prove that $E[f(X) + g(X)] = E[f(X)] + E[g(X)]$ and that $E[cf(X)] = c\,E[f(X)]$. Show that the equations in the second paragraph of question 1 are a special case of these.

3   Prove that $E[(X - E[X])] = 0$.
   What meaning is attached to the symbol $E[(X - E[X])^2]$?

4   Use the results of questions 1 and 2 to prove that

$$V[X] = E[X^2] - \mu^2 = E[X^2] - \{E[X]\}^2.$$

5   If c is constant, prove that $V[c] = 0$, $V[X + c] = V[X]$ and $V[cX] = c^2V[X]$. Interpret these equations in terms of transformations of the random variable.

6   Under what conditions is $E[X^2]$ equal to $\{E[X]\}^2$?

7   Establish the sums

$$1 \times 2 + 2 \times 3 + \ldots + n(n + 1) = \tfrac{1}{3}n(n + 1)(n + 2)$$

and

$$\frac{1}{1 \times 2} + \frac{1}{2 \times 3} + \ldots + \frac{1}{n(n + 1)} = \frac{n}{n + 1}.$$

A random variable X takes the values 1×2, 2×3, ..., $n(n + 1)$ each with probability $1/n$. Find expressions for $E[X]$ and $E[1/X]$, and verify that $E[1/X]$ is *not* equal to $1/E[X]$.

8   Prove that $E[(X - \mu)^3] = E[X^3] - 3\mu\sigma^2 - \mu^3$.
Find a similar expression for $E[(X - \mu)^4]$.

9   If X has uniform probability density over the interval $-\tfrac{1}{2}\pi \leqslant x \leqslant \tfrac{1}{2}\pi$, find the values of (a) $E[\cos X]$, (b) $E[\cos^2 X]$.

10   If X has probability density given by $\phi(x) = 2x$ over the interval $0 \leqslant x \leqslant 1$, find the values of $E[X]$ and $V[X]$, and of $E[\sqrt{X}]$ and $V[\sqrt{X}]$.

11   Two fair dice are thrown and the greater of the two scores showing (or either score if they are the same) is denoted by Y. Find the values of $E[Y]$ and $V[Y]$.
If Z is the lesser of the two scores showing (or either score if they are the same), explain why

$$P(Z = i) = P(Y = 7 - i)$$

and hence show that $E[Z] = 2.53$ (approximately) and calculate $V[Z]$.   [SMP]

12   For a standardised normal variable X, what are the values of $E[X]$ and the variance $V[X]$? Deduce the value of $E[X^2]$. Given that the probability density function of X is

$$\phi(x) = \frac{1}{\sqrt{(2\pi)}} \, e^{-\frac{1}{2}x^2},$$

show by integrating by parts that $E[X^4] = 3\,E[X^2]$.
Use the above results to find the mean and variance of the variable X^2.
                                                                        [SMP]

13   The random variable X has a Poisson distribution (for $\lambda > 0$) given by $P(X = r) = e^{-\lambda}\lambda^r/r!$, $r = 0, 1, 2, \ldots$. Show that $Y = \lambda^{-\frac{1}{2}}(X - \lambda)$ has an expected value of zero and variance of 1. By expanding $X^{\frac{1}{2}}$ as a power series in Y when λ is very large, show that $X^{\frac{1}{2}}$ has mean and variance approximately given by $\lambda^{\frac{1}{2}}$ and $\tfrac{1}{4}$ respectively.
                                                                        [MEI]

14.2 COMBINING RANDOM VARIABLES

The results in the last exercise all refer to a single random variable X, that is, a real variable with its associated probability function. An important development of the notation is to situations where there are two (or more) random variables X and Y, each with its own separate probability function, which are combined in some way. For example, one might be making a journey across town involving two buses: X could be the time of the journey by the first bus and Y the time by the second (each including the wait at the bus stop), so that the total time for the journey is $X + Y$. If the expectation and the variance for both X and Y are known, it would be useful to find the expectation and the variance for $X + Y$.

To get an idea of what is involved in answering a question of this kind, it may be helpful to begin by considering a numerical example. This has been made entirely artificial, but has been devised to highlight an important distinction.

Example 1
Fig. 1 illustrates two possibility spaces in the form of sets of 10 points. In both cases the probability associated with each point is 0.1. Calculate the expectation and the variance of X, Y, $X + Y$ and XY.

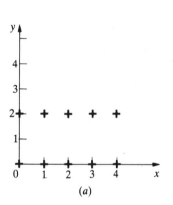
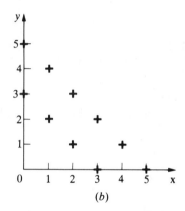

Figure 1

The procedure is to find the probability functions for each of these random variables, and then to apply the formulae for expectation and variance. See Tables 1 and 2. You should check the details of the calculations for yourself.

Value of X	Prob.	Value of Y	Prob.	Value of $X + Y$	Prob.	Value of XY	Prob.
0	0.2	0	0.5	0	0.1	0	0.6
1	0.2	2	0.5	1	0.1	2	0.1
2	0.2			2	0.2	4	0.1
3	0.2			3	0.2	6	0.1
4	0.2			4	0.2	8	0.1
				5	0.1		
				6	0.1		
$E[X] = 2$		$E[Y] = 1$		$E[X + Y] = 3$		$E[XY] = 2$	
$V[X] = 2$		$V[Y] = 1$		$V[X + Y] = 3$		$V[XY] = 8$	

Table 1:   Model (a)

Value of X	Prob.	Value of Y	Prob.	Value of X + Y	Prob.	Value of XY	Prob.
0	0.2	0	0.2	3	0.4	0	0.4
1	0.2	1	0.2	5	0.6	2	0.2
2	0.2	2	0.2			4	0.2
3	0.2	3	0.2			6	0.2
4	0.1	4	0.1				
5	0.1	5	0.1				
$E[X] = 2.1$		$E[Y] = 2.1$		$E[X + Y] = 4.2$		$E[XY] = 2.4$	
$V[X] = 2.49$		$V[Y] = 2.49$		$V[X + Y] = 0.96$		$V[XY] = 5.44$	

Table 2:   Model (b)

The purpose is now to look for connections between the various expectations and variances which have been calculated. You will notice that, for both models,

$$(1) \quad E[X + Y] = E[X] + E[Y];$$

and that, in model (a) but *not* in model (b),

$$(2) \quad E[XY] = E[X] \times E[Y],$$

and

$$(3) \quad V[X + Y] = V[X] + V[Y].$$

This provokes the question: what is the essential difference between the two models?

Now model (a) is of a type with which we are familiar; Fig. 1(a) may remind you, for example, of Fig. 3 in §2.3. It is the model which you would get if two spinners were spun simultaneously, one having five equal sectors labelled 0, 1, 2, 3, 4 (score X) and the other having two sectors labelled 0, 2 (score Y). The important feature is that the scores on the two spinners are *independent*. That is, the probability that X takes any particular value in its possibility space is unaffected by the value taken by Y in its possibility space. If this is so, then the multiplication law for probabilities (§1.3) applies: for any numbers i, j in their respective possibility spaces,

$$P((X, Y) = (i, j)) = P(X = i) \times P(Y = j).$$

Q.1   Check that this law holds in model (a).

Model (b) is clearly quite different. First, the probability of X taking a particular value depends on the value of Y with which it is paired: consider, for instance, the three conditional probabilities

$$P(X = 0 | Y = 5) = 1, \ P(X = 0 | Y = 3) = 0.5, \ P(X = 0 | Y = 4) = 0.$$

Also, the product law does not hold. For instance,

$P((X, Y) = (3, 2)) = 0.1$, whereas $P(X = 3) \times P(Y = 2) = 0.2 \times 0.2 = 0.04$.

The suggestion is obvious. Of the three relations listed above, we expect (1) to be true in every case, but we expect (2) and (3) to hold when X and Y are independent random variables, but not (necessarily) otherwise.

14.3 AN APPROACH TO PROOF

It is best to concentrate first on (1) and (2), and then to show that (3) can be deduced directly from these.

The main idea is very simple, but the difficult part is handling the notation. So, to keep this within bounds, let us first consider a model in which the random variable X takes just three possible values x_1, x_2, x_3, and Y takes just two possible values y_1, y_2. Each of the six possible pairings (x_i, y_j) will have a probability associated with it; for the present these will just be denoted by the letters r, s, t, u, v, w, as indicated in Fig. 2.

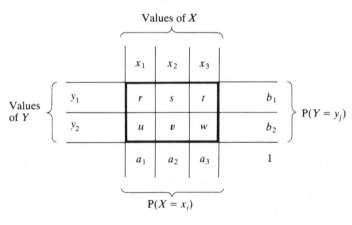

Figure 2

This diagram also shows, in the border on the right, the probabilities that Y takes the values y_1 and y_2, which are denoted by b_1 and b_2; and, in the border at the bottom, the probabilities that X takes the values x_1, x_2 and x_3, which are denoted by a_1, a_2 and a_3. The addition law for probabilities (§1.2) shows that these probabilities are the sums of the entries in the corresponding rows and columns respectively.

Q.2   Make out such diagrams for models (a) and (b) of Example 1.

Once the notation is set up, the work is as good as done; all that is needed is to write out the expressions for $E[X + Y]$ and $E[XY]$ and rearrange the terms appropriately.

(1) There are (in general) six values of $X + Y$, one for each pairing (x_i, y_j), so that

$$E[X + Y] = (x_1 + y_1)r + (x_2 + y_1)s + (x_3 + y_1)t + (x_1 + y_2)u +$$
$$(x_2 + y_2)v + (x_3 + y_2)w.$$

This can be reorganised as

$$E[X + Y] = x_1(r + u) + x_2(s + v) + x_3(t + w) + y_1(r + s + t) +$$
$$y_2(u + v + w),$$

which, by summing columns and rows, is

$$E[X + Y] = (x_1a_1 + x_2a_2 + x_3a_3) + (y_1b_1 + y_2b_2)$$

$$= E[X] + E[Y].$$

Notice that this makes no assumption about the independence of X and Y.

(2) Again there are (in general) six values of XY, and

$$E[XY] = x_1y_1r + x_2y_1s + x_3y_1t + x_1y_2u + x_2y_2v + x_3y_2w.$$

This time no further simplification is possible by purely algebraic means. But *if X and Y are independent* the product law enables us to write each of the probabilities r, s, ..., w in the form $a_i \times b_j$. The expression then becomes

$$E[XY] = x_1y_1a_1b_1 + x_2y_1a_2b_1 + x_3y_1a_3b_1 + x_1y_2a_1b_2 + x_2y_2a_2b_2 +$$
$$x_3y_2a_3b_2,$$

and this can be recognised as a product:

$$E[XY] = (x_1a_1 + x_2a_2 + x_3a_3) \times (y_1b_1 + y_2b_2)$$

$$= E[X] \times E[Y], \text{ as expected.}$$

We will return to these proofs in the next section, for there is more to be said about them. But to round off the discussion based on the observations of Example 1, we turn first to the expansion of $V[X + Y]$, which is also expected to hold when X and Y are independent.

(3) The key to the proof lies in the relation

$$V[X] = E[X^2] - \{E[X]\}^2,$$

which was obtained in Exercise 14A, question 4. Applying this to the random variable $X + Y$ gives

$$V[X \pm Y] = E[(X \pm Y)^2] - \{E[X \pm Y]\}^2$$

$$= E[X^2 + Y^2 \pm 2XY] - \{E[X \pm Y]\}^2$$

$$= E[X^2] + E[Y^2] \pm 2\,E[XY] - \{E[X] \pm E[Y]\}^2, \text{ using (1).}$$

Multiplying out the final bracket and rearranging the terms leads to

$$V[X \pm Y] = (E[X^2] - \{E[X]\}^2) + (E[Y^2] - \{E[Y]\}^2)$$
$$+ 2(E[XY] \mp E[X]E[Y]).$$

$$= V[X] + V[Y] \pm 2(E[XY] \mp E[X]E[Y]).$$

So far this is valid whether or not X and Y are independent, since only (1) has been used. However, in the special case of independence, (2) shows that the final bracket is zero, so that the equation reduces to

$$V[X + Y] = V[X] + V[Y].$$

Q.3   Check numerically that the more general expression for $V[X + Y]$ is correct for Example 1, model (b).

Exercise 14B

1   Carry out the computations of Example 1 for the space of 10 points illustrated in Fig. 3, each point having a probability of 0.1 associated with it. Investigate whether
    (a) X and Y are independent random variables,
    (b) $E[XY] = E[X]E[Y]$,
    (c) $V[X + Y] = V[X] + V[Y]$.
    Comment on your results.

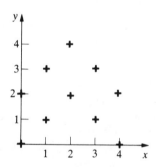

Figure 3

2   By writing $X - Y$ as $X + (-Y)$, express $V[X - Y]$ in terms of $V[X]$ and $V[Y]$, given that X and Y are independent random variables.
    A child marks off two points on a line with a ruler, at the marks for 2 cm and 10 cm respectively. At each end there is the possibility of a small random error, with mean zero and standard deviation 0.1 cm. Find the mean and standard deviation for the length of the segment of the line between the points.

3   A science student finds the mass of liquid in a container by using mass of liquid = mass of (container + liquid) − mass of container. Her measurements are each subject to an error with mean zero and standard deviation 0.7 g. Find the standard deviation of the error in the calculated mass of the liquid.

4   If X and Y are independent random single digit numbers other than zero, calculate the variance of (a) X, (b) $2X$, (c) $X + Y$, (d) $2X - Y$.   [SMP]

5   A die is thrown once and X denotes the score obtained. Calculate $E[X]$ and show that $V[X] = \frac{35}{12}$.

The die is thrown twice, and X_1 and X_2 denote the scores obtained. Tabulate the probability distribution of $Y = |X_1 - X_2|$, and find $E[Y]$.

The random variable Z is defined by $Z = X_1 - X_2$. State with reasons whether or not (a) $E[Z^2] = E[Y^2]$, (b) $V[Z] = V[Y]$.   [Cambridge]

6   Generalise equations (1), (2) and (3) to sets of three, and then n, random variables.

7   Each of the variables X_1, X_2, X_3 independently takes values from the set $\{-1, 0, 1\}$ with probablities 0.2, 0.6, 0.2 respectively; and the variable Y is defined to be the median of X_1, X_2, X_3. Show that $P(Y = -1) = 0.104$ and deduce $P(Y = 1)$ and $P(Y = 0)$.

Calculate $E[Y]$ and $V[Y]$, and determine whether the variance of Y exceeds that of the mean of X_1, X_2, X_3.   [SMP]

8   The random variable Y is distributed with mean μ and variance σ^2. An observation, y, is subject to a rounding error x, where the random variable X is distributed rectangularly with domain $-\frac{1}{2}h \leqslant x \leqslant \frac{1}{2}h$. Show that provided h is less than 11% of σ then the rounding error inflates the variance of Y by less than 0.1%, assuming that X is independent of Y. Why is the result not affected where sample means are concerned?   [MEI]

9   If the random variables $X_1, X_2, \ldots, X_n$ are independent and have variances $\sigma_1^2, \sigma_2^2, \ldots, \sigma_n^2$, show that the mean

$$\bar{X} = (X_1 + X_2 + \ldots + X_n)/n$$

has variance $(\sigma_1^2 + \sigma_2^2 + \ldots + \sigma_n^2)/n^2$.

An experimenter takes successive readings of an instrument, but owing to fatigue the variance of his readings increases linearly with each observation, so that $\sigma_r^2 = A + Br$. Find the variance of the mean of n successive readings. Show that this can never be less than a certain value however many readings he takes.

Discuss what would happen if fatigue made the experimenter's variance increase even more rapidly with each successive observation.   [SMP]

10   X and Y are independent random variables, and a, b are non-zero unequal positive numbers. Explain why

$$P(X^2 = a^2) = P(X = a) + P(X = -a),$$

and deduce that

$$P(X^2 = a^2) \times P(Y^2 = b^2) = P((X^2, Y^2) = (a^2, b^2)).$$

Say what this implies about the random variables X^2, Y^2, and deduce that

$$E[X^2 Y^2] = E[X^2]E[Y^2].$$

Deduce that, for independent random variables X, Y,

$$V[XY] = V[X]V[Y] + \{E[X]\}^2 V[Y] + \{E[Y]\}^2 V[X].$$

Check this numerically in model (a) of Example 1.

11   Rectangular sheets of card are trimmed by two guillotines, set at right angles to each other. One cuts the card to a length of 20 cm, with standard deviation 0.2 cm; the other cuts it to a width of 15 cm, with standard deviation 0.1 cm. Calculate the mean of the area, and use the result of question 10 to calculate the variance.

12   A measure of the correlation between two random variables X, Y is the *covariance* $C[X, Y]$, which is defined as $E[(X - \mu_x)(Y - \mu_y)]$, where μ_x, μ_y denote the means $E[X]$ and $E[Y]$.

(a) Prove that $C[X, Y] = E[XY] - E[X]E[Y]$, and hence that $V[X + Y] = V[X] + V[Y] + 2C[X, Y]$.

(b) Prove that, if X, Y are independent, then $C[X, Y] = 0$. Is the converse true?

(c) Write in alternative forms $C[X, X], C[aX, bY], C[X + a, Y + b], C[X, Y + Z], C[X, X + Y]$.

(d) Explain why $E[(aX + bY)^2] \geqslant 0$ for all a and b. Deduce that

$$\{E[XY]\}^2 \leqslant E[X^2]E[Y^2], \text{ and hence that } \{C[X,Y]\}^2 \leqslant C[X, X]C[Y, Y]$$

13   The variables X, Y are distributed independently with the same variance σ^2 ($\neq 0$), but with possibly different means μ, v. A linear transformation is now made to variables Z, W defined by

$$Z = aX + bY, W = cX + dY,$$

where a, b, c, d are constants. Find an expression for the covariance of Z and W in terms of (some or all of) $a, b, c, d, \mu, v, \sigma^2$ and show that $E[ZW] = E[Z]E[W]$ if, and only if, $ac + bd = 0$.   [SMP]

14   An unbiased cubical die is thrown twice. Let X_1 be the score on the first throw and X_2 the score on the second throw. Random variables Z and W are defined by

$$Z = X_1 + X_2, W = 3X_1 - 2X_2.$$

Find (a) $E[W]$, (b) $V[W]$, (c) $C[X_1, X_2]$, (d) $C[X_1, Z]$.   [Cambridge]

15   A sample consists of two observations X_1, X_2 that have been drawn independently and at random from a population with $E[X] = 0$, $E[X^2] = \mu_2$ and $E[X^4] = \mu_4$. Show that the sample variance is given by

$$S^2 = \tfrac{1}{4}(X_1 - X_2)^2.$$

By expanding this expression and its square, prove that

$$(a)\ E[S^2] = \tfrac{1}{2}\mu_2, (b)\ E[S^4] = \tfrac{3}{8}\mu_2^2 + \tfrac{1}{8}\mu_4,$$

and hence find an expression for $V[S^2]$.

Show that $V[\bar{X}^2] = \tfrac{1}{8}\mu_2^2 + \tfrac{1}{8}\mu_4$, where $\bar{X}$ is the mean of the sample $\{X_1, X_2\}$.

Verify that $S^2 + \bar{X}^2 = \tfrac{1}{2}(X_1^2 + X_2^2)$, and use this result to show that the variance of $S^2 + \bar{X}^2$ is equal to the sum of the variances of S^2 and $\bar{X}^2$ only if a certain condition holds relating μ_2 and μ_4.   [SMP]

14.4 EXTENDING AND FORMALISING

The rest of this chapter introduces no new results, but is concerned with putting the relations (1) to (3) of §14.2 on a firmer mathematical basis. You may if you wish leave this to a second reading, and go on to the applications in the following chapters.

The proofs of (1) and (2) given in §14.3 can be extended in an obvious way to discrete random variables X, Y whose possibility spaces have respectively k values $x_1, x_2, \ldots, x_k$ and l values $y_1, y_2, \ldots, y_l$, though they would look rather untidy when written out. It would obviously be more compact (though not necessarily more intelligible!) to use Σ-notation. A further advantage of doing this is that it gives an indication what modifications might be needed to the proofs when X and Y are continuous random variables or when the possibility spaces are infinite.

Most of the notation can be taken over directly from the special case dealt with earlier, in which $k = 3$ and $l = 2$. The only major change is that it is no longer practicable to use single letters r, s, t, u, v, w to denote the separate probabilities; one needs a notation which indicates clearly which probability is which. To do this, it is best to use a 'double suffix' notation, using a symbol such as c_{ij} to denote the probability that $X = x_i$ and $Y = y_j$. Fig. 4 then shows the enlarged and modified version of Fig. 2. Notice that the relations between the probabilities, obtained by summing columns and rows in Fig. 4, now take the forms

$$\sum_{j=1}^{l} c_{ij} = a_i \quad \text{and} \quad \sum_{i=1}^{k} c_{ij} = b_j.$$

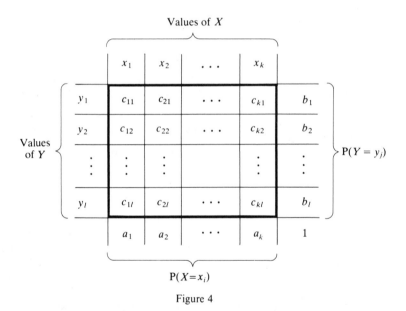

Figure 4

The proof then follows through exactly the same steps as in the special case.

Step 1. $E[X + Y]$ is defined as

$$\sum\sum (x_i + y_j)c_{ij},$$

where the symbol $\Sigma\Sigma$ indicates that summation takes place over all possible pairs of suffices i, j such that $1 \leqslant i \leqslant k$ and $1 \leqslant j \leqslant l$. This is split into two sums

$$\sum\sum x_i c_{ij} + \sum\sum y_j c_{ij}.$$

Step 2.   The first sum is found by first adding the columns (that is, j goes from 1 to l whilst i is kept constant, for each i) and then adding the column totals horizontally (that is, i goes from 1 to k). The second sum is found the other way, by first adding the rows and then adding the row totals vertically. In symbolic form,

$$E[X + Y] = \sum_{i=1}^{k} \left\{ \sum_{j=1}^{l} x_i c_{ij} \right\} + \sum_{j=1}^{l} \left\{ \sum_{i=1}^{k} y_j c_{ij} \right\}$$

Step 3.   Since x_i remains constant through the 'inner' sum in the term on the left, and y_j remains constant through the 'inner' sum on the right, these factors can be taken outside the 'bracket' (that is, the summation). The expressions can then be simplified by using the relations between the probabilities stated above.

$$E[X + Y] = \sum_{i=1}^{k} \left\{ x_i \sum_{j=1}^{l} c_{ij} \right\} + \sum_{j=1}^{l} \left\{ y_j \sum_{i=1}^{k} c_{ij} \right\}$$

$$= \sum_{i=1}^{k} x_i a_i + \sum_{j=1}^{l} y_j b_j.$$

Step 4.   All that remains to complete the proof is to recognise these sums as $E[X]$ and $E[Y]$ respectively.

This deals with (1). For (2), it is necessary to use the independence condition by noting that, in this case,

$$c_{ij} = a_i b_j,$$

so that

$$E[XY] = \sum\sum x_i y_j c_{ij} = \sum\sum x_i y_j a_i b_j.$$

This can be summed 'rows first' as

$$\sum_{j=1}^{l} \left\{ \sum_{i=1}^{k} (x_i a_i)(y_j b_j) \right\},$$

and the factor $y_j b_j$ can be taken out of the inner sum to give

$$\sum_{j=1}^{l} \left\{ y_j b_j \sum_{i=1}^{k} x_i a_i \right\},$$

which is

$$\sum_{j=1}^{l} y_j b_j E[X].$$

The factor $E[X]$ can now be taken out of this, so that finally

$$E[XY] = E[X] \sum_{j=1}^{l} y_j b_j = E[X]E[Y].$$

14.5 THE RELATIONS FOR CONTINUOUS RANDOM VARIABLES

To follow the rest of this chapter you will need to be familiar with the idea of a double integral. (Note 14.3) If you wish, the results obtained can just be assumed for the time being – they are simply extensions to continuous random variables of what has gone before. However, the notion of area probability density which is developed in this section (and which was first introduced in a special case in §12.2) will be required again in Chapter 18.

In the discrete case, if all the possible pairings of a value of X with a value of Y are represented by points with coordinates (x_i, y_j), then these will appear as isolated points forming an irregular rectangular lattice, as in Fig. 5a. But if X and Y are continuous random variables, defined on intervals U and V respectively, then the point (X, Y) can lie anywhere within a rectangle denoted by $U \times V$ (the *cartesian product* of U and V), as indicated in Fig. 5b.

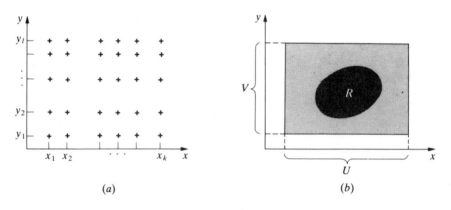

(a)   (b)

Figure 5

To describe the probability model for a random point which may vary anywhere within a region of a plane needs the idea of an "area probability density function". This is a generalisation of the probability density function for a single random variable, which is a function ϕ with the property that the probability of a random point lying within any interval I of the domain U is given by $\int_{x \in I} \phi(x)\, dx$ (see §11.3). Similarly, in two dimensions the area probability density γ associates with any region R within the domain $U \times V$ (see Fig. 5b again) the probability given by

$$\iint\limits_{(x, y) \in R} \gamma(x, y)\, dS. \quad \text{(Note 14.4)}$$

Some of the definitions associated with the idea of expectation can be extended directly to the two-dimensional case. For example, by analogy with

§14.1, the expectation of a function f of the pair of random variables X, Y is defined as

$$E[f(X, Y)] = \iint\limits_{(x, y) \,\in\, U \times V} f(x, y)\gamma(x, y) \, dS.$$

The other property which will be needed is a link between the area probability density $\gamma(x, y)$ and the one-dimensional probability densities for the separate random variables X and Y, analogous to the relations connecting c_{ij} and a_i and b_j in §14.4. To get this, let I denote any interval in the domain U of the continuous random variable X (Fig. 6). Then the probability that X lies within I is the same as the probability that (X, Y) lies within the shaded region $I \times V$ of the plane, which is

$$\iint\limits_{(x, y) \,\in\, I \times V} \gamma(x, y) \, dS.$$

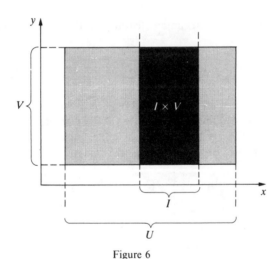

Figure 6

But because this region has the shape of a rectangle with its sides parallel to the axes, the double integral can be calculated as a repeated integral, integrating first with respect to y and then with respect to x. Symbolically,

$$P(X \in I) = \int\limits_{x \,\in\, I} \left\{ \int\limits_{y \,\in\, V} \gamma(x, y) \, dy \right\} dx,$$

where the integral inside the curly brackets is carried out first, treating x as constant. Now all that is necessary is to note that this expression inside the curly brackets is an integral of a function of x and y with respect to y over a fixed interval, so that it is a function of x alone; let it be denoted by $\alpha(x)$. Then we can write

$$P(X \in I) = \int_{x \in I} \alpha(x)\, dx.$$

But I can be any interval within U that we care to choose; so this is just the property which distinguishes the probability density function for the random variable X. And an exactly similar argument can be used for the random variable Y. So what has been shown is:

If γ is an area probability density function for a random point (X, Y) whose domain is $U \times V$, then the functions α and β defined by

$$\alpha(x) = \int_{y \in V} \gamma(x, y)\, dy \quad \text{and} \quad \beta(y) = \int_{x \in U} \gamma(x, y)\, dx$$

are probability density functions for the random variables X and Y separately.

Q.4   Write out in full the argument leading to the expression for $\beta(y)$ given above.

Everything is now set up for the proofs of the relations (1) and (2) for continuous random variables. To make the comparison with §14.4 as obvious as possible, the letters α, β and γ have been used for the probability density functions so as to correspond to the probabilities a_i, b_j and c_{ij} in the discrete case; and the steps in the proofs resemble closely those previously identified.

So, for $E[X + Y]$, we proceed as follows:

Step 1.   Using the definition of $E[f(X, Y)]$ already given,

$$E[X + Y] = \iint_{(x, y) \in U \times V} (x + y)\gamma(x, y)\, dS$$

$$= \iint_{(x, y) \in U \times V} x\gamma(x, y)\, dS + \iint_{(x, y) \in U \times V} y\gamma(x, y)\, dS.$$

Step 2.   Express the double integrals as repeated integrals, integrating first 'vertically' and then 'horizontally' in the first term, and in the opposite order in the second term:

$$E[X + Y] = \int_{x \in U} \left\{ \int_{y \in V} x\gamma(x, y)\, dy \right\} dx + \int_{y \in V} \left\{ \int_{x \in U} y\gamma(x, y)\, dx \right\} dy.$$

Step 3.   Since x is treated as constant in carrying out the 'inner' integral in the first term, and similarly for y in the second term, these can be taken as factors outside their respective integrals, to give

$$E[X + Y] = \int\limits_{x \in U} x\left\{ \int\limits_{y \in V} \gamma(x, y)\, dy \right\} dx + \int\limits_{y \in V} y\left\{ \int\limits_{x \in U} \gamma(x, y)\, dx \right\} dy;$$

and inside the curly brackets we now recognise the expressions for $\alpha(x)$ and $\beta(y)$ respectively displayed above, so that

$$E[X + Y] = \int\limits_{x \in U} x\alpha(x)\, dx + \int\limits_{y \in V} y\beta(y)\, dy.$$

Step 4.   The proof is completed by recognising these integrals as $E[X]$ and $E[Y]$ respectively.

To prove the relation (2) for $E[XY]$, one further property is needed: that if the random variables X, Y are independent, then $\gamma(x, y) = \alpha(x)\beta(y)$. This is just the ordinary multiplication law for independence, but applied to probability densities rather than probabilities. (See §12.2, where this was used in a particular case. The result can be established in general by replacing the factors $1/b$, $1/b$, $1/b^2$ in the equation by $\alpha(x)$, $\beta(y)$, $\alpha(x)\beta(y)$ respectively.) So

$$E[XY] = \iint\limits_{(x, y) \in U \times V} xy\gamma(x, y)\, dS = \iint\limits_{(x, y) \in U \times V} xy\alpha(x)\beta(y)\, dS.$$

The special feature in this case is that the expression to be integrated splits up as the product of a function of x and a function of y. So, when the double integral is written as a repeated integral,

$$E[XY] = \int\limits_{y \in V} \left\{ \int\limits_{x \in U} xy\alpha(x)\beta(y)\, dx \right\} dy,$$

the factor $y\beta(y)$ can be taken outside the 'inner' integral to give

$$E[XY] = \int\limits_{y \in V} y\beta(y)\left\{ \int\limits_{x \in U} x\alpha(x)\, dx \right\} dy$$

$$= \int\limits_{y \in V} y\beta(y)E[X]\, dy.$$

The constant factor $E[X]$ can now be taken out of this, so that finally

$$E[XY] = E[X] \int\limits_{y \in V} y\beta(y)\, dy = E[X]E[Y].$$

Again, the successive steps are essentially the same as those in the proof for the discrete case, and you would find it helpful to compare the two side by side.

14.6 INFINITE POSSIBILITY SPACES

The proofs in the last two sections have been presented for finite possibility spaces (either discrete or continuous). But we are also familiar with probability models defined over infinite possibility spaces: for example, geometric probability for which the possibility space is the set of natural numbers, or normal probability density for which it is the set of real numbers. For such examples additional questions arise, concerned with the convergence of infinite series and infinite integrals. In particular, it is not true without qualification that the order of summation (by rows and by columns) or the order of integration can be reversed without changing the value of the sum or the integral. However, there are theorems of analysis which ensure that, under certain conditions, the proofs given above remain valid in the infinite cases. It is most unlikely that you will meet probability functions in practice for which these conditions do not hold, unless you go out of your way to do so! So you can use the relations (1), (2) and (3) with confidence, even where the possibility spaces are infinite, in all ordinary situations.

Exercise 14C

1 Consider the three area probability density functions given by the expressions stated over the specified domains, and equal to zero elsewhere:
(a) $\gamma(x, y) = e^{-(x+y)}$ over the positive quadrant $x > 0$, $y > 0$;
(b) $\gamma(x, y) = x + y$ over the unit square $0 \leqslant x \leqslant 1, 0 \leqslant y \leqslant 1$;
(c) $\gamma(x, y) = 2$ over the triangle bounded by the axes and the line $x + y = 1$.
For each of these probability models,
  (i) verify that $\iint \gamma(x, y) \, dS = 1$;
  (ii) find the separate probability density functions $\alpha(x)$ and $\beta(y)$;
  (iii) calculate $E[X]$, $E[Y]$, $E[X + Y]$, $E[XY]$; $V[X]$, $V[Y]$, $V[X + Y]$, $V[XY]$.
    Comment on your answers.

2 Probability density for a single random variable can be illustrated by a graph in two dimensions in which $y = \phi(x)$ represents the density. Similarly, area probability density can be illustrated by a graph in three dimensions in which $z = \gamma(x, y)$ represents the density. For each of the three models in question 1, either draw a sketch, or make a model, or use computer graphics, to show the graph.

3 Two independent random variables X and Y have normal probability densities $N(0, \sigma_1^2)$ and $N(0, \sigma_2^2)$ respectively. Write down the expression $\gamma(x, y)$ for the area probability density of the random point (X, Y), and describe the three-dimensional graph $z = \gamma(x, y)$.
  If σ_1 and σ_2 are both equal to σ, calculate the probabilities that (X, Y) lies within the squares defined by $(a) -\sigma < X < \sigma$, $-\sigma < Y < \sigma$, $(b) -\sigma/\sqrt{2} < X < \sigma/\sqrt{2}$, $-\sigma/\sqrt{2} < Y < \sigma/\sqrt{2}$. Hence find bounds for the probability that the point (X, Y) lies inside a circle with centre $(0, 0)$ and radius σ.
  By expressing this last probability as a double integral and transforming to polar coordinates, prove that its exact value is $1 - e^{-\frac{1}{2}}$.

14.7 SUMMARY

Some of the results established in this chapter will be important later in the course, and particularly in the next chapter. It will be useful to collect them together here, for future reference.

For a single random variable X, and a constant c:

$$E[X + c] = E[X] + c \quad \text{and} \quad V[X + c] = V[X];$$

$$E[cX] = c\,E[X] \quad \text{and} \quad V[cX] = c^2 V[X].$$

For a pair of random variables X, Y:

$$E[X + Y] = E[X] + E[Y] \quad \text{and,}$$

$$\textit{if } X, Y \textit{ are independent, } V[X + Y] = V[X] + V[Y].$$

15

Estimators as random variables

The problem of choosing suitable parameters to use in a probability model has already come up on several occasions. One approach suggested was to use the extrapolation principle (introduced in §4.1, and applied more generally in §10.1); another was the maximum likelihood principle (§4.2). These are methods of "point estimation", the aim being to select values for the parameters which are, in some sense, the "best". A quite different way of tackling the problem is "interval estimation" (§8.6), in which the aim is to find intervals within which the parameters might "reasonably" lie.

One of the difficulties with point estimation is that different methods can sometimes lead to different "best estimates". The question must then be asked, whether there is some basis for preferring one to another.

We have now developed enough statistical theory to be able to deal with the problems of estimation more scientifically. In this chapter the notion of expectation, introduced in Chapter 14, will be applied to indicate how the question raised above might be answered.

15.1 ESTIMATES AND ESTIMATORS

It will be helpful to begin with an experiment. It is best if you can do this as a group; but if that is not possible, it can be adapted quite easily for working in pairs, or even by yourself.

Experiment
One member of the group should have a non-transparent plastic bag (or a sampling bottle designed to produce single samples) and some beads of two colours (black and white, say), 100 in all. The numbers of black and white beads need not be 'round numbers', but it is better if there are not too few of either colour.

She then invites each of her colleagues in turn to take a sample of 20 beads, taking one at a time and replacing it before taking the next. On this basis, and knowing that there are 100 beads in all, each colleague makes an estimate of the number of black beads in the bag. These estimates are recorded, and then compared with the actual number of black beads in the bag.

I did this in a group of seven people, whom we will call A to G. G planted 37 black and 63 white beads in her bag, and the samples and estimates of her colleagues were as follows:

	A	B	C	D	E	F
Number of black beads in sample	4	3	12	9	9	6
Estimated number of black beads in bag	20	15	60	45	45	30

It would have been very surprising if each draw had produced a sample with the same number of black beads. The number of black beads in a sample, call it I (Note 15.1), is a random variable. The values it takes will certainly depend on the number of black beads originally planted in the bag, which we will call β, but only in a probabilistic way. (Fig. 1 may help you to fix the notation in mind.)

Q.1   What is the probability of getting i black beads in a sample of 20, given that there are β black beads in the bag? What is the domain of possible values of I?

Figure 1

It is common practice to use a circumflex accent (^) to denote the estimate which one makes of any parameter on the basis of a sample; so the estimate based on the particular sample of i black beads and $(20 - i)$ white beads will be denoted by $\hat{\beta}$. (This is often read as "beta-hat"!) In this example the values of $\hat{\beta}$ given by the participants in the experiment will be just 5 times i, their particular values of I; this comes most simply by applying the extrapolation principle in the form:

> "Estimate the *proportion* of black beads in the bag to be equal to the proportion of black beads in the sample."

This leads to the equation

$$\frac{\hat{\beta}}{100} = \frac{i}{20},$$

so that

$$\hat{\beta} = 5i.$$

Q.2   Use the expression in Q.1 to show that the maximum likelihood principle leads to the same conclusion.

The important point to notice is that the rule for calculating the estimate from the number of black beads in the sample *can (and should) be specified before the start of the experiment*. One could give instructions to the experimenter in advance:

> "Find how many black beads there are in a sample of size 20, multiply this number by five, and give the answer as your estimate of the number of black beads in the bag."

This process, which can be expressed symbolically as

$$i \mapsto 5i,$$

is called the *estimator function* for the experiment. The actual numerical estimate ultimately made is the value of the estimator function obtained when the particular experimental value i is substituted.

Exercise 15A

1   In the example of the plate factory in §4.1 (see also Exercise 4A, question 2) give a formula for calculating $\hat{p}$, the estimated probability of a plate being faulty, in terms of f, the number of faulty plates in a sample of 50.

2   In Exercise 4B, question 2 give an equation to calculate $\hat{s}$, the estimated probability of a six, as a function of n, the number of sixes in 20 throws.

3   In Exercise 4B, question 4 give an equation to estimate $\hat{x}$, the estimated probability of the outcome C, as a function of r, the number of occcurrences of this outcome in a sequence of n experiments.

   Extend this to the situation in Exercise 4B, question 5 in which the numbers of occurrences on three successive days are r_1, r_2, r_3.

4   In Exercise 4B, question 11 suppose that in the second week the ecologist catches 30 squirrels, and that r denotes the number of marked squirrels amongst these. Write an equation for $\hat{n}$, her estimate of the total population, as a function of r.

Suppose that the experiment is now changed, so that in the second week she continues her hunt for marked squirrels until she has captured 4 marked ones. If to do this she has to capture s squirrels in all, write an equation for $\hat{n}$ as a function of s.

5   The number of trout in a lake, τ, is estimated by a capture-recapture experiment. On a first occasion m trout are caught, marked and returned to the lake. Some time later the lake is fished again: on this occasion s trout in all are caught, of which r are found to be marked. Each fish is returned to the lake as soon as it has been recorded (so that the sampling is "with replacement"). Write an equation for calculating $\hat{\tau}$, the estimate of the total population, as a function of r, s and m.

6   In Exercise 4B, question 6 consider the case of 11 spins, and suppose that the lemon turns up l times. Make a table of the probabilities of getting different values of l for different possible values of n from 0 to 18, and hence produce a table for finding the maximum likelihood estimate, $\hat{n}$, as a function of l. (K)

7   In the experiment of §15.1 suppose that the sampling is carried out without replacement. Prove that the likelihood, $L(\beta)$, of getting i black beads in a sample of 20 with β black beads in the bag is given by

$$L(\beta) = \binom{\beta}{i}\binom{100 - \beta}{20 - i} \bigg/ \binom{100}{20}.$$

Show that $L(\beta + 1) > L(\beta)$ if and only if $\beta < 5.05i - 1$, and deduce the maximum likelihood estimate $\hat{\beta}$ for each value of i from 0 to 20. Is the estimator function different from the one when sampling is with replacement?

8   In a raffle τ tickets are sold, numbered consecutively and starting at number 1. There are five prizes. The organisers of the raffle publish the numbers, v, w, x, y, z, of the winning tickets, but not the total number of tickets sold. Suggest some possible estimators $\hat{\tau}$ for this number as functions of v, w, x, y, z.

15.2   BIASED AND UNBIASED ESTIMATORS

An important question in statistics is: what is the connection between an estimator and the quantity it is estimating?

To explain this somewhat enigmatic question, Fig. 2 shows a graph of the values of $\hat{\beta}$ obtained by my group in the experiment described in §15.1. (You should draw the corresponding graph for your own results.) The actual value of β, which was 37, is also marked on Fig. 2, but at the time this was known only to G.

The first thing to notice is that $\hat{\beta}$ is itself a random variable. This is because I is a random variable, and $\hat{\beta}$ was chosen to be equal to 5 times the value of I. The graph shows the frequencies for a sample of six values of this random variable. These values are scattered around the actual value of β, but they are not precisely related to it in any way; for example, β is not the mean of the six values of $\hat{\beta}$.

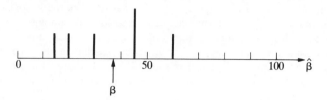

Figure 2

Q.3   Show that taking the mean of the six values of $\hat{\beta}$ is equivalent to taking a single sample of 120 beads (with replacement, of course!) and multiplying the number of black beads in the sample by $\frac{5}{6}$.

Q.4   Write a computer program to simulate the experiment described in §15.1 and run it a large number of times. Arrange for the output to be in the form of a graph similar to Fig. 2. (You may, if you wish, allow the computer to select the actual value of β randomly, and to reveal this only after the graph is completed.)

Now, as a random variable, $\hat{\beta}$ has a theoretical probability distribution, and so it has a theoretical mean $E[\hat{\beta}]$. In fact, since the value of $\hat{\beta}$ is 5 times the value of I,

$$E[\hat{\beta}] = E[5I];$$

and, by the theory developed in Chapter 14, this is equal to $5E[I]$ (see §14.7). So, if we can find $E[I]$, then $E[\hat{\beta}]$ can be calculated.

What is I? It is the number of black beads in a sample of 20, when the probability of drawing a black bead on each separate occasion is $\beta/100$ (that is, 0.37 in my group's version of the experiment). So each experiment is a Bernoulli sequence of 20 trials, and the probablity model for I is of binomial form $B(20, \beta/100)$ (see §9.6(iii)). It follows that

$$E[I] = 20 \times \beta/100 = \tfrac{1}{5}\beta.$$

Reverting now to $\hat{\beta}$, we deduce that

$$E[\hat{\beta}] = 5 \times \tfrac{1}{5}\beta = \beta.$$

That is, the theoretical mean of the estimator over all possible samples is exactly equal to the value of the quantity being estimated. Such an estimator is said to be "unbiased".

You could hardly be blamed if you did not find this very surprising! In fact, you may think that all estimators would have this property. But this is not so.

An estimator $\hat{\lambda}$ for a parameter λ is said to be *unbiased* if, averaged over all possible samples, $E[\hat{\lambda}] = \lambda$.

Q.5   Adapt the computer program which you wrote in Q.4 to calculate the mean of the values of $\hat{\beta}$ obtained when the experiment is run a large number of times. How close does this come to the theoretical mean $E[\hat{\beta}]$?

As an example of an estimator which is not unbiased, we need look no further than question 4 of Exercise 15A. On some previous occasion 20 squirrels in a wood have been marked; the ecologist now catches 30 squirrels, and finds that r of them are marked. The population n is then estimated by $\hat{n}$, calculated from the equation

$$\frac{20}{\hat{n}} = \frac{r}{30}$$

(see the solution to Exercise 4A, question 4). This gives

$$\hat{n} = \frac{600}{r}.$$

The question is now: what is the mean value of $\hat{n}$ taken over all possible samples of 30 squirrels which the ecologist might have selected from the wood?

In the actual experiment the true value of n is of course not known; but, to investigate the theory mathematically, let us suppose that there are in fact 125 squirrels in the wood. Then, since on the first expedition 20 of these were marked, the probability that a squirrel selected at random from the wood is marked will be $\frac{20}{125}$, or 0.16.

The exact analysis of the results of the second expedition depends on whether the sample of squirrels is taken with or without replacement. To simplify the calculations let us suppose that it is the former, so that each squirrel is returned to the wild immediately after it has been recorded. Then for each squirrel in the sample of 30 there is a constant probability 0.16 that it will be marked. The appropriate probability model thus has binomial form B(30, 0.16), and the probabilities for various values of r (and therefore of $\hat{n}$) can be tabulated as in Table 1.

Q.6   How would this table be altered if a different value for n (80, say) were taken?

Now, what is the theoretical mean of the estimator $\hat{n}$? The answer is surprising: since there is a non-zero probability (about 0.5%, in fact) that no marked squirrels will be caught, in which case the population would – using the rule $\hat{n} = 600/r$ – be estimated as 'infinite' in size, the mean $E[\hat{n}]$ is also infinite! So in this example $E[\hat{n}]$ is certainly not equal to n. We say that $600/r$ is a "biased" estimator for n.

An estimator $\hat{\lambda}$ for a parameter λ is said to be *biased* if, averaged over all possible samples, $E[\hat{\lambda}] \neq \lambda$.

Q.7   Write a computer program to simulate the experiment with $n = 125$, and run it a large number of times. Calculate the mean of the values of $\hat{n}$ obtained.

Number of marked squirrels in sample (r)	Population estimate ($\hat{n}$)	Probability	
0	∞ (!)	$(0.84)^{30}$	≈ 0.005
1	600	$\binom{30}{1} \times (0.84)^{29} \times (0.16)^1$	≈ 0.031
2	300	$\binom{30}{2} \times (0.84)^{28} \times (0.16)^2$	≈ 0.084
3	200	$\binom{30}{3} \times (0.84)^{27} \times (0.16)^3$	≈ 0.150
4	150	$\binom{30}{4} \times (0.84)^{26} \times (0.16)^4$	≈ 0.193
5	120	$\binom{30}{5} \times (0.84)^{25} \times (0.16)^5$	≈ 0.191
6	100	$\binom{30}{6} \times (0.84)^{24} \times (0.16)^6$	≈ 0.152
...	...	...	
...	...	...	
...	...	...	
30	20	$(0.16)^{30}$	≈ 0.000

Table 1

Exercise 15B

1 When a loaded die is rolled, the probability that a six will turn up in a single throw is s. The value of s is estimated by rolling the die 20 times, recording the number n of sixes, and using the estimator $\hat{s} = n/20$.
(a) Describe (in terms of s) the probability model for n.
(b) Give the value of $E[n]$, and hence of $E[\hat{s}]$.
(c) Is $\hat{s}$ an unbiased estimator for the probability s?

2 A certain experiment is performed n times, and the outcome C occurs on r occasions. Assuming that the succession of experiments can be modelled by a Bernoulli sequence, and denoting P(C) by x, show that $\hat{x} = r/n$ is an unbiased estimator for x.
   The experiment is performed n_1, n_2 and n_3 times respectively on three successive days, and the outcome C occurs r_1, r_2 and r_3 times. Show that $\hat{x}' = (r_1 + r_2 + r_3)/(n_1 + n_2 + n_3)$ is an unbiased estimator for x.

3 Use the table of probabilities from Exercise 15A, question 6 to investigate whether or not the maximum likelihood estimator $\hat{n}$ is biased.

4 A bag contains 10 balls of which 4 are red and 6 are white. A random sample of 3 balls is taken, without replacement, and $\hat{p}$ denotes the proportion of red balls in the sample. Tabulate the probability distribution of $\hat{p}$, and hence verify that $\hat{p}$ is an

unbiased estimate of the population proportion (i.e. the actual proportion of red balls in the bag).

Investigate whether this remains true for other mixtures of red and white balls totalling 10 in all.   [Cambridge]

5   Generalise question 4 to the case of a bag containing r red and w white balls, from which a sample of s balls is taken without replacement. Show that the probability that the sample contains x red and $s - x$ white balls can be written in the form $\binom{r}{x}\binom{w}{s-x}\bigg/\binom{r+w}{s}$. Defining $\hat{p}$ as x/s, show that $E[\hat{p}]$ can be put into the form

$$\sum \frac{\binom{r-1}{x-1}\binom{w}{s-x}}{\binom{r+w}{s}} \cdot \frac{r}{s},$$

taken over all the values of x for which the expression has meaning. By considering the coefficient of t^{s-1} in the expansion of $(1 + t)^{r-1}(1 + t)^w$, or otherwise, prove that $E[\hat{p}] = r/(r + w)$, and hence that $\hat{p}$ is an unbiased estimator for the proportion of red balls in the bag.

6   The experiment to estimate a squirrel population (see Exercise 4B, question 11 and Exercise 15A, question 4) is redesigned as follows. Instead of catching 30 squirrels on the second expedition and recording the number of these that are marked, the ecologist sets a target of catching 4 marked squirrels and recording the total number of squirrels, s, that she has to catch before reaching that target. Show that an appropriate estimator is then $\hat{n}' = 5s$.

If there are in fact 125 squirrels in the wood, of which 20 have been marked, prove that the probablity that she catches her fourth marked squirrel on the $(i + 4)$th catch is

$$\binom{i + 3}{3}(0.16)^4(0.84)^i.$$

Write an expression for $E[\hat{n}']$ in the form $\sum_{i=0}^{\infty} f(i)$, and show that this is equal to $20 \times (0.16)^4 \times (1 - 0.84)^{-5}$. What value does this give for the population estimate?

7   Generalise question 6 in terms of the situation described in Exercise 15A, question 5. Suppose that on the second occasion fishing continues until r marked trout have been caught, and that to achieve this the total number of trout that have to be caught is $s = i + r$. Using the estimator $\hat{\tau} = ms/r$, where m and r are constant and s is a random variable, obtain the equation

$$E[\hat{\tau}] = \sum_{i=0}^{\infty} \frac{m(i + r)}{r} \binom{i + r - 1}{r - 1}\left(\frac{m}{\tau}\right)^r\left(1 - \frac{m}{\tau}\right)^i.$$

Show that this sum can be converted into the form

$$m\left(\frac{m}{\tau}\right)^r\left\{1 - \left(1 - \frac{m}{\tau}\right)\right\}^{-(r+1)},$$

and deduce that $\hat{\tau}$ is an unbiased estimator for τ.

8 Buses run with an average frequency of one every s minutes, and their arrival at a certain stop is described by a Poisson probability model with $\lambda = 1/s$. The theory of §12.3 shows that the time T that a passenger has to wait has a probability density given by

$$\phi(t) = \frac{1}{s} e^{-t/s}.$$

A newcomer to the neighbourhood does not know the value of s, but estimates it as the time that she has to wait on the first occasion that she uses the service, so that she is in effect using the estimator $\hat{s} = T$. Prove that this is an unbiased estimator for s. Investigate whether $\hat{\lambda} = 1/T$ is an unbiased estimator for λ.

9 A random sample $U_1, \ldots, U_n$ comes from the distribution with probability density function

$$\phi(u) = \begin{cases} 1, & 0 \leqslant u \leqslant 1, \\ 0 & \text{otherwise.} \end{cases}$$

The sample range takes the value $l - s$, where l is the value of the largest observation and s the value of the smallest observation.

Show that $P(L \leqslant l) = l^n$ and find the cumulative distribution function of S and the probability density functions of L and S. Hence find the expected value of $L - S$. Suggest an unbiased estimator for the case where the population range is unknown.

10 In the raffle described in Exercise 15A, question 8 explain why, if v, w, x, y, z is one possible draw, then *either* $\tau + 1 - v, \tau + 1 - w, \tau + 1 - x, \tau + 1 - y, \tau + 1 - z$ is another, *or* the median of the winning numbers is $\frac{1}{2}(\tau + 1)$ and the sum of the largest and smallest winning numbers is $\frac{1}{2}(\tau + 1)$, or both.

The winning numbers (in order of drawing) are random variables V, W, X, Y, Z. From these other random variables are derived: the mean M, the median J, the largest L and the smallest S. Calculate $E[V]$, $E[M]$, $E[J]$, $E[L + S]$. Deduce that $\hat{\tau}_1 = 2M - 1$, $\hat{\tau}_2 = 2J - 1$ and $\hat{\tau}_3 = L + S - 1$ are all unbiased estimators for τ. Explain why $L - S + 1$ is not an unbiased estimator for τ.

15.3 A COMPARISON OF ESTIMATORS

The next question to ask, for any particular estimator, is: how good is it?

To illustrate this point, I wrote a computer program to simulate the raffle ticket problem in Exercise 15A, question 8 and 15B, question 10. The computer selected at random a number τ, which stood for the number of tickets sold. It then chose five different numbers at random between 1 and τ, which were the numbers of the winning tickets; and from these were calculated four other random variables: the mean M, the median J, the largest L and the smallest S. These were used to define three estimators (all unbiased) for the number of tickets:

$$\hat{\tau}_1 = 2M - 1, \quad \hat{\tau}_2 = 2J - 1, \quad \hat{\tau}_3 = L + S - 1.$$

Which of these would you expect to be the best for estimating the value of τ?

The advantage of using a computer simulation is that one can run the experiment a large number of times to build up a picture of what happens. Some of the results in one run of 100 draws with a particular value of τ are shown in Table 2.

Number of draw	Winning numbers					$\hat{\tau}_1$	$\hat{\tau}_2$	$\hat{\tau}_3$
1	89	84	48	79	87	153.8	167	136
2	109	27	54	34	70	116.6	107	135
3	16	99	77	31	69	115.8	137	114
..	..	..	..	..	..	..	..	..
..	..	..	..	..	..	..	..	..
98	5	24	77	84	65	101.0	129	88
99	48	73	101	29	53	120.6	105	129
100	97	12	43	85	60	117.8	119	108
Mean of estimator values						109.40	111.14	107.95
Standard deviation of estimator values						28.40	41.92	23.42

Table 2

It turned out that in this experiment the value of τ was 112; and you will see from the calculations at the foot of the table that the mean of all 100 values for each estimator is quite close to this. But if you just take a single value of an estimator (which is all one has to go on in a real estimation problem) then it is possible that you will be far wide of the mark.

Fig. 3 shows this spread of estimator values for the complete sequence of 100

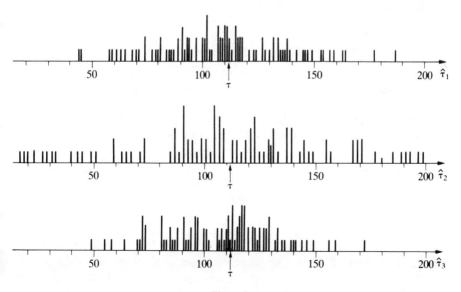

Figure 3

draws. (Note 15.2) This makes it clear that, of the three estimators, $\hat{\tau}_2$ varies more widely than the other two; and closer inspection suggests that $\hat{\tau}_1$ varies more widely than $\hat{\tau}_3$. This is confirmed by the calculation of the standard deviations in the table. To check that this was not just an accident, the experiment was run several more times, with different values for τ; in each case the standard deviations came out in the order $\hat{\tau}_3$, $\hat{\tau}_1$, $\hat{\tau}_2$ (smallest first), and in about the same ratio. This suggests that, if one makes an estimate of τ on the basis of just one draw, then using $\hat{\tau}_3$ as the estimator gives the best chance of getting close to the correct value. (Of course, this does not mean that $\hat{\tau}_3$ will *always* be closest: see, for example, draw 99 in the table, for which the closest was in fact $\hat{\tau}_2$, and $\hat{\tau}_3$ gives the worst estimate of the three.)

In this example the theoretical calculation of the standard deviation over all possible draws would be very complicated, so we have resorted to a numerical calculation. (Note 15.3) But if the standard deviation of the estimators can be found algebraically, then this will give a method of choosing between different estimators before the experiment is carried out. To save taking the square root, this principle is usually described in terms of variance rather than standard deviation:

If $\hat{\lambda}_1$, $\hat{\lambda}_2$ are two unbiased estimators for a parameter λ and if, taken over all possible samples, $V[\hat{\lambda}_1] < V[\hat{\lambda}_2]$, then $\hat{\lambda}_1$ is said to be a more *efficient* estimator than $\hat{\lambda}_2$.

The idea of using $V[\hat{\lambda}]$ as a means of answering the question "how good an estimator is $\hat{\lambda}$?" is a very important one, and plays a crucial role in the theory of sampling and estimation. To illustrate this, the sections which follow illustrate its application to two central problems of statistical inference: estimating a proportion and estimating a mean.

15.4 ESTIMATING A PROPORTION

Suppose that individuals in a population are distinguished by whether they do, or do not, have a certain property, and that we want to find out what proportion have the property. Examples would be trying to find the proportion of black beads in a bag containing both black and white beads (e.g. the quantity $\beta/100$ in the experiment described in §15.1), or the proportion of voters who intend to support a particular candidate in an election. It is in fact the basic question in assigning probabilities – which in most practical situations can only be done by finding the proportion of occurrences of a particular outcome in a sample, and using this to estimate the (actual or theoretical) proportion of occurrences in the population as a whole.

Suppose that a certain property (call it A) occurs in a proportion α of a population. If an individual is selected at random, then α is the probability that this individual will have the property A. In an experiment n individuals are sampled, one at a time. (We sample independently and with replacement, in cases where this phrase has any meaning; that is, it is assumed that the probability of an individual having property A does not change as sampling proceeds.) Then the two essential points of the argument are:

(a) The probability α is estimated by the relative frequency of occurrence of property A in the sample. That is,

$$\hat{\alpha} = I/n,$$

where I is the number of individuals in the sample having the property.

(b) The sampling process satisfies the conditions for a Bernoulli sequence (see §3.1), so that the probability model for the random variable I is the binomial model B(n, α).

The theory of expectation now gives the results:

From (a), $E[\hat{\alpha}] = \dfrac{1}{n} E[I]$ and $V[\hat{\alpha}] = \dfrac{1}{n^2} V[I]$.

From (b), $E[I] = n\alpha$ and $V[I] = n\alpha(1 - \alpha)$.

Putting these together, it follows that

$$E[\hat{\alpha}] = \frac{1}{n}(n\alpha) = \alpha,$$

which means that α is an unbiased estimator for α; and

$$V[\hat{\alpha}] = \frac{1}{n^2}\{n\alpha(1 - \alpha)\} = \frac{\alpha(1 - \alpha)}{n}.$$

If, from a population of which a proportion α has a certain property, a sample of n individuals is taken independently at random with replacement, the proportion of individuals in the sample having this property is distributed with mean α and standard deviation $\sqrt{\{\alpha(1 - \alpha)\}}/\sqrt{n}$.

It may be helpful to illustrate this theoretical (but very important) analysis with a graphical example. Suppose that 36 % of the individuals in the population have property A. (We would not of course know this in a sampling experiment.) Then $\alpha = 0.36$ and $\sqrt{\{\alpha(1 - \alpha)\}} = 0.48$, so that the estimator α has mean 0.36 and standard deviation $0.48/\sqrt{n}$. Fig. 4 shows histograms for the distribution of this estimator in the cases $n = 10$, $n = 40$ and $n = 100$. Note that, since $\hat{\alpha} = I/n$, the possibility spaces for $\hat{\alpha}$ in the three cases are $\{0, 0.1, 0.2, \ldots, 1\}$, $\{0, 0.025, 0.05, \ldots, 1\}$ and $\{0, 0.01, 0.02, \ldots, 1\}$.

The graphs show clearly that, although they are all centred round the same mean of 0.36, the estimates are clustered more tightly round this mean when n is larger – so that there is a better chance of getting close to 0.36 with a particular sample if a larger sample is taken.

Exercise 15C

1 In the numerical example at the end of §15.4, illustrated in Fig. 4, calculate the probability of getting a sample with between 31 % and 41 % having property A (a) if $n = 10$, (b) if $n = 40$, (c) if $n = 100$.

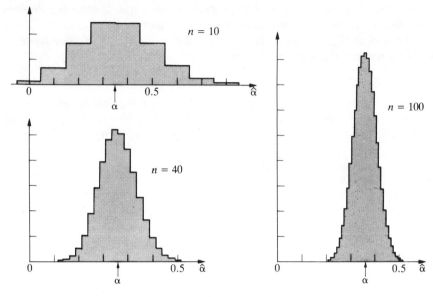

Figure 4

2   Of the adult inhabitants of a city, 20% were born there. A researcher into social mobility tries to estimate this proportion from a sample of 400 citizens selected at random. What is the probability that her estimate will be between 18% and 22%?

3   In an experiment to find the proportion of the population who have had chicken pox two samplers are used. They question n_1 and n_2 people respectively, selected independently at random. Two statisticians process the results: the first takes the average of the proportions of the two samplers, the second finds the proportion in the complete sample of $n_1 + n_2$ individuals. Show that both of these estimators are unbiased. Which is the more efficient?

4   Show that, in estimating the proportion of a population with a certain property by equating it to the proportion in a sample of size n, the standard deviation of the estimator cannot exceed $1/2\sqrt{n}$.

It is intended to estimate the proportion of votes which a candidate will get in an election by means of a poll of a sample of the electorate. If we want the estimator to have a standard deviation of not more than 1%, how large a sample will be sufficient?

5   It is desired to estimate to within 0.02 the proportion θ of the adult population of Utopia who intend to vote for the Notax party in the next election. There are r adults in a random sample of N adults who say they will do so.
   (a) Assuming these responses are independent, prove that the mean and variance of r/N are θ and $\theta(1 - \theta)/N$ respectively.
   (b) Use the result of (a), and the normal approximation to the binomial, to show that when N is large, the probability that r/N differs from θ by less than 0.02 is greater than 0.95 whenever $N > 9604\theta(1 - \theta)$.
   (c) Deduce the minimum value of N that ensures, whatever the value of θ, that r/N is within 0.02 of θ with a probability greater than 0.95.   [MEI]

6   It is desired to estimate the proportion θ of the adult population of the United Kingdom who are smokers, and a random sample of size n of this population is taken in which the proportion of smokers is p. Write down, in terms of θ, the mean and standard deviation of the probability distribution of p. Assuming n is large enough for the normal distribution to be a good approximation to the binomial distribution, find a number N such that there is at least a 95 % chance that $|p - \theta| < 0.05$ provided

$$n > N\theta(1 - \theta).$$

Hence determine the minimum sample size which ensures with 95 % confidence that p is within 0.05 of θ.   [MEI]

15.5 ESTIMATING A MEAN

The second problem arises when the statistical data take the form of measurements – lengths of elephant tusks, ages to which tortoises live, masses of cereal packets, incomes of agricultural workers – and we want to make a statement about the mean of all such measurements on the basis of a random sample of measurements of n individuals.

Suppose the mean, which we are trying to estimate, is denoted by μ; and that the n sample measurements are the random variables $X_1, X_2, \ldots, X_n$. (Note 15.4) There are various possible choices for the estimator which might be used – for example, one could take the median, or the average of the largest and smallest – but much the commonest is of course the mean, which will be denoted by M. This too is a random variable: it will take different values when different samples are selected. We have already seen that in some cases the choice of the mean can be justified by the principle of maximum likelihood (see Exercise 7C, question 17 and Exercise 13C, question 7, when the underlying probability models are Poisson and normal respectively), and it also has the advantage of being the simplest to handle algebraically.

The aim is therefore to investigate the distribution of the estimator

$$\hat{\mu} = M = \frac{1}{n}(X_1 + X_2 + \cdots + X_n).$$

Now since $\hat{\mu}$ is defined in terms of $X_1, X_2, \ldots, X_n$, its properties can only be found from those of the individual random variables. As a start, consider the variable X_1. The essential point of the argument is that this is just the measurement for a typical randomly selected individual from the population being sampled, so that

$$\mathrm{E}[X_1] = \mu \quad \text{and} \quad \mathrm{V}[X_1] = \sigma^2,$$

where σ denotes the actual (but also unknown) standard deviation of the population of measurements. And, since the sampling is independent, similar equations hold for the mean and variance of the other measurements $X_2, X_3, \ldots, X_n$.

The other part of the argument draws on results from the theory of expectation:

$$E\left[\frac{1}{n}(X_1 + X_2 + \cdots + X_n)\right] = \frac{1}{n} E[X_1 + X_2 + \cdots + X_n]$$

$$= \frac{1}{n}\{E[X_1] + E[X_2] + \cdots + E[X_n]\},$$

and (since the random variables are independent)

$$V\left[\frac{1}{n}(X_1 + X_2 + \cdots + X_n)\right] = \frac{1}{n^2} V[X_1 + X_2 + \cdots + X_n]$$

$$= \frac{1}{n^2}\{V[X_1] + V[X_2] + \cdots + V[X_n]\}.$$

Substituting the values for $E[X_1]$ and $V[X_1]$ given above (and similar ones for $X_2, X_3, \ldots, X_n$), it follows that

$$E[\hat{\mu}] = \frac{1}{n}(\mu + \mu + \cdots + \mu) = \frac{1}{n}(n\mu) = \mu,$$

so that $\hat{\mu}$ is an unbiased estimator for μ; and

$$V[\hat{\mu}] = \frac{1}{n^2}(\sigma^2 + \sigma^2 + \cdots + \sigma^2) = \frac{1}{n^2}(n\sigma^2) = \frac{\sigma^2}{n}.$$

If, from a population of measurements with mean μ and standard deviation σ, a sample of n independent measurements is taken at random, the mean of the sample is distributed with mean μ and standard deviation $\sigma/\sqrt{n}$.

Notice, just as in §15.4, the "inverse square root law" for the standard deviation of the estimator. This is a common feature of many sampling situations, and it has important practical and economic implications. The purpose of any sampling experiment is to obtain information which it is not practicable to get by inspection of the whole population. We want this information to be as accurate as possible; on the other hand, it is in the nature of random variation that perfect accuracy cannot be achieved. The import of the inverse square root law is that, to get "k times the accuracy" (more precisely, to divide the standard deviation of the estimator by k), one needs a sample k^2 times as large – which may be prohibitively time-consuming or expensive. There is an unavoidable conflict between the desire to have accurate information and the cost of obtaining it.

Exercise 15D

1   The results of IQ tests are standardised so that, in the country at large, the mean is 100 and the standard deviation is 15. In a national survey, schools are required to take a random sample of 25 ten-year-olds and to report the mean IQ of the sample. Describe the variation you would expect to find in the results.

2   Get a computer to print out a sequence of random whole numbers between 1 and 99. If the program is satisfactory, what should be the mean and standard deviation of the population of random numbers?

Modify the program to select samples of 25 of these random numbers and to calculate the mean. Repeat this a considerable number of times and make a graph of the results.

Repeat the exercise with samples of 100 numbers.

Investigate whether the variation in the sample means bears out the theory set out in §15.5.

3   Take a book (with long prose paragraphs) and estimate the number of words per line (a) by selecting a single line at random, (b) by selecting 25 lines at random and calculating the mean, (c) by selecting 100 lines at random and calculating the mean. Are the answers *necessarily* increasingly close to the mean for the whole book? If not, what is the point of going to the extra trouble of taking a large sample?

4   When the thermostat in the hot water tank is set to $\tau°$, the immersion heater raises the temperature steadily up to $(\tau + 2)°$; the current is then switched off until the temperature drops to $(\tau - 2)°$, when the heater again starts to operate. Show that over a period in which no water is drawn off, the standard deviation of the tank temperature is about $1.15°$.

In order to estimate the value of τ, I measured the water temperature for 30 days and found that the mean was $53.82°$. Using the rule of thumb that in sampling about 95% of values fall within 2 standard deviations of the mean, suggest an interval within which you can be reasonably confident that the value of τ lies.

5   One way of finding the proportion of a sample which has a property A is to regard the sampling process as a sequence of n separate trials, and to record a score of 1 each time an individual has property A and 0 otherwise. If X_i denotes the score on the ith trial, and if $P(X_i = 1) = \alpha$, prove that $E[X_i] = \alpha$ and $V[X_i] = \alpha(1 - \alpha)$.

Prove that the proportion of the sample having the property A is the mean of scores X_i, and hence obtain the results of §15.4 as a special case of those of §15.5.

6   The variables X_1 and X_2 are distributed independently with the same mean, μ, but with variances σ_1^2 and σ_2^2 respectively. Find the mean and variance of the variable X defined by

$$X = k_1 X_1 + k_2 X_2,$$

where k_1 and k_2 are constants.

Show that, in order for X to be an unbiased estimator of μ with minimum variance, k_1 must be chosen to be equal to $\sigma_2^2(\sigma_1^2 + \sigma_2^2)^{-1}$, and find the corresponding value of k_2.   [SMP]

15.6 ESTIMATING POPULATION VARIANCE

There remains one more question, which is important for later theory. We have seen that the mean M of a sample of n random measurements is distributed with mean μ; is it also true that the standard deviation S is distributed with mean σ?

A simple example shows that the answer must be "no". Imagine a game played with a coin in which you score 1 if it comes down "heads" and -1 if it comes down "tails". The theoretical mean for this game is obviously 0, and

$$\sigma^2 = \tfrac{1}{2}(-1)^2 + \tfrac{1}{2}(1)^2 = 1,$$

so that $\sigma = 1$. Now take a sample of 3 tosses: there are eight possible samples $(X_1, X_2, X_3) = (\pm 1, \pm 1, \pm 1)$, each having probability $\tfrac{1}{8}$. You can easily verify for yourself that two of these have standard deviation 0, and that the other six all have standard deviation $\tfrac{1}{3}\sqrt{8} \approx 0.94$.

We can now draw a graph to illustrate the distribution of S (Fig. 5). This makes it obvious that *no* sample has a standard deviation as large as σ; so $E[S]$ is undoubtedly less than σ!

Q.8   Calculate $E[S]$ for samples of 3 tosses. Carry out a similar analysis for samples of 4 tosses.

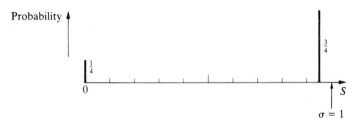

Figure 5

There is no point in continuing these calculations. Obviously the square roots involved in finding the standard deviations are a complication, even in such a simple example as this; for the general problem the algebra becomes quite prohibitive. This suggests that it might be better to ask the question about the *variance* rather than the standard deviation: that is, is the sample variance V distributed with mean σ^2?

Q.9   Draw the equivalent of Fig. 5 for the distribution of V, and prove that, for samples of 3 tosses, $E[V] = \tfrac{2}{3}$. Repeat the calculation for samples of (a) 2 tosses, (b) 4 tosses. Can you suggest and prove a generalisation of your results?

The results of Q.9 give a hint of a general rule; but note that $E[V]$ comes out smaller each time than σ^2. This may be explained in general terms by noticing that the variance is the mean squared deviation from the sample mean M; and, unless by chance M happens to be equal to μ, this is always less than the mean squared deviation from the population mean μ. (See Exercise 1A, question 7.) So if the members of the sample are 'typically' distributed, the sample variance will be in general smaller than the population variance. This intuitive argument suggests a line of approach for the calculation of $E[V]$.

The clue is to adapt the expression given in §1.1 by taking μ as a 'false origin', and calculating the variance of the random variables $X_1, X_2, \ldots, X_n$ as

$$V = \frac{1}{n} \sum_{i=1}^{n} (X_i - \mu)^2 - (M - \mu)^2.$$

Now the X_i, and therefore M and V, are random variables, but μ is constant. So, using the laws of expectation algebra,

$$E[V] = \frac{1}{n} \sum_{i=1}^{n} E[(X_i - \mu)^2] - E[(M - \mu)^2].$$

But remember that μ is the mean both of the individual random variables X_i and of their mean M. It follows that, for each i, $E[(X_i - \mu)^2] = \sigma^2$ and also that $E[(M - \mu)^2] = V[M]$, which was shown in §15.5 to be equal to σ^2/n. Substituting these values leads to the result

$$E[V] = \frac{1}{n}(n\sigma^2) - \frac{\sigma^2}{n} = \frac{n-1}{n}\sigma^2.$$

Q.10   Use this general formula to check your answers to Q.9.

Q.11   What happens when $n = 1$? Is this what you would expect?

If, from a population of measurements with variance σ^2, a sample of n independent measurements is taken at random, the variance of the sample is distributed with mean $\dfrac{n-1}{n}\sigma^2$.

This result answers in the negative the question asked at the beginning of this section. And, expressing this in the language of estimators, one immediate consequence is that:

The sample variance V is *not* an unbiased estimator for the population variance σ^2.

How, then, could we get an unbiased estimator for σ^2? Clearly we want it to relate to V and to have the same unit of measurement, so we would expect

$$\widehat{\sigma^2} = cV$$

for some constant c; and to be unbiased it is necessary that

$$E[\widehat{\sigma^2}] = \sigma^2. \text{ (Note 15.5)}$$

So

$$\sigma^2 = E[cV] = cE[V] = c\,\frac{n-1}{n}\sigma^2.$$

We must therefore choose c so that $c(n-1)/n = 1$, which gives

$$c = \frac{n}{n-1}.$$

> If the variance σ^2 of a population of measurements is to be estimated from a sample of n measurements, an unbiased estimator for σ^2 is $\dfrac{n}{n-1} V$, where V is the sample variance.

This brings us up against some fundamental questions about the problem of estimation. Suppose, for example, that a sample of five random measurements X_1, X_2, X_3, X_4, X_5 is taken from a normal parent population with unknown mean and variance. Then we have seen (Exercise 13C, question 7) that the estimators for the mean and variance which give the maximum likelihood for this sample are M and V, the mean and variance of the sample. But the expectations of these estimators (i.e. their means over all possible samples drawn from the population) are μ and $\frac{4}{5}\sigma^2$. The *unbiased* estimators for the mean and variance are M and $\frac{5}{4}V$. So there is no conflict regarding the mean; but which is the better estimator for the variance?

You may feel that this question is rather futile. With a sample of only five measurements one will get such a wide range of possible variances that any idea of deriving a reasonable estimate of σ^2 from it, either as V or as $\frac{5}{4}V$, is grossly optimistic. This is true: to get a good estimate of σ^2 you would need to take a very large sample, and then the multiplier $n/(n-1)$ is so close to 1 that it hardly matters. However, the question does have some theoretical importance, and it has had a profound effect on statistical thinking – so much so that there are two quite different sets of definitions and notations used in statistics to describe variance and standard deviation. This had better be explained, since you are likely to meet both in your reading about the subject.

15.7 A CONFLICT OF NOTATION

You will have noticed that the notation S has been used for the standard deviation of a sample, calculated in the usual way using the formula

$$S^2 = v = \frac{1}{n} \sum_{i=1}^{k} (x_i - m)^2 f(x_i). \quad \text{(See §1.1 and Note 15.4.)}$$

You may have wondered why a capital letter S is used rather than a small letter s. The reason is that s has already been appropriated: it is conventionally used to stand for the square root of the value of the unbiased variance estimator, given by

$$s^2 = \frac{n}{n-1} v = \frac{1}{n-1} \sum_{i=1}^{k} (x_i - m)^2 f(x_i).$$

So far this is confusing, but it is not inconsistent. However, worse is to come! Many statisticians prefer to *call* s the "standard deviation of the sample". That is, when dealing with a complete closed population of size N (for example, the ages at first election of British members of parliament in the nineteenth century) then the standard deviation is found by dividing the sum $\Sigma(x_i - m)^2$ by N and taking the square root; but when dealing with a sample of size n drawn randomly from such a population, then the sum is divided by $n - 1$ before taking the square root. This convention is then followed and developed throughout the whole of the theory of sampling which follows.

Clearly there is no "right" or "wrong" about this: one is free to choose definitions and notation as one finds most convenient. Devotees of $n - 1$ point out that the purpose of taking samples is to estimate population parameters, and so the notation should be moulded to reflect this. Those who prefer n claim that it is confusing to have two different formulae for quantities bearing the same name, depending on whether a collection of measurements is being considered as a population or a sample. In this book we have chosen to stick with the "n-convention"; but in an Appendix on p. 447 the two conventions are set side-by-side, to help you to transfer from one to the other. The essential thing is that, before reading a fresh book on statistics, or using a pre-programmed calculator or computer package, you should make sure that you know which convention it uses.

Exercise 15E

1   Find the variance of the scores for a single throw of a fair die.

A pair of dice is rolled, giving a random sample of two such scores. What are the possible variances for the sample, and the corresponding probabilities? Verify that the mean variance is one-half of the variance for a single throw.

2   A pencil in the shape of a hexagonal prism is used as a spinner in a game. Three of the faces show a score of 0, two a score of 1, and one a score of 2. Calculate the theoretical mean and variance of the scores when the pencil is rolled once.

The pencil is now rolled twice, and the separate scores recorded. For each of the six possible combinations of scores (disregarding the order in which they occur) calculate the probability, the mean score M and the variance V. Hence calculate $E[M]$, $V[M]$ and $E[V]$. Check your answers by reference to the general theory in §§15.5–6.

Repeat the calculations for the case in which the pencil is rolled three times.

3   In a game of chance a player can score either 0 or 1, with probabilities b and a respectively. Find the theoretical variance of the score for this game.

A player intends to play a run of four games. Write down the probability that he will score one i times and zero $4 - i$ times. Prove that in that event his mean score will be $\frac{1}{4}i$, and the variance of his scores will be $\frac{1}{16}i(4 - i)$. Hence write out in full an expression for $E[V]$, and simplify it. Verify the result proved in §15.6 for this example.

4   Generalise question 3 for a run of n games.

5   Get a computer to select samples of 25 random whole numbers between 1 and 99 and to calculate the variance. Repeat this a considerable number of times and make a graph of the results. Investigate whether the mean of the sample variances bears out the theory set out in §15.6. (Compare Exercise 15D, question 2.)

Repeat the exercise with samples of (a) 100 numbers, (b) 5 numbers.

6   An Inspector of Weights and Measures selects ten bottles of Fizzo at random and finds the contents in litres to be 1.007, 1.014, 0.992, 1.000, 0.995, 1.003, 0.989, 1.003, 1.008, 1.001. Use unbiased estimators to estimate the mean and variance of the contents in the batch as a whole.

7 A farmer wants to test the quality of a crop of peas. She selects 20 pods at random and finds that the numbers of peas in them are 12, 10, 6, 9, 10, 8, 5, 11, 9, 12, 9, 8, 10, 7, 11, 10, 8, 9, 10, 10. Use unbiased estimators to estimate the mean and variance of the numbers of peas in a pod for the whole crop.

8 Prove that s^2 can be calculated as

$$\frac{1}{n-1}\sum_{i=1}^{k} x_i^2 f(x_i) - \frac{n}{n-1} m^2.$$

9 Write a paragraph explaining the distinction between the variance of the sample mean and the mean of the sample variance.

10 In a geometric probability model the probability of getting a score of i is ab^{i-1} for $i = 1, 2, 3, \ldots$, where $a + b = 1$ (see §9.7). A random sample of two scores is taken. Write down in the form of a sum the probability that the two scores differ by r (a) when $r = 0$, (b) when $r = 1, 2, 3, \ldots$. By summing the infinite series find simpler expressions for these probabilities, and check that they add up to 1.

Show that the variance of a sample in which the scores differ by r is $\frac{1}{4}r^2$. Hence find an expression for the expectation of the sample variance, and prove that it is equal to $b/2a^2$, in accordance with the result given in §15.6.

11 Samples of size 2 are taken from a rectangular probability model whose possibility space is the interval from 0 to b (see §12.1, with $a = 0$). If a random sample is represented by a point (X_1, X_2) in a square of side b, prove that the sample variance is equal to $\frac{1}{4}r^2$, where r is the distance of the point from the diagonal joining $(0, 0)$ to (b, b). Hence show that the mean of the sample variance is equal to $\dfrac{1}{2b^2}\iint r^2 dS$ evaluated over the square.

By taking new axes parallel to the diagonals of the square, and splitting the square into two triangles, show that this double integral can be calculated as

$$\frac{1}{b^2}\cdot\int_{s=0}^{b/\sqrt{2}}\int_{r=-s}^{s} r^2 dr\,ds.$$

Hence verify that $E[V] = \dfrac{1}{2}\sigma^2$ for this model.

16

Making inferences from large samples

The twin processes of what is called "statistical inference" introduced in Chapter 8 – hypothesis testing and interval estimation – could only be carried out in rather simple situations because they were based on binomial probability, which is often complicated to apply. We have since seen, in Chapter 13, that for quite large values of n binomial probability can be approximated by normal probability. In this chapter it will be shown that this is a particular case of a much more general result, known as the "central limit theorem", which opens up the possibility of using normal probability as an approximation in a much wider range of problems. The only condition is that the samples have to be reasonably large, so that the approximations are valid.

16.1 CONFIDENCE INTERVALS

The last chapter was concerned entirely with the problem of point estimation – that is, making the "best possible estimate" of the value of a parameter on the basis of the evidence from a sample. But regarding an estimator as a random variable can also throw fresh light on the process of interval estimation – finding an interval within which we can be "reasonably confident" that the parameter lies. So we begin by picking up a thread from Chapter 8 and looking at a problem in interval estimation from a fresh viewpoint.

Example 1
A local radio station conducts an opinion poll on whether or not mathematics should be taught in schools. A researcher selects a random sample of 100 people living in the catchment area, and finds 47 in favour and 53 against. What information does this give about opinion in the region at large?

You will remember that such questions were answered by an argument involving repeated hypothesis testing. Various values for the proportion a are chosen between 0 and 1, and for each the hypothesis tested is

Hypothesis 1. The probability that a randomly selected citizen is in favour is a.

against the alternative hypothesis

Hypothesis 2. The probability that a randomly selected citizen is in favour is not a.

Taking a significance level of 5%, this involves finding whether or not the binomial probability model B(100, a) puts the result "47 in favour" inside or outside the interval which cuts off $2\frac{1}{2}$% of the probability at either end.

Trial and error methods, made simpler by using a binomial probability computer program (see §8.7, Q.11), show that hypothesis 1 is acceptable if the value of a lies between 0.369 and 0.572, but is rejected if $a > 0.572$ or $a < 0.369$. This is illustrated in Fig. 1.

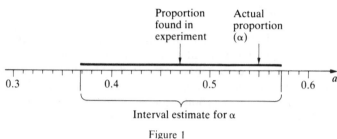

Figure 1

But of course this is only one possible experiment, and we cannot even be sure that the actual proportion lies inside this interval estimate. Indeed, if the results from ten different researchers were compared, one might get a whole set of interval estimates based on their individual findings, as illustrated in Fig. 2. Clearly the correct proportion cannot lie inside all of them!

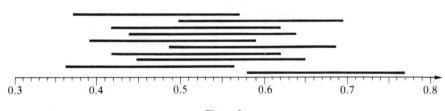

Figure 2

All the same, there must be a correct answer – the proportion of all the people in the catchment area who support the teaching of mathematics in schools. Let us denote it by α. Then the intervals shown in Fig. 2 constitute a set of "random intervals" each deduced from a random sample of 100 people in the area. The left ends of these intervals are values of a random variable which might be called the "left extreme estimate"; and on the right are values of another random variable, the "right extreme estimate".

Coming back to the researcher whose results are quoted in the example, clearly there are just two possibilities:

(1) α lies within her interval estimate,

(2) α lies outside her interval estimate.

We ought to consider the consequences of each of these possibilities for her result.

Case (1) is the one illustrated in Fig. 1. We have to remember how the interval was found – by trial and error, using many different possible values of *a*. In this process, *one* of the possible values tried might have been α itself (though the researcher would not have known this); and because α is inside the interval estimate, this proportion must have been considered acceptable. That is, "47 in favour" must be inside the 95% interval associated with the binomial probability B(100, α). This is illustrated in Fig. 3, in which everything above the line is unknown and everything below relates to the experiment.

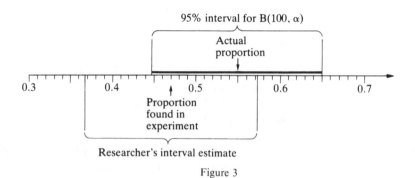

Figure 3

The conclusion is that

> Researcher's result lies within the 95% interval for B(100, α)
> ⇔ Researcher's interval estimate contains α.

This is a crucial switch of concept.

Q.1 Draw a diagram, and write out the corresponding argument, leading to the conclusion

> Researcher's result lies outside the 95% interval for B(100, α)
> ⇔ Researcher's interval estimate excludes α.

Now in Fig. 3 what is shown above the line is fixed, but what is shown below the line is random, varying from one experiment to the next. By definition, the probability that the researcher's proportion lies within the 95% interval for B(100, α) is 0.95. So there is a probability of 0.95 that the researcher's interval estimate succeeds in capturing the actual proportion α. The words used to describe this are that, on the basis of the one response of "47 out of 100 in favour", the interval $0.369 < a < 0.572$ is a "95% confidence interval for α".

The precise choice of phrase is very important here. A confidence interval does not assign a probability to the value of the unknown parameter. It would be nonsense to say that "there is a probability of 0.95 that α lies between 0.369 and 0.572"; for α is a definite number, and either it does lie within this interval (in which case the probability is 1), or it does not (so that the probability is 0). What we can say is that if, on the basis of a random sample of 100 responses, the researcher identifies an interval estimate by the method described, then there is a probability of 0.95 that this interval contains the actual proportion α.

The definition can be generalised to cover the estimation of any parameter at any significance level:

> If, in a sampling experiment to determine a parameter ζ, a random interval is defined such that there is a probability p that the interval contains ζ, then the particular interval obtained by carrying out the experiment is described as a $(100p)\%$ *confidence interval* for ζ.

16.2   APPROXIMATE METHODS

The notion of a confidence interval gives a new way of thinking about interval estimates, but it does not change the process of calculating them. In a practical example it is still necessary to carry out the laborious trial and error process of testing various hypothetical values of a, to determine the left and right extreme estimates.

However, if the sample size is reasonably large, we can get a good approximation to the confidence interval by using the fact that binomial probability $B(100, a)$ is close to normal probability density $N(100a, 100a(1 - a))$ (see §13.6). This leads to a far simpler calculation with little loss of accuracy.

This model relates, of course, to the number of favourable responses in the sample of 100. But following the line of argument in §15.4, it is rather more convenient to work with the *proportion* of favourable responses in the sample; this is just a matter of re-scaling by dividing by 100, and so is modelled by normal probability density $N(a, a(1 - a)/100)$.

To illustrate this, consider the calculation of the left extreme estimate for α in Example 1. This is based on the principle that for samples of size 100 drawn from a population with the hypothetical proportion a in favour, the probability that the sample proportion will exceed 0.47 must not be less than 0.025. (See Fig. 4. Remember that the significance level is 5%, and that the alternative hypothesis is framed in such a way that a two-tail test is appropriate.) On this hypothesis,

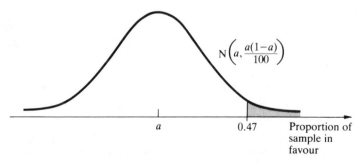

Figure 4

the proportion in favour in a random sample of size 100 is distributed with mean a and standard deviation $\sqrt{\{a(1 - a)/100\}}$. Note also that, for the standard normal probability model, the value of x such that $\Phi(x) = 0.975$ is 1.96. So the left extreme estimate has to satisfy the equation

$$\frac{0.47 - a}{\sqrt{\dfrac{a(1 - a)}{100}}} = 1.96.$$

Q.2   Write the corresponding equation for the right extreme estimate.

You will see that, when the equations for the left and right extreme estimates are squared, the same quadratic equation results. Solving this leads to the conclusion that an approximate 95 % confidence interval for α extends from 0.375 to 0.567. (Note 16.1)

This is certainly a much simpler calculation than the one based directly on binomial probability; but it still involves solving a quadratic equation, and in practice a further approximation is often introduced so as to avoid this. It depends on the fact that, if one draws the graph of $\sqrt{\{a(1 - a)\}}$ over the domain $0 \leqslant a \leqslant 1$, it is very flat over the central part of this interval. (Check this for yourself!) This means that, for proportions fairly close to $\frac{1}{2}$, we can get a reasonably good approximation by replacing the hypothetical proportion a in the expression $\sqrt{\{a(1 - a)/100\}}$ by the proportion found in the experiment, that is, 0.47 in Example 1. The equations for the left and right extreme estimates then take the forms

$$\frac{0.47 - a}{\sqrt{\dfrac{0.47 \times 0.53}{100}}} = 1.96 \quad \text{and} \quad \frac{a - 0.47}{\dfrac{0.47 \times 0.53}{100}} = 1.96,$$

giving an approximate 95 % confidence interval extending from 0.372 to 0.568. You will notice that this is still quite close to the interval found by the exact method, whose extremes were 0.369 and 0.572.

This is the justification for the rule:

If the proportion α in a population having a certain property is estimated from the proportion k in a sample of size n, where n is large and k is fairly close to $\frac{1}{2}$, then a 95 % confidence interval for α is approximately

$$k \pm 1.96 \sqrt{\frac{k(1 - k)}{n}}.$$

In making this statement the particular sample proportion 0.47 in Example 1 has been replaced by k, and the sample size of 100 by n. It could clearly be generalised further to cover other choices of significance level; the corresponding coefficients (in place of 1.96) are given in tables of the critical percentage points for normal probability in two-tail tests.

16.3   ESTIMATING A POPULATION MEDIAN

The idea of a confidence interval is in no way restricted to the estimation of proportion. The next example uses a similar argument to estimate the median of a population from sample data.

Example 2
Regarding the sample of masses at birth recorded in §11.1 as typical (Note 16.2), estimate the median mass for all babies born in this part of England at the present time.

From the detailed data, the median for the sample of 100 infants lies between 3.340 kg and 3.355 kg (the masses of the 50th and 51st babies in order of size). But because of chance variation, the median for the population as a whole might be somewhat smaller or larger than this without giving cause to doubt that this sample is "typical".

Let us denote the population median by β. Then we have to begin by asking: what is the property that characterises β? This is that just half the babies born weigh more than β, so that, if a baby is selected at random, the probability that it weighs more than β is $\frac{1}{2}$. So, in a random sample of 100 babies, we would expect about 50 to weigh more than β and 50 less. But, as with tossing a coin, a split such as "54 more and 46 less" would not surprise us, although "30 more and 70 less" would.

This suggests a basis for accepting or rejecting a hypothesis, for some mass b, that

Hypothesis 1. The median mass for the population is b.

against the alternative hypothesis

Hypothesis 2. The median mass for the population is not b.

If on hypothesis 1 the sample shows a reasonable split between "more than b" and "less than b", then the hypothesis is acceptable; if the split is unreasonable, then the hypothesis is rejected.

But this just shifts the ground of the question: what is a "reasonable" split? To answer this, we recall that, with a sample of size 100 and a probability of $\frac{1}{2}$ for each individual, the probability model for the split is the binomial $B(100, \frac{1}{2})$; and since the sample size is quite large, this is approximated closely by $N(100 \times \frac{1}{2}, 100 \times \frac{1}{2} \times (1 - \frac{1}{2}))$, or $N(50, 25)$. Taking the usual significance level of 5%, and a two-tail criterion (since we would reject a split which is too far out either way), any split will be rejected which falls more than 1.96 standard deviations away from the mean. So we calculate $50 \pm 1.96 \times 5$, which gives 59.8 or 40.2, and reject any mass b which gives a split worse than this.

However, in interpreting this rule the continuity correction should not be forgotten (see §13.6). A naive application of the above calculation would suggest that the criterion for rejection should be "60 : 40 either way, or worse". But this should be interpreted in the normal approximation as "59.5 : 40.5 either way, or worse" for which the probability is just over 5%. So when we come to convert this to a statement about masses, we should reject the masses in the sample which give splits of 61 : 39 and 39 : 61, but not those which give 60 : 40 or 40 : 60. Reference to the detailed data (shown in Fig. 2 of Chapter 11) shows that the corresponding values of b are 3.230 kg and 3.450 kg. So, erring on the conservative side, we can state with 95% confidence that the median mass of the population lies within the interval having these values at its extremities.

Q.3   State this as a general procedure for estimating a 95% confidence interval for the population median from a sample of size 100; and explain precisely what this means. Generalise the procedure to find a $(100z)$% confidence interval for the population median from a sample of size n.

Exercise 16A

1   Carry out a survey of the numbers of cars of different makes in a local car park. Taking these as a random sample of the cars in the country at large, find a 95% confidence interval for the proportion of cars licensed in Britain which are of foreign manufacture.

2   In a survey of 2000 people across the country, 920 admitted to watching "Coronation Street" on TV during the previous week. Find a 99% confidence interval for the proportion of people in the whole population who watched it.

3   A certain city has about one million adult inhabitants of whom an unknown proportion p have never spent a holiday in a foreign country. A random sample of 1000 of the inhabitants is taken, and 784 people in the sample are found never to have spent a holiday in a foreign country. Find a 95% confidence interval for p.
[Cambridge]

4   An insurance company has sold a certain specialised form of insurance to a large number of customers, and wishes to investigate the proportion p of them who are women. Records for a random sample of 100 customers are examined. Given that there are in fact 32 women in the sample, provide a two-sided 95% confidence interval for p.
[MEI]

5   It has been claimed that at least 40% of the employees of a certain large industrial firm originally sought employment there because they knew someone already employed by the firm. To check this claim, 50 employees chosen at random were interviewed, and it was found that 26 of them fell into this category.

Let θ denote the true proportion of employees in this category. Test at the 5% level of significance the null hypothesis $\theta = 0.4$ against the alternative $\theta > 0.4$. Provide also a two-sided 95% confidence interval for θ.
[MEI]

6   Before a recent general election a suitable sample of 2000 persons were asked their voting intentions. 40 per cent said that they would vote Labour, 36 per cent Conservative, 20 per cent Liberal and 4 per cent would support other parties. The firm carrying out the investigation claimed that there is a 95 per cent probability that the margin of error is within ±4 per cent of each party's share of the vote. Analyse the validity of this claim, using suitable approximate procedures.
[MEI]

7   In Example 2, what split would you need to establish a 99% confidence interval for the median?

8   In Example 2, find a procedure for determining 95% confidence intervals for the lower and upper quartiles in the population of masses.

9   Some authors are notorious for using long words. Select a page from the writings of such an author, and find a 95% confidence interval for the median number of letters in his written vocabulary.

10 Carry out a survey of car registration plates, and use it to make a histogram showing the spread of ages of cars on the road. Find a 95% confidence interval for the median age of cars on British roads.

16.4 ANOTHER APPROACH TO NORMAL PROBABILITY

The success of the methods described in the last two sections depends on the property that binomial probability approximates to normal probability density. If similar methods are to be used to find confidence intervals for other population parameters, in particular the mean, then it will have to be shown that other probability models also approximate to normal form when the sample size is large. To this end a very powerful result is available, known as the "central limit theorem"; and the rest of this chapter will be concerned with developing and applying this.

We begin with an experiment. I wrote a program to generate random digits 0, 1, 2, ..., 9 (each with probability 0.1) and to add them up in groups of four. The totals could therefore be anything between $0 + 0 + 0 + 0 = 0$ and $9 + 9 + 9 + 9 = 36$. The relative frequencies of the various totals obtained in 1000 such groups are displayed in Fig. 5.

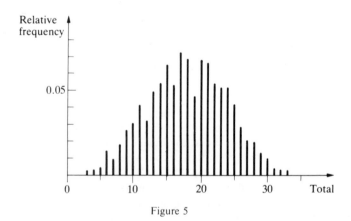

Figure 5

Now the single random digits should have occurred with almost equal frequencies; but the effect of adding four such digits is to produce a relative frequency function which is far from uniform. For example, the total 3 occurred only twice in the 1000 groups, whereas the total 17 occurred 72 times.

The reason is not difficult to find. The total 3 can only arise from a small number of selections of random digits:

0003, 0030, 0300, 3000;
0012, 0102, 1002, 0120, 1020, 1200; 0021, 0201, 2001, 0210, 2010, 2100;
0111, 1011, 1101, 1110.

There are 20 of these in all. On the other hand, there are hundreds of different ways of making a total of 17. (660, in fact. Try to count them!) Since the probability of any particular arrangement of digits is $(0.1)^4$, the probabilities of getting totals of 3 and 17 are 0.002 and 0.066 respectively. This agrees quite well with the relative frequencies of 0.002 and 0.072 found in the experiment.

If you tried to enumerate all the ways of getting a total of 17, you probably found it quite difficult. Calculating the complete set of probabilities in this way would certainly be very laborious. But fortunately there is a simpler way of doing it.

If one is to get a total of 17 with four digits, then the sum of the first *three* digits can only be 8, 9, 10, ..., 16 or 17. For example, one could get 8 with the first three digits (e.g. 233, 017, ...) and then 9 on the fourth (giving 2339, 0179, ...); or 9 on the first three and then 8 on the fourth; or 10 and then 7; ...; or 17 and then 0. In each case the probability of getting the 'right' fourth digit to make up the total of 17 is 0.1. So, if we write $p_n(t)$ to stand for the probability of getting a total of t with n digits,

$$p_4(17) = p_3(8) \times 0.1 + p_3(9) \times 0.1 + p_3(10) \times 0.1 + \cdots + p_3(17) \times 0.1$$
$$= \{p_3(8) + p_3(9) + p_3(10) + \cdots + p_3(17)\} \times 0.1.$$

Exactly the same argument can be used for any total t, and any number of digits n; so a more general version of this relationship is

$$p_{n+1}(t) = \{p_n(t-9) + p_n(t-8) + p_n(t-7) + \cdots + p_n(t)\} \times 0.1.$$

Q.4   What is $p_n(t)$ when t is a negative integer? What are the values of $p_4(3)$, $p_4(17)$, $p_n(0)$, $p_3(28)$?

A convenient way of arranging this calculation is in a table which can be built up row by row, as shown below. (The boxes pick out the application of the formula given above to the calculation of the particular values $p_3(3)$, $p_3(15)$ and $p_4(17)$.)

t	..−2 −1 0 1 2 3 4 5 6 7 8 9 10 11 12 13 14 15 16 17 · · · ·
n	
1	0.1 × 0 0 1 1 1 1 1 1 1 1 1 1 0 0 0 0 0 0 0 0 · · · ·
2	0.01 × 0 0 1 2 3 4 | 5 6 | 7 8 9 10 9 8 7 6 5 4 | 3 2 · · · ·
3	0.001 × 0 0 1 3 6 10 · · · · 45 55 63 69 73 75 75 73 69 63 · · · ·
4	0.0001 × 0 0 1 4 10 20 · · · · 660 · · · ·

Q.5 Complete this table as far as the row $n = 4$ (either by hand, or by writing a suitable computer program).

The graph of the function p_4, produced from this table, is shown in Fig. 6. It can be regarded as a theoretical probability model corresponding to the experimental data graphed in Fig. 5.

You will agree that Fig. 6 has a strikingly close resemblance to normal probability density. It is worth while investigating how close this is.

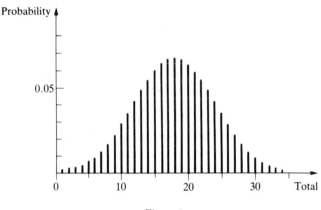

Figure 6

To do this, we need to know the mean and standard deviation of the random variable T. Now T is the sum of four random digits I_1, I_2, I_3, I_4 which should (if the random number generator is a good one) be independent; so

$$E[T] = E[I_1] + E[I_2] + E[I_3] + E[I_4],$$

and

$$V[T] = V[I_1] + V[I_2] + V[I_3] + V[I_4].$$

Each of the random digits I takes values from 0 to 9 with probability 0.1, and you can easily calculate for yourself that $E[I] = 4.5$ and $V[I] = 8.25$. So

$$E[T] = 4 \times 4.5 = 18, \text{ and } V[T] = 4 \times 8.25 = 33.$$

The probabilities in the table should therefore be compared with those given by the normal probability density function with mean 18 and standard deviation $\sqrt{33}$. The graph of this is shown in Fig. 7.

Q.6 Write down the equation of this probability density function, and compare its values with those of $p_4(t)$ (found from your answer to Q.5) for various values of t.

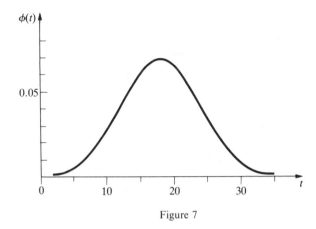

Figure 7

16.5 THE CENTRAL LIMIT THEOREM FOR TOTALS

It is time to take stock. We began with a random variable I, which had a given probability distribution. In the example in §16.4 this distribution was uniform, but it could in fact have had almost any form. (Some examples with non-uniform probability models appear in Exercise 16B, questions 6 to 9.) Suppose that I has mean μ and standard deviation σ.

A sample of several values of this random variable, $I_1, I_2, \ldots, I_n$, was then selected independently, and these were summed to give a total T. Since

$$E[T] = E[I_1] + E[I_2] + \cdots + E[I_n] = n\mu,$$
$$V[T] = V[I_1] + V[I_2] + \cdots + V[I_n] = n\sigma^2,$$

the distribution of T was compared with a normal probability model having mean $n\mu$ and standard deviation $\sqrt{n}\sigma$. It turned out that, if n is fairly large, the agreement between the two is remarkably good. (Note 16.3)

For the time being this will just be stated as an experimental observation; a justification will be given in the next chapter.

THE CENTRAL LIMIT THEOREM FOR TOTALS. If a sample of n values of a random variable, with mean μ and standard deviation σ, is summed, then when n is large the total is distributed with approximately normal probability density, with mean $n\mu$ and standard deviation $\sqrt{n}\sigma$.

It is this theorem, and its equivalent for means which is stated in §16.6, which provides the answer to the question with which this chapter began. We shall find in later chapters that normal probability density has many interesting mathematical properties; but it is the central limit theorem, with the applications to statistical sampling which this opens up, which transforms normal probability from being just one more probability model into the leading actor on the statistical stage.

Example 3

A machine fills teabags with tea. There are 25 bags in a packet, and the mean mass of tea in a bag is 4 g, with a standard deviation of 0.04 g. Between what limits will the total mass of tea in a packet lie?

If one supposes that an overweight teabag might well be as much as two standard deviations above the mean, then one bag might contain 4.08 g of tea. Twenty-five such bags would give a mass of 25×4.08 g, or 102 g. For a manufacturer this would be an unacceptable tolerance.

What the central limit theorem tells us is that it is most unlikely that the packets will vary in mass to anything like this extent.

If the fluctuations from the mean between one bag and the next are random, then the theorem predicts that the variation in the total mass of 25 bags will be described approximately by a normal probability model with mean 25×4 g $=$ 100 g and standard deviation $\sqrt{25} \times 0.04$g $= 0.2$ g. Since in normal probability only about 1 % of the population lies more than $2\frac{1}{2}$ standard deviations above or below the mean, there is a probability of 0.99 that a packet selected at random will have a mass between 99.5 g and 100.5 g, and most will be far closer to the 'target' mass of 100 g than this.

It is easy to see why. In a batch of 25 bags, it is most unlikely that all will be overweight. Usually some will be too heavy and some too light, so that the discrepancies cancel each other out.

Note how, in this example, two separate aspects of the theorem are combined to produce a very powerful result. The first is that, when the number of individuals is multiplied by n, the standard deviation of the total is multiplied only by $\sqrt{n}$. The slow growth of the square root compared with the number itself means that the total is kept within far narrower bounds than might be expected. The other feature is that the distribution of total mass approximates to a specific probability density function, the normal, which makes it possible to give a more precise statement than we could by just knowing the mean and standard deviation.

The theorem also provides support for the statement made in §13.2, that "in some experiments theoretical arguments can be suggested to justify the choice of a normal probability model". Why is it, for example, that if one makes almost any measurement of an animal, a plant, or a component produced by a machine, one does not get a constant value but a quantity whose variation appears to be described by a normal probability model? The answer might be that such measurements usually arise as the result of combining a large number of different factors. For example, the mass of a whale will be the outcome of many influences, some genetic, some environmental. The effect of any one of these influences (for example, a single gene) will probably by itself be very small; but when they are all taken together, the situation is similar to that of adding a large number of independent random variables. The central limit theorem leads us to expect a result for which the appropriate model is approximately normal. In this way, qualitatively, at least, experimental observation is in line with theoretical prediction.

Exercise 16B

1 Business executives (in full uniform, with brief cases) have an average mass of 92 kg, with standard deviation 6 kg. The proprietors of a business conference centre intend to install a new lift, with a design maximum load of 1000 kg; the lift carries a warning "maximum 10 persons". Will it be strong enough?

2 Fig. 8 gives the mileages between successive junctions on a motorway, each correct to the nearest mile. What can you say from these about the greatest and least possible lengths of the whole motorway?

What is the probability that the distance obtained by simply adding these mileages gives a value for the length of the motorway which is not more than a mile out, to the nearest mile?

Figure 8

3 A certain brand of matches has printed on the box the statement "average contents 45 matches". In fact, boxes contain 43, 44, 45, 46, 47 matches with probabilities 0.1, 0.2, 0.4, 0.2, 0.1. A customer buys a packet of 30 boxes of these matches. Calculate the probabilities that he gets (a) exactly 1350 matches, (b) between 1345 and 1355 matches (inclusive).

4 A medical practitioner has an appointments system for his walking patients. The time allotted to each patient has an expected value of five minutes with a standard deviation of two minutes. There is a fixed time of one minute for a patient to leave and the next to enter. The practitioner wishes to have a clinic lasting about $2\frac{1}{2}$ hours. How many patients should be given appointments for each day's clinic if there is not to be more than a five per cent chance of the clinic lasting more than $2\frac{3}{4}$ hours?

How short is the clinic time for which the practitioner can only expect to leave earlier on one per cent of occasions?   [MEI]

5 Repeat the experiment described in §16.4 using a set of random number tables. (If you are working in a class, it would be sensible to share the labour.) Compare the frequencies that you get for the different totals with those predicted by the theoretical model. Apply a goodness-of-fit test to see whether the discrepancy is reasonable.

6 A random variable takes the values 0, 1, 2, 3 with probabilities 0.1, 0.2, 0.3, 0.4 respectively. Calculate its mean and standard deviation.

Using $p_n(t)$ to denote the probability of getting a total of t when n values of this random variable are added, justify the equation

$$p_{n+1}(t) = p_n(t-3) \times 0.4 + p_n(t-2) \times 0.3 + p_n(t-1) \times 0.2 + p_n(t) \times 0.1.$$

Write a computer program to generate values of $p_n(t)$, and run it so as to print out the rows $n = 9$, 16 and 25. Compare the values obtained with those of the normal probability density functions as predicted by the central limit theorem.

7 A random variable takes the values 1, 0 with probabilities a, b, where $a + b = 1$. Calculate its mean and standard deviation.

A sample of n values of this random variable is taken, and the numbers added. What is the exact probability function for the sum? To what does the central limit theorem state that it approximates?

8 A continuous random variable has probability density defined by

$$\phi(x) = \begin{cases} 1 & \text{if } 0 < x < 1, \\ 0 & \text{otherwise.} \end{cases}$$

The total T of n values of this random variable has a probability density function denoted by $\phi_n(t)$. Adapt the argument in §16.4 to justify the relation

$$\phi_{n+1}(t) = \int_0^1 \phi_n(t - u) \, du.$$

Use this to obtain expressions for $\phi_2(t)$ and $\phi_3(t)$. Compare the graph of $\phi_3(t)$ with that of the approximation predicted by the central limit theorem.

9 Show that the situation described in question 8 can be extended to a general continuous random variable with probability density $\phi(x)$, leading to the relation

$$\phi_{n+1}(t) = \int_{-\infty}^{\infty} \phi_n(t - u)\phi(u) \, du.$$

Suppose that $\phi(x) = 2x$ for $0 < x < 1$ and zero otherwise. Draw, on one diagram for each part, the graphs of $\phi_1(u)$ and $\phi_1(t - u)$ in the cases (i) $0 < t < 1$, (ii) $1 < t < 2$. Deduce in each case the range of values of u for which $\phi_1(t - u)\phi_1(u) \neq 0$, and hence find formulae for $\phi_2(t)$ and sketch its graph.

10 Apply the relation at the beginning of question 9 with $\phi(x) = \dfrac{1}{\sqrt{(2\pi)}} e^{-\frac{1}{2}x^2}$ to find expressions for $\phi_2(t)$ and $\phi_3(t)$. What do your results suggest about the expression for $\phi_n(t)$? Use mathematical induction to test if your conjecture is justified.

Deduce that, if a sample of n values of a standard normal random variable is summed, then the total is distributed with *exactly* normal probability density, whether or not n is large. Extend this result to a sample of n values of any normal random variable.

11 The mass of a certain grade of potato is normally distributed with mean 50 g and standard deviation 6 g. If three potatoes are chosen at random find the probability that their total mass will exceed 135 g. [In this and the next question use the result in the second paragraph of question 10.]   [Cambridge]

12 A transport company finds that the amount of fuel that its lorries use during a week may be taken as a normal variable with mean 5000 litres and standard deviation 400 litres. Calculate the probability that in a particular four-week period more than 21 000 litres will be used, assuming that fuel consumption in any week is independent of that in other weeks.

A working year consists of 50 weeks. Calculate limits between which the company can be 95 % confident that a year's fuel consumption will lie.   [Cambridge]

13 The employees in a radio assembly plant average 42 radios each in a day, with standard deviation 2.5. These figures are used as the basis for the introduction of a new "bonus payments" scheme, whereby any employee exceeding a certain number,

N, in a 5-day week qualifies for a bonus on top of the standard wage. The scheme is to be set up in such a way that 90% of the employees may expect to get a bonus in at least 36 weeks of a 48-week working year. Assuming that the variation in performance between employees, and from one day to another, is completely random, calculate an appropriate value for N.

16.6 THE CENTRAL LIMIT THEOREM FOR MEANS

Suppose that a small firm wants to provide a pension of £20 000 a year for the managing director when he retires at age 60. What is it letting itself in for? He may only live to 62, in which case he would only cost them £40 000 in all. On the other hand, he might live to 96, committing them to a bill for nearly £$\frac{3}{4}$ m; this would place an intolerable burden on the firm's resources. The problem for the firm is that it is quite unable to forecast how long he will be drawing his pension.

The firm would therefore be wise to put the matter in the hands of an insurance company specialising in such business, which might be dealing with 100 such cases each year. The advantage is that the insurance company can base its charges on the *average* retirement life-span of these 100 people; and it can predict this with far more certainty than for a single individual.

This is a problem similar to that in §16.5, but expressed now in terms of the mean, M, rather than the total, T, of the n random variables $I_1, I_2, \ldots, I_n$. Since $M = T/n$, the equations

$$E[T/n] = \frac{1}{n} E[T] \quad \text{and} \quad V[T/n] = \frac{1}{n^2} V[T]$$

can be used to give the results

$$E[M] = \frac{1}{n}(n\mu) = \mu, \quad \text{and} \quad V[M] = \frac{1}{n^2}(n\sigma^2) = \frac{\sigma^2}{n}.$$

We have already met these equations in the previous chapter (§15.5), although there they were applied in a rather different context.

But the central limit theorem makes it possible to say more than this. Not much may be known about the probability function for the life expectancy of managing directors retiring at age 60 from small firms – though it probably has a mode in the late sixties and a long tail towards the 'older' end of the scale, which is a factor contributing to the firm's budgeting difficulties. However, since the total T is distributed with approximately normal probability density (as we saw in §16.5), and since the mean is obtained from this merely by scaling, the mean M is also distributed approximately normally. So the insurance company can use:

THE CENTRAL LIMIT THEOREM FOR MEANS. If a sample of n values of a random variable, with mean μ and standard deviation σ, is taken, then when n is large the mean is distributed with approximately normal probability density, with mean μ and standard deviation $\sigma/\sqrt{n}$.

Suppose, for example, that from records kept over a number of years it is estimated that the mean age to which managing directors live is 69, with a standard deviation of 4 years. Then the theorem tells us that the mean life expectancy of the 100 managing directors when they retire at 60 is 9 years, with a standard deviation of $4/\sqrt{100}$, or 0.4 years. If therefore the insurance company decides to base its charges on a life expectancy of 10 years (that is, $2\frac{1}{2}$ standard deviations above the mean), then there is a probability of only $1 - \Phi(2.5)$, or about 0.006, that it will be out of pocket – and of course there is a fair chance that it will make a good profit. The firm, for its part, knows that it has a certain commitment to pay £200 000, however long its managing director lives, and it can budget for the future on this basis. (Note 16.4)

16.7 THE "LAW OF AVERAGES"

If you found yourself standing behind a 190 cm (6 ft 4 in) man in a bus queue, you would probably notice that he was unusually tall, but think no more of it. But if the five men in front of you were all between 185 and 195 cm in height, you might suspect that they were a group of guardsmen or members of the police basketball team.

Once again, the central limit theorem supports our intuition. At a rough estimate, the heights of adult men in Britain have a mean of about 172 cm, with standard deviation about 9 cm. So a 190 cm man is roughly two standard deviations above the mean – unusual, but by no means rare. But if a sample of five men is taken at random, their mean height will be distributed approximately normally with mean 172 cm and standard deviation $9/\sqrt{5}$, that is about 4 cm. So for five men to have an average height as large as 190 cm, about $4\frac{1}{2}$ standard deviations above the mean, is a 'once in a blue moon' event. So it is safe to assume that the men in the bus queue are not a random sample, that is, that there is some special reason which brings five such tall men together.

This type of argument is one of the most important applications of the central limit theorem, and explains why we get much more reliable evidence by taking averages of large samples of measurements than from single measurements. What we are doing is to investigate whether a particular set of measurements could reasonably arise by random selection from a known population with mean μ and standard deviation σ. By taking n measurements, the distribution of sample means is narrowed to a standard deviation of $\sigma/\sqrt{n}$, so that any consistent abnormality in the group will show up very clearly. What is more, the distribution of means has approximately normal probability, so that tables of the normal probability function can be used to assign numerical probabilities to the selection of such a group.

Exercise 16C

1 Packets of a certain detergent have a nominal net weight of 10 ounces. They are packed in batches of 100 packets. A machine fills the packets with detergent in such a way that the weights are normally distributed with mean net weight 10.06 ounces and standard deviation 0.2 ounces. Find the probabilities (a) that a batch does not

contain any underweight packets, (b) that the mean net weight of the packets in a batch does not fall below the nominal net weight. [SMP]

2 The national average sick leave for schoolteachers during a period of 12 months was 8.4 days with a standard deviation of 2.1 days. A local authority finds that in a random sample of 100 teachers the average sick leave during the 12 months was 8.9 days. Test whether this is significantly greater than the national average.
[London]

3 The measurement of IQ is standardised so that, over the population as a whole, the mean IQ is 100 and the standard deviation 15. A class of 25 children is tested and found to have a mean IQ of 104.16. Is this evidence that it is an unusually intelligent class?

4 Rods are being produced in a factory and, over a long period, the population of their lengths is found to have a mean of 47 cm with standard deviation 2 cm. Find the probability that a random sample of 49 rods will have a mean length greater than 47.5 cm. [London]

5 A sawing machine cuts timber into planks. The lengths of the planks are normally distributed with variance $25\,\text{cm}^2$; the mean length is intended to be exactly 100 cm. A random sample of 25 planks was found to have mean length 101.2 cm. Test at the 5 % level of significance whether the mean has been correctly set.
Suppose in fact the mean has been set to 102 cm. What is the probability of accepting the null hypothesis (that the mean is 100 cm) with your test?
What would this probability be if the sample size had been 100? [MEI]

6 The diameters of eggs of the little gull are approximately normally distributed with mean 4.11 cm and standard deviation 0.19 cm. Calculate the probability that an egg chosen at random has a diameter between 3.9 and 4.5 cm.
A sample of eight little gull eggs was collected from a particular island and their diameters, in cm, were

$$4.4,\ 4.5,\ 4.1,\ 3.9,\ 4.4,\ 4.6,\ 4.5,\ 4.1.$$

Assuming that the standard deviation of the diameters of eggs from the island is also 0.19 cm, investigate, at the 1 % level, whether the results indicate that the mean diameter of little gull eggs on this island is different from elsewhere. [London]

7 A manufacturer of dice makes fair dice and also slightly biased dice which are to be used for demonstration purposes in the teaching of probability and statistics. The probability distributions of the scores for the two types of die are shown in the table.

Score	1	2	3	4	5	6
Probability for fair dice	$\frac{1}{6}$	$\frac{1}{6}$	$\frac{1}{6}$	$\frac{1}{6}$	$\frac{1}{6}$	$\frac{1}{6}$
Probability for biased dice	$\frac{1}{10}$	$\frac{1}{10}$	$\frac{1}{5}$	$\frac{1}{5}$	$\frac{1}{5}$	$\frac{1}{5}$

Calculate the expectation and variance of the score for each type of die.
Unfortunately, some dice have been made without distinguishing marks to show whether they are fair or biased. The manufacturer decides to test such dice as

follows: each die is thrown 100 times and the mean score $\bar{x}$ is calculated; if $\bar{x} > 3.7$, the die is classified as biased, but if $\bar{x} \leqslant 3.7$, it is classified as fair. Find the probability that a fair die is wrongly classified as biased as a result of this procedure.

To improve the test procedure the manufacturer increases the number of throws from 100 to N, where N is chosen to make as close as possible to 0.001 the probability of wrongly classifying a biased die as fair. Find the value of N.

[Cambridge]

8 The following experiment was carried out 100 times by each of 16 pairs of children in a class. "Each pair has an ordinary pack of cards from which one child selects a card and replaces it; the other child does likewise, and they score a point if the suit is the same for both." The average number of points scored per pair was 27.2. Test, at the 5% significance level, the hypothesis that all the cards were drawn at random.

[SMP]

9 How large a sample would you take in order to estimate the mean of a population, so that the probability is 0.95 that the sample mean will not differ from the true mean by more than 0.2 of the standard deviation of the population?   [SMP]

10 A naturalist has estimated the mean weight of a large population of field mice by measuring the mean weight of nine of the animals that he has caught at random. What is the probability that he will get an answer that is correct to within one-quarter of the population standard deviation?

What is the smallest sized sample he should take in order for this level of probability to be at least 0.95?   [SMP]

16.8 ESTIMATING A POPULATION MEAN

We can now come back once more to the problem of interval estimation, and apply the preceding theory to estimate the mean, μ, of a population of measurements from a knowledge of the mean and standard deviation of a sample. We already know, from §15.5, that the mean of the sample is an unbiased estimator for μ; the central limit theorem makes it possible to place this inside a confidence interval.

It must be said from the outset that the method described in this section is only approximate, and that it should be used only when the sample is fairly large, say 50 or more. The argument contains one not-very-satisfactory step, which needs to be recognised. In Chapter 19 an alternative method will be developed which can be used with far smaller samples – but, even then, only under certain conditions.

It is interesting to illustrate the method by applying it to the same situation as that used for the estimation of a population median, and to compare the results (see Example 2, §16.3).

Example 4
Regarding the sample of masses at birth recorded in §11.1 as typical, estimate the mean mass for all babies born in this part of England at the present time.

It was stated in §13.4 that the sample of masses of 100 babies has a mean of 3.360 kg and standard deviation 0.463 kg. So we cannot do better than to estimate the mean mass of the population to be 3.360 kg. But the question is, what reliability can be placed on this estimate? Can we be reasonably sure that it is correct to within 0.005 kg, or 0.1 kg, or what?

Now lurking in the background is the actual, fixed but unknown mean μ. The central limit theorem states that, when we take samples of 100 babies, we get sample means M whose probability distribution is normal, with mean μ and standard deviation $\sigma/\sqrt{100}$, or 0.1σ. But here lies the problem: we do not know σ!

This is where the argument becomes less than wholly satisfactory. Without knowing σ, we have reached an impasse. So the best we can do, if there is to be any further progress, is to estimate σ by using the standard deviation S of the sample; and if the sample happens to have a 'freak' standard deviation, that is just bad luck. And even this is not straightforward. For one thing, there is a choice of estimators $\hat{\sigma}$; and if we decide to go for an unbiased estimator, then the theory tells us that $\widehat{\sigma^2} = \dfrac{n}{n-1}S^2$ is an unbiased estimator for σ^2 (see §15.6), but it does not follow that $\sqrt{\dfrac{n}{n-1}}\,S$ is an unbiased estimator for σ. Nevertheless, it is the best we can hope to get; and it will turn out in Chapter 19 that there is some justification for this choice. So let us swallow our strict mathematical principles and, in this example, estimate σ to be $\sqrt{\frac{100}{99}} \times 0.463$ kg or 0.465 kg.

On this basis, the means M for samples of 100 babies are distributed with normal probability density with mean μ (still unknown) and standard deviation 0.1×0.465 kg, that is 0.0465 kg. This is illustrated in Fig. 9.

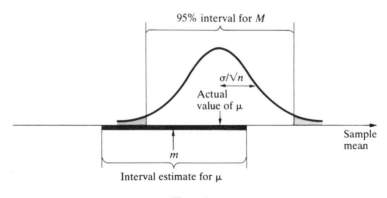

95% interval for M

$\sigma/\sqrt{n}$

Actual value of μ

Sample mean

m

Interval estimate for μ

Figure 9

The scene is now set to make some deductions about μ. Using a 5% significance level, the cut-off comes 1.96 standard deviations either side of the mean; and $1.96 \times 0.0465 \approx 0.091$. So, if a random sample of 100 babies has mean mass M, then

$$P(\mu - 0.091\,\text{kg} < M < \mu + 0.091\,\text{kg}) = 0.95.$$

The two inequalities here can each be rearranged:

$$\mu - 0.091 \text{ kg} < M \Leftrightarrow \mu < M + 0.091 \text{ kg},$$

and

$$M < \mu + 0.091 \text{ kg} \Leftrightarrow M - 0.091 \text{ kg} < \mu.$$

So the probability statement can be recast in the form

$$P(M - 0.091 \text{ kg} < \mu < M + 0.091 \text{ kg}) = 0.95.$$

Remember that this has to be read "the probability that the random interval ... contains the value of μ is 0.95", and *not* (meaninglessly) "the probability that μ lies inside the interval ... is 0.95"; it is a statement about a random measurement M, not about a fixed measurement μ.

Finally, M can be given the value found from the particular sample of 100 babies weighed, which is 3.360 kg. On the basis of this evidence, we can assert with 95% confidence that μ lies within 0.091 kg of 3.360 kg; that is, a 95% confidence interval for μ has bounds 3.269 kg and 3.451 kg. (Compare these with the bounds 3.230 kg and 3.450 kg found for the population median in Example 2.)

The argument can be summed up in algebraic terms as follows. The problem is to decide within what interval the population mean μ might reasonably be located, if a sample of n measurements drawn at random from the population has mean m and standard deviation S. The first step is to estimate σ as $\sqrt{\dfrac{n}{n-1}} S$. Then the central limit theorem states that means of samples drawn from the population are distributed approximately normally with mean μ and standard deviation $\sigma/\sqrt{n}$, for which we substitute $S/\sqrt{(n-1)}$. (Note that another way of saying this is that, if t denotes the quantity $(m - \mu)\sqrt{(n-1)}/S$, then the random variable T is distributed with approximately standard normal probability density.) It can then be argued that a 95% confidence interval for μ is bounded by $m \pm 1.96\, S/\sqrt{(n-1)}$ (with corresponding changes in the numerical factor for other significance levels).

Exercise 16D

1 In Exercise 11A, question 1 you carried out experiments to determine the distribution of a variety of measurements in a selected sample. Use your results to obtain confidence intervals for the mean values of the quantities measured, within some population of which your sample could be regarded as typical.

2 The table below gives the distribution of the age in years at marriage of 200 men.

Age (centre of interval)	17.5	22.5	27.5	32.5	37.5	42.5	47.5	52.5	57.5	62.5
Frequency	31	73	48	21	12	6	3	2	1	3

Calculate estimates of the mean and standard deviation of these ages.

If these ages may be assumed to be a random sample from a large population, obtain 95% confidence limits for the population mean, and explain carefully what your limits signify.   [Cambridge]

3   For the data in Exercise 13C, question 4, find a 95% confidence interval for the mean activity of the enzyme in normal healthy adults.

4   Use the data of Exercise 13C, question 3 to find 99% confidence intervals for the mean heights of boys and of girls aged between 7 years 3 months and 7 years 4 months in the United Kingdom at the time of the study.

5   A certain type of battery for calculators is said to last for 2000 hours. A sample of 200 of these batteries was tested; the mean life was 1995 hours and the standard deviation of the lives was 25.5 hours. Use these data to test the hypothesis that the population mean life is 2000 hours against the alternative hypothesis that it is less than 2000 hours.   [Cambridge]

16.9   COMPARING TWO SAMPLES

The processes of estimating a proportion and estimating a mean have certain common features:

(1) They depend on the principle that, for large samples, the random variable

$$\frac{\text{sample statistic} - \text{corresponding population parameter}}{\text{standard deviation of the sample statistic}}$$

is distributed with approximately standard normal probability density. (Note 16.5)

(2) The standard deviation of the sample statistic, which is a theoretical quantity depending on the parameters of the population from which the sample is taken, is not known. It is therefore replaced by an estimate, found from the statistics of the particular sample selected.

Notice that there are two separate approximations involved. The particular applications described in §§16.2 and 16.8 are summarised in Table 1.

Application	Proportion	Mean
Population	α	μ
Sample statistic (Note 16.6)	A	M
Standard deviation of sample statistic	$\sqrt{\dfrac{\alpha(1-\alpha)}{n}}$	$\dfrac{\sigma}{\sqrt{n}}$
Approximation to the standard deviation	$\sqrt{\dfrac{a(1-a)}{n}}$	$\dfrac{S}{\sqrt{(n-1)}}$

where a, S stand for the proportion, standard deviation respectively in the particular sample selected. (Note 16.7)

Table 1

Just the same general approach can be adopted with other situations in which a hypothesis has to be tested or an interval estimate is required. One group of such problems deals with the difference between the proportions, or between the means, when two separate samples are taken. There are really two different types of problem, which need to be distinguished:

(A) The point at issue may be whether or not the populations from which the samples are drawn are essentially the same. For example, suppose that in the two secondary schools in a town 41% and 28% of the pupils respectively wear spectacles; is this just an accident of the way in which the pupils were allocated to schools, or does the difference have an underlying cause? (Note 16.8) Such questions are investigated by making a "null hypothesis" that there is no essential difference, and asking whether the observed proportions might reasonably follow from that hypothesis.

(B) It may be quite clear that the samples are drawn from different populations, and the point at issue is to estimate how much difference there is. For instance, by putting an additive in feed for cattle, a farmer may be able to raise their weight at market; but to decide whether it is worth while, he needs to know by how much on average the weight is increased.

The two types of problem are tackled in slightly different ways.

The argument starts off in the same way in every case. We are sampling a population (or populations) described by a certain parameter, which we will denote by ζ; it may be a proportion, or a mean measurement. Two samples are taken, for which the parameter values are ζ_1 and ζ_2. In type A we are testing the null hypothesis $\zeta_1 = \zeta_2$, or $\zeta_1 - \zeta_2 = 0$; in type B we want to estimate $\zeta_1 - \zeta_2$.

Suppose that, when the samples are taken, the values of the sample statistics are z_1 and z_2. These are particular values of random variables Z_1 and Z_2, so we can use the properties

$$E[Z_1 - Z_2] = E[Z_1] - E[Z_2] = \zeta_1 - \zeta_2$$

and, since the samples are taken independently,

$$V[Z_1 - Z_2] = V[Z_1] + V[Z_2].$$

Applying these equations to the particular cases, it follows that for proportions

$$E[\text{difference of proportions}] = \alpha_1 - \alpha_2,$$

$$V[\text{difference of proportions}] = \frac{\alpha_1(1 - \alpha_1)}{n_1} + \frac{\alpha_2(1 - \alpha_2)}{n_2};$$

and for means

$$E[\text{difference of means}] = \mu_1 - \mu_2,$$

$$V[\text{difference of means}] = \frac{\sigma_1^2}{n_1} + \frac{\sigma_2^2}{n_2}.$$

One further piece of information is needed: that if Z_1 and Z_2 are normally distributed (which is approximately true for large samples), then $Z_1 - Z_2$ is also normally distributed. The justification of this will be found in the next chapter (see §17.5), but for the time being it will be convenient to assume it. Then, in the two applications, it will follow that

$$\frac{(A_1 - A_2) - (\alpha_1 - \alpha_2)}{\sqrt{\left\{\dfrac{\alpha_1(1 - \alpha_1)}{n_1} + \dfrac{\alpha_2(1 - \alpha_2)}{n_2}\right\}}} \quad \text{and} \quad \frac{(M_1 - M_2) - (\mu_1 - \mu_2)}{\sqrt{\left\{\dfrac{\sigma_1^2}{n_1} + \dfrac{\sigma_2^2}{n_2}\right\}}}$$

are distributed with approximately standard normal probability density.

But now we hit the same problem as before: to apply these, we need to know what values to substitute for α_1 and α_2, or for σ_1 and σ_2, in the bottom line of the fraction. The best that can be done is to estimate them from the sample values; but just how this is done differs for type A and type B problems.

In type A, the null hypothesis is that the samples come from the *same* population: so that α_1 and α_2 are both estimated as a, the proportion obtained by taking the two samples together; σ_1^2 and σ_2^2 are both estimated as $\dfrac{n}{n-1} S^2$, where S is the standard deviation of the combined sample. The hypotheses $\alpha_1 - \alpha_2 = 0$ or $\mu_1 - \mu_2 = 0$ are therefore tested on the basis that

$$\frac{A_1 - A_2}{\sqrt{\left\{a(1 - a)\left(\dfrac{1}{n_1} + \dfrac{1}{n_2}\right)\right\}}} \quad \text{or} \quad \frac{M_1 - M_2}{\sqrt{\left\{\dfrac{n}{n-1} S^2\left(\dfrac{1}{n_1} + \dfrac{1}{n_2}\right)\right\}}}$$

are distributed with approximately standard normal probability density.

This is obviously not appropriate for type B problems, and then α_1, α_2 or σ_1^2, σ_2^2 have to be estimated separately as a_1, a_2 (the proportions in the two samples) or $\dfrac{n_1}{n_1 - 1} S_1^2$, $\dfrac{n_2}{n_2 - 1} S_2^2$. So confidence intervals for $\alpha_1 - \alpha_2$ or for $\mu_1 - \mu_2$ are found on the basis that

$$\frac{(A_1 - A_2) - (\alpha_1 - \alpha_2)}{\sqrt{\left\{\dfrac{a_1(1 - a_1)}{n_1} + \dfrac{a_2(1 - a_2)}{n_2}\right\}}} \quad \text{or} \quad \frac{(M_1 - M_2) - (\mu_1 - \mu_2)}{\sqrt{\left\{\dfrac{S_1^2}{n_1 - 1} + \dfrac{S_2^2}{n_2 - 1}\right\}}}$$

are distributed with approximately standard normal probability density.

Example 5
In the sample of masses at birth of 100 babies recorded in §11.1, there were 44 boys with a mean mass of 3.480 kg, and 56 girls with a mean mass of 3.258 kg. Does this support the theory that boys weigh more than girls at birth?

Put another way, the question is: could it be that the masses of boys and of girls are typical samples from the same population, and that the difference between the means is just the result of sampling fluctuations? So this is a type A problem. We consider the null hypothesis

Hypothesis 1.   The mean masses of boys and girls are the same.

against the alternative hypothesis

Hypothesis 2.   The mean mass of boys is greater than the mean mass of girls.

It was stated in §13.4 that the combined sample of boys' and girls' masses has standard deviation 0.463 kg. So substituting this for S, and putting $n_1 = 44$, $n = 56$, $n = 100$ in the denominator of the expression for the test statistic for the difference in means gives

$$\sqrt{\left\{\frac{n}{n-1}\,S^2\left(\frac{1}{n_1}+\frac{1}{n_2}\right)\right\}} = \sqrt{\left\{\frac{100}{99}\times 0.463^2\left(\frac{1}{44}+\frac{1}{56}\right)\right\}} = 0.097\,\text{kg}.$$

The critical value at the 5 % significance level for a one-tail test is found from the tables of N(0, 1) to be 1.645. The criterion for rejecting the null hypothesis is therefore that

$$\frac{M_1 - M_2}{0.097\ \text{kg}} > 1.645,$$

that is $M_1 - M_2 > 0.154$ kg. But from the data the difference in the means of the two samples is 3.489 kg $- 3.258$ kg $= 0.231$ kg. This indicates that the null hypothesis should be rejected, and that in the whole population the mean mass of boys is greater than the mean mass of girls.

Example 6
In a national survey of mathematical attainment a test question was set to 2000 children, and 33.4 % got it right. The question was then altered by adding a diagram, and set to another 1000 children; this time 51.3 % got it right. How much difference does this suggest that adding a diagram makes to a question of this kind?

Clearly in this example there is a difference in performance between one form of the test question and the other, so this is a type B problem. Substituting $a_1 = 0.513$, $a_2 = 0.334$, $n_1 = 1000$, $n_2 = 2000$ in the approximate expression for the standard deviation of the sample statistic for the difference in proportions gives

$$\sqrt{\left\{\frac{a_1(1-a_1)}{n_1}+\frac{a_2(1-a_2)}{n_2}\right\}} = \sqrt{\left\{\frac{0.513\times 0.487}{1000}+\frac{0.334\times 0.666}{2000}\right\}} \approx 0.0190.$$

Now the critical value at the 5 % significance level for normal probability is 1.96, and the observed difference of proportions in the two samples is $0.513 - 0.334 = 0.179$. The usual argument, applied to the test statistic

$$\frac{(A_1 - A_2) - (\alpha_1 - \alpha_2)}{0.0190},$$

establishes with 95 % confidence that $\alpha_1 - \alpha_2$, the improvement in success rate in the whole population due to the provision of a diagram, lies within the interval $0.179 \pm 1.96 \times 0.0190$; that is, between 14.2 % and 21.6 %.

Q.7   Write out this "usual argument" in full.

Exercise 16E

1   At the end of term Mavis was given a random French vocabulary test, and got 58 words right out of 100. She went to France for the holidays, and at the beginning of next term she took another test and got 35 right out of 50. Could it be justifiably claimed that going to France improved her vocabulary?

2   At the outset of an election campaign, an opinion poll is published which shows that, out of a random sample of 100 electors in one constituency, 35% supported party A. Two weeks later a second poll in the same constituency showed that 38% of a random sample of 900 electors now supported party A. Analyse these figures to determine whether they supply evidence, significant at the 5% level, of a change in support for party A.   [Cambridge]

3   In the course of a survey concerning the proportion of left-handed children the following figures were obtained from two schools.

	Number of children	Proportion left-handed
School 1	620	0.284
School 2	475	0.341

Show that an approximate 95% confidence interval for the population proportion, p, of left-handed children derived from the data from School 1 is $0.25 < p < 0.32$, and calculate a corresponding interval for School 2.

Explain briefly what is wrong with the following argument: "Since these two confidence intervals overlap, we cannot reject, at the 5% significance level, the hypothesis that the populations from which the children in the two schools are samples each have the same proportion of left-handed children."

Calculate the overall proportion of left-handed children in both schools, and show that the observed difference in proportions is significant at the 5% level.
                                                            [Cambridge]

4   Two types of battery were compared for the length of time (in hours) they lasted. The data obtained are summarised in the table:

Battery type	Number tested	Sample mean	Sample standard deviation
A	200	1995	25.5
B	150	2005	32.8

Test the hypothesis that the populations from which these samples were drawn have equal means against the alternative hypothesis of unequal means.   [Cambridge]

5   For the data given in Exercise 13C, question 3 from the National Child Development Study, test the hypothesis that the excess of 0.30 inches in the mean height of the boys compared with the girls could be accounted for by the random nature of the sampling process.

If this hypothesis turns out to be untenable, find a 95% confidence interval for the excess of the mean height of boys over that of girls at this age.

6   The heights of 100 men in a random sample were measured, giving a sample mean and standard deviation of 190 cm and 10 cm respectively. Determine 95 % confidence limits for the population mean.

In another random sample the heights of 800 women were measured, giving a sample mean of 175 cm and sample standard deviation of 5 cm. Find 95 % confidence limits for the difference between the two population means.   [MEI]

7   A psychological investigation was made into the attitude of girls to the way men dress. An actor, dressed in jeans, attempted to interview 50 girls selected randomly in the streets with a dummy simulated opinion poll. Later the experiment was repeated with the same actor dressed in a smart suit. In the first stage 38 girls refused to answer the questionnaire and in the second stage 42 out of 50 girls agreed to answer. What can be said about the girls' attitude to men's dress from the results of this experiment?
                                                                                          [MEI]

Revision exercise B

1   A learner driver has constant probability k of passing the driving test at any attempt.
    (a) Find the most probable number of times that he will have to take the test.
    (b) Find the expected value of the number of times that he will have to take it.
    (c) Find the value of k which maximises the probability that he will take it exactly four times.
    (d) Find a formula for the probability that he will have to take it more than n times.
                                                                                      [SMP]

2   Each of the two ends of a domino has a number of spots between 0 and 6, and in a complete set of dominoes each possible combination occurs once. Find the mean and standard deviation for the total number of spots on a domino.
       The dominoes are said to match if they can be placed end to end so that the two touching ends have the same number of spots. Show that the probability that two dominoes (selected at random from a complete set) match is $\frac{7}{18}$.
       Given two matching dominoes neither of which is a double, with their matching ends touching, find the probability that a third domino (drawn at random from the remainder of the set) will match one or both of their free ends.   [SMP]

3   A random variable Y taking values $0, 1, 2, \ldots$ has probability distribution given by

$$P(Y = n) = ka^{-n}, \quad \text{where } a > 1.$$

Show that $k = 1 - 1/a$, and that the probability generating function for Y may be written in the form

$$G(t) = \frac{a - 1}{a - t}.$$

Deduce the mean and variance of the distribution.   [Cambridge]

4   A pack of 10 cards contains 3 red cards and 7 black cards. Two separate experiments are conducted with these cards. In experiment I, a card is drawn at random from the pack, its colour is noted and the card is then returned to the pack. The pack is shuffled, a card is drawn and its colour noted. This sequence of events is repeated until four cards have been drawn. In experiment II, four cards are drawn at random from the pack, one after the other without replacement.
    (a) Find, for each experiment, the probability that two red cards and two black cards will be obtained.
    (b) In experiment I, find the expected number of black cards that will be drawn.
    (c) In experiment II, find the expected number of cards that will be drawn in order to obtain just one black card. (Drawing ceases after the first appearance of a black card.)   [Cambridge]

5   A biased die is such that the probability of obtaining a six is 0.05, but the other numbers occur with equal probabilities. This die is thrown twice and the total score, T, is calculated. Find the expectation and variance of T.

The same die is thrown fifty times. Using a suitable approximation to the binomial distribution, obtain the probability that (a) there will be two sixes, (b) there will be more than two sixes. [Cambridge]

6 The variables X, Y are independent, and each has probability density function given by

$$\phi(t) = e^{-t} \quad (t \geqslant 0).$$

The variable U is defined to be the maximum of the variables X, Y. By considering $P(U \leqslant t)$, show that the probability density function of U is

$$2(e^{-t} - e^{-2t}) \quad (t \geqslant 0),$$

and hence find the expectation and variance of U.

Find also the probability density function of V, defined as the minimum of X and Y. [SMP]

7 On a BBC wildlife programme it was stated that when an osprey dives for a fish, it is successful on average once in every three dives; and that during the breeding season a male osprey needs to catch six fish a day to feed its family. Write down an expression for the probability that, if an osprey makes n dives, it catches its sixth fish on the last dive. Find the most probable number of dives needed for an osprey to catch exactly six fish in a day.

Write a program to compute the probability that, after n dives, an osprey will have caught fewer than six fish. How many dives must it make for this probability to be less than (a) 0.5, (b) 0.01 ?

What is the expected value of the number of dives needed for an osprey to catch six fish in a day?

8 A random variable X has a probability density function ϕ given by

$$\phi(x) = \begin{cases} cx(5 - x) & \text{if } 0 \leqslant x \leqslant 5, \\ 0 & \text{otherwise.} \end{cases}$$

Show that $c = 6/125$ and find the mean of X.

The lifetime X in years of an electric light bulb has this distribution. Given that a lamp standard is fitted with two such new bulbs and that their failures are independent, find the probability that neither bulb fails in the first year, and the probability that exactly one bulb fails within two years. [MEI]

9 The continuous random variable X has probability density function ϕ given by

$$\phi(x) = \begin{cases} kx^2(1 - x) & \text{for } 0 \leqslant x \leqslant 1, \\ 0 & \text{otherwise,} \end{cases}$$

where k is a constant.
(a) Determine the value of k, and sketch the graph of the density function.
(b) Find $E[X]$ and $V[X]$.
(c) Find $P(X < E[X])$. [Cambridge]

10 Random samples, each of unit volume, are taken from a well-mixed cell suspension in which, on average, one cell of special type is present per unit volume. Find the probability that a sample will not contain more than two of the special cells.

If ten such samples are taken, find the probability that exactly five of these will contain not more than two of the special cells.

If 100 samples are taken and only 85 of them contain two or less special cells, what would you conclude about the suspension? [London]

11 A trial consists of selecting a card at random from a pack of 52 playing cards and then replacing it. Obtain estimates for the probability that, in 104 such trials,
    (a) the ace of spades is selected at least 3 times,
    (b) at least 20 of the cards selected are spades.   [London]

12 When subjected to a dose of insecticide, a particular breed of insect will die if the dose exceeds the tolerance of the insect. For a large population of this breed of insect, the tolerance (measured in appropriate units) is normally distributed with mean 30 and variance 9. The population is subjected to a dose of insecticide of strength 27. Assuming that the effect of each dose is independent of the previous dose, show that the probability that an insect selected at random from the survivors would die when subjected to a dose of strength 34 is approximately 0.89.   [London]

13 Over a number of years an average of 40 out of every 100 who underwent a difficult operation survived. New medical techniques were then introduced and 73 out of 150 patients survived the operation. Explain whether or not the maintaining of these techniques is statistically justified.   [SMP]

14 A certain office has a stock of identical printed forms which are used independently. On any working day at most one of the forms is used, and the probability that one form is used is $\frac{1}{3}$. There are 250 working days in the year. Using a suitable approximation, calculate the number of forms that must be in stock at the beginning of the year if there is to be a 95% probability that they will not all be used before the end of the year.
    If one form in 100 is unusable through faulty printing, and these faults occur at random, calculate the probability that in a batch of 250 forms there will be not more than one that is unusable.   [Cambridge]

15 The weights (in grams) of male wrens are distributed normally with mean 17 and variance 4, and the weights of female wrens are also distributed normally with mean 12 and variance 1. Sketch the distributions, marking the mean value in each case, of
    (a) the weights of the population of male wrens,
    (b) the weights of the population of female wrens,
    (c) the weights of a population of which half are male and half are female wrens.
    Find the probability that a wren drawn at random from population (c) will have a weight of less than 12 g.   [London]

16 A machine in an amusement arcade works as follows. The player inserts 1p and then fires a ball at a target. There is a probability 0.1 that the ball hits the bullseye, in which case the machine pays out 2p. The ball hits the outer part of the target with probability 0.4, and if this happens the player receives no payout but has another shot free. Otherwise the ball misses the target completely and the machine pays out nothing. A trial consists of the player inserting 1p and playing until the ball either hits the bullseye or else misses the target completely. Show that the player will in the long run get back an average of $\frac{1}{3}$p per trial.
    On a given day a total of £8 is paid into the machine. Estimate the probability that the owner of the machine makes a profit of more than £5 that day.   [SMP]

17 Show that the mean number of squares to which a knight placed at random on an (otherwise empty) 8×8 chessboard can move is $5\frac{1}{4}$.
    In a game two players, A and B, independently and at random select one square each on a chessboard. If they both choose the same square, there is no score. If a

knight on B's square threatens A's square, then A pays B 10p. Otherwise B pays A 1p. Show that the probability that B threatens A's square is $\frac{21}{256}$. Find also the mean and the standard deviation for the amount of money B pays A.

Estimate the probability that B makes a profit in a sequence of 100 games.

[SMP]

18   In a capture-recapture experiment (see Exercise 4A, question 4) 40 animals were caught and marked on the first occasion. Subsequently 60 were caught, of which 15 were found to be marked. The population was therefore *estimated* as 160. Consider, however, the possibility that the population of the colony was in fact 200. Taking this as a working hypothesis, find the probability that 15 or more marked animals would have been caught in the second sample of 60. On the basis of this calculation, discuss whether you consider it reasonable on the evidence that the population might have been as large as 200.

Investigate similarly the hypothesis that the population might have been as small as 100.   [SMP]

19   In a triangular taste test a food taster is presented with a triangular tray that has on it three identical bowls. Two of these bowls contain samples of a given foodstuff, while the third bowl contains a sample of a second foodstuff that differs from the first only in taste. The taster tastes each bowl and correctly identifies the second foodstuff on three occasions out of a series of five triangular taste tests. Test the hypothesis that he is unable to distinguish between the two substances.

It is decided to use a series of 20 repetitions of the triangular taste test for a trainee tester. What number of correct identifications should the teacher demand in order to be sure at the 5% significance level that the trainee is genuinely able to detect a taste difference?   [SMP]

20   In a certain large population, heights are distributed normally about a mean of 180 cm with standard deviation 5 cm. Random samples are taken with three in each sample and their heights are arranged in increasing order. In 1000 such samples, approximately how many will have
(a) the middle height under 175 cm;
(b) the least height less than 175 cm;
(c) the least height between 175 and 180 cm?   [SMP]

21   The playing time was measured for each of 1000 cassettes chosen at random. The following results were obtained.

Playing time (min)	less than 60	60–	61–	62–	63–	64 or more
Frequency	33	225	380	280	78	4

Carry out a chi-squared test to determine whether these frequencies are consistent with the hypothesis that the playing time is normally distributed with mean 61.5 minutes and standard deviation 1 minute.   [Cambridge]

22   It was suspected that candidates from schools with small sixth forms did not have a fair chance of getting into a certain university. A study was therefore made of the 60 applicants for one faculty; the following list gives the size of sixth form for each applicant's school and whether they were successful (s) or unsuccessful (u) in gaining a place:

204 s	157 s	245 s	89 s	301 u	161 s	60 s	196 s	196 u	113 s
48 s	238 s	302 u	335 s	150 s	67 u	301 s	206 s	45 u	78 u
215 s	335 u	128 u	56 u	126 s	223 s	88 s	215 u	302 s	28 u
60 s	124 u	255 u	137 s	192 u	229 s	68 s	136 s	343 s	45 s
39 u	109 s	38 u	218 u	207 s	310 s	229 s	218 u	178 s	199 s
70 u	77 u	192 u	302 s	146 u	69 s	39 u	94 u	124 s	84 s

Taking a 'small' sixth form to be one with fewer than 100 pupils, analyse the data statistically and discuss whether they give support to the suspicion of unfairness.

Present the information in the table in a suitable graphical form to show the degree of success in schools with sixth forms of various sizes.   [SMP]

23 A firm makes two different brands of similar electronic components, A and B. The life of brand A has mean 23 hours, standard deviation 2 hours; the life of brand B has mean 25 hours, standard deviation 5 hours. Their lives are assumed to be distributed according to a normal probability model. Which brand is more likely to break down over a period of (a) 22 hours, (b) 20 hours?

Replacing such a component in the course of a certain job causes expensive delay, so a new component is fitted before starting the job. If the component lasts for x hours, it ensures a profit £$F(x)$, where

$$F(x) = \begin{cases} -100, & 0 < x < 20; \\ 20, & 20 \leqslant x \leqslant 25; \\ 40, & x \geqslant 25. \end{cases}$$

Which brand gives the greater expected profit?   [SMP]

24 A chemical plant has regular chemical analyses carried out on it for the purposes of quality control. If one of these analyses ever results in an observation that differs from what is thought to be the correct mean value by more than 3 standard deviations, then the plant is shut down until appropriate remedial action can be taken. An observation of the above type is therefore said to "fall in the action category". Suppose now that the mean value were suddenly to shift by 1 standard deviation (without any change in the standard deviation itself). Show that the probability that a given subsequent observation will fall into the action category is 0.023, approximately.

If, following this change in mean value, X denotes the number of observations that are made before the first 'actionable' observation occurs, find the probability generator for X. Hence show that E[X] lies between 42 and 43.   [SMP]

25 An unbiased die is thrown repeatedly until a 5 and a 6 have been obtained. The random variable M denotes the number of throws required. Show that E[M] = 9 and calculate V[M].

26 A man maintains a check on the balance in his current bank account to the nearest pound; that is, after each transaction in or out of the account the record of the balance is adjusted, after ignoring fractions of a pound up to 49p and counting all fractions from 50p to 99p as one pound. If all fractions are equally likely, calculate the expected bias in his record and, using a normal approximation, the probability that after two transactions into the account and one hundred transactions out of the account there is a cumulative error of £5.00 or more.   [MEI]

27 The weekly demand for petrol, X, measured in thousands of gallons, at a small petrol station is given by a random variable whose density function is

$$\phi(x) = \begin{cases} 12x^2(1-x) & \text{if } 0 \leqslant x \leqslant 1, \\ 0 & \text{elsewhere.} \end{cases}$$

Sketch the graph of this function. Find the mean and variance of the distribution of X. What is the most likely value of X?

The station's storage tank is filled up with petrol once a week, at the beginning of the week. It is required that the probability of meeting the weekly demand shall be at least 95%. Estimate from your graph the minimum size of storage tank necessary, and improve this estimate by one application of Newton's iterative formula.

Assuming that the weekly demands for petrol are mutually independent, use a normal approximation to find the probability that in a year (52 weeks) the total demand for petrol exceeds 35 000 gallons.

28 The consultation time, in minutes, in a doctor's surgery is distributed with probability density function

$$\phi(x) = \begin{cases} \alpha e^{-0.208x} & \text{if } x \geqslant 0, \\ 0 & \text{otherwise.} \end{cases}$$

Determine α and find the probability that a consultation lasts for more than ten minutes.

No patient arrives late and there is always at least one patient waiting for the doctor until the last patient goes in. The consultation times for patients are independent. Use a normal approximation to find the probability that the surgery lasts for more than 2 hours 15 minutes if appointments have been made for 20 patients.   [MEI]

29 The variable X takes the values $1, -1, 0$ with probabilities p, q and $1 - p - q$. Show that $E[X] = p - q$ and that the variance $V[X]$ is $p + q - (p - q)^2$.

The variable Y is defined by

$$Y = (X_1 + X_2 + \ldots + X_n)/n,$$

where the variables $X_1, X_2, \ldots, X_n$ are independent and all have the distribution defined above. Find $E[Y]$ and $V[Y]$.

An opinion pollster samples n people (with repetitions allowed) in an attempt to obtain information about the proportions p, q and $1 - p - q$ of people who support one of three political parties A, B and C. It is known in advance that p and q are both close to 0.4, and the main quantity of interest is $p - q$. If n_A, n_B and $n - n_A - n_B$ are the numbers in the sample supporting parties A, B and C, show that

$$E\left[\frac{n_A - n_B}{n}\right] = p - q, \quad V\left[\frac{n_A - n_B}{n}\right] \approx \frac{0.8}{n}.$$

Use the central limit theorem to estimate the smallest value of n that would be needed for a sample of the above type to be 95% certain of correctly forecasting which of the parties A, B was the more popular, when p exceeds q by 0.01.
                                                                [SMP]

30 The continuous random variable X has probability density function

$$\phi(x) = \begin{cases} \lambda e^{-\lambda x} & \text{if } x > 0, \\ 0 & \text{elsewhere,} \end{cases}$$

where $\lambda > 0$. Find, in terms of λ, numbers l and u such that $P(X < l) = 0.05$ and $P(X > u) = 0.05$. Deduce that

$$0.90 = P(0.334X < \lambda^{-1} < 19.496X).$$

Hence write down a 90% confidence interval for λ^{-1} given a single observation on X having value 10.0.

$\bar{X}$ denotes the mean of a random sample of 100 observations on X. State the approximate distribution of $\bar{X}$, and hence show that, using this approximation,

$$0.90 = P(0.859\bar{X} < \lambda^{-1} < 1.197\bar{X})$$

and give a 90% confidence interval for λ^{-1} given that the value of the sample mean is 10.0.   [MEI]

Project exercises B

B1 TORTOISE RACE

Children play a game in which model tortoises are moved forward on a board marked out in unit squares, according to the number thrown on a die. Each tortoise begins on square zero.

1   Find the expected value, and the variance, of the number occupied by any one of the tortoises after 10 throws. What can you say about the probability distribution for the number of this square?

2   Deduce an approximate value for the probability of being on or beyond square 40 after 10 throws.

3   Repeat questions 1 and 2 for other numbers of throws.

4   Suppose that square 40 is the 'finish' (but that there is no requirement in the rules to throw exactly at the end – it is good enough to get 'past the post'). What is the possibility space for the number of moves needed to complete the course?

5   Investigate in numerical terms the approximate probability function for the number of moves it takes to complete the course.

6   Write a computer program to play this game and run it a large number of times, recording on each occasion the number of moves it takes to reach square 40. Compare the frequencies of different numbers of moves with the expected frequencies suggested by your probability function.

B2 TWO COLLECTING GAMES

Game 1.   On a touring holiday a family collects car numbers, beginning with the number 1, then 2, then 3, and so on. The aim is to get up to the number 50 by the end of the holiday.

Game 2.   A petrol company produces picture cards of "Great Athletes"; there are 50 different cards altogether. Each time a customer buys 10 litres of petrol he is given one of these cards, chosen at random. The customer's aim is to collect a complete set of the cards.

1   Assuming that all cars have numbers between 1 and 999, and that these occur with equal probability, find the expectation and variance of the number of car sightings the family will have to make in game 1 in order to get the number 1.

2   Find the expectation and variance of the number of car sightings the family will have to make to get all the numbers from 1 to 50 in turn.

3   How many sightings would they have to make to have an 80% chance of reaching their target? Are they likely to see that many cars on a family touring holiday?

4   In game 2, find the expectation and variance of the number of 10-litre purchases which would be necessary in order to get (*a*) the first card, (*b*) the second card (different from the first), (*c*) the third card, (*d*) the rth card.

5   Find the expectation and variance of the number of 10-litre purchases which would be necessary in order to get the complete set of cards.

6 In game 2, would you expect the probability model for the number of games needed to get a complete set to be approximately normal? Investigate this probability model by simulating the game on a computer and running it a large number of times.

B3 HAPHAZARDS

The haphazards are a family of insects all of which have similar life-styles. By day they remain completely stationary, but each night they transfer their position by 1 metre exactly in a straight line in some direction selected at random. The species differ, however, in the number of random directions available to them.

1 Most primitive are the "linear haphazards", which spend their whole life in one straight line, making nocturnal displacements of $+1$ and -1 with equal probabilities. If X denotes the insect's displacement from its starting-place after n nights, find a probability generator for the random variable X. Deduce from this that $E[X^2] = n$.

2 The "plane haphazards" live entirely in one plane, on which two possible perpendicular directions of motion are available. The insects make nocturnal displacements of $\begin{bmatrix} 1 \\ 0 \end{bmatrix}$, $\begin{bmatrix} -1 \\ 0 \end{bmatrix}$, $\begin{bmatrix} 0 \\ 1 \end{bmatrix}$, or $\begin{bmatrix} 0 \\ -1 \end{bmatrix}$, all with equal probabilities. If X denotes the insect's displacement from its starting-place after n nights in one of these directions, and R denotes its distance from its starting-place, show that $E[X^2] = \frac{1}{2}n$ and that $E[R^2] = n$.

3 "Space haphazards" have three possible directions of motion, all perpendicular to each other, along which they can move in either sense; all the six displacements have equal probabilities. Show that, for these insects too, $E[R^2] = n$.

4 There is even a species of haphazard which lives in m-dimensional space, having m possible mutually perpendicular directions of motion along which they can move in either sense. Carry out the same investigation for this species.

5 More advanced are the free-ranging haphazards, which are not restricted to particular directions of motion. The "free-ranging plane haphazards" are restricted to a plane, but can make their displacements in any direction with equal probability. "Free-ranging space haphazards" have a similar behaviour in 3-dimensional space. It turns out that these species also have the property that $E[R^2] = n$. Prove this.

B4 BEETLE

In the game of "Beetle" players compete against each other to be the first to complete the drawing of a picture like this:

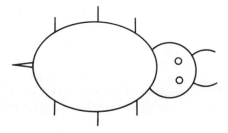

They may draw in the various components when they throw the right score on a die: 6 for the body, 5 for the head, 4 for the tail, 3 for a leg, 2 for a feeler, 1 for an eye. The body must be drawn first, and no feelers or eyes may be put in until the head has been drawn.

1   For each of the 'partial beetles' (a) to (d), find the probability that a player will need to throw the die r times before the picture is *at least* as complete as this.

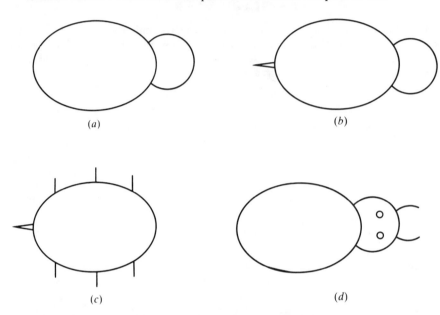

(a)   (b)

(c)   (d)

2   Find the expected numbers of throws needed to get pictures which are at least as complete as those shown in Figs. (a) to (d).

3   A similar theoretical analysis for the complete beetle would be very complicated, but it is possible to simulate the game using a computer. Write a suitable program, and by running it many times obtain a theoretical estimate for the expected number of throws needed to draw a complete beetle.

4   Calculate a 95% confidence interval for this number.

B5 INVESTIGATING AN UNFAIR DIE

An unfair die has a probability p of coming up 'six'. An experiment is carried out to try to determine the value of p. In this experiment the die is rolled n times, and the number of occasions on which it comes up 'six' is denoted by R.

1   Show that $\hat{p}_1 = R/n$ is an unbiased estimator for p, and explain how this estimator can be derived using the principle of maximum likelihood. Find an expression for the variance of $\hat{p}_1$.

2   If in fact p has the value 0.2, use tables of normal probability to calculate approximately, for various values of n and δ of your choice, the probabilities that the relative frequency R/n obtained from the experiment will be within δ of the value of p. In what sense can one say that the relative frequency "tends to the value of p as n tends to infinity"?

3   In a second experiment the die is rolled repeatedly until a 'six' comes up, and the number of throws for this to happen is recorded as X_1; the process is then re-started, and the number of throws for a 'six' recorded as X_2; and so on, for k sequences in all. Write down the possibility space and the probability function for each of the random variables $X_1, X_2, \ldots, X_k$. Hence prove that, if $M = (X_1 + X_2 + \cdots + X_k)/k$, then $E[M] = 1/p$.

4   Misled by this result, the experimenter uses $\hat{p}_2 = 1/M$ as an estimator for p. Write down the possibility space and the probability function for $1/M$. From these show, for the cases $k = 1$ and $k = 2$, that $\hat{p}_2$ is *not* an unbiased estimator for p.

5   Show, however, that $\hat{p}_3 = (k - 1)/(kM - 1)$ *is* an unbiased estimator for p; and that, when k is large, $\hat{p}_3$ is not very different from $\hat{p}_2$. Is $\hat{p}_3$ larger or smaller than $\hat{p}_2$?

6   Write and run programs to simulate these experiments on a computer, using a random number input. The program should make provision for a 'concealed' probability p to be fed in, and for estimators $\hat{p}_1$ and $\hat{p}_3$ to be evaluated and subsequently compared with the value of p.

7   Extend the program to demonstrate the variances of the two estimators. If n and k are chosen so that $n = 6k$ (so that in the long run the same number of throws will be made in each experiment), which estimator has the smaller variance?

B6 CHEBYSHEV'S INEQUALITY

This exercise develops a result first published in 1867 by the Russian mathematician Pafnutii Lvovitch Chebyshev, who lived from 1821 to 1894. (His name is transcribed into English in many different ways: various books have the spellings Tchebychef, Tchebycheff, Tchebysheff, etc.) An English translation of his original paper is given in D. E. Smith, *Source Book in Mathematics* (McGraw-Hill).

The notation in this exercise is that used in §1.1, where the standard deviation S of n measurements $x_1, x_2, \ldots, x_k$ with frequencies $f(x_1), f(x_2), \ldots, f(x_k))$ is defined by the equation

$$nS^2 = \sum_{i=1}^{k} (x_i - m)^2 f(x_i),$$

m being the mean. If λ is any positive number, then the k values of the measurement X can be separated into two sets, according as $|x_i - m| < \lambda S$ or $|x_i - m| \geq \lambda S$. Denote these sets by I and E respectively.

1   State the meaning of these two inequalities in words. ⇐ *range divided up into 2 bits*

2   The equation defining S can now be rewritten   *Sqre ⟹ ≥ 0*

$$nS^2 = \sum_{x_i \in I} (x_i - m)^2 f(x_i) + \sum_{x_i \in E} (x_i - m)^2 f(x_i). \qquad ——①$$

——②

Explain why the first term on the right of this equation is non-negative, and the second term is greater than or equal to $\lambda^2 S^2 \sum_{x_i \in E} f(x_i)$. ⇐ $(x_i - m)^2 \geq \lambda^2 s^2 \Rightarrow \sum_E (x_i - m)f \geq \lambda^2 s^2 \sum f$

3   Denoting $\sum_{x_i \in E} f(x_i)$ by n_E, deduce that   ① & ② ⟹ $nS^2 \geq \lambda^2 s^2 \sum f$

$$\frac{n_E}{n} \leq \frac{1}{\lambda^2}.$$

Restate this result in words. $\frac{1}{\lambda^2}$ *mmt lie above* $m - \lambda s$ *to* $m + \lambda s$.
both hold.

At the top margin, handwritten notes:
$$p(\text{unsh}...) \geqslant 1 - \frac{1}{\lambda^2}$$
$$\Rightarrow p(|x-m| < \lambda s) \geqslant 1 - \frac{1}{\lambda^2}$$

4 Suppose now that the n measurements form a complete population from which single samples are drawn at random. If X denotes the measurement drawn, prove that

$$P(|X - m| < \lambda S) \geqslant 1 - \frac{1}{\lambda^2}.$$

This result is often called *Chebyshev's inequality* in statistics. (Be warned, however, that there is a quite different inequality in algebra which goes by the same name: see, for example, G. H. Hardy, J. E. Littlewood and G. Polya, *Inequalities* (Cambridge University Press), p. 43.)

5 In previous chapters you have been asked a number of times, in connection with various probability models, "what is the probability of getting a value of the random variable which lies within λ standard deviations of the mean?" for some numerical value of λ. Investigate this question for a number of probability models of your choice, and compare the results with each other and with the prediction given by Chebyshev's inequality.

6 Apply Chebyshev's inequality to the problem of estimating the mean of a population of measurements by the mean M of a sample of n values. Prove that, if δ denotes a desired standard of accuracy for the estimate,

$$P(|M - \mu| > \delta) < \sigma^2/n\delta^2.$$

Deduce that, although there is always the risk that a random sample may turn up whose mean differs from μ by a large margin, the probability of getting a sample mean which differs from the population mean by more than δ can be made as small as we please by taking a large enough sample. (This is sometimes called the *weak law of large numbers*.)

7 Restate the result of question 6 when it is applied to the estimation of the proportion α in a population which possesses a certain attribute by means of the proportion in a sample of size n. (The result is then called *Bernoulli's theorem*.)

B7 A COMPARISON OF ESTIMATORS

A random variable X is known to be distributed with uniform probability density over an interval of positive real numbers from 0 to α. The value of α is not known, and cannot be measured directly; it is therefore decided to estimate α by carrying out a statistical experiment. The procedure used is to take a random sample of n values of X, denoted by $x_1, x_2, \ldots, x_n$, and to find an estimator α which is a function of the random variables $X_1, X_2, \ldots, X_n$.

1 Suppose that we regard α as known and that a sample of size 5 is taken, giving the following values of X correct to two places of decimals:

$$x_1 = 3.74, \ x_2 = 5.90, \ x_3 = 1.62, \ x_4 = 4.17, \ x_5 = 0.33.$$

Write down, in terms of α, the probability of drawing this particular sample (a) if $\alpha > 5.905$, (b) if $\alpha < 5.895$. What value of α maximises this probability?

2 Consider the problem in general, where the sample values are $x_1, x_2, \ldots, x_n$ with a measurement tolerance in each case of h (so that a measurement of x_1 means that the value is between $x_1 - \frac{1}{2}h$ and $x_1 + \frac{1}{2}h$). What is the maximum likelihood estimator for α? Let this estimator be denoted by $\hat{\alpha}_1$. Can you suggest any obvious shortcomings of $\hat{\alpha}_1$ as an estimator for α?

3   If t is a number between 0 and α, and δt is the measurement tolerance for x_1, write down the probability that the random variable X_1 lies between $t - \frac{1}{2}\delta t$ and $t + \frac{1}{2}\delta t$ and that $X_2, X_3, \ldots, X_n$ are all less than t. Deduce the probability that the largest of X_1, X_2, $\ldots$, X_n lies between $t - \frac{1}{2}\delta t$ and $t + \frac{1}{2}\delta t$. Hence prove that $E[\hat{\alpha}_1] = n\alpha/(n+1)$, and find $V[\hat{\alpha}_1]$.

4   Find an estimator $\hat{\alpha}_2$ which is a multiple of $\hat{\alpha}_1$ and which is unbiased. Calculate $V[\hat{\alpha}_2]$.

5   If M is the mean of $X_1, X_2, \ldots, X_n$, prove that $E[M] = \frac{1}{2}\alpha$. Hence show that another unbiased estimator for α is $\hat{\alpha}_3$, defined as twice the mean of the sample values. Calculate $V[\hat{\alpha}_3]$.

6   Finally, one might use as an estimator $\hat{\alpha}_4$, defined as twice the median of the sample values. (To simplify the situation, take n to be an odd number, writing $n = 2k + 1$. You may find it simpler to begin by taking the special case $n = 5$.) Write down the probability that X_1 lies between $t - \frac{1}{2}\delta t$ and $t + \frac{1}{2}\delta t$ and that $X_2 < t$, $X_3 < t$, $\ldots$, $X_{k+1} < t$, $X_{k+2} > t$, $\ldots$, $X_{2k+1} > t$. Deduce the probability that the median of the sample lies between $t - \frac{1}{2}\delta t$ and $t + \frac{1}{2}\delta t$. Hence calculate $E[\hat{\alpha}_4]$ and $V[\hat{\alpha}_4]$.

7   Place the unbiased estimators $\hat{\alpha}_2$, $\hat{\alpha}_3$, $\hat{\alpha}_4$ in decreasing order of efficiency (see §15.3).

17

Moment generators – a basis for theory

Most chapters in this book develop some theory and apply it to actual statistical problems. This chapter is rather different, in that the theory is used to produce other theoretical results, whose application will mostly be found in other chapters. Readers whose main interest lies in using statistics to solve real-life problems may prefer to pass over this chapter quickly and take the results on trust. But if you are interested in knowing why the central limit theorem works, or in proving results which will later be used to justify the t-test, then this chapter is an important one.

We have already seen how, by introducing more abstract notions which appear to be remote from the data from which they originate, powerful results may follow. For example, probability generators made possible the investigation of more complicated probability models, and expectation notation provided a basis for discussing problems of estimation. Moment generators represent a further stage in this process of abstraction; you may at first wonder why one should ever want to introduce such a definition, but hopefully by the end of the chapter you will be convinced by seeing how much can be achieved with them.

17.1 GENERATORS AND MOMENTS

You have already met one kind of generator in this course, the probability generator (see §9.7). For example, the expression $G(t) = e^{\lambda(t-1)}$ is said to generate the Poisson probabilities

$$e^{-\lambda}, \frac{\lambda}{1!}e^{-\lambda}, \frac{\lambda^2}{2!}e^{-\lambda}, \ldots$$

because its expansion in powers of t gives

$$G(t) = e^{\lambda t}e^{-\lambda} = e^{-\lambda} + \frac{\lambda}{1!}e^{-\lambda}t + \frac{\lambda^2}{2!}e^{-\lambda}t^2 + \ldots,$$

and the probabilities of $0, 1, 2, \ldots$ occurrences in unit time are the coefficients of $t^0, t^1, t^2, \ldots$ in this expansion.

You have also met examples of moments, though not by name. In calculating means and variances, for example, the expressions

$$E[X] = \sum_{i=1}^{k} x_i p(x_i) \quad \text{or} \quad \int_{-\infty}^{\infty} x\phi(x)\,dx,$$

$$E[X^2] = \sum_{i=1}^{k} x_i^2 p(x_i) \text{ or } \int_{-\infty}^{\infty} x^2\phi(x)\,dx \quad (\text{see §14.1})$$

have been used and applied to various discrete or continuous probability models. These are called the *first and second moments* (about the origin).

It is no great step to generalise this, and to define the rth moment (about the origin) as

$$E[X^r] = \sum_{i=1}^{k} x_i^r p(x_i) \quad \text{or} \quad \int_{-\infty}^{\infty} x^r \phi(x) \, dx.$$

We shall need a notation for this quantity: it is usually denoted by μ_r (where μ stands for "moment" and the suffix r indicates which moment is under discussion).

Q.1   What meaning should be given to μ_0?

Q.2   Write the mean and variance of the random variable X using this notation.

The word "moment" is most familiar in its mechanical sense, as the turning effect of a force; and its use in statistics is in some ways similar. If we think of the probability p_i of a particular value x_i as a kind of 'mass' located at x_i, as indicated in Fig. 1a, then $x_i p_i$ can be compared to the turning effect due to its weight about the axis $x = 0$. The sum $\mu_1 = \Sigma x_i p_i$ measures the total turning effect; and since the total probability is 1, this can be thought of as the turning effect due to the whole weight at a distance μ_1 from the axis (Fig. 1b). So μ_1 is equivalent to the coordinate of the centre of mass.

The second moment μ_2 is a measure of the spread of the random variable about the axis. In the special case where $\mu_1 = 0$ it is just the variance of X. This also has an analogy in mechanics, as the moment of inertia for a body of total mass 1. In fact, the relation

$$\sigma^2 = E[X^2] - \mu^2 = \mu_2 - \mu_1^2$$

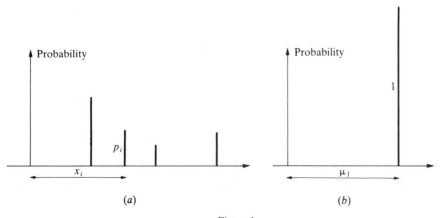

(a)   (b)

Figure 1

corresponds precisely to the "parallel axes theorem" often used in calculating moments of inertia.

It is not so easy to see what μ_3 signifies; perhaps this is most simply shown by a numerical example. The probability function illustrated in Fig. 2 has for its mean

$$\mu_1 = \tfrac{2}{3}(-1) + \tfrac{1}{3}(2) = 0,$$

so that it is 'balanced' about the origin. But for this function

$$\mu_3 = \tfrac{2}{3}(-1)^3 + \tfrac{1}{3}(2)^3 = 2.$$

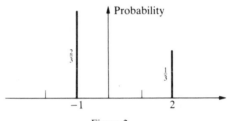

Figure 2

The positive value is an indication that the random variable is 'more spread out' on the positive side than the negative, even though the actual probability on that side is smaller. We say that such a probability function is skewed to the right, or "positively skewed".

With μ_4 it is again the spread away from the origin which is important, but in this case large values of the random variable on both the positive and negative sides contribute positively to the moment. This is strikingly illustrated in Fig. 3,

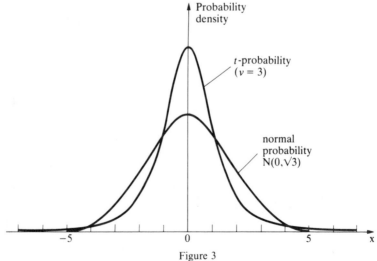

Figure 3

which shows graphs of probability density for normal probability and for t-probability with $v = 3$ (see Chapter 19); the normal graph has been scaled so that both models have the same variance of 3. The equations are respectively

$$\phi_1(x) = \frac{1}{\sqrt{(6\pi)}} e^{-x^2/6} \quad \text{and} \quad \phi_2(x) = \frac{6\sqrt{3}}{\pi} \frac{1}{(3 + x^2)^2}.$$

It can be shown that the corresponding fourth moments are 27 and ∞! The feature responsible for this remarkable difference is the nature of the 'tails' of the two graphs. Although both $\phi_1(x)$ and $\phi_2(x)$ tend to zero as $|x| \to \infty$, the exponential in $\phi_1(x)$ causes it to tail off much more rapidly, so that the contribution to $\int x^4 \phi(x) \, dx$ in the tails is much smaller for ϕ_1 than for ϕ_2.

Exercise 17A

1   Calculate the first four moments about the origin for the probability function defined by the table:

x_i	−2	0	1	5
p_i	0.4	0.2	0.3	0.1

2   Calculate the first four moments about the origin for the random variable defined by the probability density function

$$\phi(x) = \begin{cases} \frac{2}{9}(x + 2) & \text{for } -2 < x < 1, \\ 0 & \text{otherwise.} \end{cases}$$

3   Verify that $\phi(x) = \frac{12}{625}(x + 3)^2(2 - x)$ over the domain $-3 < x < 2$ defines a probability density function with mean zero. Sketch its graph, and decide on the basis of the graph whether you expect the third moment to be positive or negative. Verify your conjecture by direct calculation.

4   Fig. 4 shows the graph of a probability density function. Given that the mean is zero, express b in terms of a. Calculate the second and third moments in terms of a.

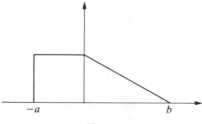

Figure 4

5   Sketch the graph of the probability density function given by

$$\phi(x) = \begin{cases} \lambda e^{-(\lambda x + 1)} & \text{for } x > -1/\lambda, \\ 0 & \text{otherwise.} \end{cases}$$

Verify that the first moment is zero, and calculate the second and third moments.

6   Fig. 5 shows graphs of two probability density functions. If these have the same second moment, express b in terms of a. In that case, which would you expect to have the larger fourth moment? Verify your conjecture by direct calculation.

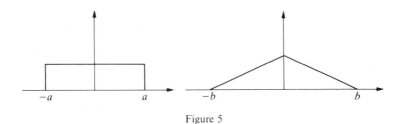

Figure 5

7   Two probability density functions, with domains $-a < x < a$ and $-b < x < b$ respectively, have equations

$$\phi_1(x) = k_1(a^2 - x^2) \quad \text{and} \quad \phi_2(x) = k_2(b^2 - x^2)^2.$$

If their second moments are equal, compare their fourth moments.

8   Verify the values stated for the variances and fourth moments for the functions ϕ_1 and ϕ_2 in §17.1.

17.2   MOMENT GENERATORS

The scene is now set for a definition. For a given probability model we have a sequence of moments $\mu_0(=1)$, μ_1, μ_2, ... Also, the generator of a sequence c_0, c_1, c_2, ... has been defined as a function whose expansion as a power series has these numbers as coefficients. In this chapter the letter u will be used for the variable (to distinguish moment generators from probability generators, for which the letter t was used); so the generator is a function with expansion $c_0 + c_1 u + c_2 u^2 + \ldots$

There is just one additional complication. For a reason which will become clear later in the chapter, it is more convenient not to identify the coefficient c_r directly with the rth moment, but to take it to be the moment divided by $r!$, so that

$$c_0 = \frac{\mu_0}{0!}(=1), \; c_1 = \frac{\mu_1}{1!}, \; c_2 = \frac{\mu_2}{2!}, \text{ and so on.}$$

Thus the *moment generator* (about the origin) is defined as the sum

$$1 + \frac{\mu_1}{1!}u + \frac{\mu_2}{2!}u^2 + \cdots + \frac{\mu_r}{r!}u^r + \cdots$$

In this way all the information about the moments for a particular probability function is encapsulated in one single function.

Example 1
Find the moment generator for a random variable having rectangular probability given by

$$\phi(x) = \begin{cases} \frac{1}{2} & \text{for } -1 < x < 1, \\ 0 & \text{otherwise.} \end{cases}$$

From the definition of rth moment for a continuous random variable,

$$\mu_r = \int_{-1}^{1} x^r . \tfrac{1}{2} \, dx,$$

which is equal to 0 if r is odd and to $1/(r + 1)$ if r is even. So the moment generator is

$$1 + \frac{1}{3}\frac{1}{2!} u^2 + \frac{1}{5}\frac{1}{4!} u^4 + \cdots + \frac{1}{2s + 1}\frac{1}{(2s)!} u^{2s} + \cdots$$

$$= 1 + \frac{u^2}{3!} + \frac{u^4}{5!} + \cdots + \frac{u^{2s}}{(2s + 1)!} + \cdots$$

(writing $r = 2s$ when r is even).

However, this is not the usual way of finding moment generators. Often it is quite complicated to get the individual moments, but there is an alternative method which gives the whole generator as a single function. To obtain this, we begin by writing μ_r as $E[X^r]$, so that the generator becomes

$$1 + E[X]\frac{u^1}{1!} + E[X^2]\frac{u^2}{2!} + \cdots + E[X^r]\frac{u^r}{r!} + \cdots;$$

which, by the usual rules, can be written as

$$E\left[1 + \frac{X^1 u^1}{1!} + \frac{X^2 u^2}{2!} + \cdots + \frac{X^r u^r}{r!} + \cdots\right].$$

Notice that in doing this the "dummy variable" u is treated as if it were a constant. The expression in the square brackets is one which you will recognise (see result (3) of §7.1); and it follows that the moment generator can be written very concisely as

$$E[e^{Xu}]$$

It is not at all clear what 'meaning' one could attach to this expression; it seems very remote from the 'real life situations' which probability was invented to model. But if we do not concern ourselves too much with meaning, and simply treat it as a formula, it certainly provides an effective means of calculation. Applied to Example 1, for instance, since the random variable is continuous,

$$E[e^{Xu}] = \int_{-1}^{1} e^{xu} \cdot \tfrac{1}{2} \, dx.$$

Remembering that u is treated as if it were a constant, this is evaluated as

$$\left[\frac{1}{2u} e^{xu} \right]_{-1}^{1}$$

$$= \frac{1}{2u}(e^u - e^{-u}), \quad \text{or} \quad \frac{1}{u} \sinh u.$$

Q.3   Use the power series expansion for sinh u to show that this agrees with the answer obtained previously.

Example 2
A spinner is spun three times, the probabilities of getting "banana" and "apple" on each occasion being b and a respectively, where $a + b = 1$. Find the moment generator for the number of times that "apple" comes up.

Here the random variable is discrete, so that the expression $E[e^{Xu}]$ takes the form $\Sigma \, e^{x_i u} p(i)$. In the given situation the random variable takes values 0, 1, 2, 3 with probabilities

$$b^3, \; 3b^2 a, \; 3ba^2, \; a^3.$$

The corresponding forms for e^{Xu} are

$$e^0 = 1, \; e^u, \; e^{2u}, \; e^{3u}.$$

The moment generator (about the origin) is therefore

$$b^3 + e^u \cdot 3b^2 a + e^{2u} \cdot 3ba^2 + e^{3u} \cdot a^3,$$

which can be written

$$b^3 + 3b^2(ae^u) + 3b(ae^u)^2 + (ae^u)^3,$$

or

$$(b + ae^u)^3.$$

The answers to both these examples draw attention to the important fact that the moment generator is just a function of the dummy variable u. The random variable X which appears in the expression $E[e^{Xu}]$ is a variable of summation or integration; when we sum over all the x_i in the possibility space, or integrate over the domain of integration, the random variable is 'absorbed'. So the moment generator can be denoted simply by $M(u)$, without reference to X.

The function $M(u)$, defined as

$$E[e^{Xu}] = \sum_{i=1}^{k} e^{x_i u} p(i), \quad \text{or} \quad \int_{-\infty}^{\infty} e^{xu} \phi(x)\, dx,$$

is called the *moment generator* (about the origin) of the random variable X. The coefficient of u^r in the expansion of $M(u)$ in powers of u is $\mu_r/r!$, where $\mu_r = E[X^r]$ is the rth moment (about the origin) of X.

Exercise 17B

1   A spinner has its surface divided into 5 equal sectors, numbered with the scores -4, $-2, 0, 2, 4$. Write down the moment generator for the score when it is spun. Use the formula for the sum of a geometric progression to show that the moment generator can be written as $\frac{1}{5} \sinh 5u/\sinh u$.

2   A gambler tosses a coin repeatedly until it comes up tails. He gets £1 for each head that comes up before that happens, and pays back £1 for the tail. Find the moment generator for his winnings and show that it can be written in the form $1/(2e^u - e^{2u})$. Find a third order polynomial approximation to this expression. Hence show that it is a fair game, find the variance, and determine whether the probability function is positively or negatively skewed.

3   A counter is placed at the origin on a number line. A coin is spun; if it comes down heads the counter is moved one unit in the positive direction; if it comes down tails the counter is moved one unit in the negative direction. The coin is then spun again, and the process is repeated until a *different* face comes up; when that happens, the counter remains where it is and the game stops. Find the moment generator for the number on which the counter ends up. By expanding it in powers of u as far as the term in u^4, find the second and fourth moments about the origin for this random variable.

4   Example 2 shows that for the binomial probability model with $n = 3$, for which the probability generator is $(b + at)^3$, the moment generator is $(b + ae^u)^3$. By comparing the definitions of the probability generator and the moment generator for a general discrete random variable, show that if the probability generator is $G(t)$, then the moment generator (about the origin) is $G(e^u)$. Hence state the moment generator for the general binomial probability model.

5   Use the result $M(u) = G(e^u)$ (see question 4) to write down the moment generators for (i) the geometric probability model with $p(i) = ab^{i-1}$ for $i = 1, 2, 3, \ldots$, (ii) the Poisson probability model with $p(i) = (\lambda^i/i!)e^{-\lambda}$ for $i = 0, 1, 2, \ldots$. By expanding these generators in powers of u as far as the terms in u^2, verify the expressions for the mean and variance of each of these models given in Table 1 of §9.7.

6   Explain why $\mu_1 = M'(0)$, $\mu_2 = M''(0)$, and in general $\mu_r = M^{(r)}(0)$. Use this and the result $M(u) = G(e^u)$ (see question 4) to prove that $\mu_1 = G'(1)$ and $\mu_2 = G''(1) + G'(1)$. Obtain similar expressions for μ_3 and μ_4.

7   Find the moment generators for the two probability density functions illustrated in Fig. 6. In (b), show that the moment generator can be written as $\left(\frac{1}{u} \sinh u\right)^2$.

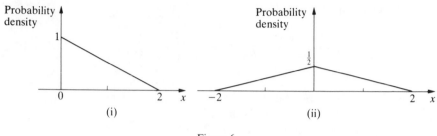

Figure 6

8 Find the moment generator for the negative exponential probability model, for which the probability density function is

$$\phi(x) = \begin{cases} \lambda e^{-\lambda x} & \text{for } x > 0, \\ 0 & \text{otherwise.} \end{cases}$$

Use this to find μ_1 and μ_2, and deduce the variance.

9 Points are distributed over the interior of a circle of radius r with uniform area probability density. Find the moment generator for the distance of a random point from the centre.

10 Repeat question 9 for points distributed over the interior of a sphere with uniform volume probability density.

17.3 SOME THEORY

The next step is to establish some theoretical results about moment generators. These are concerned with the effect of performing certain transformations on the random variable, or of combining two random variables.

(1) *Scaling up the random variable.* The problem is: given a moment generator $M(u)$ for a random variable X, what is the moment generator for the variable cX, where c is a constant?

To answer this, it is sufficient to notice that

$$e^{(cX)u} = e^{X(cu)},$$

so that

$$E[e^{(cX)u}] = E[e^{X(cu)}],$$

which from the definition is just $M(cu)$. It follows that:

The moment generator for cX is obtained from that of X by replacing the letter u by cu.

Example 3
Find the moment generator for the errors in the mileages given on motorway signs.

It was shown in §11.3, Example 1, that this random variable has rectangular probability over the interval $-\frac{1}{2} < x < \frac{1}{2}$, with probability density 1. The error variable is therefore related to the random variable in Example 1 of this chapter (see §17.2) by a scale change of factor $\frac{1}{2}$. Since the moment generator for Example 1 was $\dfrac{1}{u}$ sinh u, the moment generator for the mileage error is

$$\frac{1}{\frac{1}{2}u} \sinh \tfrac{1}{2}u, \quad \text{or} \quad \frac{2}{u} \sinh \tfrac{1}{2}u.$$

Q.4 Use this moment generator to check the mean and variance for the mileage error found in Exercise 11C, question 1.

(2) *Increasing the random variable by a constant.* This problem is similar to (1), but this time the random variable X is changed to $X + b$, where b is a constant. The moment generator therefore becomes

$$E[e^{(X+b)u}] = E[e^{Xu}e^{bu}] = e^{bu}E[e^{Xu}],$$

since in finding the generator u is treated as constant. This can be recognised as $e^{bu}M(u)$, so that:

> The moment generator for $X + b$ is obtained from that of X by multiplying by e^{bu}.

(3) *Adding two independent random variables.* Denote the random variables by X and Y. The fact that these are independent means that e^{Xu} and e^{Yu} are independent; so the rule for the expectation of a product (§14.2) can be applied in the form

$$E[e^{Xu}e^{Yu}] = E[e^{Xu}]E[e^{Yu}].$$

Now the expression on the right is the product of the moment generators for X and Y separately; and on the left we have

$$E[e^{(X+Y)u}],$$

which is the moment generator for $X + Y$. This shows that:

> The moment generator for the sum of two independent random variables is the product of the moment generators for the two variables separately.

Notice the similarity between this result and the multiplication property for probability generators found in §9.8. Either could, in fact, be derived from the other by using the fact that $M(u) = G(e^u)$ (see Exercise 17B, question 4). But note how much simpler the proof becomes now that expectation notation is available; the underlying idea may be more abstract, but the algebra is far less complicated.

This important property is one of the main reasons for defining the moment generator in terms of the coefficients $\mu_1/1\,!$, $\mu_2/2\,!$, ... rather than simply μ_1, μ_2, ... This is investigated further in Exercise 17C, question 12.

Exercise 17C

1   In Example 1 of §14.2, write down for each model the moment generators for the random variables X, Y and $X + Y$. Investigate whether the multiplication property (3) holds.

2   If independent random variables X, Y have moment generators $M_1(u)$, $M_2(u)$, what is the moment generator for the random variable $X - Y$?

3   Use the results established in §17.3 to find the moment generators for
   (a) a rectangular probability model defined on the interval $0 < x < b$;
   (b) a triangular probability model defined on the interval $0 < x < 2b$, with its maximum at $x = b$.

4   Use the multiplication property (3) to show that, if X and Y are independent, $V[X + Y] = V[X] + V[Y]$.

5   The idea of moments about the origin can be generalised to moments about any value d, defined as $E[(X - d)^r]$.
   (a) Prove that the moments about d are generated by $e^{-du}M(u)$.
   (b) Use (a) to find expressions for the first four moments about d in terms of the moments about the origin.
   (c) Simplify your answers to (b) in the case where $d = \mu_1$.

6   Explain why the rth moment has dimensions which are the rth power of the unit in which the random variable is measured.
   The rth moment about the mean is denoted by μ_r^*. Explain why $\mu_1^* = 0$, and state the significance of μ_2^*. Show that the quantity $\mu_3^*/\mu_2^{*\frac{3}{2}}$ is dimensionless, and justify the use of this as a measure of 'skewness' of a probability model.

7   Prove that the generator for the moments about the mean na of the binomial probability function is $(be^{-au} + ae^{bu})^n$. By expanding this in powers of u as far as the term in μ^4, find the values of μ_2^*, μ_3^*, μ_4^* (using the notation of question 6).
   Deduce an expression for the skewness, and show that it tends to zero as $n \to \infty$. What is the implication of this result?

8   Find the generator for the moments about the mean of the geometric probability function, and deduce an expression for the skewness (see question 6).

9   Repeat question 8 for (a) the Poisson probability function, (b) the negative exponential probability density function.

10   In §12.5 it was shown that the negative exponential probability model can be derived from the geometric probability model by a change of scale in the random variable with factor $1/n$, writing $na = \lambda$, and finally letting $n \to \infty$. Starting with the moment generator (about the origin) for geometric probability (Exercise 17B, question 5(i)), carry out this sequence of transformations to obtain the moment generator for negative exponential probability (Exercise 17B, question 8).

11   Show that the probability generator $G(t)$ for a discrete random variable can be expressed, using expectation notation, as $E[t^X]$. Use this
   (a) to justify the multiplication property of probability generators for independent random variables;
   (b) to devise a definition for the probability generator for a continuous random variable;
   (c) to find a probability generator for the random variable defined in Example 1 (§17.2).

12   Show that the moments $\mu_1, \mu_2, \ldots$ (without factorials in the denominators) would be generated by $E[1/(1 - Xu)]$, but that this generator would not have the multiplicative property (3).

    Evaluate this generator for the probability model defined in Example 1 (§17.2), and verify that the expansion of this function in powers of u gives the correct values for the moments.

13   Evaluate the generator $E[1/(1 - Xu)]$ (see question 12) for the probability density function defined by

$$\phi(x) = \begin{cases} 2x & \text{for } 0 < x < 1, \\ 0 & \text{otherwise.} \end{cases}$$

Expand the generator in powers of u, and verify that the coefficients give the correct values for the moments.

    What is the moment generator (as usually defined) for this function?

17.4 THE MOMENT GENERATOR FOR NORMAL PROBABILITY

Many important applications of moment generators relate to the normal probability model. So the next question is: what form does the moment generator take for normal probability?

The results of §17.3 become immediately useful here. Since we know how to adjust moment generators for change of scale and increase by a constant, we can begin with the much easier problem of finding the moment generator for standard normal probability $N(0, 1)$, with probability density

$$\phi(x) = \frac{1}{\sqrt{(2\pi)}} e^{-\frac{1}{2}x^2}.$$

Substituting this in the expression $\int_{-\infty}^{\infty} e^{xu}\phi(x)\, dx$ gives

$$M(u) = \int_{-\infty}^{\infty} e^{xu} \cdot \frac{1}{\sqrt{(2\pi)}} e^{-\frac{1}{2}x^2}\, dx$$

$$= \int_{-\infty}^{\infty} \frac{1}{\sqrt{(2\pi)}} e^{(xu - \frac{1}{2}x^2)}\, dx.$$

To find this integral, the trick is to write the quadratic expression in a different form by completing the square:

$$xu - \tfrac{1}{2}x^2 = \tfrac{1}{2}u^2 - \tfrac{1}{2}(x - u)^2,$$

so that

$$e^{(xu - \frac{1}{2}x^2)} = e^{\frac{1}{2}u^2} e^{-\frac{1}{2}(x - u)^2}.$$

So, remembering that in the integration u is treated as constant, the expression for the moment generator can be written

$$M(u) = e^{\frac{1}{2}u^2} \int_{-\infty}^{\infty} \frac{1}{\sqrt{(2\pi)}} e^{-\frac{1}{2}(x - u)^2}\, dx.$$

Now comes the really neat part of the argument. The integrand in this last expression is just the probability density function for a normal random variable with mean u and standard deviation 1. This means that the value of the integral must be 1, so that the moment generator simplifies to

$$M(u) = e^{\frac{1}{2}u^2}.$$

All that remains to be done is to generalise this to find the moment generator for the normal random variable $N(\mu, \sigma^2)$. This merely involves scaling up the standard normal random variable by σ, and then increasing it by μ (see §13.2, Fig. 4). This is effected by first replacing u by σu in the expression for $M(u)$ (using (1) of §17.3), and then multiplying by $e^{\mu u}$ (using (2)). For general normal probability, therefore,

$$M(u) = e^{\mu u}e^{\frac{1}{2}(\sigma u)^2}.$$

The result is very important:

The moment generator (about the origin) for the normal random variable $N(\mu, \sigma^2)$ is $e^{\mu u + \frac{1}{2}\sigma^2 u^2}$.

17.5 ADDING NORMAL RANDOM VARIABLES

As an illustration of the use of the moment generator for normal probability, consider the following problem.

Suppose that poles for a tent are made in two parts, with a designed total length of 1 m. There will be, as always, some variation in the lengths of the components actually produced; but it is specified that the tolerance allowed on the total length is ± 1 cm. Suppose further that the variations in the lengths of the two sections can be modelled by normal probability, with means 55 cm and 45 cm and standard deviations 0.5 cm and 0.4 cm respectively. If the two parts are matched together randomly, what proportion of the poles resulting will fall within the prescribed tolerance limits?

Some information about this problem can be found by using expectation algebra. Denoting the lengths of the sections by X and Y, we know that

$$E[X + Y] = E[X] + E[Y] = 55\,\text{cm} + 45\,\text{cm} = 100\,\text{cm};$$

and, since X and Y are independent,

$$V[X + Y] = V[X] + V[Y] = (0.5\,\text{cm})^2 + (0.4\,\text{cm})^2 = 0.41\,\text{cm}^2,$$

so that the standard deviation of $X + Y$ is $\sqrt{0.41}$ cm, or about 0.64 cm.

But to complete the solution, we lack one essential piece of information: how is $X + Y$ distributed? You might guess that the answer would be "normally", since that is how X and Y are distributed. You would in fact be right: but we need the moment generator to prove it.

Q.5 Complete the solution on the assumption that $X + Y$ is normally distributed.

Using the result found in §17.4, the moment generators for X and Y are

$$e^{55u + \frac{1}{2}(0.25)u^2} \quad \text{and} \quad e^{45u + \frac{1}{2}(0.16)u^2}. \quad \text{(Note 17.1)}$$

It follows from the multiplication property of moment generators that, since X and Y are independent, the moment generator for $X + Y$ is

$$e^{55u + \frac{1}{2}(0.25)u^2} \quad e^{45u + \frac{1}{2}(0.16)u^2} = e^{100u + \frac{1}{2}(0.41)u^2};$$

and we recognise this as the generator for the normal random variable with mean 100 cm and variance 0.41 cm^2.

Are we entitled to take this last step backwards, and to conclude that $X + Y$ is normally distributed? That is, does the moment generator define the probability function uniquely? For the time being we will assume that this is true; if so, then the proof is complete. But this is a question to which we will return at the end of the chapter.

With this proviso, the result of this numerical example can be generalised:

If independent random variables X and Y have normal probability $N(\mu, \sigma^2)$ and $N(\mu', \sigma'2)$, then $X + Y$ has normal probability $N(\mu + \mu', \sigma^2 + \sigma'^2)$.

Q.6   Use moment generators to prove this general result.

17.6 SAMPLING FROM A NORMAL DISTRIBUTION

Another question which can be investigated in a similar way is the distribution of the mean M of a sample of n independent values of a random variable X, where X has the normal distribution $N(\mu, \sigma^2)$.

If the n values are denoted by $X_1, X_2, \ldots, X_n$, then in this case the moment generators for each of these variables are the same, that is

$$e^{\mu u + \frac{1}{2}\sigma^2 u^2}.$$

So by an extension of the multiplication property, the moment generator for $X_1 + X_2 + \ldots + X_n$ is

$$\{e^{\mu u + \frac{1}{2}\sigma^2 u^2}\}^n.$$

To get the generator for M from this, the random variable $X_1 + X_2 + \ldots + X_n$ has to be scaled down by a factor $c = 1/n$; and in §17.4(1) it was seen that this is done by replacing u in the moment generator by u/n. So the moment generator for M is

$$\{e^{\mu(u/n) + \frac{1}{2}\sigma^2(u/n)^2}\}^n.$$

You should check for yourself that this can be simplified to

$$e^{\mu u + \frac{1}{2}(\sigma^2/n)u^2};$$

and this is the moment generator for a random variable with the normal distribution $N(\mu, \sigma^2/n)$.

Of course, the values of the mean and variance were known already from the work of Chapter 15. But what we could not prove before was that, if the original distribution is normal, then so – *exactly* – is the distribution of M, however large or small the sample.

The conclusion is again based on the assumption that the moment generator defines the probability function uniquely. With this proviso, we have established:

> If a random variable has the normal distribution $N(\mu, \sigma^2)$, then the mean of a sample of n independent values of the random variable has the normal distribution $N(\mu, \sigma^2/n)$.

Exercise 17D

1 With the notation of Exercise 17C, question 6, show that the quantity μ_4^*/μ_2^{*2} is dimensionless. Use the moment generator to prove that, for normal probability, this quantity has the value 3.

    The quantity $\mu_4^*/\mu_2^{*2} - 3$, called the "kurtosis", is used to compare other probability models with normal probability (along the lines suggested in §17.1, Fig. 3). Use the results of Exercise 17C, question 7, to find the kurtosis for the binomial probablity function. What is its limiting value as $n \to \infty$?

2 Write an expression for the moment μ_r for standard normal probability $N(0, 1)$ as an integral. Use integration by parts to obtain the recurrence relation $\mu_r = (r - 1)\mu_{r-2}$. Hence obtain the result $M(u) = e^{\frac{1}{2}u^2}$ directly from the moments.

3 If independent random variables X and Y have normal probability $N(\mu, \sigma^2)$ and $N(\mu', \sigma'^2)$, find the probability distribution for the random variable $aX + bY$.

4 The lengths of bricks are normally distributed with mean 215 mm and standard deviation 5 mm, and the heights of the bricks are normally distributed with mean 65 mm and standard deviation 0.5 mm. The lengths and heights of bricks may be regarded as statistically independent.

    For storage, the bricks are stacked one on top of the other on shelves, the bricks being laid lengthwise on the shelves. Find the minimum height required between shelves to ensure that, with probability at least 99 %, five bricks may be stacked.

    The mortar joints between bricks have thicknesses normally distributed with mean 10 mm and standard deviation 2 mm; the thicknesses of the joints may be regarded as statistically independent of each other and of the dimensions of the bricks. A finished row of bricks consists of five bricks laid lengthwise with four mortar joints between them. Find the probability that the length of a finished row is between 1100 and 1125 mm.   [MEI]

5 A factory has two machines, one making round pegs to a nominal diameter of 8 mm and the other punching round holes to a nominal diameter of 8.4 mm, into which the pegs are expected to fit. If the output of the peg machine is modelled by normal probability with mean 8 mm and standard deviation 0.2 mm, and that of the hole punch by normal probability with mean 8.4 mm and standard deviation 0.3 mm, and if pegs are matched to holes at random, what proportion of the output will be unacceptable?

6 The length of thread is measured on each of a large number of reels of two brands of thread A and B. For brand A the length is found to have mean 102 m and variance 1.25 m^2, and for brand B the corresponding values are 101 m and 1 m^2. Assuming that

both distributions are normal, calculate the probability that if one reel of each brand is taken at random, there will be less thread on the reel of brand A. [Cambridge]

7 The marks of two classes, one of boys and one of girls, in an examination may be assumed to be distributed independently and normally. The mean mark and standard deviation for the boys are 45 and 16 respectively, and for the girls are 48 and 13. One boy and one girl are chosen at random. Calculate the probabilities that
(a) the boy's mark is less than the girl's;
(b) the boy's mark is at least 20 marks less than the girl's. [MEI]

8 A random variable X has probability density function ϕ, defined on the interval $x > 0$ by

$$\phi(x) = Kx^{\alpha-1}e^{-\lambda x},$$

where $\lambda > 0$ and α is a positive integer. Prove that $K = \lambda^{\alpha}/(\alpha - 1)!$. Investigate the graphs of this function for various values of α and λ. (This model, and particularly the special case with $\lambda = 1$, is called *gamma probability*.)

Find the moment generator about the origin.

This function with $\alpha = 1$ defines the negative exponential probability model. Find the moment generator for the sum of n independent values of the negative exponential random variable, and deduce the probability distribution for this sum.

17.7 JUSTIFICATION OF THE CENTRAL LIMIT THEOREM

The exact result proved in §17.6 is mathematically attractive, but it is of limited use; for it is rare to be able to assert with confidence that the original probability distribution is normal. Far more useful is the fact that, whatever (almost) the original probability distribution, the sample mean has approximately normal probability when n is large.

As before, the proof begins by writing down the moment generator for the sample values $X_1, X_2, \ldots, X_n$; but now we can only do this in a very general form. To keep the algebra simple, it is best to choose the origin from which the measurements are made to be the mean of the original distribution. If we do this, then the first moment $\mu_1 = 0$, and the second moment $\mu_2 = \sigma^2$, so that the moment generator can be written as an infinite series beginning

$$M(u) = 1 + \frac{1}{2}\sigma^2 u^2 + \frac{1}{6}\mu_3 u^3 + \ldots.$$

(We have to assume that σ^2 and all the higher moments are finite. There are some probability functions for which this is not true, but they are of little importance in this context. For an example, see Exercise 17F, question 4.)

The argument now proceeds exactly as in §17.6. To get the distribution of the mean, we raise $M(u)$ to the power n and then replace u by u/n. This gives the moment generator

$$\{M(u/n)\}^n = \left(1 + \frac{\sigma^2 u^2}{2n^2} + \frac{\mu_3 u^3}{6n^3} + \ldots\right)^n.$$

What is then needed is a simple approximation to this when n is large.

At this stage it is worth stopping to consider what answer we expect to get.

This should be the moment generator for normal probability with mean 0 and variance σ^2/n, which is $e^{\frac{1}{2}(\sigma^2/n)u^2}$. This form suggests that it might be easier to find an approximation to the *logarithm* of the moment generator, which should come to $\frac{1}{2}(\sigma^2/n)u^2$. So the next step is to write

$$\ln\{M(u/n)\}^n = n \times \ln\left(1 + \frac{\sigma^2 u^2}{2n^2} + \frac{\mu_3 u^3}{6n^3} + \cdots\right),$$

which can be expanded, using the standard Taylor series for $\ln(1 + h)$, as

$$n \times \left\{\left(\frac{\sigma^2 u^2}{2n^2} + \frac{\mu_3 u^3}{6n^3} + \cdots\right) - \frac{1}{2}\left(\frac{\sigma^2 u^2}{2n^2} + \frac{\mu_3 u^3}{6n^3} + \cdots\right)^2 + \cdots\right\}.$$

When multiplied out, the first term has n in the denominator, but all the other terms have powers at least as high as n^2. Therefore, when n is large, the first term is the dominant one, and it follows that

$$\ln\{M(u/n)\}^n \approx \frac{\sigma^2 u^2}{2n},$$

or

$$\{M(u/n)\}^n \approx e^{\frac{1}{2}(\sigma^2/n)u^2},$$

the moment generator for $N(0, \sigma^2/n)$. Since the mean of the original distribution was taken as origin, this is the result predicted by the central limit theorem.

17.8 OTHER APPROXIMATELY NORMAL MODELS

Apart from the central limit theorem, there are some other examples of probability functions which in certain circumstances approximate to normal form. We will discuss just one example in detail, which is related to the *Wilcoxon signed rank test*, a statistical test which belongs to the category known as "non-parametric", or "distribution free", because it does not depend on any prior assumption about the distribution of the scores. (Note 17.2) A typical situation to which it can be applied is as follows.

Two Wednesday afternoon golfers, Alf Mashie and Bert Niblick, meet to play 18 holes once a week. Over one period of three months their scores are:

Alf	104	90	88	85	100	81	98	93	87	80	82	77
Bert	83	95	79	86	85	88	78	81	91	96	90	91
Difference												
(A – B)	+21	−5	+9	−1	+15	−7	+20	+12	−4	−16	−8	−14

Which would you say is the better player?

At first glance Alf seems to be marginally (though certainly not significantly) better, since he won 7 times to Bert's 5. (Remember that the player who goes round in the smaller number of strokes is the winner, so that a negative difference indicates a win for Alf.) But notice that Alf's wins are often by quite small margins, whilst when Bert wins the differences are generally bigger. This might alter our judgement about the two golfers.

One way of taking account of this is to list the two matches in order of the differences between the scores, smallest first, without regard to sign. A "rank" can then be assigned to each difference, from 1 (for the smallest) to 12 (for the largest). Finally, the ranks for all the *positive* scores are added up. In this way, greater weight is given to the big differences than to the small ones.

Q.7   What is the sum of the ranks of *all* the differences? If the two players were equally good, what would you expect the sum of the ranks of just the positive differences to come to? Generalise your answer for the case when there are n matches rather than 12.

Q.8   If a simple count of the number of Bert's wins is used to compare the two players, show that this can be calculated by assigning a weight of 1 to each positive difference and 0 to each negative difference. If the performance of the golfers were totally random, what would be the probability distribution for the sum of these weights (*a*) in 12 matches, (*b*) in n matches? To what normal probability model would this approximate when n is large?

Here is the calculation:

Difference (in order)	-1	-4	-5	-7	-8	$+9$	$+12$	-14	$+15$	-16	$+20$	$+21$
Rank	1	2	3	4	5	⑥	⑦	8	⑨	10	⑪	⑫

(Circled ranks indicate those for positive differences.)

Sum of ranks for positive differences $= 6 + 7 + 9 + 11 + 12 = 45$.

Notice that the smallest value that this rank sum can have is 0 (if all the differences are negative, that is if Alf always wins); and the largest value is $1 + 2 + \ldots + 12 = 78$ (if Bert always wins). So 45 is well up the scale, suggesting that perhaps Bert is really the better player.

But by now you know enough about statistical testing to be wary of jumping to such a conclusion. A rank sum of 45 is above average, but is it large enough to be "significant"?

To answer this, we need to set up a proper probability model, which will enable the rank sum to be tested using the customary procedure. First, a null hypothesis must be stated:

Hypothesis.   Alf and Bert are equally good golfers.

By this we mean that, if a match is selected at random, there is a probability $\frac{1}{2}$ that Alf will win, and a probability $\frac{1}{2}$ that Bert will win. (In practice a draw is also possible. But in applying the Wilcoxon test, drawn games are deleted from the record before the differences are ranked. So these probabilities of $\frac{1}{2}$, $\frac{1}{2}$ are appropriate for any match in which one or other player wins.)

With the scores used in the illustration, the signs of the differences in the various ranks were

$$- \quad - \quad - \quad - \quad - \quad + \quad + \quad - \quad + \quad - \quad + \quad +$$

and the contributions of these results to the rank sum were

$$0 \quad 0 \quad 0 \quad 0 \quad 0 \quad 6 \quad 7 \quad 0 \quad 9 \quad 0 \quad 11 \quad 12.$$

But on the hypothesis that Alf and Bert are equally good, the sign of the difference in each rank could equally well have been positive or negative, each with probability $\frac{1}{2}$. So, if the symbol X_i is used to denote the contribution of the ith ranked difference to the rank sum, then X_i can take either of the two values i or 0, each with probability $\frac{1}{2}$. It follows that the moment generator for the random variable X_i is

$$\mathrm{E}[e^{X_i u}] = \tfrac{1}{2} e^{iu} + \tfrac{1}{2} e^{0u} = \tfrac{1}{2}(e^{iu} + 1). \quad \text{(Note 17.3)}$$

Now the rank sum T is simply the sum of the random variables X_1, X_2, ..., X_n (where we have now written n in place of 12, since the method applies equally well however many games are played). So, by the multiplication property for moment generators, the moment generator for T is

$$\mathrm{M}(u) = \tfrac{1}{2}(e^u + 1) \times \tfrac{1}{2}(e^{2u} + 1) \times \ldots \times \tfrac{1}{2}(e^{nu} + 1).$$

It turns out that, when n is large, the probability model with this generator is approximately normal.

To show this, it helps to notice first that the expression $\tfrac{1}{2}(e^{iu} + 1)$ can be written as

$$e^{\frac{1}{2} iu} \times \tfrac{1}{2}(e^{\frac{1}{2} iu} + e^{-\frac{1}{2} iu}), \quad \text{or} \quad e^{\frac{1}{2} iu} \cosh \tfrac{1}{2} iu.$$

So another way of writing $\mathrm{M}(u)$ is

$$e^{\frac{1}{2} u} \cosh \tfrac{1}{2} u \times e^{\frac{1}{2}(2u)} \cosh \tfrac{1}{2}(2u) \times \ldots \times e^{\frac{1}{2} nu} \cosh \tfrac{1}{2} nu$$

$$= e^{\frac{1}{2}(1 + 2 + \ldots + n)u} \cosh \tfrac{1}{2} u \cosh \tfrac{1}{2}(2u) \ldots \cosh \tfrac{1}{2} nu$$

$$= e^{\frac{1}{4} n(n+1)u} \prod_{i=1}^{n} \cosh \tfrac{1}{2} iu.$$

The first factor in this expression can be removed straight away by taking the moments about $\tfrac{1}{4} n(n+1)$ instead of 0. This is in fact the mean (see Q.7); and by §17.3(2) the moment generator then becomes

$$\mathrm{M}^*(u) = e^{-\frac{1}{4} n(n+1)u} \mathrm{M}(u) = \prod_{i=1}^{n} \cosh \tfrac{1}{2} iu.$$

Next, the reason given in §17.7 for using the logarithm of the moment generator, rather than the moment generator itself, still applies. This converts the product into a sum:

$$\ln M^*(u) = \sum_{i=1}^{n} \ln \cosh \tfrac{1}{2} iu.$$

The desired result will then come by expanding this as a series of powers of u.

There is no well known formula for the expansion of $\ln \cosh x$ in powers of x. But the first few coefficients can be found by using the expansion of $\cosh x$, writing

$$\ln \cosh x = \ln\left(1 + \frac{1}{2} x^2 + \frac{1}{24} x^4 + \dots\right)$$

and then using the Taylor series for $\ln(1 + h)$ to give

$$\ln \cosh x = \left(\frac{1}{2} x^2 + \frac{1}{24} x^4 + \dots\right) - \tfrac{1}{2}\left(\frac{1}{2} x^2 + \frac{1}{24} x^4 + \dots\right)^2 + \dots.$$

In fact only the first coefficient is needed exactly; the rest can simply be left as unknown constants, so that

$$\ln \cosh x = \tfrac{1}{2} x^2 + a_4 x^4 + a_6 x^6 + \dots.$$

Substituting this in the expression above,

$$\ln M^*(u) = \sum_{i=1}^{n} \{\tfrac{1}{2}(\tfrac{1}{2} iu)^2 + a_4(\tfrac{1}{2} iu)^4 + a_6(\tfrac{1}{2} iu)^6 + \dots\}$$

$$= \frac{1}{8} u^2 \sum_{i=1}^{n} i^2 + \frac{1}{16} a_4 u^4 \sum_{i=1}^{n} i^4 + \frac{1}{64} a_6 u^6 \sum_{i=1}^{n} i^6 + \dots.$$

If the symbol S_r is used to stand for the sum of the rth powers of the whole numbers from 1 to n,

$$\ln M^*(u) = \frac{1}{8} S_2 u^2 + \frac{1}{16} a_4 S_4 u^4 + \frac{1}{64} a_6 S_6 u^6 + \dots.$$

Now in all this detail it is important not to lose sight of the ultimate aim, which is to show that the distribution is approximately normal when n is large. In fact, it is best at this stage to make a change of scale, so as to obtain *standard* normal probability N(0, 1) as the limit; and we know that for this the logarithm of the moment generator must be $\tfrac{1}{2} u^2$. So, to convert the first term $\tfrac{1}{8} S_2 u^2$ into this form, the variable u must be replaced by $u/\sqrt{(\tfrac{1}{4} S_2)}$. By §17.3(1), this means scaling the random variable $T - \tfrac{1}{4} n(n + 1)$ by dividing it by $\sqrt{(\tfrac{1}{4} S_2)}$, which is $\sqrt{\{\tfrac{1}{24} n(n + 1)(2n + 1)\}}$. Then, for this new random variable, the logarithm of the moment generator is

$$\frac{1}{8} S_2 \left(\frac{u}{\sqrt{(\tfrac{1}{4} S_2)}}\right)^2 + \frac{1}{16} a_4 S_4 \left(\frac{u}{\sqrt{(\tfrac{1}{4} S_2)}}\right)^4 + \frac{1}{64} a_6 S_6 \left(\frac{u}{\sqrt{(\tfrac{1}{4} S_2)}}\right)^6 + \dots$$

$$= \tfrac{1}{2} u^2 + a_4(S_4/S_2^2)u^4 + a_6(S_6/S_2^3)u^6 + \dots.$$

We are home at last! Although the general formula for S_r is not easy to find, it is well known that it is a polynomial in n with highest power n^{r+1}. (Note 17.4) So the expression S_4/S_2^2 is a ratio of polynomials with n^5 in the numerator and n^6 in the denominator; S_6/S_2^3 has n^7 in the numerator and n^9 in the denominator; and so on. All these ratios clearly tend to 0 as $n \to \infty$. So all that is then left is the first term $\frac{1}{2}u^2$. Since this is the logarithm of the moment generator, the generator itself is $e^{\frac{1}{2}u^2}$.

If T is the sum of ranks calculated in Wilcoxon's signed rank test, then on the null hypothesis of equal probabilities, the random variable $\{T - \frac{1}{4}n(n+1)\}/\sqrt{\{\frac{1}{24}n(n+1)(2n+1)\}}$ is distributed with approximately standard normal probability when n is large.

Although this may seem a complicated and bewildering argument the first time you meet it, every step in fact follows a standard pattern. It can be applied, with only changes of detail, to several other probability distributions. It therefore repays the effort of mastering it.

Finally, to return to the golfers. In that illustration n had the value 12, so that the random variable which is approximately N(0, 1) is $(T - 39)/\sqrt{162.5}$, or $(T - 39)/12.75$. Taking the alternative hypothesis that the players are not equally good (so that a two-tail test is appropriate) this would mean that, at 5 % significance level, only values of T outside the range $39 \pm 1.96 \times 12.75$ would be regarded as significant. This gives $T < 14$ or $T > 64$. So the value 45 obtained from the given data, although marginally favouring Bert, certainly does not provide support for rejecting the null hypothesis.

Exercise 17E

1   If X is a Poisson random variable with mean λ, find the moment generator for the random variable $(X - \lambda)/\sqrt{\lambda}$. By expanding the logarithm of this generator as a series of powers of u, show that the distribution of this random variable is approximately N(0, 1) when λ is large.

3   In Exercise 17D, question 8 you obtained the moment generator $\{\lambda/(\lambda - u)\}^n$ for the sum of n independent values of the negative exponential random variable. By suitable shift of origin and re-scaling, show that when n is large the distribution of the sum is approximately N$(n/\lambda, n/\lambda^2)$.

3   An alternative way of applying the Wilcoxon signed rank test would be to calculate the rank sum as the sum of all the ranks, but with the appropriate sign attached (so that, in the illustration in §17.8, the rank sum would be taken to be $-1 - 2 - 3 - 4 - 5 + 6 + 7 - 8 + 9 - 10 + 11 + 12 = 12$). Denoting by W this alternative rank sum, find the distribution of W when n is large.

4   Find the moment generator for binomial probability B(n, a) about the mean, and expand its logarithm in powers of u as far as the term in u^4. By appropriate re-scaling and letting $n \to \infty$, show that B(n, a) is approximately N(na, nab) when n is large.

5   In an examination in mathematics, there are two papers each marked out of 100. For a class of 20 pupils the marks obtained were:

Paper 1	75	63	60	53	45	29	25	68	52	77
Paper 2	65	59	67	37	67	29	39	38	54	77
Paper 1	33	55	71	67	50	50	31	60	84	70
Paper 2	41	73	48	47	39	23	32	45	78	51

Investigate whether these marks justify the conclusion that one of the papers is harder than the other.

6   It is widely believed that wives are generally younger than their husbands. Investigate this hypothesis, using for data the relative ages of a sample of married couples known to you (for example, the parents of all the members of your group).

17.9   A MATHEMATICAL POSTSCRIPT

Finally, we come back to the question raised earlier, on which the validity of many of the proofs in this chapter depends: if the moment generator is given, is the probability function uniquely determined ?

In a trivial sense, the answer to this question must be "no". This can be illustrated by the rectangular probability density function in Example 1 (§17.2). Consider the two functions:

$$\phi_1(x) = \begin{cases} \tfrac{1}{2} & \text{for } -1 < x < 1 \\ 0 & \text{otherwise} \end{cases} \quad \text{and} \quad \phi_2(x) = \begin{cases} \tfrac{1}{2} & \text{for } -1 \leqslant x \leqslant 1, \\ 0 & \text{otherwise.} \end{cases}$$

Technically these are two different functions, since they differ in value at the two points $x = \pm 1$. But in both cases $M(u)$ is given by $\int_{-\infty}^{\infty} \tfrac{1}{2} e^{xu} dx = (\sinh u)/u$.

But are these two functions essentially different as density functions? Surely not: one cannot imagine a situation for which one would be an appropriate probability model and the other not. And they have identical cumulative probability functions, whose gradient is of course discontinuous at the points ± 1. So it seems sensible to regard two probability density functions as really the same if they differ only at isolated points. With this modification of the problem, the assumption that $M(u)$ defines $\phi(x)$ uniquely can be justified.

We can go even further, and describe how $\phi(x)$ can be obtained from $M(u)$. To do this, it is convenient to introduce a new form of moment generator which uses complex numbers. Instead of $M(u) = E[e^{Xu}]$ we use the *characteristic function*, defined as

$$K(u) = E[e^{Xuj}] = \sum_{i=1}^{k} e^{x_i uj} p(x_i), \quad \text{or} \quad \int_{-\infty}^{\infty} e^{xuj} \phi(x)\, dx.$$

This has two important advantages. (Note 17.5)

Q.9 Show that $K(u)$ generates the sequence $1, \mu_1 j, -\mu_2/2!, -\mu_3 j/3!, \ldots$.

Q.10 Show that $K(u)$ can be written down directly by replacing u in the expression for $M(u)$ by uj. Hence write down the characteristic function for (a) the rectangular probability model in Example 1, (b) the standard normal probability model $N(0, 1)$.

The first is that it avoids problems about convergence of series or integrals. One of the problems with the moment generator is that it involves the factor e^{xu}, which (for any value of u other than 0) tends to infinity either when $x \to \infty$ or when $x \to -\infty$. But the corresponding factor in the characteristic function is e^{xuj}, which always has modulus 1 when x and u are real. Now there is a property of infinite integrals that, if $\int_{-\infty}^{\infty} |f(x)| \, dx$ is convergent, then $\int_{-\infty}^{\infty} f(x) \, dx$ is convergent. (It is then said to be "absolutely convergent".) Now, for the integral expression for the characteristic function,

$$\int_{-\infty}^{\infty} |e^{xuj}\phi(x)| \, dx = \int_{-\infty}^{\infty} 1 \times \phi(x) \, dx \text{ (because probability density is never negative)}$$

$$= 1.$$

So the integral defining $K(u)$ is absolutely convergent.

The other benefit is that with the characteristic function one can apply a result known as the *Fourier transform inversion theorem*. This had its origins in the investigation of the differential equations which arise in the theory of heat conduction and elasticity; but it turns out to be just what is needed to solve this problem in probability theory. It states that, if

$$K(u) = \int_{-\infty}^{\infty} e^{xuj}\phi(x) \, dx,$$

then at points where $\phi(x)$ is continuous,

$$\phi(x) = \frac{1}{2\pi} \int_{-\infty}^{\infty} e^{-xuj}K(u) \, du.$$

So, to obtain the probability density $\phi(x)$ from the moment generator $M(u)$, the procedure is first to convert the moment generaor into a characteristic function by replacing u by uj, and then to apply the inversion theorem. Notice that the condition about ϕ being continuous deals precisely with the trivial breakdown of uniqueness mentioned above. So in this way the whole theory is tied up. (Note 17.6)

Exercise 17F

Note. Several of the questions in this exercise depend on a knowledge of particular definite integrals, which are found by means of an advanced technique in complex variable theory known as "contour integration". These integrals are given in the respective questions, so that they can be applied to situations involving characteristic functions.

1   A random variable can take either of two values, -1 and $+1$, each with probability $\frac{1}{2}$. Find the characteristic function in its simplest form.
      What is the characteristic function for the mean of a sample of n independent values of this random variable?

2   Find the characteristic function for the negative exponential probability model (see Exercise 17B, question 8).

3   Use the Fourier transform inversion theorem to show that, if $K(u) = e^{-\frac{1}{2}u^2}$, then $\phi(x)$ is the standard normal probability density function. (Compare Q.10(b).)

4   The Cauchy probability density function is defined by

$$\phi(x) = \frac{1}{\pi(1 + x^2)}.$$

   (a) Show that the variance is infinite.
   (b) Show that the integral defining the moment generator is not convergent unless $u = 0$.
         It can be proved that, if u is real, then

$$\int_{-\infty}^{\infty} \frac{e^{xuj}}{1 + x^2}\, dx = \pi e^{-|u|}.$$

   (c) State the characteristic function for this probability model.
   (d) Verify the Fourier transform inversion theorem in this case.
   (e) Prove that, if samples of n independent values of a Cauchy random variable are taken, then the mean is distributed with the same probability density.
   (f) Why does the central limit theorem not apply in this case?

5   It can be proved that, if $\lambda > 0$, then

$$\int_{-\infty}^{\infty} \frac{e^{x(\lambda - uj)}}{\lambda - uj}\, du = \begin{cases} 2\pi & \text{if } x > 0, \\ 0 & \text{if } x < 0. \end{cases}$$

   Use this to find the probability density function for a random variable whose moment generator is $M(u) = \lambda/(\lambda - u)$.

6   It can be proved that

$$\int_{-\infty}^{\infty} \frac{\sin u}{u}\, du = \pi.$$

   Deduce the value of $\int_{-\infty}^{\infty} (\sin cu)/u\, du$, (a) if $c > 0$, (b) if $c < 0$.
      Hence find the probability density function for a random variable whose characteristic function is $K(u) = (\sin u)/u$. (Compare Q.10(a).)

7   Use a method similar to that of question 6 to find the probability density function for a random variable whose characteristic function is

$$K(u) = \cos u\, \frac{\sin(hu)}{hu},$$

   where h is a positive number less than 1.
      By considering the limiting situation as $h \to 0$, find the probability function for a random variable whose characteristic function is $\cos u$.

18

Chi-squared probability

Tables of chi-squared probability have already been used, in Chapters 6 and 10, to test theoretical probability models against experimental evidence. At that stage, however, the reasoning had to be based largely on 'hunch', and the tables themselves could be justified only by numerical approximation. Now we are in a position to define precisely what is meant by chi-squared probability, and to explain why it provides a good approximation for the distribution of the discrepancy between observed and expected frequencies in these applications.

18.1 WHAT IS CHI-SQUARED PROBABILITY?

If you look at the chi-squared probability tables, it is very unlikely that you will recognise the entries as having a connection with any other probability tables. So it may surprise you to be told that the first line of the chi-squared table (for $v = 1$) is just a selection from the table of cumulative normal probability in another form!

If the standard normal random variable N(0, 1) is denoted by X, then the table of cumulative normal probability gives the values of $P(X < x)$ for various values of x. This is the probability we need if a hypothesis is being tested using a one-tail test (see §8.5). But with a two-tail test the question that has to be asked is: "What is the probability that the random variable differs from the mean by at least a certain amount?" And if (for reasons which will appear very soon) this "certain amount" is denoted by the symbol χ (greek letter "chi"), then it is easy to see from Fig. 1 that the answer is

$$P(|X| \geqslant \chi) = 2(1 - \Phi(\chi)),$$

where Φ denotes the standard normal cumulative probability function. Some typical values of the probability and of χ are:

$P(\lvert X \rvert \geqslant \chi)$	0.1	0.05	0.01	0.001
χ		1.64	1.96	2.58	3.29

Q.1 Check these statements for yourself. Show that $P(|X| \geqslant \chi)$ can be written also as $P(X^2 \geqslant \chi^2)$. Make a table of this probability against values of χ^2, and then check that what you have done is to construct part of the first line of the table of chi-squared probability. Use the same method to check the other entries in that line of the table.

What Q.1 shows is that, if X is a standard normal random variable, then for $v = 1$ the table of chi-squared probability associates with certain values of χ^2 the probability that X^2 exceeds χ^2.

This is the clue to the interpretation of the whole of the chi-squared probability table; but for the general line with v degrees of freedom, we are dealing with v independent random variables rather than just one.

Take for example the case $v = 2$. This relates to two independent random variables X and Y, each having standard normal probability $N(0, 1)$. You could imagine, for example, a fairground game in which customers throw darts at a board to try to hit a point marked O, and in which the errors both horizontally and vertically are distributed with standard normal probability (in units of decimetres, say). Then the holes on the board would form a pattern which would look something like Fig. 2, which was, in fact, made by simulating the throws of 1000 such darts on a computer.

You will notice that the distribution of these holes appears to have more or less circular symmetry. By looking at the pattern, you cannot tell which were the

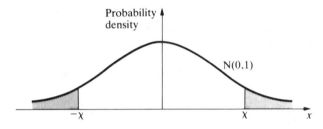

Figure 1

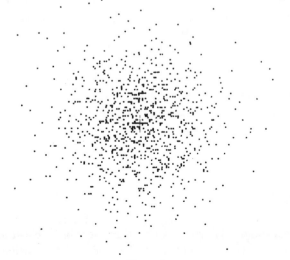

Figure 2

horizontal and vertical directions on the board. The reason for this can be found by calculating the area probability density for the distribution. If you follow through the argument of §12.2, but with standard normal probability densities for X and Y rather than rectangular probability densities $1/b$, the area probability density for the point (X, Y) is seen to be

$$\frac{1}{\sqrt{(2\pi)}} e^{-\frac{1}{2}x^2} \times \frac{1}{\sqrt{(2\pi)}} e^{-\frac{1}{2}y^2} = \frac{1}{2\pi} e^{-\frac{1}{2}(x^2 + y^2)}.$$

(This is a particular case of the relation $\gamma(x, y) = \alpha(x)\beta(y)$ used in the calculation of $E[XY]$ for independent random variables in §14.5.) This can be written as

$$\frac{1}{2\pi} e^{-\frac{1}{2}r^2},$$

where r denotes the distance of the point (x, y) from O. So the area probability density is the same for all points at the same distance from O; that is, it has circular symmetry about O.

Q.2 Make up a problem corresponding to the case $v = 3$. Representing the random variables by points of three-dimensional space, find an expression for the volume probability density and show that it has spherical symmetry about O.

The appearance of Fig. 2 suggests the name "swarm" for a probability model of this kind; and bearing in mind how this example arose, we will call it a "two-dimensional standard normal swarm". Similarly, the model obtained in Q.2 is a three-dimensional standard normal swarm. When v is greater than three, it becomes impossible to produce an actual spatial representation. But the strength of mathematics is that it is created in the mind, and is not limited by what can be constructed in the physical world. So if we have n independent standard normal random variables, denoted by $X_1, X_2, \ldots, X_n$, then it is not difficult to imagine the coordinates $(X_1, X_2, \ldots, X_n)$ defining a random "point" in n-dimensional space, and the "distance" R of that point from the origin (itself a random variable) being defined by

$$R^2 = X_1^2 + X_2^2 + \cdots + X_n^2.$$

It will then follow, exactly as in the two- and three-dimensional cases, that an n-dimensional standard normal swarm has n-dimensional probability density

$$\frac{1}{(2\pi)^{\frac{1}{2}n}} e^{-\frac{1}{2}r^2}.$$

With these definitions, we are now in a position to extend the meaning of chi-squared probability given above for $v = 1$ to the complete table:

If R denotes the distance from the origin of a random point of an n-dimensional standard normal swarm, then the table of chi-squared probability associates with certain values of χ^2 the probability that R^2 exceeds χ^2, for $v = n$.

Later in this chapter we will investigate mathematical consequences of this definition. First, however, it will be helpful to consider some applications.

18.2   DIRECT APPLICATIONS

One example of a standard normal swarm arises when the random variables X_1, $X_2, \ldots, X_n$ represent the first, second, $\ldots$, nth measurements of a sample drawn from a standard normal distribution.

Example 1
A seed potato merchant claims that the mean weight of crop from each tuber of a certain variety is 1.5 kg, and that the weight is distributed normally with standard deviation 0.25 kg. A grower selects five plants at random for a test dig, and finds the yields to be 1.24 kg, 1.93 kg, 1.07 kg, 0.91 kg, 1.80 kg. Are these in line with the merchant's claim?

To apply chi-squared probability, the random variable must be standardised to a mean of zero and a standard deviation of 1. So the weights W kg are converted to standardised values using the transformation $X = (W - 1.5)/0.25$. The hypothesis to be tested then becomes:
 $-1.04, +1.72, -1.72, -2.36, +1.20$ form a random sample of independent values of a standard normal variable.
To test this hypothesis, we calculate

$$R^2 = (-1.04)^2 + (+1.72)^2 + (-1.72)^2 + (-2.36)^2 + (+1.20)^2 = 14.008,$$

and use chi-squared probability tables with $v = 5$ to find the probability of getting a value of R^2 as large as this by random sampling. For a probability of 5%, the critical value of χ^2 is 11.07; since 14.008 is greater than this, the hypothesis is rejected at the 5 % significance level.

Exercise 18A

1   The heights of recruits to the Ruritanian army are distributed normally with mean 175 cm and standard deviation 5 cm. A sample of four, said to be drawn at random, have heights 180 cm, 180 cm, 184 cm, 179 cm. Is this unusual?

2   Children's IQs are supposed to form a normal population with mean 100 and standard deviation 15. A gang of five children have IQs 95, 105, 124, 130 and 133. Do they form a particularly unrepresentative group?

3   Six samples of 180 men under forty were drawn at random from a large population to test the hypothesis that one-sixth of them have black hair. The numbers observed were 40, 35, 30, 30, 25, 20. Is there evidence against the hypothesis?

4   Resistors are being produced in bulk, with nominal resistance 100 ohms; the resistances are in fact distributed with probability N(100, 2^2). In a sample of ten, the sum of the squared deviations from 100 was 74. Is this unusual?

5   In question 2, a class of 40 children is found to have a mean IQ of 95 and standard deviation 12. Do they form a particularly unrepresentative group? Is the mean, considered by itself, significantly low?

6 Make a model of the surface with equation $z = f(x, y)$, where f is the area probability density function for a two-dimensional standard normal swarm, by cutting drinking straws to an appropriate length and placing them over the nails of a geoboard, then covering the model with a sheet of cling-film. What feature of your model represents the chi-squared probability?

7 Use chi-squared probability to decide whether, at 1 % significance level, the eight eggs whose diameters are given in Exercise 16C, question 6, could come from a normal distribution with mean 4.11 cm and standard deviation 0.19 cm.

Compare this test with the one you used in Chapter 16.

18.3 THE GOODNESS-OF-FIT PROBLEM

At this stage you may be thinking that the application of chi-squared probability illustrated by Example 1 is quite different from the ways in which we have previously used chi-squared probability tables (in Chapters 6 and 10). So the next question to ask is: how does the definition of chi-squared probability given in §18.1 relate to its application to goodness-of-fit problems?

Let us recap how chi-squared probability was used to test the fit of a probability model. The situation is that we have an experiment for which there are k possible outcomes, the probabilities of these being $a, b, c, \ldots$ respectively. The experiment is repeated n times, so that the expected frequencies of these outcomes are $na, nb, nc, \ldots$. However, when the experiment is carried out the frequencies are observed to be $f, g, h, \ldots$. The discrepancy is then calculated as

$$\frac{(f - na)^2}{na} + \frac{(g - nb)^2}{nb} + \frac{(h - nc)^2}{nc} + \cdots;$$

and the fit of the observations to the model is judged on the basis that the discrepancy is distributed with chi-squared probability. The situation is illustrated in Fig. 3. (If one tries to describe this in general, one clearly soon runs out of alphabet; so it would be better to use a suffix notation, writing the probabilities as $a_1, a_2, \ldots, a_k$ and the frequencies as $f_1, f_2, \ldots, f_k$. But since there

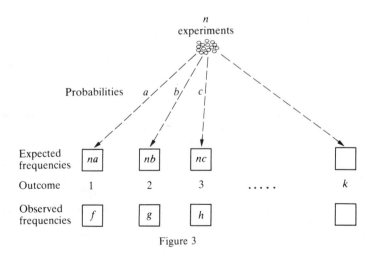

Figure 3

is some quite formidable algebra to come, it may be simpler to meet it first
without the complication of suffix notation. Once you have grasped the essential
argument, expressing it in the more general notation will present no difficulty;
see Q.5.)

Why may the observed frequencies differ from the expected frequencies? This
is because, at each individual experiment, a random process is involved. So the
allocation of an outcome to each experiment can only be expressed in terms of
probabilities. Since the probabilities remain constant and the experiments are
independent of each other, we have a Bernoulli type of situation; and the
probability of getting the observed frequencies f, g, h, ... is given by the
multinomial probability model (Exercise 3B, question 13) as

$$\frac{n!}{f!\,g!\,h!\ldots}\,a^f b^g c^h \ldots,$$

where we have to remember that $a + b + c + \ldots = 1$ and $f + g + h + \ldots = n$.

Here is a clue to the link between chi-squared probability and the goodness-
of-fit problem. For we have described chi-squared probability as a development
of normal probability; and we know that normal probability is an approximation to binomial probability when n is large. This suggests that the technique
used to establish that approximation in §13.5 might also work here. So, using
Stirling's approximation $n! \approx \sqrt{(2\pi)}n^{n+\frac{1}{2}}e^{-n}$, the probability of getting the
observed frequencies can be written approximately as

$$\frac{\sqrt{(2\pi)}n^{n+\frac{1}{2}}e^{-n}}{\sqrt{(2\pi)}f^{f+\frac{1}{2}}e^{-f} \times \sqrt{(2\pi)}g^{g+\frac{1}{2}}e^{-g} \times \sqrt{(2\pi)}h^{h+\frac{1}{2}}e^{-h} \times \ldots}\,a^f b^g c^h \ldots.$$

This probability has then to be associated somehow with the discrepancy given
by the expression quoted above.

This is clearly going to be quite complicated, so it may be best to start by
looking at the problem first with only a small number of outcomes.

The two-outcome case
It will help to begin by looking back at §13.5; for with two outcomes you will see
that the expressions for the probability and its approximation are exactly the
same as those given in the earlier chapter for p(i), with the sole modification that
the letters i and j are replaced by f and g. So a lot of the algebraic work carries
over directly from §13.5 to the present problem.

The main difference arises when we bring in the discrepancy, which you will
notice can be written as

$$\left(\frac{f - na}{\sqrt{(na)}}\right)^2 + \left(\frac{g - nb}{\sqrt{(nb)}}\right)^2.$$

This suggests that, instead of the change of variable made in §13.5, a more
appropriate transformation would be to write

$$x = \frac{f - na}{\sqrt{(na)}} \quad \text{and} \quad y = \frac{g - nb}{\sqrt{(nb)}}. \quad \text{(Note 18.1)}$$

These have to be turned round into the forms

$$f = na + x\sqrt{(na)} \quad \text{and} \quad g = nb + y\sqrt{(nb)}.$$

There are now several points to notice:

(1) There are $n + 1$ possible pairs of values of f and g, from $f = 0, g = n$ to $f = n$, $g = 0$; and there are therefore $n + 1$ pairs of values of x and y.

(2) Adding the expressions for f and g, and using the relation $a + b = 1$, all the values of x and y satisfy the equation

$$x\sqrt{(na)} + y\sqrt{(nb)} = 0.$$

Properties (1) and (2) are shown geometrically in Fig. 4

(3) The discrepancy is $x^2 + y^2$, the square of the displacement of a point from the origin. As before, it is convenient to denote this by r^2.

(4) The probability

$$\frac{\sqrt{(2\pi)n^{n+\frac{1}{2}}e^{-n}}}{\sqrt{(2\pi)f^{f+\frac{1}{2}}e^{-f}} \times \sqrt{(2\pi)g^{g+\frac{1}{2}}e^{-g}}} a^f b^g$$

can be simplified using the relation $f + g = n$ to the form

$$\frac{1}{\sqrt{(2\pi)}} \frac{1}{\sqrt{(nab)}} \frac{(na)^{f+\frac{1}{2}}(nb)^{g+\frac{1}{2}}}{f^{f+\frac{1}{2}}g^{g+\frac{1}{2}}};$$

and substitution for f and g in terms of x and y converts this into

$$\frac{1}{\sqrt{(2\pi)}} \frac{1}{\sqrt{nab}} \frac{1}{Q_1 Q_2},$$

where

$$Q_1 = \left(\frac{f}{na}\right)^{f+\frac{1}{2}} = \left(1 + \frac{x}{\sqrt{(na)}}\right)^{na+x\sqrt{na}+\frac{1}{2}},$$

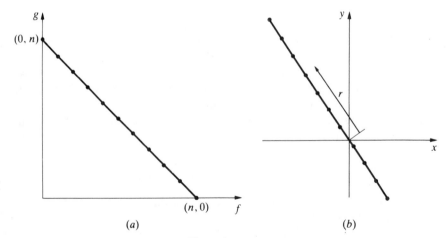

(a)   (b)

Figure 4

and similarly

$$Q_2 = \left(1 + \frac{y}{\sqrt{(nb)}}\right)^{nb + y\sqrt{(nb)} + \frac{1}{2}}.$$

You should check all these details for yourself.

Now notice that Q_1 is just the expression for P_1 in §13.5 with b put equal to 1; so we can save ourselves some work by quoting the approximation for $\ln P_1$ when n is large found there, and deduce (putting $b = 1$) that

$$\ln Q_1 \approx x\sqrt{(na)} + \tfrac{1}{2}x^2.$$

And similarly

$$\ln Q_2 \approx y\sqrt{(nb)} + \tfrac{1}{2}y^2.$$

Adding these two equations gives

$$\ln(Q_1 Q_2) = \ln Q_1 + \ln Q_2 = (x\sqrt{(na)} + y\sqrt{(nb)}) + \tfrac{1}{2}(x^2 + y^2)$$
$$= \tfrac{1}{2}r^2,$$

using (2) and (3). So $Q_1 Q_2 \approx e^{\frac{1}{2}r^2}$, and the approximate expression for the probability can be written

$$\frac{1}{\sqrt{(2\pi)}} \frac{1}{\sqrt{(nab)}} e^{-\frac{1}{2}r^2}.$$

We are obviously getting very close to normal probability! Just one last step remains – to re-interpret this as a probability *density* rather than a probability. It is clear from Fig. 4b that the displacement r takes only discrete values; but by enclosing each point of the possibility space within an interval, whose length we denote by δr, the probability function can be approximated by a probability density function over a continuous possibility space. Fig. 5 shows a part of this possibility space on a large scale; δr is the hypotenuse of a right-angled triangle whose other sides, δx and δy, are the changes in x and y when f is increased by 1

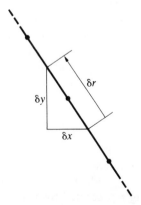

Figure 5

(so that g is decreased by 1). So, from the definitions of x and y,

$$\delta x = \frac{1}{\sqrt{(na)}} \quad \text{and} \quad \delta y = \frac{-1}{\sqrt{(nb)}}.$$

Therefore

$$(\delta r)^2 = (\delta x)^2 + (\delta y)^2 = \frac{1}{na} + \frac{1}{nb} = \frac{b+a}{nab} = \frac{1}{nab}.$$

This is just the expression whose square root appears in the probability function. So finally that probability can be put into the form

$$\frac{1}{\sqrt{(2\pi)}} e^{-\frac{1}{2}r^2} \delta r$$

– familiar territory!

What then does all this prove? The crucial points of the argument to fix on are:

(1) When the two outcomes of the Bernoulli-type experiment are distributed randomly according to their probabilities, the discrepancy between the observed and expected frequencies is a random variable R^2.

(2) R is a standard normal random variable (which we can describe as a "one-dimensional standard normal swarm") approximately if n is large.

Putting these two facts together with the interpretation of chi-squared probability given in §18.1 leads to the conclusion:

If n is large, the table of chi-squared probability associates approximately with certain values of χ^2 the probability that the discrepancy exceeds χ^2, for $\nu = 1$.

This is a precise description of the way in which chi-squared probability was used in Chapter 6 when there are just two outcomes in the experiment.

The three-outcome case

A great deal of the work put into the two-outcome case can be extended directly to larger values of k. When there are three outcomes the expression for the discrepancy has a third term, which can be written as z^2, where $z = (h - nc)/\sqrt{(nc)}$. The expression for the probability can be simplified just as before, leading to the approximation

$$\frac{1}{2\pi} \frac{1}{n\sqrt{(abc)}} e^{-\frac{1}{2}r^2}.$$

It is left to you to write out in detail the argument leading to this result.

What is not quite so straightforward is to convert this probability into a probability density. The equivalent of Fig. 4a is now three-dimensional, the possible frequencies being represented by a triangular lattice of points all lying in the plane $f + g + h = n$. When transformed, as in Fig. 4b, these points are mapped to a triangular lattice (but not necessarily an equilateral one) in the plane $x\sqrt{(na)} + y\sqrt{(nb)} + z\sqrt{(nc)} = 0$. The probability function therefore has to be reinterpreted as an area probability density function. To do this, we shall have to find a pattern of regions tessellating the plane, with just one point of the possibility space inside each region. The area of the region will then correspond to the length δr of the interval in the two-outcome case.

Q.3   How many points are there in the possibility space?

The clue is provided by Fig. 6. There are six triangles of the lattice surrounding a typical point of the possibility space, and the centroids of these triangles lie at the vertices of a hexagon. The hexagons surrounding the points (x, y, z) fit together (like the bases of a set of basalt columns) to cover the relevant part of the plane.

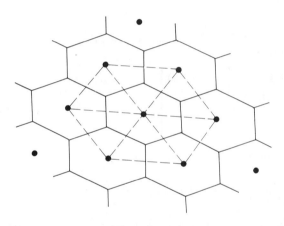

Figure 6

Q.4   Draw your own copy of Fig. 6, and prove that the area δS of any one of the hexagons is twice the area of one of the basic triangles of the lattice.

The problem is now to calculate δS in terms of a, b, c and n. To do this, note that a triangle of the lattice in the (x, y, z)-plane is derived from an equilateral triangle in the plane $f + g + h = n$ by means of the transformation

$$x = (f - na)/\sqrt{(na)}, \quad y = (g - nb)/\sqrt{(nb)}, \quad z = (h - nc)/\sqrt{(nc)}.$$

Note also that, between any two neighbouring points of the equilateral triangle lattice in the plane $f + g + h = n$, one of the coordinates f, g, h is unchanged, one increases by 1 and one decreases by 1. It follows that the analogue of Fig. 5 for the three-outcome case is Fig. 7, where the magnitudes of $\delta x, \delta y, \delta z$ are $1/\sqrt{(na)}, 1/\sqrt{(nb)}, 1/\sqrt{(nc)}$. We need to calculate the area of the triangle ABC. There are various ways of doing this; one of the simplest is to use the idea of

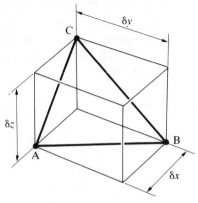

Figure 7

vector area. (Note 18.2) For the triangle ABC, this is $\frac{1}{2}\mathbf{AB} \times \mathbf{AC}$, which can be written in component form as

$$
\frac{1}{2}
\begin{bmatrix}
-1/\sqrt{(na)} \\
1/\sqrt{(nb)} \\
0
\end{bmatrix}
\times
\begin{bmatrix}
-1/\sqrt{(na)} \\
0 \\
1/\sqrt{(nc)}
\end{bmatrix}
=
\frac{1}{2}
\begin{bmatrix}
1/n\sqrt{(bc)} \\
1/n\sqrt{(ac)} \\
1/n\sqrt{(ab)}
\end{bmatrix}
=
\frac{1}{2n\sqrt{(abc)}}
\begin{bmatrix}
\sqrt{a} \\
\sqrt{b} \\
\sqrt{c}
\end{bmatrix}.
$$

So the area of the triangle has magnitude

$$
\frac{1}{2n\sqrt{(abc)}}\sqrt{(a+b+c)} = \frac{1}{2n\sqrt{(abc)}}, \text{ since } a+b+c = 1.
$$

Using Q.4, this means that the area δS of a hexagon is $1/n\sqrt{(abc)}$, which is just the factor which appears in the approximate expression for the probability. The probability can therefore be written as

$$
\frac{1}{2\pi} e^{-\frac{1}{2}r^2}\, \delta S;
$$

and this ties in as expected with chi-squared probability with $v = 2$.

The general case

You will have noticed that the discussion of the two- and three-outcome cases has fallen into two parts: first, the use of algebra to obtain an approximate expression for the probability; and second, its interpretation as a probability density, and the linking of this to chi-squared probability as defined in §18.1.

There is no difficulty about generalising the first of these steps to the case where there are k outcomes. The only additional complication is one of notation.

Q.5   Using the suffix notation suggested at the beginning of this section, obtain an approximation to the probability of getting frequencies $f_1, f_2, \ldots, f_k$ in the form

$$\frac{1}{(2\pi)^{\frac{1}{2}(k-1)}}\frac{1}{n^{\frac{1}{2}(k-1)}\sqrt{(a_1 a_2 \ldots a_k)}}\, e^{-\frac{1}{2}r^2},$$

where $r^2 = x_1^2 + x_2^2 + \ldots + x_k^2$ and, for $i = 1, 2, \ldots, k, x_i = (f_i - na_i)/\sqrt{(na_i)}$.

The second step presents more difficulty, since it involves geometrical reasoning in k rather than two or three dimensions. You might think that it was rather lucky that the constants worked out in such a way that the second factor in the expression for the probability could be identified exactly with δr or δS. But in fact this was bound to happen because, over the complete possibility space, the probabilities have to add up to 1, both in the discrete situation and in the continuous approximation. And this has to apply whether the number of outcomes is 2, 3 or k. So the final result can be generalised with confidence:

If a goodness-of-fit procedure is applied to the results of an experiment of Bernoulli type repeated a large number of times, and if the number of possible outcomes is k, then the discrepancy is distributed approximately according to the chi-squared probability model with $v = k - 1$.

18.4 THE EFFECT OF THE APPROXIMATIONS

Several approximations were made in the course of the theory linking the goodness-of-fit test to chi-squared probability, and these have implications when we come to apply the method. Two of these need to be discussed in some detail.

(1) *Large differences*
The first approximation came in when Stirling's formula was used to approximate $n!$; but this in fact is not very important. For one thing, the errors are surprisingly small. Even when $n = 1$, it gives the value $\sqrt{(2\pi)}/e$, or about 0.922, an error of less than 8%; and this quickly improves further (less than 2% when $n = 5$). In any case, these errors occur only at the fringes, when one of the f_i is very small; and we should expect some trouble here, since the normal probability curve extends to infinity, whereas the multinomial probabilities do not exist if any of the f_i are negative.

A more important approximation arises in the use of the Taylor polynomial

$$\ln(1 + z) \approx z - \tfrac{1}{2}z^2$$

later on in the calculation of $\ln Q_i$. This was used with z replaced by $x_i/\sqrt{(na_i)}$, which is $(f_i - na_i)/na_i$.

Q.6 Compute the percentage errors in using this Taylor approximation for various z from -0.9 to 1.0. Between what values of z is this error less than 10%?

This suggests that if $|f_i - na_i|$ is greater than about $\frac{1}{2}na_i$ for any of the entries (that is, if the actual frequencies differ from the expected frequencies by more than about 50%), then there may be quite a serious error in the probabilities predicted by the theory.

Actually, the situation is not quite as bad as it seems since the chi-squared tables give cumulative probabilities, and the errors in the probabilities are therefore errors in the *increments* towards the right of the table. Nevertheless, the inaccuracies are there; and this should be a warning to users of chi-squared tables who draw conclusions about the value of the discrepancy being "significant" or "not significant" based on hair's breadth variations on one side or the other of a tabulated value. The general conclusion is, therefore, that if one or more of the observed frequencies differs very markedly from the expected frequency (say, by more than about 50%), then special caution should be used in drawing conclusions from calculations based on chi-squared probability. (Note 18.3)

(2) *The continuity approximation*
The approximation that is usually more important is the replacement of a probability function for a discrete possibility space by a probability density function.

This is an issue which has been discussed once already, in Example 3 of §13.6, where normal probability tables were used to obtain approximate answers to a binomial probability problem. The question was whether, in a sequence of 100 trials with a probability 0.2 of success, a 27:73 split in the ratio of successes to failures might reasonably occur, using a one-tail test at 5% significance level. Now this is an example which could also be investigated using chi-squared probability: the discrepancy from the expected frequencies of 20 and 80 is

$$\frac{(27 - 20)^2}{20} + \frac{(73 - 80)^2}{80} = 3.06,$$

which is just over the critical value at the 10% level for chi-squared probability with $v = 1$. This fits in with the conclusion reached before, since the chi-squared test does not distinguish between deviations above or below the expected split; so chi-squared corresponds to a two-tail test, and a one-tail probability of 5% produces the same cut-off as a two-tail probability of 10%.

But it was pointed out in §13.6 that, because a discrete possibility space had been replaced by a continuous one, the result "27:73 or worse" should really be interpreted as "$26\frac{1}{2}:73\frac{1}{2}$ or worse". If we apply the same interpretation in the chi-squared test, then the discrepancy becomes

$$\frac{(26\frac{1}{2} - 20)^2}{20} + \frac{(73\frac{1}{2} - 80)^2}{80} = 2.64.$$

which is just *below* the 10% critical value. So, at this significance level, the hypothesis of random choice would not be rejected.

This is the same conclusion as was arrived at in §13.6, and this is not surprising, since we have already seen that using chi-squared probability to tackle the goodness-of-fit problem with two outcomes is based on the replacement of a binomial model by the equivalent normal model. The procedure can be put into the form of a rule:

> When chi-squared probability with $v = 1$ is used in a goodness-of-fit test with one degree of freedom, more accurate results are obtained by moving each of the observed frequencies by $\frac{1}{2}$ closer to the expected frequencies before calculating the discrepancies.

This is called a *continuity correction*.

One might ask whether similar corrections can be made in the three-outcome, ..., k-outcome cases. The answer is unfortunately no. This is not that the problem doesn't then exist; but that, because of the larger number of degrees of freedom, there is no simple way of making allowance for it. This re-inforces once again the danger of attaching too much precision to the values of chi-squared when using them in goodness-of-fit tests.

There is, however, one other situation with one degree of freedom to which a similar continuity correction can usefully be applied. This is when the frequencies can be set out in a 2×2 contingency table, as described in §§10.3–4, and we are testing for the independence of two properties. We shall see in §18.6 that in this case too the possibility space is in reality restricted to one dimension, so the reasoning underlying the use of the correction is the same as before. (Note 18.4)

Example 2

Over the Christmas period one year the police in Humberside and Greater Manchester reported on the number of drivers breathalysed with positive and negative results. The figures were:

	Positive	Negative	Total
Humberside	53	121	174
Greater Manchester	150	225	375
Total	203	346	549

Is the difference in the proportions between the two regions significant?

From the totals, the expected frequencies are calculated to be:

64.3	109.7	174
138.7	236.3	375
203	346	549

So the discrepancy is calculated using observed frequencies amended by the continuity correction:

53.5	120.5	174
149.5	225.5	375
203	346	549

This gives a discrepancy of

$$\frac{(53.5 - 64.3)^2}{64.3} + \frac{(149.5 - 138.7)^2}{138.7} + \frac{(120.5 - 109.7)^2}{109.7} + \frac{(225.5 - 236.3)^2}{236.3}$$
$$= 4.21.$$

With $v = 1$ this would occur by chance with a probability of less than 5%; so, at this significance level, there is evidence that the ratios of positive to negative breath tests are different in the two regions.

Q.7 Why might this be so?

Q.8 What would be the value of the discrepancy without the continuity correction? Would this make much difference to the estimate of the probability?

Exercise 18B

1 Use chi-squared probability, with a continuity correction, to answer Exercise 13D, questions 3 and 5.

2 Rework Exercise 10B, questions 4 and 6, using a continuity correction.

3 In the two-outcome case of the goodness-of-fit problem, show that the discrepancy can be written as $(f - na)^2/nab$. Interpret this directly in relation to the binomial probability model B(n, a), and hence approximately in relation to N(0, 1). Hence relate this directly to chi-squared probability.

4 In the two-outcome case of the goodness-of-fit problem, show that the effect of the continuity correction on the value of the discrepancy is to reduce it by about $1/q$ of its uncorrected value, where q is the difference between the observed and the expected frequency for either of the two outcomes.

   Does a similar result hold for the 2×2 contingency table?

18.5 THE MATHEMATICS OF CHI-SQUARED PROBABILITY

The definition at the end of §18.1 explains what chi-squared probability is. The next step is to find out how it can be calculated. Again it will be helpful to consider some particular small values of v before tackling the question in general.

In fact $v = 1$ is rather special (see Exercise 18C, question 1); but $v = 2$ and $v = 3$ also have the advantage that geometrical arguments can be used to illustrate the probability calculations.

(1) The case $v = 2$.

We saw in §18.1 that the chi-squared probability table gives the probability that a random variable R exceeds χ, where R is the distance from the origin of a point of a 2-dimensional standard normal swarm, with area probability density $(1/2\pi)e^{-\frac{1}{2}r^2}$ at a distance r from the origin. Calculating this involves a process of 'summation' over the region of the plane which lies outside the circle given by

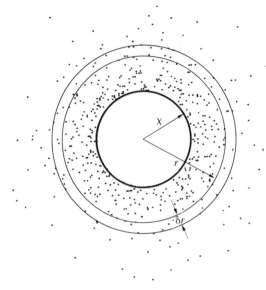

Figure 8

$r = \chi$; this is illustrated in Fig. 8, which selects from Fig. 2 just the part lying outside the circle.

Because of the circular symmetry, the best way to do this is to split the region up into 'rings' of radius r thickness δr, whose area can be taken to be $2\pi r \times \delta r$. (Note 18.5) This gives, for the chi-squared probability,

$$P(R^2 \geqslant \chi^2) = P(R \geqslant \chi)$$
$$= \int_\chi^\infty \frac{1}{2\pi} e^{-\frac{1}{2}r^2} \times 2\pi r \, dr$$
$$= \int_\chi^\infty r e^{-\frac{1}{2}r^2} \, dr$$
$$= [-e^{-\frac{1}{2}r^2}]_\chi^\infty$$
$$= e^{-\frac{1}{2}\chi^2}.$$

The fact that this integral can be found exactly is a bonus – as is the fact that χ^2 appears in the formula. It means that the function tabulated in the chi-squared probability tables for $\nu = 2$ is simply

$$\chi^2 \mapsto e^{-\frac{1}{2}\chi^2};$$

and this is the quantity denoted by $P/100$, where P is the percentage significance level.

Q.9   Draw the graph of this function, with χ^2 as the independent variable.

Q.10   Express χ^2 as a function of P, and hence verify the entries in the second line of the chi-squared probability table.

(2) The case $v = 3$

The argument is very similar to that for $v = 2$; the only differences are that the standard normal swarm now has a *volume* probability density $(1/2\pi)^{3/2}e^{-\frac{1}{2}r^2}$, and that the region outside the sphere given by $r = \chi$ is split into 'shells' whose volume can be taken to be $4\pi r^2 \delta r$. So the chi-squared probability becomes

$$P(R^2 \geqslant \chi^2) = \int_\chi^\infty \frac{1}{(2\pi)^{3/2}} e^{-\frac{1}{2}r^2} \times 4\pi r^2 \, dr$$

$$= \int_\chi^\infty \frac{2}{\sqrt{(2\pi)}} r^2 e^{-\frac{1}{2}r^2} \, dr.$$

But here the similarity stops. This time the integral cannot be evaluated directly (though it can be computed with the help of tables of cumulative normal probability; see Exercise 18C, question 4). Another inconvenience is that it gives the probability in terms of χ, rather than χ^2. However, this drawback can be overcome by making the substitution $r^2 = s$ in the integral. It is left to you to verify that this converts the integral into the form

$$P(R^2 \geqslant \chi^2) = \int_{\chi^2}^\infty \frac{1}{\sqrt{(2\pi)}} s^{\frac{1}{2}} e^{-\frac{1}{2}s} ds.$$

(3) The general case

To go beyond $v = 3$, we need to exercise our imagination to extend the geometrical reasoning into more than three dimensions. But it is not difficult to see in outline how the argument should be generalised. The 'density' for a v-dimensional standard normal swarm is

$$\frac{1}{(2\pi)^{\frac{1}{2}v}} e^{-\frac{1}{2}r^2};$$

and to find what proportion of the swarm lies outside a 'hypersphere' of radius χ, one must integrate by means of 'hypershells', whose v-dimensional 'volume' is given by a formula of the type

$$A_v r^{v-1} \, \delta r,$$

where A_v is some numerical constant, at present unknown.

Q.11   What are the values of A_2 and A_3?

The same argument as before then gives

$$P(R^2 \geqslant \chi^2) = \int_\chi^\infty \frac{A_v}{(2\pi)^{\frac{1}{2}v}} r^{v-1} e^{-\frac{1}{2}r^2} \, dr;$$

and to express this in terms of χ^2 rather than χ, we can again make the substitution $r^2 = s$, so that

$$P(R^2 \geqslant \chi^2) = \int_{\chi^2}^\infty \frac{\frac{1}{2}A_v}{(2\pi)^{\frac{1}{2}v}} s^{\frac{1}{2}v-1} e^{-\frac{1}{2}s} \, ds.$$

We may as well use a single symbol B_v to denote the complicated constant, and write

$$P(R^2 \geqslant \chi^2) = \int_{\chi^2}^{\infty} B_v s^{\frac{1}{2}v-1} e^{-\frac{1}{2}s} ds.$$

But the problem remains that we do not know B_v (or, what comes to the same thing, A_v). There are two ways of completing the calculation. The most obvious is to explore the possibilities of generalising the ideas of surface area and volume to a v-dimensional hypersphere (see Exercise 18C, question 6). But we have a trump card up our sleeve, and it is simpler to play that. It is that since the integral represents a probability, and $P(R^2 \geqslant 0)$ must equal 1, then

$$\int_0^{\infty} B_v s^{\frac{1}{2}v-1} e^{-\frac{1}{2}s} ds = 1.$$

If we can work out this integral (and luckily we can, for this is a standard result) then B_v falls out as a by-product. The details are set for investigation in Exercise 18C, question 2.

Once this is done, the integral for $P(R^2 \geqslant \chi^2)$ is completely known, and from this the complete table of chi-squared probability can be constructed. There are still difficulties in the way: the integral cannot always be found exactly, and even when found it gives an expression for $P/100$ in terms of χ^2 – whereas in the table we really want to find χ^2 for given values of $P/100$. These, however, are mathematical issues; from the statistical point of view, the problem can be regarded as solved.

Exercise 18C

1   The case $v = 1$, which was omitted in §18.5, has certain special features. Using the results of Q.1 in §18.1, write $P(X^2 \geqslant \chi^2)$ as an integral in this case; and by making the substitution $x^2 = s$ show that this fits in with the general formula found in §18.5(3). What values does this suggest should be taken for B_v and A_v when $v = 1$?

2   Using the symbol I_v to denote the integral

$$\int_0^{\infty} s^{\frac{1}{2}v-1} e^{-\frac{1}{2}s} ds,$$

apply the method of integration by parts to express I_v in terms of I_{v-2}. Hence prove that (in the notation of §18.5(3))

$$B_v = \frac{1}{v-2} B_{v-2}.$$

Write down the values of B_2 and B_3, and hence find B_4, B_5 and a general expression for B_v. Does this relation also give a correct value for B_1 (see question 1)? Deduce a general expression for A_v.

3   Explain why the derivative of the integral $\int_w^{\infty} f(s) ds$ with respect to the variable w is $-f(w)$. Hence, by replacing χ^2 by w in the expression for chi-squared probability in

§18.5(3), show that the probability density function for chi-squared probability with v degrees of freedom is given by

$$w \mapsto B_v w^{\frac{1}{2}v-1} e^{-\frac{1}{2}w}.$$

Draw graphs of this function for various numbers of degrees of freedom. Where appropriate, find the value of χ^2 for which the probability density is a maximum.

4 Use integration by parts to show that chi-squared probability is given by the expressions

$$2(1 - \Phi(\chi)) + \sqrt{\frac{2}{\pi}}\, \chi e^{-\frac{1}{2}\chi^2} \quad \text{when } v = 3,$$

$$e^{-\frac{1}{2}\chi^2}(1 + \tfrac{1}{2}\chi^2) \qquad \text{when } v = 4.$$

Use these to check the third and fourth lines of the chi-squared probability table. Plot these as functions of χ^2.

5 Use the result of question 3 to write the moment generator for chi-squared probability in the form

$$\int_0^\infty B_v w^{\frac{1}{2}v-1} e^{-\frac{1}{2}(1-2u)w}\, dw.$$

By means of the substitution $(1 - 2u)w = s$, show that this is equal to $(1 - 2u)^{-\frac{1}{2}v}$. Hence find the mean and variance for chi-squared probability.

Show that, when v is large, $(\chi^2 - v)/\sqrt{(2v)}$ is distributed approximately as standard normal probability $N(0, 1)$. Use this to check the values given in the last line of the chi-squared probability table.

If two random variables X and Y are distributed independently with chi-squared probability density with α and β degrees of freedom respectively, how is $X + Y$ distributed?

6 Another way of calculating the constants A_v, and hence B_v, is to generalise the geometrical ideas of 'surface content' and 'volume content' to a hypersphere of v dimensions. (These refer, for example, to surface area and volume if $v = 3$, but to circumference and area if $v = 2$; what would they signify if $v = 1$?) Explain why A_v is the constant in the surface content formula

$$S_v = A_v r^{v-1}.$$

If the volume content formula is

$$V_v = C_v r^v,$$

justify the relationships

(a) $dV_v/dr = S_v$, and hence $A_v = vC_v$;

(b) $\displaystyle\int_{-1}^{1} C_{v-1}(r^2 - x^2)^{\frac{1}{2}(v-1)}\, dx = C_v r^v.$

(It may help to begin by considering the special cases $v = 3$ and $v = 2$.)

Using the substitution $x = r \sin \theta$, and noting that

$$\int_{-\frac{1}{2}\pi}^{\frac{1}{2}\pi} \cos^v\theta\, d\theta = \frac{v-1}{v} \int_{-\frac{1}{2}\pi}^{\frac{1}{2}\pi} \cos^{v-2}\theta\, d\theta,$$

prove that $(v - 2)A_v = 2\pi A_{v-2}$. Check this against the values obtained for A_v in question 2.

18.6 THE EFFECT OF ADDITIONAL CONSTRAINTS

The theory worked out in §18.3 shows why, when the goodness-of-fit procedure is used, the number of degrees of freedom is one less than the number of possible outcomes. Also, diagrams such as Figs. 4 and 6 demonstrate this geometrically: with two outcomes, the points representing possible values of x and y are restricted to a line through the origin, and with three outcomes the points are restricted to a plane through the origin.

But in some applications, such as those which are described in Chapter 10, the number of degrees of freedom is reduced still further because there are additional constraints on the possibility space. In the rest of this chapter the theory will be taken further to cover such situations.

It will help to begin with a numerical illustration. Here are two scenarios in which we might find ourselves using a goodness-of-fit test:

(a) A sample of 200 men from amongst the inhabitants of a town is taken. The probabilities of picking at random an Englishman, a Scotsman, a Welshman or an Irishman are 0.72, 0.08, 0.18, 0.02. Are the numbers of each nationality in the sample consistent with these probabilities?

(b) Of the 200 people staying in a hotel 160 are British, and 180 are adults. Does the proportion of children depend on nationality?

You will notice that in each case there are four possible outcomes, and the frequencies f_i can be assigned as in the tables:

(a) English	Scottish	Welsh	Irish	Total
f_1	f_2	f_3	f_4	200

(b)		Adult	Child	Total
	British	f_1	f_2	160
	non-British	f_3	f_4	40
	Total	180	20	200

You can easily check that, in both examples, the expected frequencies are 144, 16, 36 and 4 (using the hypothesis of independence in (b)).

Now clearly in both cases the frequencies f_i satisfy

$$f_1 + f_2 + f_3 + f_4 = 200.$$

But in (b) there are two more conditions:

$$f_1 + f_2 = 160,$$
$$f_1 + f_3 = 180.$$

(Of course, it is also true that $f_3 + f_4 = 40$ and $f_2 + f_4 = 20$; but these two equations tell us nothing new, since they are dependent on the first three.)

If we follow through the theory in §18.3, making the substitutions $x_i = (f_i - na_i)/\sqrt{(na_i)}$, so that

$$x_1 = \frac{f_1 - 144}{12}, \quad x_2 = \frac{f_2 - 16}{4}, \quad x_3 = \frac{f_3 - 36}{6}, \quad x_4 = \frac{f_4 - 4}{2},$$

we get

$$(12x_1 + 144) + (4x_2 + 16) + (6x_3 + 36) + (2x_4 + 4) = 200;$$

and, in case (b), also

$$(12x_1 + 144) + (4x_2 + 16) = 160 \quad \text{and} \quad (12x_1 + 144) + (6x_3 + 36) = 180.$$

That is,

$$6x_1 + 2x_2 + 3x_3 + x_4 = 0; \qquad \text{(A)}$$

and, in case (b),

$$3x_1 + x_2 = 0 \quad \text{and} \quad 2x_1 + x_3 = 0. \qquad \text{(B, C)}$$

What do these equations signify geometrically? We have to imagine (x_1, x_2, x_3, x_4) as the coordinates of a point in space of four dimensions. But the equation (A) means that in fact all the points lie in a three-dimensional subspace (a 'hyperplane').

Q.12   By substituting for x_4 in terms of x_1, x_2, x_3, find a basis for this subspace.

In case (b) things are even simpler, since the three equations (A, B, C) have the effect of reducing the original four-dimensional space to just one dimension – that is, a line.

Q.13   Show that in case (b) the equations have solution $(x_1, x_2, x_3, x_4) = \lambda(1, -3, -2, 6)$, where λ can take any value.

In this way we can give a geometrical meaning to the idea of "degrees of freedom". Given the actual frequencies f_i, the discrepancy can be calculated, and tables can then be used to test the appropriate hypotheses. In (a) these would be the tables for three degrees of freedom, corresponding to the fact that the points (x_1, x_2, x_3, x_4) lie in a three-dimensional space. But in (b) we use the tables for one degree of freedom, and this corresponds to the fact that the points lie in a one-dimensional space, that is a line through the origin.

Q.14   By considering general situations of the kind exemplified by (a) and (b), show that the property that the origin satisfies all these equations follows from the fact that the expected frequencies (na_1, na_2, na_3, na_4) satisfy the same conditions as do the observed frequencies (f_1, f_2, f_3, f_4).

18.7 RESTRICTING A NORMAL SWARM TO A SUBSPACE

What then is the effect on a standard normal swarm of requiring the points to be confined to a subspace? For example, suppose that (x, y, z) is a point of a three-dimensional standard normal swarm, but that it is restricted to lie in a plane $\alpha x + \beta y + \gamma z = 0$ through the origin. The problem is, to find the area probability density distribution over the plane.

This is the sort of situation we have met before. It is essentially a problem of conditional probability (see §1.3), and it can be investigated by applying the definition

$$P(A \mid B) = \frac{P(A \text{ and } B)}{P(B)},$$

where the event B is the restriction of the point to the given plane.

Notice first that, since the normal swarm has spherical symmetry, the mathematics can be simplified by rotating the axes from $Oxyz$ to a new position denoted by $Ox'y'z'$, chosen in such a way that the given plane has for its equation $z' = 0$. This is illustrated in Fig. 9.

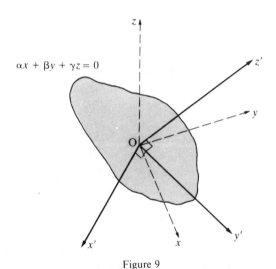

Figure 9

There is just one small difficulty to contend with. Since the three-dimensional swarm has a volume probability *density*, the probability that a random point lies in the plane $z' = 0$ (or any other given plane) is zero! To get round this, we can replace the plane by a thin layer (let us call it L) of thickness $\delta z'$ surrounding the plane. Now take a small region of the plane with area δS. The events A and B are then defined as follows:

A: A point (x', y', z') of the space lies inside the cylinder through this region in the direction of the axis Oz'. (That is, the projection of the point, $(x', y', 0)$, lies in the region.)

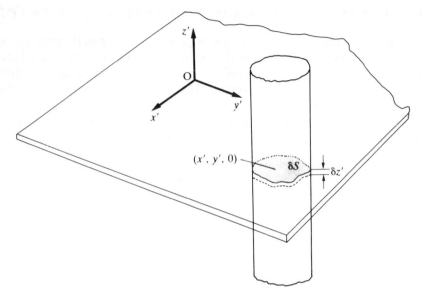

Figure 10

B: The point (x', y', z') lies inside L.

These definitions are illustrated in Fig. 10.

It now follows that P(A and B) is the probability that a point of the three-dimensional swarm lies inside the disc of volume $\delta S \times \delta z'$ around the point $(x', y', 0)$, which is approximately

$$\frac{1}{(2\pi)^{3/2}} e^{-\frac{1}{2}(x'^2 + y'^2 + 0^2)} \delta S \, \delta z'.$$

Also, P(B) is the probability that a point of the swarm lies within the layer L, which is

$$\iiint \frac{1}{(2\pi)^{3/2}} e^{-\frac{1}{2}(x'^2 + y'^2 + z'^2)} dx' dy' dz'$$

integrated over L. And since $\delta z'$ is small, the probability density within the layer varies very little from its value when z' is put equal to zero; so this integral is approximately

$$\left\{ \iint \frac{1}{2\pi} e^{-\frac{1}{2}(x'^2 + y'^2 + 0^2)} dx' dy' \right\} \times \frac{1}{(2\pi)^{\frac{1}{2}}} \delta z',$$

where in the double integral x' and y' both run from $-\infty$ to ∞. But this double integral is just the total probability for a two-dimensional standard normal swarm; it therefore has the value 1. We deduce that, approximately,

$$P(B) = \frac{1}{(2\pi)^{\frac{1}{2}}} \delta z'.$$

So

$$P(A \mid B) = \frac{P(A \text{ and } B)}{P(B)} = \frac{1}{(2\pi)^{3/2}} e^{-\frac{1}{2}(x'^2 + y'^2 + 0^2)} \delta S \, \delta z' \bigg/ \frac{1}{(2\pi)^{\frac{1}{2}}} \delta z'$$

$$= \frac{1}{2\pi} e^{-\frac{1}{2}(x'^2 + y'^2)} \, \delta S,$$

and this is the probability for a two-dimensional standard normal swarm in the plane $z' = 0$. Finally, letting $\delta z' \to 0$, the approximations become exact.

So we have proved a special case (with $n = 3$, $m = 2$) of the result:

If an n-dimensional standard normal swarm is restricted to an m-dimensional subspace, the resulting conditional probability is that of an m-dimensional standard normal swarm.

This puts the finishing touches to the theory of chi-squared probability, by justifying the procedure for dealing with additional constraints: that, when there are extra linear constraints on the frequencies, one may continue to use the tables of chi-squared probability, but with a reduction by 1 in the value of v for each independent constraint.

Exercise 18D

1   There is doubt whether the electronic game in the Students' Union is playing consistently, so 100 students volunteer to play it 5 times each, with the following results:

Number of wins	0	1	2	3	4	5
Frequency	73	12	9	4	2	0

The probability of winning on a particular play has to be inferred from the data. Do these results support the hypothesis that the game is playing fairly?

Write down two equations which should be satisfied by both the observed and expected frequencies in applying the goodness-of-fit test. Does this in fact happen?

2   In a study of accident-proneness forty 16-year-old boys were asked how many times they had broken bones as a result of accidents during their childhood. The results were as follows:

Number of occasions	0	1	2	3	4	5	6
Frequency		1	5	10	11	6	4	3

The researcher suggests that broken bones occur to children quite randomly, and so decides to investigate this hypothesis by comparing the data with the expected frequencies given by a Poisson probability model with the same mean. Write down two equations which should be satisfied by both the expected frequencies and the observed frequencies. Does this happen when the goodness-of-fit test is carried out in practice?

3   Write out proofs of the result stated at the end of §18.7 for the cases (a) $n = 2, m = 1$; (b) $n = 3, m = 1$.

19

Sampling from a normal population

The method we have used so far to find an interval estimate for the mean of a population from measurements of a sample, described in §16.8, is not entirely satisfactory. In the first instance, it is based on the central limit theorem, which is only an approximation. More important, it depends on using an estimate of the standard deviation of the population, and with some samples this estimate will be badly out. We do not even have the means of finding how far out it might be. All these drawbacks are diminished if a large sample is used, though they cannot be completely eliminated. The trouble is that we have been too ambitious: we have been trying to find a method which will work for any population, however it is distributed. This means that there are so many possibilities that no conclusions can be drawn with any precision.

In this chapter it will emerge that one can make much firmer estimates, even with small samples, if the population from which the sample is taken can be described by a normal probability model. This is, of course, a major restriction; but we have seen that it is not an unreasonable assumption for many of the populations which interest us in practice. We have already seen (see §17.6) that the central limit theorem can then be stated as an exact result. The approach used in this chapter will lead to an alternative proof of this, and will then suggest a new test (the t-test) which gets round the difficulty of having to use an estimate of the standard deviation. As a by-product it will also produce a method of making an interval estimate for the value of the standard deviation.

It must be stressed that these procedures are only valid on the assumption that the population is normal. But the methods are so powerful that it is well worth while developing the theory for application in those cases when the assumption is justified.

19.1 A GEOMETRICAL VIEW OF SAMPLING

A sample of measurements is made up of values of n independent random variables $X_1, X_2, \ldots, X_n$. If n is equal to 3, then these values can be taken to be the coordinates of a point in space. This means that a random sample is represented by a random point. (Notice that the coordinates of the point are an *ordered* triple of measurements: the first coordinate is the first sample value taken, and so on.) This is illustrated in Fig. 1.

How can the mean of this sample be shown on the diagram? The mean M is defined by the equation

$$X_1 + X_2 + X_3 = 3M.$$

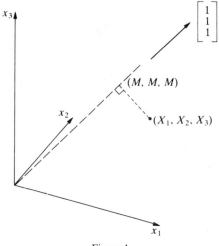

Figure 1

The mean M is also, of course, a random variable; but suppose for a moment we think of it as a constant in this equation. Then the equation could be interpreted geometrically as meaning that the random point (X_1, X_2, X_3) lies in a plane whose equation is

$$x_1 + x_2 + x_3 = 3M.$$

(In this chapter it will be more convenient to denote coordinates by (x_1, x_2, x_3) rather than (x, y, z), as was done occasionally in Chapter 18.) This is a plane with

normal vector $\begin{bmatrix} 1 \\ 1 \\ 1 \end{bmatrix}$; and it meets the line with equation $x_1 = x_2 = x_3$,

which is the line through the origin in the direction of this normal vector (shown as a broken line in Fig. 1) in the point (M, M, M). So the mean M of the random sample is represented by the coordinates of the foot of the perpendicular from the random point onto this line. In Fig. 2 the random sample is represented by the point R, and the mean by the point N.

Q.1 Write, as an equation involving a scalar product, the condition for the line

joining (X_1, X_2, X_3) to (M, M, M) to be perpendicular to $\begin{bmatrix} 1 \\ 1 \\ 1 \end{bmatrix}$.

Show that, when multiplied out, it is the same as the equation given above.

If the right-angled triangle ONR is completed, then it is easily seen that

$$ON = \sqrt{(M^2 + M^2 + M^2)} = M\sqrt{3},$$

and that

$$NR = \sqrt{\{(X_1 - M)^2 + (X_2 - M)^2 + (X_3 - M)^2\}}.$$

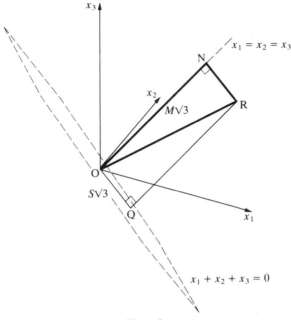

Figure 2

Inside the curly brackets in this second equation you will recognise the expression which occurs in the formula for the variance,

$$S^2 = \frac{(X_1 - M)^2 + (X_2 - M)^2 + (X_3 - M)^2}{3}.$$

It follows that

$$NR = \sqrt{(3S^2)} = S\sqrt{3}. \quad \text{(Note 19.1)}$$

There is another, rather more convenient, way of showing the length $S\sqrt{3}$ on the diagram. Fig. 2 shows also the plane with equation $x_1 + x_2 + x_3 = 0$, which is the plane through the origin perpendicular to the vector $\begin{bmatrix} 1 \\ 1 \\ 1 \end{bmatrix}$. If the line RQ is drawn perpendicular to this plane, then RQ is parallel to NO and so ONRQ is a rectangle. This means that the length OQ is equal to NR, so that $OQ = S\sqrt{3}$. Notice that this is the projection of OR on the plane.

Q.2   Represent a sample of two measurements by a random point R in a plane. Write down expressions for the mean and standard deviation, and verify that the projections of OR on the lines $x_1 = x_2$ and $x_1 + x_2 = 0$ are $M\sqrt{2}$ and $S\sqrt{2}$.

To extend these ideas to samples of more than three measurements, you have to be prepared to accept the idea that one might do geometry in more than three dimensions, and that concepts such as line, plane, vector, length and right angle can still be given meanings in this geometry. Vector algebra (including an algebraic definition of scalar product) provides a natural means for carrying out this generalisation. The results which have been proved for the cases $n = 2$ and $n = 3$ then take the general form:

> If a random sample of measurements is represented by the point R with coordinates $(X_1, X_2, \ldots, X_n)$, and if M and S denote the sample mean and standard deviation, then the projections of OR on the line $x_1 = x_2 = \ldots x_n$ and on the 'hyperplane' $x_1 + x_2 + \ldots + x_n = 0$ are respectively $M\sqrt{n}$ and $S\sqrt{n}$.

Q.3 In Fig. 2, express OR^2 in terms of the coordinates of R, and then write the equation obtained by applying Pythagoras's theorem to the triangle ONR. In what context have you met this equation before?

Q.4 Suppose that the sample X_1, X_2, X_3 is taken from a population whose mean is μ. By adding a point C with coordinates (μ, μ, μ) to Fig. 2, and applying Pythagoras's theorem to the triangle CNR, obtain the result

$$V = \frac{1}{3} \sum_{i=1}^{3} (X_i - \mu)^2 - (M - \mu)^2 \quad \text{(compare §15.6)}.$$

19.2 APPLICATION TO A NORMAL POPULATION

The purpose of taking the sample X_1, X_2, X_3 is to find out something about the population of measurements from which it is taken. Let us now introduce the assumption that this population can be described by the normal probability model $N(\mu, \sigma^2)$, where the values of μ and σ are unknown. The sample values then provide a means for estimating these two parameters.

Since the probability density for a single random measurement X is

$$\frac{1}{\sigma\sqrt{(2\pi)}} e^{-(x-\mu)^2/2\sigma^2},$$

the argument used in §12.2 can be applied to give, for the random point (X_1, X_2, X_3), the volume probability density

$$\frac{1}{\sigma\sqrt{(2\pi)}} e^{-(x_1-\mu)^2/2\sigma^2} \times \frac{1}{\sigma\sqrt{(2\pi)}} e^{-(x_2-\mu)^2/2\sigma^2} \times \frac{1}{\sigma\sqrt{(2\pi)}} e^{-(x_3-\mu)^2/2\sigma^2}$$

$$= \frac{1}{\sigma^3(2\pi)^{\frac{3}{2}}} e^{-\{(x_1-\mu)^2+(x_2-\mu)^2+(x_3-\mu)^2\}/2\sigma^2}.$$

This can be written

$$\frac{1}{\sigma^3(2\pi)^{\frac{3}{2}}} e^{-r^2/2\sigma^2},$$

where r is the distance of the particular sample point (x_1, x_2, x_3) from the point (μ, μ, μ), which we call C.

This is very much like the standard normal swarm introduced in Chapter 18, but rather more general, since it has its centre at a point C on the line $x_1 = x_2 = x_3$ rather than at the origin, and it is scaled up in the ratio σ to 1. It will be called a "normal swarm with centre C and size σ". This is illustrated in Fig. 3.

The property of the normal swarm that is of particular importance here is its perfect spherical symmetry: the probability density at any point R depends only on the distance of R from C. This means that, having put the swarm together by combining three independently varying measurements represented by coordinates in three perpendicular directions (the directions of the axes), we can now take it to pieces in a different way, using three other perpendicular directions. The obvious way of doing this is to take one of these directions along the line $x_1 = x_2 = x_3$, and the other two in the plane $x_1 + x_2 + x_3 = 0$ (we need not specify these precisely). It then follows that the same volume probability density would have been obtained by the independent combination of

one-dimensional normal probability along the line OC with standard deviation σ,

and

a two-dimensional normal swarm in the plane $x_1 + x_2 + x_3 = 0$ with centre O and size σ.

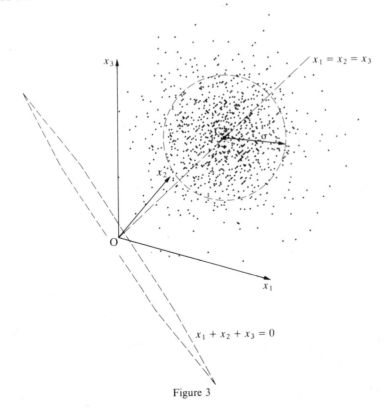

Figure 3

These describe the distributions of the points N and Q in Fig. 2.

Before these results can be used practically, it is necessary to change the origin and scale so that we can use the normal and chi-squared probability tables, which are based on normal probability centred at the origin with standard deviation 1. Then, using the fact that the distances OC, ON and NR are $\mu\sqrt{3}$, $M\sqrt{3}$ and $S\sqrt{3}$ respectively, it follows that:

(1) The distribution of $M\sqrt{3} - \mu\sqrt{3}$ has normal probability density with standard deviation σ, so that the distribution of $(M - \mu)\sqrt{3}/\sigma$ has standard normal probability density.

(2) $S\sqrt{3}/\sigma$ is the distance from the origin of points distributed in a two-dimensional swarm of size 1, so that (by the definition in §18.1) the distribution of $(S\sqrt{3}/\sigma)^2$ has chi-squared probability with 2 degrees of freedom.

The whole of this argument can be extended easily to samples of size n rather than 3, although you will then have to imagine the geometry of space of n dimensions. The n-dimensional probability density of the normal swarm is

$$\frac{1}{\sigma^n (2\pi)^{\frac{1}{2}n}} e^{-r^2/2\sigma^2},$$

and the distances OC, ON and NR contain the factor $\sqrt{n}$ rather than $\sqrt{3}$. Also the 'hyperplane' $x_1 + x_2 + \ldots + x_n = 0$ has $n - 1$ dimensions. The general results are then:

> If a sample of n independent measurements is taken from a normal population with mean μ and standard deviation σ, and if a random sample has mean M and standard deviation S, then
> (1) $(M - \mu)\sqrt{n}/\sigma$ is distributed with standard normal probability density;
> (2) nS^2/σ^2 is distributed with chi-squared probability density with $\nu = n - 1$.

The first of these is, of course, already familiar (see §17.6); but the second is new. Notice that this is a quite different application of chi-squared probability from any that we have met previously. This is a good example of the power of mathematics, in that the same model can be applied to the solution of problems which are apparently unconnected with each other.

19.3 A CONFIDENCE INTERVAL FOR STANDARD DEVIATION

In tackling sampling problems in earlier chapters, the expression $S\sqrt{\{(n/(n-1)\}}$ has been used to estimate the standard deviation of a population; but it was recognised that this was of very limited usefulness, since the value of S was found to vary considerably from one sample to another. The theory in §19.2 makes it possible to say something about the extent of this variation.

Example 1

A sample of nine cooking apples was picked at random from a tree, and the masses (in grams) were found to be

$$170, \quad 115, \quad 140, \quad 120, \quad 135, \quad 155, \quad 160, \quad 145, \quad 140.$$

What can be said about the standard deviation of the whole crop?

To begin with, we have to make an assumption: that the masses of the apples on the tree from which the sample is taken are distributed normally. This we cannot prove; it is an assumption based entirely on past experience of populations of this kind. But without it, we could not make any further progress.

The problem, then, is to find an interval of masses within which it is reasonable to think that the standard deviation, σ grams, might lie. An obvious first step is to calculate the mean and standard deviation, m grams and S grams, of the sample; these come to 142.22 grams and 16.85 grams respectively. The trouble is that we have no idea whether this is a fairly typical sample, or whether it is exceptionally close-packed or exceptionally spread out.

However, if σ were known (which of course it is not), then the result (2) proved in §19.2 tells us that the quantity $9S^2/\sigma^2$ is distributed with chi-squared probability with 8 degrees of freedom. If we decide to work on a basis of 95% confidence, then the relevant columns of the chi-squared probability table are those headed $P = 97.5$ and $P = 2.5$, since these cut off the extreme $2\frac{1}{2}\%$ at either side; and the corresponding values of χ^2 with $\nu = 8$ are 2.18 and 17.53. So, for a given σ, there is a 95% probability that a sample S will be selected such that

$$2.18 < \frac{9S^2}{\sigma^2} < 17.53;$$

that is,

$$0.492\sigma < S < 1.396\sigma.$$

Let us suppose, then, that our sample for which S is equal to 16.85 is one of this "middle 95%" of samples. It would then follow that

$$\sigma < \frac{16.85}{0.492} \quad \text{and that} \quad \sigma > \frac{16.85}{1.396};$$

that is, that

$$12.1 < \sigma < 34.2.$$

This defines a 95% confidence interval for σ.

It is important to emphasise again just what this statement does and does not mean. It certainly does not signify that "there is a 95% probability that the standard deviation of the crop lies between 12.1 grams and 34.2 grams". That would be a totally meaningless statement: σ is a quite specific quantity, and one cannot make a probability statement about its value. What it does signify is that, if σ were to lie within this interval, then the sample of apples picked is a reasonably typical one from the point of view of its standard deviation; any hypothesis about σ lying within this interval would not be rejected (at the 5% level) on the evidence of this sample. (Note 19.2)

Finally, it is worth noticing how wide the interval is. The formula $S\sqrt{\{(n/(n-1)\}}$ gives for the estimate of the standard deviation the value

$16.85 \times \sqrt{\frac{9}{8}} = 17.9$ grams; but for all its apparent precision, it is clear that an estimate of standard deviation based on a sample of only nine apples is extremely unreliable.

19.4 t-PROBABILITY

Although the theory in §19.2 makes it possible to find a confidence interval for standard deviation, it gets us no further forward with the more important problem of finding a confidence interval for the mean. In this respect, we are in almost the same situation as that described in §16.8. That is, the theory tells us that $(M - \mu)\sqrt{n}/\sigma$ is distributed with standard normal probability; but we cannot use this, since not only do we not know μ, but also we do not know σ. The best we have been able to do is to replace σ in this expression by its estimate $S\sqrt{\{n/(n-1)\}}$, giving a different random variable $(M - \mu)\sqrt{v}/S$, where $v = n - 1$, and to hope that the distribution of this is not too different from standard normal probability. The only new feature when the population is normal is that the distribution of $(M - \mu)\sqrt{n}/\sigma$ is known exactly rather than approximately; but this is the least of our worries.

The real breakthrough when the population is normal is that it becomes possible to extend the theory in §19.2 so as to give a precise description, not only of the distribution of $(M - \mu)\sqrt{n}/\sigma$, but also of the distribution of $(M - \mu)\sqrt{v}/S$. This involves inventing a new probability density function, called t-probability, which is similar to but different from standard normal probability. With the use of tables of t-probability, an exact confidence interval for the mean can be found.

Before we develop the theory, it will help to see how t-probability is used in practice.

Example 2
What can be said about the mean mass of the crop of cooking apples from which the sample described in Example 1 was picked?

For this sample $n = 9$, so that $v = 8$; and the theory tells us that $(M - \mu)\sqrt{8}/S$ has t-probability. There is, however, an important difference between tables of t-probability and those of standard normal probability, which is that t-probability is conventionally tabulated for application in two-tail tests. That is to say, the quantity tabulated is the value of t such that $P(|M - \mu|\sqrt{v}/S > t)$ is equal to the critical percentage. So, if we decide to work at the 5% significance level, for which the tables give the value $t = 2.31$ when $v = 8$, then $2\frac{1}{2}\%$ of the area under the probability density graph is cut off in each tail. This means that there is a 95% probability of getting a sample for which $(M - \mu)\sqrt{8}/S$ lies between -2.31 and 2.31.

This is just the information we need to find the 95% confidence interval. It was found in Example 1 that $m = 142.22$ and $S = 16.85$ for the given sample. So it can be stated with 95% confidence that

$$-2.31 < \frac{(142.22 - \mu)\sqrt{8}}{16.85} < 2.31,$$

that is
$$-13.76 < 142.22 - \mu < 13.76.$$

A 95% confidence interval for the mean mass of the apples in the crop from which the sample was taken is from 128.5 grams to 156.0 grams.

Example 3
Two soporific drugs, A and B, were tested out on ten patients. The number of additional hours of sleep which resulted were as follows:

Patient	1	2	3	4	5	6	7	8	9	10
Drug A	1.9	0.8	1.1	0.1	−0.1	4.4	5.5	1.6	4.6	3.4
Drug B	0.7	−1.6	−0.2	−1.2	−0.1	3.4	3.7	0.8	0.0	2.0

Is this convincing evidence for thinking that drug A is more effective than drug B?

This is one of the illustrations used by W. S. Gosset (who always published his papers under the pen-name of "Student") in his original paper in *Biometrika* in the year 1908 which introduced the idea of *t*-probability. Gosset, who worked for the firm of Guinness, made many important contributions to the application of statistics to industrial problems.

In the present example, it certainly seems as if drug A produces more additional hours of sleep than drug B; this is shown up by calculating the differences in the corresponding rows in the table:

$$1.2 \quad 2.4 \quad 1.3 \quad 1.3 \quad 0.0 \quad 1.0 \quad 1.8 \quad 0.8 \quad 4.6 \quad 1.4$$

These times have a mean of 1.58 hours and a standard deviation of 1.17 hours.

However, before jumping to conclusions it is necessary to set up a proper statistical test. The null hypothesis would be that drug A and drug B are equally effective; in that case the mean difference (over the whole population) in the amount of additional sleep produced by the two drugs would be zero. One therefore tests:

Hypothesis 1. The mean difference (hours from drug A − hours from drug B) is zero.

against the alternative hypothesis:

Hypothesis 2. The mean difference is positive.

Now, on the null hypothesis $\mu = 0$, the random variable $M\sqrt{9}/S$ would have *t*-probability with $\nu = 9$. Suppose that we choose a significance level of 1%; then since in this instance the test is one-tailed, we look for a probability in the *two* tails together of 2%. The critical value for *t* is then found from the table to be 2.82.

For the sample tested, the value of $M\sqrt{9}/S$ comes to 4.05; and this is well above the critical value. So we deduce that drug A is significantly better than drug B at the 1% level of significance.

An application of this kind is sometimes called a "paired difference test", since for each individual tested a pair of experimental values is measured, and we are interested in the difference between the two measurements.

Exercise 19A

1   A machine is producing components to a nominal dimension of 1.500 cm. The dimensions of components in a random sample of eight are found to be 1.502, 1.501, 1.504, 1.498, 1.503, 1.499, 1.505, 1.504. Give 95% confidence limits for the mean component dimension. Is the result consistent with the nominal dimension?

2   The annual rainfall at Marlborough in Wiltshire over the five-year period 1961–5, measured in millimetres, was:

Year	1961	1962	1963	1964	1965
Rainfall	736	752	793	555	746

Use these data to give a 95% confidence interval for the mean annual rainfall.

It is known that in fact the mean annual rainfall over the 100-year period 1865–1964 was 832 mm. Do the figures suggest that 1961–5 was a particularly dry period?

3   Fifteen observations were taken from a population as follows:

   1.41,   1.41,   0.23,   0.36,   −0.01,   0.07,   −0.10,   2.20, −0.62,   −0.66,
   0.30,   0.07,   −0.16,   0.02,   0.66.

Test the hypothesis that the mean of the population is zero, and give 95% confidence limits for the mean.

4   Some research was carried out by Hope Simpson on measles in households of two people. The figure given is the number of days between the onset of the two cases.

Days	4	5	6	7	8	9	10	11	12	13	14	15	16	17	18	21
Frequency	1	2	4	11	5	25	37	38	26	12	15	6	3	1	3	1

What can you deduce about the mean interval between the onset of the two cases in such households generally?

5   An industrial process usually operates at a process level, μ, of 80 units per hour. The process has been altered with the intention of increasing output and a sample of observations of the units per hour was taken randomly as follows:

   78.5, 84.9, 83.4, 82.6, 82.7, 78.7, 85.0, 79.3, 82,0, 78.7, 84.9.

Test the null hypothesis $\mu = 80$ against the alternative hypothesis $\mu > 80$ at the 2.5% level.   [MEI]

6   With the data in question 3, give 95% confidence limits for the standard deviation of the normal population from which the sample was taken.

7   With the data in question 4, give 95% confidence limits for the standard deviation of the distribution from which the sample was taken.

8   A jam manufacturer uses a machine to fill jam jars. The machine is usually set so that the mean mass of jam delivered is 504 grams, with standard deviation 2 grams; it

can be assumed that the masses are normally distributed. One morning a random sample of 25 jars is selected, and they are found to have a mean content of 505 grams, with standard deviation 2.5 grams. Is (a) the standard deviation, (b) the mean of the sample unacceptably large?

9 Over a long period a machine has been cutting aluminium rods with mean length 15.20 cm and standard deviation 0.5 cm. One day an inspector finds that a batch of 20 rods has mean length 15.35 cm and standard deviation 0.7 cm. Should this give cause for concern?

10 An experiment was performed to compare two methods of analysing the percentage impurity in a chemical. Tests were made on twelve different samples of the chemical, each sample being analysed by both methods. The results of the experiment were:

Sample number	1	2	3	4	5	6	7	8	9	10	11	12
% impurity { Method A	2.12	2.56	2.43	2.51	2.42	2.44	2.45	2.41	2.41	2.46	2.43	2.38
Method B	2.26	2.65	2.46	2.44	2.55	2.56	2.45	2.36	2.50	2.52	2.48	2.42

Test the hypothesis that on average the two methods of analysis are equivalent.

11 Ten equal strips of metal were each divided into two, and one member of each pair was coated with a special lacquer intended to prevent corrosion. The specimens were left exposed to urban air for two years, and then the percentage change in weight was noted for each of the twenty pieces. Analyse the data.

Strip number	1	2	3	4	5	6	7	8	9	10
Treated	5.0	3.9	3.4	4.8	6.3	6.1	5.2	4.3	5.0	4.2
Untreated	4.6	4.6	4.7	5.1	7.5	5.0	6.4	5.7	5.9	3.1

12 In order to investigate the possible differences between two strains of a plant, two seedlings, one of each strain, were planted in each of eight pots and their heights measured after a period of growth. Is there evidence from the results that the strains differ in respect of height?

Pot	1	2	3	4	5	6	7	8
Strain A (height in cm)	21	28	19	11	14	20	24	19
Strain B (height in cm)	23	21	20	14	9	16	23	18

[MEI]

13 Two types of motor fuel are compared by running ten engines on each type of fuel

Octane number ratings

Engine number	1	2	3	4	5	6	7	8	9	10
Fuel A	100.5	99.8	101.0	100.5	101.0	101.4	102.4	99.5	102.8	103.6
Fuel B	98.3	98.5	100.0	99.5	101.8	100.5	102.3	99.8	100.8	102.0

and noting the octane number on each run. Test the difference in octane number between fuels A and B for significance and comment.

Give a 95% confidence interval for the difference, and say how you would explain to an automobile engineer the meaning of the interval that you have calculated.

[MEI]

14   An experiment was performed in order to compare a standard chemical method (S) of determining the glucose content of human blood in mg/100 ml with a new method (R) based on the optical properties of glucose solution.

Ten outpatients in a diabetes clinic were selected randomly and both methods were applied to blood samples, one from each patient. The following data were obtained. Use the data to estimate the expected difference between the new method and the standard method. Obtain a 95% confidence interval for this bias.

Glucose levels in blood										
Patient number	1	2	3	4	5	6	7	8	9	10
Method S	147	165	72	95	83	172	140	131	178	193
Method R	142	160	87	90	81	163	145	137	180	198

[MEI]

15   Write a computer program to select samples of size n at random from a standard normal probability distribution, to calculate the values of M and S for each sample, and from these to calculate $M\sqrt{n}$ and $M\sqrt{v}/S$ (which are the forms taken by $(M - \mu)\sqrt{n}/\sigma$ and $(M - \mu)\sqrt{v}/S$ when $\mu = 0$ and $\sigma = 1$). Develop this program to show the distribution of these random variables graphically, either as a histogram or as a cumulative probability graph. Investigate how the graphs for the two random variables compare for different values of n.

19.5 THE THEORY OF t-PROBABILITY

Now that we have seen how the table of t-probability is used, it is appropriate to ask how it is constructed. The theory is a development of the argument used in §19.2, and depends essentially on the spherical symmetry of the normal swarm in Fig. 3. In order to be able to use geometrical ideas, it is simplest if for the most part the discussion is restricted to samples of size 3 (or even 2); but the results remain true for all values of n.

Fig. 4 (for the case $n = 3$) shows the same situation as Fig. 2, but the point $C(\mu, \mu, \mu)$ has been added to the figure. As before, R is a random point representing a sample drawn from the distribution $N(\mu, \sigma^2)$, and the point N with coordinates (M, M, M) represents the mean of the sample.

Since t-probability is about the distribution of $(M - \mu)\sqrt{v}/S$, we begin by asking how the quantity $(M - \mu)/S$ can be shown in the diagram. The obvious approach is to concentrate on the vector **CR**, whose projections along and perpendicular to the line OD, with direction vector $\begin{bmatrix} 1 \\ 1 \\ 1 \end{bmatrix}$, are CN = $(M - \mu)\sqrt{3}$ and NR = $S\sqrt{3}$ respectively. So $(M - \mu)/S$ is the cotangent of the angle DCR, marked as θ in the figure.

Note that this is true in any number of dimensions, since in general $CN = (M - \mu)\sqrt{n}$ and $NR = S\sqrt{n}$, but this still gives (see Fig. 5)

$$\cot \theta = \frac{M - \mu}{S}.$$

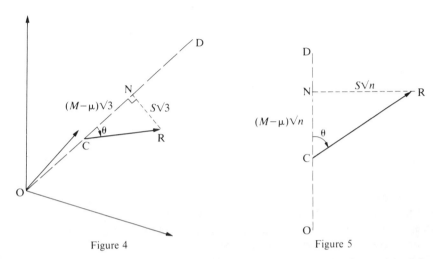

Figure 4   Figure 5

This was in fact the form of the random variable used in Gosset's original paper on t-probability. (Note 19.3) He supported some incomplete analysis (though it produced the correct probability density function) with a series of simulations, an unusual but impressive use of a technique which today the computer is bringing into greater prominence. It was the great mathematical statistician R. A. Fisher who, in the 1920s, made Gosset's work fully rigorous; and Fisher too was responsible for introducing the extra factor $\sqrt{\nu}$ into the random variable. But Fisher's form, $(M - \mu)\sqrt{\nu}/S$, is still often referred to as "Student's t", in honour of the originator.

So what we have to investigate is the probability function for $\sqrt{\nu} \cot \theta$, where $\nu = n - 1$, when the sample points R are distributed in a normal swarm with centre C and size σ. What makes this quite a simple problem is that this normal swarm has spherical (or circular, when $n = 2$) symmetry. Remarkably, this is the only property we need to use: the equation of normal probability will not appear again in this chapter!

(1) *The case $n = 2$*
Notice first that, when $n = 2$, $\sqrt{(n - 1)} = 1$, so that $\sqrt{\nu} \cot \theta$ reduces simply to $\cot \theta$.

It is probably simplest to ask the question in terms of the cumulative probability function rather than the probability density function:

> If R is a random point of a circular normal swarm, what is the probability that $\cot \theta$ is less than a given number t?

And the answer can be read off directly from Fig. 6, in which the shaded region is

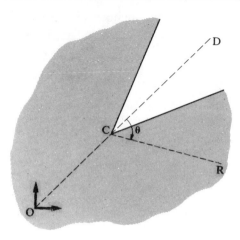

Figure 6

bounded by the two radii making angles of $\cot^{-1}t$ with C. For $\cot\theta$ to be less than t, R must lie inside this shaded region (remember that $\cot\theta$ *decreases* as θ increases!). And because of the circular symmetry of the normal swarm about C, the probability that R lies in the shaded region is

$$\frac{2\pi - 2\cot^{-1}t}{2\pi},$$

which simplifies to

$$1 - \frac{1}{\pi}\cot^{-1}t.$$

Notice that, as t increases from $-\infty$ to ∞, $\cot^{-1}t$ decreases from π to 0, so that this probability increases from 0 to 1 as expected.

Q.5   Draw the graph of this function, and compare it with the graph of the cumulative standard normal probability function. (K)

(2) *The case $n = 3$*
Since $\sqrt{(n-1)} = \sqrt{2}$, we now have to find the probability function for $\sqrt{2}\cot\theta$. Apart from this, the question and the argument are essentially the same as when $n = 2$; but now, since we require C to be placed so that $\sqrt{2}\cot\theta < t$, the shaded region lies outside a conical beam of vertical semi-angle $\cot^{-1}(t/\sqrt{2})$, which we denote by α (Fig. 7). The problem is, what fraction of the 'solid angle' surrounding C does this occupy?

To answer this, a digression into solid geometry will be necessary. What follows is an outline of the argument; it is left to you to fill in the details of the calculation.

(*a*) In two dimensions, angles are measured (in radians) by drawing a circle of unit radius round the vertex and finding the length of arc cut off by the arms

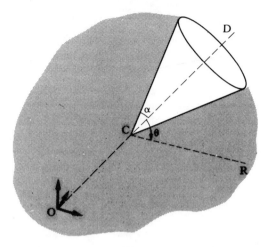

Figure 7

of the angle. In three dimensions, solid angles are measured (in steradians) by drawing a sphere of unit radius round the vertex and finding the surface area cut off by the boundary of the angle.

(b) Since the surface area of a sphere is $4\pi r^2$, the solid angle which completely surrounds the vertex measures 4π steradians. (This is the equivalent of a 'complete revolution' of 2π radians in a plane.)

(c) A conical beam of vertical semi-angle α cuts off on the unit sphere a spherical cap of 'thickness' $1 - \cos \alpha$.

(d) The formula of Archimedes for the area cut off on the surface of a sphere by a pair of parallel planes,

$$\text{area} = 2\pi r \times \text{distance between the planes,}$$

applies in particular to a spherical cap, taking the distance between the planes to be the thickness of the cap. (One of the parallel planes is then a tangent plane to the sphere.)

(e) It follows from (c) and (d) that the solid angle of a conical beam of vertical semi-angle α is $2\pi(1 - \cos \alpha)$.

Q.6 Verify this formula for the special cases $\alpha = 0, \frac{1}{2}\pi, \pi$.

This formula is all that is needed to identify the cumulative probability function, $P(\sqrt{2} \cot \theta < t)$, when $n = 3$. By our definition, $\alpha = \cot^{-1}(t/\sqrt{2})$, so that $t = \sqrt{2} \cot \alpha$ (see Fig. 7). Since, for $\cot \theta$ to be less than t, the random point R has to lie inside the shaded region outside the conical beam, the cumulative probability is

$$\frac{4\pi - 2\pi(1 - \cos \alpha)}{4\pi} = \tfrac{1}{2}(1 + \cos \alpha).$$

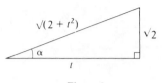

Figure 8

Fig. 8 shows that this can be expressed in terms of t as

$$\tfrac{1}{2}\left\{1 + \frac{t}{\sqrt{(2 + t^2)}}\right\}.$$

Q.7   Check that, as t increases from $-\infty$ to ∞, this probability increases from 0 to 1. Add its graph to the diagram which you drew in Q.5.

(3) The general case
There is no immediately obvious connection between the two cumulative probability functions found in (1) and (2), which might form the basis of a generalisation. However, if we look at the corresponding probability density functions, which are found by differentiating the cumulative functions (see §11.8), a remarkable similarity emerges. It is left to you to carry out the two differentiations; you should then find that both your derivatives fit the formula

$$\frac{C}{(n - 1 + t^2)^{\frac{1}{2}n}},$$

where the constant C has the values $1/\pi$ and 1 respectively.

Two examples are very flimsy evidence on which to make a generalisation! But in this instance it is in fact justified, and it turns out that this formula is valid for all values of n. You may be prepared to take this on trust for the time being; but it can be proved by generalising the geometrical argument into n dimensions, and you can follow the details by working through Exercise 19C.

This formula is usually quoted in terms of the number $v = n - 1$ rather than n. This has already been referred to as the number of "degrees of freedom", and the geometrical argument provides an explanation why this term is used in connection with t-probability. For although the sample point R is determined by n coordinates, we have only taken account of the direction of the vector **CR**, not its length, in discussing the distribution of the ratio $(M - \mu)/S$; and this ratio is completely specified by $n - 1$ angular coordinates. (For example, to line up a telescope on a star, you need only select the correct bearing and elevation, so that two angles will fix it on any point in three-dimensional space.) The probability function is therefore usually described and tabulated in terms of the number of degrees of freedom:

The *t-probability density function* with v degrees of freedom is defined, for all real values of t, by the equation

$$\phi_v(t) = \frac{C_v}{(v + t^2)^{\frac{1}{2}(v+1)}},$$

where the constant C_v is chosen so that $\displaystyle\int_{-\infty}^{\infty} \phi_v(t) \, dt = 1$.

In passing, it is worth noting that statisticians sometimes name functions by the letter conventionally used for the variable. One such example is the χ^2-probability density function, and t-probability is another. The symbol ϕ_v used here is not a standard one; but it is useful to have a notation for the function itself, and ϕ_v is quite a suitable choice since (as shown in Exercise 19B, question 8) $\phi_v(t)$ tends to normal probability density $\phi(t)$ as $v \to \infty$. Similarly it is convenient to use $\Phi_v(t)$ for the cumulative probability function, defined by

$$\Phi_v(t) = \int_{-\infty}^{t} \phi(u) \, du. \quad \text{(Note 19.4)}$$

Thus the results in (1) and (2) can be stated in the form

$$\Phi_1(t) = 1 - \frac{1}{\pi} \cot^{-1}t \quad \text{and} \quad \Phi_2(t) = \frac{1}{2}\left\{1 + \frac{t}{\sqrt{(2 + t^2)}}\right\}.$$

The application of t-probability to sampling from a normal distribution can now be summarised in terms of this function:

If a sample of n independent measurements is taken from a normal population with mean μ, and if a random sample has mean M and standard deviation S, then $(M - \mu)\sqrt{v}/S$ is distributed with t-probability density with v degrees of freedom, where $v = n - 1$.

As explained in §19.4, the tables of t-probability do not give $\Phi_v(t)$ directly, but are based on two-tail applications. The probability usually denoted by $P/100$ is the sum of the probabilities in the two tails taken together, so that

$$\frac{P}{100} = 2\{1 - \Phi_v(t)\}, \quad \text{where} \quad t > 0.$$

As with the chi-squared probability tables, what is then actually tabulated is the inverse function; that is, the tables give the values of t corresponding to certain critical values of the probability.

Exercise 19B

1 Assuming the formula for $\phi_3(t)$, find the value of C_3, and verify that

$$\Phi_3(t) = 1 - \frac{1}{\pi}\left\{\cot^{-1}(t/\sqrt{3}) - \frac{t\sqrt{3}}{3 + t^2}\right\}.$$

Add the graph of this function to those which you drew in Q.5 and Q.7.

2 Use the formulae for $\Phi_\nu(t)$ when $\nu = 1$, 2 and 3 given in the text and in question 1 to check the entries in the first three rows of the table of t-probability.

3 Verify that the quantity t_P tabulated in the table of t-probability is defined by

$$\frac{P}{100} = \int_{t_P}^{\infty} (\nu + t^2)^{-\frac{1}{2}(\nu+1)} dt \bigg/ \int_0^{\infty} (\nu + t^2)^{-\frac{1}{2}(\nu+1)} dt.$$

4 Use the substitution $u = \sqrt{\nu} \cot \theta$ in the integral $\Phi_\nu(t) = \int_{-\infty}^{t} \phi_\nu(u) \, du$ to show that

$$\Phi_\nu(t) = 1 - \int_0^{\alpha} C_\nu \nu^{-\frac{1}{2}\nu} \sin^{\nu-1}\theta \, d\theta, \text{ where } \alpha = \cot^{-1}(t/\sqrt{\nu}).$$

5 Deduce from the result of question 4 that

$$\int_0^{\pi} C_\nu \nu^{-\frac{1}{2}\nu} \sin^{\nu-1}\theta \, d\theta = 1.$$

It is well known (and can be proved by integration by parts, combined with the relation $\cos^2\theta = 1 - \sin^2\theta$) that, for $k \geqslant 2$,

$$\int_0^{\pi} \sin^k\theta \, d\theta = \frac{k-1}{k} \int_0^{\pi} \sin^{k-2}\theta \, d\theta.$$

Use this to obtain the expressions

$$C_\nu = \begin{cases} \nu^{\frac{1}{2}\nu}\left(\dfrac{\nu-1}{\nu-2} \cdot \dfrac{\nu-3}{\nu-4} \cdots \dfrac{2}{1}\right)\dfrac{1}{\pi} & \text{if } \nu \text{ is odd,} \\[2ex] \nu^{\frac{1}{2}\nu}\left(\dfrac{\nu-1}{\nu-2} \cdot \dfrac{\nu-3}{\nu-4} \cdots \dfrac{3}{2}\right)\dfrac{1}{2} & \text{if } \nu \text{ is even,} \end{cases}$$

where the expressions in brackets are taken to be equal to 1 if $\nu = 1$ or $\nu = 2$. Check that this gives the correct value for C_3 as found in question 1.

6 Using the values of C_ν found in question 5, draw on the same diagram graphs of $\phi_\nu(t)$ for a selection of values of ν, together with the graph of the normal probability density function.

7 Express the variance of the t-probability density function with ν degrees of freedom in the form of an integral. Use integration by parts, combined with the relation $t^2 = (\nu + t^2) - \nu$, to show that, if $\nu > 2$, this variance is $\nu/(\nu - 2)$.
   What happens in the cases $\nu = 1$ and $\nu = 2$?

8 Show that $\phi_\nu(t)$ can be written in the form

$$\frac{K_\nu}{(1 + t^2/\nu)^{\frac{1}{2}\nu}} \cdot \frac{1}{(1 + t^2/\nu)^{\frac{1}{2}}}.$$

Deduce that, as $\nu \to \infty$,

$$\phi_\nu(t) \to K e^{-\frac{1}{2}t^2}, \text{ where } K = \lim K_\nu.$$

Use the result of question 5 to express K_ν in terms of ν.
   Explain why

$$\int_0^{\pi} \sin^{\nu+1}\theta \, d\theta < \int_0^{\pi} \sin^\nu\theta \, d\theta < \int_0^{\pi} \sin^{\nu-1}\theta \, d\theta.$$

By evaluating these integrals (as in question 5) when v is even, obtain the inequalities

$$\frac{v}{v+1} < \frac{1}{v}\left(\frac{v-1}{v-2}\cdot\frac{v-3}{v-4}\cdots\frac{3}{2}\right)^2\frac{\pi}{2} < 1.$$

Deduce that, as v tends to infinity through even values,

$$K_v \to \frac{1}{\sqrt{(2\pi)}}.$$

Carry out a similar investigation when v is odd.
   What do you deduce from this analysis?

Exercise 19C

The purpose of this exercise is to indicate how the geometrical derivation of the formula for t-probability can be extended to samples for which $n > 3$. It takes for its starting point the cumulative probability function

$$\Phi_v(t) = 1 - \frac{\text{solid angle within a conical beam of vertical semi-angle } \alpha}{\text{total solid angle around the vertex}},$$

where $t = \sqrt{v}\cot\alpha$, with the context of solid angle generalised to apply in geometry of n dimensions. As before, $v = n - 1$.

The case $n = 3$

1   In §19.5 the ratio of the solid angles was found as the ratio of the areas on the surface of a unit sphere with centre C. Explain why it can also be found as the ratio of the volume within the unit sphere inside the conical beam to the total volume of the sphere. (You may find it helpful to begin by going down one dimension, and noting that for a circle the ratio of an arc to the whole circumference is equal to the ratio of the area of the corresponding sector to the whole area.)

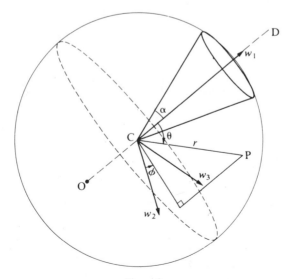

Figure 9

2   Fig. 9 is based on Fig. 7 of §19.5, and shows the position of the point P defined by cartesian coordinates (w_1, w_2, w_3) with origin C, and also by spherical polar coordinates (r, θ, ϕ), where $r = CP$. (Note that, unconventionally, the axis Cw_1 is taken along the line OD; Cw_2, Cw_3 can be any pair of perpendicular lines in the plane at right angles to Cw_1. Also, the angle θ is measured from Cw_1. The reason for this is to make the later generalisation easier.) Obtain the equations

$$w_1 = r \cos \theta,$$

$$w_2 = r \sin \theta \cos \phi,$$

$$w_2 = r \sin \theta \sin \phi.$$

What inequalities involving r, θ, ϕ restrict the point P to (a) the interior of the unit sphere, (b) the part of the interior of the unit sphere which lies inside the conical beam?

3   If $\mathscr{S}$ denotes the interior of the unit sphere and $\mathscr{C}$ denotes the interior of the conical beam, prove that the ratio of the solid angles in the definition is

$$\iiint\limits_{P \in \mathscr{S} \cap \mathscr{C}} dw_1 dw_2 dw_3 \bigg/ \iiint\limits_{P \in \mathscr{S}} dw_1 dw_2 dw_3.$$

4   Prove that the jacobian determinant $\det \dfrac{\partial(w_1, w_2, w_3)}{\partial(r, \theta, \phi)}$ is equal to $r^2 \sin \theta$.

5   By expressing the triple integrals in question 3 as multiple integrals in spherical polar coordinates, prove that the ratio of the solid angles reduces to

$$\int_0^\alpha \sin \theta \, d\theta \bigg/ \int_0^\pi \sin \theta \, d\theta.$$

Hence derive the expression for $\Phi_2(t)$.

The case n = 4

6   In geometry of four dimensions, the notion of spherical polar coordinates can be generalised, so that the coordinates of any point can be written as

$$w_1 = r \cos \theta,$$

$$w_2 = r \sin \theta \cos \phi,$$

$$w_3 = r \sin \theta \sin \phi \cos \psi,$$

$$w_4 = r \sin \theta \sin \phi \sin \psi.$$

What inequalities involving r, θ, ϕ, ψ restrict the point to (a) the interior of the unit 'sphere', (b) the part of the interior of the unit 'sphere' which lies inside the 'conical' beam?

7   Prove that $\det \dfrac{\partial(w_1, w_2, w_3, w_4)}{\partial(r, \theta, \phi, \psi)}$ is equal to $r^3 \sin^2\theta \sin \phi$.

8   Prove that the ratio of the 'solid' angles reduces to

$$\int_0^\alpha \sin^2\theta \, d\theta \Big/ \int_0^\pi \sin^2\theta \, d\theta.$$

Hence derive the expression for $\Phi_3(t)$.

The general case

9   Develop the details of the case $n = 5$ for yourself, and derive the expression for $\Phi_4(t)$. By differentiating this, verify the formula given for $\phi_4(t)$ in §19.5.

10   Prove that, in general,

$$\Phi_\nu(t) = 1 - \int_0^\alpha \sin^{\nu-1}\theta \, d\theta \Big/ \int_0^\pi \sin^{\nu-1}\theta \, d\theta, \text{ where } t = \sqrt{\nu}\cot\alpha.$$

Deduce the general expression for $\phi_\nu(t)$ given in §19.5.

19.6   A MORE ABSTRACT VIEW OF t-PROBABILITY

If the only use of t-probability were in problems of locating the population mean, it would still be important but it would not occupy the central place in statistical theory that it is now given. But this is only one example of a whole range of situations to which it can be applied.

To understand this, let us summarise the three results which have been established about samples of size n drawn from the normal distribution $N(\mu, \sigma^2)$:

(1)   The random variable $U = (M - \mu)\sqrt{n}/\sigma$ has standard normal probability.
(2)   The random variable $W = nS^2/\sigma^2$ has chi-squared probability with ν degrees of freedom, where $\nu = n - 1$.
(3)   The random variable $T = (M - \mu)\sqrt{\nu}/S$ has t-probability with ν degrees of freedom.

Now it is a simple matter to eliminate σ between the equations in (1) and (2); and it is left to you to check that, when this is done, we get the equation

$$T = \frac{U\sqrt{\nu}}{\sqrt{W}}.$$

The crucial step is now to concentrate on the properties of the three random variables U, W and T, and to forget about their relationship to the sampling problem. That is, we let U be *any* random variable having standard normal probability, and W be *any* random variable having chi-squared probablity with ν degrees of freedom. Just one other condition is required: that U and W should vary *independently*. It then follows that:

> If U and W are independent random variables, U having standard normal probability and W having chi-squared probability with ν degrees of freedom, then the random variable $U\sqrt{\nu}/\sqrt{W}$ has t-probability with ν degrees of freedom.

This can be shown by building up the usual geometrical diagram of a normal swarm from the data. For example, if $v = 2$, then W can be represented as the square of the distance from the origin of a random point Q of a standard plane normal swarm; and U can be represented as the coordinate of a random point N distributed with standard normal probability along a line perpendicular to the plane (Fig. 10). Since U and W are independent, the three-dimensional probability density describing the distribution of R is the product of the one- and two-dimensional probability densities describing N and Q; and this produces a standard normal swarm centred on O. Thus

$$\frac{U\sqrt{v}}{\sqrt{W}} = \sqrt{v} \cot \theta;$$

and this has t-probability with v degrees of freedom.

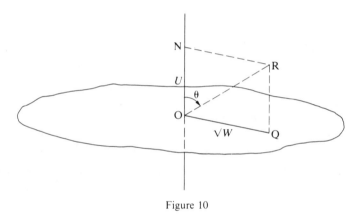

Figure 10

The example in the next section illustrates how this abstract principle can be turned to practical use.

Q.8 Show that, if the unbiased variance estimator $s^2 = \dfrac{n}{n-1} S^2$ is used instead of the sample variance S^2 (see §15.7), then the random variables in (2) and (3) take the forms $W = vs^2/\sigma^2$ and $T = (M - \mu)\sqrt{n}/s$.

19.7 COMPARING THE MEANS OF TWO SAMPLES

Example 4 is based on a well-known set of data about the eggs laid by cuckoos in the nests of two host species – hedge sparrows and wrens. On average hedge sparrows lay bigger eggs than wrens, and it was conjectured that cuckoos made allowance for this, by laying bigger eggs in the nests of hedge sparrows than in the nests of wrens. We can use the more general form of t-probability given in §19.6 to examine conjectures of this kind.

Example 4
In 1902, Latter gave the lengths of cuckoos' eggs found in the nests of hedge sparrows and wrens. Is there evidence in these figures that cuckoos can adapt the size of their eggs to that of the host species?

Host nest	Lengths of eggs in mm
Hedge sparrow	22.0, 23.9, 20.9, 23.8, 25.0, 24.0, 23.8, 21.7,
	22.8, 23.1, 23.5, 23.0, 23.0, 23.1
Wren	19.8, 22.1, 21.5, 20.9, 22.0, 21.0, 22.3, 21.0,
	20.3, 20.9, 22.0, 22.0, 20.8, 21.2, 21.0

There are two hypotheses which we might make about this situation:

Hypothesis 1 (the "null hypothesis"). The size of cuckoos' eggs does not depend on the choice of host species. That is, the figures for hedge sparrow hosts and wren hosts represent two independent samples taken at random from a single normal parent population, with mean μ mm and standard deviation σ mm.

Hypothesis 2 (the "alternative hypothesis"). Cuckoos lay larger eggs in the nests of host species whose eggs are larger. That is, the figures represent samples taken from two different normal populations, that for hedge sparrows having a larger mean than that for wrens.

As usual, we shall examine the data on the basis of the first hypothesis, and accept the second only if the figures suggest that the first is unreasonable.

Let m_1, S_1 denote the mean and standard deviation of a sample of size $n_1 = 14$ (which is the number of sparrows' nests examined), and m_2, S_2 those of a second sample of size $n_2 = 15$ (the number of wrens' nests). Then, on this hypothesis, we know that:

The random variables $(M_1 - \mu)\sqrt{14}/\sigma$ and $(M_2 - \mu)\sqrt{15}/\sigma$ are both distributed with standard normal probability.

The random variables $14S_1^2/\sigma^2$ and $15S_2^2/\sigma^2$ are both distributed with chi-squared probability, having degrees of freedom $v_1 = 14 - 1 = 13$ and $v_2 = 15 - 1 = 14$ respectively.

To be able to use t-probability, we need to find two independent random variables U and W which have respectively standard normal probability and chi-squared probability distributions. Also, $U\sqrt{v}/\sqrt{W}$ must not involve the unknown parameters μ and σ.

To identify U, we can find the distributions of $M_1 - \mu$ and $M_2 - \mu$, and then subtract to eliminate μ. Now we know that

$$X_1 = M_1 - \mu \text{ has probability distribution } N\left(0, \frac{\sigma^2}{14}\right),$$

$$X_2 = M_2 - \mu \text{ has probability distribution } N\left(0, \frac{\sigma^2}{15}\right).$$

So (using the result in Exercise 17D, question 3 with $a = 1$ and $b = -1$)

$$X_1 - X_2 = M_1 - M_2 \text{ has probability distribution } N\left(0, \frac{\sigma^2}{14} + \frac{\sigma^2}{15}\right),$$

or $N(0, 0.138\sigma^2)$.

We therefore take U to be $(M_1 - M_2)/\sqrt{(0.138\sigma^2)}$, or $(M_1 - M_2)/0.372\sigma$, which has probability distribution $N(0, 1)$.

For W, we can use the result of Exercise 18C, question 5 that, if Y_1 and Y_2 independently have chi-squared probability distributions with v_1 and v_2 degrees of freedom respectively, then $Y_1 + Y_2$ is distributed with chi-squared probability with $v_1 + v_2$ degrees of freedom. This can be applied directly in this example with $Y_1 = 14S_1^2/\sigma^2$ and $Y_2 = 15S_2^2/\sigma^2$ respectively. It follows that

$$Y_1 + Y_2 = \frac{14S_1^2 + 15S_2^2}{\sigma^2} \text{ has chi-squared probability distribution with}$$

$13 + 14 = 27$ degrees of freedom.

This is the random variable which we take as W.

All is now set to apply the result of §19.6. (The independence of U and W follows from the independence of M_1, S_1 and of M_2, S_2.) This shows that

$$T = \left(\frac{M_1 - M_2}{0.372\sigma}\right)\sqrt{27} \bigg/ \sqrt{\left(\frac{14S_1^2 + 15S_2^2}{\sigma^2}\right)} \text{ has } t\text{-probability distribution}$$

with 27 degrees of freedom.

Notice that things have been so arranged that σ cancels out in the expression for T. In fact,

$$T = \frac{(M_1 - M_2)\sqrt{27}}{0.372\sqrt{(14S_1^2 + 15S_2^2)}}.$$

At this stage we test out the hypothesis by substituting in this expression the particular values of M_1, M_2, S_1 and S_2 for the samples in the data. We find that

$$m_1 = 23.11, \quad m_2 = 21.25, \quad S_1^2 = 1.023, \quad S_2^2 = 0.481.$$

so that the random variable T takes the value

$$t = \frac{1.86 \times \sqrt{27}}{0.372 \times \sqrt{21.53}} = 5.60.$$

Now it is time to consult the table of t-probability. As the alternative hypothesis has been formulated, a one-tail test is appropriate; so to test the hypothesis at a significance level of 5%, we look at the column headed $P = 10$. This gives a value $t = 1.70$ when $v = 27$ (Note 19.5), so that 5.60 is far above this critical value. We deduce that the null hypothesis must be rejected; that is, the evidence supports the theory that cuckoos are able to adapt the size of the eggs they lay to match the eggs of the host species. (In fact, the value $t = 5.60$ is so large that it is significant even at the 0.1% level. So the evidence supports the theory very strongly indeed.)

You should notice the difference between this example and Example 3. In both cases one is testing a hypothesis that the means of the distributions from which the two samples are taken are the same; but the nature of the data is different. In Example 3 the same ten patients were used to try out both drugs, so that the sample values were paired off. But in Example 4 there is no such pairing: each of the 29 sample measurements comes from a different nest. The statistical analysis is therefore totally different, even though both examples use t-probability as the basis for testing the hypothesis. It is very important, in any statistical analysis aimed at detecting whether or not there is a significant difference between the means of two populations, to be quite clear whether the sample data are paired or unpaired, and then to select the appropriate method. (The same is true when a non-parametric method is being used; compare §17.8 and Project exercise C4, between which there is a similar distinction.)

Q.9   Write a general expression, in terms of M_1, M_2, S_1, S_2, n_1, n_2 for the random variable T in Example 4.

Q.10   Show that, in terms of the unbiased variance estimators s_1, s_2 (see Q.8), the random variable T in Example 4 can be written as

$$\frac{(M_1 - M_2)\sqrt{n}}{s}, \quad \text{where} \quad \frac{1}{n} = \frac{1}{n_1} + \frac{1}{n_2} \quad \text{and} \quad s^2 = \frac{v_1 s_1^2 + v_2 s_2^2}{v_1 + v_2}.$$

(This last quantity is sometimes called the "pooled variance estimator".)

19.8   COMPARING THE VARIANCES OF TWO SAMPLES

The example in §19.7 shows that, to answer the question "Could these two samples, with different means m_1 and m_2, reasonably come from the same normal population?", it is not necessary to invent a new probability model: the method is simply another application of t-probability. Sometimes, however, we want to ask a similar question about the variances: "Could these two samples, with different variances S_1^2 and S_2^2, reasonably come from the same normal population?" To investigate this a new probability model, known as F-probability, has to be devised.

There is a small complication to be disposed of before explaining the model. This is that the theory of F-probability has been developed, not to compare variances directly, but to compare the population variance estimates $\widehat{\sigma^2}$, which were denoted in §15.7 by $s^2 = \dfrac{n}{n-1} S^2$. So the statement

$$W = \frac{nS^2}{\sigma^2} \quad \text{has chi-squared probability with } v = n - 1 \text{ degrees of freedom}$$

is rewritten (see Q.8) in the form

$$W = \frac{v s^2}{\sigma^2} \quad \text{has chi-squared probability with } v \text{ degrees of freedom.}$$

Suppose now that two separate samples are drawn independently from a single normal population. Then if they are of sizes n_1, n_2 respectively, and if their variance estimators are s_1^2, s_2^2, then

$$W_1 = \frac{v_1 s_1^2}{\sigma^2} \text{ and } W_2 = \frac{v_2 s_2^2}{\sigma^2} \text{ both have chi-squared probability, with}$$

$$v_1 = n_1 - 1 \text{ and } v_2 = n_2 - 1 \text{ degrees of freedom respectively.}$$

The unknown parameter σ can be eliminated from the two equations by dividing:

$$\frac{W_1}{W_2} = \frac{v_1 s_1^2}{v_2 s_2^2},$$

so that

$$\frac{s_1^2}{s_2^2} = \frac{v_2 W_1}{v_1 W_2}.$$

It is the cumulative probability for this random variable which is given in tables of F-probability:

If W_1, W_2 are random variables distributed with chi-squared probability with v_1, v_2 degrees of freedom respectively, then the random variable $v_2 W_1 / v_1 W_2$ is distributed with F-probability with v_1, v_2 degrees of freedom.

This probability model forms the basis of the *variance ratio test*. It is applied in the usual way, using the following result:

If independent random samples, of sizes n_1, n_2 with variances S_1^2, S_2^2, are drawn from the same normal distribution (or from two different normal distributions having the same variance), then the ratio of the variance estimators $s_1^2/s_2^2 = \dfrac{n_1}{n_1 - 1} S_1^2 \Big/ \dfrac{n_2}{n_2 - 1} S_2^2$ is distributed with F-probability with $n_1 - 1, n_2 - 1$ degrees of freedom.

When we apply this result, it obviously does not matter which of the two samples has suffix 1 and which has suffix 2. Tables, however, usually only give values of the ratio greater than 1; so it is customary to assign the suffix 1 to the sample with the larger variance estimate. (Note 19.6)

Example 5
Do the figures for the lengths of cuckoos' eggs quoted in Example 4 support the theory that the eggs laid in hedge sparrows' nests vary more than those laid in wrens' nests?

The hypothesis that all the eggs could be regarded as coming from a single population has already been ruled out by Example 4. However, it might still be that:

Hypothesis 1. The distributions of the lengths of eggs laid in the nests of the two host species have the same variance.

The alternative hypothesis is:

Hypothesis 2. Lengths of eggs laid in hedge sparrows' nests have a greater variance than lengths of eggs laid in wrens' nests.

With this form of alternative hypothesis a one-tail test is appropriate; and it should be noted that tables of F-probability are usually constructed in one-tail form. For a 5% significance level and 13, 14 degrees of freedom these give a value $F = 2.55$. So if the variance estimator ratio exceeds this value the null hypothesis will be rejected in favour of the alternative hypothesis.

The variances of the two samples were calculated in Example 4, and from these we can calculate

$$s_1^2/s_2^2 = \left(\frac{14}{13} \times 1.023\right)\Big/\left(\frac{15}{14} \times 0.481\right) = 2.14.$$

Since this falls below the critical value of 2.55, there is insufficient evidence to reject the null hypothesis, that the variances of the two distributions are the same.

Exercise 19D

1 In 1959 Dowdeswell published the results of an earthworm count. He measured the number of worms per unit area in samples from two plots, one well manured and the other not. Is there evidence that earthworms prefer manured ground?

| Manured plot: | 5, | 9, | 12, | 9, | 10, | 7, | 5, | 8, | 4 |
| Non-manured plot: | 4, | 3, | 6, | 8, | 5, | 3, | 4, | 5 | |

2 The breaking strengths in tension of five steel specimens taken from each of two consignments A and B were given in $Nm^{-2} \times 10^{12}$ in the following table. Use the t-test to compare the mean breaking strengths of the two consignments.

A: 0.4751, 0.4828, 0.4951, 0.4720, 0.4735
B: 0.4936, 0.5029, 0.4982, 0.4951, 0.4789

3 One group of mice was fed a normal diet and another group was fed a test diet. Examine the following data on body weight in grams for differences in the average weight in the two groups.

Normal diet 40, 30, 41, 41, 41, 42, 31
Test diet   34, 28, 41, 38, 34, 41, 35

4 Suppose that in Example 3 (§19.4) the data for drug A related to one group of 10 patients selected at random, and the data for drug B to a different group of 10 patients. Would this make any difference to the conclusion which you would draw from the data?

5 In a training session, two groups of hockey players practised shooting at goal. In five minutes the five players in one group scored 23, 31, 19, 40 and 27 goals respectively, while the seven players in the second group scored 42, 36, 25, 28, 45, 27 and 35 goals respectively. Carry out a t-test to determine whether the means of the numbers of goals scored by each group differ significantly. [Cambridge]

6   In §16.9 Example 5 an approximate method based on normal probability was used
to analyse the data about masses of infants at birth, with the aim of testing support
for the theory that boys weigh more than girls at birth. Rework this analysis using
the method described in §19.7, given that the 56 girls in the sample had a mean mass
of 3.258 kg and variance 0.1473 kg², whilst the 44 boys had a mean mass of 3.489 kg
and variance 0.2675 kg².

7   A study of the effect of weathering on the radioactivity of granite was made by
selecting a random sample of weathered rocks and another random sample of freshly
exposed rocks. Measurements were made of the amount of radioactivity emitted in
periods of one minute and the following data were obtained. Examine the data for
evidence of the effect of weathering and find a 95% confidence interval for the
difference in mean radioactivity.

| Fresh rocks | 225 | 188 | 165 | 211 | 178 | 171 | 199 | counts per minute |
| Weathered rocks | 177 | 170 | 140 | 132 | 168 | 172 | 170 | counts per minute |

[MEI]

8   The abstract definition of t-probability given in §19.6 leads to an alternative method
of deriving the algebraic expression for the probability density function. It is
convenient to write $\sqrt{W}$ as R, so that R^2 has chi-squared probability with v degrees
of freedom.
(a) Taking (r, u) as cartesian coordinates in a plane, explain why the area
probability density associated with this point has the form

$$\text{constant} \times r^{v-1}e^{-\frac{1}{2}r^2}e^{-\frac{1}{2}u^2},$$

where the constant depends only on the value of v.
(b) Show that the complete possibility space for points corresponding to the
random variables R and U is the half-plane on the positive side of the u-axis; and
that the points for which $T < t$ lie in the part of that half-plane cut off below the

line with equation $u = \dfrac{t}{\sqrt{v}} r$.

(c) Write the probability $P(T < t)$ as a double integral in the variables r and u. (It is
not necessary to find the exact form of the constant factor.)

(d) Show that the transformation $r = x$, $u = \dfrac{1}{\sqrt{v}} xy$ converts the probability into an
integral of the form

$$\text{constant} \times \int_{y=-\infty}^{t} \int_{x=0}^{\infty} x^v e^{-\frac{1}{2}x^2(1+y^2/v)} \, dx \, dy.$$

(e) By making the substitution $ax = z$, where $a > 0$, show that

$$\int_0^\infty x^v e^{-\frac{1}{2}a^2x^2} \, dx$$

has the form constant $\times a^{-(v+1)}$, where the constant depends only on v.

(*f*) Deduce that

$$P(T < t) = \text{constant} \times \int_{-\infty}^{t} (1 + y^2/v)^{-\frac{1}{2}(v+1)}\, dy.$$

(*g*) Hence find the density for *t*-probability, as given in §19.5 (3).

9 A method similar to that in question 8 can be used to find the probability density function for *F*-probability.

(*a*) Taking (w_1, w_2) as cartesian coordinates in a plane, explain why the area probability density associated with this point has the form

$$\text{constant} \times w_1^{\frac{1}{2}v_1 - 1} e^{-\frac{1}{2}w_1} w_2^{\frac{1}{2}v_2 - 1} e^{-\frac{1}{2}w_2},$$

where the constant depends only on the values of v_1, v_2.

(*b*) Show that the complete possibility space for points corresponding to the random variables W_1 and W_2 is the positive quadrant; and that the points for which $v_2 W_1/v_1 W_2 < F$ lie in the part of the quadrant cut off above the line with equation $Fv_1 w_2 = v_2 w_1$.

(*c*) Write the probability $P(v_2 W_1/v_1 W_2 < F)$ as a double integral in the variables w_1 and w_2.

(*d*) Show that the transformation $w_1 = v_1 xy/v_2$, $w_2 = y$ converts the probability into an integral of the form

$$\text{constant} \times \int_{x=0}^{F} \int_{y=0}^{\infty} x^{\frac{1}{2}v_1 - 1} y^{\frac{1}{2}(v_1 + v_2) - 1} e^{-\frac{1}{2}y(1 + xv_1/v_2)}\, dx\, dy.$$

(*e*) By making the substitution $ay = z$, where $a > 0$, show that

$$\int_0^{\infty} y^{\frac{1}{2}(v_1 + v_2) - 1} e^{-\frac{1}{2}ay}\, dy$$

has the form constant $\times a^{-\frac{1}{2}(v_1 + v_2)}$, where the constant depends only on v_1 and v_2.

(*f*) Deduce that

$$P(v_2 W_1/v_1 W_2 < F) = \text{constant} \times \int_0^{F} x^{\frac{1}{2}v_1 - 1}(v_2 + xv_1)^{-\frac{1}{2}(v_1 + v_2)}\, dx.$$

(*g*) Hence find the form of the density function for *F*-probability.

10 Using the figures given in question 6 as evidence, investigate the hypothesis that baby boys vary more widely in mass than baby girls at birth.

11 Using the figures given in question 7 as evidence, investigate the hypothesis that the amount of variation in the radioactivity of freshly exposed rocks is greater than that of weathered rocks.

20

Correlation

Do tall people have large dogs? Can you predict the height of a beech tree from its girth? Are mathematicians musical?

These are, of course, statistical questions. There would be no great difficulty in finding a tall man with a dachshund, or a tone-deaf professor of mathematics. Implied in the questions are words like "in general" or "on average". This chapter describes ways of thinking about such questions.

We saw in §10.3 that, when we are dealing with distinct categories (men/women, smokers/non-smokers, English/Welsh/Scottish) then chi-squared probability can help us to decide whether the evidence is strong enough to suggest a connection between two characteristics. But quantities such as height, size of dog, girth, mathematical and musical ability, etc, do not split up conveniently like this. So the problem is to find a way of indicating a connection between two quantities which are measured numerically. For such a connection the word commonly used is "correlation".

It is important to understand that the existence of correlation between two quantities does not necessarily mean that one causes the other. For example, in recent years there has been a sharp increase in the number of people capable of using computers; there has also been a drop in the consumption of animal fats. So a statistical survey might well reveal a correlation between computer literacy and fat consumption. But nobody would suggest that computer usage turns people off fat, or that eating fat hinders one's capacity to learn about computers. Of course, where there is a causal connection there is likely to be a statistical correlation; but the converse of this statement is not true.

20.1 MEASURING CORRELATION

Suppose that for each individual two separate quantities are measured, and that the measurements are represented by random variables X and Y. (The word "individual" may apply to a person, but it may equally well be a tree, a motor car, or a married couple depending on the nature of the investigation.) A sample of n individuals will give rise to n pairs of values $(x_1, y_1), (x_2, y_2), \ldots, (x_n, y_n)$. (Note 20.1) The obvious way of representing this is by a set of n points having these pairs as coordinates. Such a diagram is called a *scatter diagram*. Three typical scatter diagrams are shown in Fig. 1.

The appearance of Figs. 1*a* and 1*c* suggests a rather loose connection between X and Y. In (*a*), they are said to be *positively correlated*: in general terms, X and Y increase together. In (*c*) they are *negatively correlated*: larger values of X tend

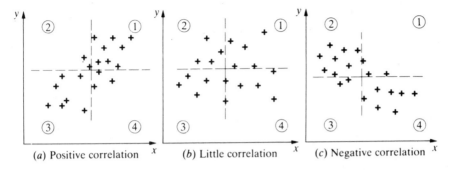

(a) Positive correlation   (b) Little correlation   (c) Negative correlation

Figure 1

to go with smaller values of Y. Fig. 1b suggests a situation where there is no obvious connection between X and Y.

A first aim is to find a way of measuring correlation numerically, and Fig. 1 suggests one way in which this might be done. The broken lines in the figures have been drawn to indicate the mean values of X and Y in the sample. These means will be denoted by m_x and m_y. The clue is then to look at the four quadrants into which the plane is divided by these broken lines, and to examine where most of the points in the scatter diagram are located:

In (a) there are many points in quadrants 1 and 3, few in quadrants 2 and 4.

In (b) the points are distributed almost equally amongst the four quadrants.

In (c) there are many points in quadrants 2 and 4, few in quadrants 1 and 3.

Now in quadrant 1, the quantities $x - m_x$ and $y - m_y$ are both positive, whilst in quadrant 3 they are both negative; in either case the product $(x - m_x)(y - m_y)$ is positive. But in quadrants 2 and 4, one of these factors is positive and the other negative, so the product is negative. Considering the sum of these products for all the points in the sample, we would therefore expect:

In (a), positive terms outweigh negative terms.

In (b), positive and negative terms almost cancel each other out.

In (c), negative terms outweigh positive terms.

This suggests that the mean value of the product $(x - m_x)(y - m_y)$, taken over all pairs of measurements in the sample, might give an indication of the correlation between the two quantities. This is called the *covariance*; it will be denoted by C_{xy}, so that

$$C_{xy} = \frac{1}{n} \sum_{i=1}^{n} (x_i - m_x)(y_i - m_y). \quad \text{(Note 20.2)}$$

Q.1 Write down the expression for the covariance C_{xx} of x with itself. What is this usually called?

Q.2 Prove that C_{xy} is unaltered if all the x_i are increased by a constant a, and all the y_i are increased by a constant b. What would be the effect of this transformation on Fig. 1?

Q.3 What would be the effect on C_{xy} if all the x_i were doubled and all the y_i were trebled?

By itself, C_{xy} is not in fact a good measure of correlation, because it is 'dimensional'. For example, if x and y were quantities of length and mass measured in metres and kilograms, then the products $(x_i - m_x)(y_i - m_y)$, and hence also the covariance C_{xy}, would be measured in m kg. But correlation is essentially a dimensionless concept. To put the point another way, if all the x_i were doubled and all the y_i were trebled, the number representing the correlation should be unaffected; but Q.3 shows that C_{xy} would be multiplied by 6. We therefore want to divide it by some other quantity which would be multiplied by the same factor. On the other hand, we would not want this quantity to be changed if the x_i or the y_i were simply increased by a constant, as in Q.2. The obvious choice is therefore to use the standard deviations, S_x and S_y, of the measurements in the sample. If x is doubled and y is trebled, then S_x is doubled and S_y is trebled, so that the product $S_x S_y$ is mutiplied by 6, as required. This reasoning leads us to define the *coefficient of correlation*, r, between the sample measures as

$$r = \frac{C_{xy}}{S_x S_y}. \quad \text{(Note 20.3)}$$

This coefficient is not affected by either a change of origin or a change of scale in x and y, and is a pure number whatever units x and y are measured in.

It will appear later (see Exercise 20A, question 5) that r always lies between -1 and $+1$, and that these extreme values are achieved only when all the points representing the sample lie on a straight line. A value of r near to 1 indicates strong positive correlation between the quantities; a value near to -1 indicates strong negative correlation.

Exercise 20A

1   Prove that an alternative expression for the covariance is

$$C_{xy} = \frac{1}{n} \sum_{i=1}^{n} x_i y_i - m_x m_y.$$

What are the computational advantages of this form?

2   Calculate the coefficient of correlation between the mass of the heart and the mass of the liver in mice, using the following data. (K)

Mass of organs (in units of 0.01 g)

Heart	20	16	20	21	26	24	18	18
Liver	230	126	203	241	159	230	140	242

3 Seventeen pupils took an examination in mathematics, which was compared with their marks for work done during the term. Draw a scatter diagram and find the coefficient of correlation. (K)

Exam mark	155	148	146	135	135	128	127	126	122	118	113	113	110	110	108	106	91
Term mark	88	79	84	99	80	72	56	68	56	69	63	61	65	54	74	73	49

4 Write a computer program to read in pairs of sample values of X and Y and then calculate the coefficient of correlation. (K)

5 Prove that, if the numbers a_i, b_i are real, then the expressions

$$(a_1^2 + a_2^2)(b_1^2 + b_2^2) - (a_1 b_1 + a_2 b_2)^2$$

and

$$(a_1^2 + a_2^2 + a_3^2)(b_1^2 + b_2^2 + b_3^2) - (a_1 b_1 + a_2 b_2 + a_3 b_3)^2$$

are either positive or zero. Under what conditions are they zero? Generalise these results. (This is known as *Cauchy's inequality*, or sometimes as the Cauchy-Schwarz inequality.)

Use Cauchy's inequality to prove that, for a sample of n pairs (x_i, y_i), $C_{xy}^2 \leqslant S_x^2 S_y^2$. In what circumstances does equality occur? Deduce that the correlation coefficient r always lies between -1 and 1.

6 The notation in §20.1 assigns the suffix i to just one sample pair, the ith sample pair selected; if the same pair occurs twice, two different suffixes will be used. But if the sample is large, and the possibility space is finite, then it is sometimes more convenient to let $\{x_1, x_2, \ldots, x_k\}$ denote the possibility space for X and $\{y_1, y_2, \ldots, y_l\}$ the possibility space for Y, and to denote the frequency of the pair (x_i, y_j) by $f(x_i, y_j)$. Write expressions for n, m_x, S_x^2, C_{xy} and r in this notation.

7 With the notation of question 6, write a computer program to read in the values of x_i, y_j and $f(x_i, y_j)$ as arrays and to calculate the coefficient of correlation. (K)

Use your program to find the coefficient of correlation between birthweight and period of gestation in Table 1, a large sample of children studied by Tanner. (The imperial units of weight used in the actual experiment have been retained.)

Birth-weight	Gestation in weeks								
	up to 28	29–30	31–32	33–34	35–36	37–38	39–40	41–42	over 42
up to 2 lb	11	10	3	4	2				
2–3 lb	16	20	13	14	4			1	
3–4 lb	2	12	21	23	27	11	4	1	1
4–5 lb		1	28	38	63	79	59	32	2
5–6 lb	1	1	10	38	142	393	540	180	27
6–7 lb		1	3	14	120	752	2048	944	107
7–8 lb			2	13	60	565	2705	1546	202
8–9 lb				1	24	209	1360	1091	112
9–10 lb					4	48	343	360	37
over 10 lb					2	3	52	66	12

Table 1

8   If, as in the numerical example quoted, the values of x_i and y_j in question 7 are in arithmetical progression, then by a suitable transformation these measurements can be replaced by the numbers 1, 2, 3, ... In this case it is only necessary to input the frequencies into the computer program. Amend your program in this way, and run it again with the numerical data provided. (K)

9   In some experiments (for example, in education or psychology) the actual measurements have little meaning in themselves, but the order in which the individuals are ranked can be regarded as reliable. In this case it is possible to define a coefficient of rank correlation between sample pairs. (The coefficient described in this question is known as *Spearman's coefficient of rank correlation*. A different coefficient of rank correlation, devised by M. G. Kendall, is described in Project exercise C3.)

In a "beautiful baby contest" the babies are numbered 1, 2, ..., n. There are two judges. Judge A assigns to these babies the ranks $x_1, x_2, ..., x_n$ (so that the numbers x_i are a rearrangement of the numbers 1, 2, ..., n). Judge B assigns the ranks $y_1, y_2, ..., y_n$. The difference in the rankings by the two judges of baby number i is denoted by d_i, so that $d_i = x_i - y_i$.

(a) Prove that for each judge the mean and variance of the ranks are $\frac{1}{2}(n+1)$ and $\frac{1}{12}(n+1)(n-1)$.

(b) Prove that $\sum_{i=1}^{n} d_i^2 = \frac{1}{3}n(n+1)(2n+1) - 2\sum_{i=1}^{n} x_i y_i$.

(c) Write down an expression for the covariance of the ranks, and deduce that

$$r = 1 - \frac{6 \sum d_i^2}{n(n^2 - 1)}.$$

(d) Explain why it is reasonable for correlation to be measured by $\sum d_i^2$. Verify that the formula gives the expected value for r (i) when the judges are in complete agreement, (ii) when they are in complete disagreement.

10 In a beauty competition, there were ten candidates and the marks awarded by two judges, A and B, are shown in the table. Draw a scatter diagram of the data. Calculate also Spearman's rank correlation coefficient. (See question 9.)

Competitor	1	2	3	4	5	6	7	8	9	10
Judge A	36	34	24	38	20	37	22	28	30	32
Judge B	20	26	8	30	13	19	17	11	15	25

[London]

11 Ten varieties of tea, labelled A, B, C, ..., J, were tasted by two groups of people, and were ranked from best to worst as in the table.

Group 1:	G	H	C	D	A	E	B	J	I	F
Group 2:	C	B	H	G	J	D	I	E	F	A

Calculate a coefficient of rank correlation for the data.

A Spearman rank correlation coefficient calculated from ten pairs of results is significant at the level stated if its modulus exceeds the appropriate entry in the table.

Significance level	0.01	0.02	0.05	0.10
Coefficient	0.79	0.73	0.64	0.56

Determine whether there is significant agreement between the rankings in the tea-tasting experiment. [Cambridge]

12 It is believed that a patient who absorbs a drug well on one occasion will do so on another occasion. Tests on ten patients gave the results shown in the table, for the percentage of drug absorbed on two days. Calculate a rank correlation coefficient, and use it to decide whether the belief appears to be justified. (See the second table in question 11.)

Percentages of drug absorbed										
Patient	1	2	3	4	5	6	7	8	9	10
Day A	35.5	16.6	13.6	42.5	37.0	28.5	29.5	39.0	19.7	42.0
Day B	27.6	15.1	12.9	30.5	23.1	14.5	35.5	27.5	16.1	18.9

Calculate also the product-moment correlation coefficient (see Note 20.3).
[London]

13 Obtain a rank correlation coefficient for the data given in the table, and hence, for these data, discuss the validity of the commonly held belief that, if a locality has a low annual rainfall (R), then it has a high number of hours of sunshine each year (S).

Locality	1	2	3	4	5	6	7	8	9	10
R (cm)	93	126	118	45	102	57	93	71	95	57
S (hours)	1629	1714	1727	1521	1490	1636	1687	1851	1669	1907

Calculate also the product-moment correlation coefficient. [London]

14 Two random variables have theoretical covariance $C[X, Y]$ (see Exercise 14B, question 12), and a random sample of n independent pairs is denoted by (X_1, Y_1), (X_2, Y_2), ..., (X_n, Y_n). The covariance C_{xy} is then a random variable, and its expectation can be investigated in a manner similar to that of the variance V in §15.6.
(a) Explain why $C[X_i, Y_j] = C[X, Y]$ if $i = j$, and 0 if $i \neq j$.
(b) Prove that $C[M_x, M_y] = (1/n) C[X, Y]$.
(c) Justify the equation

$$C_{xy} = \frac{1}{n} \sum_{i=1}^{n} (X_i - \mu_x)(Y_i - \mu_y) - (M_x - \mu_x)(M_y - \mu_y),$$

and use it to prove that

$$E[C_{xy}] = \frac{n-1}{n} \, C[X, Y].$$

(d) Deduce that $\dfrac{n}{n-1} \, C_{xy}$ is an unbiased estimator of $C[X, Y]$.

20.2 THE METHOD OF LEAST SQUARES

We tend to think of statistics as a branch of mathematics linked to the social and biological sciences, with applications in fields such as insurance, demography, medicine and industrial processes. However, it also has an important part to play in the study of physical science. An early example of this was the use of statistical techniques around the year 1800 to improve the accuracy with which the orbits of planets and comets could be described – a process which led to Gauss's location of the minor planets and later, in 1845, to the discovery of the planet Neptune. The problem was that each astronomical observation was subject to random error, and so a range of possible orbits could be calculated consistent with the data. How could one decide which was the 'best' estimate of the orbit? This was especially difficult with comets, which could only be observed over the short period of time when they were close to the earth. In 1805 the French mathematician Legendre published a paper in which he described what he called the "method of least squares" as a way of tackling this problem; and he pointed out that this method could be applied not just to comet orbits, but to other estimation questions as well. (Note 20.4)

One simple example arises in calculating the variance of a sample of measurements $x_1, x_2, \ldots, x_n$. We know that, if a 'false origin' p is chosen from which to make the measurements, then the variance v is given by

$$v = \frac{1}{n} \sum_{i=1}^{n} (x_i - p)^2 - (m - p)^2.$$

This can be rearranged as

$$\frac{1}{n} \sum_{i=1}^{n} (x_i - p)^2 = v + (p - m)^2.$$

Now think of this equation in a different way, by regarding p as a variable. The left side is then the mean of the squared deviations of the n sample points from p; and the right side shows that this is a quadratic function of p, whose minimum value is v when $p = m$. That is, the sample mean is the point of the scale at which the mean of the squared deviations is least. This is illustrated in Fig. 2.

Notice in passing that this last equation can be thought of as splitting the mean squared deviation from p into two parts: one due to the variance within the sample itself, the other due to the squared deviation of p from the mean of the sample. This idea forms the basis of a statistical technique known as "analysis of variance". The general theory is not covered in this book, but some indication of the procedure is given in Exercise 20B, question 13.

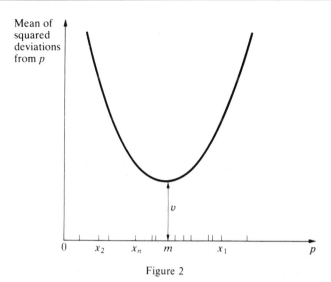

Figure 2

The immediate purpose of introducing the equation, and the accompanying Fig. 2, is that it suggests yet another approach to the problem of estimating a population parameter from a sample of measurements. We saw in §15.5 that, if $x_1, x_2, \ldots, x_n$ are regarded as sample measurements drawn from a population with mean μ, then the sample mean can be used to estimate μ. The "minimum mean square deviation" property can be thought of as a justification for this. It can be formulated more generally as follows:

THE LEAST SQUARES PRINCIPLE OF ESTIMATION. Given a sample of measurements from which it is desired to estimate a population parameter, we select as estimator that value for which the mean of the squared deviations from the sample values is least.

This principle will now be applied to samples of pairs of measurements, as described in §20.1, to estimate the coefficients in a relation between the random variables.

20.3 REGRESSION

A problem which A-level examiners sometimes have to cope with is how to make allowance for a candidate who has sat Paper 1 and then missed Paper 2 through illness. (It should be pointed out that this is a practice which is only followed sparingly; but on occasions it is the fairest way to proceed.) The practicability of doing this depends on there being good correlation between the marks on the two papers for the candidates as a whole. But when this exists, it should be possible to make a reasonable estimate of the likely Paper 2 mark on the basis of the Paper 1 mark. How should this be done?

Let x, y denote the Paper 1 and Paper 2 marks respectively. Fig. 3 shows a scatter diagram for the marks of the candidates from the centre in question who have sat both papers. This seems to indicate fair correlation; in fact, r is just under 0.6. It also suggests, and this is important for the method to be effective, that when 'averaged out' there might be a reasonably straight line relationship between the marks, having an equation of the form.

$$y = a + bx.$$

Of course, this is not an exact relationship, but an approximate one subject to statistical variation. A possible such straight line is drawn in Fig. 3. If its equation could be found, then it could be used to suggest the allowance to be made to the absent candidate. So the question is, how can a and b be estimated?

Notice that, by asking the question in this way, the symmetry between x and y has been thrown overboard. The intention is to use the graph with x as the "independent variable" to calculate y - not the other way round. So it is natural to ask, if a typical pair of marks (x_i, y_i) is taken from the sample, how far out one would be if one were to calculate y from this equation. The answer is given by the vertical arrow in Fig. 3; the point on the line has coordinates $(x_i, a + bx_i)$ instead of (x_i, y_i); so the deviation for this sample pair is $|y_i - a - bx_i|$.

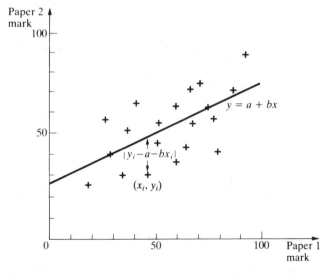

Figure 3

The scene is now set to apply the least squares principle. There are two coefficients to find, a and b, and we shall select these by making the mean of the squared deviations as small as possible. Now this mean is

$$\frac{1}{n} \sum_{i=1}^{n} (y_i - a - bx_i)^2,$$

which when expanded can be written as

$$\frac{1}{n}\sum y_i^2 + a^2 + b^2\left(\frac{1}{n}\sum x_i^2\right) - 2a\left(\frac{1}{n}\sum y_i\right) - 2b\left(\frac{1}{n}\sum x_i y_i\right) + 2ab\left(\frac{1}{n}\sum x_i\right).$$

(The limits $i = 1$ to n in the sums are omitted to simplify the appearance.) Now each of the expressions in brackets can be written in terms of the sample statistics m_x, m_y, S_x, S_y, $C_{xy} = rS_xS_y$. You should check for yourself that the mean of the squared deviations then becomes

$$(S_y^2 + m_y^2) + a^2 + b^2(S_x^2 + m_x^2) - 2am_y - 2b(C_{xy} + m_xm_y) + 2abm_x,$$

which can be rearranged as

$$(m_y^2 + a^2 + b^2m_x^2 - 2am_y - 2bm_xm_y + 2abm_x) + (b^2S_x^2 - 2brS_xS_y + S_y^2).$$

In this last line, the expression in the first bracket is a perfect square, and the second is a quadratic function of b which can be rewritten by the standard process of completing the square. This gives the final form for the mean of the squared deviation as

$$(m_y - a - bm_x)^2 + (bS_x - rS_y)^2 + (1 - r^2)S_y^2.$$

The intention is to choose a and b so that this is as small as possible. Since the first two terms are squares involving these variables, whilst the third term is just a constant, the way to do this is to choose a and b so that the first two terms are zero; that is,

$$m_y = a + bm_x \quad \text{and} \quad b = rS_y/S_x.$$

It is interesting that both these equations have simple geometrical interpretations. The first states that the line $y = a + bx$ should be chosen so that it passes through the point (m_x, m_y); we might have guessed this, since we are looking for a kind of 'average line'. The second equation gives the gradient of the line. So the whole procedure can be summarised in the statement:

> For a sample of pairs of values of two quantities x and y, the straight line relationship which best predicts y for given values of x (according to the principle of least squares) passes through the point (m_x, m_y) and has gradient rS_y/S_x. This is called the *line of regression of y on x*, and the gradient is the *coefficient of regression of y on x*.

Notice in passing that, when this line is chosen as the estimated linear relationship, the actual value of the minimum mean square deviation is $(1 - r^2)S_y^2$. As we should expect, this is small (and therefore the linear relationship can be used reliably) when r is close to $+1$ or to -1; that is, when there is good correlation between the measurements.

Q.4   Use this to give another proof that r always lies between -1 and $+1$. Under what conditions does r take one or other of these extreme values?

The inclusion of the words "of y on x" in the above statement stresses the important point that the process described is not symmetrical as between the two variables. To illustrate this, let us return to the problem of the A-level candidate with which this section began. The line of regression of y on x can be used to estimate the most appropriate Paper 2 mark from a known mark on Paper 1; but it should not be used in reverse to estimate a Paper 1 mark for a candidate who sat only Paper 2. For this purpose, what is needed is the line of regression of x on y, and this is a different line. To find it, we need not go through the algebra again; the result must be similar to the one already found, but with x and y interchanged. This would suggest that the line also passes through the 'mean point' (m_x, m_y), and that its gradient should now be rS_x/S_y; *but care is needed in interpreting this!* For the word "gradient" used here has to be understood in relation to the vertical (y) axis rather than the horizontal (x) one. Fig. 4 should help to make this clear: the relation corresponding to

$$\tan \alpha = rS_y/S_x \quad \text{(for the line of regression of } y \text{ on } x)$$

is

$$\tan \beta = rS_x/S_y \quad \text{(for the line of regression of } x \text{ on } y).$$

But the word "gradient" is usually reserved for the reciprocal of this, namely

$$\tan \gamma = \frac{1}{r}(S_y/S_x).$$

The essential thing to understand is that, in reading off a value of y for given x, the line of regression of y on x should be used; but to read off a value of x for

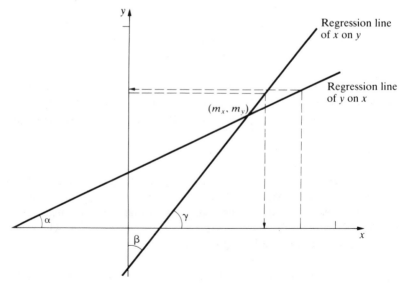

Figure 4

given y, it is necessary to use the line of regression of x on y. This is indicated by the broken arrows in Fig. 4.

Exercise 20B

1 The table gives the altitude x (in metres) above sea level, and mean air temperature y (in °C), for 10 weather stations.

x	2	7	12	40	76	99	135	163	235	307
y	9.7	10.7	9.9	10.4	9.5	9.2	9.2	9.4	8.7	7.5

Calculate the equation of the regression line of y on x.
Estimate the mean air temperature at a place 200 m above sea level. (K)
[Cambridge]

2 The ages, x years, and heights, y cm, of 10 boys were as follows:

x	6.6	6.8	6.9	7.5	7.8	8.2	10.1	11.4	12.8	13.5
y	119	112	116	123	122	123	135	151	141	141

Calculate the equation of the regression line of y on x, and use it to estimate the height of a boy 9.0 years old.
State the value of y given by the regression line when $x = 30$ and comment upon your answer. (K)
[Cambridge]

3 For the data in Exercise 20A, question 3, find the lines of regression of the examination mark on the term mark, and of the term mark on the examination mark. Add these lines to your scatter diagram.
What *total* mark would you suggest would be appropriate for
(a) a pupil who scored 82 marks during the term but missed the examination;
(b) a pupil who was absent for most of the term but scored 105 marks in the examination? (K)

4 Adapt the computer program which you wrote in Exercise 20A, question 4 so that it draws a scatter diagram of the data and superimposes the two lines of regression on it.

5 Adapt the computer program which you wrote in Exercise 20A, question 7 so that it calculates also the equations of the two lines of regression.

6 Show that, with the notation of Fig. 4, $r^2 = \tan\alpha/\tan\gamma$. What does this tell us about the two lines of regression?
Can the two lines of regression ever be the same?

7 For a given bivariate distribution (that is, a probability model with two random variables) the equation of the line of regression of Y on X is $5y + 2x = 25$. The equation of the line of regression of X on Y is $2y + x = 11$. Find the means of X and Y, and the value of the linear correlation coefficient between X and Y.
[Cambridge]

8 If the random variables in a bivariate distribution are scaled so that they have the same variance, and a diagram similar to Fig. 4 is then drawn, prove that the coefficient of correlation is $\tan(\frac{1}{4}\pi - \frac{1}{2}\lambda)$, where λ is equal to $\gamma - \alpha$, the angle between the two regression lines.

Explain why, in particular, this is true for the calculation of Spearman's rank correlation coefficient (see Exercise 20A, question 9).

9 Obtain the coefficients a and b in the equation for the line of regression of y on x by finding the partial derivatives of $\Sigma(y_i - a - bx_i)^2$ with respect to a and b, and putting these equal to zero.

10 Sometimes there is reason to think that the approximate relationship between x and y might have some form other than $y = a + bx$. Express the coefficients in terms of the sample values if the relatonship is taken to have the form (i) $y = bx$, (ii) $y = a + bx + cx^2$, using the princple of least squares.

11 The rate of growth y of a particular organism is thought to depend in some way on the temperature t. The table shows the results of 10 experiments.

t (in °C)	6	9	11	14	17	22	26	29	32	34
Rate of growth	5	13	15	21	20	24	19	16	10	7

Calculate the value of the linear correlation coefficient.

Represent the data on a suitable diagram and comment upon the statement: "The linear correlation coefficient does not differ significantly from zero, and thus y does not depend in any way upon t." [Cambridge]

12 If a sample of n measurements $x_1, x_2, \ldots, x_n$ is used to estimate the mean of a population which is known to have normal probability density, show that the maximum likelihood and the least squares principles of estimation are equivalent to each other. (See Exercise 13C, question 7.)

13 In three schools A, B, C a test is taken by classes of n children, and the marks are collected together. The mean marks for the three schools are m_A, m_B, m_C and the standard deviations are S_A, S_B, S_C. The mean mark for the three schools taken together is m, and the standard deviation is S. Denoting the marks of the individual children by a_i, b_i, c_i (where $i = 1, 2, \ldots, n$), write down an expression for S^2. Show, by writing S_A^2 in the form

$$\frac{1}{n} \Sigma (a_i - m)^2 - (m_A - m)^2,$$

and similarly for S_B and S_C, that

$$S^2 = \tfrac{1}{3}(S_A^2 + S_B^2 + S_C^2) + \tfrac{1}{3}\{(m_A - m)^2 + (m_B - m)^2 + (m_C - m)^2\}.$$

Explain how this can be interpreted as the sum of a term indicating the variation of marks within the classes and a term indicating the variation of marks between the classes.

Generalise this expression to the case where there are different numbers of children (n_A, n_B, n_C) in the three classes.

14   If the variables x and y in the regression problem are standardised using the sample means and standard deviations, writing $x' = (x - m_x)/S_x$ and $y' = (y - m_y)/S_y$, show that the coefficient of correlation is the gradient of the line of regression of y' on x'. How are the two lines of regression (of y' on x', and of x' on y') then related? Demonstrate the relationship between these two lines as r decreases in value from $+1$ to -1.

20.4 HOW ACCURATE IS THE LINE OF REGRESSION?

We are now faced with the usual statistical problem. The coefficients a and b found in §20.3 were obtained from a particular sample of pairs of measurements (x, y). If a different sample had been taken, the coefficients would have been different. So a and b cannot be treated as absolute, but only as estimates of coefficients α and β in a theoretical linear relationship connecting x and y, of the form

$$y = \alpha + \beta x.$$

Before we can use the method with confidence, we need to know how good these estimates are.

What is the status of this theoretical equation? That has to depend on the type of problem it is being applied to. In a physics experiment (for example, if x is the temperature of a copper rod and y is its length) then we think of the equation as "exact", and any deviation from it as due to "experimental error". But in the example of the two examination papers in §20.3, one would not expect the marks on Paper 2 to be exactly related to those on Paper 1 (or there would be no point in having two papers!); so y is a kind of "idealised average" Paper 2 mark for a candidate who gets x marks on Paper 1. But whatever the reason, for each sample value of x the corresponding value of y will deviate somewhat from that given by the theoretical equation. This can be expressed by writing, for the ith sample pair,

$$y_i = \alpha + \beta x_i + e_i,$$

where e_i is an "error term".

To derive any practical use from this idea, it will be necessary to make some assumption about the error terms e_i. One possible model is to suppose that they are distributed normally, at random and independently of the value of x_i. In that case, if the theoretical regression line is a good one, we would expect the mean of this distribution to be zero, and the standard deviation will be denoted by σ. In a physics experiment σ would hopefully be small, but for the examination marks it could be quite large.

Before getting involved in the theory, it is worth remarking that, when finding the regression line of y on x, the values x_i are regarded as 'fixed' and the variability is ascribed to errors in y_i. This means that the mean m_x is also fixed; and we saw in §20.3 that this mean appears in the equation of the sample line of regression. Because of this, it is helpful to make two modifications in the notation:

(i) Instead of writing the theoretical line of regression as $y = \alpha + \beta x$, it is simpler to write it in the form

$$y = \kappa + \beta(x - m_x),$$

and to work in terms of the constants κ and β rather than α and β.

(ii) The measurements y_i are treated as random variables, being subject to the random sampling errors e_i. It is therefore appropriate to use capital letters for these variables (but *not* for the x_i), writing

$$Y_i = \kappa + \beta(x_i - m_x) + E_i.$$

The coefficients in the sample line of regression, now written in the form $y = k + b(x - m_x)$, are then also random variables, and will therefore be given capital letters K and B, where (from §20.3)

$$K = M_y = \frac{1}{n} \sum_{i=1}^{n} Y_i$$

and

$$B = C_{xy}/S_x^2 \quad \text{with} \quad C_{xy} = \frac{1}{n} \sum_{i=1}^{n} (x_i - m_x)(Y_i - M_y).$$

These random variables are estimators for the constants κ and β in the theoretical equation, so in the usual way we write

$$\hat{\kappa} = K, \quad \hat{\beta} = B.$$

The question that has to be answered is: how are $\hat{\kappa}$ and $\hat{\beta}$ distributed? Since the model is based on an assumption about the error terms, we begin by writing K and B in terms of E_i rather than Y_i:

$$K = \frac{1}{n} \sum_{i=1}^{n} \{\kappa + \beta(x_i - m_x) + E_i\}$$

$$= \kappa + \frac{1}{n} \sum_{i=1}^{n} E_i,$$

since κ and β are constants and $\sum_{i=1}^{n} (x_i - m_x) = 0$. Also,

$$C_{xy} = \frac{1}{n} \sum_{i=1}^{n} \{(x_i - m_x)Y_i - (x_i - m_x)M_y\}$$

$$= \frac{1}{n} \sum_{i=1}^{n} (x_i - m_x)\{\kappa + \beta(x_i - m_x) + E_i\} - \frac{1}{n} M_y \sum_{i=1}^{n} (x_i - m_x)$$

$$= \frac{\beta}{n} \sum_{i=1}^{n} (x_i - m_x)^2 + \frac{1}{n} \sum_{i=1}^{n} (x_i - m_x)E_i$$

$$= \beta S_x^2 + \frac{1}{n} \sum_{i=1}^{n} (x_i - m_x)E_i,$$

so that

$$B = \beta + \frac{1}{n} \sum_{i=1}^{n} (x_i - m_x)E_i/S_x^2.$$

It is now a simple matter to say how K and B are distributed. Since each E_i has distribution $N(0, \sigma^2)$, the result of §17.6 shows that $(1/n)\Sigma_{i=1}^{n} E_i$ has distribution $N(0, \sigma^2/n)$; so K has distribution $N(\kappa, \sigma^2/n)$. Also, since the multipliers $(x_i - m_x)$ are constant, $\Sigma_{i=1}^{n} (x_i - m_x)E_i$ is distributed normally; and it follows that C_{xy}, and therefore B, is normally distributed. Moreover, using the rules summarised at the end of Chapter 14,

$$E[C_{xy}] = \beta S_x^2 + \frac{1}{n} \sum_{i=1}^{n} (x_i - m_x)E[E_i]$$

$$= \beta S_x^2,$$

since each $E[E_i] = 0$; and

$$V[C_{xy}] = \frac{1}{n^2} \sum_{i=1}^{n} (x_i - m_x)^2 V[E_i]$$

$$= \frac{\sigma^2}{n^2} \sum_{i=1}^{n} (x_i - m_x)^2 = \frac{\sigma^2}{n} S_x^2.$$

So

$$E[B] = \beta S_x^2/S_x^2 = \beta, \quad V[B] = \frac{\sigma^2}{n} S_x^2/S_x^4 = \frac{\sigma^2}{nS_x^2}.$$

The whole argument can be summarised as follows:

Suppose that the theoretical regression line of y on x is written as

$$y = \kappa + \beta(x - m_x),$$

where the coefficients κ and β are estimated from the corresponding coefficients in the equation of the sample regression line based on sample values (x_i, y_i) for $i = 1, 2, \ldots, n$. Then, if the differences between the sample values of y and the theoretical values are distributed independently as $N(0, \sigma^2)$, the estimators $\hat{\kappa}$ and $\hat{\beta}$ are distributed as $N(\kappa, \sigma^2/n)$ and $N(\beta, \sigma^2/nS_x^2)$ respectively.

Q.5 If the equation of the regression line is written as $y = \alpha + \beta x$, how is the estimator $\hat{\alpha}$ distributed?

Although these results have emerged from some rather complicated algebra, you will notice that they are very much in line with what we would expect. Thus both estimators are unbiased (that is, $E[\hat{\kappa}] = \kappa$ and $E[\hat{\beta}] = \beta$); also the variances are proportional to σ^2, have the correct dimensions and include the usual factor of $1/n$.

Unfortunately, they are not of much use! This is because, in any particular application, we do not know the value of σ^2.

But this is a situation we have been in before. You will remember that, in trying to find a confidence interval for the mean μ of a normal population from a sample of n measurements, we had at one stage proved that the sample mean M is distributed as $N(\mu, \sigma^2/n)$; but this could not be used because σ^2 was unknown. In that case, the procedure was to replace $\sigma^2 = E[(X - \mu)^2]$ by the unbiased variance estimator $\dfrac{n}{n-1} S^2$, where $S^2 = (1/n)\Sigma_{i=1}^n (X_i - M)^2$. So, instead of using the test statistic $\dfrac{M - \mu}{\sigma/\sqrt{n}}$ (with distribution $N(0, 1)$), we used $\dfrac{M - \mu}{S/\sqrt{(n-1)}}$, which is distributed with t-probability (see §19.4).

This procedure can be taken over almost directly into the regression line problem. In this case, by definition,

$$\sigma^2 = E[E^2] = E[(Y - \alpha - \beta X)^2].$$

But since α and β are unknown, they are replaced by their estimates a and b, giving a sample error variance of

$$S^2 = \frac{1}{n} \sum_{i=1}^{n} (y_i - a - bx_i)^2.$$

Now this is just the "mean square deviation" investigated in §20.3; and when a and b are chosen to minimise this, the minimum value was found to be

$$S^2 = (1 - r^2)S_y^2$$
$$= S_y^2 - C_{xy}^2/S_x^2.$$

However, it turns out (as in the single variable case) that, when the Y_i (and therefore also the coefficients A and B) are regarded as random variables, then the minimum square deviation S^2 is not an unbiased estimator for σ^2. In fact, it can be shown that

$$E[S^2] = \frac{n-2}{n} \sigma^2.$$

It is left to you to prove this (see Exercise 20C, question 5). (Note 20.5)

To get an unbiased estimator for σ^2, we therefore use the quantity $\dfrac{n}{n-2} S^2$.

And the suggestion then is that the test statistics $\dfrac{K - \kappa}{\sigma/\sqrt{n}}$ and $\dfrac{B - \beta}{\sigma/S_x\sqrt{n}}$ (which are both distributed as $N(0, 1)$) should be replaced by $\dfrac{K - \kappa}{S/\sqrt{(n-2)}}$ and $\dfrac{B - \beta}{S/S_x\sqrt{(n-2)}}$. It can be proved, though the details are too difficult to go into here, that both of these are distributed with t-probability.

With how many degrees of freedom? In the single variable case, when σ is replaced by $S\sqrt{\{n/(n-1)\}}$ (whose calculation involves the sample mean m), the number of degrees of freedom is reduced from n to $n-1$. It would be a reasonable guess that for the regression line, when σ is replaced by $S\sqrt{\{n/(n-2)\}}$ (whose calculation involves the two sample coefficients a and b), the number of degrees of freedom is reduced from n to $n-2$. This guess is in fact correct.

If the constants κ and β in the equation of the theoretical regression line of y on x are estimated from the coefficients k and b in the equation of the sample regression line, and if S^2 denotes the minimum mean sum of squares $(1-r^2)S_y^2$, then the random variables $\dfrac{K-\kappa}{S/\sqrt{(n-2)}}$ and $\dfrac{B-\beta}{S/S_x\sqrt{(n-2)}}$ are both distributed with t-probability with $v = n-2$.

Q.6 Find a corresponding result for the constant α in the equation $y = \alpha + \beta x$.

Example 1
Readings were taken in a sample of 37 patients with diabetic acidosis of serum chloride in milliequivalents per litre (x) and blood non-protein nitrogen (azotemia) (y):

x	76	87	92	92	93	93	95	98	99	99	105	105	101	80	89	91	92	93	94	95
y	39	76	71	40	43	69	84	38	41	30	22	38	37	90	42	39	43	51	79	33

x	99	99	104	105	110	86	90	91	92	93	95	97	99	99	105	105	94
y	33	50	30	32	24	59	31	70	67	59	76	30	27	23	41	35	54

Investigate the dependence of y on x.
We calculate

$$m_x = 95.46, \quad m_y = 47.19; \quad S_x^2 = 49.22, \quad S_y^2 = 347.45, \quad C_{xy} = -70.09;$$

giving the coefficients in the sample regression line

$$k = m_y = 47.19 \quad \text{and} \quad b = C_{xy}/S_x^2 = -1.42.$$

The equation of the regression line is therefore

$$y = 47.19 - 1.42(x - 95.46) = 182.7 - 1.42x.$$

But it is important to know how much reliability can be placed on these coefficients. For this purpose, we calculate also $S_x = \sqrt{49.22} = 7.02$ and

$$S^2 = S_y^2 - C_{xy}^2/S_x^2 = 247.65,$$

so that $S = 15.74$; and we note that, at the 5% significance level, the critical value of t when $v = 37 - 2 = 35$ is 2.03. Using the theory summarised above, it then follows that the sample readings are consistent with any values of κ and β satisfying the inequalities

$$-2.03 < \frac{47.19 - \kappa}{15.74/\sqrt{35}} < 2.03$$

and

$$-2.03 < \frac{-1.42 - \beta}{15.74/7.02\sqrt{35}} < 2.03.$$

This gives, for the 95% confidence intervals,

$$41.8 < \kappa < 52.6 \quad \text{and} \quad -2.19 < \beta < -0.65.$$

You may think that these intervals are so wide that the equation found for the regression line in this example has little value. However, if you try drawing the scatter diagram from the data, you will see that the points are so spread out that it would be unreasonable to expect a very accurate answer. If greater precision is wanted, the only way of getting it is to carry out the experiments on a much larger sample of patients.

Exercise 20C

1   Repeat Example 1 for the line of regression of x on y.

2   For the data in Exercise 20B, question 1, find 95% confidence intervals for the coefficients κ and β, and for the mean air temperature at a place 200 m above sea level.

3   For the data in Exercise 20B, question 2, find 95% confidence intervals for the coefficients κ and β, and for the height of a typical boy 9.0 years old.

4   Find confidence intervals for your answers to the questions in Exercise 20B, question 3 (a) and (b).

5   Work through the following argument to establish the result $E[S^2] = \dfrac{n-2}{n} \sigma^2$ quoted in §20.4.

(a) Use the expressions for $E[C_{xy}]$ and $V[C_{xy}]$ given in the text to find an expression for $E[C_{xy}^2]$, and deduce that

$$E[C_{xy}^2/S_x^2] = \frac{\sigma^2}{n} + \beta^2 S_x^2.$$

(b) Show that $E[S_y^2] = (1/n)\Sigma_{i=1}^{n} E[(Y_i - M_y)^2]$.

(c) Prove that

$$Y_i - M_y = \beta(x_i - m_x) + \left(1 - \frac{1}{n}\right)E_i - \frac{1}{n}\sum_{j \neq i} E_j,$$

and deduce from this that

$$E[Y_i - M_y] = \beta(x_i - m_x) \quad \text{and} \quad V[Y_i - M_y] = \frac{n-1}{n} \sigma^2.$$

Hence find an expression for $E[(Y_i - M_y)^2]$.

(*d*) Use the result of (*c*) to prove that

$$E[S_y^2] = \frac{n-1}{n}\,\sigma^2 + \beta^2 S_x^2.$$

(*e*) Deduce that $E[S^2] = \frac{n-2}{n}\,\sigma^2.$

20.5 A TWO-VARIABLE NORMAL PROBABILITY MODEL

The line of regression of *y* on *x* is found on the basis that the *x*-measurements are exactly known. But a complete analysis of a two-variable situation needs to take account of the variation in both measurements equally. In this section we will construct one particular model of this kind, in which the random variables *X* and *Y* are both distributed normally.

To keep the algebra as simple as possible, we will begin by restricting *X* and *Y* to standard normal random variables, with distribution N(0, 1). You are already familiar with one such probability model, the standard normal swarm (see §18.1) with area probability density

$$\frac{1}{2\pi}\,e^{-\frac{1}{2}(x^2+y^2)}.$$

But this is too special for the present purpose, since it was based on the assumption that the random variables *X* and *Y* are independent; that is to say, there is no correlation between them. The problem is to generalise it in such a way that *X* and *Y* remain standard normal variables, but with the possibility that they may be correlated.

An important feature of a normal swarm is its circular symmetry, but the diagrams in Fig. 1 (§20.1) suggest that for correlated variables the pattern of circles might be replaced by a pattern of ellipses. One way of achieving this transformation is by a shear parallel to the *y*-axis; Fig. 5*a* shows such a shear, with angle θ, applied to the unit circle. The equation of this shear is

$$\begin{bmatrix} x' \\ y' \end{bmatrix} = \begin{bmatrix} 1 & 0 \\ \tan\theta & 1 \end{bmatrix} \begin{bmatrix} x \\ y \end{bmatrix};$$

or, in its inverted form,

$$\begin{bmatrix} x \\ y \end{bmatrix} = \begin{bmatrix} 1 & 0 \\ -\tan\theta & 1 \end{bmatrix} \begin{bmatrix} x' \\ y' \end{bmatrix}.$$

If this substitution is made in the expression for the probability density of a standard normal swarm, then it takes the form

$$\frac{1}{2\pi}\,e^{-\frac{1}{2}\{x'^2+(y'-x'\tan\theta)^2\}}$$

$$= \frac{1}{2\pi}\,e^{-\frac{1}{2}(x'^2\sec^2\theta - 2x'y'\tan\theta + y'^2)}.$$

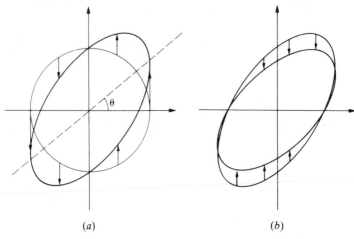

(a)   (b)

Figure 5

Notice that, since shearing does not affect areas, the total probability remains equal to 1; so this expression still defines an area probability density model. Also, since none of the values of x have changed, the random variable X' is still distributed as N(0, 1). But there is one snag: the values of y have changed, so that the variance of Y' is no longer 1, but is in fact increased to $\sec^2\theta$.

Q.7 By integrating with respect to x' from $-\infty$ to ∞, prove that Y' is distributed as N(0, $\sec^2\theta$).

A correction therefore has to be made which, whilst not affecting the values of x, reduces the values of y in the ratio $\cos\theta:1$ (see Fig. 5b). That is, we write $x'' = x'$, $y'' = y'\cos\theta$; or, in inverted form, $x' = x''$, $y' = y''\sec\theta$. But this transformation, a squash, does affect areas by reducing them in the ratio $\cos\theta:1$. So this time the probability density also has to be multiplied by $\sec\theta$ in compensation. The final form for the probability density is therefore

$$\frac{\sec\theta}{2\pi}\, e^{-\frac{1}{2}(x''^2\sec^2\theta - 2x''y''\sec\theta\tan\theta + y''\sec^2\theta)}.$$

As a check, notice that this expression is symmetrical between x'' and y''. Since neither of the transformations changes the values of x, the distribution of X'' is certainly N(0, 1). So, by symmetry, the distribution of Y'' is also N(0, 1), as required.

The transformations used to find this probability density also enable us to find the line of regression of y'' on x'' for this model. Since the original random variables X and Y were independent, the line of regression of y on x simply has the equation $y = 0$. The transformations convert this first to $y' = x'\tan\theta$, and then to $y''\sec\theta = x''\tan\theta$; or, more simply, $y'' = x''\sin\theta$. By symmetry, the line of regression of x'' on y'' is $x'' = y''\sin\theta$. (Note 20.6)

Lastly, we can obtain a theoretical coefficient of correlation for the model. To do this, notice that for the sample statistics in §20.3 the coefficients of regression of y on x, and of x on y, are respectively rS_y/S_x and rS_x/S_y; so the product of the two regression coefficients is r^2. Carrying this over to the probability model, where the regression coefficients are both equal to $\sin \theta$, we can define a "theoretical coefficient of correlation", ρ, given by the equation $\rho^2 = \sin^2\theta$. Also, Fig. 5 shows that positive values of ρ correspond to values of θ between 0 and $\frac{1}{2}\pi$, and negative values of ρ to values of θ between $-\frac{1}{2}\pi$ and 0. So taking square roots leads to the result

$$\rho = \sin \theta.$$

All this can be summarised (dropping the dashes, which are now superfluous):

The area probability density function

$$\phi(x, y) = \frac{\sec \theta}{2\pi} e^{-\frac{1}{2}(x^2 \sec^2\theta - 2xy \sec \theta \tan \theta + y^2 \sec^2\theta)}$$

represents a probability model in which the separate random variables X and Y each have standard normal probability density, and the coefficient of correlation between these variables is $\sin \theta$.

Q.8   Write down the equation of the area probability density function in which the random variables X, Y are distributed as $N(\mu_x, \sigma_x^2)$ and $N(\mu_y, \sigma_y^2)$, and the coefficient of correlation between them is ρ.

What use can be made of the model described in Q.8? Suppose that we have a population of pairs of random variables, for example, the heights of husbands and wives, where it would be reasonable to assume that both populations separately have a normal distribution, and which we suspect may be correlated, though we do not know how strongly. Such a population needs five parameters to describe it completely: μ_x, μ_y, σ_x, σ_y and ρ. The only practical way of estimating these is by making measurements of the heights in a sample of married couples, and calculating the sample statistics m_x, m_y, S_x, S_y and r. The theory in Chapter 20 of sampling from a normal population provides methods of estimating, within a confidence interval, the first four of these from the sample means and standard deviations. The hope is that a theoretical study of sampling from the two-variable model might lead, in the same way, to a confidence interval for the parameter ρ.

Exercise 20D

The questions in this exercise all refer to the model described in §20.5.

1   Write down an expression for the probability density $\alpha(x)$ for the random variable X. (The notation is that used in §14.5.) Deduce that the *conditional* probability of Y given X, defined as $\phi(x, y)/\alpha(x)$, is that of the normal probability model $N(\rho x, 1 - \rho^2)$.

How does this fit in with the assumption made in §20.4 about the distribution of errors?

2 In the expression for $\phi(x, y)$, show that the expression in brackets can be written as $(x - y \sin \theta)^2 \sec^2\theta + y^2$. Hence show that the total probability over the whole of the (x, y)-plane can be expressed in the form

$$\int_{y=-\infty}^{\infty} \frac{\sec \theta}{2\pi} e^{-\frac{1}{2}y^2} \left\{ \int_{x=-\infty}^{\infty} e^{-\frac{1}{2}(x - y \sin \theta)^2 \sec^2\theta} \, dx \right\} dy.$$

Explain why the integral within the curly brackets (evaluated treating y as constant) is equal to

$$\int_{-\infty}^{\infty} e^{-\frac{1}{2}x^2 \sec^2\theta} \, dx,$$

and give the value of this. Hence check that the repeated integral for the total probability has the value 1.

3 Comparison with the definition of the sample coefficient of correlation in §20.1 suggests that, in the notation of Exercise 14B, question 12, the theoretical coefficient of correlation could be defined as $C[X, Y]/\sigma_x\sigma_y$. For the given probability model, write this expression in the form of a repeated integral. Evaluate this by a method similar to that used in question 2, and hence verify that for this model ρ is equal to $\sin \theta$.

20.6 TESTING FOR THE EXISTENCE OF CORRELATION

The complete programme outlined at the end of the last section turns out to be difficult mathematically, and it would be too ambitious to attempt it here. (Note 20.7) But it is possible to tackle a simplified version of the problem, and to ask: how can we tell, from a sample of pairs drawn from two normal populations, whether they are correlated or not?

This may seem a foolish question: surely one merely calculates r, and if this comes out to be positive one deduces that the populations are positively correlated. But things are not as simple as this; and to demonstrate the nature of the problem, it is worth while carrying out a small experiment. (If you are working in a class, it is a good idea for each person to do the experiment separately with different random numbers, giving an opportunity to compare results.)

Take two rows of 50 random digits each (or generate them with a computer) and split each row into five groups of 10 digits. Add together the numbers in each group, and then designate the five sums in the two groups as x_1, x_2, x_3, x_4, x_5; y_1, y_2, y_3, y_4, y_5. From the five pairs (x_i, y_i), calculate the correlation coefficient r. What would you expect the answer to be? Is this what you get?

The point of taking the sums of 10 digits in each group is that, by the central limit theorem, these sums are expected to be distributed approximately normally. We have therefore simulated the selection of 5 pairs at random from two normal populations. But unless there is something disturbingly wrong with the random numbers we have used, these two populations should be uncorrelated.

So the theoretical correlation coefficient ρ should be zero. But it is likely that some members of your class will obtain values of r which are very different from zero. The purpose of the experiment is to throw some light on the "sampling distribution" of the correlation coefficient.

Q.9   In this experiment, what is the probability model for the random pair (X, Y)? Illustrate your results by plotting them on squared paper; show how they are related to the theoretical mean.

The question dealt with in the next few pages is: if samples of n pairs are drawn from two uncorrelated normal populations, what values of r might one reasonably get? Or, put another way, how large would r have to be for us to reject the hypothesis that the populations are uncorrelated?

20.7 AN ALTERNATIVE REPRESENTATION OF CORRELATION

It turns out that the geometrical approach used in Chapter 19 also provides an effective method of dealing with the question of correlation. But in order to use this, we shall need to devise a different way of showing n sample pairs geometrically from that introduced in §20.1. There we used a two-dimensional diagram, with each of the n pairs (x_i, y_i) represented by a separate point. The alternative is to work in n-dimensional space (that is, one dimension for each pair), and to represent the sample by a pair of points in this space. Here the description will be given for $n = 3$, so as to keep the geometry familiar; but the results can be extended quite generally for any value of n. The two points then have coordinates (x_1, x_2, x_3) and (y_1, y_2, y_3).

Now recall the definitions

$$C_{xy} = \frac{1}{n}\sum (x_i - m_x)(y_i - m_y), \quad S_x^2 = \frac{1}{n}\sum (x_i - m_x)^2, \quad S_y^2 = \frac{1}{n}\sum (y_i - m_y)^2.$$

These suggest that we might consider the vectors

$$\mathbf{x} = \begin{bmatrix} x_1 - m_x \\ x_2 - m_x \\ x_3 - m_x \end{bmatrix}, \quad \mathbf{y} = \begin{bmatrix} y_1 - m_y \\ y_2 - m_y \\ y_3 - m_y \end{bmatrix}.$$

Then all three of the definitions can be recast in the form of scalar products:

$$C_{xy} = \tfrac{1}{3}\mathbf{x}.\mathbf{y}, \quad S_x^2 = \tfrac{1}{3}\mathbf{x}.\mathbf{x} = \tfrac{1}{3}|\mathbf{x}|^2, \quad S_y^2 = \tfrac{1}{3}\mathbf{y}.\mathbf{y} = \tfrac{1}{3}|\mathbf{y}|^2;$$

and it follows that

$$r = \frac{C_{xy}}{S_x S_y} = \frac{\mathbf{x}.\mathbf{y}}{|\mathbf{x}||\mathbf{y}|}.$$

But this is a form which you will recognise. If ψ is the angle between the vectors $\mathbf{x}$ and $\mathbf{y}$, then the definition of scalar product gives

$$\mathbf{x} \cdot \mathbf{y} = |\mathbf{x}||\mathbf{y}| \cos \psi. \quad \text{(Note 20.8)}$$

The argument generalises from the special case $n = 3$ in the obvious way:

If a sample of n pairs (x_i, y_i) is represented by a pair of n-dimensional vectors with components $x_i - m_x$, $y_i - m_y$ respectively, then the coefficient of correlation is equal to $\cos \psi$, where ψ is the angle between the vectors.

This result provides the clue to the analysis of the distribution of the correlation coefficient.

20.8 SAMPLING PAIRS FROM INDEPENDENT NORMAL POPULATIONS

We must now bring in the fact that the populations from which the measurements x_i, y_i are drawn have normal probability. To do this, we can make use of a diagram similar to that used to study samples from a single normal population in Chapter 19. But now two normal swarms have to be represented on the same figure, with their centres at points C_x and C_y with coordinates $(\mu_x, \mu_x, \ldots, \mu_x)$ and $(\mu_y, \mu_y, \ldots, \mu_y)$ and with standard deviations σ_x and σ_y.

(1) *The case n = 3*
The diagram for this case is shown in Fig. 6; the points are labelled so as to correspond to Figs. 2–4 of Chapter 19, with suffixes x and y to distinguish the two measurements. Thus the sample x-values are represented by the point $\mathbf{R}_x$ with coordinates (x_1, x_2, x_3), and their mean by the point $\mathbf{N}_x (m_x, m_x, m_x)$ which lies on the 'central line' OD, so that $\mathbf{R}_x \mathbf{N}_x$ is perpendicular to OD. Notice now that the displacement $\mathbf{N}_x \mathbf{R}_x$ is equivalent to the vector

$$\begin{bmatrix} x_1 \\ x_2 \\ x_3 \end{bmatrix} - \begin{bmatrix} m_x \\ m_x \\ m_x \end{bmatrix} = \begin{bmatrix} x_1 - m_x \\ x_2 - m_x \\ x_3 - m_x \end{bmatrix},$$

which is the vector $\mathbf{x}$ in §20.7. A similar interpretation can be put on the point $\mathbf{R}_y$ of the normal swarm representing the sample y-values, with the displacement $\mathbf{N}_y \mathbf{R}_y$ equivalent to the vector $\mathbf{y}$.

Since the vectors $\mathbf{x}$, $\mathbf{y}$ are to be compared, it is convenient to locate them both in the 'base plane' through the origin at right angles to the central line OD, so that they are equivalent to the displacements $\mathbf{OQ}_x$ and $\mathbf{OQ}_y$. If ψ is the angle between these vectors in the base plane, we know from §20.7 that $r = \cos \psi$.

This completes the geometrical interpretation of the correlation coefficient for a particular sample. Now we need to take into account the hypothesis that the random variables X and Y are independent (as explained in §20.6), and that the samples drawn from these are random. Since the normal swarms in Fig. 7 both have rotational symmetry about the central line OD, this means that the vectors $\mathbf{x}$ and $\mathbf{y}$ vary independently and have no preferred directions in the base plane.

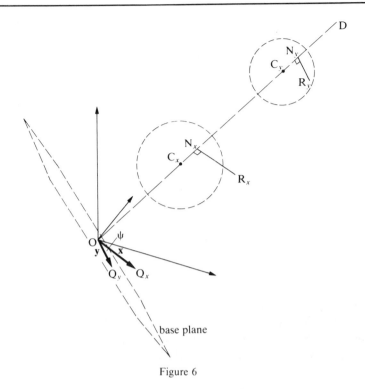

Figure 6

As far as their directions are concerned, we can imagine the vectors to be radii drawn on discs, each free to rotate independently about O. And the problem is, in that case, to find the probability distribution of the random variable $R = \cos \psi$.

Put in this form, the problem would seem at first sight to have two degrees of freedom, since both x and y can rotate arbitrarily. However, the situation can be simplified by imagining oneself to be sitting on the disc which rotates with the vector x, and then considering the rotation of the y-disc relative to the x-disc. This means that any angle ψ between the radii (where $-\pi < \psi < \pi$) is equally likely, and that there is in effect only one degree of freedom.

It is simplest to find the cumulative probability function for R: that is, $P(R < r)$, where r is a particular number between -1 and 1. If we write $r = \cos \alpha$, then this probability can be expressed as $P(|\psi| > \alpha)$; and from Fig. 7 it is clear that this probability is

$$\frac{2\pi - 2\alpha}{2\pi} = 1 - \frac{\alpha}{\pi}, \quad \text{or} \quad 1 - \frac{1}{\pi} \cos^{-1} r.$$

The probability density function can then be found simply by differentiating, which gives the expression

$$\frac{1}{\pi \sqrt{(1 - r^2)}}$$

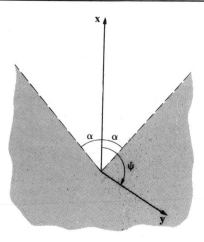

Figure 7

This is an extraordinary result, as you will see if you draw the graph of this function, which has vertical asymptotes at ± 1. This shows that, if a sample of three pairs is taken at random from two independent normal populations, it is more probable that you will get a value of r near to ± 1 than one near to zero!

Q.10   Test this out experimentally, by repeating the random digit experiment in §20.6 with 30 pairs of random digits, split into three groups of ten.

(2) *The case n = 4*
To extend the method to a sample of four pairs, four dimensions will clearly be needed; but apart from this complication, the diagram of the two swarms carries over directly. An essential difference is then that perpendicular to the central line one has a "base hyperplane" through the origin; and the diagram showing possible positions of **x** and **y** has spherical rather than circular symmetry. In place of Fig. 7 we therefore have Fig. 8, and we have to ask: if **y** can take any direction in 3-space relative to **x** with equal probability density, what is the probability that it makes an angle ψ with **x** greater than α?

    This is most easily answered by finding what portion of the surface of a sphere lies outside a cone of semi-angle α. And since the area of the surface of a zone of a sphere is proportional to its height, this probability is

$$\frac{1 + \cos \alpha}{2}.$$

So, with $n = 4$, the cumulative probability function for R is

$$\frac{1 + r}{2}.$$

Differentiation then gives the probability density as $\frac{1}{2}$. That is, for samples of

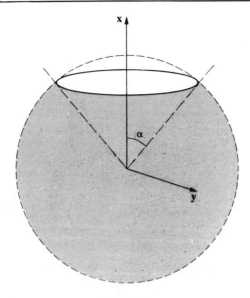

Figure 8

four pairs drawn at random from independent normal populations, all values of the correlation coefficient r are equally likely.

(3) *The general case*
By now you will have realised that we have been repeating, with only slight differences, the arguments used in §19.5 which led to the identification of the functions of t-probability. The only essential changes are:
(a) Instead of the relation $\cot \alpha = t/\sqrt{v}$ we have the relation $\cos \alpha = r$.
(b) The analysis of the case $n = 2$ for t-probability (based on circular symmetry) corresponds to the analysis of the case $n = 3$ for correlation; and the analysis of $n = 3$ for t-probability corresponds to the analysis of $n = 4$ for correlation.
    This means that it is unnecessary to go through all the mathematics again to find the distribution of R. All that is required is to make the substitution

$$t = \sqrt{v} \cot \alpha = \sqrt{v} \, \frac{\cos \alpha}{\sqrt{(1 - \cos^2 \alpha)}} = \sqrt{v} \, \frac{r}{\sqrt{(1 - r^2)}},$$

and replace the equation $v = n - 1$ for t-probability by $v = n - 2$ for correlation.

So, using the notation of §19.5, the probability of getting a value of the coefficient of correlation less than r is given by

$$\Phi_v\left(\frac{r\sqrt{v}}{\sqrt{(1 - r^2)}}\right);$$

and the corresponding probability density function is

$$\phi_v\left(\frac{r\sqrt{v}}{\sqrt{(1-r^2)}}\right) \times \frac{d}{dr}\left(\frac{r\sqrt{v}}{\sqrt{(1-r^2)}}\right)$$

$$= \frac{C_v}{\left(v + \dfrac{r^2 v}{1-r^2}\right)^{\frac{1}{2}(v+1)}} \times \frac{\sqrt{v}}{(1-r^2)^{\frac{3}{2}}}$$

$$= (C_v/v^{\frac{1}{2}v})(1-r^2)^{\frac{1}{2}v-1}.$$

Finally, substituting $v = n - 2$ and writing $D_n = C_v/v^{\frac{1}{2}v}$, we obtain:

If n sample pairs are drawn at random from two independent normal populations, then the correlation coefficient is distributed with probability density $D_n(1 - r^2)^{\frac{1}{2}n-2}$, where the constant D_n is chosen so as to make $\int_{-1}^{1} D_n(1 - r^2)^{\frac{1}{2}n-2}\, dr = 1$.

Some books of statistical tables provide cumulative probability tables for this probability model, which can be used directly to test whether a calculated value of r is or is not statistically significant. However, the link with t-probability means that, if such tables are not available, then tables of t-probability can be used instead. The example which follows illustrates this.

Example 2
A sample of 20 pairs of measurements is taken, and a correlation coefficient of 0.25 is calculated. Does this provide evidence that the quantities are in fact positively correlated?

The approach is to test the hypothesis $\rho = 0$ against the alternative hypothesis $\rho > 0$. A one-tail test is therefore appropriate.

With $v = 20 - 2 = 18$, the value $r = 0.25$ corresponds to

$$t = \frac{0.25 \times \sqrt{18}}{\sqrt{(1 - 0.0625)}} = 1.095.$$

Referring to tables of t-probability with $v = 18$, the value of t corresponding to a two-tail probability of 0.2 (that is, a one-tail probability of 0.1) is 1.33. So there is a probability of well over 0.1 that chance variation will produce a correlation coefficient as large as 0.25. Clearly the sample provides no significant evidence of correlation.

How large a value of r would be needed to convince one that two random variables are positively correlated? If we take a 5% level of significance (that is, a two-tail probability of 10%) the critical value of t is 1.73. This corresponds to

$$r = \cos(\cot^{-1}(1.73/\sqrt{18})) = 0.38.$$

Any value of r less than this could reasonably occur by the accident of sampling even if the random variables are completely independent.

This shows the danger of jumping uncritically to conclusions about the connection between two quantities on the basis of the coefficient of correlation, unless the sample is large or the coefficient is close to $+1$ or -1.

Exercise 20E

1   Investigate whether the data in Exercise 20A, question 2 provide significant evidence that the masses of heart and liver in mice are positively correlated.

2   For the data of Example 1 (§20.4), calculate the sample correlation coefficient and discuss its significance.

  Use the result set out in Note 20.7 to find an approximate 95% confidence interval for the value of ρ.

3   By collecting your own sample data of the heights of husbands and wives, investigate the evidence of correlation between them. Using the result in Note 20.7, find a confidence interval for the population correlation coefficient.

4   Find explicit expressions for the constant D_n in §20.8, distinguishing odd and even values of n. Hence draw graphs (or display them using a computer) of the probability density functions for the distribution of the coefficient of correlation.

5   Show that, if the method of §20.4 is used to test the hypothesis $\beta = 0$, then the test used is essentially the same as that used to test the hypothesis $\rho = 0$.

6   Draw a graph to show how the critical value of r, on the hypothesis $\rho = 0$, varies for different sample sizes, taking a 10% (two-tail) level of significance.

  On the same diagram, draw similar graphs for other levels of significance. Write a brief instruction to a non-mathematician for the use of this chart.

7   Prove that the standard deviation for the probability density function of the distribution of r is $1/\sqrt{(n-1)}$. Explain how this can be used to make an approximate judgement about the significance of the correlation coefficient for samples of a given size.

8   If X and Y are uncorrelated random variables with the same variance, and c is constant, prove that the theoretical correlation coefficient between X and $Y + cX$ is $c/\sqrt{(1 + c^2)}$. Hence devise a simulation experiment, using tabulated or computer generated random digits, to draw samples from a two-variable probability model in which both variables are (approximately) normally distributed and the coefficient of correlation between them is ρ.

  Run this experiment for a substantial number of samples with a chosen value of ρ. Calculate the sample coefficient of correlation each time, and comment on your results.

21

Probability chains

In this final chapter we return to some themes of probability theory which were introduced earlier in the book, but which it is now possible to explore in greater depth by using more advanced mathematical techniques. The chapter is quite independent of those which immediately precede it, and you could read it at any time once you are familiar with the pure mathematics (mainly linear algebra) on which it relies.

The starting point is the distinction made in Chapter 3 between sequences of Bernoulli and Markov type. You will recall that, in a Bernoulli sequence,

(a) the probability of each outcome is independent of the result on previous occasions,

(b) the probability of each outcome is the same on each occasion.

The conditions for a Markov sequence are rather more general:

(a) the probability of each outcome is conditional only on the result on the immediately preceding occasion,

(b) the conditional probability of each outcome is the same on each occasion.

When events occur at random in continuous time, rather than as the result of discrete experiments, then the model which corresponds to a Bernoulli sequence is Poisson probability. In Chapter 7 the equations of Poisson probability were derived as limiting cases of those for Bernoulli sequences. But they can also be obtained directly using calculus methods, and with this approach the assumptions underlying this model stand out more clearly. The section in this chapter on Poisson probability therefore combines revision with some new insights into the model.

21.1 BERNOULLI SEQUENCES

The simplest Bernoulli sequence is one with two possible outcomes, A and B, with probabilities a and b of occurring each time the experiment is repeated. If we use the symbol A_n to denote "the outcome A occurs on the nth occasion", and similarly for B, then we can draw a "transition diagram" for the sequence in the form of Fig. 1.

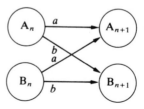

Figure 1

One of the most important questions we ask about Bernoulli sequences is: how many times does the outcome A occur in n repetitions of the experiment? The answer to this question may be any one of $0, 1, 2, \ldots, n$; and if we use the symbol i_n to denote "the outcome A occurs i times in n repetitions of the experiment", then we can draw a different transition diagram in the form of Fig. 2.

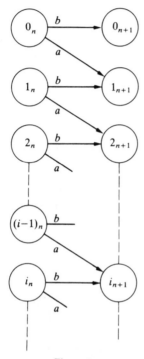

Figure 2

You might think that Fig. 2 resembles a Markov transition diagram rather than a Bernoulli one! In fact,

$$P(i_{n+1} \,|\, i_n) = b \quad \text{and} \quad P(i_{n+1} \,|\, (i-1)_n) = a,$$

and $P(i_{n+1} \,|\, s_n) = 0$ unless $s = i$ or $i - 1$. So the probabilities in this chain are generated by the equation

$$P(i_{n+1}) = bP(i_n) + aP((i-1)_n).$$

Q.1   What meaning would you give to $P(i_n)$ if i is an integer less than 0 or greater than n? With this extension of the notation, show that the above equation holds for all integral values of i, not just those for which i lies between 0 and n.

Q.2   Verify that this equation is satisfied by $P(i_n) = \binom{n}{i} a^i b^{n-i}$, where $\binom{n}{i}$ is defined as in §3.3. Convert your verification into a proof, using mathematical induction, of the correctness of this expression for $P(i_n)$.

21.2 POISSON PROBABILITY

The representation of the discrete Bernoulli sequence in Fig. 2 gives a clue to the way in which continuous Poisson probability can be tackled. But instead of finding the probabilities of 0, 1, 2, ... occurrences of a certain outcome in n repetitions of an experiment, we want expressions for the probabilities of 0, 1, 2, ... occurrences in a given interval of time.

Notice that there are two variables involved: how many times the event occurs, and in what period of time. So a notation will be needed which involves both of these. It is convenient to use a symbol

$p_i(t)$ = the probability that the event occurs i times in an interval of duration t. (Note 21.1)

This is more general than the notation p_i used in Chapter 7, which was the probability that the event occurs i times in *unit* time; we would now call this $p_i(1)$. The notation also makes it possible to cope with the question "how long will it be before the event next occurs?"; for $p_0(t)$ is the probability that the event will *not* occur within a time-interval of duration t, so $1 - p_0(t)$ is the probability that it occurs at least once in that time.

What then are the essential features of the Poisson model? In §7.4 the words used were: "If a certain event occurs randomly, singly and independently at a uniform average rate of λ occurrences per unit of time, then ..." Let us take this to pieces to see just what is involved.

The first word to pick on is "independently". This means that what happens in any interval is in no way influenced by what has happened previously. So consider two successive intervals, of duration t and t^* respectively, making up a single composite interval of duration $t + t^*$. This is illustrated in Fig. 3, in which the various outcomes shown are the numbers of occurrences of the event since the start of the first interval. The probabilities associated with the arrows on the left are then what we have called $p_i(t)$ for $i = 0, 1, 2, 3, \ldots$; and those associated with the arrows on the right are $p_i(t^*)$ for $i = 0, 1, 2, 3, \ldots; 0, 1, 2, \ldots; 0, 1, \ldots; 0, \ldots$ The important point is that these probabilities $p_i(t^*)$ do not depend on the outcomes after time t.

But the probabilities of the outcomes on the right can also be described as $p_i(t + t^*)$ for $i = 0, 1, 2, 3, \ldots$ So we can write a sequence of equations, of which the first two are

$$p_0(t^*)p_0(t) = p_0(t + t^*),$$

$$p_1(t^*)p_0(t) + p_0(t^*)p_1(t) = p_1(t + t^*).$$

Q.3 Write the next two equations in the sequence, and then use Σ-notation to write a general equation. (K)

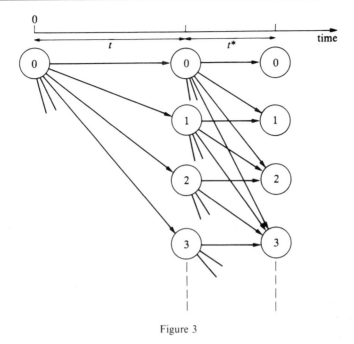

Figure 3

The next phrase that needs interpretation is "at a uniform average rate of λ occurrences per unit of time". How can this be expressed in terms of the notation $p_i(t)$?

In Chapter 7, to make sense of the idea of "average rate of occurrence" in a probability context, we found it necessary to think in terms of very short time-intervals (see §7.2). With this restriction, it seems reasonable to take the phrase to mean that, if t is very small, then the *probability* of the event occurring within a time-interval of duration t is approximately λt. This can be expressed graphically, that the graph of $p_1(t)$ near the origin has the form of Fig. 4a, where the tangent to the graph at the origin has gradient λ. So this condition can be summarised in the equation

$$p_1'(0) = \lambda. \quad \text{(Note 21.2)}$$

Q.4   Give a reason why it cannot be true that $p_1(t) \approx \lambda t$ except when t is small.

The last word to consider is "singly". This does not rule out the possibility of the event occurring twice within a very short space of time; but it does imply that, if one takes a short enough time-interval, then the probability of getting two occurrences within that interval is very small compared with the probability of getting one. More precisely, $p_2(t)/p_1(t)$ tends to zero as $t \to 0$. So the graph of $p_2(t)$ near the origin has the form shown in Fig. 4b; and this can be summarised in the equation

$$p_2'(0) = 0.$$

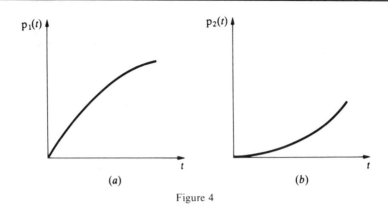

Figure 4

And clearly this is true even more strongly for the probabilities of 3, 4, ... occurrences. So we can write

$$p'_i(0) = 0 \text{ for } i = 2, 3, 4, \ldots.$$

In what follows we shall also need the value of $p'_0(0)$, but this can be deduced from the other values of $p'_i(0)$ already found. Clearly, for any particular duration t, the outcomes "0, 1, 2, 3, ... occurrences" are exclusive and exhaustive. This means that the equation

$$p_0(t) + p_1(t) + p_2(t) + p_3(t) + \ldots = 1$$

holds identically for all values of t. It can therefore be differentiated to give

$$p'_0(t) + p'_1(t) + p'_2(t) + p'_3(t) + \ldots = 0.$$

Putting $t = 0$, and using the values of $p'_i(0)$ already found,

$$p'_0(0) + \lambda + 0 + 0 + \ldots = 0,$$

so that

$$p'_0(0) = -\lambda.$$

The argument now takes a new direction. So far we have been concerned with the process of modelling: that is, interpreting the data in the form of mathematical equations. The next step is to solve these equations so as to find expressions for $p_i(t)$.

Since some of the data involves $p'_i(t)$, one step that is obviously indicated is to differentiate the equations found earlier for $p_i(t + t^*)$. These equations involve the two variables t and t^*; and the trick is to regard t as fixed to begin with, and to differentiate with respect to t^* alone. This gives, for the first two equations:

$$p'_0(t^*)p_0(t) = p'_0(t + t^*),$$

$$p'_1(t^*)p_0(t) + p'_0(t^*)p_1(t) = p'_1(t + t^*).$$

Q.5   Use your answers to Q.3 to write the next two equations, and the general equation. (K)

Next, we make the substitution $t^* = 0$, and use the values for $p_i'(0)$ already found:

$$-\lambda p_0(t) = p_0'(t),$$

$$\lambda p_0(t) - \lambda p_1(t) = p_1'(t);$$

and, in general,

$$\lambda p_{i-1}(t) - \lambda p_i(t) = p_i'(t).$$

Q.6   From your general equation in Q.5 for $p_i'(t + t^*)$, check this last equation.

It is again time to stand back and think. What we have here is a sequence of differential equations for the functions $p_i(t)$. The first equation can be solved directly for $p_0(t)$ alone. Once this is known, it can be substituted in the second equation, which is then a differential equation for $p_1(t)$ alone. This can then be substituted in the next equation of the sequence (for $i = 2$), which can then be solved for $p_2(t)$ ... and so on.

But the situation is even simpler than this. If we imagine ourselves carrying out this programme, then the differential equation for $p_i(t)$ will be

$$p_i'(t) + \lambda p_i(t) = \lambda p_{i-1}(t),$$

in which the function on the right will already have been found. Now this is a standard type of differential equation – a first order linear equation (Note 21.3) – which is solved by multiplying by an integrating factor $e^{\lambda t}$:

$$e^{\lambda t} p_i'(t) + \lambda e^{\lambda t} p_i(t) = \lambda e^{\lambda t} p_{i-1}(t),$$

which can be written

$$\frac{d}{dt} (e^{\lambda t} p_i(t)) = \lambda e^{\lambda t} p_{i-1}(t).$$

What is interesting about this equation is that it connects two functions of the same form: $e^{\lambda t} p_i(t)$ and $e^{\lambda t} p_{i-1}(t)$. This suggests making the substitution

$$e^{\lambda t} p_i(t) = q_i(t);$$

and the differential equation then takes the specially simple form

$$q_i'(t) = \lambda q_{i-1}(t).$$

This means that all that has to be done to find $q_i(t)$, once $q_{i-1}(t)$, is known, is to "multiply by λ and integrate". So carrying out this process repeatedly starting from $q_0(t)$, all the functions $q_i(t)$ can be found in turn, and from these $p_i(t)$ can be written down.

There are just a few details to be filled in before doing this. First, the solution to the differential equation requires knowledge of the initial conditions: that is, the values of $q_i(0)$. Now clearly, from the definition of $p_i(t)$,

$$p_0(0) = 1 \quad \text{and} \quad p_i(0) = 0 \text{ for } i = 1, 2, 3, \ldots.$$

(That is, in a time-interval of duration 0, the event occurs no times.) So, from the definition of $q_i(t)$ in terms of $p_i(t)$,

$$q_0(0) = 1 \quad \text{and} \quad q_i(0) = 0 \text{ for } i = 1, 2, 3, \ldots .$$

This set of equations determines the constants of integration.

It also needs to be noted that the first of the equations, in terms of the functions $q_i(t)$, is simply

$$q_0'(t) = 0.$$

So the first integral is

$$q_0(t) = 1;$$

and the procedure "multiply by λ and integrate" then gives in succession

$$q_1(t) = \lambda t, \quad q_2(t) = \tfrac{1}{2}\lambda^2 t^2, \quad q_3(t) = \tfrac{1}{6}\lambda^3 t^3, \ldots, q_i(t) = \frac{1}{i!}\lambda^i t^i.$$

That is,

$$p_i(t) = q_i(t)e^{-\lambda t} = \frac{\lambda^i t^i}{i!} e^{-\lambda t}.$$

This is the most general form of the equations for Poisson probabilities (see Exercise 7C, question 18), obtained by an argument which reveals precisely the assumptions on which it is based:

THE POISSON PROBABILITY MODEL.   If a certain event occurs repeatedly, singly and independently, at randomly distributed instants of time, at a uniform average rate of λ occurrences per unit of time, the probability that the event will occur i times within a time-interval of duration t is $\dfrac{(\lambda t)^i}{i!} e^{-\lambda t}$.

Exercise 21A

1 If the random variable I denotes the number of occurrences of a Poisson event in a given time t, prove that

$$E[I] = \lambda t.$$

What light does this throw on the description of λ as "the average rate of occurrence of the event"?

2 A boy is sitting by the side of a road counting the cars which pass him. If λ is the average number of cars passing in one minute, under what conditions would the number of cars passing in an arbitrary one-minute interval be given by the Poisson probability model? State, in this case, the probability $p_0(t)$ that no cars would pass the boy in the time-interval $[0, t]$ (the time t being measured in minutes).

Let the continuous variable T denote the time that elapses (after some initial instant) before the boy observes his first car. If $\phi(t)$ is the probability density function of T, prove that $\phi(t) = \lambda e^{-\lambda t}$ for $t \geqslant 0$.

Evaluate the conditional probability $P(T \geqslant s + t \mid T \geqslant s)$, showing that it is independent of the parameter s. Give an interpretation of this result in the context of the boy waiting for his first car to arrive. [SMP]

3 The leaves of a certain type of fruit tree are often infected by a pest, and an agricultural research station is carrying out an investigation into this phenomenon. The pest reveals its presence by eating small holes in the leaves. A large number of leaves having such holes have been brought to the research station, and it has been found that the random variable

$$X = \text{number of holes per leaf}$$

follows a Poisson distribution with parameter λ, except that the only values X can take are 1, 2, 3, ... since cases having $X = 0$ will not be found amongst the leaves brought in. Show that

$$P(X = x) = \frac{e^{-\lambda}\lambda^x}{x!(1 - e^{-\lambda})} \quad \text{for } x = 1, 2, 3, \dots.$$

Write down the corresponding expression for $P(X = x)$ for a case where neither $X = 0$ nor $X = 1$ will be found. [MEI]

4 The number of female elephants on a game reserve is known to follow a Poisson distribution with mean λ. In a certain year each animal has a probability p of producing a single offspring and zero probability of producing more than one offspring. Suppose that at the end of the year there are S offspring in the field. Prove that the probability that S is equal to s is given by

$$\sum_{n=s}^{\infty} \frac{p^s(1 - p)^{n-s}}{s!(n-s)!} \lambda^n e^{-\lambda}.$$

By writing $m = n - s$, evaluate the sum and hence show that S has a Poisson distribution with mean λp. [SMP]

21.3 SOME MARKOV SEQUENCES

The rest of this chapter will be devoted to a more detailed study of sequences of Markov type, and it will be helpful to begin by illustrating the definition with a number of examples. First, the example already discussed in §3.4:

Example 1
In the boat race model, the probability that an Oxford win in year n would be followed by an Oxford win in year $n + 1$ is $\frac{3}{5}$; and the probability that a Cambridge win in year n would be followed by a Cambridge win in year $n + 1$ is $\frac{2}{3}$.

This was represented by a transition diagram (Fig. 5a), which was then regarded as just one link of a chain (Fig. 5b) of indefinite length.

There may, of course, be more than two possible outcomes to the experiment in a Markov model:

Example 2
Don Giovanni, in Mozart's opera, had three girl friends: Anna, Elvira and Zerlina. He might have organised his evenings like this. If he went out with Anna

Outcome
in year . . .

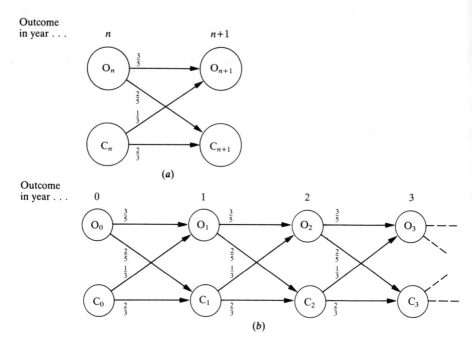

(a)

(b)

Figure 5

one evening, then he tossed a coin to decide whether to go out with Elvira or Zerlina the next. If he spent an evening with Elvira, then he drew a card from a pack; if it was a heart, then he took Zerlina out the next evening, otherwise he took out Anna. If he spent an evening with Zerlina, then he rolled a die; if it came up six, then he went out with Zerlina again; otherwise he went out with Anna.

Using the notation A_n to denote the event "he went out with Anna on the nth evening", and similarly E_n, Z_n for Elvira and Zerlina, the transition diagram is shown in Fig. 6.

Outcomes
on evening . . .

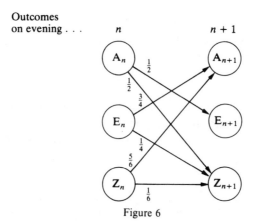

Figure 6

Q.7   Extend Fig. 6 to a chain, as in Fig. 5*b*.

The next example will be found to develop in a different way:

Example 3
A pegboard has four holes in line, labelled A, B, C, D. The rules of the game are that, on each round, the peg must be moved to an adjacent hole: if there is a choice, the player tosses a coin to decide which way to move it.

The transition diagram is shown in Fig. 7.

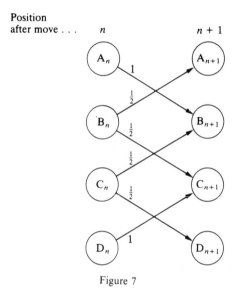

Figure 7

Q.8   Extend Fig. 7 to a chain, as in Fig. 5*b*.

Example 4
One of the side-shows at the village fete is a tortoise race. There are five tortoises in each race, each with an equal chance of winning. Spectators are invited to put 10p on the tortoise of their choice; if it comes in first, the backer wins a goldfish and gets her money back. Lucy goes to the fete with 50p in her pocket, and puts 10p at random on each race until her money runs out; after that she just stands by and watches.

If this is to be regarded as a Markov situation, we must be clear just what is meant by the 'outcome' of any particular race. If the outcomes are simply "Lucy wins" and "Lucy loses", then (for as long as she continues to play) they form a Bernoulli sequence. But if they are taken to be "Lucy has 50p, 40p, ..., 10p, nothing in her pocket", then the outcome of each race depends on how much she had before. You can check that, with this interpretation, the transition diagram has the form of Fig. 8.

There is a close similarity between this diagram and that for binomial

Money left
after race . . . n $n + 1$

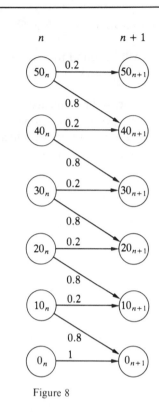

Figure 8

probability in Fig. 2 of §21.1. It is only after the fifth race, by which time Lucy may be out of funds, that the two diverge from each other.

Q.9   Extend Fig. 8 to a chain, as in Fig. 5b.

The last introductory example is a particular case of a famous problem known as the "random walk":

Example 5
A customer leaves the pub at closing time. His home is three doors up the road, and the jail is two doors down the road. Uncertain of his direction, he makes his way from door to door; after trying each door, he moves to the next door either up or down the road, with equal probabilities. However, if he reaches home or the jail, he is taken in for good. Trace the course of his walk.

If each walk from one door to the next is regarded as an experiment, then the outcome of that experiment is the door at which he lands up. Fig. 9 shows the transition diagram for one stage of the walk: X and Y are the houses between the pub P and his home H, and Z is the house between the pub and jail J. The broken lines are in a sense artificial, since once he reaches H or J there are no more 'steps' in his walk. However, it simplifies the analysis to insert them; perhaps he goes on walking in his dreams!

House after
stage . . .   *n*   *n* + 1

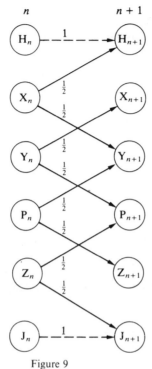

Figure 9

21.4 PATTERNS OF LONG-RUN BEHAVIOUR

One of the most interesting questions that arise with Markov sequences is, what happens to the probabilities of the various outcomes if we go on indefinitely, that is, "as *n* tends to infinity". Before reading on, look back at Examples 1 to 5 and try to decide for yourself (without doing any detailed calculation) how they behave in this respect.

We have already seen in §3.5 that the boat race model gives probabilities which approach steady values: $\frac{5}{11}$ for Oxford and $\frac{6}{11}$ for Cambridge. The model for the Don's girl friends (Example 2) is more complicated, and the long-run probabilities are more difficult to predict; but later (see §21.5) we shall see that this also gives probabilities which approach steady values.

But Example 3 is very different. To see this, suppose first that the peg starts at A. Where can it be after 1, 2, 3, . . . moves? It is easy to discover that after an odd number of moves it can only be at B or D, and that after an even number it can only be at A or C. So the probabilities certainly cannot settle down to limiting steady values; the model is said to be *periodic*, with period 2. (This is investigated in more detail in Exercise 21C, question 12.)

Q.10   Redraw Fig. 7 with the outcomes in the order A, C, B, D. How does this show up the periodicity?

The curious thing is that a steady situation, in which the probabilities remain constant, is in fact possible! Using the method described in §3.5 to find a set of steady probabilities, denoted by P*(A), P*(B), P*(C), P*(D) gives the equations (see Fig. 7)

$$P^*(A) = \tfrac{1}{2} \times P^*(B),$$

$$P^*(B) = 1 \times P^*(A) + \tfrac{1}{2} \times P^*(C),$$

$$P^*(C) = \tfrac{1}{2} \times P^*(B) + 1 \times P^*(D),$$

$$P^*(D) = \tfrac{1}{2} \times P^*(C).$$

These lead to the ratios

$$P^*(A):P^*(B):P^*(C):P^*(D) = 1:2:2:1.$$

Combining these with the requirement

$$P^*(A) + P^*(B) + P^*(C) + P^*(D) = 1$$

gives the solution

$$P^*(A) = P^*(D) = \tfrac{1}{6}, \quad P^*(B) = P^*(C) = \tfrac{1}{3}.$$

Q.11   Put these probabilities into Fig. 7 and verify that they give a steady situation.

So if the game starts with these probabilities (for example, by the player rolling a die and assigning the peg initially to A, B, C, D according as the die shows 1, [2 or 3], [4 or 5], 6) then *before the die is rolled* the probabilities for the position of the peg after 1, 2, 3, ... moves are all the same, and equal to the initial probabilities. (But of course, once the die has been rolled and the initial position of the peg settled, these probabilities no longer apply, and we are into the periodic situation.)

Examples 4 and 5 are different again. The contents of Lucy's pocket (Example 4) can clearly be steady in only one way: when her cash is exhausted, and remains so. In this example the outcome "0p" has the property that, when once attained, there is no escape from it. For this reason it is called an *absorbing outcome* of the system. In Example 5 there are two such absorbing outcomes: home and the jail.

Taken as a whole, the other houses in Example 5 (X, Y, P and Z) form a set with the opposite property: that once left, there is no returning to it. Such a set of outcomes is called a *transient class*. (It is important to note that this is a property of the set as a whole, not of the individual outcomes in the set. For example, the customer might return to the pub many times during his walk, so long as he stays within the transient class.)

Similarly, in Example 4 the outcomes 50p, 40p, 30p, 20p, 10p taken together make up a transient class. In this case it is a simple matter to calculate the probabilities of Lucy having each of these amounts in her pocket after *n* races (see Exercise 21B, question 5), and to show that the probability of staying indefinitely within the transient class as a whole is zero. (Put this last statement into "Lucy language".) This doesn't mean that it is *impossible*; Lucy might just possibly have a very lucky day on the tortoises. But the probability tends to zero as $n \to \infty$.

It is not so obvious in Example 5 that the customer will land up eventually either at home or in jail; that is, that the probability of remaining for ever within the transient class tends to zero. It can be shown, however, that this is so.

But even these examples do not exhaust all the possibilities. For instance, the Markov model illustrated in Fig. 10 has a single-outcome transient class A, feeding into a two-outcome class {B, C} which, once reached, can never be left. It is easy to see that $P^*(A) = 0$, and that $P^*(B) = P^*(C) = \frac{1}{2}$. In this case the outcomes B and C taken together are said to form a *closed class*.

Q.12 Make up a story to fit Fig. 10.

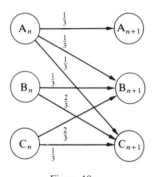

Figure 10

Q.13 What name do we give to a single-outcome closed class?

Fig. 11 is an attempt to summarise these ideas in a diagram. The thick arrows indicate only transfer between the classes, not between the individual states. For example, the figure might be a 'global' representation of the system shown in Fig. 12; if so, then all three dotted arrows in Fig. 12 are incorporated in the single oblique arrow in Fig. 11, all five broken arrows in Fig. 12 are incorporated in the lower horizontal arrow in Fig. 11, and all four full continuous arrows in Fig. 12 are incorporated in the upper horizontal arrow in Fig. 11. It is important to add that the arrows in Fig. 11 do not have numerical probabilities attached to them; they merely indicate the possibility of movement from one class to another. This figure shows a system with just one class of each type; it is possible to have more than one closed class (see Example 5) or more than one transient class, or to have no transient class at all (Examples 1, 2, 3).

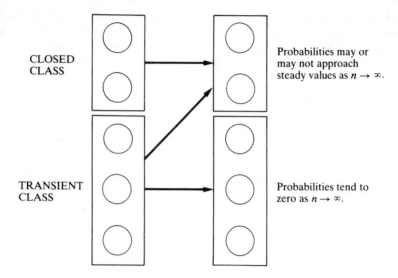

CLOSED
CLASS

Probabilities may or
may not approach
steady values as $n \to \infty$.

TRANSIENT
CLASS

Probabilities tend to
zero as $n \to \infty$.

Figure 11

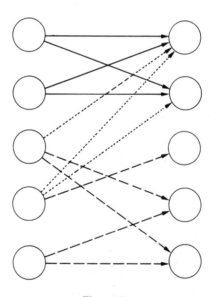

Figure 12

Exercise 21B

1   Suppose that, in Example 2, the Don goes out with Anna on Sunday evening. What
are the probabilities that he will go out with her again on (a) Monday, (b) Tuesday,
(c) Wednesday? Which of Elvira and Zerlina will he see more frequently in the long
run?

2 Four points on a horizontal line are labelled A, B, C, D, reading from left to right. A counter is placed on one of these points, and its movement on the line is determined by tossing two coins. If two heads fall, the counter moves one place to the right, unless it is at D when it stays put. If two tails are thrown, the counter moves one place to the left, unless it is at A in which case it moves to B. Otherwise the counter does not move. Draw a transition diagram for the movement of the counter.

If it is placed at A, what is the probability that it is at D after five tosses?

3 Adapt Example 3 to the case of pegboards with (a) three, (b) five holes in a row. Describe the long-term behaviour, and investigate whether a set of steady probabilities is possible.

4 A red and a green bag contain respectively three white and three black balls. At each move one ball is drawn at random from each bag, and each ball is replaced in the other bag. Draw an appropriate transition diagram, and investigate the long-run behaviour of the system.

5 In Example 4, write down the probabilities that, after n races, Lucy has 50p, 40p, ..., 10p, nothing in her pocket. What are the limiting values of these various probabilities as $n \to \infty$? Draw graphs showing the probabilities of the various outcomes as n varies.

6 My pattern of TV watching is as follows. If I have ITV on one evening, then the probabilities that I will have ITV, BBC or nothing the next evening are $\frac{1}{6}, \frac{1}{2}, \frac{1}{3}$ respectively; if I have BBC on one evening, then the corresponding probabilities for the next evening are $\frac{1}{4}, \frac{1}{4}, \frac{1}{2}$. If I miss television entirely one evening, then the next evening I shall be certain to watch BBC. I never change channels during an evening. Assuming that in the long run my pattern of watching settles down to a steady state, find in what proportions I shall watch ITV, BBC or nothing.

If the probabilities of watching ITV, BBC or nothing on the nth night of the year are p_n, q_n, r_n prove that, except perhaps for the first night ($n = 1$) of this pattern of watching, $r_n = 2p_n$. Deduce that, if x_n denotes $10p_n - 3q_n$, then, for $n \geqslant 2$, $x_{n+1} = kx_n$, where k is constant. Hence show that, whatever happens on the first night, my pattern of watching is bound to settle down in time to a steady state. [SMP]

7 Draw diagrams illustrating Markov models with
   (a) two transient classes and one closed class,
   (b) one transient class and two closed classes, just one of which consists of a single absorbing outcome.
   In each case make up a situation which would be represented by your model.

8 For the transition diagrams in Fig. 13, identify the closed and transient classes. Then re-draw the transition diagrams, placing the outcomes in the same class next to each other. (K)

9 The probability of the local football team winning the next match depends only on the results of the two previous games. This probability is
   (a) 0.9 if both previous matches were won,
   (b) 0.7 if the last match was won, and the one before was drawn or lost,
   (c) 0.6 if the last match was drawn or lost, and the one before was won,
   (d) 0.2 if both previous matches were drawn or lost.
   Model this problem by a four-stage Markov process whose four states correspond to (a), (b), (c), (d) respectively.

Suppose the team won both of its last two matches; calculate the probabilities that they will win (i) the next match but one, (ii) the next match but two. [SMP]

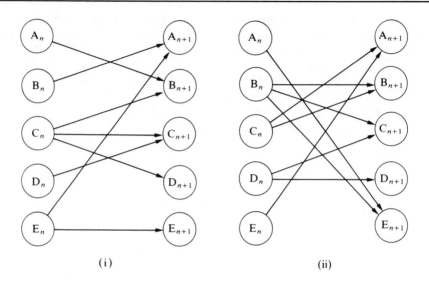

(i)   (ii)

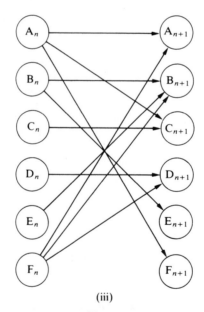

(iii)

Figure 13

21.5 MATRIX METHODS

The idea of a transition matrix and an outcome probability matrix, used in §3.6 for the boat race model, can be extended to Markov models with any number of outcomes. This opens up the whole range of possibilities of investigating the properties of such models using results from matrix algebra.

As an illustration, look again at Example 2 in §21.3. To calculate $P(A_{n+1})$, note that the outcome A_{n+1} must have been preceded by one of A_n, E_n or Z_n. The probability is therefore given by

$$P(A_{n+1} | A_n) \times P(A_n) + P(A_{n+1} | E_n) \times P(E_n) + P(A_{n+1} | Z_n) \times P(Z_n),$$

leading to the equation

$$0 \times P(A_n) + \tfrac{3}{4} \times P(E_n) + \tfrac{5}{6} \times P(Z_n) = P(A_{n+1}).$$

Similarly,

$$\tfrac{1}{2} \times P(A_n) + 0 \times P(E_n) + 0 \times P(Z_n) = P(E_{n+1}),$$

$$\tfrac{1}{2} \times P(A_n) + \tfrac{1}{4} \times P(E_n) + \tfrac{1}{6} \times P(Z_n) = P(Z_{n+1}).$$

In matrix form, these are written as the single equation

$$
\begin{bmatrix} 0 & \tfrac{3}{4} & \tfrac{5}{6} \\ \tfrac{1}{2} & 0 & 0 \\ \tfrac{1}{2} & \tfrac{1}{4} & \tfrac{1}{6} \end{bmatrix}
\begin{bmatrix} P(A_n) \\ P(E_n) \\ P(Z_n) \end{bmatrix}
=
\begin{bmatrix} P(A_{n+1}) \\ P(E_{n+1}) \\ P(Z_{n+1}) \end{bmatrix}
$$

The square matrix, whose elements are the conditional probabilities, is the transition matrix, denoted by $\mathbf{T}$; and the column matrices are the outcome probability matrices, denoted by $\mathbf{p}_n$ and $\mathbf{p}_{n+1}$. With this notation, the equation again has the simple form

$$\mathbf{T}\mathbf{p}_n = \mathbf{p}_{n+1};$$

and every Markov model can be represented in a similar way.

Two important properties of these matrices should be noted straight away:
(1) The entries are all numbers between 0 and 1 (inclusive).
(2) The sum of the numbers in any column is 1.
On the basis of these properties it is possible to build up a general theory of Markov models.

Q.14 Write down the transition matrices for Examples 3, 4 and 5. Check that they have the properties (1) and (2) just stated.

From the matrix form of the transition equation it follows at once that the sequence $\mathbf{p}_0$, $\mathbf{p}_1$, $\mathbf{p}_2$, ... of outcome probability matrices forms a 'geometric progression' with matrix multiplier $\mathbf{T}$, so that the general term can be written as

$$\mathbf{p}_n = \mathbf{T}^n\mathbf{p}_0.$$

So to solve the problem completely, assuming that the initial probabilities in $\mathbf{p}_0$ are known, it is sufficient to be able to calculate $\mathbf{T}^n$. And we can often do just this by using the theory of eigenvectors. (Note 21.4)

Example 6
Investigate the Markov sequence with transition matrix

$$\begin{bmatrix} \frac{1}{3} & \frac{1}{2} & \frac{1}{2} \\ \frac{1}{3} & \frac{1}{2} & \frac{1}{3} \\ \frac{1}{3} & 0 & \frac{1}{6} \end{bmatrix}.$$

Q.15 Make up a situation having this transition matrix, and illustrate it with a transition diagram.

This matrix has been chosen because it has simple eigenvalues and eigenvectors, so that the theory can be explained without too much numerical complication. It is left to you to check that

$$\mathbf{T}\begin{bmatrix} 15 \\ 14 \\ 6 \end{bmatrix} = \begin{bmatrix} 15 \\ 14 \\ 6 \end{bmatrix}, \quad \mathbf{T}\begin{bmatrix} 0 \\ 1 \\ -1 \end{bmatrix} = \frac{1}{6}\begin{bmatrix} 0 \\ 1 \\ -1 \end{bmatrix}, \quad \mathbf{T}\begin{bmatrix} 1 \\ 0 \\ -1 \end{bmatrix} = -\frac{1}{6}\begin{bmatrix} 1 \\ 0 \\ -1 \end{bmatrix};$$

so the eigenvalues are $1, \frac{1}{6}, -\frac{1}{6}$ with corresponding eigenvectors

$$\mathbf{e}_1 = \begin{bmatrix} 15 \\ 14 \\ 6 \end{bmatrix}, \quad \mathbf{e}_2 = \begin{bmatrix} 0 \\ 1 \\ -1 \end{bmatrix} \quad \mathbf{e}_3 = \begin{bmatrix} 1 \\ 0 \\ -1 \end{bmatrix}.$$

Then it is standard knowledge that, if $\mathbf{U}$ denotes the matrix whose columns are $\mathbf{e}_1, \mathbf{e}_2, \mathbf{e}_3$ (often written $\mathbf{U} = [\mathbf{e}_1 \vdots \mathbf{e}_2 \vdots \mathbf{e}_3]$), and if Λ is the diagonal matrix whose entries are the eigenvalues,

$$\Lambda = \begin{bmatrix} 1 & 0 & 0 \\ 0 & \frac{1}{6} & 0 \\ 0 & 0 & -\frac{1}{6} \end{bmatrix},$$

then $\mathbf{TU} = \mathbf{U}\Lambda.$

You can check this yourself for the matrix under discussion. It follows that we can write $\mathbf{T}$ as $\mathbf{U}\Lambda\mathbf{U}^{-1}$, so that

$\mathbf{T}^n = (\mathbf{U}\Lambda\mathbf{U}^{-1}) \ldots (\mathbf{U}\Lambda\mathbf{U}^{-1})$ (with n factors)

$\quad = \mathbf{U}\Lambda^n\mathbf{U}^{-1}$ (by re-grouping the product and using $\mathbf{U}^{-1}\mathbf{U} = \mathbf{I}$).

And now the problem is solved, since it is easily checked that

$$\Lambda^n = \begin{bmatrix} 1 & 0 & 0 \\ 0 & (\frac{1}{6})^n & 0 \\ 0 & 0 & (-\frac{1}{6})^n \end{bmatrix}.$$

Of course, it is necessary to know $\mathbf{p}_0$ to get an explicit formula for $\mathbf{p}_n$; but if the initial probabilities to be assigned to the outcomes A, B, C are known, then this expression for $\mathbf{T}^n$ enables us to find formulae for $P(A_n)$, $P(B_n)$, $P(C_n)$. The results are not very interesting!

What is far more interesting is the limiting form as $n \to \infty$. Because $(\frac{1}{6})^n$ and $(-\frac{1}{6})^n$ both tend to zero, Λ^n is then replaced by the matrix

$$\mathbf{L} = \begin{bmatrix} 1 & 0 & 0 \\ 0 & 0 & 0 \\ 0 & 0 & 0 \end{bmatrix}.$$

This gives the limit of $\mathbf{T}^n$ as

$$\mathbf{ULU}^{-1} = \begin{bmatrix} 15 & 0 & 1 \\ 14 & 1 & 0 \\ 6 & -1 & -1 \end{bmatrix} \begin{bmatrix} 1 & 0 & 0 \\ 0 & 0 & 0 \\ 0 & 0 & 0 \end{bmatrix} \cdot \frac{1}{35} \begin{bmatrix} 1 & 1 & 1 \\ -14 & 21 & -14 \\ 20 & -15 & -15 \end{bmatrix}$$

$$= \frac{1}{35} \begin{bmatrix} 15 & 15 & 15 \\ 14 & 14 & 14 \\ 6 & 6 & 6 \end{bmatrix}.$$

It is left to you to check that the inverse is as stated (by multiplying out $\mathbf{UU}^{-1}$) and that the final product has been correctly evaluated. (Note 21.5)

This is a very extraordinary result. Notice first that it has the property that each column sums to 1. This is not surprising, since it is the limit of $\mathbf{T}^n$, which is itself a transition matrix (from outcome 0 to outcome n in one jump). More remarkable is the fact that the columns are all the same: the matrix is in fact $\frac{1}{35}[\mathbf{e}_1 \quad \mathbf{e}_1 \quad \mathbf{e}_1]$, where $\mathbf{e}_1$ was the eigenvector we found corresponding to the eigenvalue 1. The significance of this is that, when the product $(\lim \mathbf{T}^n)\mathbf{p}_0$ is formed, where $\mathbf{p}_0$ is *any* initial outcome probability matrix, the result is

$$\frac{1}{35} \begin{bmatrix} 15 & 15 & 15 \\ 14 & 14 & 14 \\ 6 & 6 & 6 \end{bmatrix} \begin{bmatrix} P(A_0) \\ P(B_0) \\ P(C_0) \end{bmatrix}, \quad \text{which equals} \quad \begin{bmatrix} \frac{15}{35} \\ \frac{14}{35} \\ \frac{6}{35} \end{bmatrix}$$

because $P(A_0) + P(B_0) + P(C_0) = 1$. That is, the limiting outcome probabilities are the same whatever probabilities are assigned to the various outcomes in the first place.

Finally, what is this limiting outcome probability vector? Since it is proportional to $\mathbf{e}_1$, an eigenvector satisfying $\mathbf{Te}_1 = \mathbf{e}_1$, it is itself an eigenvector with the same property. (Remember that eigenvectors are not unique, but are arbitrary to the extent of a constant of proportion.) And since it is also an outcome probability vector, it is in fact just the 'steady' outcome probability vector

$$\mathbf{p^*} = \begin{bmatrix} P^*(A) \\ P^*(B) \\ P^*(C) \end{bmatrix}.$$

Probably this is what we would have expected; but reference back to Example 3 should be enough to remind us that the steady outcome probability matrix is not *always* a limiting outcome probability matrix. So this is something which needs investigating in more detail; Example 3 must exhibit some feature which makes it an exception to the general method described in Example 6. (See Exercise 21C, question 12.)

You may think that Example 6 was rather carefully contrived. Was it a matter of luck that one of the eigenvalues was equal to 1 and that the others ($\frac{1}{6}$ and $-\frac{1}{6}$) were both less than 1, so that their nth powers tended to zero? It was certainly very convenient!

The answer to this question is "no". This is because of two important properties which are common to all transition matrices:

(3) One eigenvalue of any transition matrix is always equal to 1.

(4) No eigenvalue of a transition matrix can have modulus greater than 1.

These properties are a consequence of conditions (1) and (2) stated above. (See Exercise 21C, questions 8 and 9.) This means that, provided that $\mathbf{T}$ has a full clutch of linearly independent eigenvectors, and that apart from the simple eigenvalue 1 it has no other eigenvalues with modulus 1, then it is always possible to write $\mathbf{T}$ as $\mathbf{U \Lambda U^{-1}}$, where

$$\mathbf{\Lambda}^n \rightarrow \begin{bmatrix} 1 & 0 & 0 & .. & .. \\ 0 & 0 & 0 & .. & .. \\ 0 & 0 & 0 & .. & .. \\ .. & .. & .. & .. & .. \end{bmatrix};$$

and then the analysis will always proceed as in Example 6.

If, in a Markov model with k outcomes, the transition matrix $\mathbf{T}$ has k independent eigenvectors, and the only eigenvalue with modulus 1 is the simple eigenvalue 1 itself, then as $n \rightarrow \infty$ the outcome probability matrix after n steps tends to the steady outcome probability matrix $\mathbf{p^*}$ satisfying $\mathbf{Tp^*} = \mathbf{p^*}$, whatever the values of the initial probabilities.

This is a very powerful result, which describes the 'typical' behaviour of Markov models (however many possible outcomes there are). A special point to be made is that, unless the actual formulae for the outcome probabilities after n steps are needed (and they are not often of much interest), it is not necessary to go through the steps of actually calculating the eigenvector matrix $\mathbf{U}$ and its inverse – often a tedious procedure unless the numbers have been specially arranged to come out nicely. Instead, one can just quote the general theory and go direct to the limiting probabilities.

Example 2 offers a good illustration of this. The transition matrix for the Don's dating rule is

$$\begin{bmatrix} 0 & \frac{3}{4} & \frac{5}{6} \\ \frac{1}{2} & 0 & 0 \\ \frac{1}{2} & \frac{1}{4} & \frac{1}{6} \end{bmatrix},$$

whose eigenvalues are 1 and $\frac{1}{12}(\pm\sqrt{19}-5)$. These awkward numbers make it quite complicated to calculate the eigenvectors. But if the Don is just interested in the relative long-run frequencies of his evenings with Anna, Elvira and Zerlina, he can find these from the much simpler equations for the steady probability. The theory then guarantees that these are also the limiting probabilities.

Q.16 Verify that these are $\frac{4}{9}, \frac{2}{9}, \frac{1}{3}$.

However, although this is typical of Markov models, it must be emphasised that there are exceptions, such as Example 3 to which reference has already been made. This is because the conditions of the theory may not be satisfied. For example, the characteristic equation for **T** may have 1 as a repeated root, or there may be roots other than 1 with modulus 1, or there may be some other repeated eigenvalue with only one corresponding eigenvector. Some of these possibilities are explored in Exercise 21C.

Exercise 21C

1 Investigate, in the manner of Example 6, the Markov models with transition matrices

$$(a)\ \begin{bmatrix} \frac{2}{3} & \frac{3}{4} \\ \frac{1}{3} & \frac{1}{4} \end{bmatrix};\quad (b)\ \begin{bmatrix} 0 & \frac{1}{2} & \frac{3}{4} \\ \frac{1}{2} & 0 & 0 \\ \frac{1}{2} & \frac{1}{2} & \frac{1}{4} \end{bmatrix};\quad (c)\ \begin{bmatrix} \frac{1}{2} & \frac{1}{4} & 0 & 0 \\ \frac{1}{2} & \frac{3}{4} & 0 & 0 \\ 0 & 0 & \frac{2}{5} & \frac{1}{3} \\ 0 & 0 & \frac{3}{5} & \frac{2}{3} \end{bmatrix}.$$

2 In Example 4, suppose that Lucy goes to the fete with just 10p in her pocket. Write down the transition matrix in this case, and use the method described in the text to investigate the subsequent probabilities of having either 10p or nothing in her pocket.

3 Write down the transition matrix for the situation described in Exercise 21B, question 6. Use the method described in Example 6 to find expressions for the probabilities p_n, q_n, r_n in terms of the first night probabilities p_1, q_1, r_1. Hence verify the relations $r_n = 2p_n$ and $x_{n+1} = kx_n$, where $x_n = 10p_n - 3q_n$, quoted in the earlier question. Find also the limiting values of these probabilities.

4   Find the eigenvalues and eigenvectors for the transition matrices in
(a) Example 4, adapted so that Lucy goes to the fete with just 20p in her pocket;
(b) Example 3, adapted so that the pegboard has just three holes in line.
Explain, in each case, why the method described in Example 6 breaks down.

5   Consider a very simple 'random walk' problem (Example 5) in which the pub lies
immediately between the customer's home and the jail. Write down the transition
matrix $\mathbf{T}$ and find its eigenvalues. Prove that $\mathbf{T}^2 = \mathbf{T}$, and explain what this implies
about the calculation of the subsequent probabilities.

6   Consider a version of the random walk problem (see Example 5) in which home is
two doors up the road from the pub, and the jail is next door down the road. Write
down the transition matrix, and show that it has 1 as a multiple eigenvalue, but that
there is a full clutch of linearly independent eigenvectors. Apply the method
described in the text to this matrix, and find the probabilities of being at each of the
four possible locations after n steps. Evaluate these probabilities numerically for the
first few values of n, and verify from a transition diagram that these are what you
would expect.

7   In a three-outcome Markov model, with transition matrix $\mathbf{T}$, $\mathbf{e} = \begin{bmatrix} x \\ y \\ z \end{bmatrix}$ is an

eigenvector corresponding to the eigenvalue λ. The row matrix $[1 \quad 1 \quad 1]$ is denoted
by $\mathbf{r}$. Prove that $\mathbf{rT} = \mathbf{r}$.
By multiplying both sides of the equation $\mathbf{Te} = \lambda \mathbf{e}$ on the left by $\mathbf{r}$, prove that
either $\lambda = 1$ or $x + y + z = 0$. Verify that this is true in Example 6.
Generalise this result to a k-outcome model.

8   If $\mathbf{T}$ is a transition matrix, show that the matrix $\mathbf{T} - \mathbf{I}$ has the property that the sum
of the numbers in each column is zero. Deduce that $\det(\mathbf{T} - \mathbf{I}) = 0$, and hence that 1
is an eigenvalue of $\mathbf{T}$.

9   Suppose that $\mathbf{T} = \begin{bmatrix} a & d & g \\ b & e & h \\ c & f & i \end{bmatrix}$ is a transition matrix and that $\begin{bmatrix} x \\ y \\ z \end{bmatrix}$ is an

eigenvector corresponding to an eigenvalue λ. Show that

$$a|x| + d|y| + g|z| \geqslant |\lambda||x|.$$

(Use the property that, if α, β are real or complex numbers, $|\alpha| + |\beta| \geqslant |\alpha + \beta|$.)
From this, and two similar equations, deduce that $|\lambda| \leqslant 1$.
Does this property generalise to a k-outcome transition matrix?

10   In a k-outcome Markov model with transition matrix $\mathbf{T}$, the eigenvalues are denoted
by $\lambda_1, \lambda_2, \ldots, \lambda_k$ (possibly with repetitions). Explain why

$$\det(\mathbf{T} - \lambda \mathbf{I}) = (\lambda_1 - \lambda)(\lambda_2 - \lambda) \ldots (\lambda_k - \lambda),$$

and deduce that

$$\det \mathbf{T} = \lambda_1 \lambda_2 \ldots \lambda_k.$$

Combining this with the result of question 9, prove that the determinant of a
transition matrix cannot exceed 1 in absolute value.

11   In Example 6, verify that the fact that the columns of the limiting matrix $\mathbf{ULU}^{-1}$ are
all the same depends on the fact that the entries in the first row of the matrix $\mathbf{U}^{-1}$

are all equal to $1/s$, where s is the sum of the entries in the column eigenvector corresponding to the eigenvalue 1.

Suppose that in a Markov model with three outcomes the transition vector has just one simple eigenvalue with modulus 1 (that is, the value 1 itself), and a full clutch of linearly independent eigenvectors. The matrix of eigenvectors $\mathbf{U}$ is denoted by $\begin{bmatrix} p & u & x \\ q & v & y \\ r & w & z \end{bmatrix}$, with the first column corresponding to the eigenvalue 1; and the entries in the first row of its inverse $\mathbf{U}^{-1}$ are denoted by l, m, n. Using the equation $\mathbf{U}^{-1}\mathbf{U} = \mathbf{I}$, write down three equations for l, m, n; and show (using the results of question 7) that they are all satisfied by taking $l = m = n = 1/s$.

Deduce that the property referred to at the beginning of this question in respect of Example 6 is true in general for Markov models satisfying these conditions.

12 Write a transition matrix for Example 3 (§21.3) and show that two of its eigenvalues have modulus equal to 1. Show that, although $\lim \mathbf{T}^n$ does not exist, the sequences of matrices $\mathbf{T}^{2m}$ and $\mathbf{T}^{2m+1}$ considered separately tend to limits. Hence find the limiting probabilities, after even and odd numbers of steps, if the peg is placed initially in the position A.

13 Indicate the form of the transition matrices corresponding to the transition diagrams in Exercise 21B, question 8, using the symbol * to indicate any non-zero entry.

Repeat this with the redrawn transition diagrams, in which outcomes in the same class are placed next to each other. What feature of the matrices distinguishes (a) a closed class, (b) a transient class?

14 Show that the Markov model illustrated in Fig. 10 has a transition matrix $\mathbf{T}$ which can be rearranged and partitioned into the form $\begin{bmatrix} \mathbf{P} & \vdots & \mathbf{Q} \\ \hline \mathbf{O} & \vdots & \mathbf{R} \end{bmatrix}$, where $\mathbf{P}$ and $\mathbf{R}$ are square matrices and the matrix $\mathbf{O}$ consists entirely of zeros. Write down the matrices $\mathbf{T}^2, \mathbf{T}^3$ and $\mathbf{T}^4$, and suggest the limiting form of $\mathbf{T}^n$. Can you prove that this is correct?

15 Show that the Markov model illustrated in Fig. 11 has a transition matrix $\mathbf{T}$ which can be partitioned into the form $\begin{bmatrix} \mathbf{P} & \vdots & \mathbf{Q} \\ \hline \mathbf{O} & \vdots & \mathbf{R} \end{bmatrix}$, where $\mathbf{P}$ and $\mathbf{R}$ are square matrices, the matrix $\mathbf{O}$ consists entirely of zeros, and at least one of the columns of $\mathbf{R}$ has a sum less than 1. Write down expressions for $\mathbf{T}^2$ and $\mathbf{T}^3$. What does this suggest about the form of $\mathbf{T}^n$?

21.6 A GEOMETRICAL INTERPRETATION

The representation of outcome probabilities in column matrices leads to the suggestion that they might be shown diagrammatically by points having these matrices as position vectors. Suppose, for example, that a model has three possible outcomes A, B, C; then the probabilities after n steps can be represented by a 3-dimensional vector with components $\begin{bmatrix} P(A_n) \\ P(B_n) \\ P(C_n) \end{bmatrix}$. Since the sum of the three probabilities is 1, the point having this as a position vector must lie in the plane $x + y + z = 1$; and since the probabilities are all positive or zero, the

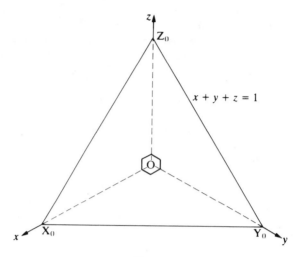

Figure 14

point is restricted to that part of the plane in the positive octant, which is bounded by an equilateral triangle denoted by $X_0 Y_0 Z_0$ in Fig. 14.

The points X_0, Y_0, Z_0 themselves correspond to the outcome matrices $\begin{bmatrix} 1 \\ 0 \\ 0 \end{bmatrix}$,

$\begin{bmatrix} 0 \\ 1 \\ 0 \end{bmatrix}$, $\begin{bmatrix} 0 \\ 0 \\ 1 \end{bmatrix}$, and can be thought of as three possibilities for the initial

probability vector $\mathbf{p}_0$. But in fact they enable us to follow what happens with *any* initial probability vector, since

$$\begin{bmatrix} P(A_0) \\ P(B_0) \\ P(C_0) \end{bmatrix} = P(A_0) \begin{bmatrix} 1 \\ 0 \\ 0 \end{bmatrix} + P(B_0) \begin{bmatrix} 0 \\ 1 \\ 0 \end{bmatrix} + P(C_0) \begin{bmatrix} 0 \\ 0 \\ 1 \end{bmatrix},$$

which is the centroid of 'masses' $P(A_0)$ at X_0, $P(B_0)$ at Y_0, $P(C_0)$ at Z_0. If the linear transformation $\mathbf{T}$ takes X_0, Y_0, Z_0 to X_1, Y_1, Z_1, then $\mathbf{p}_1 = \mathbf{T}\mathbf{p}_0$ is simply represented by the centroid of the same masses located at X_1, Y_1, Z_1 – and so on at each subsequent step. So it is enough to follow the points X_0, Y_0, Z_0 through the sequence of transformations, and then to put them together at the end by finding the centroid appropriate to the given initial probabilities.

As an illustration, let us apply the method with the transition matrix in

Example 6 (see §21.5). At the first step the vectors $\begin{bmatrix} 1 \\ 0 \\ 0 \end{bmatrix}$, $\begin{bmatrix} 0 \\ 1 \\ 0 \end{bmatrix}$, $\begin{bmatrix} 0 \\ 0 \\ 1 \end{bmatrix}$ are transformed to $\begin{bmatrix} \frac{1}{3} \\ \frac{1}{3} \\ \frac{1}{3} \end{bmatrix}$, $\begin{bmatrix} \frac{1}{2} \\ \frac{1}{2} \\ 0 \end{bmatrix}$, $\begin{bmatrix} \frac{1}{2} \\ \frac{1}{3} \\ \frac{1}{6} \end{bmatrix}$. Taking these as position vectors gives the

points X_1, Y_1, Z_1 shown in Fig. 15. (You should check for yourself that you understand how the plotting is carried out on this triangular grid. For convenience, the sides of the small triangles are $\frac{1}{36}$ of those of the large triangle $X_0 Y_0 Z_0$, so that for the first two steps all the points representing outcome probabilities are located at points of the grid.)

Notice that, because all the numbers in the matrix T are between 0 and 1, the transformation has the effect of closing up the 'orthogonal trihedron' $OX_0 Y_0 Z_0$ bounded by the three coordinate planes into a trihedron $OX_1 Y_1 Z_1$ which is much more sharp-pointed at O.

What happens at the next stage? When the transformation T is applied again, the points X_1, Y_1, Z_1 (which form a triangle inside $X_0 Y_0 Z_0$) move to points X_2, Y_2, Z_2 inside the triangle $X_1 Y_1 Z_1$. This is also shown in Fig. 15; notice that, in

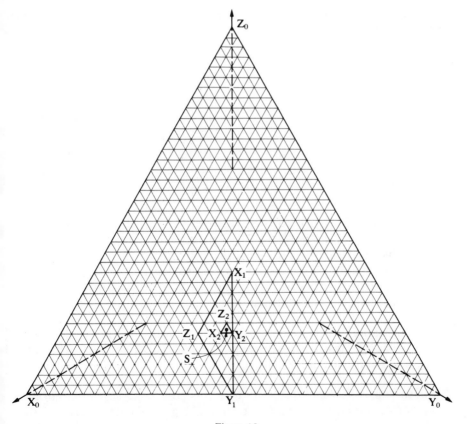

Figure 15

the sense of affine geometry (that is, properties involving ratios and parallels) $X_2Y_2Z_2$ is related to $X_1Y_1Z_1$ in just the same way as $X_1Y_1Z_1$ is to $X_0Y_0Z_0$. For example, Y_1 is the mid-point of X_0Y_0, and Y_2 is the mid-point of X_1Y_1.

Q.17   How is the point X_1 related to triangle $X_0Y_0Z_0$, and X_2 to $X_1Y_1Z_1$? Which sides of triangle $X_1Y_1Z_1$ are parallel to sides of $X_0Y_0Z_0$, and which sides of $X_2Y_2Z_2$ are parallel to sides of $X_1Y_1Z_1$?

As this process goes on, we get a sequence of smaller and smaller triangles, each inside the one before, converging eventually on a single point S which represents the steady probabilities $\frac{15}{35}$, $\frac{14}{35}$, $\frac{6}{35}$. It is clear from this picture why the limiting probabilities do not depend on the initial probabilities in this example; for since the original triangle closes down on to a single point, the centroid of masses $P(A_0)$, $P(B_0)$, $P(C_0)$, which lies inside the original triangle, must also converge to that point.

It is interesting to go further, and to put some numerical values on the relative areas of the triangles $X_0Y_0Z_0$, $X_1Y_1Z_1$, $X_2Y_2Z_2$, ... Since the tetrahedron $OX_0Y_0Z_0$ is transformed by **T** into $OX_1Y_1Z_1$, the volume of the latter is det **T** times the volume of the former. But, regarding O as the apex of each tetrahedron, and the plane $x + y + z = 1$ as the base, they both have the same perpendicular height. So the area of triangle $X_1Y_1Z_1$ is det **T** times the area of the triangle $X_0Y_0Z_0$ – and similarly from each triangle to the next as the sequence progresses.

Now the value of det **T** is equal to the product of the eigenvalues (see Exercise 21C, question 10), which in this example are 1, $\frac{1}{6}$ and $-\frac{1}{6}$; so det $\mathbf{T} = -\frac{1}{36}$. Each triangle is therefore $\frac{1}{36}$ of its predecessor in area.

Q.18   What is the significance of the negative sign in this example? How does it show up in Fig. 15?

One last point which it is interesting to note is that, if at any stage in the sequence a triangle is reached which is *strictly inside* the original triangle (as $X_2Y_2Z_2$ is in Fig. 15, but not $X_1Y_1Z_1$), then convergence to a single steady point is inevitable. The only way in which one can get the exceptional behaviour which has been noted in some examples is by having a sequence of triangles in which at least one vertex of each triangle lies on the perimeter of the original triangle $X_0Y_0Z_0$. This property can be stated:

If in a Markov model some power of the transition matrix contains no zeros amongst its entries, then the probabilities converge to the values of the steady probabilities.

However, the converse of this is not true: it is possible to have a zero in every power of **T** but for the probabilities still to converge. (See Exercise 21D, question 3(*b*).)

Exercise 21D

1 Illustrate Example 2 (see §21.3) with a diagram like Fig. 15. What is the smallest power of the transition matrix which contains no zeros?

2 Illustrate the situation described in Exercise 21B, question 6 with a diagram like Fig. 15.

3 Draw diagrams to illustrate the Markov models with the following transition matrices:

$$(a) \begin{bmatrix} 0 & \frac{1}{2} & \frac{3}{4} \\ \frac{1}{2} & 0 & 0 \\ \frac{1}{2} & \frac{1}{2} & \frac{1}{4} \end{bmatrix}; \quad (b) \begin{bmatrix} \frac{1}{2} & 0 & 0 \\ \frac{1}{4} & \frac{3}{4} & \frac{1}{2} \\ \frac{1}{4} & \frac{1}{4} & \frac{1}{2} \end{bmatrix}; \quad (c) \begin{bmatrix} 1 & 0 & 0 \\ 0 & \frac{3}{4} & \frac{1}{2} \\ 0 & \frac{1}{4} & \frac{1}{2} \end{bmatrix}; \quad (d) \begin{bmatrix} 0 & 1 & 0 \\ 0 & 0 & 1 \\ 1 & 0 & 0 \end{bmatrix}$$

For which of these models is it true that the outcome probabilities tend to a limit which is independent of the initial probabilities?

4 Draw diagrams to illustrate:
(a) Lucy's visit to the fete (Example 4) if she goes with just 20p in her pocket;
(b) Example 3 if there are just three holes in the pegboard;
(c) the random walk problem (Example 5) if the pub lies immediately between home and the jail.

5 With a four-outcome model the equilateral triangle $X_0 Y_0 Z_0$ is replaced by an equilateral tetrahedron $W_0 X_0 Y_0 Z_0$ (a section of four-dimensional space intersected by the hyperplane $w + x + y + z = 1$). Use a sequence of tetrahedra to illustrate:
(a) Lucy's visit to the fete if she goes with just 30p in her pocket;
(b) Example 3 with four holes in the pegboard;
(c) the random walk problem if home is two doors up the street from the pub and the jail is next door to the pub down the street.

21.7 GLOBAL METHODS

In the random walk problem (§21.3, Example 5) there were two absorbing outcomes (see §21.4): home and jail. When the customer leaves the pub at closing time, what are the probabilities that he will reach each of these destinations?

With a six-outcome model such as this, the methods described so far in this chapter would not be at all pleasant to handle; and in any case the transition matrix turns out to have a repeated eigenvalue 1, and there is not a unique steady vector. So there is a strong incentive to find a method of solution which avoids having to find formulae for the outcome probabilities.

One way of doing this is to select a particular outcome, H say, and find equations for the probabilities that he will end up there (rather than in jail) from each of the other houses. For example, when he is at the pub there is a certain probability (which we will denote by h_p) that he will eventually reach H from P. The important point is that this probability is the same each time he arrives at the pub in the course of his walk, since by definition our customer has no memory! Similarly, there are probabilities h_X, h_Y, h_Z that he will eventually reach home from X, Y and Z. (But note that there is no need to define h_j; if he reaches the jail, he has no chance at all of sleeping in his own bed that night. Or, put another way, h_J can be defined as zero; and by a similar convention, $h_H = 1$.)

Now, referring to Fig. 9, his next walk from the pub takes him to either Y or Z, each with probability $\frac{1}{2}$. Fig. 16 shows the relevant part of the Markov chain. So the probability that he reaches home from the pub can be calculated as

P(next call is Y) × P(he reaches home from Y)
+ P(next call is Z) × P(he reaches home from Z).

That is,

$$h_P = \tfrac{1}{2}h_Y + \tfrac{1}{2}h_Z.$$

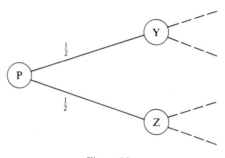

Figure 16

There is nothing special about the pub, and a similar argument can be used for each of the houses X, Y, Z. This gives the equations

$$h_X = \tfrac{1}{2}h_H + \tfrac{1}{2}h_Y = \tfrac{1}{2} + \tfrac{1}{2}h_Y \qquad \text{(since } h_H = 1\text{),}$$
$$h_Y = \tfrac{1}{2}h_X + \tfrac{1}{2}h_P,$$
$$h_Z = \tfrac{1}{2}h_P + \tfrac{1}{2}h_J = \tfrac{1}{2}h_P \qquad \text{(since } h_J = 0\text{).}$$

There are now four equations for the four unknowns h_X, h_Y, h_P, h_Z and it is a straightforward matter to find the solutions

$$h_X = 0.8, \; h_Y = 0.6, \; h_P = 0.4, \; h_Z = 0.2.$$

Q.19   Write and solve similar equations for j_X, j_Y, j_P, j_Z, the probabilities that the customer will eventually land up in jail from X, Y, P, Z.

How long will the customer take to reach his destination (whichever it is)? This question can be dealt with by a similar argument. Of course, the time (measured in numbers of moves from one location to the next) is a random variable, so the answer will have to be expressed in terms of expectation rather than as a definite number.

Referring again to Fig. 16, it takes him one move more to get indoors from P than it does from Y or Z, whichever door he knocks at next. So, denoting the number of moves from P until he is tucked up (either in his own bed or in his cell) by M_P, and similarly for the other starting points, we have the equation

$$E[M_P] = 1 + \tfrac{1}{2}E[M_Y] + \tfrac{1}{2}E[M_Z].$$

Just the same kind of argument can be used for walks starting from the other doors. Since $M_S = M_J = 0$, this leads to the equations

$$E[M_X] = 1 + \tfrac{1}{2}E[M_Y],$$
$$E[M_Y] = 1 + \tfrac{1}{2}E[M_X] + \tfrac{1}{2}E[M_P],$$
$$E[M_Z] = 1 + \tfrac{1}{2}E[M_P].$$

These four equations give the solutions $E[M_X] = E[M_Z] = 4$, $E[M_Y] = E[M_P] = 6$. So, starting from the pub, the expected number of doors the customer will call at in his walk is six.

Exercise 21E

1   In a game between two tennis players, the server has probability $\tfrac{3}{4}$ of winning each point. In one game the score reaches deuce. Show that after each subsequent point the score can be in any one of five possible states, and write down the transition matrix for the probabilities before and after a point is played. What is the probability that the server will eventually win the game?

   What is the expected number of points that will need to be played before the game is finished?

2   In Example 4 (§21.3) how many races can Lucy hope to bet on before she runs out of money? How many goldfish will she expect to take home?

3   In Example 2 (§21.3), when the Don says goodnight to Anna on Sunday evening, how many evenings does he expect to pass before he sees her again?

4   Write the four equations in §21.7 connecting the probabilities h_H, h_X, h_Y, h_P, h_Z, h_J, together with the two trivial equations $h_H = h_H$ and $h_J = h_J$, in a matrix form.

   If T denotes the transition matrix for this example, and **h** denotes the row matrix $[h_H \ h_X \ h_Y \ h_P \ h_Z \ h_J]$, show that $\mathbf{hT} = \mathbf{h}$.

5   When a stake of k pence is put into a certain gaming machine the machine pays out $2k$ pence with probability $\tfrac{1}{4}$ (and otherwise pays out nothing). I have twopence in my pocket and decide to gamble with it, in units of 1p, either until I have lost all my money or until I have fourpence in my pocket. Denoting by $S_n (0 \leqslant n \leqslant 4)$ the state of having n pence in my pocket, write down the transition matrix **T** between S_0, S_1, ..., S_4.

   If $x_n (0 \leqslant n \leqslant 4)$ denotes the probability of my eventually reaching state S_4, given that I started in S_n, explain why $x_0 = 0$ and $x_4 = 1$. Prove that

$$[x_0 \ x_1 \ x_2 \ x_3 \ x_4]\mathbf{T} = [x_0 \ x_1 \ x_2 \ x_3 \ x_4].$$

   Use these equations to calculate x_2. Hence show that, if I start in state S_2, I would do better to stake all my money in a single bet, rather than gamble in units of 1p.

   [SMP]

6   A biological population consists of individuals who have three different types T_1, T_2, T_3 of genetic make-up (which are independent of the sex of the individual

concerned). Thus six different mating combinations M_1, M_2, ..., M_6 are possible between pairs of individuals, as listed in the following table. The table also gives, for each mating combination, the probabilities of the types of offspring that can result from the mating.

		Offspring probabilities		
Mating	Parents	T_1	T_2	T_3
M_1	T_1, T_1	1	0	0
M_2	T_1, T_2	$\frac{1}{2}$	$\frac{1}{2}$	0
M_3	T_1, T_3	0	1	0
M_4	T_2, T_2	$\frac{1}{4}$	$\frac{1}{2}$	$\frac{1}{4}$
M_5	T_2, T_3	0	$\frac{1}{2}$	$\frac{1}{2}$
M_6	T_3, T_3	0	0	1

Suppose now that when these offspring reach maturity they mate randomly, but only with partners who had the same type of parents as themselves. Show that the offspring of an M_4 mating would then be involved in matings of types M_1, M_2, ..., M_6 with probabilities $\frac{1}{16}, \frac{1}{4}, \frac{1}{8}, \frac{1}{4}, \frac{1}{4}, \frac{1}{16}$ respectively. Interpreting these probabilities as being the elements in the appropriate column of the transition matrix of a Markov process with states $M_1, M_2, ..., M_6$, complete the remaining columns of this matrix.
   If $x_k (k = 1, 2, ..., 6)$ denotes the probability that, starting from a mating of type M_k, the process will eventually end up with matings all of type M_1, explain why $x_1 = 1$ and $x_6 = 0$. Show that

$$x_2 = \tfrac{1}{4}x_1 + \tfrac{1}{2}x_2 + \tfrac{1}{4}x_4.$$

Write down three more equations of this type, and hence evaluate the remaining probabilities $x_k (k = 2, 3, 4, 5)$. [SMP]

7 A Markov model with three possible outcomes A, B, C has initial outcome probabilities 0, 0, 1 and transition matrix

$$T = \begin{bmatrix} 1 & 0.1 & 0.2 \\ 0 & 0.3 & 0.6 \\ 0 & 0.6 & 0.2 \end{bmatrix}, \text{ which can be partitioned as } \begin{bmatrix} 1 & * & * \\ 0 & & \\ 0 & & Q \end{bmatrix}.$$

(a) Identify the transient class and the absorbing outcome.
(b) Evaluate T^2 and T^3, and show that T^n has the form

$$\begin{bmatrix} 1 & * & * \\ 0 & & \\ 0 & & Q^n \end{bmatrix}.$$

(c) Introduce the notation

$$\begin{bmatrix} 1 & * & r_n \\ 0 & * & \uparrow \\ 0 & * & \begin{matrix} s_n \\ \downarrow \end{matrix} \end{bmatrix}$$

for $\mathbf{T}^n$; so that, starting from C, r_n is the probability that after n steps the outcome is A, and s_n is the probability that it is B or C. Prove that the probability that the absorbing outcome is reached at the nth step is $1 - s_1$ when $n = 1$, and $s_{n-1} - s_n$ when $n > 1$.

(d) Prove that the expected number of steps before the absorbing outcome is reached is $1 + s_1 + s_2 + \dots$, and that this is the sum of the elements in the column corresponding to the outcome C in the matrix $\mathbf{I} + \mathbf{Q} + \mathbf{Q}^2 + \dots$

(e) Explain why the infinite series of matrices in (d) has sum $(\mathbf{I} - \mathbf{Q})^{-1}$.

(f) For the given transition matrix $\mathbf{T}$, find $(\mathbf{I} - \mathbf{Q})^{-1}$, and hence find the expected number of steps required to reach the absorbing outcome.

(g) Check your answer to (f) by using the method described at the end of §21.7.

8 Apply the method outlined in question 7 to find the number of races Lucy can expect to bet on in Example 4 (§21.3) in the cases where Lucy goes to the fete with (a) just 20p in her pocket, (b) just 30p in her pocket.

9 By partitioning the transition matrix for Example 5 (§21.3) in the form

$$
\begin{bmatrix}
1 & \vdots & * & * & * & * & \vdots & 0 \\
\hline
0 & \vdots & & & & & \vdots & 0 \\
0 & \vdots & & & & & \vdots & 0 \\
0 & \vdots & & \mathbf{Q} & & & \vdots & 0 \\
0 & \vdots & & & & & \vdots & 0 \\
\hline
0 & \vdots & * & * & * & * & \vdots & 1
\end{bmatrix},
$$

show that the procedure outlined in question 7 can be extended to this example in which there are two absorbing outcomes. Use this method to obtain the values of $E[M_X]$, $E[M_Y]$, $E[M_P]$, $E[M_Z]$ found at the end of §21.7.

10 Apply the method outlined in questions 7 and 9 to the problem in the second paragraph of question 1.

21.8 MORE APPLICATIONS OF THE TRANSITION MATRIX

Some of the questions in Exercise 21E (4–5 and 7–10 respectively) suggest how the two problems discussed in §21.7 can be tackled using the transition matrix. We end this chapter with general statements of the procedures used in these questions.

In a Markov model with more than one absorbing outcome, the probabilities of arriving finally at a particular absorbing outcome from various states in the transient class(es) are elements of a row matrix $\mathbf{x}$ (with one element for each possible outcome) satisfying the equation

$$\mathbf{x}\mathbf{T} = \mathbf{x}$$

where the element of $\mathbf{x}$ corresponding to the chosen absorbing outcome is 1, and the elements for the other absorbing outcomes are 0.

In a Markov model with at least one absorbing outcome (or closed class), let $\mathbf{Q}$ denote the minor matrix of $\mathbf{T}$ containing only the rows and columns corresponding to outcomes in the transient class(es). Then the expected number of steps needed to reach an absorbing outcome (or closed class) from one of these states is given by the sum of the elements in the appropriate column of the matrix $(\mathbf{I} - \mathbf{Q})^{-1}$.

Revision exercise C

1   In a certain population, the heights of men are normally distributed with mean
    172 cm and standard deviation 10 cm, and the heights of women are normally
    distributed with mean 165 cm and standard deviation 8 cm. Calculate the probabi-
    lity that
    (a) a man chosen at random is taller than 180 cm,
    (b) a man and a woman chosen at random are both taller than 180 cm,
    (c) of a man and a woman chosen at random neither is taller than 180 cm,
    (d) a man chosen at random is taller than a woman chosen at random.
                                                                            [Cambridge]

2   The heights of men can be assumed to be normally distributed with standard
    deviation 0.11 m.
        In 1928 the mean height of men in a certain city was 1.72 m. In a survey in 1978 the
    mean height of a random sample of 16 men from the same city was 1.77 m. On the
    hypothesis that the population mean height has not changed, calculate the probabi-
    lity of obtaining a sample mean height greater than that measured.
        In another survey in 1978 the mean height of a random sample of 32 men from a
    second city was 1.73 m. Assuming that the population mean heights are the same in
    the two cities, calculate the probability that a difference in sample mean heights
    greater than that measured would be obtained.   [MEI]

3   Two machines, A and B, fill sugar bags. The bags from machine A have mean mass
    1005 g with standard deviation 1.5 g; those from machine B have mean mass 1006 g
    with standard deviation 2.0 g. The masses of the bags from each machine have a
    normal distribution. A bag is taken at random from each machine. Calculate the
    probability that the bag from machine B is the lighter.
        Bags are packed into cases, with 25 bags from each machine being put into every
    case. Calculate 99 % probability limits for the total mass of contents of a case.
                                                                            [Cambridge]

4   The number of vehicles passing a given point on one of the carriageways of a
    motorway in any one-minute interval may be modelled by a Poisson distribution.
    The unknown parameter λ of this distribution may be estimated by keeping count of
    the numbers of vehicles that pass in several one-minute intervals. In a traffic survey
    60 such observations were made, and their mean was found to be 20.1 vehicles per
    minute. Let λ_1 be the smallest estimate, and λ_2 the largest estimate of λ that would be
    consistent, each at the $2\frac{1}{2}$ % probability level, with this observed mean passage rate.
    Prove that λ_1, λ_2 are the roots of a quadratic equation of the form

$$x^2 - 2(a + b)x + a^2 = 0.$$

    Show that, for these values of a and b, the roots are given to a good approximation
    by $x \approx (a + b) \pm \sqrt{(2ab)}$, and hence find λ_1 and λ_2.
        About how many additional observations would be required to reduce the
    difference $\lambda_2 - \lambda_1$ between the estimates to 2?   [SMP]

5   The continuous random variable X has probability density function

$$\phi(x) = \begin{cases} 30x^2(1-x)^2 & \text{for } 0 \leqslant x \leqslant 1, \\ 0 & \text{elsewhere.} \end{cases}$$

Sketch the graph of $\phi(x)$, and find the mean of X. Obtain also the variance of X.
    Find the probability that X takes a value within 0.1 of its mean. Find also the probability that the mean of 20 independent observations from this distribution takes a value within 0.1 of its mean. [MEI]

6   The probability density function of χ^2 with four degrees of freedom is $Cxe^{-x/2}$ $(0 \leqslant x < \infty)$. Find the value of C. If χ_0^2 satisfies

$$\int_0^{\chi_0^2} Cxe^{-x/2}\, dx = 0.95,$$

show that $(2\chi_0^2 + 4)\exp(-\tfrac{1}{2}\chi_0^2) = 0.2$, and verify that an approximate solution of this equation is $\chi_0^2 = 9.49$. Explain the usefulness of this result.
    A group of 300 people is classified according to their occupations and smoking habits while at work. The results are shown in the table.

	Cigarette smoker	Cigar or pipe smoker	Non-smoker
Manual worker	36	10	74
Office worker	23	16	61
Executive	22	25	33

Test at the 95% level of significance whether there is any association between occupation and smoking habits, and comment on your answer. [MEI]

7   A factory manufactures a certain type of machine. During one week the numbers of machines produced each day were 37, 40, 43, 39, 36. Assuming this to be a random sample from a normal distribution, calculate symmetrical 95% confidence limits for the mean daily production.
    Some time later a new production method was tried, and over a ten-day period the numbers of machines produced were 38, 45, 47, 45, 39, 38, 43, 45, 42, 38. Carry out a significance test on the two sets of production figures to determine whether the new production rate is significantly different from the old. [Cambridge]

8   A machine is producing a continuous wire. If δt is small, the probability of a length δt m containing a defect is $0.005\,\delta t$. The probabilities of any two sections having a defect are independent. By considering a long length x m, explain why the probability of 0, 1, 2, ... defects in that long length is given by a Poisson process of parameter $0.005x$.
    Find the probability of the tenth fault being more than 3100 m from the start. [SMP]

9   Past experience has shown that a certain machine, which can cut hacksaw blades to any required length, produces blades whose lengths are normally distributed with variance $0.003\,\text{cm}^2$. An order for hacksaw blades of length 18 cm is received, and the first four blades produced when the machine is set to 18 cm have lengths 17.98, 17.82, 17.91 and 18.09 cm. Test whether the machine setting is giving significantly low values. [SMP]

10 A man on holiday spends his nights at camps A, B, C or D. Each day he walks out and either returns or goes to another camp for the next night. The probabilities of his movements are given by the transition matrix

$$\begin{bmatrix} \frac{2}{3} & \frac{1}{2} & \frac{1}{4} & \frac{1}{3} \\ \frac{1}{3} & 0 & 0 & 0 \\ 0 & \frac{1}{2} & \frac{3}{4} & 0 \\ 0 & 0 & 0 & \frac{2}{3} \end{bmatrix}.$$

Name (a) any closed classes, and (b) any transient classes, which exist in this system.

Find the expected number of consecutive nights he will spend at A if he has just arrived there. [SMP]

11 At a certain weather station a simplified record of the weather is kept in which, at the end of each day, the day's weather is recorded as fine (F), dull (D), or wet (W). The record for 44 consecutive days was

FFFF FFFD DDFD WDDW WDFF FDDD DFFD DFDD DWDF
DDWW WWDW.

By using a model in which each day's weather depends on, and only on, that of the day before, and in which the transition probabilities are taken directly from the observed proportions, show that the probabilities of a previously fixed day displaying each type of weather when the previous day's weather is not known, are given by $F : \frac{5}{17}$, $D : \frac{8}{17}$ and $W : \frac{4}{17}$. Discuss, without formal tests, the degree of agreement between the frequencies expected from these probabilities and the observed frequencies of each type of weather.

Calculate also the expected number of nights to elapse between the recording of a fine day and the recording of the next wet day. [SMP]

12 The following is a model of a simple diffusion process. The hollow vessels A, B contain a total of n molecules of gas. The vessels are connected by a narrow tube through which one molecule at a time is able to pass from one vessel to the other. When there are n_A molecules in vessel A, the probability that the next molecule to change vessels moves from A to B is equal to n_A/n. If S_r denotes the state defined by $n_A = r$ $(r = 0, 1, \ldots, n)$, write down the matrix of transition probablities between S_0, $S_1, \ldots, S_n$.

Deduce that if $u_0, u_1, \ldots, u_n$ are the stationary probabilities for the process then

$$u_1 = nu_0,$$
$$ru_r = nu_{r-1} - (n + 2 - r)u_{r-2} \quad \text{for } 2 \leqslant r \leqslant n - 1,$$
$$nu_n = u_{n-1}.$$

Verify that these equations are satisfied by

$$u_r = \binom{n}{r}u_0 \quad \text{for} \quad 0 \leqslant r \leqslant n,$$

and deduce that

$$u_r = \binom{n}{r}2^{-n}.$$

Show that if $n = 10^6$ then, after this stationary probability distribution has been set up, the probability of n_A differing from 500 000 by more than 1000 is somewhat less than 5%. [SMP]

Project exercises C

C1 IT ALWAYS RAINS ON THURSDAY

The following letter appeared in *The Times* some years ago:

"Sir,
The title 'wettest day of the week' stays with Thursday as my 20-year rainfall totals 1954/73 show:

Thursday	74.03 inches
Saturday	71.57 inches
Monday	70.90 inches
Tuesday	70.35 inches
Sunday	68.36 inches
Wednesday	63.34 inches
Friday	62.20 inches
	480.76 inches

Yours faithfully, G. NICHOLSON, Teddington, Middlesex."

A possible model for the daily rainfall at Teddington might be as follows. There is a probability $1 - \lambda$ that a day is completely dry, and a probability λ that some rain falls; and on a day when it rains, the probability density for the amount of rain that falls (X inches) is proportional to $x^2 e^{-ax}$ (the constant of proportion being chosen to make the total probability equal to 1).

1   Explain why this might be a reasonable model. On this basis, show that the mean and variance of the daily rainfall are $3\lambda/a$ and $3\lambda(4 - 3\lambda)/a^2$.

2   It seems not unreasonable to assume that the rainfall on any Yday (where Y is a variable which may take the values Sun, Mon, Tues, Wednes, Thurs, Fri or Satur) is independent of that on any other Yday. On this assumption, taking Mr Nicholson's 20 years to consist of 1043 complete weeks, what does the model suggest for the mean and variance (in terms of a and λ) of the total rainfall over all the Ydays of the period of his observations?

3   Guessing that λ has the value 0.4, and equating the mean daily rainfall in the model to the actual mean daily rainfall over the 20-year period, find numerical values for the mean and variance of the total rainfall over all the Ydays of this period.

4   Regarding the seven possible values of Y as providing a sample of seven values of the mean Yday rainfall, calculate the bounds within which the variance of such a sample might reasonably lie.

5   What comment would you make on the implications of Mr Nicholson's letter in the light of these calculations?

6   Investigate the effect of making a different guess for the value of λ.

440

C2 ONE HYPOTHESIS TEST FOR THE PRICE OF TWO

Two driving schools both prepare novice drivers for the driving test. School A has 300 learners, and a 27% pass rate; school B has 200 learners, of whom 34% pass. Assuming that, at the outset, all the customers have an equally good chance of reaching pass standard, do these figures justify a claim by school B that its teaching is more effective?

1   This is one of the types of problem discussed in §16.9. Use the method described there to test the hypothesis that, when they take the driving test, there is no difference in the probability of passing for candidates from school A and those from school B. (Use a two-tail test.)

2   The hypothesis could also be tested by making a two-way table for the numbers of candidates who pass and fail from each of the schools, and using chi-squared probability tables. Does this lead to the same conclusion?

3   Find an arithmetical connection between the value of the test-statistic which you calculated in question 1 and the discrepancy which you calculated in question 2. Use the definition of chi-squared probability (with one degree of freedom) given in §18.1 to show that the two methods give the same probability that the result recorded could have occurred by chance.

4   The results of questions 1–3 suggest that the two methods used to solve this problem may be equivalent to each other. To investigate this in general, suppose that school A has n_1 customers, of which a proportion p_1 pass and a proportion q_1 ($= 1 - p_1$) fail; and that for school B the corresponding statistics are n_2, p_2, q_2.
(a) Express the test-statistic you used in question 1 algebraically.
(b) Express the discrepancy you calculated in question 2 algebraically.

5   Use the answers to 4(a) and (b) to complete the argument that the same probability of chance occurrence will always be found by the two methods.

C3 KENDALL'S COEFFICIENT OF RANK CORRELATION

A method of measuring the correlation between two different rankings of a set of individuals, due to the psychologist C. Spearman, was introduced in Exercise 20A, questions 9–13. More recently the statistician M. G. Kendall proposed another way of measuring rank correlation, based on a totally different idea. One advantage of Kendall's method is that it is easier to investigate the significance of the value of his coefficient.

The process of ranking may be regarded as making a judgement on relative merit between each pair of individuals in the set. For example, if a taster is ranking four wines A,B,C,D, then she is making a preference of one wine or the other within each of the pairs

A,B ; A,C ; A,D ; B,C ; B,D ; C,D.

If there are two tasters, then on each of the pair preferences they may either agree or disagree. For example, if for one taster the order of merit is ABCD, and for the other it is BDAC, then they can be compared as follows:

Agreements   A,C ; B,C ; B,D
Disagreements   A,B ; A,D ; C,D

Let us denote the difference

number of agreements − number of disagreements

by the symbol δ.

1 If there were n wines, how many pairs would there be? What would be the largest and smallest possible values of δ? How must the two rankings be related to give these values of δ?

2 Consider the special cases where there are just (i) 2, (ii) 3, (iii) 4 wines. Suppose that for one taster the ranking is (i) AB, (ii) ABC, (iii) ABCD. Write down in each case all the possible rankings for the other taster, and for each of these calculate the value of δ. Show that the numbers of occurrences of the various possible values of δ are:

Value of δ:	-6	-5	-4	-3	-2	-1	0	1	2	3	4	5	6	Total
$n = 2$							1	1						2
$n = 3$				1		2		2		1				6
$n = 4$	1		3		5		6		5		3		1	24

3 To see how this table can be built up, it is helpful to extend it by inserting zeros to right and left. Verify that each line can then be calculated from the line above as illustrated in the diagram below:

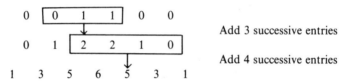

Add 3 successive entries

Add 4 successive entries

Assuming that this rule can be continued, calculate the rows for $n = 5$ and $n = 6$.

4 Note that, from each of the six possible arrangements of the letters A,B,C when $n = 3$, four arrangements of the letters A,B,C,D when $n = 4$ can be obtained, as illustrated by the following example:

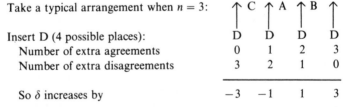

Take a typical arrangement when $n = 3$:	↑ C	↑ A	↑ B	↑
Insert D (4 possible places):	D	D	D	D
Number of extra agreements	0	1	2	3
Number of extra disagreements	3	2	1	0
So δ increases by	-3	-1	1	3

Use this argument to justify the method of building up the table suggested in question 3.

5 It is conventional to define coefficients of correlation so that the values lie between -1 (perfect negative correlation) to 1 (perfect positive correlation). With this in mind, *Kendall's coefficient of rank correlation*, usually denoted by τ, is defined as

$$\tau = \frac{\delta}{\frac{1}{2}n(n-1)}.$$

Draw graphs to show the probability distribution of τ for $n = 2, 3, \ldots, 6$, if the first taster places her wines in alphabetical order and the second taster allocates his rankings at random.

6 Show that the probability distributions in question 5 are given by the probability generators

$$G(t) = \frac{t^{-\alpha} + t^{\alpha}}{2} \quad \text{when } n = 2,$$

$$G(t) = \frac{t^{-\alpha} + t^{\alpha}}{2} \times \frac{t^{-2\alpha} + t^0 + t^{2\alpha}}{3} \quad \text{when } n = 3,$$

$$G(t) = \frac{t^{-\alpha} + t^{\alpha}}{2} \times \frac{t^{-2\alpha} + t^0 + t^{2\alpha}}{3} \times \frac{t^{-3\alpha} + t^{-\alpha} + t^{\alpha} + t^{3\alpha}}{4} \quad \text{when } n = 4,$$

where $\alpha = 1/\{\frac{1}{2}n(n-1)\}$. Explain this in terms of the method of building up the table described in question 3.

7 Show that, in general,

$$G(t) = \frac{(t^{2\alpha} - t^{-2\alpha})(t^{3\alpha} - t^{-3\alpha}) \dots (t^{n\alpha} - t^{-n\alpha})}{n! \, (t^{\alpha} - t^{-\alpha})^{n-1}}.$$

8 Deduce from question 7 an expression for the moment generator for Kendall's rank correlation coefficient. Dividing each factor by $2\alpha u$, show that this can be written in the form

$$M(u) = \prod_{i=1}^{n} \left(\frac{\sinh i\alpha u}{i\alpha u}\right) \bigg/ \left(\frac{\sinh \alpha u}{\alpha u}\right)^n.$$

[The symbol Π means "the product of factors such as ..."; that is, it is the analogue for products of the symbol Σ for sums.]

9 The point of expressing $M(u)$ in the form given in question 8 is to make it possible to use the Taylor approximation

$$\ln \frac{\sinh x}{x} \approx \frac{1}{6}x^2 - \frac{1}{180}x^4 \quad \text{when } x \text{ is small.}$$

Prove this result, and use it to find a Taylor approximation (as far as the term in u^4) for $\ln M(u)$. [You will probably find it useful to know the result $\Sigma_{i=1}^n i^4 - n = \frac{1}{30}n(n-1)(6n^3 + 21n^2 + 31n + 31).$]

10 Deduce that, when n is large,

$$\tau \sqrt{\frac{9n(n-1)}{2(2n+5)}}$$

is distributed with approximately standard normal probability density. By referring back to question 5, find how good this approximation is when $n = 6$.

11 Rework Exercise 20A, questions 10–13, using Kendall's coefficient of rank correlation rather than Spearman's.

C4 WILCOXON'S RANK SUM TEST

In Chapter 19, Example 4, a t-test was used to determine, from two samples of measurements, whether the mean of one population is significantly different from the mean of another. It is sometimes useful to try to answer a similar question from data which are in the form of rankings rather than actual measurements. An appropriate test to use is then *Wilcoxon's rank sum test*. (Notice that this test is used when the samples are "unpaired"; a test for paired samples, also associated with the name of Wilcoxon, was described in §17.8.)

Suppose that in a school there are two parallel classes, A and B. Class A has m pupils and class B has n pupils. They are all given a test, and the $m + n$ children are ranked in order of merit on the results. The sum of the ranks of the children in class A is calculated, and denoted by the letter T.

1   Explain why this sum might be used to determine how, *as a class*, the children in class A compare with those in class B.

2   In how many ways is it possible to arrange m As and n Bs in a row? What are the least and the greatest possible values for T? How many different values of T might one get?

As an example, suppose that $m = 5$ and $n = 3$. [As a check on your answers to the questions above, there are then 56 possible arrangements of As and Bs, and there are 16 possible values for T.] One possible ranking arrangement is

Rank	1	2	3	4	5	6	7	8
Class	A	B	A	A	A	B	B	A

The value of T is then $1 + 3 + 4 + 5 + 8 = 21$. This arrangement could be represented in a diagram:

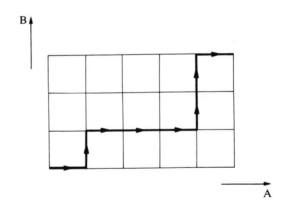

Make a copy of this diagram, and mark on it the points at the right end of each of the 'A' vectors. Write down the coordinates of these five points, and the ranks to which they correspond: how are these related? Use your answer to this question to verify that T can be calculated as

$$(1 + 2 + 3 + 4 + 5) + (0 + 1 + 1 + 1 + 3)$$
$$= 15 + (0 + 1 + 1 + 1 + 3).$$

Carry through a similar calculation for some other arrangements of five As and three Bs.

3   In general, show that T can be calculated as $\frac{1}{2}m(m + 1) + U$, where U is the sum of the total number of Bs to the left of each A (i.e. the sum of the "y-coordinates" of the points you have marked). (This quantity U is used as the basis of the "Mann-

Whitney U-test", which is an alternative form of the rank sum test.) If the number of Bs to the left of the ith A is denoted by b_i, then $U = \Sigma_{i=1}^n b_i$. Show that the b_i satisfy the conditions

$$0 \leqslant b_1 \leqslant b_2 \leqslant \ldots \leqslant b_{m-1} \leqslant b_m \leqslant n,$$

and deduce that $0 \leqslant U \leqslant mn$. Draw on your diagram the paths corresponding to the extreme values 0 and mn of U.

4   Write out in full each of the possible sequences b_i in the case $m = 5, n = 3$. Hence find the probability model for the value of U on the hypothesis that all arrangements of As and Bs are equally likely, and represent it graphically.

5   Write out in full all the possible sequences b_i in the cases $m = 4, n = 3$; $m = 3, n = 3$; $m = 2, n = 3$; $m = 1, n = 3$. Using these as examples, show that:
   (a) Any sequence for particular values of m and n which begins with $b_1 = 0$ corresponds directly to a similar sequence (beginning with b_2) for $m - 1$ and n with the same value of U.
   (b) Any sequence for particular values of m and n which begins with $b_1 = 1$ corresponds to a sequence (beginning with $b_2 = 1$) for $m - 1$ and $n - 1$ with the sum $U - m$. (For example, the sequence 1,1,2,3,3 with $m = 5$, $n = 3$ and $U = 10$ corresponds to 0,1,2,2 with $m = 4$, $n = 3$ and $U = 5$.)
   (c) More generally, any sequence for particular values of m and n which begins with $b_1 = r$ corresponds to a sequence (beginning with $b_2 = r$) for $m - 1$ and $n - r$ with the sum $U - rm$.

6   Let us now introduce the symbol $[U:m, n]$ to denote the number of arrangements of As and Bs that give a sum of U. Make tables of values, for the relevant values of U, for $[U:5,3]$, $[U:4,3]$, $[U:3,3]$, $[U:2,3]$ and $[U:1,3]$.
   Prove that

$$[U:m,n] = [U:m-1,n] + [U-m:m-1,n-1] + [U-2m:m-1,n-2] + \ldots$$

How far does this sum go on?
   Prove also that

$$[U:1,n] = \begin{cases} 1 & \text{if } 0 \leqslant U \leqslant n \\ 0 & \text{if } U > n; \end{cases}$$

and that

$$[0:m,n] = 1.$$

7   The next step is to define a generator for the *number of ways* (not yet for the probabilities) of getting a total of U. So we define a polynomial $G(t:m, n)$ to stand for

$$[0:m,n] + [1:m,n]t + [2:m,n]t^2 + \ldots + [mn:m,n]t^{mn}.$$

Use the results of question 6 to prove that

$$G(t:m,n) = G(t:m-1,n) + t^m G(t:m-1,n-1) + t^{2m} G(t:m-1,n-2) + \ldots + t^{nm} G(t:m-1,0),$$

and that

$$G(t:1,n) = \frac{1 - t^{n+1}}{1 - t}.$$

8 Deduce from the results of question 7 that

$$G(t:2,n) = \frac{(1 - t^{n+1})(1 - t^{n+2})}{(1 - t)(1 - t^2)}.$$

This suggests the generalisation

$$G(t:m, n) = \frac{(1 - t^{n+1})(1 - t^{n+2})\ldots(1 - t^{n+m})}{(1 - t)(1 - t^2)\ldots(1 - t^m)}.$$

Show that putting $m = 5$, $n = 3$ leads to the results you found in question 6 for $[U:5, 3]$.

9 The obvious way to try to prove the generalisation is to use mathematical induction (on the value of m). This is a difficult piece of algebra, so to lead into it try to prove the result for $m = 3$ from that for $m = 2$. Show that this involves establishing the subsidiary result

$$(1 - t^{n+1})(1 - t^{n+2}) + t^3(1 - t^n)(1 - t^{n+1}) + \ldots + t^{3n}(1 - t)(1 - t^2)$$
$$= \frac{(1 - t^{n+1})(1 - t^{n+2})(1 - t^{n+3})}{1 - t^3},$$

and prove this by induction (on the value of n).

By a similar argument, use mathematical induction to prove the full generalisation.

10 Show that a generator for the *probabilities* of getting the various possible values of U can be written in the form

$$t^{\frac{1}{2}mn} \prod_{i=1}^{m} \frac{t^{\frac{1}{2}(n+i)} - t^{-\frac{1}{2}(n+i)}}{n + i} \bigg/ \prod_{i=1}^{m} \frac{t^{\frac{1}{2}i} - t^{-\frac{1}{2}i}}{i}.$$

11 Write down a moment generator $M(w:m,n)$ for the random varible U, on the hypothesis that all arrangements of As and Bs are equally likely. (The letter w is used on this occasion for the dummy variable rather than the more usual u, to avoid confusion with U.) Show that

$$\ln M(w:m,n) = \tfrac{1}{2}mnw + \sum_{i=1}^{n} \left\{\ln \frac{\sinh \tfrac{1}{2}(n + i)w}{\tfrac{1}{2}(n + i)w} - \ln \frac{\sinh \tfrac{1}{2}iw}{\tfrac{1}{2}iw}\right\}.$$

Expand this in powers of w as far as the term in w^4, using the Taylor approximation for $\ln \dfrac{\sinh x}{x}$ given in Project exercise C3, question 9.

12 Show that for large values of m and n, on the hypothesis that all possible arrangements of As and Bs are equally likely,

$$\frac{U - \tfrac{1}{2}mn}{\sqrt{\{\tfrac{1}{12}mn(m + n + 1)\}}}, \text{ which is the same as } \frac{T - \tfrac{1}{2}m(m + n + 1)}{\sqrt{\{\tfrac{1}{12}mn(m + n + 1)\}}},$$

is distributed with approximately standard normal probability.

13 Use the result of question 12 to answer Exercise 19D, question 5 by an alternative method.

Appendix
Definitions and notation for sample statistics

It was explained in §15.7 that two alternative conventions are in use amongst statisticians for certain definitions concerning samples. They are sometimes described as the "n-convention" and the "$(n-1)$-convention", since they differ in dividing by n or by $n-1$ in the definition of the variance of a sample. The choice of convention then has consequences for the application of some statistical tests. In this book the n-convention has been adopted; but before using any other book, a calculator or a computer program it is important to find out which convention it is based on. Some of the differences between the two conventions are listed below.

n-convention	*(n − 1)-convention*
The variance of a sample is defined as	The variance of a sample is defined as
$$S^2 = \frac{1}{n} \sum_{i=1}^{k} (x_i - m)^2 f(x_i).$$	$$s^2 = \frac{1}{n-1} \sum_{i=1}^{k} (x_i - m)^2 f(x_i).$$
The standard deviation S is defined as the square root of the variance.	The standard deviation s is defined as the square root of the variance.
The unbiased variance estimator $\widehat{\sigma^2}$ is equal to $\dfrac{n}{n-1} S^2$.	The unbiased variance estimator $\widehat{\sigma^2}$ is equal to s^2.
When sampling from a normal population nS^2/σ^2 is distributed with chi-squared probability, and	When sampling from a normal population vs^2/σ^2 is distributed with chi-squared probability, and
$$(M - \mu)\sqrt{v}/S$$	$$(M - \mu)\sqrt{n}/s$$
is distributed with t-probability, both with $v = n - 1$ degrees of freedom.	is distributed with t-probability, both with $v = n - 1$ degrees of freedom.
For a sample of n pairs (x_i, y_i), the sample covariance is defined as	For a sample of n pairs (x_i, y_i), the sample covariance is defined as
$$C_{xy} = \frac{1}{n} \sum_{i=1}^{n} (x_i - m_x)(y_i - m_y).$$	$$c_{xy} = \frac{1}{n-1} \sum_{i=1}^{n} (x_i - m_x)(y_i - m_y).$$
The sample correlation coefficient $r = C_{xy}/S_x S_y$.	The sample correlation coefficient $r = c_{xy}/s_x s_y$.

Notes on the text

1.1 For example, SMP *Revised Advanced Mathematics, Books 1* and *2* (Cambridge University Press), Chapters 11 and 15.

1.2 These are dealt with in other books in the Further Mathematics series, particularly *Linear Algebra and Geometry* and *Extensions of Calculus*.

1.3 Sometimes it is more convenient to use $x_1, x_2, \ldots, x_k$ to denote all the *possible* measurements, whether or not they are actually taken by members of the sample. In this case k may be greater than n, and some of the $f(x_i)$ may be zero. For example, a die may be rolled five times, giving scores of 3,6,3,2,6; but it seems sensible to take $x_i = i$ for $i = 1,2,3,4,5,6$, so that $f(x_1) = f(x_4) = f(x_5) = 0, f(x_2) = 1, f(x_3) = f(x_6) = 2$, and $k = 6$, $n = 5$. The remaining definitions and formulae given in §1.1 still hold if this notation is adopted.

1.4 You should be warned that many statisticians prefer to define "sample variance" by dividing the sum by $n - 1$ rather than n, denoting the result by s^2 and calling s the "sample standard deviation". This is the reason for using capital letter S in this text. Some calculator and computer programs are based on this alternative definition, so it is important to beware of this complication. The reason will be seen later in §15.7.

1.5 You can read an English translation of this correspondence in D. E. Smith, *Source Book in Mathematics* (McGraw-Hill).

1.6 We use capital letters P, F for the probability or frequency of an "outcome" or "event", and small letters p, f for the probability or frequency of a "measurement" or "score". Compare the use of F(C) in §1.2 with that of $f(x_i)$ in §1.1. If the letter X is used to describe the measurement being made (we shall later call this a "random variable"), then "$X = x_i$" is an outcome, so that we can write $F(X = x_i) = f(x_i)$ and $P(X = x_i) = p(x_i)$.

1.7 Sir Harold Jeffreys, *Scientific Inference* (Cambridge University Press).

2.1 Professor Richard Stone, in an article on models of the national economy in the *Operational Research Quarterly* for 1963, described the idea of a model in the following words: "Every model is an abstraction designed to analyse a slice of life with the object of understanding it better and, if it is at all controllable, adapting it better to our wishes." The article is reprinted as Chapter 6 of his book *Mathematics in the Social Sciences* (Chapman & Hall).

2.2 It is not universally understood that "dice" is a plural word; the singular equivalent is "die" (as in the phrases "the die is cast" and "straight as a die").

2.3 Damon Runyon makes this point in his short story "Blood pressure" in *Guys and Dolls*: "The odds in any country in the world that a guy does not make a ten with a pair of dice before he rolls seven, is 2 to 1."

3.1 In Britain at the present time, there are rather more male than female births: between 51 % and 52 % of children born are boys. But these proportions vary from country to country, and may change over time.

3.2 The Bernoulli family could be described as "the Bachs of mathematics"; they produced distinguished mathematicians over three generations. An interesting account of their achievements is given in E. T. Bell, *Men of Mathematics* (Penguin).

3.3 Some writers restrict the use of the description "Bernoulli type" to sequences of experiments with only two outcomes, but there seems to be no advantage in making this limitation.

3.4 See, for example, SMP *Revised Advanced Mathematics, Book 1* (Cambridge University Press), Chapters 1 and 9, for a discussion of geometric progressions.

3.5 Label the k positions in which the objects are to be placed as $P_1, P_2, P_3, \ldots, P_k$. Any of the k objects can be placed in P_1; this leaves a choice of $k - 1$ to be placed in P_2, which in turn leaves a choice of $k - 2$ to be placed in P_3, and so on. When one reaches the final position P_k, there is only one object left to place in it. So the total number of arrangements is $k \times (k - 1) \times (k - 2) \times \ldots \times 3 \times 2 \times 1$.

3.6 See, for example, SMP *Revised Advanced Mathematics, Book 3* (Cambridge University Press), Chapter 30.

3.7 Although commonly attributed to Pascal (a French mathematician and philosopher who lived from 1623 to 1662), he was not the first person to make this diagram; he himself used it in his calculations on probability. In Carl B. Boyer, *History of Mathematics* (Wiley) its invention is traced back to a Chinese mathematician of the Sung dynasty, Chu Shih-chieh, in a work entitled "Precious Mirror" in 1303. About 100 years later it was used by the Arab al-Kashi in Samarkand, and it first appeared in the west in Germany on the title page of Peter Apian's "Rechnung" in 1527.

3.8 In using this illustration we have ignored the fact that there have been breaks in the record: in its early history the race was not rowed every year, and there were gaps during the two world wars when the race did not take place. Also, dead heats have been omitted from the list.

3.9 The experiment was carried out using a sequence of two-digit random numbers, and assigning the outcome A or B according as the number was between 00 and 45 or between 46 and 99. This technique is described in Chapter 5. To obtain a direct comparison with the boat race results, a block of random numbers was selected which gave almost the same frequencies of the outcomes A and B as the numbers of Oxford and Cambridge wins.

3.10 In this book the outcome probability matrices are written in column form, so that transition matrices have columns whose elements add to 1. This convention has been chosen because it is more likely to be familiar to those who have studied matrices at school. In specialised treatments of Markov chains, however, it is more common to write the equations in transposed form, so that outcome probabilities are presented in row matrices and transition matrices have row sums equal to 1. Thus the equation in the text would be set out in the form

$$[P(O_{n+1})\ P(C_{n+1})] = [P(O_n)\ P(C_n)] \begin{bmatrix} \dfrac{3}{5} & \dfrac{2}{5} \\ \dfrac{1}{3} & \dfrac{2}{3} \end{bmatrix}.$$

4.1 See, for example, SMP *Revised Advanced Mathematics, Books 1* and *2* (Cambridge University Press), Chapters 13 and 16. Alternatively, in this example, you could express the likelihood in terms of b, as

$$1225(1 - b)^2 b^{48} = 1225(b^{48} - 2b^{49} + b^{50}),$$

which can be differentiated directly as a polynomial function.

5.1   An informative article about the operation of ERNIE is J. L. Field, E. A. Johnston & J. C. Poole, "The mathematics of Premium Savings Bonds", *Bulletin of the Institute of Mathematics and its Applications*, vol. 15, nos. 5/6, May/June 1979.

5.2   You can see this method in use when the draw for the F.A. Cup is televised. Each team is given a number, and the fixtures are then decided by drawing numbered balls out of a bag.

5.3   Tables of random numbers are included, for example, in the *SMP Advanced Tables* and in the *Formulae for Advanced Mathematics with Statistical Tables*, both published by Cambridge University Press.

5.4   Computer programs are set out in a version of BASIC, although some details will vary according to the particular machine being used, so that readers may have to adapt the instructions for their own use. In operation it will, of course, be necessary for the lines to be numbered. The symbol RND(6) is used to stand for "a random number between 1 and 6".

6.1   The reason why the new critical values are not exactly 100 times as large is simply that, since l^2 is always a whole number, it was sufficient in §6.3 to give the critical values as the whole number next below the ones suggested by the theoretical probability model.

6.2   You will sometimes see or hear the discrepancy referred to as "chi-squared", and denoted by the symbol χ^2, but this is not really correct usage. This symbol should be reserved for the random variable in the theoretical probability model, which will be defined in Chapter 18.

6.3   This method was first published in 1900 by Karl Pearson (1857–1936), who was Professor of Applied Mathematics at University College, London, and later the first Galton Professor of Eugenics. His paper, which appeared in the *Philosophical Magazine*, was entitled "On the criterion that a given system of deviations from the probable in the case of a correlated system of variables is such that it can be reasonably supposed to have arisen from random sampling". Pearson was the leading member of the group of English statisticians who laid the foundations of the modern study of the subject in the early years of this century.

6.4   A much fuller version of this table is given in the *SMP Advanced Tables* and in the *Formulae for Advanced Mathematics with Statistical Tables* (Cambridge University Press).

6.5   Commander (later Baron) Stephen King-Hall, who used to broadcast on *Children's Hour* in the 1930s.

6.6   The probability of getting at least one block in class (E) out of 100 blocks is $1 - (0.999)^{100}$, which is just below 0.1 – so on the 10% criterion it is by itself an improbable event.

7.1   For example, SMP *Revised Advanced Mathematics, Book 3* (Cambridge University Press), Chapter 29.

7.2   In practice, of course, the problem would be the other way round: one would know the number of soft oranges in the sample, and infer from this the proportion in the consignment, as described in Chapter 4.

8.1   We need to take great care over the wording here. There would be nothing wrong in saying, as a hypothesis, that "he can distinguish real ale from keg with probability 75%" (although, in the text, this hypothesis was not in fact discussed). This would mean that, when he is presented with a glass of beer, there is a probability of 0.75 that he will identify it correctly. It is quite different from the meaningless assertion that "there is a 75% probability that he can distinguish real ale from keg".

8.2 We could, of course, ask the question "what is the probability, on this hypothesis, of getting two or fewer faulty plates?" (i.e. consider only the cumulative probability from the left); this would be equivalent to taking the alternative hypothesis as "the probability of a plate being faulty is less than 0.08", and a one-tail test would be involved. But then a different alternative hypothesis would have to be taken for hypotheses about probabilities below 0.04 from those about probabilities above 0.04. The procedure described in the text enables us to discuss all hypothetical probabilities in the same terms, whether they are above or below the sample proportion.

8.3 Small rounding errors may accumulate when calculating the cumulative probabilities, but these are not often important.

8.4 Because of the infinitely long tail in the Poisson model, there is a special advantage in this case of using the fact that

$$P(i \text{ or more As}) = 1 - P((i - 1) \text{ or fewer As});$$

that is, the cumulative probability from the right corresponding to "i faulty" is 1 minus the cumulative probability from the left for "$(i - 1)$ faulty".

9.1 It is convenient to adopt the practice of using letters from the ordinary alphabet to denote statistics calculated from actual data, and greek letters for the corresponding theoretical quantity in a probability model.

9.2 There is no letter in the standard greek alphabet corresponding to our v; so theoretical variance is usually denoted by σ^2, to correspond with S^2.

9.3 For many functions the nth Taylor approximation (see, for example, SMP *Revised Advanced Mathematics*, Book 2, p. 556 (Cambridge University Press)) tends to the function as a limit as n tends to infinity. The resulting infinite series is then called the power series expansion of the function.

9.4 See, for example, SMP *Revised Advanced Mathematics*, Book 1, p. 77 (Cambridge University Press).

9.5 Note that the outcomes A and B, and the probabilities a and b, have been interchanged from the description of the model given in §3.2.

9.6 You should be warned that the process of differentiating infinite series is not always straightforward. Suppose, for example, that p(i) is taken to be $\dfrac{1}{i(i-1)}$ for $i = 2, 3, 4, \ldots$. Then the probability generator G(t) is properly defined, and by writing p(i) in partial fractions as $\dfrac{1}{i-1} - \dfrac{1}{i}$, it can be seen that G(1) = 1 as required. However, the expressions $G'(t) = \Sigma_{i=2}^{\infty} \dfrac{1}{i-1} t^{i-1}$ and $G''(t) = \Sigma_{i=2}^{\infty} t^{i-2}$ do not converge when t is put equal to 1. For more information about this difficulty you must consult a book on mathematical analysis; but there are very few instances in probability theory where such problems arise.

9.7 The omission of any mention of the set of natural numbers from this statement is not an oversight. The argument developed in §§9.6-7 does not depend in any essential on the scores being drawn from this set; but attention has been confined to this special case because it is in this form that probability generators are most often used, and the restriction has made it possible to adopt a more straightforward notation. However, the result quoted remains true for any (finite or countably infinite) set of scores $x_1, x_2, \ldots$ with G(t) defined as $\Sigma \, \mathrm{p}(x_i) t^{x_i}$.

9.8   If the possibility space is infinite, the justification for this process depends on a theorem in mathematical analysis. However, it turns out that the conditions of this theorem are always satisfied when the infinite series represent probability generators.

10.1 There are small rounding errors in the calculation of the expected frequencies.

10.2 The figures are for students entering the university in 1981 who obtained honours, derived from the *Cambridge University Reporter* for 22 August 1984.

11.1 Often the outcome of a statistical experiment does not appear directly as a real number. For example, the result of tossing a coin five times might be HTHHT; to get a real number out of this (for example, so as to calculate an average) it is necessary to apply a mapping such as

outcome of five tosses → number of heads.

A random variable is for this reason sometimes defined as "a mapping from the set of outcomes of an experiment to the real numbers".

11.2 The words "under normal conditions" entitle us to exclude one baby girl with a birth mass of 1.000 kg born after 31 weeks gestation. For some statistical purposes it would be important to include such a measurement in the data; but since the present aim is to give a description of normal births, it has been excluded. The data have been kindly supplied by Dr G. D. Starte.

11.3 Since these masses have clearly only been measured to the nearest 5 grams, there will soon be repetitions in the data to this degree of accuracy; in this sense, the masses as measured constitute a discrete possibility space. However, more accurate measurement would show that two masses which appear to be equal are in fact slightly different.

11.4 Some statisticians prefer to adopt the convention that a random variable can only be a real number, not a measurement with a unit attached – in which case relative frequency density is also a pure number. However, the present writer believes that the concepts are easier to grasp if the random variable is allowed to be a measurement on some occasions.

11.5 There is some ambiguity whether the mass of one baby girl recorded as 3.000 kg should be assigned to the interval from 2.5 to 3.0 kg, or from 3.0 to 3.5 kg. It has been arbitrarily placed in the second of these intervals; but if the measurements had been made with statistical analysis in view, it would have been better to record them in the form "between 3.000 and 3.005 kg" rather than as "3.000 kg to the nearest 5 grams", so as to avoid this difficulty.

11.6 These probabilities would only be appropriate for babies born at a given period in a particular locality. The probability model for babies born in the south of England in the fifteenth century, or for babies born in Ethiopia at the present time, would certainly be very different.

11.7 On the principle of using greek letters for theoretical models and corresponding english letters for statistical populations, the greek letter ϕ has been chosen for probability density functions in this book. However, the letter f is often used for this purpose; we have preferred to reserve this for frequency functions.

11.8 See, for example, SMP *Revised Advanced Mathematics, Book 3* (Cambridge University Press), Chapter 31.

11.9 The name "distribution function" is also sometimes used.

11.10 If f is used to denote probability density (see Note 11.7), then F is normally used for the cumulative probability function.

11.11 There is a problem of notation here, since we do not want to use the same letter x

for the upper end of the interval of integration and for the "dummy variable" in the integral. Since it does not matter what symbol is used for the dummy variable, the letter t has been chosen arbitrarily.

11.12 See, for example, SMP *Revised Advanced Mathematics, Book 1* (Cambridge University Press), Chapter 10.

12.1 The process described will give numbers ranging from 0.000000 to 0.999999. It is better still to add 0.0000005 to each random 6-digit decimal, so that the theoretical mean is exactly 0.5 – as it is in the rectangular model being simulated.

12.2 For the inverse Φ^{-1} to exist, the function Φ should be *strictly* increasing; that is, its graph should not contain any horizontal line-segments. If the modification suggested in Note 12.1 is adopted, there is no problem about $\Phi^{-1}(0)$ or $\Phi^{-1}(1)$, since the random decimal number can then never take the values 0 or 1. If there is a number b between 0 and 1 such that $\Phi(x) = b$ over an interval of values of x, then in theory the method described in the text breaks down; but in practice it is usually a simple matter to find an expedient for circumventing the difficulty.

12.3 There will be a problem if the domain of the probability density function extends to infinity, as happens for example with negative exponential probability (Fig. 6). But the error will not be serious if one chops off the tail, provided that the probability associated with this tail (that is, the area under the graph) is small.

12.4 You may recall that the same device was used in §7.6 to obtain Poisson probabilities as a limiting form of binomial probabilities.

13.1 Abraham de Moivre, though born in France, took refuge in London at the age of 18 to escape the suppression of the Huguenots, and remained there until his death in 1754. He was already 66 years old when he announced the equation of normal probability. Both his account and that of Laplace are given in D. E. Smith, *Source Book in Mathematics* (McGraw-Hill). According to Sir Harold Jeffreys, it was Karl Pearson, the inventor of chi-squared probability, who proposed the name "normal" for this function; see H. Jeffreys, *Scientific Inference* (Cambridge University Press), p. 44.

13.2 The theory underlying this calculation is given in Chapter 20.

13.3 Normal probability is so important that in some books the symbols ϕ and Φ are reserved for this model alone, some other letters (f, F for example) being used for probability density and cumulative probability in general. In this chapter, wherever ϕ, Φ occur they refer to normal probability.

13.4 You should notice, however, that some sets of tables give $\Phi(x) - \frac{1}{2}$, or $2\Phi(x) - 1$, rather than $\Phi(x)$. Draw graphs of normal probability density indicating the areas represented by these quantities, and describe in words what they stand for. In some books $2\Phi(x) - 1$ is denoted by the symbol erf(x); "erf" is an abbreviation for "error function", and reminds us that normal probability is sometimes called the "law of errors".

13.5 You will notice that the normal probability paper reproduced in Fig. 6 has the cumulative relative frequencies printed in the margin on the right in the form of percentages. The corresponding values of the measurement are called "percentiles", and the 25 % and 75 % measurements are called "quartiles".

13.6 A quite different method of deriving normal probability density from binomial probability is given in SMP *Revised Advanced Mathematics, Book 3* (Cambridge University Press), Chapter 39; you may find it interesting to compare the two. The approach using Stirling's approximation will be used again in Chapter 18 to develop the theory of chi-squared probability.

13.7 See, for example, the book *Extensions of Calculus* in this series.

13.8   For greater accuracy when using tables of cumulative normal probability to test hypotheses, some books of tables provide a separate table of values of the argument at critical percentage points, such as 95 %, 97.5 %, 99 %, etc. These are in effect tables of the inverse function Φ^{-1}. See, for example, *Formulae for Advanced Mathematics with Statistical Tables* (Cambridge University Press).

13.9   Of course, we cannot be quite sure of this, since normal probability is only approximately equal to binomial probability – but we have no way of assessing this, short of carrying out the binomial calculation exactly. So here we treat the normal model as if it were exact rather than approximate.

14.1   The notations $E(X)$ and $E[x]$ are also used for the expectation. In his book *Statistics and probability* (Cambridge University Press), J. H. Durran argues interestingly for these as alternative abbreviations for the complete form $E_X([x])$; however, there are practical advantages in the form $E[X]$ adopted here.

14.2   The notation var$[X]$ is sometimes used for the variance.

14.3   See, for example, the book *Extensions of Calculus* in this series.

14.4   The symbol "dS" stands for an "element of area" in the plane. The use of the letter S has nothing to do with its statistical meaning of standard deviation in this context!

15.1   The capital letter I is used here to signify that it is a random variable; a particular value is denoted by i. Although this convention is used in the chapter where practicable, it is not possible to adhere to it rigidly on all occasions.

15.2   To make comparison easier, values of $\hat{t}_1$ have been rounded to the nearest integer in drawing Fig. 3. Notice that, more exactly, $\hat{t}_1$ is always an odd multiple of 0.2; $\hat{t}_2$ is always an odd integer, and $\hat{t}_3$ an integer (odd or even).

15.3   An approximation, replacing the discrete possibility space $1, 2, \ldots, \tau$ by the interval of real numbers from $\frac{1}{2}$ to $\tau + \frac{1}{2}$ and ignoring the possibility of repetitions in the draw, leads to the conclusion that the standard deviations of $\hat{t}_1$, $\hat{t}_2$ and $\hat{t}_3$ are approximately $\tau/\sqrt{15} \approx 0.258\tau$, $\tau/\sqrt{7} \approx 0.378\tau$ and $\tau/\sqrt{21} \approx 0.218\tau$. These are very close to the standard deviations found from the experimental run of 100 draws, which are 0.254τ, 0.374τ and 0.209τ with $\tau = 112$.

15.4   The notation $X_1, X_2, \ldots, X_n$ for the random measurement in the first, second, ..., nth sample must be clearly distinguished from the notation $x_1, x_2, \ldots, x_k$ used in previous chapters for the possible values which can be taken by a discrete random variable X. The second notation only appears in this chapter in §15.7.

15.5   Note that the correct notation is $\widehat{\sigma^2}$, not $\hat{\sigma}^2$. An unbiased estimator for the variance is not the square of an unbiased estimator for the standard deviation.

16.1   In order to avoid excessive complication the continuity correction has not been included in this argument. If this is taken into account, then the numerators of the left sides of the equations for the left and right extreme estimates become $0.465 - a$ and $a - 0.475$, leading to solutions of 0.370 and 0.572, which are even closer to the exact values. Using $k = 0.465$ and 0.475 in the approximate method which follows gives for the left and right extreme estimates respectively 0.367 and 0.573, compared with 0.369 and 0.572 given by the exact method.

16.2   The sample of 100 consecutive births within one practice could by no means be called "random". In many actual sampling experiments one has to forgo the strict requirement of randomness, and use instead a sample that is "typical", in the sense that there is no reason to think that deductions from it would be different from those obtained from a genuine random sample.

16.3   The question always arises, how large is large? It is impossible to give a general answer. Figs. 6 and 7 show that, starting with a uniform distribution, even $n = 4$

may give a remarkably good approximation. But if the original distribution is very uneven, it may be necessary to take n to be around 100 before the distribution for the totals begins to look normal. It is interesting to investigate this question experimentally using a computer program.

16.4   In practice insurance calculations are of course vastly more complicated than this. No mention has been made of inflation, or of investing the money subscribed, or of a service charge, or of VAT. All the same, the general principle of risk-sharing, based on the central limit theorem, is at the root of the insurance business.

16.5   The standard deviation of the sample statistic is often called the "standard error", especially in older literature.

16.6   Capital letters A, M are used here to emphasise that, in this argument, the sample statistic is a random variable.

16.7   In §16.2 the letter k was used rather than a, since a played a different role in the discussion. It is now simpler to revert to a.

16.8   Questions of this kind can also be answered by using chi-squared probability (see §10.3). It can be shown that the two methods are equivalent to each other mathematically; see Project exercise C2.

17.1   Since in this illustration the random variable is a physical quantity (length measured in cm), notionally a dimension of cm^{-1} should be assigned to the variable u, so that the exponents in these expressions are dimensionless. See Note 11.4.

17.2   Besides the examples referred to in this chapter and its exercises, one may mention Kendall's rank correlation coefficient and Wilcoxon's rank sum for unpaired samples (see Project exercises C3 and C4), chi-squared probability (see Exercise 18C, question 5) and t-probability (see Exercise 19B, question 8).

17.3   Readers who are accustomed to using the symbol i for $\sqrt{(-1)}$ should beware: in this expression i is an integer between 1 and n. In this book $\sqrt{(-1)}$ is denoted by j (see §17.9).

17.4   This is easily shown by using the method outlined in SMP *Revised Advanced Mathematics, Book 1* (Cambridge University Press), Chapter 9, §3.3.

17.5   An early example of the use of a characteristic function is in Laplace's proof (dated about 1820) of normal probability for the distribution of the mean error when a large number of observations is made. For an English translation of his paper, see D. E. Smith, *Source book in mathematics* (McGraw-Hill).

17.6   Strictly, the inversion theorem deals only with continuous random variables. When the random variable is discrete, more sophisticated arguments are needed. See Exercise 17F, question 7 for an example.

18.1   This is sometimes referred to as a "Poisson transformation", in contrast to the "binomial transformation" in §13.5, because a Poisson probability model with mean na has standard deviation $\sqrt{(na)}$ whereas the binomial model has standard deviation $\sqrt{(nab)}$.

18.2   See, for example, *Mechanics and Vectors* in this series.

18.3   The rule is sometimes given that the procedure should be modified, by amalgamating classes, when the expected frequency for an outcome is less than 5 (see §6.8). The analysis here suggests that as a rule of thumb this is rather crude; there may be some occasions when the expected frequency is much smaller than this but quite reliable conclusions can still be drawn from the test.

18.4   When applied in this context, the continuity correction is sometimes referred to as "Yates's correction", after the British statistician F. Yates.

18.5   See, for example, SMP *Revised Advanced Mathematics, Book 3* (Cambridge

University Press), Chapter 31, §2. The result may also be obtained by writing the probability in cartesian coordinates as a double integral, and then transforming this to polar coordinates.

19.1 Although the "capital letter convention" enables us to distinguish M, the random variable, from m, the mean of the particular sample, the notation explained in §15.7 prevents the same convention being adopted for S. For standard deviation the capital letter has to fulfil both functions.

19.2 Since the population from which this sample was drawn is finite, it is not quite accurate to describe the given sample as "random". To apply this theory, the sample should be chosen in some way which allows the same apple to be included more than once; that is, the sampling should be with replacement.

19.3 "On the probable error of a mean", published in *Biometrika*, volume 6.

19.4 See Note 11.11. Here for obvious reasons the letter t is not available for use as the dummy variable, so the letter u is used instead.

19.5 With some sets of tables it may be necessary to estimate this value of t by interpolation between two tabulated values, e.g. for $v = 20$ and $v = 30$.

19.6 Tables of F-probability are included, for example, in F. C. Powell, *Cambridge Mathematical and Statistical Tables* (Cambridge University Press). This probability model is important in a statistical procedure called "analysis of variance". It was given the letter F by the American statistician G. W. Snedecor in honour of R. A. Fisher (see §19.5).

20.1 Compare Note 15.4. In this chapter it is most convenient to let (x_i, y_i) denote the values of X and Y in the ith sample pair selected; this means that there is a possibility of repetitions. The alternative notation indicated in Exercise 20A, questions 6 and 7 is occasionally useful when handling discrete or grouped data, but this is exceptional. Capital letters (X_i, Y_i) will be used when the values are considered as random variables.

20.2 There is a close parallel between covariance and variance; and just as in sampling it is $\{n/(n-1)\}S^2$ rather than S^2 which gives an unbiased estimator for the population variance, so $\{n/(n-1)\}C_{xy}$ gives an unbiased estimator for the population covariance (see Exercise 20A, question 14). It is convenient to take the analogy further, and to use the notation c_{xy} for $\{n/(n-1)\}C_{xy}$. Some statisticians actually call this the "sample covariance", but in this book the term "unbiased covariance estimator" is preferred. See the Appendix, in which the two alternative notation systems are compared.

20.3 This is sometimes called the "product-moment correlation coefficient" or the "coefficient of linear correlation", to distinguish it from other measures of correlation. Note that, in the alternative notation (see Note 20.2), r can also be written as $c_{xy}/s_x s_y$.

20.4 An English translation of Legendre's paper is included in D. E. Smith, *Source Book in Mathematics* (McGraw-Hill).

20.5 Notice that if there are only two sample pairs, then the best fitting straight line is just the line joining the two points, so that S^2 is always zero. This makes the presence of the factor $(n-2)$ in the expression for $E[S^2]$ plausible. Compare Q.11 in §15.6.

20.6 The argument to find the line of regression of y'' on x'' by transforming the line of regression of y on x is perhaps a little too glib; for you will notice that the line of regression of x on y (which is the y-axis) is not transformed into the line of regression of x'' on y''. It is left to you to consider why not.

20.7 R. A. Fisher, in a paper published in the journal *Biometrika* in 1915, showed that if one works in terms of a statistic $z = \tanh^{-1}r$, writing $\zeta = \tanh^{-1}\rho$, then $(z - \zeta)\sqrt{(n - 3)}$ has approximately standard normal probability when n is large. This can be used to find a confidence interval for the parameter ζ, and hence for ρ. Notice that the function $\tanh^{-1}$ can be evaluated directly on most scientific calculators.

20.8   See, for example, SMP *Revised Advanced Mathematics*, Book 2 (Cambridge University Press), Chapter 18. In the geometry of more than three dimensions, this equation can be used as a *definition* of angle.

21.1   Extending the notation used in §21.1, it might seem more natural to use the notation $P(i_t)$. The alternative form, $p_i(t)$, has been chosen here because it will be important to emphasise that it is a function of t.

21.2   Strictly, $p'_1(0)$ must indicate only the derivative of $p_1(t)$ *on the right* at $t = 0$, since the functions $p_i(t)$ are only defined for $t > 0$. A similar comment applies throughout the argument which follows.

21.3   See, for example, *Differential Equations and Numerical Analysis* in this series.

21.4   See, for example, *Linear Algebra and Geometry* in this series.

21.5   You will find the labour of working exercises in this section much reduced if you have access to a set of computer programs for matrix manipulation.

Answers, hints and comments on questions in the text

Chapter 1

Q.2 $\Sigma (x_i - m)f(x_i) = \Sigma x_i f(x_i) - m \Sigma f(x_i) = mn - mn = 0$. The factor $(x_i - m)$ is the displacement of x_i from the mean, and $\Sigma (x_i - m)f(x_i)$ is the equivalent of the sum $\Sigma x_i f(x_i)$ used in calculating m if displacements are measured from the mean rather than the origin. To take an analogy from mechanics, the sum of the 'moments' about the mean is zero.

Q.4 $\Sigma (x_i - m)^2 f(x_i) = \Sigma x_i^2 f(x_i) - 2m \Sigma x_i f(x_i) + m^2 \Sigma f(x_i)$
$$= \Sigma x_i^2 f(x_i) - 2m(mn) + m^2 n = \Sigma x_i^2 f(x_i) - m^2 n.$$

Q.8 It is helpful to suppose that the dice can be distinguished by their colours (white and black, say). Then the 36 different outcomes "i on the white die, j on the black die", where i and j take separately the values 1, 2, 3, 4, 5, 6, are all equally likely provided that the dice are unbiased.

Q.10 If in the figure d, e, f denote the frequencies corresponding to the regions, then $F(A \text{ or } B) = d + e + f$, $F(A) = d + e$, $F(B) = e + f$, $F(A \text{ and } B) = e$. The probability law (using the empirical definition) follows by dividing by n.

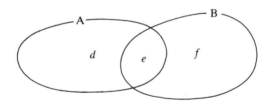

Q.11 $\frac{11}{36}, \frac{6}{36}, \frac{1}{36}, \frac{16}{36}$, assuming that the dice are unbiased.

Q.13 $P(\sim A \text{ and } B) = P(\sim A|B) \times P(B)$, $P(A \text{ and } \sim B) = P(A| \sim B) \times P(\sim B)$,
$P(\sim A \text{ and } \sim B) = P(\sim A| \sim B) \times P(\sim B)$.

Q.15 $\frac{1}{6}, \frac{5}{6}, \frac{1}{3}, \frac{2}{3}$.

Q.16 "A and B_1", "A and B_2", "A and B_3", ... is a set of exclusive outcomes, and A can be split up as "A and B_1" or "A and B_2" or "A and B_3" or ...

Q.17 (a) $P(A) = P(A|B) \times P(B) + P(A|\sim B) \times P(\sim B)$
$= P(A|B) \times P(B) + P(A|B) \times P(\sim B)$
$= P(A|B) \times \{P(B) + P(\sim B)\} = P(A|B)$.
(b) $P(A \text{ and } \sim B) = P(A) - P(A \text{ and } B)$, so that

$$P(A \text{ and } B) = P(A) \times P(B) \Rightarrow P(A \text{ and } \sim B) = P(A) \times \{1 - P(B)\}$$
$$= P(A) \times P(\sim B).$$

Therefore
$$P(A|B) = P(A \text{ and } B)/P(B) = P(A),$$
$$P(A| \sim B) = P(A \text{ and } \sim B)/P(\sim B) = P(A).$$

Q20. $\frac{5}{29}, \frac{24}{29}$.

Chapter 2

Q.2 Outcomes such as [45] have twice the probability of doubles such as [66].

Q.3 All these outcomes have the same probability.

Q.4 $P((4, 5)) = P((6, 6)) = \frac{1}{36}$; $P([45]) = \frac{1}{18}$, $P([66]) = \frac{1}{36}$.

Q.5 The probabilities go up steadily from $\frac{1}{36}$ to $\frac{6}{36}$ for a seven, then go down steadily.

Q.6 875; 1.18.

Chapter 3

Q.3 Once the genetic mechanism of sex determination is understood, a basis for a theory of sex distribution becomes available. Without such a theory, the evidence can only be empirical. The situation is more complicated for the creatures in the second list, where large numbers of offspring are conceived at the same time. What does the question mean then?

Q.2 (a), (c) and (d) give examples of Bernoulli sequences. In (b) the sequence is only of Bernoulli type if the beads are returned to the bag after the colour has been recorded. (e) would only satisfy the conditions if the proportions of each colour at each light are the same and the lights are randomly timed, whilst in (f) the requirement of independence is unlikely to be met.

Q.6 $a, ab, ab^2, ab^3, \ldots, ab^{i-1}, \ldots$ Notice that the probability of a run length of 2 is the same for each outcome.

Q.7 b^5, a^5.

Q.8 $b^5, 5ab^4, 10a^2b^3, 10a^3b^2, 5a^4b, a^5$.

Q.10 1, 3, 4, 2, 5; 1, 4, 3, 2, 5; 3, 1, 4, 2, 5; 3, 4, 1, 2, 5; 4, 1, 3, 2, 5; 4, 3, 1, 2, 5; 1, 3, 4, 5, 2; 1, 4, 3, 5, 2; 3, 1, 4, 5, 2; 3, 4, 1, 5, 2; 4, 1, 3, 5, 2; 4, 3, 1, 5, 2. The first six of these combine the six different orderings of $\{1, 3, 4\}$ with one of the orderings of $\{2, 5\}$; the second six combine the same six orderings of $\{1, 3, 4\}$ with the other ordering of $\{2, 5\}$. Clearly this gives $6 \times 2 = 12$ of the orderings of $\{1, 2, 3, 4, 5\}$ in all. The other partitionings can be dealt with in just the same way.

Q.11 $(b + a)^5 = b^5 + 5b^4a + 10b^3a^2 + 10b^2a^3 + 5ba^4 + a^5$. Compare the solution to Q.8.

Q.12 $i! \times j! = j! \times i!$, where $j + i = n$. The result is illustrated by the symmetry of Pascal's triangle (see Exercise 3B, question 12).

Q.13 Apart from morale, some of the crew will have been in last year's winning boat, and there is probably the same coach.

Q.14 The last win must be omitted from the columns (because the result of the next race is not known), and the first win from the rows (because there was no previous race).

Q.15 See §3.7 for one answer.

Q.17 0.457, 0.543; 0.455, 0.545. After this the probabilities remain the same to three decimal places.

Q.18 0.333, 0.667; 0.422, 0.578; 0.445, 0.555; and so on.

Q.19 Because of the complication referred to in Q.14, the probabilities are not exactly equal to the proportions of wins, but $\frac{5}{11}$ and $\frac{6}{11}$ of 125 are very close to the numbers of Oxford and Cambridge wins.

Q.20 The columns are the probabilities calculated in Q.17 (and the preceding text) and Q.18, and the limit is a matrix both of whose columns are the steady long-run probabilities.

Q.21 The points represented by the vectors all lie on a line (since their coordinates add to 1). The steady probability vector is left unchanged by the transformation.

Q.22 Choose an example where the entries in the leading diagonal of the transition matrix are small.

Chapter 4
Q.3 0.10.

Chapter 6
Q.1 $F_e(C) = P(C) \times n$.

Q.2 $F_e(\text{blue}) = 10$ for everyone, but $F_o(\text{blue})$ depends on you.

Q.3 $\sum_{i=1}^{k} F_o(C_i)$ and $\sum_{i=1}^{k} F_e(C_i)$ are both equal to n. We shall see later that it is often necessary to calculate $F_o(C_i) - F_e(C_i)$ for each outcome; this equation then provides a useful check on the computations.

Q.6 $(b - 10)^2 + (g - 10)^2 + (r - 10)^2$
$= \{F_o(\text{blue}) - F_e(\text{blue})\}^2 + \{F_o(\text{green}) - F_e(\text{green})\}^2 + \{F_o(\text{red}) - F_e(\text{red})\}^2$.
The sum of the components is always zero (see Q.3).

Q.8 $\dfrac{30!}{11! \times 8! \times 11!}(\tfrac{1}{3})^{11}(\tfrac{1}{3})^{8}(\tfrac{1}{3})^{11} \approx 0.0201$. Similarly for $(8, 11, 11)$ and $(11, 11, 8)$. The others are $(9, 9, 12)$, $(9, 12, 9)$ and $(12, 9, 9)$, each with probability 0.0204.

Q.9 0.0010. Any permutation of 17, 6, 7 or of 3, 14, 13 gives $I^2 = 74$, so $P(I^2 = 74) = 0.0010 \times 6 + 0.0004 \times 6 \approx 0.008$.

Q.10 $P(\text{all blue}) = P(\text{all green}) = P(\text{all red}) = (\tfrac{1}{3})^{30} \approx 4.9 \times 10^{-15}$. $I^2 = 600$.

Q.12 Besides those mentioned in Q.8, there are $(10, 10, 10)$ and the six permutations of 9, 10, 11 for which $I^2 = 2$. $P(I^2 \leqslant 6) \approx 0.296$.

Q.18 $\dfrac{\{F_o(\text{blue}) - F_e(\text{blue})\}^2}{F_e(\text{blue})} + \cdots + \cdots$

Q.19 (a) $\dfrac{30!}{15! \times 5! \times 10!}(\tfrac{1}{2})^{15}(\tfrac{1}{6})^{5}(\tfrac{1}{3})^{10} \approx 0.0310$; (b) 0.009; (c) 0.004.

Q.20 (a) 2.27; (b) 3.87.

Q.23   (1460, 520, 1020).

Q.25   For example: (*a*) If cards are dealt from a pack one at a time (with replacement), the probability that the discrepancy between the frequencies of the four suits and the expected frequencies is greater than 6.25 is 0.1. (*b*) Similarly, with frequencies of the various scores on a die when it is rolled repeatedly.

Q.27   The probabilities would be replaced by conditional probabilities, given that at least one child in the family is a girl; they would therefore be $\frac{3}{7}, \frac{3}{7}, \frac{1}{7}$. Also, since the "all boys" category is empty, the value of v is reduced to 2.

Q.28   The only possibilities are (in order of birth) BBB, BBG, GGB, GGG, and the expected frequency of each would be 18.

Q.29   The discrepancies are 0.05, 0.074 and 0.152. None of these are significantly close at the 1 % level, but the first two are significant at the 5 % level and might therefore be regarded with some suspicion.

Q.30   The discrepancy is 0.6, which is certainly not significant. Indeed, it was shown in Q.12 that the probability of being as close to (10, 10, 10) as this is nearly 0.3.

Chapter 7

Q.1   0.1955, 0.1956, 0.1565

Q.3   0.0182139 ..., 0.0183156 ...

Q.5   0.0183, 0.0732, 0.1465, 0.1954, 0.1954, 0.1563, ...

Chapter 8

Q.2   For example, decide the contents of each successive glass by tossing a coin: heads for real ale, tails for keg.

Q.3   For the probability in the second line of the table, a stick graph would be used, and the criterion for rejection would be that the sum of the heights of the sticks corresponding to 9, 10, 11 and 12 right should be less than 0.05. But for the probability reckoned cumulatively, as in the last line, one would use a graph of isolated points (perhaps joined by dotted lines to indicate the trend), and the criterion for rejecting the null hypothesis would be that the point corresponding to 9 right should lie below a horizontal line at a height of 0.05 above the axis.

Q.4   (*a*) 10,   (*b*) 11.

Q.5   (*a*) $\frac{1}{37} \approx 0.027$, (*b*) $\frac{1}{36} \approx 0.028$, both less than 0.05. The fact that an event is unlikely to happen does not mean that it cannot happen; it is important to be aware that we may from time to time be rejecting a hypothesis on the grounds that it is unlikely to lead to the experimental result observed, when the hypothesis is in fact true.

Q.6   This instance points to the need to use common sense in interpreting statistical data. If these figures had been used in support of an experiment to test the hypothesis "more girls than boys are born in Cambridge", then the procedures described in the text would lead one to come down in favour of the hypothesis at the 1 % significance level. But in this case it is clear that the August 1975 figures represent one of those occasional aberrations which are an inevitable consequence of statistical variability. See Q.5.

Q.7   The fact that the result of an experiment is "not statistically significant" does not mean that the experiment is a failure. In this case, it indicates that the mock examination was predicting more successfully than the teacher had thought.

Q.9   On the basis of the null hypothesis, the probabilities that the number of plates in a sample of 50 found to be faulty is (a) i or fewer, (b) i or more, where i is the entry in the top line of the table.

Q.10   At the 5% significance level, all the hypothetical probabilities in Table 1 give reasonable estimates: in each row of the table, the probability of 2 or fewer faulty plates, and the probability of 2 or more faulty plates, both exceed 0.025. Reasonable estimates range from about 0.0048 (for which the probability of 2 or more faulty plates is about 0.025) to 0.137 (for which the probability of 2 or fewer faulty is about 0.025).

Chapter 9

Q.1   (a) 0.632,   (b) 0.264.

Q.2   1.

Q.4 $\Sigma (x_i - \mu)^2 p(x_i) = \Sigma x_i^2 p(x_i) - 2\mu \Sigma x_i p(x_i) + \mu^2 \Sigma p(x_i)$
$= \Sigma x_i^2 p(x_i) - 2\mu^2 + \mu^2 = \Sigma x_i^2 p(x_i) - \mu^2.$

Q.5   Uniform; geometric; possibly Poisson; binomial.

Q.6   (a) $0, \frac{1}{6}, \frac{1}{6}$;   (b) $\frac{1}{16}, \frac{1}{4}, 0$.

Q.8   (a) $1 + 2t + 4t^2 + \cdots + 2^{n-1}t^{n-1}$, (b) $2^n t^n$. $A = 1, B = 1 - 2t, Q, R$ are answers to (a), (b).

Q.10   (a) $1, 2, 3, \ldots$;   (b) $1, 1, 2, 3, 5, \ldots$ (the Fibonacci sequence).

Q.11 $0, 1, \frac{1}{2}, \frac{1}{3}, \frac{1}{4}, \cdots$

Q.13 $p(i) = ab^i$. $G(t) = a/(1 - bt)$. (Notice that, in this case, $i = 0, 1, 2, 3, \ldots$)

Q.17 $\frac{1}{36}, \frac{2}{36}, \frac{3}{36}, \frac{4}{36}, \frac{5}{36}, \frac{6}{36}, \frac{5}{36}, \frac{4}{36}, \frac{3}{36}, \frac{2}{36}, \frac{1}{36}$. All further coefficients are 0.

Q.18   (a) $\frac{1}{216}, \frac{3}{216}, \frac{6}{216}, \frac{10}{216}, \frac{15}{216}, \frac{21}{216}, \frac{25}{216}, \frac{27}{216}, \frac{27}{216}, \frac{25}{216}, \ldots$, descending symmetrically.
(b) $\frac{1}{1296}, \frac{4}{1296}, \frac{10}{1296}, \frac{20}{1296}, \frac{35}{1296}, \frac{56}{1296}, \frac{80}{1296}, \frac{104}{1296}, \frac{125}{1296}, \frac{140}{1296}, \frac{146}{1296}, \frac{140}{1296}, \cdots$
For an alternative derivation of (a), see Exercise 2B, question 3(a).

Chapter 10

Q.3   There is a small complication here because of the amalgamation of the last four classes. Without this, one could write

$$\frac{F_o(1) + 2F_o(2) + 3F_o(3) + \cdots}{100} = \frac{F_e(1) + 2F_e(2) + 3F_e(3) + \cdots}{100},$$

both sides being equal to 0.9. With the classes for $i = 3, 4, 5, 6$ combined into a single class "3 or more", the corresponding equation is only approximately true.

Chapter 11
Q.1 For the 20 babies, 0.1, 0.1, 0.57 kg^{-1}; for the 100 babies, 0.1, 0.06, 0.59 kg^{-1}.

Q.2 1.

Q.5 (*a*) 1, (*b*) 0.5, (*c*) 0.1, (*d*) 0.2.

Q.7 Discontinuities in the cumulative graph correspond to the sticks in Fig. 1.

Q.12 At $x = \pm 0.5$, both the height of the probability density graph and the gradient of the cumulative probability graph are undefined.

Chapter 12
Q.1 $\Phi(x) = 0$ if $x < a$, $\Phi(x) = (x - a)/(b - a)$ if $a \leqslant x \leqslant b$, $\Phi(x) = 1$ if $x > b$.

Q.2 Mean $= \frac{1}{2}(a + b)$, standard deviation $= \dfrac{1}{2\sqrt{3}}(b - a)$.

Q.3 The graphs consist of horizontal lines at heights $0, \frac{1}{6}, \frac{2}{6}, \frac{3}{6}, \frac{4}{6}, \frac{5}{6}, 1$ and $0, \frac{1}{36}, \frac{3}{36}, \frac{6}{36}, \frac{10}{36}, \frac{15}{36}, \frac{21}{36}, \frac{26}{36}, \frac{30}{36}, \frac{33}{36}, \frac{35}{36}, 1$ respectively.

Q.7 Although in the Poisson model the event occurs at a uniform average rate, it becomes less and less likely that an event occurring in a given time-interval is the *next* occurrence.

Chapter 13
Q.9 The experiment cannot *prove* either of these statements; the best one can assert is that it does not exclude the possibility that the first statement (and therefore, of course, the second) is true. But the data would also be consistent with the hypothesis that the masses have a normal probability distribution with various other values for μ and σ.

Q.10 It is possible (though not very likely) that one might find some other normal probability model, with a different mean and standard deviation, with which the experimental data are consistent.

Q.12 The second and third factors tend to e^1 and 1 respectively as $n \to \infty$.

Chapter 15
Q.1 $\dbinom{20}{i}\left(\dfrac{\beta}{100}\right)^i\left(1 - \dfrac{\beta}{100}\right)^{20-i}, 0 \leqslant i \leqslant 20.$

Q.8 $1/\sqrt{2}, (3 + 2\sqrt{3})/8.$

Q.9 (*a*) $\frac{1}{2}$. (*b*) $\frac{3}{4}$.

Chapter 16
Q.4 $0; 0.002, 0.066, 10^{-n}, 0.$

Q.6 $\phi(t) = \dfrac{1}{\sqrt{(66\pi)}} e^{-(t-18)^2/66}.$

Chapter 17

Q.1 $\mu_0 = 1$.

Q.2 $\mu_1, \mu_2 - \mu_1^2$.

Q.5 88%.

Q.7 78; 39. $\frac{1}{2}n(n + 1)$; $\frac{1}{4}n(n + 1)$.

Q.8 (a) B(12, $\frac{1}{2}$), (b) B(n, $\frac{1}{2}$); N($\frac{1}{2}n$, $\frac{1}{4}n$).

Q.10 (a) Since $\sinh uj = j \sin u$, $K(u) = \frac{1}{u} \sin u$. (b) $e^{-\frac{1}{2}u^2}$.

Chapter 18

Q.2 $1/(2\pi)^{\frac{1}{2}}e^{-\frac{1}{2}r^2}$.

Q.3 $\frac{1}{2}(n + 1)(n + 2)$.

Q.6 Between about -0.50 and 0.58.

Q.8 4.61. This would change the probability by about 1%, though in this example it would not affect the significance at either the 5% or 1% level.

Q.10 $-2 \ln(P/100)$.

Q.11 2π, 4π.

Q.12 $(1, 0, 0, -6)$, $(0, 1, 0, -2)$, $(0, 0, 1, -3)$.

Chapter 19

Q.3 See the equation in Q.4, with $\mu = 0$. This is the familiar alternative method of calculating variance given in §1.1.

Q.9 $$\frac{M_1 - M_2}{\sqrt{\left(\dfrac{1}{n_1} + \dfrac{1}{n_2}\right) \cdot \sqrt{\dfrac{n_1 S_1^2 + n_2 S_2^2}{n_1 + n_2 - 2}}}}.$$

Chapter 20

Q.1 $C_{xx} = S_x^2$, the variance of X.

Q.2 The means m_x and m_y are increased by a and b respectively, so the products $(x_i - m_x)(y_i - m_y)$ are unaltered.

Q.3 C_{xy} is multiplied by 6.

Q.5 $\hat{\alpha} = \hat{\kappa} - \hat{\beta}m_x$, so A, or $\hat{\alpha}$, is distributed as $N(\kappa - \beta m_x, (\sigma^2/n)(1 + m_x^2/S_x^2))$.

Q.6 $\dfrac{A - \alpha}{S\sqrt{(1 + m_x^2/S_x^2)}/\sqrt{(n - 2)}}$ is distributed with t-probability with $v = n - 2$.

Q.7 Completing the square gives $x'^2 \sec^2 \theta - 2x'y' \tan \theta + y'^2 = (x' \sec \theta - y' \sin \theta)^2 + y'^2 \cos^2\theta$. Note that (treating y' as fixed), $\dfrac{1}{\cos \theta \sqrt{(2\pi)}} \displaystyle\int_{-\infty}^{\infty} e^{-\frac{1}{2}(x' - y' \sin \theta \cos \theta)^2/\cos^2\theta} dx'$

$= 1$. This gives probability density for y' as $\dfrac{1}{\sec \theta \sqrt{(2\pi)}} e^{-\frac{1}{2}y'^2/\sec^2\theta}$.

Q.8 $\dfrac{1}{2\pi\sigma_x\sigma_y\sqrt{(1-\rho^2)}}\exp\left(-\left\{\dfrac{(x-\mu_x)^2}{\sigma_x^2}-2\dfrac{(x-\mu_x)(y-\mu_y)}{\sigma_x\sigma_y}+\dfrac{(y-\mu_y)^2}{\sigma_y^2}\right\}\Big/2(1-\rho)^2\right).$

Q.9 Both X and Y separately are distributed as N(45, 82.5), so the area probability density for the random points is $(1/165\pi)e^{-\{(x-45)^2+(y-45)^2\}/165}$.

Chapter 21

Q.1 Adopt the convention $P(i_n) = 0$ if $i > n$ or $i < 0$.

Q.2 Use the result of Exercise 3B, question 12. For a proof by induction, assume the expression to be correct *for* $n = k$ *and all* i, and deduce that it holds *for* $n = k + 1$ *and all i.* If one adopts the convention that $\binom{n}{i} = 0$ if $i > n$ or $i < 0$, together with the convention in Q.1, it is not necessary to consider the extreme values of i separately.

Q.3 $\sum_{r=0}^{i} P_{i-r}(t^*)p_r(t) = p_i(t + t^*).$

Q.4 Eventually $p_1(t)$, which is a probability, would become greater than 1.

Q.5 $\sum_{r=0}^{i} p'_{i-r}(t^*)p_r(t) = p'_i(t + t^*).$

Q.13 An absorbing outcome.

Q.14
$$\begin{bmatrix} 1 & \frac{1}{2} & 0 & 0 \\ 0 & 0 & \frac{1}{2} & 0 \\ 0 & \frac{1}{2} & 0 & 0 \\ 0 & 0 & \frac{1}{2} & 1 \end{bmatrix},\quad \begin{bmatrix} 0.2 & 0 & 0 & 0 & 0 & 0 \\ 0.8 & 0.2 & 0 & 0 & 0 & 0 \\ 0 & 0.8 & 0.2 & 0 & 0 & 0 \\ 0 & 0 & 0.8 & 0.2 & 0 & 0 \\ 0 & 0 & 0 & 0.8 & 0.2 & 0 \\ 0 & 0 & 0 & 0 & 0.8 & 1 \end{bmatrix},\quad \begin{bmatrix} 1 & \frac{1}{2} & 0 & 0 & 0 & 0 \\ 0 & 0 & \frac{1}{2} & 0 & 0 & 0 \\ 0 & \frac{1}{2} & 0 & \frac{1}{2} & 0 & 0 \\ 0 & 0 & \frac{1}{2} & 0 & \frac{1}{2} & 0 \\ 0 & 0 & 0 & \frac{1}{2} & 0 & 0 \\ 0 & 0 & 0 & 0 & \frac{1}{2} & 1 \end{bmatrix}.$$

Q.17 X_1 is the centroid (intersection of the medians) of $X_0Y_0Z_0$; X_2 is the centroid of $X_1Y_1Z_1$. Y_1Z_1 is parallel to Y_0Z_0, X_1Z_1 to Z_0X_0; Y_2Z_2 is parallel to Y_1Z_1, X_2Z_2 to Z_1X_1.

Q.18 The orientation of the triangle is reversed in the transformation; following the order of the letters, anticlockwise becomes clockwise.

Q.19 The equations and solutions are similar to those for $h_H, h_X, \ldots, h_J$ but with the order of the houses H, X, Y, P, Z, J reversed.

Answers, hints and comments on the exercises

Exercise 1A

1 For $X = 1, 2, 3, 4, 5, f(X) = 16, 8, 4, 2, 2$; mean $= 1.94$, variance $= 1.43$.

2 Σ (displacement from mean)$^2 = 120$ on Monday, 125 on Tuesday; standard deviation $= 2.2$ minutes.

3 Mean $= 58$. For the trained boys, $\sum (x_i - 58)^2 f(x_i) = 30(100 + 16)$, using $S^2 = (1/n) \sum (x_i - c)^2 f(x_i) - (m - c)^2$ with $c = 58$; a similar calculation for the untrained boys. The total variance is therefore $\frac{1}{50}\{30(100 + 16) + 20(144 + 36)\} = 141.6$, giving a standard deviation of 11.90.

For the remaining 49 boys, mean $= 59.16$, standard deviation $= 8.77$.

4 Mean $= 48.6\,^\circ$F, standard deviation $= 2.7\,^\circ$F. See question 5 for the general theory.

5 If f, g are the frequency functions for X and Y, $y_i = a + bx_i$ and $f(x_i) = g(y_i)$. So

$$m_Y = (1/n) \sum y_i g(y_i) = (1/n) \sum (a + bx_i) f(x_i) = a + bm_X,$$

$$S_Y^2 = (1/n) \sum (y_i - m_Y)^2 g(y_i) = (1/n) \sum b^2 (x_i - m_X)^2 f(x_i) = b^2 S_X^2.$$

$b = 3$, $a = -70$.

6 There is no advantage in calculating the frequencies and amalgamating all the x_i into a single term $x_i f(x_i)$; it is simpler to read in each measurement as it arises. Call the n values (with possible repetitions) $a_1, a_2, \ldots, a_n$ and use the formulae

$$m = (1/n) \, \Sigma_{i=1}^n \, a_i, \quad v = (1/n) \, \Sigma_{i=1}^n \, a_i^2 - m^2.$$

(Note that this form for v is simpler than $(1/n) \, \Sigma \, (a_i - m)^2$, since the value of m is unknown at the time when the a_i are input.) Some method is needed to indicate when all the data have been input; you may either input n separately before the a_i, or (if you do not know how many measurements there will be at the beginning) insert a 'phoney' $(n + 1)$th entry to indicate when all the measurements have been input.

7 This shows that the mean is the point from which the mean of the squared differences has its smallest value (that is, v). A generalisation of this idea is used to find the best fitting line to a sample of experimental readings: see Chapter 20.

8 In the first case $(p < 0)$, $r = \frac{1}{10}\{1(-p) + 4(10 - p) + 3(25 - p) + 2(30 - p)\} = 17.5 - p$. In the other four intervals, $r = 17.5 - 0.8p$, $r = 9.5$, $r = -5.5 + 0.6p$, $r = -17.5 + p$. Note that the minimum of r occurs throughout the interval $10 \leqslant p \leqslant 25$, which is the 'median interval' in which there is the same number of measurements to the left as to the right.

9 Note that $|p - x_i| = p - x_i$ if $x_i < p$, that is if $i \leqslant u$; and $|p - x_i| = x_i - p$ if $p < x_i$, that is if $i \geqslant u + 1$. So

$$r = \frac{1}{n}\left\{\sum_{i=1}^u (p - x_i) f(x_i) + \sum_{i=u+1}^k (x_i - p) f(x_i)\right\},$$

which has the form $a + bp$ with b as given in the question. If $p < x_1$, $r = m - p$; if $p > x_k$, $r = p - m$.

If p is to the left of the median value (or the 'median interval' between the two middle measurements if these are different; see question 8) then $\sum_{i=1}^{u} f(x_i) < \sum_{i=u+1}^{k} f(x_i)$, so that r decreases with p; if p is to the right of the median, r increases with p. So r is least when p is at the median; the minimum value of r is called the *mean deviation* of the sample of measurements. This result should be compared with that for q, the mean of the squared differences, in question 7.

Exercise 1B

1   Probability that 2 is the same as 1 but 3 is different is $\frac{1}{6} \times \frac{5}{6} = \frac{5}{36}$. Similarly for the other two arrangements, so P(double) $= \frac{5}{12}$. Alternatively, P(triple) $= \frac{1}{6} \times \frac{1}{6}$ and P(all different) $= \frac{5}{6} \times \frac{4}{6}$, so P(double) $= 1 - \frac{1}{36} - \frac{20}{36}$.

2   (a) 0.4;   (b) $\frac{1}{2} \times 0.4 + \frac{1}{2} \times 0.6 = 0.5$;   (c) $0.6 \times 0.6 + 0.4 \times 0.4 = 0.52$.

3   Assuming that the probability of the third pair of twins is also $\frac{1}{8}$ (and it seems unlikely that it would be smaller), the probability of three pairs of twins in a row would be $\frac{1}{80} \times \frac{1}{8} \times \frac{1}{8} = \frac{1}{5120}$. This may appear large, but it assumes that, having already produced twins, the parents decide to enlarge the family further; many couples after the first pair of twins (and even more after the second) might not wish to tempt providence yet again. The element of personal choice makes it especially difficult to investigate statistically human behaviour.

4   $\frac{3}{13}s + \frac{10}{13}(1 - s) = \frac{1}{13}(10 - 7s)$. This is a useful technique for researching sensitive questions; if the proportion of "yes" answers is y, then s can be estimated by solving the equation $\frac{1}{13}(10 - 7s) = y$.

5   (a) $\frac{1}{10}$;   (b) $\frac{1}{5}$.

6   The probability should be $1 - (1 - p_1)(1 - p_2)(1 - p_3)(1 - p_4)$, but since the p_i are small it is reasonable to approximate to this as $p_1 + p_2 + p_3 + p_4$.

7   P(A or B) $\neq$ P(A) + P(B); P(A and B) $= 0.67 \neq$ P(A) $\times$ P(B).

8   P(C) $= \frac{1}{4}$, so that P(B and C) $= \frac{1}{6} + \frac{1}{4} - \frac{3}{8}$, which equals P(B) $\times$ P(C).

9   (a) P(M or E) $= 90\%$, so P(M and E) $= 60\%$;   (b) P(E|M) $= 75\%$.

10   $\frac{1}{45}$. Denote P(B and L) by x, and express P(B and $\sim$L) and P($\sim$B and L) in terms of x. It may help to set out the data in a 'contingency table' of probabilities, thus:

	L	$\sim$L
B	x	
$\sim$B		$\frac{4}{5}$

11   Show (perhaps using a contingency table, as in question 10), that P(diseased and reacts) $= 0.05$. Then P(reacts|diseased) $= \frac{5}{7}$.

12 $P(RRR) + P(BBB) + P(WWW) = \frac{12}{24} \times \frac{11}{23} \times \frac{10}{22} + \cdots + \cdots = \frac{35}{253}$.
$P(RBW) = \frac{12}{24} \times \frac{8}{23} \times \frac{4}{22}$, and similarly for the other five arrangements, so P(all different) $= \frac{48}{253}$.

13 $P(\text{all different}) = \dfrac{N-1}{N} \times \dfrac{N-2}{N} \times \ldots \times \dfrac{N-M+1}{N} = \dfrac{(N-1)!}{N^{M-1}(N-M)!}$;
P(at least one repeat) $= 1 - P(\text{all different})$.

14 (*a*) 0.504 (see question 13); (*b*) $6 \times 0.072 = 0.432$ (the pair can occur in any of six places); (*c*) $3 \times 0.009 = 0.027$ (the pairing can occur in three ways); (*d*) $4 \times 0.009 = 0.036$; (*e*) 0.001. These probabilities form the basis of the 'poker test' for randomness (see §6.8).

15 The direct approach leads to infinite geometric progressions:

$P(A \text{ wins}) = \frac{1}{3} + (\frac{2}{3} \times \frac{1}{3} \times \frac{1}{3})\frac{1}{3} + (\frac{2}{3} \times \frac{1}{3} \times \frac{1}{3})^2\frac{1}{3} + \ldots = \frac{9}{25}$.
and by a similar calculation $P(B \text{ wins}) = \frac{12}{25}$, $P(C \text{ wins}) = \frac{4}{25}$. Another method is to use a tree diagram:

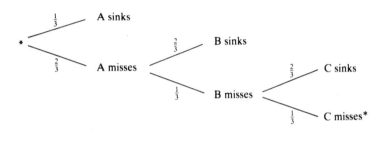

The probability of any player winning is the same at both points marked *. So if P(A wins) $= a$, etc,

$a = \frac{1}{3} + \frac{2}{3} \times \frac{1}{3} \times \frac{1}{3}a, \quad b = \frac{2}{3} \times \frac{2}{3} + \frac{2}{3} \times \frac{1}{3} \times \frac{1}{3}b, \quad c = \frac{2}{3} \times \frac{1}{3} \times \frac{2}{3} + \frac{2}{3} \times \frac{1}{3} \times \frac{1}{3}c.$

16 $\frac{4}{15}, \frac{4}{15}, \frac{3}{15}; \frac{1}{4}, \frac{1}{4}, \frac{1}{4}, \frac{1}{4}.$

17 Any such run must begin either T ... or HT ..., and the probabilities of these initial results are $\frac{1}{2}$ and $\frac{1}{4}$. So

P(no HH in *n* tosses) $= \frac{1}{2} \times$ P(no HH in $n-1$ tosses) $+ \frac{1}{4} \times$ P(no HH in $n-2$ tosses).

Also $a_2 = \frac{3}{4}$, $a_3 = \frac{5}{8}$, from which $a_5 = \frac{13}{32}$.

18 In bridge there are 4 players, conventionally described by their positions round the table:

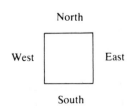

Each player has 13 cards. One player (South, say) is 'declarer', and his partner (North) lays her cards face up on the table, so that he can see 26 of the cards. One of the four suits is called 'trumps'. In this question the 26 cards which South cannot see are shared between his two opponents (East and West), and 4 of these are trumps. We need only consider the cards held by one of them (East, say), since if these are known so are those held by the other; it helps to think of them in the order in which they are dealt.

(a) To find P(East holds 2 trumps), note that the probability that the first two cards dealt to East are trumps and the rest non-trumps is $(\frac{4}{26} \times \frac{3}{25})(\frac{22}{24} \times \frac{21}{23} \times \frac{20}{22} \times \cdots \times \frac{12}{14}) = \dfrac{3}{25 \times 23}$; and similarly if the trumps come in any of the 78 possible positions. So the probability that the trumps fall 2–2 is $\frac{234}{575} \approx 0.407$.

(b) P(East holds 1 trump) $= (\frac{4}{26})(\frac{22}{25} \times \frac{21}{24} \times \frac{20}{23} \times \cdots \times \frac{11}{14}) \times 13 = \frac{143}{575}$, and P(East holds 3 trumps) = P(West holds 1 trump) is the same. So the probability that the trumps fall 1–3 or 3–1 is $\frac{286}{575} \approx 0.497$.

(c) P(East holds no trumps) $= \frac{22}{26} \times \frac{21}{25} \times \frac{20}{24} \times \ldots \times \frac{10}{14} = \frac{55}{1150}$, and P(East holds 4 trumps) = P(West holds no trumps) is the same. So the probability that the trumps fall 0–4 or 4–0 is $\frac{55}{575} \approx 0.096$.

Exercise 1C

1   $\frac{1}{4} \times 0.02\% + \frac{3}{4} \times 0.004\% = 0.008\%$; $\frac{0.00005}{0.00008} = \frac{5}{8}$.

2   0.38; $\frac{9}{19}$.

3   0.106; $\frac{1}{894} \approx 0.11\%$.

4   (a) $\frac{17}{240}$;   (b) $\frac{10}{17}$;   (c) $\frac{133}{223}$.

5   $P(B_s|A_r) \times P(A_r) / \sum_{i=1}^{m} P(B_s|A_i) \times P(A_i)$.

Exercise 2A

1   (a) P(same suit) $= 4 \times \frac{1}{17} \approx 0.24$; P(different suits) $= 6 \times \frac{13}{102} \approx 0.76$.
    (b) P(two red) = P(two black) $= \frac{1}{2} \times \frac{25}{51} \approx 0.245$; P(one of each) $= \frac{26}{51} \approx 0.510$.

2   (a) P(all same suit) $= \frac{12}{51} \times \frac{11}{50} \approx 0.052$; P(two the same) $= 3 \times \frac{12}{51} \times \frac{39}{50} \approx 0.551$; P(all different) $= \frac{39}{51} \times \frac{26}{50} \approx 0.398$.
    (b) P(three red) = P(three black) $= \frac{1}{2} \times \frac{25}{51} \times \frac{24}{50} \approx 0.118$; P(two red, one black) = P(one red, two black) $= 3 \times \frac{1}{2} \times \frac{25}{51} \times \frac{26}{50} \approx 0.382$.

3   (a) $(\frac{3}{4})^{10} \approx 0.056$.
    (b) The probability of the given pattern is $\frac{3}{4} \cdot \frac{1}{4} \cdot \frac{3}{4} \cdot \frac{3}{4} \cdot \frac{3}{4} \cdot \frac{1}{4} \cdot \frac{1}{4} \cdot \frac{1}{4} \cdot \frac{3}{4} \cdot \frac{1}{4}$, and similarly for every other arrangement with five diamonds, so the probability is $252 \times (\frac{1}{4})^5 (\frac{3}{4})^5 \approx 0.058$.
    It is usual to regard probabilities above 5% (0.05) as signifying nothing out of the ordinary, so the suspicions are not justified.

4   (a) $\frac{2}{15}, \frac{8}{15}, \frac{1}{3}$;   (b) $\frac{1}{30}, \frac{3}{10}, \frac{1}{2}, \frac{1}{6}$;   (c) $\frac{1}{210}, \frac{4}{35}, \frac{3}{7}, \frac{8}{21}, \frac{1}{14}$;   (d) $0, \frac{1}{42}, \frac{5}{21}, \frac{10}{21}, \frac{5}{21}, \frac{1}{42}$.

5   $\frac{91}{228}, \frac{105}{228}, \frac{15}{114}, \frac{1}{114}$.

Exercise 2B

Note. To avoid repetitive printing of fractions, tables of probabilities are often set out with all probabilities multiplied by their least common denominator.

2 (*a*)

$X - Y$	-5	-4	-3	-2	-1	0	1	2	3	4	5
Prob. $\times$ 36	1	2	3	4	5	6	5	4	3	2	1

This could be obtained by a diagram similar to Fig. 4 in the text, but tilting Fig. 3 through 45° in the opposite sense; lines for which $X - Y$ is constant are at right angles to those for which $X + Y$ is constant.

(*b*)

$|X - Y|$	0	1	2	3	4	5
Prob. $\times$ 18	3	5	4	3	2	1

(*c*)

XY	1	2	3	4	5	6	8	9	10	12	15	16	18	20	24	25	30
Prob. $\times$ 36	1	2	2	3	2	4	2	1	2	4	2	1	2	2	2	1	2

(*d*)

max(X, Y)	1	2	3	4	5	6
Prob. $\times$ 36	1	3	5	7	9	11

(*e*)

Number of sixes	0	1	2
Prob. $\times$ 36	25	10	1

3 (*a*)

$X + Y + Z$	3	4	5	6	7	8	9	10	11	12	13	14	15	16	17	18
Prob. $\times$ 216	1	3	6	10	15	21	25	27	27	25	21	15	10	6	3	1

The dots lying in the planes $X + Y + Z = c$ form triangles from $c = 3$ to 8 and from $c = 13$ to 18, and the entries in the table are the so-called 'triangular numbers'. Between $c = 9$ and $c = 12$ the dots form a hexagon pattern, and can be counted as a large triangle less three small triangles.

(*b*)

max(X, Y, Z)	1	2	3	4	5	6
Prob. $\times$ 216	1	7	19	37	61	91

Note that $7 = 2^3 - 1^3$, $19 = 3^3 - 2^3$, etc. Compare the answer to question 2(*d*).

(*c*)

Number of sixes	0	1	2	3
Prob. $\times$ 216	125	75	15	1

4 (*a*) 28.

(*b*)

Total	0	1	2	3	4	5	6	7	8	9	10	11	12
Prob. $\times$ 28	1	1	2	2	3	3	4	3	3	2	2	1	1

It is interesting to draw a diagram similar to Fig. 3 in the text for the possibility space of primitive outcomes; the crosses form a triangle rather than a square. The probability model for the totals can then be constructed by a method similar to that shown in Fig. 4.

5   The successive terms of the series are n^2 times the probabilities of getting totals of 2, 3, 4, ..., 2n. The probability model for rolling two dice is the same as the special case with $n = 6$.

6   (a)

Product	0	1	2	4
Prob.	$\frac{11}{36}$	$\frac{1}{9}$	$\frac{1}{3}$	$\frac{1}{4}$

(b)

Product	0	1	2	4	8
Prob.	$\frac{91}{216}$	$\frac{1}{27}$	$\frac{1}{6}$	$\frac{1}{4}$	$\frac{1}{8}$

7

Total	2	3	4	5	6	8
Prob (a)	$\frac{12}{72}$	$\frac{24}{72}$	$\frac{6}{72}$	$\frac{16}{72}$	$\frac{12}{72}$	$\frac{2}{72}$
Prob. (b)	$\frac{16}{81}$	$\frac{24}{81}$	$\frac{9}{81}$	$\frac{16}{81}$	$\frac{12}{81}$	$\frac{4}{81}$

Exercise 2C

2   In case last year's tables are not available, the following summary of results for the 1982–3 season may be used:

	Division				
	1	2	3	4	Total
Home win	255	220	297	283	1055
Away win	96	98	118	127	439
Draw	111	144	137	142	534
Total number of matches	462	462	552	552	2028

With these figures the probabilities are (a) 2.31×10^{-5}, (b) 1.52×10^{-4}.

3   The probability that a randomly selected client will make no claim in a month is 0.991, so the probability that he makes no claim in 36 months is $(0.991)^{36}$. The expected number of such entitlements is therefore about 14400.

Exercise 3A

1   (i) 0.5, 0.25, 0.125, 0.0625, ... for each outcome.
     (ii) 0.2, 0.16, 0.128, 0.1024, ... for A; 0.8, 0.16, 0.032, 0.0064 for B.

2   Note the infinite geometric progression $1 + a + a^2 + \cdots$ has sum $1/(1 - a) = 1/b$. P(run has length less than 5) $= b(1 + a + a^2 + a^3) = b(1 - a^4)/(1 - a) = 1 - a^4$, which is $1 - $ P(the first four outcomes after the first A are also A).

3 $(0.7)^2 \times 0.3 = 0.147$; $1 - (0.7)^{10} \approx 0.97$.

4 $\frac{1}{6}, \frac{5}{36}, \frac{25}{216}, \frac{125}{1296}, \ldots$; $0, \frac{1}{36}, 2 \times \frac{5}{216}, 3 \times \frac{25}{1296}, \ldots$ (note that, for example, the second six can occur on the fourth throw by rolling any of the sequences SNNS, NSNS, NNSS).

5   (i) $(b + c)a^{i-1}$,   (ii) $(1 - ab)(ab)^{i-1}$,   (iii) $(1 - abc)(abc)^{i-1}$,
     (iv) $(1 - a^2b)(a^2b)^{i-1}$, for $i = 1, 2, 3, \ldots$

Exercise 3B

1 $\binom{6}{3}(\frac{1}{2})^3(\frac{1}{2})^3 = 20 \times \frac{1}{64} = \frac{5}{16}$.

2 P(one six) $= 10 \times 5^9/6^{10}$; P(two sixes) $= 45 \times 5^8/6^{10} = 9 \times 5^9/6^{10}$; so one six is more probable. A general result, of which this is a special case, is given in question 16.

3 $(90 + 15 + 1)/4^5 \approx 0.10$.

4 P(0 hurdles) + P(1 hurdle) + P(2 hurdles) ≈ 0.80. But notice that, since stride pattern is affected by knocking down a hurdle, the events may not be independent.

5 $1 - $ P(0 or 1 Rhesus negative) ≈ 0.34.

6 0.29.

7 Imagine that the people sampled have no sense of taste whatsoever, and that they select merely on the toss of a coin: heads they choose Brand A, tails Brand B. Then the binomial probability model gives the probability that *at least* four out of the five choose Brand A as $\frac{3}{16}$, which is nearly 20%. If a result which is apparently so favourable to Brand A can occur by chance with such a high probability, the fact that in the test four out of five chose Brand A is of no significance.

This type of argument is typical of the process of "hypothesis testing", which is an important part of statistics; in this case the hypothesis is that "people prefer Brand A to Brand B". This topic is discussed in detail in Chapter 8, and the question has been inserted here to give a foretaste of things to come.

8 It is possible to answer the question laboriously by calculating

$$\sum_{i=1}^{3} \text{P}(i \text{ tails on first three throws}) \times \text{P(fewer than } i \text{ tails on last three throws)}.$$

But it is neater to note that there must be either (*a*) fewer, (*b*) the same number, or (*c*) more tails on the first three throws than on the last three. By symmetry, (*a*) and (*c*) have the same probability (since "fewer tails" implies "more heads", and in any toss H and T have the same probability). Also, we can argue that the probability of any sequence is unchanged if, on the last three throws, we call a head a "tail" and a tail a "head" (what's in a name?); so the probability of a sequence such as THH HTH, which is an example of (*b*), is the same as that of THH THT, which has the same number of heads as tails – and the probability of three heads and three tails in six tosses is $\frac{5}{16}$ (compare question 1). So the probability of (*a*) is $\frac{1}{2}(1 - \frac{5}{16}) = \frac{11}{32}$.

9 (*a*) $\frac{64}{243}$, (*b*) $\frac{256}{729}$. $\frac{64}{729} \times 6(0.8)^5(0.2) + \frac{64}{243} \times (0.8)^5 \approx 0.12$.

10 $(n - i)/(i + 1)$.
Begin by setting PROB as b^n, then for $i = 0$ to n follow the sequence
   PRINT i, PROB
   PROB $=$ PROB $* (n - i)/(i + 1) * a/b$.

11 Choose $a = b = \frac{1}{2}$, then multiply by 2^n. You can verify the result by adding along the rows of Pascal's triangle (see question 12).

12 The result of question 10, with $i - 1$ in place of i, gives

$$\binom{n}{i} = \frac{n - i + 1}{i} \times \binom{n}{i - 1},$$

so that the left side of the relation to be proved is

$$\left(1 + \frac{n-i+1}{i}\right) \times \binom{n}{i-1} = \frac{n+1}{i} \times \frac{n!}{(i-1)!(n-i+1)!} = \frac{(n+1)!}{i!(n+1-i)!}$$

$$= \binom{n+1}{i}.$$

13 $P(2A, 1B, 2C) = 30a^2bc^2$.

14   Using the result of question 10,

$$\binom{7}{i}\left(\frac{2}{3}\right)^i\left(\frac{1}{3}\right)^j < \binom{7}{i+1}\left(\frac{2}{3}\right)^{i+1}\left(\frac{1}{3}\right)^{j-1} \Leftrightarrow \frac{1}{3} < \frac{7-i}{i+1}\cdot\frac{2}{3} \Leftrightarrow 3i < 13.$$

So $P(0A, 7B) < P(1A, 6B) < \cdots < P(5A, 2B)$, but
$P(5A, 2B) > P(6A, 1B) > P(7A, 0B)$.

15   Replacing 7 by 8 in question 14 leads to the inequality $3i < 15$, or $i < 5$. The reverse inequality holds if $i > 5$. But if $i = 5$ the two probabilities are equal, so that $P(5A, 3B) = P(6A, 2B)$ are the largest probablities.

16   If $(n + 1)a$ is not a whole number, then the largest whole number i which satisfies $i < (n + 1)a - 1$ is $i = [(n + 1)a] - 1$.

Exercise 3C

1   (a) $\frac{5}{8}$,   (b) $\frac{77}{128}$; twice.

2   4 evenings in 11.

3 $\frac{23}{144}$.

4 $P(A_{n+1}) = 0.2P(A_n) + 0.6P(B_n)$, $P(B_{n+1}) = 0.8P(A_n) + 0.4P(B_n)$. 0.4, 0.6; 0.44, 0.56; 0.424, 0.567; 0.4304, 0.5696; approaching steady values $\frac{3}{7}$, $\frac{4}{7}$, which are the elements of each column in the limiting value of T^n.

5 $P(R_{n+1}) = \frac{1}{3}P(R_n) + \frac{4}{9}P(G_n)$, $P(G_{n+1}) = \frac{2}{3}P(R_n) + \frac{5}{9}P(G_n)$,   with $P(R_0) = 0.4$, $P(G_0) = 0.6$. Since these initial probabilities are also the steady probabilities, $P(R_n) = 0.4$ and $P(G_n) = 0.6$ for all n.

6   "I have a die and a pack of cards. First I roll the die. If it is not a six, I roll again; if it is a six, I take a card. If the card is not a spade, I take another; if it is a spade, I roll the die." The steady probabilities 0.6, 0.4 give the proportions of occasions on which I roll the die or draw the card in the long run.

7   Note that $x_0 = 1 - \frac{5}{11} = \frac{6}{11}$, so that $x_n = \frac{6}{11}\left(\frac{4}{15}\right)^n$.

8 $u_0 = 1$, so $x_0 = \dfrac{q}{q+s}$, $x_n = (p - s)^n x_0$ and $u_n = \dfrac{s}{q+s} + \dfrac{q}{q+s}(p - s)^n$, which approaches the value $s/(q + s)$.

9 $P(H_n) = P(T_n) = \frac{1}{2}$. Transition matrix $\begin{bmatrix} 0 & 1 \\ 1 & 0 \end{bmatrix}$, a reflection in the line with direction $\begin{bmatrix} 1 \\ 1 \end{bmatrix}$.

10 (a) $P(H_n) = P(T_n) = \frac{1}{2}$; $\begin{bmatrix} 1 & 0 \\ 0 & 1 \end{bmatrix}$. (b) $P(H_n) = 1 - (\frac{1}{2})^{n+1}$, $P(T_n) = (\frac{1}{2})^{n+1}$; $\begin{bmatrix} 1 & \frac{1}{2} \\ 0 & \frac{1}{2} \end{bmatrix}$.

12 0.3, 0.2, 0.5; 0.45, 0.10, 0.45; 0.395, 0.110, 0.495; approaching 0.4, 0.1, 0.5, so there is a probability 0.9 that the car will be free on March 1 (since after 28 days the probabilities are almost equal to the steady probabilities).

13 Probabilities $\frac{8}{27}, \frac{8}{27}, \frac{11}{27}; \frac{25}{81}, \frac{28}{81}, \frac{28}{81}$.

14 $\begin{bmatrix} 0.6 & 0.2 & 0.2 \\ 0.3 & 0.6 & 0.4 \\ 0.1 & 0.2 & 0.4 \end{bmatrix}$; $\frac{1}{3}, \frac{11}{24}, \frac{5}{24}$.

Exercise 3D

1

Run length		1	2	3	4	5	6	7	8	9
Probability	O	0.40	0.24	0.14	0.09	0.05	0.03	0.02	0.01	0.01
	C	0.33	0.22	0.15	0.10	0.07	0.04	0.03	0.02	0.01
	A	0.54	0.25	0.11	0.05	0.02	0.01	0.01	0.00	0.00
	B	0.46	0.25	0.13	0.07	0.04	0.02	0.01	0.01	0.00

2 (a) If he rolls a black, use die 2 next time; if he rolls white, use die 1.
(b) If he rolls a black, use die 1 next time; if he rolls white, use die 2.
(c) Always use die 2 (Bernoulli sequence).

Run length			1	2	3	4	5	6	7	8	9
Probability	(a)	B	0.25	0.19	0.14	0.11	0.08	0.06	0.04	0.03	0.03
		W	0.25	0.19	0.14	0.11	0.08	0.06	0.04	0.03	0.03
	(b)	B	0.75	0.19	0.05	0.01	0.00	0.00	0.00	0.00	0.00
		W	0.75	0.19	0.05	0.01	0.00	0.00	0.00	0.00	0.00
	(c)	B	0.25	0.19	0.14	0.11	0.08	0.06	0.04	0.03	0.03
		W	0.75	0.19	0.05	0.01	0.00	0.00	0.00	0.00	0.00

Exercise 4A
1 (a) Even in a large county, the statistics for a single month (based perhaps on about 100 births) might give a fairly unreliable estimate.
(b) Such an estimate would not allow for possible geographical or seasonal variations, or the peculiarities of a particular year; it would be better to randomise the sample.
(c) Our astronauts are highly selected physically, and untypical of the population as a whole; the same probably goes for Martian astronauts.

2 There is no evidence of a steady trend for the proportion to increase or decrease, so it is reasonable to assume the probability remains constant, and to base the estimate on the sample of 200 plates, of which 10 are faulty, giving a probability of 0.05.

3 (i) 0.58; (ii) $\frac{10}{21} \approx 0.48$. (The sequence was in fact produced from an experiment in which $P(A) = 0.6$. Estimation based on a sample of this size is not very reliable.)

4 Suppose that the proportion of marked animals in the whole population is equal to the proportion of marked animals in the sample recaptured, i.e.

$$\frac{\text{number of animals marked}}{\text{total population}} = \frac{\text{number of marked animals recaptured}}{\text{total number captured second time}}.$$

Exercise 4B

1 $L(a) = \binom{50}{5} a^5 (1 - a)^{45}$, so $L'(a) = Ca^4 (1 - a)^{44}(1 - 10a)$ where C is constant.

2 $L(s) = \binom{20}{3} s^3 (1 - s)^{17}$, giving the estimate 0.15 for s.

3 0.05.

4 $L(x) = \binom{n}{r} x^r (1 - x)^{n-r}$, leading to the estimate r/n for x. The maximum likelihood principle can therefore be used to give a theoretical justification for the empirical estimate of probability as $F(C)/n$.

5 $L(x) = \text{constant} \times x^{r_1 + r_2 + r_3}(1 - x)^{n_1 - r_1 + n_2 - r_2 + n_3 - r_3}$, giving the estimate $(r_1 + r_2 + r_3)/(n_1 + n_2 + n_3)$. Note that this can be written as

$$\left(n_1 \cdot \frac{r_1}{n_1} + n_2 \cdot \frac{r_2}{n_2} + n_3 \cdot \frac{r_3}{n_3} \right) / (n_1 + n_2 + n_3),$$

which is the weighted mean of the estimates r_1/n_1, r_2/n_2, r_3/n_3 for the three days separately. Question 3 gives a numerical example of this result.

6 With nine spins, $L(n) = \binom{9}{2} \left(\frac{n}{18}\right)^2 \left(1 - \frac{n}{18}\right)^7$. It is not strictly proper to use calculus to find the maximum, since the variable n can only take integer values. But if n is replaced by continuous variable x, we find that $L(x)$ has a maximum when $x = 4$; so $n = 4$ must give the greatest value of $L(n)$.

In (*a*) the corresponding value of x is 3.6, so $L(n)$ must be greatest either when $n = 3$ or $n = 4$. A numerical check shows that the maximum likelihood estimate is 4. In (*b*) we find $x = 3.27$ for the maximum, and a numerical check then gives an estimate of 3.

7 At each draw the probability of a white bead is $w/100$, so that the likelihood $L(w) = \binom{10}{4} \left(\frac{w}{100}\right)^4 \left(1 - \frac{w}{100}\right)^6$. This is greatest when $w = 40$.

8 $L(w + 1) > L(w) \Leftrightarrow \dfrac{w + 1}{w - 3} > \dfrac{100 - w}{94 - w} \Leftrightarrow w < 39.4$, so that $w = 40$ maximises the likelihood.

9 For sampling with replacement, the calculus method (replacing w by a continuous variable x) gives a maximum when $x = 37.5$, so that the maximum likelihood must occur either when $w = 37$ or $w = 38$; numerical substitution gives a marginally higher value when $w = 38$. For sampling without replacement, $L(w + 1) > L(w) \Leftrightarrow w < 36.875$, so that $w = 37$ gives the greatest likelihood.

11 Two approaches are possible, according as the sampling on the second occasion is carried out with or without replacement; that is, whether or not the same squirrel can be counted twice.

If it is with replacement, then the probability of a squirrel selected at random being marked is $20/n$, where n is the total population. The likelihood of the outcome recorded, four marked in a sample of 30, is then $L(n) = \binom{30}{4}\left(\dfrac{20}{n}\right)^4\left(1 - \dfrac{20}{n}\right)^{26} =$ constant $\times (n - 20)^{26}n^{-30}$. Replacing the integer n by a continuous variable x,

$$L'(x) = \text{constant} \times (x - 20)^{25}x^{-31}(600 - 4x),$$

so the maximum of $L(x)$ is at $x = 150$; since this is an integer, it is the maximum likelihood esxtimate for n.

If it is without replacement, the likelihood is $\binom{20}{4}\binom{n - 20}{26}\Big/\binom{n}{30}$. Then

$$L(n + 1) > L(n) \Leftrightarrow \frac{n - 19}{n - 45} > \frac{n + 1}{n - 29} \Leftrightarrow n < 149,$$

and $L(n)$ takes its maximum equally when $n = 149$ or 150.

The extrapolation principle gives an estimate of $\frac{30}{4} \times 20 = 150$.

12 The probability that the fifth six occurs on the nth throw is

$$P(4 \text{ sixes in the first } n - 1 \text{ throws}) \times P(n\text{th throw is a six})$$

$$= \binom{n - 1}{4}\left(\frac{1}{6}\right)^4\left(\frac{5}{6}\right)^{n-5} \times \left(\frac{1}{6}\right) = \binom{n - 1}{4}\left(\frac{1}{6}\right)^5\left(\frac{5}{6}\right)^{n-5},$$

which is the likelihood $L(n)$. Since $L(n + 1) > L(n) \Leftrightarrow n < 24$, $L(n)$ is greatest when $n = 24$ or 25.

13 When $a = 0.12$, P(2 or fewer faulty) $\approx 0.002 + 0.011 + 0.038 = 0.051$. When $a = 0.007$, P(2 or more faulty) $\approx 1 - (0.704 + 0.248) = 0.048$. So (i) and (ii) are less then 0.05 respectively when a is greater than 0.12 and less than 0.007, approximately. More accurate answers can be found by using algebraic expressions for (i) and (ii), as $(1 - a)^{48}(1 + 48a + 1176a^2)$ and $1 - (1 - a)^{49}(1 + 49a)$. This gives an interval of "reasonable" values $0.0072 < a < 0.1206$.

This question looks forward to an alternative approach to the problem of estimation, which is developed more fully in Chapter 8.

Exercise 5A

2 (*b*) If by a 'double' we mean that the random digit is the same as its predecessor, then a sequence such as 444 would count as two doubles, and 8888 as three. Then, if there are $n + 1$ random digits in all, we should expect to get about $\frac{1}{10}n$ doubles in the sequence.

3 (*b*) One possible coding would be to take the random digits in groups of three, and to make the correspondence "odd" $\rightarrow$ "boy", "even" $\rightarrow$ "girl" for each digit in the group.

4 (a) Use three-digit random numbers and take the remainder after division by 250.
(b) Use three-digit numbers and take the remainder after division by 200, counting a zero remainder as 200.
(c) Use four-digit numbers and proceed as in (b) using 80 as divisor.
(d) Use two-digit numbers, divide by 25 and add 34 to the remainder.

6 Since $9996 = 98 \times 102$, the random numbers 102, 1, 2, 3 occur once more amongst all the 10000 remainders than the others. So [CC] can arise in 591 ways, compared with 588 for [DD], [HH] and [SS]; the probabilities are respectively 0.0591 and 0.0588, compared with the correct value of $\frac{6}{102} = 0.05882\ldots$ Similarly, in the simulation [HS] can arise in 1275 ways, compared with 1274 for the other mixed pairs, giving probabilities of 0.1275 and 0.1274, compared with the correct value of 0.12745... One way of evening up the probabilities is to ignore the random numbers 9996, 9997, 9998, 9999 if they arise in the sequence.

7 Since $0.0588 < \frac{6}{102} < 0.0589$, $0.1176 < \frac{12}{102} < 0.1177$, all the random numbers from 0000 to 0588 will yield the outcome [CC], and those from 0589 to 1176 will yield [DD]. Thus the probabilities of these two outcomes are 0.0589 and 0.0588 respectively. Similarly, [HH] and [SS] have probabilities 0.0588; [CD], [CS] and [DS] have probabilities 0.1275; and [CH], [DH] and [HS] have probabilities 0.1274.

9 (c) One method would be to use four-digit random numbers, and to determine the suit from the first two digits (00 to 24 → C, 25 to 49 → D, etc.) and the card value from the last two (by one of the methods described in §5.2).

Exercise 5B

4 It will be necessary to retain each random digit in a store long enough for it to be compared with the next random digit generated, using an instruction for counting doubles such as

IF SCORE = LASTSCORE THEN COUNT = COUNT + 1.

5 The algorithm may lead one into undesirable loops: for example, numbers of the form ab00 or 00ab reproduce their own kind. The sequence does not therefore have the desired random properties.

6 The sum and the sum of the squares of the scores should be accumulated within the loop, using a set of instructions such as

```
FOR THROW = 1 TO n
S = RND(q)
SUM = SUM + S
SUMSQUARE = SUMSQUARE + S↑2
NEXT THROW
```

and the mean and variance then calculated from the final values of the variables SUM and SUMSQUARE.

7 The most interesting method is to write the graphics into the program so that the sticks are built up cumulatively within the loop.

9 See Note 3.9.

10   The probability that the random number contains a 7 is 0.19, so in the long run we would expect 3.8 in every 20 to have this property. The sticks in the graph should have heights which are roughly proportional to binomial probabilities with $a = 0.19$, $b = 0.81$ and $n = 20$ (see Exercise 3B, question 10).

Exercise 5C

1   Using the table of random numbers suggested, there are only 26 calls on day 2, with total duration of $60\frac{1}{2}$ hours, but six fire engines are needed.

Exercise 6A

2   (*a*) 25,   (*b*) 25,   (*c*) 50.

3   5, 10, 15, 20, 25, 30, 25, 20, 15, 10, 5.

4   Discrepancy = 6.81, $v = 2$: significant at the 5 % level, not at the 1 % level.

5   Discrepancy = 4.33, $v = 2$: not significant at the 10 % level.

7   Discrepancy = 20.46, $v = 5$. Significant at the 1 % level (and almost at 0.1 %).

9   Discrepancy = $\Sigma\{F_o(C_i)\}^2/F_e(C_i) - 2\Sigma F_o(C_i) + \Sigma F_e(C_i)$
          $= \Sigma\{F_o(C_i)\}^2/F_e(C_i) - 2n + n$ (see Q.3).

This form simplifies the calculation considerably if a calculator is used; the main drawback is that it does not draw attention to the terms which make the biggest contribution to the discrepancy. It may be compared with the alternative form for calculating the variance of a sample (see §1.1).

10   Although this is not a *proof* of the expression for the discrepancy, the argument developed in the question does go some way to making it mathematically plausible. It is developed here in the context of the experiment described in the text, but it can be generalised to apply to any sequence of trials with unequal probabilities.

Exercise 6B

1   The discrepancy is 1.28, with $v = 10$. This is significant at the 1 % level; the teacher has strong grounds for his suspicion.

2   A discrepancy of 0.52, with $v = 3$, is not significantly close at the 5 % level.

3   The discrepancies are (*a*) 0.47, (*b*) 3.73, (*c*) 9.91. With $v = 3$, the first two are not significant at either end of the scale, but the third is large enough to be significant at the 5 % level; however, this single piece of evidence would certainly not be strong enough to discredit the theory. (Some of Mendel's own figures are, in fact, uncomfortably close to the theoretical expected frequencies, and it has been suggested that one of his assistants may have distorted or suppressed some readings in order to make the evidence fit the theory better; at any rate, the readings recorded by one of his assistants appear notably more 'successful' than those recorded by the others.

4   The probabilities of the five outcomes are 0.6561, 0.2916, 0.0486, 0.0036, 0.0001; so with a hundred or two blocks the expected frequencies for the last two classes will be very small, and it would be prudent to combine (*c*), (*d*) and (*e*) into a single class, "two or more nines".

5 Theoretically the probabilities of runs of lengths 1, 2, 3, 4, ... are $\frac{1}{2}, \frac{1}{4}, \frac{1}{8}, \frac{1}{16}, \ldots$ and there is no end to this sequence. So it will be essential to combine all the frequencies beyond a certain point onto class, for "runs of length ... or more".

6 Taking four classes, "no sixes", "one six", "two sixes", "three or more sixes", gives a discrepancy of 7.89 with $v = 3$, which is just significant at the 5 % level.

7 It is best to combine the two classes at either end of each distribution. This then gives discrepancies of 2.15, 1.23 and 2.97 with $v = 3, 4, 5$ respectively, none of which is significantly large; there is no reason to question the appropriateness of the binomial probability model.

Exercise 7A

1 For example, $x = 2$ gives $(1 + x/n)^n = 7.374657 \ldots$ when $n = 2^{10}$, and $7.389032 \ldots$ when $n = 2^{20}$, compared with $e^2 = 7.389056 \ldots$

2 The sum can be computed with a program such as:

```
SUM = 1
TERM = 1
For I = 1 TO 10
TERM = TERM * X/I
SUM = SUM + TERM
NEXT I
```

4 $y = e^{-x}$ is the reflection of $y = e^x$ in the y-axis; $y = e^{2x}$ is obtained from $y = e^x$ by a squash of ratio $\frac{1}{2}$ parallel to the x-axis.

5 Denoting the sum by $s(x)$, $s'(x) = s(x) - x^k/k!$; so that, if k is large, $s'(x) \approx s(x)$.

6 Note that $f'(x) = f(x)/(1 + x/n)$, and the divisor is approximately 1 when n is large.

7 For example, the coefficient of x^2 is $\dfrac{n(n-1)}{2!} \cdot \dfrac{1}{n^2} = \dfrac{1}{2!}\left(1 - \dfrac{1}{n}\right)$, which is approximately $\dfrac{1}{2!}$ when n is large.

Exercise 7B

1 The probability is $3/60 = 0.05$. Probabilities 0.046, 0.145, 0.226, 0.230, ...

2 Using 2-digit random numbers, let 00, 01, 02, 03, 04 (for example) stand for "a customer arrives in the given second", and 05 to 99 stand for "no customer arrives".

3 1/600: 0.904, 0.091, 0.004, ...

Exercise 7C

1 0.548, 0.329, 0.099, 0.020, 0.003, ...

2 Using the distributive law, the sum is $e^\lambda \cdot e^{-\lambda} = 1$.

3 $1 - 5e^{-2} = 0.323$.

4 0.125.

5 0.184. The switchboard is fully loaded if 12 or more calls have come in during the previous 3 minutes; since the mean rate is 9 per 3-minute interval, the probability is 0.197.

6 We require P(k or fewer sold) > 0.98, so that $1 + 2 + \dfrac{2^2}{2!} + \cdots + \dfrac{2^k}{k!} > 0.98\,e^2$. By trial, k must be at least 5.

7 $\dfrac{\lambda^{i-1}}{(i-1)!}\,e^{-\lambda} < \dfrac{\lambda^i}{i!}\,e^{-\lambda}$ provided that $i < \lambda$, so the largest probability is when i is the largest integer less than λ, which is written $[\lambda]$. When λ is an integer, $i = \lambda - 1$ and $i = \lambda$ give equally the largest probability.

8 It is simplest to use the method of computing the probabilities illustrated in Example 1.

9 20, 60, 90, 90, 67, 40, 33. (a) £1260, (b) £1340, (c) £1286.

10 The Poisson probabilities are 0.050, 0.149, 0.224, 0.224, ... so you could use 3-digit random numbers and then code them as follows:

Random number	000 to 049	050 to 198	199 to 422	423 to 646 ...
Number of arrivals in the minute	0	1	2	3 ...

11 The probabilities can be worked out in either of two ways. The two units may be considered separately, giving (a) $p_0 p_0$, (b) $p_1 p_0 + p_0 p_1$, (c) $p_2 p_0 + p_1 p_1 + p_0 p_2$, (d) $p_3 p_0 + p_2 p_1 + p_1 p_2 + p_0 p_3$, which come to (a) $e^{-2\lambda}$, (b) $2\lambda e^{-2\lambda}$, (c) $2\lambda^2 e^{-2\lambda}$, (d) $\frac{4}{3}\lambda^3 e^{-2\lambda}$. Alternatively, work with a doubled unit of time, in which the average rate of occurrences is 2λ, and calculate the probabilities as $\dfrac{(2\lambda)^i}{i!}\,e^{-2\lambda}$ for $i = 0, 1, 2, 3$.

12 Again the probabilities can be worked out in two ways. The Poisson probabilities for the women and men can be found separately, as $p_0, p_1, p_2, \ldots$ and $q_0, q_1, q_2, \ldots$, in which case the probabilities are (a) $p_0 q_0$, (b) $p_1 q_0 + p_0 q_1$, etc. Alternatively the average rates can be combined to give a single average rate of $\lambda_1 + \lambda_2$ for people entering the shop.

13 The combined rate of breakdown is $1 + \frac{1}{2}$ per day. (a) 0.223,   (b) 0.191.

14 (a) 0.102, (b) 0.285 (note that on average 6 drinks are sold in a 3-minute period), (c) 0.696 (calculated as a conditional probability, P(3 coffees sold)/P(3 drinks sold)).

15 0.066.

16 0.287 (over a period of $1\frac{2}{3}$ months, $\lambda = 1.25$ for B), 0.271.

17 P(7 cases on day 1) $= \dfrac{\lambda^7}{7!}\,e^{-\lambda}$. P(4 cases on day 2) $= \dfrac{\lambda^4}{4!}\,e^{-\lambda}$, etc. Because of independence, the probability for the ten days on this hypothesis (i.e. the likelihood of the outcome) is as given. The numerical factors can be ignored; to maximise $f(\lambda) = \lambda^{39} e^{-10\lambda}$, put $f'(\lambda) = \lambda^{38}(39 - 10\lambda)e^{-10\lambda}$ equal to zero.

In the general case, the likelihood is $\dfrac{\lambda^{\Sigma a_i}}{a_1!a_2!\dots a_n!}e^{-n\lambda}$, which has a maximum when $\lambda = \Sigma a_i/n$, the mean of the daily numbers recorded. (For a note on the notation used, see the solution to Exercise 1A, question 6.)

18 $\dfrac{(\lambda t)^{i-1}}{(i-1)!}e^{-\lambda t} < \dfrac{(\lambda t)^i}{i!}e^{-\lambda t}$ provided that $i < \lambda t$; so if $i < \lambda t < i + 1$, the most probable number of cases is i.

Exercise 7D

1 0.668, 0.272, 0.053, 0.006.

2 For example, with $a = 0.02$ the probabilities are 0.368, 0.368, 0.184, 0.061, 0.015, 0.003, 0.001, vs.

3 $1 - (1 + 5)e^{-5} = 0.960$.

4 (a) $e^{-1} = 0.368$, (b) $1 - 2e^{-1} = 0.264$.

5 P(a success) $= 0.01$, so $\lambda = na = 2$. P(more than 4 successes) $= 0.053$.

6 $(0.99)^{200} + 200(0.99)^{199}(0.01) + 19900(0.99)^{198}(0.01)^2 + 1313400(0.99)^{197}(0.01)^3 + 64684950(0.99)^{196}(0.01)^4$

$$\approx \text{(far more simply) } \left(1 + 2 + \frac{2^2}{2!} + \frac{2^3}{3!} + \frac{2^4}{4!}\right)e^{-2} \approx 0.947.$$

P(5 or more abnormalities) $= 0.053$, or more than 1 in 20; so a week with five abnormalities is a bad week, but to be expected from time to time.

7 Mean $= 0.5$. P(3 or more) $= 0.014$.

8 228, 211, 98, 30, 7, 2 (for 5 or more).

9 (a) 0.779, 0.002; (b) $e^{-N/10^7} > 0.999$, so that $N < 10^4$ approximately.

Exercise 8A

1 Take a null hypothesis that "the support for Anna is still 40%", with an alternative hypothesis that "the support is greater than 40%"; and show that, on the basis of the null hypothesis, the probability that Anna would get eight or more votes in the magazine poll is 0.012. So taking a significance level of 5%, the null hypothesis is rejected; the magazine poll suggests a significant increase in her support.

2 Take a null hypothesis that the probability of selecting yellow is $\frac{1}{3}$. The probability that 10 or more children will select yellow is 0.092, which is greater than 0.05; so the null hypothesis is not rejected, which means that the researcher's conclusion is not justified.

3 The appropriate probability model is Poisson. With $\lambda = 10$, the probability of four or fewer attacks in a year is 0.029, which is below the 5% significance level. So reject the null hypothesis that tablets do no good, and accept the alternative hypothesis that they are effective in reducing the frequency of attacks.

4 With $\lambda = 5$, P(10 or more eruptions in a year) $= 0.032$. Deduce that the increase in activity is significant.

5 Either method gives P(2 or more colour-blind) = 0.09, so two out of 50 is not significantly high.

6 With $\lambda = 8$, P(4 or fewer accidents) = 0.100. No significant improvement.

7 With an average annual rate of 0.2 fatalities per year per 100 miles, P(3 or more fatalities) = 0.001, so there is a strong case for additional protection.

8 For an unbiased die, P(7 or more sixes) = 0.037, so 7 sixes out of 20 are sufficient to suggest bias.

However, it is not difficult to calculate that, in the three computer simulations, the probabilities of getting fewer than 7 sixes are respectively 0.913, 0.608 and 0.058. So it was very likely that in (a), even though a biased die was being simulated, the test would not show up the bias; there was a good chance that this would also happen in (b); and even in (c) the probability of not detecting the bias is greater than 5%.

This illustrates the two types of risk which are inescapable when carrying out statistical tests. On the one hand, there is the possibility that the die is not biased, but that (using the "7 or more" rule) we claim that it is; on the other hand, the die may in fact be biased, but our rule may not show this up, so that we accept the die as fair. Statisticians refer to these two errors as being of "Type I" and "Type II" respectively. Notice that if we make the criterion stiffer, say by requiring 9 sixes out of 20 as evidence of bias, then the probability of making a Type I error goes down, but the probability of a Type II error becomes bigger.

9 A two-tail test is needed. The coin can be rejected if it comes up 13 or more heads *or* 13 or more tails (probability $2 \times 0.0037 = 0.0074$).

10 The lobby will object if there are 11 or more women (probability 0.007) or 10 or more men (probability 0.010); any split between 9 men and 3 women, and 2 men and 10 women, will avoid objection. (Remember that the 5% excluded tails are conventionally split as $2\frac{1}{2}$% at either end.)

11 Between 2 and 12.

Exercise 8B

1 Between about 44.5% and 97.5%.

2 Between 27 and 87. (Compare Exercise 4B, question 7.)

3 Between about 4.3% and 48.1%.

4 It is the choice of between 46% and 88% of the population.

5 Between 2.9 and 14.4 (directly from Fig. 3; the relevant probability model in this case is Poisson).

6 Between 0.022 and 0.204.

7 Between 0.4% and 1.7%.

Revision exercise A

1 (a) $\frac{45}{1024}$, (b) $\frac{7}{128}$. 5 or more.

2 $\frac{1}{2}$. ± 3, probabilities $\frac{1}{8}$ each, ± 1, $\frac{3}{8}$ each. (a) 1, (b) 2, (c) 3, (d) 4. Least when $p = \frac{1}{2}$.

3 $\frac{1}{15}, \frac{7}{40}, \frac{3}{10}, \frac{5}{12}, \frac{1}{2}, \frac{21}{40}, \frac{7}{15}, \frac{3}{10}$ (for 2 to 9 bad in the box).

4 (a) $\frac{1}{10}$, (b) $\frac{1}{25}$, (c) $\frac{1}{4}$. 0.014, 0.015.

5 $\frac{1}{7} < p < \frac{4}{21}$.

6 (a) $\frac{1}{8}$, (b) $\frac{5}{32}$. $\frac{385}{1024}$. $3\frac{1}{4}\%$, $2\frac{1}{2}\%$. $\frac{10}{13}$.

7 P(no winner) $= 0$.

8 $1 - 2(\frac{5}{6})^n + (\frac{4}{6})^n$. Limit $= 1$.

9 (a) $\frac{1}{9}$, (b) $\frac{8}{81}$.

10 $\begin{bmatrix} 0.3 & 0.8 \\ 0.7 & 0.2 \end{bmatrix}$. (a) 0.4, (b) 0.5.

11 (a) 0.991, 0.977.
(b) 335, 402, 201, 54, 8, (1), 0 (replace 1 by 0 to ensure a total of 1000).
(c) Discrepancy is 42.3, a highly significant difference with 4 degrees of freedom (combining the last three entries).

12 (a) 0.050, (b) 0.318, (c) 0.423. $e^{-3}\left(1 + \dfrac{2}{(1!)^2} + \dfrac{2^2}{(2!)^2} + \dfrac{2^3}{(3!)^2} + \cdots\right)$

13 (a) 0.084, (b) 0.007.

14 (i) (a) 0.238, (b) 0.841, (ii) 0.083.

15 (a) 0.076, (b) 0.679, (c) 0.606, (d) 0.073.

16 (a) 0.939, (b) 0.938. 0.879.

17 Both have probability $\frac{1}{8}$. The second.

18 (a) 0.267, (b) 0.191. No (probability 0.135, not significant).

Exercise 9A

1 Mean loss £1.50 in each case; variances $(£)^2$ 42.25, 12.25, 22.25.

2 6.7 p.

3 4.47, 1.97.

4 Sector with score i has angle $(24i)°$. 3.67, 1.56.

5 3.5, 2.92, 1.71; 7, 5.83, 2.42 (mean and variance both doubled); 12.25 ($= 3.5^2$), 79.97, 8.94.

6 $\frac{1}{2}(n + 1)$, $\frac{1}{12}(n^2 - 1)$.

7 2.5, 1.25, 1.12; for n pennies, $\frac{1}{2}n$, $\frac{1}{4}n$, $\frac{1}{2}\sqrt{n}$.

8 $\frac{5}{6}$, $\frac{25}{36}$, $\frac{5}{6}$; for n dice, $\frac{1}{6}n$, $\frac{5}{36}n$, $\frac{1}{6}\sqrt{(5n)}$.

9 2.5; in the Poisson model the variance is equal to the mean (see §9.4).

10 a, ab; $2a$, $2ab$; for n trials, na, nab.

11 0.787. 13.15.

Exercise 9B

1    $1/a$, b/a^2.

2   na, $\sqrt{(nab)}$.

Exercise 9C

1    $0.4, 0.24, 0.144, \ldots, 0.4(0.6)^{i-1}$. $0.4t/(1 - 0.6t)$. 2.5, 1.94.

2   (a) 1.43×10^{-5},   (b) 1.13×10^{-35},   (c) 1.78×10^{-4},   (d) $\binom{50}{i}(0.8)^{50-i}(0.2)^i$.
     $(0.8 + 0.2t)^{50}$. 10, 2.83.

3   (a) $t(\frac{1}{3} + \frac{1}{6}t)/(1 - \frac{1}{2}t^2)$;   (b) $\frac{1}{4}t(1 + t)/(1 - \frac{1}{2}t^2)$.   (a) $3\frac{1}{3}$,   (b) $3\frac{1}{2}$.

4   (a) 100,   (b) 9.95.

5   (a) 16.2 weeks;   (b) 37.7 p.

6   (i) $\mu = 3.6$, $\sigma = 1.2$. Probability $= 0.588$. Median $= 4$, mode $= 4$.
     (ii) $\mu = 14.4$, $\sigma = 2.4$. Probability $= 0.595$ (0.694 if inclusive). Median $= 14$,
     mode $= 14$ or 15.
     (iii) $\mu = 5.76$, $\sigma = 2.4$. Probability $= 0.697$. Median $= 6$, mode $= 5$.
     (iv) $\mu = 5$, $\sigma = 4.47$. Probability $= 0.867$. Median $= 4$, mode $= 1$.

8    $\frac{1}{2}\{1 - G(-1)\}$. $0.2t/(1 - 0.8t)$. $\frac{5}{9}$.

9   Write $G(t)$ as $\left(1 + \dfrac{\lambda(t - 1)}{n}\right)^n$ and use property (2) of §7.1.

10   Probability is $1 - \{1 - (\frac{1}{2})^n\}^2$. If this is u_n, then $P(N = n) = u_{n-1} - u_n$. $\frac{8}{3}$, $\frac{8}{3}$.

11   The probability of a score less than or equal to n. The probabilities q(i) do not refer
     to exclusive events, so K(t) is not a probability generator in the usual sense.

12   The summation gives $G(t) - 1 = \frac{5}{6}tG(t) + \frac{1}{6}\left(\dfrac{t}{1 - t} - tG(t)\right)$.

13   $1, 0, \frac{1}{2}, \frac{1}{2}$.

Exercise 9D

1

Points	0	1	2	3	4	5	6
Probability	0.10	0.19	0.06	0.31	0.19	0	0.15

2   (a) $\frac{1}{2} + \frac{1}{2}t$,   (b) $(\frac{1}{2} + \frac{1}{2}t)^2$,   (c) $(\frac{1}{2} + \frac{1}{2}t)^n$.

3   (a) $(\frac{3}{4} + \frac{1}{4}t)^2$,   (b) $(\frac{3}{4} + \frac{1}{4}t)^3$,   (c) $(\frac{3}{4} + \frac{1}{4}t)^n$.

4    $b + at$, $(b + at)^n$. This shows that the binomial probability model is a consequence of
     the multiplicative property.

5   (a) $3^{3(t-1)}$,   (b) $e^{2(t-1)}$,   (c) $e^{5(t-1)}$,   (d) $e^{120(t-1)}$.

7   (a) $t/(6 - 5t)$,   (b) $t^2/(6 - 5t)^2$,   (c) $t^r/(6 - 5t)^r$.   (d) 0.058,   (e) 0.032. $6r$,
     $\sqrt{(30r)}$.

8 $(\frac{1}{6}t + \frac{1}{3}t^2 + \frac{1}{2}t^3)^5$. $\frac{1}{2}\{1 + G(-1)\} = \frac{121}{243}$ (see Exercise 9C, question 7).

9 $\frac{19}{125}$.

10   First method 20, 64; second method 0, 100.

11   The sum of the generators has no useful interpretation. Note that $G(1) + H(1) \neq 1$.

12 $K(t) = \{G(t)\}^n$. Mean $= n\mu$, variance $= n\sigma^2$.

13   From $K(t) = G(t)H(t)$ deduce $K'(1) = G'(1) + H'(1)$ and $K''(1) = G''(1) + 2G'(1)H'(1) + H''(1)$.

Exercise 10A

1   Mean $= 2$. $n = 6$, $a = \frac{1}{3}$; 17.56, 52.67, 65.84, 43.90, 16.46, 3.29, 0.27. Combining the last two classes gives a discrepancy of 0.90 with $\nu = 4$: a good fit.

2 $p = 0.6$; 5.12, 30.72, 69.12, 69.12, 25.92.
    Discrepancy $= 0.133$ with $\nu = 3$, which is smaller than the critical value 0.352 for 95%. The hypothesis "the student obtained the results from a random experiment" is therefore rejected; it is likely that he made up the frequencies from the theory without carrying out the experiment at all.

3   The hypothesis $a = \frac{1}{6}$ gives a discrepancy between observed and expected frequencies of 7.89 (combining the last three classes), which is just significant with $\nu = 3$ at the 5% level; we conclude that the die is biased.
    The probability suggested by the data is 0.2, which leads to a discrepancy of 0.04. This is smaller than the critical value at 95% with $\nu = 2$, suggesting that the figures in the question (which comes from an examination paper) may have been made up rather than obtained experimentally.

4   Mean $= 3.023$; 2.14, 6.47, 9.78, 9.86, 7.45, 4.50, 3.84 (for 6 or more).
    The discrepancy 1.13 with $\nu = 5$ is not significant, so that the hypothesis of a Poisson model is acceptable. (You may be interested to investigate the hypothesis using a more recent set of results.)

5   Fitting a Poisson model with mean 2 gives a discrepancy between observed and expected frequencies of 9.24 (combining "5 or more" into a single class), which is below the critical value for 5% with $\nu = 4$. The model is not therefore rejected.

6   Combining "4 or more" into a single class, a Poisson model with mean 0.62 gives a discrepancy of 16.1, which is almost significant at the 0.1% level with $\nu = 3$; the Poisson model does not give an acceptable fit. (Notice, though, that the weakness lies in the figures for 3, 4, ... visits; if "3 or more" is combined into a single class, the discrepancy falls to 0.74, which with $\nu = 2$ indicates a good fit.)

7   Discrepancy $= 1.35$, with $\nu = 2$; a good fit.

8   3, 3. Discrepancy $= 5.69$, with $\nu = 6$; Poisson model is acceptable.

9   (*a*) 2.5, 1.48.
    (*b*) 8.21, 20.52, 25.65, 21.38, 13.36, 6.68, 4.20 (for 6 or more). Discrepancy $= 2.89$, with $\nu = 5$; Poisson model is acceptable.
    (*c*) The variance is somewhat low. For a Poisson model the mean and variance are equal, but the data have mean 2.5 and variance 2.19.

Exercise 10B

1   Discrepancy = 428.2, with $\nu = 2$; the hypothesis of independence is strongly rejected. (Education students have been omitted from the data; there is a disproportionate number of women reading education, for special local reasons.)

2   Discrepancy = 4.88, with $\nu = 1$; significant at the 5% level, so there is evidence of association.

3   Discrepancy = 28.72, with $\nu = 1$; the age distribution is significantly different in the epidemic year.

4   Discrepancy = 1.47, with $\nu = 1$; not significant.

6   Discrepancy = 7.15, with $\nu = 1$; the difference of behaviour is significant.

7   Discrepancy = 1.77, with $\nu = 3$; no significant difference.

8   Discrepancy = 9.28, with $\nu = 6$; no significant difference in the pattern of results between divisions.

Exercise 11A

2   The proportion (a) can be found exactly as the sum of the areas of the corresponding rectangles, but (b) can only be estimated approximately in this way because 2.8 is not a point of subdivision in the histogram.

3   The problem is that there is a certain number of days on which the rainfall is exactly 0 mm; to analyse the data, one wants to combine the relative frequency at 0 mm with the relative frequency *density* over intervals for the days when some rain falls. The only satisfactory way of showing this in a histogram is to begin with a very short interval (say 0 to 1 mm) including all the rain-free days, which would give a very tall narrow rectangle.

4   This presents a similar problem to question 3, since there will be some occasions when it is possible to cross immediately.

Exercise 11B

1   (a) 0.648,   (b) 0.544.

2   0.146.

3   0.39.

4   $\dfrac{3\sqrt{5}}{100}$.   (a) 0.07,   (b) 0.20.

5   $\dfrac{c}{\pi}(c^2 + x^2)^{-1}$.

Exercise 11C

1   0 miles, $\frac{1}{12}$ miles^2.

2   6 m.

3   4 minutes. (Note that $te^{-\frac{1}{4}t}$ tends to 0 as $t \to \infty$.)

4   $\frac{20}{7} \approx 2.86$ km, $\frac{200}{147} \approx 1.36$ km^2. (Use the substitution $x = 5 - u^2$.)

5   $k = 20$. Mean $= \frac{2}{3}$, variance $= \frac{2}{63}$. $P(\mu - \sigma < X < \mu + \sigma) \approx 0.65$.

6   $k = 1$. Mean $= 1$, variance $= 1$. $P(\mu - \sigma < X < \mu + \sigma) = 1 - e^{-2} \approx 0.86$.

7   (a) $1/\pi$,   (b) $\frac{1}{2}$,   (c) $\frac{1}{3}$.

8   Mean $= 0$, standard deviation $= b/\sqrt{5}$. The ratio $c/b = x$ satisfies $3x - x^3 = 1.9$, and the relevant solution can be found by trial and error as $x = 0.811$, giving $c = 1.81\sigma$.

9   $k = \lambda^2$. Probability $\displaystyle\int_0^{(2 + 2\sqrt{2})/\lambda} \phi(x)\,dx = 1 - (3 + 2\sqrt{2})e^{-(2 + \sqrt{2})} \approx 0.81$.

10   (a) The value of x such that $\phi(x)$ is a maximum.   (b) The number v such that $\displaystyle\int_0^v \phi(x)\,dx = \frac{1}{2}$.

For question 5, mode $= \frac{3}{4}$, median satisfies $5v^4 - 4v^5 = \frac{1}{2}$, $v \approx 0.69$.
For question 6, mode $= 0$, median $= \ln 2 \approx 0.69$.

11   (i) 0.62,   (ii) 0.38.

12   $\displaystyle\int_a^b \phi(r)\,dr = \frac{1}{100}(b^2 - a^2)$, giving $\phi(r) = \frac{1}{50}r$. Mean $= \frac{20}{3}$ miles, variance $= \frac{50}{9}$ miles^2.

13   By a method similar to question 12, $\phi(r) = 3r^2/c^3$. Mean $= \frac{3}{4}c$, variance $= \frac{3}{80}c^2$.

16   (i) $\displaystyle\int_a^b \phi(x)\,dx = 1$.   (ii) Centre of mass, moment of inertia.   (iii) Radius of gyration.   (iv) Parallel axes rule.

17   Mean $= 20\,\text{s}$. (This is based on the assumption that the times are evenly spread over each interval, so that they can be supposed for the purposes of calculation to be located at the centre of the interval. In this example it is likely that they will be concentrated more densely towards the left of each interval, so that this value for the mean is probably an over-estimate.)
$A = \lambda$.

Choose $\lambda = 0.05$. The probability of a time interval between a seconds and b seconds is, on this model, $e^{-\lambda a} - e^{-\lambda b}$, giving expected frequencies 63.3, 29.9, 14.1, 6.7, 3.2, 2.8. The discrepancy is 2.88 with $v = 4$, indicating satisfactory agreement between the experimental data and the model.

18   $\lambda = 0.01$. Expected frequencies 196.7, 119.3, 72.4, 43.9, 26.6, 16.1, 9.8, 5.9, 3.6, 2.2, 3.4. Discrepancy $= 4.75$ with $v = 9$, indicating satisfactory agreement.

Exercise 11D

2   $\pounds x = \pounds 68.80$, $\pounds y = \pounds 90.20$.

3   Mean $= 6\,\text{kg}$, variance $= 7.7\,\text{kg}^2$.

Exercise 11E

1   $\Phi(x) = \frac{1}{2}(1 - \cos x)$.

2   $\phi(x) = ke^{-kx}$.

3   $0.004x^3 - 0.0003x^4$.

6 $\dfrac{1}{\mu}e^{-t/\mu}$. Probability $= e^{-2} \approx 0.14$. Mean lifetime must exceed 4997 hours.

7 (a) $\frac{3}{32}$. (b) $\frac{11}{16}$. (c) $\phi(x) = \frac{3}{32}(4 - x^2)$ for $-2 < x < 2$, 0 otherwise. (d) Mean $= 0$, variance $= 0.8$.

8 (i) x/b. (ii) P(score $< x$) = P(all three shots $< x$) $= (x/b)^3$. (iii) $\phi(x) = 3x^2/b^3$ for $0 < x < b$, 0 otherwise.

9 (a) x^2/r^2. (b) P(best shot $< x$) $= 1 - $ P(all shots $> x$) $= 1 - (1 - x^2/r^2)^5$. $\phi(x) = \dfrac{10x}{r^2}(1 - x^2/r^2)^4$ for $0 < x < r$, 0 otherwise.

10 P$(0 < Y < y)$ = P$(-\sqrt{y} < X < \sqrt{y}) = \dfrac{2}{\pi}\tan^{-1}(\sqrt{y})$. $1/\pi\sqrt{y}(1 + y)$ for $y > 0$.

11 Integrate $\displaystyle\int_a^b x\Phi'(x)\,dx$ by parts to obtain $\mu = b - \displaystyle\int_a^b \Phi(x)\,dx$. When $b > 0 > a$, the mean is the difference between the area above the curve to the right of the vertical axis and the area below the curve to the left of the axis. The median is the value of x for which $\Phi(x) = \frac{1}{2}$; the mode is where the gradient is steepest.

Exercise 12A

1 $\Phi(s) = \frac{1}{2}(1 + s)^2$, $1 - \frac{1}{2}(1 - s)^2$ and $\phi(s) = 1 + s$, $1 - s$ for $-1 < s \leqslant 0$, $0 < s < 1$ respectively.

2 $\Phi(g) = g^2/b^2$, $\phi(g) = 2g/b^2$ for $0 < g < b$.

3 (i) $\Phi(q) = \frac{1}{2}q$, $\phi(q) = \frac{1}{2}$; (ii) $\Phi(q) = 1 - 1/(2q)$, $\phi(q) = 1/(2q^2)$.

4 $\phi(t) = \dfrac{1}{b^2}\ln\left(\dfrac{b^2}{t}\right)$ for $0 < t < b^2$.

6 $\Phi(s) = \dfrac{s^2}{2bc}$, $\dfrac{2s - b}{2c}$, $1 - \dfrac{(b + c - s)^2}{2bc}$ and $\phi(s) = \dfrac{s}{bc}$, $\dfrac{1}{c}$, $\dfrac{b + c - s}{bc}$ for $0 < s \leqslant b$, $b < s \leqslant c$, $c < s < b + c$ respectively.

7 Mean $= b$, standard deviation $= b/\sqrt{6}$. (i) $2/\sqrt{6} - \frac{1}{6} \approx 0.650$, (ii) $4/\sqrt{6} - \frac{2}{3} \approx 0.966$.

8 The relevant regions of the cube in the three cases may be regarded as a right-angled tetrahedron, a right-angled tetrahedron less three smaller right-angled tetrahedra, and a cube less a right-angled tetrahedron.

$$\Phi(s) = \dfrac{s^3}{6b^3}, \quad \dfrac{s^3}{6b^3} - \dfrac{(s - b)^3}{2b^3}, \quad 1 - \dfrac{(3b - s)^3}{6b^3} \quad \text{and} \quad \phi(s) = \dfrac{s^2}{2b^3}, \quad \dfrac{s^2 - 3(s - b)^2}{2b^3},$$

$\dfrac{(3b - s)^2}{2b^3}$ respectively. Mean $= \frac{3}{2}b$, standard deviation $= \frac{1}{2}b$.

9 $\alpha = \frac{1}{2}b$, $\beta = \dfrac{b}{2\sqrt{3}}$, the mean and standard deviation for a single rectangular random variable (see answer to Q.2). This is a special case of a general result; other examples have already been encountered in Exercise 9A, questions 5, 7, 8 and 10. The general theory is developed in Chapter 15.

Exercise 12B

2 In (a) the first method can be used, with $\Phi^{-1}(y) = \cos^{-1}(1 - 2y)$.

3 $\Phi^{-1}(y) = \sqrt{(2y)}$ for $0 < y \leqslant \frac{1}{2}$, $2 - \sqrt{\{2(1 - y)\}}$ for $\frac{1}{2} < y < 1$.

4 $\Phi^{-1}(y) = \tan \pi(1 - y)$; if the modification suggested in Note 12.1 is adopted, then the first method of simulation cannot give a value of X greater than $\tan(0.4999995\pi) \approx 6.4 \times 10^5$, which is large but far from "infinite". It does, however, give a far more extensive range of values for the random variable than the second method. For example, if one chops off the tail as suggested in Note 12.3 outside the interval $-20 < x < 20$, one will still lose more than 3% of the values of the random variable; but over such a wide interval, more than 92% of all the random points would have to be discarded in applying the method.

This is in fact a somewhat extreme example of the difficulties of applying the second method to a probability density function with an infinite tail. This model, often called the *Cauchy probability density function*, is peculiar in having infinite variance.

5 The mean of the random variable S is 3, whereas the means of T are (a) 2, (b) 3, (c) 4. The probability model for S is an example of a class of models called *gamma probability models*; more generally, these are described by probability density functions of the form $\psi(s) = (1/n!)s^n e^{-s}$.

Exercise 12C

3 $\phi(x) = \frac{1}{2}\pi \sin(\pi x)$.

Exercise 13A

1 0.309.

2 (a) 0.136, (b) 0.433, (c) 0.452, (d) 0.532, (e) 0.092.

3 0.67.

4 $\phi''(x) = \dfrac{1}{\sqrt{(2\pi)}}(x^2 - 1)e^{-\frac{1}{2}x^2}$, so inflections are at $(\pm 1, 0.242)$.

5 Note that $\displaystyle\int_{-\infty}^{\infty} x^2 e^{-\frac{1}{2}x^2}dx = [-xe^{-\frac{1}{2}x^2}]_{-\infty}^{\infty} + \int_{-\infty}^{\infty} e^{-\frac{1}{2}x^2}dx$, and $xe^{-\frac{1}{2}x^2} \to 0$ as $x \to \infty$.

6 0.682, 0.954, 0.997.

Exercise 13B

1 (a) 13.6%, (b) 38.2%.

2 0.91.

3 4.5 days.

4 0.004. (a) $\mu = 230.64$ g; (b) $\sigma = 1.29$ g.

5 63 g.

6 (a) 0.091. (b) 0.538. (c) 0.347. 8.28 a.m.

7 0.22.

8 (a) 8.48 a.m., (b) 5 minutes. 118 pupils. 8% of pupils arrive during the peak minute, so that 4 entrances are needed.

9 $\mu + 1.28\sigma = 10$, $\mu + 0.525\sigma = 9$, so that $\sigma = 1.325$, $\mu = 8.305$.

10 $\sigma = 25\,\text{mm}$, $\mu = 53\,\text{mm}$.

11 $7.51\frac{3}{5}$ a.m.

12 $\mu = 74.4$, $\sigma = 3.2$. (a) 0.76, (b) 0.24.

13 When plotted on normal probability paper, there appears to be considerable deviation from the straight line graph. However, see §13.4.

14 The cumulative probability functions are $\dfrac{1}{\pi}\tan^{-1}x + \frac{1}{2}$ and $\dfrac{2}{\pi}\tan^{-1}(e^x)$ respectively.

For more general models x can be replaced by $(x - \mu)/\alpha$, where μ and α are constants; μ is the mean, but α is not the standard deviation for the model. (In fact, the first model has infinite standard deviation, whilst for the second the standard deviation $\displaystyle\int_{-\infty}^{\infty} \dfrac{x^2}{\pi\cosh x}\,dx$ is difficult to evaluate exactly.)

15 This expresses the fact that for the general normal probability model the cumulative frequency is $\Phi\left(\dfrac{x - \mu}{\sigma}\right)$.

Exercise 13C

1 Expected frequencies are 5.5, 4.8, 7.7, 12.1, 16.9, 22.8, 28.6, 33.0, 36.7, 37.8, 36.0, 32.7, 27.2, 21.7, 16.1, 11.0, 7.0, 9.5. (Take the dividing marks between the ranges as $10\frac{1}{2}$, $20\frac{1}{2}$, etc.) This gives a discrepancy of 44.7 with $\nu = 18 - 3 = 15$, which is far above the 5% critical value of 25.00. The hypothesis that the marks fit a normal model is rejected. (Marks in a selective examination such as A-level often depart significantly from a normal probability model.)

2 Mean $= 89.39\,\text{cm}$, standard deviation $= 7.80\,\text{cm}$. Taking a normal model with this mean and standard deviation gives expected frequencies of 3, 13.5, 40.5, 81.5, 122, 116.6, 74.5, 32, 9.5, 2 (this last figure for the number too large for waist 110). This gives a discrepancy of 11.1 with $\nu = 7$, below the critical value of 14.07 at the 5% level. (There is, however, a minor difficulty about the calculation of the mean and standard deviation. Apart from the need to assign all the measurements in each group to the middle measurement of the interval, it should be noted that if 110 cm is the largest size stocked by the store, any potential customers larger than this will have gone away dissatisfied and will not therefore contribute to the data.)

3 The calculations (with appropriate grouping of classes at the extremes) give:

	Number	Mean	Standard deviation	Discrepancy	Degrees of freedom
Boys	2157	48.01	2.45	159.4	12
Girls	2088	47.71	2.53	161.5	13

In both cases the discrepancy is far in excess of the critical values at 5% level in tables of chi-squared probability. The hypothesis that the heights are distributed normally is rejected.

4 There is acceptable agreement with a normal model having mean 6.81 and standard deviation 2.23. Note, however, that there is also acceptable agreement with a Poisson model having mean 6.81.

5 With mean 155.6 and standard deviation 62.2 the discrepancy is 14.73 with $v = 4$. At 5% significance level the hypothesis of a normal model is rejected. (If the values $\mu = 156$, $\sigma = 59$ suggested by Fig. 6 are tested, the normal model is still rejected.)

6 The discrepancy from the normal frequencies is 2.71 with $v = 4$. This is not small enough to reject the hypothesis that the departure from the normal model is due to random variation; the critical value for $P = 95$ is 0.711. (It is of interest to note that the figures were made up from a normal model with $\mu = 1280$ and $\sigma = 100$, with no frequency changed by more than 1.)

7 Denoting $h\phi((x_i - \mu)/\sigma)$ by p_i, the expression is $p_1 p_2 \ldots p_n$. Note that $S^2 = (1/n)\Sigma(x_i - \mu)^2 - (m - \mu)^2$ (see §1.1). As μ is varied, the expression is clearly greatest when $\mu = m$. It is therefore required to maximise $\sigma^{-n}e^{-nS^2/2\sigma^2}$; by differentiation this leads to $\sigma = S$. This justifies using the mean and standard deviation of the sample as the estimate of the mean and standard deviation of the normal model, on the basis of the maximum likelihood principle (see §4.2).

Exercise 13D

1 Use a normal approximation with mean $= 10\,000 \times 0.1$ and standard deviation $\sqrt{(10\,000 \times 0.1 \times 0.9)}$. (a) The probability of 1030 or fewer appearances (using a continuity correction) is $\Phi(30.5/\sqrt{90}) \approx 0.9993$.   (b) $\Phi(-19.5/\sqrt{90}) \approx 0.02$.

2 Probability of 439 or fewer is $\Phi(-10.5/\sqrt{45}) \approx 0.058$. The yield is not significantly lower than usual at the 5% level.

3 On the hypothesis that male and female births occur in equal numbers, the probability of a split 13 or more away from the expected half-and-half ratio is $2\{1 - \Phi(12.5/\sqrt{25.5})\} \approx 0.013$. The occurrence is worthy of remark, but not very unusual; one would expect such an imbalance of the sexes in one or two months each decade.

4 On the hypothesis that the lateness was due solely to external factors, the probability of 35 or more late runs in 100 journeys is about 0.014; the bus company's claim is not sustained.

5 The probability of such a result arising by chance is 0.0015. The guesswork hypothesis is rejected at the 5% level (and, indeed, at the 1% level).

6 (a) $\Phi(4.425)$, or near certainty;   (b) 0.98.

7 0.18. The sample size must satisfy the inequality $(0.014N + 0.5)^2 > 0.6759N$, giving $N > 3377$; with such a large sample the effect of the continuity correction is negligible, and it is sufficient to solve $(0.014N)^2 > 0.6759N$.

8 $n = 30$, $y = 24$.

9 The normal approximation gives 0.0997, 0.0457, 0.0044. From the binomial formula the values are 0.0993, 0.0439, 0.0052.

10 0.736. Using the continuity correction the probability for a single page is $\Phi(0.91) - \Phi(0.59)$ rather than $\Phi(0.9) - \Phi(0.6)$.

11 $\Phi(2.5)$ gives the probability of an IQ greater than $137\frac{1}{2}$; but since IQ is an integer this is interpreted (using the continuity correction) as "138 or more". In a class of 30, probability of at least one such child is 0.165.

12 $n/50$, $7\sqrt{n/50}$. 1407.

Exercise 14A

1 $E[c] = c$.

3 Since $E[X] = \mu$, the expressions are simply $E[X - \mu]$ and $E[(X - \mu)^2] = V[X]$.

4 $E[(X - \mu)^2] = E[X^2] - 2\mu E[X] + E[\mu^2]$, and $E[X] = \mu$.

5 $V[X + c] = E[(X + c)^2 - \{E[X + c]\}^2$
$\qquad = (E[X^2] + 2cE[X] + c^2) - (E[X] + c)^2 = E[X^2] - \{E[X]\}^2$

6 Only if $V[X] = 0$; that is, if X takes a single value with probability 1.

7 $E[X] = \frac{1}{3}(n + 1)(n + 2)$, $E[1/X] = 1/(n + 1)$.

8 $E[X^4] - 4\mu E[X^3] + 6\mu^2\sigma^2 + 3\mu^4$.

9 (a) $2/\pi$, (b) $\frac{1}{2}$.

10 $\frac{2}{3}$, $\frac{1}{18}$; $\frac{4}{5}$, $\frac{3}{75}$.

11 4.47, 1.97. $E[Z] = \sum_{i=1}^{6} i\,p(7 - i) = \sum_{j=1}^{6} (7 - j)p(j) = 7 - E[Y]$; $V[Z] = V[Y]$.

12 $E[X] = 0$, $V[X] = 1$, $E[X^2] = 1$. Mean $= 1$, variance $= 2$.

13 From §9.4, $E[X] = \lambda$, $V[X] = \lambda$. For large λ, $X^{\frac{1}{2}} \approx \lambda^{\frac{1}{2}} + \frac{1}{2}Y$, so that $E[X^{\frac{1}{2}}] \approx \lambda^{\frac{1}{2}}$, $V[X^{\frac{1}{2}}] \approx V[\frac{1}{2}Y] = \frac{1}{4}$ (neglecting negative powers of λ).

Exercise 14B

1 $E[X] = 2$, $E[Y] = 1.8$, $E[X + Y] = 3.6$, $E[XY] = 3.8$, $V[X] = 2$, $V[Y] = 1.56$, $V[X + Y] = 3.56$, $V[XY] = 11.44$. (a) is false but (b) and (c) are true. This shows that, although independence is a sufficient condition for properties (2) and (3) to hold, it is not a necessary condition.

2 $V[X - Y] = V[X] + V[Y]$. Mean $= 8$ cm, standard deviation $= 0.14$ cm.

3 $\sqrt{(0.98)}\,\text{g} \approx 1.0\,\text{g}$.

4 (a) $\frac{20}{3}$, (b) $\frac{80}{3}$, (c) $\frac{40}{3}$, (d) $\frac{100}{3}$.

5 $E[X] = 3.5$. Y takes values 0, 1, 2, 3, 4, 5 with probabilities $\frac{3}{18}$, $\frac{5}{18}$, $\frac{4}{18}$, $\frac{3}{18}$, $\frac{2}{18}$, $\frac{1}{18}$. $E[Y] = \frac{35}{18}$. (a) is true, since $Y^2 = Z^2$, but not (b) (using Exercise 14A, question 4, since $E[Y] \neq E[Z]$).

7 $E[Y] = 0$, $V[Y] = 0.208$. Also $V[\bar{X}] = \frac{1}{9}(V[X_1] + V[X_2] + V[X_3]) = 0.133$.

8 $V[X] = \frac{1}{12}h^2 < 0.001\sigma^2$, and $V[Y + X] = \sigma^2 + V[X]$.

9 $A/n + \frac{1}{2}(1 + 1/n)B$, which is always greater than $\frac{1}{2}B$.

10 Because X and Y are independent, $P(X = a) \times P(Y = b) = P((X, Y) = (a, b))$, and similarly with $-a$ for a and/or $-b$ for b. Also

$$P((X^2, Y^2) = (a^2, b^2)) = P((X, Y) = (a, b) \text{ or } (a, -b) \text{ or } (-a, b) \text{ or } (-a, -b)).$$

The conclusion is that, if X and Y are independent, so are X^2 and Y^2. Therefore $E[X^2 Y^2] = E[X^2]E[Y^2]$, so
$V[XY] + \{E[XY]\}^2 = (V[X] + \{E[X]\}^2)(V[Y] + \{E[Y]\}^2)$.

11 300 cm^2, 13.0004 cm^4.

12 (b) The converse is false; see question 1. (c) $V[X]$, $abC[X, Y]$, $C[X, Y]$, $C[X, Y] + C[X, Z]$, $V[X] + C[X, Y]$. (d) The final deduction is especially simple if $E[X]$ and $E[Y]$ are zero, since then $C[X, Y] = E[XY]$, $C[X, X] = E[X^2]$, $C[Y, Y] = E[Y^2]$. In general, prove the result for the random variables $X' = X - \mu_x$, $Y' = Y - \mu_y$, and note that $C[X', Y'] = C[X, Y]$ from the third part of (c).

13 $C[Z, W] = E[ZW] - E[Z]E[W] = (ac + bd)\sigma^2$.

14 (a) $\frac{7}{2}$, (b) $\frac{455}{12}$, (c) 0, (d) $\frac{35}{12}$.

15 $V[S^2] = \frac{1}{8}\mu_4 + \frac{1}{8}\mu_2^2$. The condition is $\mu_4 = 3\mu_2^2$. Note from Exercise 14A, question 12 that this holds for standard normal probability; it will transpire later that, for this probability model, the mean and variance are independent random variables.

Exercise 14C

1 (a) (ii) e^{-x}, e^{-y}; (iii) 1, 1, 2, 1; 1, 1, 2, 3.
(b) (ii) $x + \frac{1}{2}$, $y + \frac{1}{2}$; (iii) $\frac{7}{12}$, $\frac{7}{12}$, $\frac{7}{6}$, $\frac{1}{3}$; $\frac{11}{144}$, $\frac{11}{144}$, $\frac{5}{36}$, $\frac{1}{18}$.
(c) (ii) $2(1 - x)$, $2(1 - y)$; (iii) $\frac{1}{3}$, $\frac{1}{3}$, $\frac{2}{3}$, $\frac{1}{12}$; $\frac{1}{18}$, $\frac{1}{18}$, $\frac{1}{18}$, $\frac{1}{240}$.

3 $\dfrac{1}{2\pi\sigma_1\sigma_2} e^{-(x^2/2\sigma_1^2 + y^2/2\sigma_2^2)}$. (a) $(0.682)^2 \approx 0.465$, (b) $(0.520)^2 \approx 0.270$. In polar coordin-

ates the probability that the point lies inside the circle is

$$\int_{\theta=0}^{2\pi} \int_{r=0}^{\sigma} \frac{1}{2\pi\sigma^2} e^{-r^2/2\sigma^2} \times r d\theta \, dr.$$

Exercise 15A

1 $\hat{p} = f/50$.

2 $\hat{s} = n/20$.

3 $\hat{x} = r/n$; $\hat{x} = (r_1 + r_2 + r_3)/(n_1 + n_2 + n_3)$.

4 $\hat{n} = 600/r$; $\hat{n} = 5s$.

5 $\hat{\tau} = ms/r$.

6

l	0	1	2	3	4	5	6	7	8	9	10	11
n	0	2	3	5	6	8	10	12	13	15	16	18

7 $\hat{\beta}$ is the integer next greater than $5.05i - 1$. This in fact gives the same values for the estimator function as in the case of sampling with replacement.

8   See Exercise 15B, question 10.

Exercise 15B

1   (a) B(20, s).   (b) 20s, s.   (c) Yes.

2   Probability model for R is B(n, x), so that $E[\hat{x}] = E[R]/n = (nx)/n = x$. $E[\hat{x}'] = (E[R_1] + E[R_2] + E[R_3])/(n_1 + n_2 + n_3) = (n_1x + n_2x + n_3x)/(n_1 + n_2 + n_3) = x$.

3   No. For example, using the probabilities in the table, we can calculate that when $n = 2$, $E[\hat{n}] = 0.274 \times 0 + 0.376 \times 2 + 0.235 \times 3 + 0.088 \times 5 + 0.022 \times 6 + 0.004 \times 8 + \ldots$, which is approximately 2.06.

4   Probabilities for $p = 0, \frac{1}{3}, \frac{2}{3}, 1$ are $\frac{1}{6}, \frac{1}{2}, \frac{3}{10}, \frac{1}{30}$, so that $E[\hat{p}] = \frac{4}{10}$.

5   Note first that $x\binom{r}{x} = r\binom{r-1}{x-1}$. The coefficient of t^{s-1} in the expansion is $\sum \binom{r-1}{x-1}\binom{w}{s-x}$; this must equal the coefficient of t^{s-1} in $(1 + t)^{r+w-1}$, which is $\binom{r+w-1}{s-1}$.

6 $f(i) = 5(i + 4)\binom{i+3}{3}(0.16)^4(0.84)^i = 20(0.16)^4\binom{i+4}{i}(0.84)^i$.

8 $E[\hat{s}] = \int_0^\infty t \cdot \frac{1}{s} e^{-t/s}\, dt$, which equals s. $E[\hat{\lambda}] = \int_0^\infty \frac{1}{t} \cdot \frac{1}{s} e^{-t/s}\, dt$, which is infinite, so that $E[\hat{\lambda}] \neq \lambda$.

9 $P(S \leq s) = 1 - (1 - s)^n$; nl^{n-1}, $n(1 - s)^{n-1}$; $E[L - S] = \dfrac{n-1}{n+1}$. Estimator for range $= \dfrac{n+1}{n-1}(L - S)$.

10 $\frac{1}{2}(\tau + 1)$ in each case. The greatest value which $L - S + 1$ can have is τ, so that $E[L - S + 1] < \tau$.

Exercise 15C

1   (a) This occurs only with 4 out of 10 having property A, probability = 0.24.
   (b) This occurs with 13, 14, 15 or 16 out of 40, probability = 0.49.
   (c) This is ambiguous, since it is not clear whether "between" is exclusive or inclusive; using a normal approximation (with continuity correction) gives probabilities of 0.65 or 0.75 according to the interpretation.

2   0.68.

3 The variances are $\frac{1}{4}k\left(\dfrac{1}{n_1} + \dfrac{1}{n_2}\right)$ and $\dfrac{k}{n_1 + n_2}$ respectively, where $k = \alpha(1 - \alpha)$. Since $(n_1 + n_2)^2 > 4n_1 n_2$ (unless $n_1 = n_2$), the second estimator is more efficient.

4 2500.

5 2401.

6 1537; 385.

Exercise 15D

1 Mean 100, standard deviation 3.

4 Between $53.40°$ and $54.22°$.

Exercise 15E

1 $\frac{35}{12}$. 0, $\frac{1}{4}$, 1, $2\frac{1}{4}$, 4, $6\frac{3}{4}$ with probabilities $\frac{1}{6}$, $\frac{5}{18}$, $\frac{4}{18}$, $\frac{3}{18}$, $\frac{2}{18}$, $\frac{1}{18}$.

2 $\frac{2}{3}$, $\frac{5}{9}$; $\frac{2}{3}$, $\frac{5}{18}$, $\frac{5}{18}$; $\frac{2}{3}$, $\frac{5}{27}$, $\frac{10}{27}$.

3 ab; $4ab^3 \times \frac{3}{16} + 6a^2 b^2 \times \frac{1}{4} + 4a^3 b \times \frac{3}{16} = \frac{3}{4}ab$.

4 $E[V] = \sum \dbinom{n}{i} \dfrac{i(n - i)}{n^2} a^i b^{n-i}$. Notice that $\dbinom{n}{i} \dfrac{i(n - i)}{n^2} = \dbinom{n - 2}{i - 1} \dfrac{n - 1}{n}$.

6 1.0012, 0.000058.

7 9.2, 3.33.

10 (a) $\sum_{i=1}^{\infty} a^2 b^{2i-2} = a^2/(1 - b^2)$; (b) $\sum_{i=1}^{\infty} 2a^2 b^{2i-2+r} = 2a^2 b^r/(1 - b^2)$. To sum $\sum r^2 b^{r-1}$, note that $r^2 = r(r - 1) + r$.

Exercise 16A

2 Using the approximate method, the proportion lies between $0.46 \pm 2.5758 \times \sqrt{\dfrac{0.46 \times 0.54}{2000}}$, that is between 0.431 and 0.489.

3 Between 0.758 and 0.810.

4 Between 0.23 and 0.41.

5 On the null hypothesis, the probability that 26 or more fall into this category is 0.056; taking a 5% significance level, the null hypothesis is acceptable. Between 0.38 and 0.66.

6 The approximate method gives margins of error of 2.1%, 2.1%, 1.8% respectively for the three parties, well within the 4% claimed.

7 36:64 (giving a median mass between 3.185 kg and 3.470 kg).

8 Take a split between 16:84 and 34:66. (This gives a lower quartile between 2.920 kg and 3.155 kg, and an upper quartile between 3.495 kg and 3.840 kg.)

Exercise 16B

1 The probability that the maximum is exceeded is $1 - \Phi(4.22)$, which is about 10^{-5}.

2   The error cannot exceed 6 miles, so that the distance is between 91 miles and 103 miles. But the probability of being no more than one mile out, to the nearest mile, is $2\Phi(1.5) - 1$, that is 0.866.

3   (a) 0.066, (b) 0.64. Note that the first of these probabilities, calculated (using a continuity correction) as $2\Phi(0.5/6) - 1$, can also be approximated as $\frac{1}{6}\phi(0)$, that is

$$\frac{1}{6\sqrt{(2\pi)}}.$$

4   Choose n so that $6n - 1 + 3.29\sqrt{n}$ is less than 150, giving $n = 22$ or fewer. With 22 patients, he has only a 1 % chance of getting away in under 109 minutes.

6   Mean $= 2$, standard deviation $= 1$. The central limit theorem predicts a probability density function approximating to $\dfrac{1}{\sqrt{(2\pi n)}}e^{-(t-2n)^2/2n}$ for large n, even though the original distribution is strongly skewed.

7   Mean $= a$, standard deviation $= b$. This provides an alternative way of thinking about binomial probability, since the total t is simply the number of occurrences of the outcome (A) with probability a. The result that binomial probability approximates to normal probability for large n is then just a special case of the central limit theorem.

8   The probability that the total of $n + 1$ values of the random variable X lies between t and $t + \delta t$ is approximately $\phi_{n+1}(t)\delta t$, if δt is small. Regard this total as made up of the sum S of the first n random variables $X_1, X_2, \ldots, X_n$ and the random variable $U = X_{n+1}$; then we want to find the probability that $t < S + U < t + \delta t$. Now the probability that U lies between u and $u + \delta u$, and that s lies between $t - u$ and $t - u + \delta t$ is approximately $\phi(u)\delta u \times \phi_n(t - u)\delta t$; and integrating this over all possible values of U (between 0 and 1) gives

$$\phi_{n+1}(t)\delta t = \int_0^1 \phi(u)\phi_n(t - u)\,du \times \delta t.$$

Since $\phi(u) = 1$ for values of u between 0 and 1, this gives the relation required.

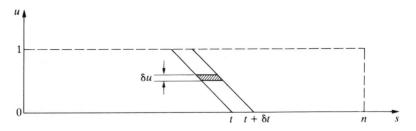

The diagram may help to make this argument clear. The oblique strip contains the points whose coordinates (S, U) satisfy $t < S + U < t + \delta t$, and the area probability density at the point (s, u) is $\phi(u)\phi_n(t - u)$, where $s = t - u$.

Now clearly $\phi_1(t)$ is the same as $\phi(t)$, so that $\phi_2(t) = \displaystyle\int_0^1 \phi(t - u)\,du$. In calculating this integral, t is treated as a constant; and we note that $\phi(t - u) = 1$ for values of u

between $t - 1$ and t, but 0 otherwise. It follows that if $0 < t < 1$, then $\int_0^1 \phi(t - u)\,du = \int_0^t 1\,du = t$; but if $1 < t < 2$, then $\int_0^1 \phi(t - u)\,du = \int_{t-1}^1 1\,du = 2 - t$. For all other values of t, $\phi_2(t) = 0$. This is just the triangular probability model introduced in §12.2, in the special case with $b = 1$; the argument corresponds to the second method described in that section.

Similarly, to find $\phi_3(t) = \int_0^1 \phi_2(t - u)\,du$, it is necessary to consider separately the intervals $0 < t < 1$, $1 < t < 2$, $2 < t < 3$. Suppose for example that $1 < t < 2$. Then if u lies between 0 and $t - 1$, $t - u$ lies between 1 and t, so that $\phi_2(t - u) = 2 - (t - u)$; but if u lies between $t - 1$ and 1, then $t - u$ lies between $t - 1$ and 1, so that $\phi_2(t - u) = t - u$. So, over this interval, $\phi_3(t) = \int_0^{t-1} (2 - t + u)\,du + \int_{t-1}^1 (t - u)\,du$, which comes to $-\frac{3}{2} + 3t - t^2$. Over the other intervals, if $0 < t < 1$, $\phi_3(t) = \frac{1}{2}t^2$; and if $2 < t < 3$, $\phi_3(t) = \frac{1}{2}t^2 - 3t + \frac{9}{2}$.

9 For the general theory, see the solution to question 8.

$\phi_2(t) = \frac{2}{3}t^3$ if $0 < t < 1$, $-\frac{8}{3} + 4t - \frac{2}{3}t^3$ if $1 < t < 2$.

$\phi_3(t) = \frac{1}{15}t^5$ if $0 < t < 1$, $-\frac{2}{15}t^5 + 2t^3 - 4t^2 + 3t - \frac{4}{5}$ if $1 < t < 2$,

$\frac{1}{15}t^5 - 2t^3 + 4t^2 + 3t - \frac{36}{5}$ if $2 < t < 3$.

It is noteworthy that, even with an original distribution which is strongly skewed, the total of as few as 3 values has a distribution which already exhibits the humped shape which is characteristic of normal probability.

10 $\phi_2(t) = \int_{-\infty}^{\infty} \frac{1}{2\pi} e^{-\frac{1}{2}(t-u)^2} e^{-\frac{1}{2}u^2}\,du = \int_{-\infty}^{\infty} \frac{1}{2\pi} e^{-\frac{1}{2}(2u^2 - 2tu + t^2)}\,du$. Complete the square to give $2u^2 - 2tu + t^2 = \{\sqrt{2}(u - \frac{1}{2}t)\}^2 + \frac{1}{2}t^2$, and make the substitution $v = \sqrt{2}(u - \frac{1}{2}t)$. The result $\int_{-\infty}^{\infty} \frac{1}{\sqrt{(2\pi)}} e^{-\frac{1}{2}v^2}\,dv = 1$ can then be used, giving $\phi_2(t) = \frac{1}{\sqrt{(4\pi)}} e^{-\frac{1}{4}t^2}$, which is the equation for $N(0, 2)$. Similarly, the equation for $\phi_n(t)$ is that corresponding to $N(0, n)$. Notice that the result is exact; there is no approximation involved.

11 $1 - \Phi\left(\dfrac{135 - 150}{6\sqrt{3}}\right) = 0.925$. Note that it is necessary to specify that the masses are distributed normally, since $n = 3$ which is not large enough to apply the central limit theorem reliably.

12 0.106. Between 244 500 litres and 255 500 litres (to the nearest 100 litres).

13 Suppose that for any individual employee the probability of getting a bonus in any one week is p. In 48 weeks the expected number of bonuses is $48p$, and the standard deviation $\sqrt{\{48p(1 - p)\}}$. We need to find p so that the probability that this number exceeds 35.5 (using a continuity correction) is 0.9; this gives $p = 0.8118$. Now the number of radios produced in one week has expected value 210, with standard deviation $2.5 \times \sqrt{5}$; the number N is to be chosen so that the probability that this number exceeds $N - \frac{1}{2}$ (again using a continuity correction) is 0.8118. Giving the employees the benefit of the rounding correction, the appropriate value of N is 205.

Exercise 16C

1 (a) 1.3×10^{-21}, (b) 0.9987.

2 The probability of a mean of 8.9 or more is 0.0087, so that the recorded average is significantly greater at the 1 % level.

3 Not significant; probability of a mean as great as 104.16 is 0.083.

4 0.04.

5 There is no reason to suspect an incorrect setting; P(|mean length $-$ 100| > 1.2) is 0.23. 0.484; 0.021.

6 0.846. The mean of the sample is significantly greater.

7 3.5, 2.92; 3.9, 2.49, 0.121. $N = 594$.

8 The probability of a mean score as high as 27.2 is only 0.021, so the hypothesis of randomness is rejected.

9 97.

10 0.546.   62.

Exercise 16D

2 26.925, 8.648.   Between 25.7 and 28.1 years.

3 Between 6.37 and 7.25.

4 For boys, between 47.87 and 48.15 inches; for girls, between 47.57 and 47.85 inches.

5 Significant at the 1 % level; probability of a mean life as low as 1995 is 0.0029.

Exercise 16E

1 No. On the null hypothesis, the probability of an improvement in test results as good as that recorded is 0.077.

2 On purely random sampling, the probability of an increase of this magnitude is 0.088; the improvement is not significant.

3 $0.30 < p < 0.38$. The probability of a difference as large as that recorded on the null hypothesis is 0.043.

4 The standard deviation of the combined sample is 29.26 hours. On the null hypothesis, the probability of a difference of 10 or more in the sample means is $2\{1 - \Phi(3.16)\}$, which is less than 0.002.

5 The difference in mean heights is highly significant. On average, boys of this age are between 0.15 and 0.45 inches taller than girls.

6 Between 188 and 192 cm. Between 13 and 17 cm.

7 A 95 % confidence interval for the proportion of girls who are influenced by the interviewer's dress is between 44.4 % and 75.6 %.

Revision exercise B

1 (a) 1. (b) $1/k$. (c) $\frac{1}{4}$. (d) $(1-k)^n$.

2 6, 3. $\frac{11}{26}$.

3 $1/(a-1)$, $a/(a-1)^2$.

4 (a) 0.2646, 0.3. (b) 2.8. (c) 1.375.

5 3.15, 2.3275. (a) 0.257, (b) 0.456.

6 1.5, 1.25. $2e^{-2t}$.

7 $\binom{n-1}{5}\left(\frac{2}{3}\right)^{n-6}\left(\frac{1}{3}\right)^6$. 15 or 16. (a) 17, (b) 35. 18.

8 2.5. 0.803, 0.456.

9 (a) 12. (b) 0.6, 0.04. (c) 0.4752.

10 0.9197. 5.5×10^{-4}. Probability of 85 or fewer is 0.0087, so conclude that the suspension is not well-mixed.

11 (a) 0.323, (b) 0.929.

13 Probability of the result occurring randomly is 0.0188, so new technique is significantly better.

14 97. 0.287.

15 Mean of $(c) = 14.5$ g. 0.253.

16 0.94.

17 0.0820p, 3.016p. 0.394.

18 0.21, so 200 is a reasonable estimate. With 100, the probability of catching 15 or fewer marked is 0.0125, so this is not a reasonable estimate.

19 Probability $= 0.21$, not significant. 11.

20 (a) 68, (b) 405, (c) 470.

21 On the normal hypothesis frequencies are 67, 242, 381, 242, 61, 6. Discrepancy of 30.82 with $v = 5$, so hypothesis is rejected.

22 Discrepancy $= 2.81$ with $v = 1$, not significant.

23 (a) A, (b) B. A (£15.14 compared with £10.92).

24 $0.023/(1 - 0.977t)$.

25 36.

26 0.091.

27 0.6, 0.04. $\frac{2}{3}$. 902 gallons. 0.004.

28 0.208; 0.125. 0.035.

29 217.

30 $0.0513/\lambda$, $2.996/\lambda$. Between 3.34 and 194.96. Between 8.59 and 11.97.

Exercise 17A

1   0, 4.4, 9.6, 69.2.

2   0, 0.5, -0.2, 0.6.

3 $\mu_3 = -14.88$.

4 $b = a\sqrt{3}$. $\mu_2 = \dfrac{\frac{1}{3} + \frac{1}{4}\sqrt{3}}{1 + \frac{1}{2}\sqrt{3}}a^2 \approx 0.411a^2$, $\mu_3 = \dfrac{\frac{1}{5}}{1 + \frac{1}{2}\sqrt{3}}a^3 \approx 0.107a^3$.

5 $\mu_2 = 1/\lambda^2$, $\mu_3 = 2/\lambda^3$.

6 $b = a\sqrt{2}$. Fourth moments are $\frac{1}{5}a^4$ and $\frac{1}{15}b^4 = \frac{4}{15}a^4$.

7 $b^2 = \frac{7}{5}a^2$; the fourth moments are $\frac{3}{35}a^4$ and $\frac{1}{21}b^4 = \frac{7}{75}a^4$, so that ϕ_2 has the larger fourth moment.

Exercise 17B

1 $\frac{1}{5}e^{-4u} + \frac{1}{5}e^{-2u} + \frac{1}{5} + \frac{1}{5}e^{2u} + \frac{1}{5}e^{4u}$.

2 $\frac{1}{2}e^{-u} + \frac{1}{4} + \frac{1}{8}e^{u} + \cdots$. $M(u) \approx 1 + u^2 + u^3$.   Mean $= 0$,   variance $= 2$,   positively skewed.

3 $\frac{1}{4}e^{u}/(1 - \frac{1}{2}e^{u}) + \frac{1}{4}e^{-u}/(1 - \frac{1}{2}e^{-u}) = (2\cosh u - 1)/(5 - 4\cosh u)$. $\mu_2 = 6$, $\mu_4 = 150$.

4 $(b + ae^{u})^n$.

5   (i) $ae^{u}/(1 - be^{u})$; (ii) $e^{\lambda(e^{u} - 1)}$.

6 $\mu_3 = G'''(1) + 3G''(1) + G'(1)$, $\mu_4 = G^{iv}(1) + 6G'''(1) + 7G''(1) + G'(1)$.

7   (a) $(e^{2u} - 1 - 2u)/2u^2$; (b) $(e^{2u} - 2 + e^{-2u})/4u^2$.

8 $\lambda/(\lambda - u) = (1 - u/\lambda)^{-1}$. $\mu_1 = 1/\lambda$, $\mu_2 = 2/\lambda^2$; variance $= 1/\lambda^2$.

9 $(2/r^2u^2)\{(ru - 1)e^{ru} + 1\}$.

10 $(3/r^3u^3)\{(r^2u^2 - 2ru + 2)e^{ru} - 2\}$.

Exercise 17C

1   (a) $(0.2 + 0.2e^{u} + 0.2e^{2u} + 0.2e^{3u} + 0.2e^{4u})(0.5 + 0.5e^{2u})$
    $= 0.1 + 0.1e^{u} + 0.2e^{2u} + 0.2e^{3u} + 0.2e^{4u} + 0.1e^{5u} + 0.1e^{6u}$.
   (b) $(0.2 + 0.2e^{u} + 0.2e^{2u} + 0.2e^{3u} + 0.1e^{4u} + 0.1e^{5u})^2 \neq 0.4e^{3u} + 0.6e^{5u}$.

2   By (1), the generator for $-Y$ is $M_2(-u)$; so, by (3), the generator for $X - Y$ is $M_1(u)M_2(-u)$.

3   (a) $(2/bu)\sinh \frac{1}{2} bu \cdot e^{\frac{1}{2}bu} = (e^{bu} - 1)/bu$.   (b) $(e^{bu} - 1)^2/b^2u^2$.

5   (b) $\mu_1 - d$, $\mu_2 - 2d\mu_1 + d^2$, $\mu_3 - 3d\mu_2 + 3d^2\mu_1 - d^3$,
    $\mu_4 - 4d\mu_3 + 6d^2\mu_2 - 4d^3\mu_1 + d^4$.
    These results may, of course, also be obtained using the methods of Chapter 14.
   (c) 0, $\mu_2 - \mu_1^2$, $\mu_3 - 3\mu_1\mu_2 + 2\mu_1^3$, $\mu_4 - 4\mu_1\mu_3 + 6\mu_1^2\mu_2 - 3\mu_1^4$.

7 $\mu_2^* = nab$, $\mu_3^* = nab(b - a)$, $\mu_4^* = nab(a^2 - ab + b^2) + 3n(n - 1)a^2b^2 = nab(1 - 6ab) + 3n^2a^2b^2$. Skewness $= (b - a)/\sqrt{(nab)}$; this tends to zero, confirming the observation based on numerical computation in §13.1.

8 $a/(e^{bu/a} - be^{u/a})$. Skewness $= (1 + b)/\sqrt{b}$.

9 (a) $e^{\lambda(e^u - 1 - u)}$. Skewness $= 1/\sqrt{\lambda}$. (b) $e^{-u/\lambda}/(1 - u/\lambda)$. Skewness $= 2$.

10 The moment generator becomes successively $ae^u/(1 - be^u)$, $ae^{u/n}/(1 - be^{u/n})$, $(\lambda/n)e^{u/n}/\{1 - (1 - \lambda/n)e^{u/n}\} = \lambda/\{\lambda - n(1 - e^{-u/n})\}$, which tends to $\lambda/(\lambda - u)$.

11 (b) $G(t) = \int_{-\infty}^{\infty} t^x \phi(x)\,dx$. (c) $\int_{-1}^{1} \frac{1}{2} t^x\,dx = (t - 1/t)/(2 \ln t)$.

12 $\int_{-1}^{1} \frac{1}{2}/(1 - xu)\,dx = (1/2u)\ln\{(1 + u)/(1 - u)\}$.

13 $-(2/u^2)\ln(1 - u) - 2/u$; $(2/u^2)\{(u - 1)e^u + 1\}$.

Exercise 17D

1 $(1 - 6ab)/nab$.

3 $N(a\mu + b\mu', a^2\sigma^2 + b^2\sigma'^2)$.

4 327.6 mm; 0.70.

5 The difference between the diameters, which has to be positive, is distributed with probability $N(0.4, 0.13)$; 13.3 % of the pairs are unacceptable.

6 0.25.

7 (a) 0.548; (b) 0.212.

8 $\{\lambda/(\lambda - u)\}^\alpha$. $\{\lambda/(\lambda - u)\}^n$, gamma probability with $\alpha = n$.

Exercise 17E

1 In the answer to Exercise 17C, question 9(a) replace u by $u/\sqrt{\lambda}$. The logarithm of the moment generator is then expanded as $\frac{1}{2}u^2 + \frac{1}{6}u^3/\sqrt{\lambda} + \cdots$ This is a very useful result, since it means that problems involving Poisson probability when λ is large can be solved more simply by using tables of standard normal probability density.

3 $N(0, \frac{1}{6}n(n + 1)(2n + 1))$.

4 $\frac{1}{2}nabu^2 + \frac{1}{6}nab(b - a)u^3 + \frac{1}{24}nab(a^2 - 4ab + b^2)u^4 + \cdots$ Replace u by $u/\sqrt{(nab)}$.

5 Discarding the two cases of equality, the sum of the ranks for positive differences (Paper 1 – Paper 2) is 121. With $n = 18$ this sum is distributed, on the null hypothesis, approximately as $N(85.5, 527.25)$; this gives critical values, in a two-tailed test, of 40 and 130 at 5 % level.

Exercise 17F

1 $\cos u$.

2 $\lambda/(\lambda - uj)$.

3 We know from Q.10(b) that $\displaystyle\int_{-\infty}^{\infty} e^{xuj} \cdot \frac{1}{\sqrt{(2\pi)}} e^{-\frac{1}{2}x^2}\,dx = e^{-\frac{1}{2}u^2}$. Replacing u by $-u$,

interchanging x and u, and multiplying by $1/\sqrt{(2\pi)}$ gives the result

$$\frac{1}{2\pi} \int_{-\infty}^{\infty} e^{-xuj} e^{-\frac{1}{2}u^2}\,du = \frac{1}{\sqrt{(2\pi)}} e^{-\frac{1}{2}x^2}.$$

4 (a) Note that $x^2\phi(x)$ approaches $1/\pi$ as $x \to \pm\infty$.

(c) $e^{-|u|}$.

(d) $\dfrac{1}{2\pi}\left\{\displaystyle\int_{-\infty}^{0} e^{-xuj}e^{u}du + \int_{0}^{\infty} e^{-xuj}e^{-u}du\right\} = \dfrac{1}{2\pi}\left(\dfrac{1}{1-xj} + \dfrac{1}{1+xj}\right) = \phi(x)$.

(e) The moment generator for the mean is $(e^{-|u/n|})^n = e^{-|u|}$.

(f) The central limit theorem requires the moments to be finite (see §17.7).

5 $\lambda e^{-\lambda x}$ if $x > 0$, 0 if $x < 0$; that is, negative exponential probability density.

6 (a) π, (b) $-\pi$. In the expression for $\phi(x)$ write $e^{-xuj} = \cos(xu) - j\sin(xu)$; the imaginary part is zero because the integrand is an odd function of u. For the real part write $\cos(xu)\sin u = \frac{1}{2}\{\sin(x+1)u - \sin(x-1)u\}$ and consider separately the cases $x < -1$, $-1 < x < 1$, $x > 1$.

7 $\phi(x) = 1/4h$ if $-1-h < x < -1+h$ or $1-h < x < 1+h$, 0 otherwise. For the limiting form, see question 1. This illustrates a way in which the inversion theorem can be extended to apply to a discrete random variable.

Exercise 18A

1 $R^2 = 5.88$ with $v = 4$. Not significant at the 5% level. (However, a test on the sample mean shows that to be significantly high. Compare question 5.)

2 $R^2 = 11.62$ with $v = 5$. Using a 5% significance level, the group is unrepresentative.

3 The hypothesis is $B(180, \frac{1}{6})$, which is approximated by $N(30, 25)$. So take for X_i the values $2, 1, 0, 0, -1, -2$, giving $R^2 = 10$. Not significant at the 5% level.

4 $R^2 = 18.5$ with $v = 10$. Significant at the 5% level.

5 The expression for variance at the end of §1.1 gives $12^2 = \frac{1}{40}\Sigma(a_i - 100)^2 - (95 - 100)^2$, and $x_i = (a_i - 100)/15$. So in applying chi-squared probability the value $R^2 = 30.04$ is tested, with $v = 40$; this is not significant at the 5% level. However, the mean is distributed with standard deviation $15/\sqrt{40}$, so a mean of 95 is 2.11 standard deviations below the population mean, significant at the 5% level.

7 $R^2 = 20.96$ with $v = 8$, which is significant at the 1% level. The hypothesis that the eggs come from a different population is therefore rejected on the basis of two separate tests: the mean is significantly greater, and R^2 is significantly high.

Exercise 18B

1 Discrepancy $= 6.13$, significant at the 5% but not the 1% level; discrepancy $= 9.19$, significant at the 1% level.

2 Discrepancies are changed to 1.23, 7.02.

4 The numerators in the discrepancy are all reduced from q^2 to $(q - \frac{1}{2})^2$, that is by $q - \frac{1}{4} \approx q$; so the proportional reduction is approximately $1/q$. This argument applies to both types of application.

Exercise 18C

1 $2\int_{x}^{\infty}\frac{1}{\sqrt{(2\pi)}}e^{-\frac{1}{2}x^2}dx = \int_{x^2}^{\infty}\frac{1}{\sqrt{(2\pi)}}s^{-\frac{1}{2}}e^{-\frac{1}{2}s}ds.\ B_1 = \frac{1}{\sqrt{(2\pi)}},\ A_1 = 2.$

2 $I_v = (v-2)I_{v-2}.$ Note that $B_v I_v = 1.$ $B_2 = \frac{1}{2},\ B_3 = 1/\sqrt{(2\pi)},$ so $B_4 = \frac{1}{2}B_2 = \frac{1}{4},$

$B_5 = \frac{1}{3}B_3 = \frac{1}{3\sqrt{(2\pi)}}.$ In general $B_v = \frac{1}{(v-2)(v-4)\dots 2}\times\frac{1}{2}$ if v is even,

$\frac{1}{(v-2)(v-4)\dots 3}\times\frac{1}{\sqrt{(2\pi)}}$ if v is odd; $A_v = \frac{(2\pi)^{\frac{1}{2}v}}{(v-2)(v-4)\dots 2} = \frac{2\pi^{\frac{1}{2}v}}{(\frac{1}{2}v-1)!}$ if v is

even, $\frac{2(2\pi)^{\frac{1}{2}(v-1)}}{(v-2)(v-4)\dots 3} = \frac{2^v\pi^{\frac{1}{2}(v-1)}(\frac{1}{2}(v-1))!}{(v-1)!}$ if v is odd.

3 Note that the cumulative probability is $P(R^2 < \chi^2) = 1 - P(R^2 \geqslant \chi^2),$ and so is

represented by $1 - \int_{w}^{\infty} B_v s^{\frac{1}{2}v-1}e^{-\frac{1}{2}s}ds.$ For $v > 2,$ the probability density is at its

maximum when $\chi^2 = v - 2.$ Notice that chi-squared probability density is a special case of gamma probability density as defined in Exercise 17D, question 8, with $\lambda = \frac{1}{2}$ and $\alpha = \frac{1}{2}v.$

5 Mean $= v,$ variance $= 2v.$ Notice that, even for $v = 60,$ the approximation is not very close. $X + Y$ has chi-squared probability density with $\alpha + \beta$ degrees of freedom.

Exercise 18D

1 The appropriate model is B(100, 0.1) so the expected frequencies are 59.049, 32.805, 7.290, 0.810, 0.045, 0.001. Combining the last four classes (to avoid small expected frequencies) gives a discrepancy of 22.26 with $v = 3 - 2 = 1;$ the hypothesis is strongly rejected. The frequencies should satisfy the equations $f_0 + f_1 + f_2 + f_3 + f_4 + f_5 = 100$ and $f_1 + 2f_2 + 3f_3 + 4f_4 + 5f_5 = 50$ (since the means have been made the same). This is true for the frequencies as originally found; but note that when the classes are combined, the second equation is no longer satisfied by either the observed or the actual frequencies. Thus the process of combining the classes (which is necessary to avoid too large errors in the approximation) actually renders the theory strictly inapplicable! There is nothing that can be done about this; it simply emphasises further that the application of chi-squared probability to goodness-of-fit questions is inevitably imprecise.

2 $f_0 + f_1 + f_2 + f_3 + f_4 + f_5 + f_6 + \cdots = 40,$ $f_1 + 2f_2 + 3f_3 + 4f_4 + 5f_5 + 6f_6 + \cdots = 120.$ The same problem arises, however, as in question 1 but to an even greater degree; for with a Poisson model (where theoretically there are infinitely many classes) some of the classes must be combined, and then the second equation will cease to hold exactly.

Exercise 19A

1 With $m = 1.502,$ $S = 0.002345$ and $v = 7,$ the confidence limits are $1.502 \pm 2.36(0.002345/\sqrt{7})$ cm; that is, between 1.4999 cm and 1.5041 cm.

2 Between 601 mm and 832 mm. It might seem that the mean rainfall of 832 mm is just consistent with the interval estimate obtained from the sample. However, the confidence interval is based on a two-tail criterion. But to test the hypothesis

"1961–5 was a typical period" against "1961–5 was drier than a typical period", a one-tail test would be used; this means, for a 5% significance test, taking the value of t corresponding to $P = 10$. On this basis, the null hypothesis would be rejected if the mean rainfall is below 744 mm for the five-year period. The actual mean was 716.4 mm, so the conclusion is that 1961–5 was an unusually dry period.

3 $(m - 0)\sqrt{14}/S = 1.55$, which is less than $t = 2.14$ (at 5% level) when $v = 14$; so the hypothesis $\mu = 0$ is acceptable. Between -0.133 and 0.821.

4 A 95% confidence interval for the mean is from 10.56 to 11.29 days.

5 $(m - 80)\sqrt{10}/S = 2.36$. The critical value of t with $v = 10$ is 2.23 (since 2.5% on a one-tail test is equivalent to 5% on a two-tail test). Conclude that $\mu > 80$.

6 Between 0.63 and 1.36.

7 Since no table of chi-squared probability is available for $v = 189$, use the fact that for large v chi-squared probability is approximated by $N(v, 2v)$ (see Exercise 18C, question 5). This suggests, for $P = 2.5$ and 97.5, the values $\chi^2 = 189 \pm 1.96 \times \sqrt{378}$, that is 227.1 and 150.9. This gives confidence limits for σ between 2.34 and 2.87 days.

8 Test the hypothesis $\mu = 504$ and $\sigma = 2$, and use one-tail tests.
  (*a*) For the given sample, $25S^2/4 = 39.1$, which is greater than the value $\chi^2 = 36.4$ for $P = 5$. The standard deviation is unacceptably large.
  (*b*) $(m - 504)\sqrt{24}/S = 1.96$, which is greater than the value $t = 1.71$ when $P = 10$ (for a 5% one-tail test). The mean is unacceptably large.

9 On the hypothesis $\mu = 15.2$ and $\sigma = 0.5$, the values of $(m - \mu)\sqrt{v}/S$ and nS^2/σ^2 for the sample inspected are 0.93 and 39.2 respectively. The former compares favourably with the value $t = 1.73$ when $P = 10$ (for a 5% one-tail test), but the latter exceeds the value $\chi^2 = 30.1$ when $P = 5$. The sample measurements do not suggest that the machine is incorrectly set, but they indicate that it is functioning too erratically.

10 For the differences (method B–method A) $m = 0.0525$ and $S = 0.2834$, so that $m\sqrt{11}/S = 0.61$. Comparing this with the value $t = 2.20$ when $P = 5$, the hypothesis is acceptable.

11 $m\sqrt{9}/S = 1.54$, compared with $t = 2.26$ when $P = 5$. The effectiveness of the lacquer in reducing corrosion is not established.

12 $m\sqrt{7}/S = 1.58$, compared with $t = 2.36$ when $P = 5$. The difference in mean height is not significant.

13 $m\sqrt{9}/S = 2.92$. If the alternative hypothesis is "fuel A has a higher octane rating than fuel B", then compare this value with $t = 1.83$ with $P = 10$ (for a 5% one-tail test); the null hypothesis is rejected. A 95% confidence interval for the difference is between $0.9 \pm \dfrac{2.26 \times 0.924}{\sqrt{9}}$, that is from 0.20 to 1.60.

14 The reading using the new method exceeds that by the old method by between -4.5 and $+5.6$.

Exercise 19B
1 $C_3 = 6\sqrt{3}/\pi$.

7 When $v = 1, 2$ the variance is infinite. With $v = 1$ t-probability has the form of Cauchy probability (see Exercise 17F, question 4).

8 This shows that t-probability approaches normal probability as $v \to \infty$.

Exercise 19C

2 (a) $0 \leqslant r < 1, 0 \leqslant \theta \leqslant \pi, 0 \leqslant \phi < 2\pi$. (b) As (a) except that $0 \leqslant \theta < \alpha$.

6 To get all 16 possible combinations of sign for the coordinates, take the inequalities as in question 2 except that $0 \leqslant \phi \leqslant \pi, 0 \leqslant \psi < 2\pi$.

7 Denote the general jacobian determinant by J_n. It is helpful to find a method of evaluating J_n which can be applied generally. Starting from J_4, carry out the following steps in turn:
(1) Multiply row 3 by $\cos \psi$; this multiplies the determinant by $\cos \psi$.
(2) Add $\sin \psi \times$ row 4 to row 3; this leaves the determinant unchanged.
(3) Expand the determinant from the bottom row, and cancel the factor $\cos \psi$. This gives the relationship $J_4 = \sin \theta \sin \phi J_3$.

Exercise 19D

1 The test-statistic has the value 2.68 which, with $v = 15$, is significant at the 5% level.

2 The test-statistic has the value 2.39, with $v = 8$. The consignments have significantly different mean breaking strengths, at the 5% level.

3 The test-statistic has the value 0.82, with $v = 12$. The difference in weight is not significant.

4 The test-statistic has the value 1.86, with $v = 18$. The difference is not significant. (Notice that it is more difficult to establish a significant difference in the mean values with an unpaired sample test than in a paired sample test.)

5 The test-statistic has the value 1.43, with $v = 12$. The difference is not significant.

6 The test-statistic has the value 2.54, with $v = 98$. Taking as the alternative hypothesis that "baby boys weigh more than baby girls", so that a one-tail test is appropriate, and taking normal probability as a good enough approximation to t-probability with this value of v, the difference in mean masses is significant, so the theory is supported (in fact, at the 1% level).

7 To apply the theory described in §19.7, it is necessary to assume that the counts for the two types of rock have the same variance. The confidence limits are 29.71 $\pm$ 2.18 $\times \sqrt{\frac{2}{7}} \times$ 19. 88, that is between 6.5 and 52.9 counts per minute.

9 (g) Constant $\times F^{\frac{1}{2}v_1 - 1}(v_2 + Fv_1)^{-\frac{1}{2}(v_1 + v_2)}$.

10 $s_1^2/s_2^2 = 1.83$. Tables give the critical value of F at the 5% level for 43, 55 degrees of freedom as about 1.70 (using interpolation). So the observed variance ratio is significant at this level, which supports the stated hypothesis.

11 $s_1^2/s_2^2 = 1.55$. The critical value of F for 6, 6 degrees of freedom at 5% level is 4.28. The observed variance ratio is not large enough to reject the null hypothesis.

Exercise 20A

2 0.23. (It is simplest to calculate this using the result of question 1.)

3 0.71.

4 The program is much simpler if you use the result of question 1.

5 The expressions are $(a_1b_2 - a_2b_1)^2$ and $(a_1b_2 - a_2b_1)^2 + (a_1b_3 - a_3b_1)^2 + (a_2b_3 - a_3b_2)^2$ respectively. These are zero only if $a_1:a_2:a_3:\ldots = b_1:b_2:b_3:\ldots$. To apply this to the correlation coefficient write $a_i = x_i - m_x$, $b_i = y_i - m_y$.

6 For example, $n = \sum\limits_{i=1}^{k}\sum\limits_{j=1}^{l} f(x_i,\, y_j)$, $\quad m_x = \dfrac{1}{n}\sum\sum x_i f(x_i,\, y_j)$,

$$C_{xy} = \frac{1}{n}\sum\sum (x_i - m_x)(y_j - m_y)f(x_i,\, y_j) = \frac{1}{n}\sum\sum x_i y_j f(x_i,\, y_j) - m_x m_y.$$

7 0.44.

10 0.76.

11 0.48, which is not significant at any of the levels tabulated.

12 0.67, which is significant at the 5% level. $r = 0.62$.

13 It is necessary to adapt Spearman's coefficient to take account of equal rankings, since two pairs of localities have the same rainfall. The usual procedure is, for each pair, to assign to each place an "average ranking" ($5\frac{1}{2}$ and $8\frac{1}{2}$ respectively), so that the sum of all the ranks remains the same. This gives a rank correlation coefficient of 0.07, which is not significant evidence of correlation. Compare this with the value $r = -0.06$.

Exercise 20B

1 $y = 9.42 - 0.007\,85(x - 107.6)$, or $y = 10.26 - 0.007\,85x$. When $x = 200$, $y = 8.69$.

2 $y = 128.3 + 4.46(x - 9.16)$, or $y = 87.4 + 4.46x$. For a boy aged 9.0 years this gives a height of 127.6 cm. Substituting $x = 30$ gives $y = 221$, a ridiculous value for the height; the linear relationship clearly does not extend to age 30.

3 $e = 123 + 0.905(t - 70)$; $t = 70 + 0.553(e - 123)$. (a) 216,   (b) 165.

6 $|\tan\alpha| \leqslant |\tan\gamma|$, so the line of regression of x on y is at least as steep as the line of regression of y on x. If the lines coincide, $r = \pm 1$.

7 5, 3; $r = 2/\sqrt{5} \approx 0.89$.

8 $\tan\lambda = (1 - r^2)/2r$; so if $r = \tan\theta$, $\tan\lambda = \cot 2\theta$.

9 Differentiation gives $-2\sum(y_i - a - bx_i) = 0$ and $-2\sum x_i(y_i - a - bx_i) = 0$. Dividing by n gives $m_y = a + bm_x$ and $(C_{xy} + m_x m_y) = am_x + b(S_x^2 + m_x^2)$, so that $b = C_{xy}/S_x^2$.

10 (i) Minimising $\sum(y_i - bx_i)^2$ gives $b = \sum x_i y_i / \sum x_i^2$.
(ii) Minimising $\sum(y_i - a - bx_i - cx_i^2)$ gives $\sum y_i - na - b\sum x_i - c\sum x_i^2 = 0$,
$\sum x_i y_i - a\sum x_i - b\sum x_i^2 - c\sum x_i^3 = 0$, $\sum x_i^2 y_i - a\sum x_i^2 - b\sum x_i^3 - c\sum x_i^4 = 0$.

11 $r = -0.018$. But the points make a good fit to a quadratic function. The method of question 10(ii) suggests the equation: Growth rate $= -0.09 + 3.70t - 13.95t^2$.

12 From Exercise 13C, question 7, μ is estimated by minimising $nS^2 + n(m - \mu)^2$, which is $\sum(x_i - \mu)^2$.

13 $(n_A S_A^2 + n_B S_B^2 + n_C S_C^2)/N + \{n_A(m_A - m)^2 + n_B(m_B - m)^2 + n_C(m_C - m)^2\}/N$,
where $N = n_A + n_B + n_C$.

14 $y' = rx'$ and $x' = ry'$ make equal angles $\tan^{-1} r$ with the axes.

Exercise 20C

1 $x = \kappa' + \beta'(y - 47.19)$, where $93.4 < \kappa' < 97.5$, $-0.31 < \beta' < -0.09$.

2   Confidence limits for κ and β are 9.42 ± 0.26, -0.00785 ± 0.00264 respectively. The
value of y when $x = 200$, which is $m_x + 92.4$, denoted by λ, is estimated by
$L = K + 92.4B$, which is distributed as $\mathrm{N}(\kappa + 92.4\beta,\ \dfrac{\sigma^2}{n}(1 + 92.4^2/S_x^2))$. So, by an

argument similar to that in the text, $\dfrac{L - \lambda}{S\sqrt{(1 + 92.4^2/S_x^2)}/\sqrt{(n - 2)}}$ has t-probability
with $\nu = n - 2$. Substituting $S_x^2 = 9586.44$, $S = 0.3611$, $n = 10$ gives 95% confidence
limits for λ of 8.69 ± 0.41.

3 128.3 ± 4.3; 4.46 ± 1.73; 127.6 ± 4.3.

4 95% confidence limits are (*a*) 208 to 224, (*b*) 153 to 167.

Exercise 20D

1 $\alpha(x) = \dfrac{1}{\sqrt{(2\pi)}} e^{-\frac{1}{2}x^2}$,

so the conditional probability density for Y given X can be written as

$$\frac{1}{\sqrt{(2\pi)}\cos\theta} e^{-\frac{1}{2}(y - x \sin\theta)^2/\cos^2\theta},$$

which is $\mathrm{N}(x \sin\theta, \cos^2\theta)$, or $\mathrm{N}(\rho x, 1 - \rho^2)$. Notice that the variance is independent
of x, as in the model postulated in §20.4.

2   The integral has the value $\sqrt{(2\pi)}\cos\theta$.

3 $\rho = \displaystyle\int_{y=-\infty}^{\infty} \int_{x=-\infty}^{\infty} xy\phi(x, y)\, dx\, dy.$

Exercise 20E

1   Consider the null hypothesis $\rho = 0$ against the alternative hypothesis $\rho > 0$. With
$n = 8$ (that is, $\nu = 6$) the critical value of t for a one-tail probability of 5% (that is,
$P = 10$) is 1.94; and this gives $r = \cos(\cot^{-1}(1.94/\sqrt{6})) = 0.62$. The measured value
$r = 0.23$ is clearly not significant.

2 $r = -0.536$. Testing the hypothesis $\rho = 0$ against the alternative hypothesis $\rho < 0$, at
the 1% (one-tail) significance level, gives a critical value $r = -0.38$; so the measured
sample correlation coefficient is significant at this level.
    The value of $z = \tanh^{-1} r$ is -0.598, so a 95% confidence interval for ζ is given by
$-1.96 < (-0.598 - \zeta)\sqrt{34} < 1.96$, that is $-0.9346 < \zeta < -0.2623$; so the confidence interval for $\rho = \tanh\zeta$ is $-0.73 < \rho < -0.26$.

4 $\left(\dfrac{n-3}{n-4} \cdot \dfrac{n-5}{n-6} \cdots \dfrac{2}{1}\right)\dfrac{1}{\pi}$ if n is odd, $\left(\dfrac{n-3}{n-4} \cdot \dfrac{n-5}{n-6} \cdots \dfrac{3}{2}\right)\dfrac{1}{2}$ if n is even; for $n = 3$ and $n = 4$,
interpret the expressions within the brackets as having the value 1.

5   Putting $\beta = 0$, the theory states that $B/\{S/S_x\sqrt{(n-2)}\}$ is distributed with t-probability with $v = n - 2$. Writing $B = C_{xy}/S_x^2$, $S = S_y\sqrt{(1-r^2)}$ and $C_{xy}/S_x S_y = r$, it follows that $r\sqrt{v}/\sqrt{(1-r^2)}$ is distributed with t-probability, as shown in §20.8.

7   The approximate "two standard deviation" rule suggests that, if $\rho = 0$, there is a probability of about 95 % that the sample value of r will have absolute value less than $2/\sqrt{(n-1)}$.

8   Choose $c = \rho/\sqrt{(1-\rho^2)}$, and adapt the experiment in §20.6 using two rows, each with n groups of 10 digits added together, recording the values of X and $Y + cX$.

Exercise 21A

1   See §9.4 (in particular Q.7), but with λt in place of λ.

2   The criteria for Poisson probability are likely to be met provided that the traffic density is low enough, so that cars do not appreciably influence each others' motion. $p_0(t) = e^{-\lambda t}$; $\Phi(t) = 1 - p_0(t)$, so that $\phi(t) = -p_0'(t)$. The conditional probability is $e^{-\lambda(s+t)}/e^{-\lambda s} = e^{-\lambda t}$; so the probability function for the arrival of the first car is the same whenever he begins his observations.

3   The probability is $P(X = x | X \neq 0) = P(X = x \text{ and } X \neq 0)/P(X \neq 0)$. In the second case, $P(X = x) = e^{-\lambda}\lambda^x/x!(1 - e^{-\lambda} - \lambda e^{-\lambda})$ for $x = 2, 3, 4, \ldots$.

4   The probability that there are n female elephants in all is $\lambda^n e^{-\lambda}/n!$, and the probability that just s of these produce offspring is $\binom{n}{s}p^s(1-p)^{n-s}$. After writing n as $m + s$, extract the factor $(p\lambda)^s e^{-\lambda}/s!$ from the summation; the remaining factor is then $e^{\lambda(1-p)}$, giving a probability $(\lambda p)^s e^{-\lambda p}/s!$.

Exercise 21B

1   (a) 0,   (b) $\frac{19}{24}$,   (c) $\frac{25}{144}$.   Zerlina.

2 $\frac{55}{512}$.

3   (a) Suppose that the peg starts at A. Then after an odd number of tosses it is always at B, after an even number it is at A or C each with probability $\frac{1}{2}$.
   (b) If the peg starts at A, then after an odd number of tosses it is always at B or D, after an even number it is at A, C or E. There are steady probabilities after alternate moves: after an odd number these are $\frac{1}{2}$ each at B and D, after an even number they are $\frac{1}{2}$ at C and $\frac{1}{4}$ each at A and E.

4   The transition diagram has a form similar to Fig. 7, but with probabilities $\frac{1}{3}, \frac{2}{3}$ from B_n to A_{n+1} and C_{n+1} respectively, and similarly from C_n to D_{n+1} and B_{n+1} (where A denotes the state www/bbb, B denotes wwb/bbw, etc). Steady probabilities are $\frac{1}{8}, \frac{3}{8}, \frac{3}{8}, \frac{1}{8}$. (Note that these are the probabilities one would get if the balls were distributed in the bags randomly.)

5   For 50 p, 40 p, $\ldots$, 10 p the probabilities are the same as the binomial probabilities, $\binom{n}{i}(0.8)^{n-i}(0.2)^i$ for $i = 0, 1, 2, 3, 4$. (Note the similarity between Fig. 8 and Fig. 2.) The probability of having nothing is such as to make the sum of all the probabilities equal to 1; that is, it is the sum of all the remaining coefficients in the expansion of $(0.8 + 0.2t)^n$, for values of $n \geqslant 5$. In the limit, the probabilities tend to 0, 0, 0, 0, 0, 1.

6 $x_{n+1} = 10(\frac{1}{6}p_n + \frac{1}{4}q_n) - 3(\frac{1}{2}p_n + \frac{1}{4}q_n + r_n) = \frac{1}{6}p_n + \frac{7}{4}q_n - 3r_n$; using $r_n = 2p_n$, this is $-\frac{35}{6}p_n - \frac{7}{4}q_n = -\frac{7}{12}x_n$, which tends to zero. The steady probabilities are $\frac{3}{19}, \frac{10}{19}, \frac{6}{19}$.

8 (i) {A, B} closed, {C, D} transient, {E} transient.
(ii) {A, E} closed, {B, C} transient, {D} transient.
(iii) {C} closed, {D} closed, {B, E} closed, {A, F} transient.
Notice, though, that although the answers to (i) and (ii) look similar, the two chains have different structures. This is shown in the figure, which indicates the possible ways of moving from one class to another; in (i) it is impossible to move into either of the transient classes from outside, whereas in (ii) it is possible to move into one of the transient classes from the other. Closed classes are always at the end of the line, but transient classes are not necessarily at the beginning.

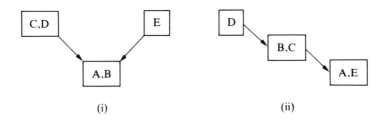

(i)   (ii)

9 (i) 0.87,   (ii) 0.833.   These correspond to the probabilities of "(a) or (b)" after (i) 2, (ii) 3 steps in the chain.

Exercise 21C

1 (a) $U = \begin{bmatrix} 9 & 1 \\ 4 & -1 \end{bmatrix}$, $\Lambda = \begin{bmatrix} 1 & 0 \\ 0 & -\frac{1}{12} \end{bmatrix}$, $U^{-1} = \frac{1}{13}\begin{bmatrix} 1 & 1 \\ 4 & -9 \end{bmatrix}$. Limit $= \frac{1}{13}\begin{bmatrix} 9 \\ 4 \end{bmatrix}$.

(b) $U = \begin{bmatrix} 2 & 1 & 1 \\ 1 & -1 & -2 \\ 2 & 0 & 1 \end{bmatrix}$, $\Lambda = \begin{bmatrix} 1 & 0 & 0 \\ 0 & -\frac{1}{2} & 0 \\ 0 & 0 & -\frac{1}{4} \end{bmatrix}$, $U^{-1} = \frac{1}{5}\begin{bmatrix} 1 & 1 & 1 \\ 5 & 0 & -5 \\ -2 & -2 & 3 \end{bmatrix}$.

Limit $= \begin{bmatrix} 0.4 \\ 0.2 \\ 0.4 \end{bmatrix}$.

(c) $U = \begin{bmatrix} 1 & 1 & 0 & 0 \\ 2 & -1 & 0 & 0 \\ 0 & 0 & 5 & 1 \\ 0 & 0 & 9 & -1 \end{bmatrix}$, $\Lambda = \begin{bmatrix} 1 & 0 & 0 & 0 \\ 0 & \frac{1}{4} & 0 & 0 \\ 0 & 0 & 1 & 0 \\ 0 & 0 & 0 & \frac{1}{15} \end{bmatrix}$, $U^{-1} = \begin{bmatrix} \frac{1}{3} & \frac{1}{3} & 0 & 0 \\ \frac{2}{3} & -\frac{1}{3} & 0 & 0 \\ 0 & 0 & \frac{1}{14} & \frac{1}{14} \\ 0 & 0 & \frac{9}{14} & -\frac{5}{14} \end{bmatrix}$.

A limiting matrix $L = \begin{bmatrix} 1 & 0 & 0 & 0 \\ 0 & 0 & 0 & 0 \\ 0 & 0 & 1 & 0 \\ 0 & 0 & 0 & 0 \end{bmatrix}$ exists, leading to the result

$$\lim \mathbf{T}^n = \mathbf{ULU}^{-1} = \begin{bmatrix} \frac{1}{3} & \frac{1}{3} & 0 & 0 \\ \frac{2}{3} & \frac{2}{3} & 0 & 0 \\ 0 & 0 & \frac{5}{14} & \frac{5}{14} \\ 0 & 0 & \frac{9}{14} & \frac{9}{14} \end{bmatrix}.$$

This does not have all its columns the same, and so does not give a unique limiting outcome probability vector. In fact, if the initial probabilities are a, b, c, d, the limiting probabilities are $\frac{1}{3}(a + b)$, $\frac{2}{3}(a + b)$, $\frac{5}{14}(c + d)$, $\frac{9}{14}(c + d)$. It is easy to see that this is a steady set of probabilities. The reason for this behaviour is shown up at once by the transition diagram. Algebraically the standard method goes astray because there are two eigenvalues equal to 1, although there is still a full clutch of eigenvectors.

2 $\mathbf{T} = \begin{bmatrix} 0.2 & 0 \\ 0.8 & 1 \end{bmatrix}$, $\mathbf{U} = \begin{bmatrix} 0 & 1 \\ 1 & -1 \end{bmatrix}$, $\mathbf{\Lambda} = \begin{bmatrix} 1 & 0 \\ 0 & 0.2 \end{bmatrix}$, $\mathbf{U}^{-1} = \begin{bmatrix} 1 & 1 \\ 1 & 0 \end{bmatrix}$, $\mathbf{p}_n = \begin{bmatrix} (0.2)^n \\ 1 - (0.2)^n \end{bmatrix}$.

3 $\begin{bmatrix} \frac{1}{6} & \frac{1}{4} & 0 \\ \frac{1}{2} & \frac{1}{4} & 1 \\ \frac{1}{3} & \frac{1}{2} & 0 \end{bmatrix}.$

$p_n = \frac{1}{133}\{(21 - 2(-\frac{7}{12})^{n-1})p_1 + (21 - 21(-\frac{7}{12})^{n-1})q_1 + (21 + 36(-\frac{7}{12})^{n-1})r_1\}$,

$q_n = \frac{1}{133}\{(70 + 6(-\frac{7}{12})^{n-1})p_1 + (70 + 63(-\frac{7}{12})^{n-1})q_1 + (70 - 108(-\frac{7}{12})^{n-1})r_1\}$,

$r_n = \frac{1}{133}\{(42 - 4(-\frac{7}{12})^{n-1})p_1 + (42 - 42(-\frac{7}{12})^{n-1})q_1 + (42 + 72(-\frac{7}{12})^{n-1})r_1\}$.

$\frac{3}{19}, \frac{10}{19}, \frac{6}{19}.$

4   (a) 1, 0.2 (double); $\begin{bmatrix} 0 \\ 0 \\ 1 \end{bmatrix}$, $\begin{bmatrix} 0 \\ 1 \\ -1 \end{bmatrix}$. Only two linearly independent eigenvectors.

(b) 1, -1, 0; $\begin{bmatrix} 1 \\ 2 \\ 1 \end{bmatrix}$, $\begin{bmatrix} 1 \\ -2 \\ 1 \end{bmatrix}$, $\begin{bmatrix} 1 \\ 0 \\ -1 \end{bmatrix}$. Two eigenvalues have modulus 1.

5 $\begin{bmatrix} 1 & \frac{1}{2} & 0 \\ 0 & 0 & 0 \\ 0 & \frac{1}{2} & 1 \end{bmatrix}$, eigenvalues 1 (double), 0. After the first move the customer is at one of the absorbing outcomes, so the probabilities are fixed from then on.

6 $\begin{bmatrix} 1 & \frac{1}{2} & 0 & 0 \\ 0 & 0 & \frac{1}{2} & 0 \\ 0 & \frac{1}{2} & 0 & 0 \\ 0 & 0 & \frac{1}{2} & 1 \end{bmatrix}$; eigenvalues 1 (double), $\frac{1}{2}$, $-\frac{1}{2}$;

eigenvectors $\begin{bmatrix} 1 \\ 0 \\ 0 \\ 0 \end{bmatrix}$, $\begin{bmatrix} 0 \\ 0 \\ 0 \\ 1 \end{bmatrix}$, $\begin{bmatrix} 1 \\ -1 \\ -1 \\ 1 \end{bmatrix}$, $\begin{bmatrix} 1 \\ -3 \\ 3 \\ -1 \end{bmatrix}$.

$\frac{1}{3} - \frac{1}{2}(\frac{1}{2})^n + \frac{1}{6}(-\frac{1}{2})^n$, $\frac{1}{2}(\frac{1}{2})^n - \frac{1}{2}(-\frac{1}{2})^n$, $\frac{1}{2}(\frac{1}{2})^n + \frac{1}{2}(-\frac{1}{2})^n$, $\frac{2}{3} - \frac{1}{2}(\frac{1}{2})^n - \frac{1}{6}(-\frac{1}{2})^n$.

8   Note that the eigenvalues are solutions of the equation $\det(\mathbf{T} - \lambda\mathbf{I}) = 0$.

9 Apply the "triangle inequality" given (extended to three terms) to the expression $ax + dy + gz$ (which is equal to λx) and note that, since $a \geqslant 0$, $|ax|$ can be written as $a|x|$. Adding the inequality to those formed similarly from the second and third rows of **T** gives $|x| + |y| + |z| \geqslant |\lambda|(|x| + |y| + |z|)$.

12
$$
\begin{bmatrix}
0 & \frac{1}{2} & 0 & 0 \\
1 & 0 & \frac{1}{2} & 0 \\
0 & \frac{1}{2} & 0 & 1 \\
0 & 0 & \frac{1}{2} & 0
\end{bmatrix} =
$$

$$
\begin{bmatrix}
1 & 1 & 1 & 1 \\
2 & -2 & 1 & -1 \\
2 & 2 & -1 & -1 \\
1 & -1 & -1 & 1
\end{bmatrix}
\begin{bmatrix}
1 & 0 & 0 & 0 \\
0 & -1 & 0 & 0 \\
0 & 0 & \frac{1}{2} & 0 \\
0 & 0 & 0 & -\frac{1}{2}
\end{bmatrix}
\cdot \frac{1}{6}
\begin{bmatrix}
1 & 1 & 1 & 1 \\
1 & -1 & 1 & -1 \\
2 & 1 & -1 & -2 \\
2 & -1 & -1 & 2
\end{bmatrix}.
$$ Limiting

probabilities are $\frac{1}{3}, 0, \frac{2}{3}, 0$ after an even number of steps, $0, \frac{2}{3}, 0, \frac{1}{3}$ after an odd number.

13 (i)

	A	B	C	D	E
A	0	*	0	0	*
B	*	0	*	0	0
C	0	0	*	*	0
D	0	0	*	0	0
E	0	0	0	0	*

.

(ii)

	A	B	C	D	E
A	0	0	*	0	*
B	0	*	*	0	0
C	0	*	0	*	0
D	0	0	0	*	0
E	*	*	0	0	0

,

	A	E	B	C	D
A	0	*	0	*	0
E	*	0	*	0	0
B	0	0	*	*	0
C	0	0	*	0	*
D	0	0	0	0	*

(iii)

	A	B	C	D	E	F
A	*	0	0	0	0	*
B	0	*	0	0	*	*
C	*	0	*	0	0	0
D	0	0	0	*	0	*
E	0	*	0	0	0	0
F	*	0	0	0	0	0

,

	C	D	B	E	A	F
C	*	0	0	0	*	0
D	0	*	0	0	0	*
B	0	0	*	*	0	*
E	0	0	*	0	0	0
A	0	0	0	0	*	*
F	0	0	0	0	*	0

.

The closed classes have zeros in the rest of their columns, the transient classes can be arranged with all zeros on the left.

14

	B	C	A
B	$\frac{1}{3}$	$\frac{2}{3}$	$\frac{1}{3}$
C	$\frac{2}{3}$	$\frac{1}{3}$	$\frac{1}{3}$
A	0	0	$\frac{1}{3}$

; T^n has limiting form
$$
\begin{bmatrix}
\frac{1}{2} & \frac{1}{2} & \frac{1}{2} \\
\frac{1}{2} & \frac{1}{2} & \frac{1}{2} \\
0 & 0 & 0
\end{bmatrix}.
$$

Exercise 21D

1 The cube.

3 (a) Converges to a point inside the triangle, corresponding to steady probabilities $\frac{2}{5}, \frac{1}{5}$, $\frac{2}{5}$. (b) Converges to a point on the side $Y_0 Z_0$, corresponding to steady probabilities 0, $\frac{2}{3}, \frac{1}{3}$. (c) The triangle collapses not into a point but into a line; if one starts at X_0 (with initial probabilities 1, 0, 0) then the limiting probabilities are 1, 0, 0; but if one starts at Y_0 or Z_0, the limiting probabilities are 0, $\frac{2}{3}, \frac{1}{3}$ (as in (b)). Notice that the fact that the area of the triangle $X_n Y_n Z_n$ tends to zero does not ensure convergence to a point. (d) The matrix merely permutes the vertices of the triangle; although there is a set of steady probabilities $\frac{1}{3}, \frac{1}{3}, \frac{1}{3}$, with any initial probabilities other than these there is no convergence.

Exercise 21E

1 The states are server wins (W), advantage server (V), deuce (D), advantage against server (K), server loses (L). It is convenient to insert in the transition diagram the notional broken lines, as in Fig. 9. Denote the probabilities of winning from these states by $w_W(=1)$, w_V, w_D, w_K, $w_L(=0)$; and the number of points before reaching a result from the states by $M_W(=0)$, M_V, M_D, M_K, $M_L(=0)$. Typical equations are $w_D = \frac{3}{4}w_V + \frac{1}{4}w_K$, $E[M_D] = 1 + \frac{3}{4}E[M_V] + \frac{1}{4}E[M_K]$, and similarly for other states: $w_D = 0.9$, $E[M_D] = 3.2$.

2 6.25, 1.25.

3 He expects to see her again 2.25 nights later.

4 Note that if the probabilities are written as a column matrix, the multiplier is the transpose of $\mathbf{T}$; so transposing the equation, which arranges the probabilities as a row matrix, produces the given equation.

5
$$\begin{bmatrix} 1 & \frac{3}{4} & 0 & 0 & 0 \\ 0 & 0 & \frac{3}{4} & 0 & 0 \\ 0 & \frac{1}{4} & 0 & \frac{3}{4} & 0 \\ 0 & 0 & \frac{1}{4} & 0 & 0 \\ 0 & 0 & 0 & \frac{1}{4} & 1 \end{bmatrix} .$$
$x_2 = 0.1$, compared with a probability of 0.25 in a single bet.

6
$$\begin{bmatrix} 1 & \frac{1}{4} & 0 & \frac{1}{16} & 0 & 0 \\ 0 & \frac{1}{2} & 0 & \frac{1}{4} & 0 & 0 \\ 0 & 0 & 0 & \frac{1}{8} & 0 & 0 \\ 0 & \frac{1}{4} & 0 & \frac{1}{4} & \frac{1}{4} & 0 \\ 0 & 0 & 0 & \frac{1}{4} & \frac{1}{2} & 0 \\ 0 & 0 & 0 & \frac{1}{16} & \frac{1}{4} & 1 \end{bmatrix} . \frac{3}{4}, \frac{1}{2}, \frac{1}{2}, \frac{1}{4}.$$

7 (a) $\{B, C\}, \{A\}$. (b)
$$\begin{bmatrix} 1 & 0.25 & 0.3 \\ 0 & 0.45 & 0.3 \\ 0 & 0.3 & 0.4 \end{bmatrix}, \begin{bmatrix} 1 & 0.355 & 0.41 \\ 0 & 0.315 & 0.33 \\ 0 & 0.33 & 0.26 \end{bmatrix} .$$

(c) The probabilities are $r_1, r_2 - r_1, r_3 - r_2, \ldots$, and $r_n = 1 - s_n$.
(e) Note that $(\mathbf{I} - \mathbf{Q})(\mathbf{I} + \mathbf{Q} + \mathbf{Q}^2 + \cdots + \mathbf{Q}^{n-1}) = \mathbf{I} - \mathbf{Q}^n$, and since $\{B, C\}$ is a transient class $\mathbf{Q}^n$ tends to zero.
(f) $\begin{bmatrix} 4 & 3 \\ 3 & 3.5 \end{bmatrix}$, 6.5 steps.

8   (*a*) Partitioning **T** as $\begin{bmatrix} \mathbf{Q} & \vdots & 0 \\ & \vdots & 0 \\ \hline 0 & 0.8 & \vdots & 1 \end{bmatrix}$; $(\mathbf{I} - \mathbf{Q})^{-1} = \begin{bmatrix} 1.25 & 0 \\ 1.25 & 1.25 \end{bmatrix}$, 2.5 steps.

    (*b*)   3.75 steps.

Revision exercise C

1   (*a*) 0.212,   (*b*) 0.130,   (*c*) 0.764,   (*d*) 0.707.

2   0.034; 0.234.

3   0.345. Between 50.243 kg and 50.307 kg.

4 $a = 20.1$, $b = 0.032$; 19.00, 21.27. About 17 more.

5   0.5, 0.0357; 0.365, 0.982.

6 $C = \frac{1}{4}$. Discrepancy = 20.16, significant.

7   Between 35.6 and 42.4. Test-statistic = 1.766, not significant.

8   0.055.

9   Probability is 0.034, significant at the 5 % level. (Note however, that a chi-squared test on the data gives a value 16.33 for the test-statistic, which is significant at the 1 % level.)

10   (*a*) {A, B, C},   (*b*) {D}.   3 nights.

11   9 nights. (Notice that this can be found either by the method described in §21.7, or using the matrix method given in §21.8 by re-interpreting "wet" as an absorbing outcome.)

Index